Juvenile Delinquency

Peter C. Kratcoski • Lucille Dunn Kratcoski
Peter Christopher Kratcoski

Juvenile Delinquency

Theory, Research, and the Juvenile Justice Process

Sixth Edition

 Springer

Peter C. Kratcoski
Sociology/Justice Studies
Kent State University
Tallmadge, OH, USA

Lucille Dunn Kratcoski
Tallmadge, OH, USA

Peter Christopher Kratcoski
Williams, Welser & Kratcoski LLC
Kent, OH, USA

ISBN 978-3-030-31454-5   ISBN 978-3-030-31452-1   (eBook)
https://doi.org/10.1007/978-3-030-31452-1

This Springer imprint is published by the registered company Springer Nature Switzerland AG
The registered company address is: Gewerbestrasse 11, 6330 Cham, Switzerland

This book is dedicated to three generations of the Kratcoski and Dunn families, who encouraged and supported our academic and professional endeavors.

Preface

Publication of this sixth edition of *Juvenile Delinquency* provided an opportunity to reflect on the changes in the amount and types of juvenile misbehavior and the juvenile justice response to it that have taken place since the first edition was published more than 35 years ago. The cyclical nature of delinquency and the increased formalization of juvenile court procedures and juvenile justice system approaches became apparent in this examination. However, we have seen a renewed emphasis on diversion and treatment of youths with special needs.

The first edition explored the problems of youth deviance and unlawful behavior in the Unites States at the close of the 1970s and the methods used at that time to inhibit, detect, punish, deter, or reduce this activity. It reported trends and developments in the amount and nature of delinquency that are still occurring, including increased similarities in the amount and types of offenses committed by males and females; involvement of younger age groups in delinquent activity; and increases in middle-class, suburban, and rural youths' misbehavior, gang activity, and substance abuse. It was noted that treatment strategies had moved beyond the "medical model" and had begun to focus on minimization of penetration into the system, community treatment, deinstitutionalization, and the "right to punishment."

The second edition focused on delinquency in the mid-1980s. The continuing narrowing of the gap between the rates of male and female offending and overrepresentation of minority group members in arrests for property crime and violent crime were important trends. Key issues were the pressures for removal of both status offenders (those who commit offenses that are unlawful only for juveniles) and serious violent delinquents from juvenile court jurisdiction and revision of juvenile codes to formalize processing of serious offenders and mandate their referral to adult criminal courts or specialized youth courts. For other offenders, the emphasis was on diversion, community treatment, and deinstitutionalization.

At the beginning of the 1990s, the third edition noted increases in arrests of juveniles for offenses relates to substance abuse and substantial increases in gang activity, which was regarded as a serious threat to safety in the schools and inner-city neighborhoods. As a result of policies for separate handling of delinquent and status offenders at all levels of the juvenile justice system, the debate over status offenders had largely subsided. Increased attention was given to physical and sexual abuse as threats to the welfare of children, and the juvenile court procedures for dealing with these problems became important. Firmer handling of serious offenders and more severe dispositions for habitual, serious offenders had been initiated, leading to increases in the number of juveniles held in long-term institutions. Treatment in institutions now focused on education, job skills, and preparation for return to the community rather than on the personal problems of the offenders. For other offenders, restitution, community service, and intensive probation were used. Privatization of juvenile corrections was a new trend.

When the fourth edition appeared in the mid-1990s, increases in arrests of juveniles for serious and violent crimes and overrepresentation of minority group youths in these types of offenses, new surges in gang activity and expansion in the age ranges of gang members, and rapid increases in female delinquency were noted. These trends were seen as creating an identity crisis for the juvenile courts. Many states lowered the upper age of juvenile court jurisdiction so that older adolescent offenders could be referred directly to adult courts. Juvenile court procedures were formalized, and there were new pressures for complete removal of status offenders from juvenile court jurisdiction. Increases in the number of abuse, neglect, and dependency cases required the juvenile courts to devote more attention to these cases. The demands for harsher penalties for serious juvenile offenders resulted in waiver of more cases to adult criminal courts. The trend toward more severe dispositions for habitual, serious offenders continued, with increases in the number of institutionalized juveniles and close supervision of them when they were released. Institutional treatment continued to focus on the skills needed for reintegration into the community. Privatization of juvenile corrections increased. The schools began to take greater responsibility for delinquency prevention programming.

When the fifth edition of *Juvenile Delinquency* appeared at the beginning of the twenty-first century, it was apparent that the problems of youth had not changed appreciably over the years since the first edition, but certain trends were identified. Juvenile arrests for both violent and property crimes declined considerably in the late 1990s, but offenses related to the personal, family, and community behavior of youths, including substance abuse, offenses against family, and disorderly conduct, increased. School-related violence and gang activity continued to capture the headlines, minority group youths were still overrepresented in every facet of the juvenile justice system, and involvement of females in gang activity and serious and violent delinquencies showed strong increases. The reductions in arrests for violent and property crimes were attributed to the strong economy in the late 1990s, harsher dispositions for and closer supervision of serious offenders, and the institutionalization of many habitual serious offenders. However, as the economy declined in the early 2000s, serious and violent delinquency began to increase again, underlining the connection between poverty and lack of opportunities and delinquency. The formalization of juvenile court procedures had continued, and some legal scholars questioned the wisdom of having a separate juvenile justice system. Many states lowered the upper age of juvenile court jurisdiction so that older adolescent offenders were referred directly to adult courts. Judicial waiver (transfer of juveniles' cases to adult criminal courts), statutory exclusion (giving criminal courts original jurisdiction over certain offenses by juveniles, so that they are automatically excluded from the juvenile court), and concurrent jurisdiction (both the juvenile and criminal courts have jurisdiction, but the prosecutor has the discretion to file the case in either type of court) resulted in the removal of many serious delinquency cases from the juvenile courts. The renewed call for removal of status offenders from juvenile court jurisdiction was seen as a challenge to the purposes of the court, which was originally designed to intervene in and touch the lives of any youths believed to be disposed toward unacceptable or inappropriate conduct.

More severe dispositions for habitual, serious offenders frequently took the form of institutionalization. Treatment strategies in institutions that focus on preparing the incarcerated youths for return to the community were described. Such programs as restitution, community service, and intensive probation promoted greater involvement of the community in delinquency prevention control.

Police and the courts developed diversion programs and intensive supervision possibilities based on the "balanced approach," which gives equal consideration to protecting the community and rehabilitating offenders. The schools become a focal point for meeting the needs of many children who had no other agency contacts. They developed programs to feed needy children during the school day, reach out to their families, and provide for their safety as they travel to and from school, through patrol of areas near the schools and by use of in-school police officers, who present classes on drug and alcohol abuse prevention and avoiding sexual exploitation. Schools also offered opportunities for teenage mothers to continue their education, and peer influence groups were formed to encourage youths to stay in school and avoid gang influences.

The title of the sixth edition has been changed to *Juvenile Delinquency: Theory, Research, and the Juvenile Justice Process*, to emphasize the importance of using the findings from "evidence-based" research in the enactment of laws, developments of policies, and implementation of programs in the processing and treatment of juvenile offenders. Several of the theories of delinquency causation that were discarded because they were considered to be not relevant to contributing to our understanding of the behavior of youths, particularly that of delinquent youths, now have received renewed interest as a result of having the technology and assessment tools needed to complete large-scale research.

The conditions early theorists associated with delinquency, such as poverty, crowded living conditions, and lack of educational opportunities, can still be accepted as explanations for a portion of delinquent behavior, but they have little validity in explaining middle-class delinquency. The influence of portrayals of violent and morally permissive subject matter in the mass media, violent video games, lack of supervision of young people brought on by the need for both parents to contribute to the family income or parents' desires for self-fulfillment, rootlessness and lack of extended family ties, the impersonality of large school systems, and the lack of opportunities for meaningful work for teenagers, or various combinations of these factors, have been demonstrated to be conditions that contribute to the misbehavior of certain young people. It is apparent that delinquency is still a complex phenomenon that defied easy explanations.

In addition, greater emphasis is placed on the influence of communications by way of the internet as it is related to the victimization of youth, violence in the schools and the family, and conflict in the community.

In this sixth edition, these matters and many others related to juvenile delinquency in contemporary society were examined with the help of professionals in the juvenile justice field, including juvenile court judges, probation and aftercare officers, police officers, youth leaders, social workers, researchers, and those involved in special diversion or community treatment programs. Their candor, assistance, and encouragement helped us to develop *Juvenile Delinquency's* sixth edition into a book that we believe presents a picture of delinquency and the juvenile justice system as they were, as they are, and as they may exist in the future.

Tallmadge, OH, USA   Peter C. Kratcoski
Tallmadge, OH, USA   Lucille Dunn Kratcoski
Kent, OH, USA   Peter Christopher Kratcoski

Acknowledgments

The writing of this book would not have been possible without the assistance of many individuals who contributed their time and ideas and who provided invaluable information.

In addition to including the most recent developments in theories of delinquency causation and the latest research on young people who violate the laws and those who are victims of crime, we enlisted the aid of numerous professionals and the help of adults and juveniles who were willing to share their experiences with the juvenile justice system. Their insights and willingness to "tell it as it is" helped the authors develop an understanding of the operation of the juvenile justice system. These individuals include:

Robert Berger, Judge, Portage County, Ohio Court of Common Pleas, Juvenile Division

Daniel Cody, Magistrate, Summit County, Ohio Court of Common Pleas, Juvenile Division

Rory Franks, Chief Probation Officer, Portage County, Ohio Court of Common Pleas, Juvenile Division

Lisa Green, Administrator, New Philadelphia Girls' Group Home, Multi-County Juvenile Attention System, New Philadelphia, Ohio

Kristine Pytash, Ph.D., Kent State University College of Education, Health, and Human Services

Troy Reeves, Attorney at Law, Kent, Ohio

Lenny Sorboro, Director of Youth Rehabilitation, Portage County, Ohio Court of Common Pleas, Juvenile Division

Linda Tucci Teodosio, Judge, Summit County, Ohio Court of Common Pleas, Juvenile Division

Lisa Testa, Ph.D., Kent State University College of Education, Health, and Human Services

We also wish to acknowledge many others who contributed to this work through assisting with the research and typing the manuscript. They include Dawn McMurdo,

Administrative Assistant, Williams, Kratcoski & Can, LLC, and Emma Samuels, Kent State University Paralegal Intern.

Special thanks to Judith Newlin, Social and Behavior Sciences Editor, Springer Publishing, who provided assistance to the authors throughout the process and Ms. Kala Palanisamy, Project Manager and Contents Solutions, who provided assistance with the production of the book.

Contents

About the Authors

Peter C. Kratcoski earned a PhD in sociology from Pennsylvania State University, University Park, Pennsylvania; an MA in sociology from the University of Notre Dame, Indiana; and a BA in sociology from King's College, Wilkes-Barre, Pennsylvania. He was selected for several postdoctoral grants by the National Science Foundation. He taught at the College of St. Thomas, St Paul, Minnesota, and at the Pennsylvania State University before assuming the position of assistant professor of sociology at Kent State University, Kent, Ohio, in 1969. He retired as professor of criminal justice studies and chair of the Department of Criminal Justice Studies at Kent State University, where he is currently a professor emeritus and adjunct professor. He has published many books, chapters in books, and journal articles in the areas of juvenile delinquency, juvenile justice, international policing, crime prevention, corrections, and victimology. His most recent writing and research have centered on juvenile delinquency, juvenile justice, collaborative policing, correctional counseling, financial crimes, corruption and fraud, and victimization of the elderly.

Lucille Dunn Kratcoski was awarded a Bachelor of Arts degree from Marywood College, Scranton, Pennsylvania, and a master's degree from Pennsylvania State University, University Park, Pennsylvania. She has numerous years of teaching experience at the elementary, high school, and university levels. She coauthored *Juvenile Delinquency* and many book chapters and journal articles on the subjects of social issues, victims of crime, juvenile delinquency, and juvenile justice.

Peter Christopher Kratcoski was awarded a Bachelor of Arts degree in political science from The Ohio State University and a Juris Doctorate degree from The Ohio State University College of Law. He is the managing partner at the law firm Williams, Kratcoski & Can where he has been practicing law since 1988. In addition to his law practice, he has taught as an adjunct professor at several colleges and universities for over 30 years. He currently teaches as an adjunct professor in the paralegal program at Kent State University, teaching various law-related courses. He has coauthored two books related to experiential education in law, coauthored chapters of books, and has presented papers at professional meetings.

Part I
Definition, Scope, and Trends in Juvenile Delinquency

Juvenile delinquency may be legally defined as any action by a person in a specified age category (generally the lower age is not specified and the upper age is below the 18th birthday) who commits an act that is defined as criminal if committed by an adult. Most young persons are involved in some form of unlawful behavior during their adolescent years, but escape detection, apprehension, or court involvement. Only those who have been officially adjudicated as such by a juvenile court are normally designated "juvenile delinquents."

Chapter 1 traces the role of the child in previous societies and the manner in which society responded to the misbehavior of children. Juvenile deviation from societal norms has existed throughout history and is usually tolerated unless the behavior becomes so extreme that the common good is threatened. As behavior becomes more seriously antisocial, sanctions may be applied by parents, the school, or by the police in an unofficial manner. If such methods fail, arrest and referral to the courts may follow.

Juveniles are referred to the courts for two broad types of offenses. Acts that would be illegal for adults are termed delinquent offenses, and violations of regulations that apply only to children are labeled status offenses.

The actual amount of delinquent and status offending is unknown, since so much of it is not reported to the police or made known to the courts. However, estimates can be made based on the results of self-report surveys and reports based on information collected from official justice agencies.

Chapter 2 presents major theories of crime and delinquency causation developed in the past, including heredity, low intelligence, and other biological based theories related to the causation of deviant behavior. Research and theory relating to the biosocial perspective are also covered in this chapter.

The classical theorists, such as Beccaria and Bentham, believed that the decision to become involved in criminal behavior was a rational one, and that this behavior can be deterred by establishing a system of sure and immediate punishment.

In contrast to the freedom of choice stressed by the classical and neoclassical theorists, the biological theorists believe that offenders are predetermined, or at least predisposed, toward criminality by features of their biological makeup, and

that certain physical characteristics can be noted in individuals who have this predisposition. Those who promote heredity-based theories follow a similar line of
reasoning, claiming that the tendency toward delinquency and other aberrations
such as mental illness and alcoholism is generically transmitted from parents to
children.

The development of sophisticated methods to research some of the basic assumptions underlying the bio-social theories of delinquency and criminal causation led to
a new wave of research in this area, and some of the research is presented in
Chapter 2.

Chapter 3 focuses on the developmental cognitive, moral, psychological, and
socialization processes of children. Social-psychological theories of delinquency
causation focus on personality development. Researchers concerned with moral
development of the child emphasize the importance of the internalization of moral
values in a gradual, developmental sequence.

Cognitive development theorists maintain that the ability to make appropriate
choices and judgments is a gradual maturation process, related to perceived costs
and rewards.

Personality trait theorists have identified several personality traits that are found
to be prevalent and conducive to deviant behavior. Also, in this chapter research is
presented on those persons labeled psychopaths and sociopaths, as well as those
found to have other personality disorders.

Chapter 4 presents a social organization perspective on delinquency causation by
focusing on youths' experiences in the family, environment, and community.

Social disorganization, which is the breakdown of conventional institutional controls within a community and the inability of organizations, groups, or individuals
who live in these communities to solve common problems, is an important influence
on delinquency. Environmental theorists regard the conditions of poverty, deteriorated and crowed housing, family disorganization, educational deprivation, and lack
of opportunity as important factors contributing to the delinquency of the youths
living in these depressed areas.

Chapter 5 focuses on the interpersonal relationships in the family. Theories and
research on the effects of living in a functional family, in contrast to living in a dysfunctional family, are presented in this chapter.

A number of changes that occurred, beginning in the early twentieth century and
continuing up to the present time, have been identified as affecting the structure and
practices of American families. These include urbanization, industrialization,
mobility, complex communication networks, and changes in traditions and values.
Most notable among observed changing values are the relaxation of sexual standards, the acceptance of divorce and varied marriage styles, same gender marriages,
a turning away from child-centered family life, and new views on the appropriate
roles for women in the family unit and in the larger society.

The effects of the psychological disruption of the family through alcoholism,
mental illness, emotional disruption of parent-child interaction, or home atmospheres characterized by internal conflict and tension have been identified as factors
related to delinquency causation.

Chapter 6 focuses on the influence of peer groups relating to substance abuse, sexually deviance, involvement in gangs, and other types of deviance.

A review of the history of gang development reveals that gangs have existed in the urban areas in the United States from the time cities became large enough to develop slum areas. Conflict over control of territory was a chief concern of the earlier gangs. While such conflict still is a major problem at the present time, in many cases the areas in which the conflict occurs have moved from the neighborhoods into the schools or shopping malls. In addition, the motive for conflict is no longer protection of one's territory, but such matters as drug trafficking and other criminal activities. The levels of gang violence have escalated markedly in the early twenty-first century, with an increase in the use of firearms and the number of homicides that are recorded each year that are attributed to delinquent gangs.

Approaches to gang control may be proactive or reactive. Proactive efforts focus on preventing gang formation by developing community and school activities and programs to meet the needs of youths who might fall prey to the gang's appeal. Reactive approaches may take the form of collection of intelligence or attempting to destroy the gang's solidity by isolating the leaders through arrest and institutionalization and by debunking the romanticized versions of gang behavior often presented by the mass media.

Chapter 7 provides several perspectives relating to delinquency and violence in the schools. Factors relating to bullying, physical abuse, and sexual abuse of youths within the school setting are considered. In addition, the measures taken by school authorities and the community to control such problems are described.

When delinquency is school related, it may be the result of socialization difficulties experienced in the schools. Some children from disadvantaged backgrounds may come to school without having mastery of the basic skills needed to succeed there. Others may come to school hungry and wearing clothing that is so different from that worn by the other children that they immediately become targets for ridicule.

Fear of physical violence going to and coming from school or within the school grounds may contribute to truancy, absenteeism, or a climate that makes both teaching and learning difficult.

Learning disabilities, including dyslexia, aphasia, and hyperkinesis, have been noted in a large number of delinquent children. Although a causal link has not been established between learning disabilities and delinquency, their presence in a substantial number of delinquent children has led to the establishment of efforts to identify these problems and establish remedial programs by a number of juvenile courts.

Chapter 1
The Transition of Child to Adult

1.1 Introduction

Juvenile misbehavior occurs in every city, town, and rural area throughout the United States. It can also be said with a high degree of certainty that this statement holds true for every country throughout the world. Statistics are available on the amount and types of delinquent acts that are committed by youths in the United States. The violent, aggressive acts by juveniles capture the spotlight, but juvenile delinquency extends beyond these acts and it encompasses a wide range of inappropriate activities by young people. Those who have completed research on the causes of deviant behavior by young persons have formulated several theories of causation that seek to explain the causes for a large portion of delinquency, but for some youths who engage in deviant acts the motivation for their behavior seems to fall outside of the scope of any theory.

In this chapter, we will explore what types of acts committed by children were considered deviant in past societies as well as in present societies. In addition, we will touch on the various methods authorities have used to punish children confined as deviant and trace the development of the juvenile justice system. Definitions of juvenile delinquency, the extent of delinquency and the types of delinquent acts committed by youths in the United States will be given.

1.2 Societal Reaction to Youthful Misbehavior

Concern about the behavior of the youths of a country is a universal phenomenon, regardless of the society in question or the period of history being considered. In some societies, cultural values, beliefs, customs, and material possessions do not change much from one generation to another, while in other societies the change is very rapid. But no matter how stable or traditional a society appears to be, people do

© Springer Nature Switzerland AG 2020
P. C. Kratcoski et al., *Juvenile Delinquency*,
https://doi.org/10.1007/978-3-030-31452-1_1

not remain exactly the same from one generation to the next. New challenges to the welfare of the society often result in changes in the attitudes, behavior, and values of the people. The younger population often introduces these changes, and they are not always readily accepted by those who have established a comfortable way of life and do not want to accept anything that is viewed as a threat to it. Those in power are likely to develop rules and laws designed to punish those who violate the existing norms and values of the society.

The large majority of laws designed to regulate the behavior of the members of a society, including the youths, were generally based in the customs and traditions of the society. Although these rules and laws were unwritten, they were nevertheless understood as the proper way for children to behave and were taught to children by their parents and other authority figures in the community, such as religious leaders, teachers, and government officials. These authority figures also had the responsibility to punish those children who violated the norms and traditions of the society. There are a few examples of written codes that specifically spell out the acts that constitute violations, and the punishments given for those youths who violate the codes. For example, Lawrence and Hemmens (2008, p. 20) note, "The Code of Hammurabi some 4,000 years ago (2270 B.C.) included reference to runaways, children who disobeyed their parents, and sons who cursed their fathers." The authors continue by stating that Roman civil law and canon (church) law 2000 years ago distinguished between juveniles and adults based on the idea of "age of responsibility." The unwritten "common law" developed in England in the eleventh and twelfth centuries was an integration of the traditional laws of the Anglo Saxons, canon law, and Roman law. These laws were generally not codified. If there was confusion on the meaning of the law, judges would provide the interpretation. English laws held children as young as 10 who committed criminal acts subject to the same penalties as adult offenders. Shoemaker (2009, p. 13) mentioned that children as young as seven could be held responsible for their behavior. Based on the common law, children who reached the age of seven were generally considered to know the difference between right and wrong and thus could make a moral judgement on an action. Portman (1982, p. 13) contends that the age of seven was selected as the age that children could make moral judgments because this was the age that children had command of speech. Portman suggests that age seven was the end of the period of innocence in a child's development and responsibility for one's actions started at this age.

The term "juvenile delinquent" commonly refers to a young person, usually a teenager, who has committed acts at variance with the laws or norms of a particular group or area. The idea of considering "juvenile delinquents" somehow different from adult lawbreakers has been in vogue only since the middle of the nineteenth century and is closely related to the contemporary conception of childhood and adolescence as periods of life distinct from adulthood. Before the mid-nineteenth century, children who came into contact with the police or the courts were housed with, and given punishments similar to those given adult offenders. The juvenile court, a unique American creation designed to serve as a "benevolent parent" safeguarding the well-being of children and adolescents, has been in existence for more than a century.

1.2.1   Children in the Middle Ages

The division of the human life cycle into periods of childhood, adolescence, adulthood, middle age and old age is a social phenomenon of relatively recent vintage. According to Rojek and Jensen (1982, p. 25), the life span and life expectancy levels remained rather constant at 25 or 30 years until the fifteenth century, with the majority of babies and young children succumbing to the ravages of such diseases as smallpox or diphtheria or falling victim to malnutrition. The number of children was further controlled and reduced by infanticide and child abandonment, with illegitimate or defective children and even female children being the victims of these fates.

Certain child-care practices also contributed to infant mortality. These included swaddling and wet-nursing. The swaddling procedure is documented in the biblical account of the birth of Jesus Christ, when his mother wrapped him in swaddling clothes and laid him in a manger. Swaddling involves the tight wrapping of the infant's body in cloths, making it virtually impossible for the baby to move its limbs. Explanations for the reasons for this practice include the notion that a child had to be keep warm or the direct sunlight was bad for the baby's skin, but the practice may have been used as a matter of convenience, since it prevented the child from moving away from the spot where it was placed. The dangers to children in this practice, in addition to the possible retardation of the physical development of the child because of the restrictions in body movement, were the health hazards caused by infrequent washing and changing of the waste materials discharged by the infant (Robertson 1974, p. 411).

The use of wet nurses, another common practice during the late middle ages, was practiced by those families having the wealth to afford either hiring a woman for this role or using a servant. The child was nursed by the substitute parent almost from birth. The seeming lack of interest by the parents of both the upper classes and the lower social-economic classes having close contact with their children during the middle ages can be accounted for by a number of factors, including being totally preoccupied with providing the food, clothing, and shelter to survive, as well as not expecting the child to live beyond childhood and thus developing a psychological defense mechanism to protect them from the grief if the child were to die. The birth of many children and the probability that quite a number of them would die before reaching adulthood was accepted as a matter of fact. During the middle ages, and also during other periods of history in various societies, many children grew up with and were socialized by persons other than members of their immediate family. Similar practices were used in the American South up until the Civil War, when children on large plantations were nursed and cared for by slaves and spent a great deal of time growing up in their company.

During the medieval period of European history, various historians have documented that children were generally perceived as young adults in terms of work, play, and relationships. The male head of the family had almost complete control of all of the members of the family, including his wife, and punishment of the children in the family for deviant behavior, including most acts that were considered criminal, was given by the family head. Punishments were generally harsh, consisting of corporal punishment and even death in extreme cases.

The value of children in the Middle Ages was often viewed in material terms. Land-holding families were controlled and governed by the fathers, who had authority over the entire family. Sons were needed to work the land that would someday be inherited by a son or distributed to all of the sons. Daughters in contrast, could be a drain on the family's wealth, especially in those families in which a dowry was expected to be given to the husband when the daughter married. Empey (1982, p. 30) notes that the growth of cities, industrialism, and the development of a middle class resulted in many male children from the lower social-economic stratum being apprenticed to tradesmen and merchants and some having the opportunity to rise above their station by entering the priesthood. Beginning at the age of seven, children were "bound out" and sent into the homes of others to work and learn skills. This practice extended to all social classes, separated a child from the family of kinship for very long periods of time, and further weakening the bond between parents and child. Children who did not serve as apprentices worked the land or, in the case of the female children, assumed household duties similar to those performed by the adult women.

In the Middle Ages, children were not shielded or protected from the realities or difficulties of everyday living. The innocence of children in matters of sex was not safe guarded and there is documented evidence that children were frequently the objects of sexual abuse. The socialization of young children, including those of the well-to-do families, who lived in crowded dwellings, made them almost certain to be exposed to sexual activity at an early age. Children who failed to work, or who were found to be disobedient or rebellious, were subjected to beatings. If they were found to have committed a serious crime, they were subjected to an authority other than the male head of the household. If convicted, the punishment received could very likely be similar to that of an adult convicted of a crime of the same gravity.

1.2.2   The Renaissance and the Development of Interest in Children

Historians note that an increased interest in children can be detected beginning in the thirteenth century and becoming apparent in the fifteenth century, the age of the Renaissance. The historical indicators include the introduction into various languages of words describing children as separate or different from adults and the depiction of children in paintings in a realistic manner, rather than as small bodies with adult faces. The many realistic representations of the Madonna and Child in Renaissance art are examples of this change. As the Renaissance and the Enlightenment progressed, a renewed interest in learning and the extension of the privilege of education to persons other than nobles and the clergy created a desire to begin formal education as early as possible and to set aside a period of a youth's life for schooling.

The variety of ideas discussed and debated at the time of the Protestant Reformation also had an influence on the handling and treatment of children. The concept of original sin was stressed, highlighting the need to shape an individual's moral development virtually from the moment of birth. This created an interest in training children at much earlier ages than was formerly the case. Their instruction involved not only moral training, but also education and discipline. Children began to be viewed as different from adults and in need of intensive supervision and attention.

Shoemaker (2009, p. 13) notes that societal views of children changed in seventeenth century Europe. He states, "Now, instead of being viewed as miniature adults, so to speak, children were beginning to be seen as young innocents, and their moral and spiritual development became matters of concern and importance to adults and leaders. Off-color jokes and displays of sexual body parts were considered immoral and were to be avoided in European countries. Sexual modesty was becoming the norm for juveniles. Children were considered weak and in need of guidance and adult supervision."

The movement from an agrarian to an industrialized society also contributed to the emergence of a concept of childhood. The differentiation of skills and occupations created a need for better educated and skilled workers, so public education began to be introduced. Young people placed in schools were removed from the constant association and identification with adults that had been the norm under the apprenticeship system. Industrialization created an urbanizing trend, with families forsaking life on the land to move to cities. Parents brought their children with them to the cities and kept them in their own households for longer periods of time, creating more intense and prolonged contact between parents and children. Although children were used as workers in factories and mines beginning at very early ages, continued urbanization provided large numbers of adults who competed for these jobs. As the mechanization of tasks became more complex, a number of the activities performed by children were no longer needed. Many children were subsequently removed from the labor force and placed in schools, where they were differentiated by age and status from adults. The notion that the activities of children should be different from those of adults was further reinforced.

The ideals of democracy, as expressed by the leading figures of the French and American Revolutions, also contributed to patterns of behavior that resulted in the conception of childhood and adolescence as distinct and privileged periods. Education was seen as the vehicle by which children rich and poor could be given equal opportunities for virtually unlimited social, esthetic, political, and moral achievement.

1.2.3 Childhood in Colonial America

In Puritan society, the handling of children was dominated by the belief that a child is a creature whose tendency to mischief and sin must be repressed by careful training and discipline. Children and servants were viewed in the same manner in this regard. The family had the responsibility for seeing that they conformed to norms. If the family failed, the church or the community intervened through the use of publicly applied punishments and sanctions. The Massachusetts Stubborn Child Law, enacted in 1646, detailed severe punishments for youths who were disobedient toward their parents, for rude or disorderly children, and for children who profaned the Sabbath. Whipping was the most commonly applied punishment, and parents could be fined if their children were found guilty of stealing (Thornton, James, & Doerner, 1982, p. 8). Incorrigibility was viewed as a capital offense for certain children. The Connecticut Blue Laws of 1650 contained the following legal remedy for such behavior:

> If any man have a stubborne and rebellious sonne of sufficient years and understanding which will not obey the voice of his father or the voice of his mother, and that when they have chastised him will not harken unto them, then may his father and mother lay hold of him and bring him to the Magistrates assembled in Courte, and testify unto them that their sonne is stubborn and rebellious and will not obey their voice and Chastisement, but lives in sundry notorious Crimes, such a sonne shall be put to death (Cole, 1974, p. 13).

Work was the chief activity of Puritan children, and they were introduced to it early in life. The Puritans brought the apprenticeship system with them from England, but gradually the more affluent families abandoned its use for their children in favor of schooling. There were few dependent or homeless children. Social control of all children was handled within the family or the local community.

Methods of controlling children throughout the American colonies were similar to those used in New England, although the other colonies had no special punishments or laws that applied only to children. Youths involved in serious offenses received the same penalties as adults, and children could be put to death for certain offenses. Disobedience to parents was regarded as evidence that a child was on the path to a life of waywardness and sin. Benjamin Wadsworth, author of a popular treatise of child rearing, "The Well Ordered Family," published in 1712, noted,

> When children are disobedient to parents, God is often provoked to leave them to those sins which bring them to the greatest shame and misery…. When person have been brought to die at the gallows, how often have they confessed that disobedience to parents led them to those crimes (Rothman, 1971, p. 16).

Execution sermons were used as a powerful warning to all citizens of the consequences of sin, and execution of children had particular significance for the young. On one such occasion in Connecticut, the minister stated the message clearly:

> Let all children… beware of disobedience…. Appetites and passions unrestricted in childhood become furious in youth; and ensure dishonor, disease, and an untimely death (Rothman, 1971, p. 17).

During the Colonial period, the emphasis on a strong family life, religion, and the work ethic fostered a climate of rigid social control of children.

1.2.4 Childhood During the Period of Industrialization and Immigration

Feld (1999, p. 5) claims that economic development in the United States during the nineteenth century resulted in changes in the perspective on the role of children. He states, "Economic modernization during the nineteenth century brought with it changes in family structure, altered the function of the family in society, and fostered a new cultural conception of childhood. Families became more private, women's roles more domestic, and childhood and adolescence emerged as distinct developmental stages." During the late nineteenth century and early twentieth century. Industrialism continued to develop, as well as urbanization in the United States as well as in Europe. Millions of immigrants came to the United States from all corners of the globe. They were seeking employment and a better standard of living than that which they experienced in "the old country." During this period in American history, a social and political movement referred to as the Progressive Movement emerged. In reference to this movement, Feld (1999, p. 5) states, "Progressivism encompassed a host of ideologies and addressed issues ranging from economic regulation to criminal justice and social and political reform." The notion that the state could cure many of the maladies that confronted American society at that time, including those than afflicted the poor families of recent immigrants, resulted in the "Child Savers" movement and eventually the establishment of a justice system for children separate from that of the justice system for adults.

During the nineteenth century, the United States experienced an expansion in population that made the closely knit family life of small towns and rural communities experienced in earlier periods during the development of the United States difficult to maintain. After the American Revolution, waves of immigrants from Europe came to the new country and predominately settled in the urban centers of the Northeast and Midwest. Between 1850 and 1900, the urban population increased by 700%. Those in positions of control viewed the resulting overcrowding, poverty, and increase in crime with alarm, feeling that the ideals of the stable family and community life were threatened. Children who lived in crowded city tenement buildings could not be assigned the types of work so readily available in rural settings. It appeared to the "established generation" that the children of the recent immigrants were lazy, lacked ambition, unruly, and lacking in moral training. Those juvenile lawbreakers who were arrested, even if the offense was minor, were tried in the criminal courts, housed with adult offenders in jails, and imprisoned with adult criminals. The harsh response to juvenile misbehavior resulted in the physical and sexual exploitation of children housed in jails and prisons as well as the fostering of their learning how to become a successful criminal. As the number of homeless children increased, the need to provide for their care and supervision promoted one of the key movements in the history of the control of children—the creation of the "Houses of Refuge."

1.3 Houses of Refuge

New York was the first state to respond to the pressures for removing children from prisons and jails and for establishing places of residence for homeless youths. In 1824, the New York legislature granted a charter to the Society for the Reformation of Juvenile Delinquents, authorizing it to build and maintain a House of Refuge. The goals of the Society were twofold: to rescue children of the poor, whether deviant or homeless, from the influence of adult criminals encountered in the courts and jails, and to provide them with "homelike" care and discipline to arrest and reverse their movement toward criminality (Lerman, 1970, pp. 12–14). Houses of Refuge were soon built in Philadelphia, Boston, and other major cities. They were viewed as the panacea for correcting the evils afflicting youths in a changing society. Private orphan asylums were also established. By 1810, New York State alone had 27 public and private childcare institutions (Rothman, 1971, p. 207).

Admission to an orphan asylum or a House of Refuge was not contingent upon proved deviant behavior or lack of parental control.

> The trustees quickly spread their nets to catch a wide variety of dependent children. They admitted the abandoned as well as the orphaned child and those whose widowed or deserted mothers, hard pressed to make ends meet, had little time for supervision. They accepted minors whose parents were quite alive but very poor and those from families that seemed to be morally, if not financially, inadequate to their tasks... [The House of Refuge], like the orphan asylum, maintained a flexible admissions policy, prepared to accept the commitment decisions of a judicial body, the less formal recommendations of overseers of the poor, or the personal inclination of the head of a household. Its administrators expressed no fear about a possible miscarriage of justice.... A good dose of institutionalization could only work to the child's benefit (Rothman, 1971, pp. 207–209).

Once a child was committed to an orphanage or House of Refuge, his or her release was dependent upon the judgment of the institution's administrators that the child had been reformed or properly trained according to the prevailing moral and ethical precepts. Obedience and conformity were required in these institutions, and strictly applied discipline was considered the best method for preparing children for productive lives. We shall see that the use of indeterminate stays in institutions until youths were judged ready for release by administrators became an established practice of juvenile corrections that has continued to the present time.

1.4   Compulsory Education

The movement toward compulsory education for all children was also important in differentiating childhood and adolescence as distinct life stages. Massachusetts and New York passed compulsory education laws early in the nineteenth century, and by the century's close, compulsory public education for those between the ages of 6 and 16 was the law in many states (Bakan, 1982, pp. 30–31). Public school officials enforced attendance laws and had the right to suspend, expel, or punish students for improper behavior. Compulsory schooling removed young people from their homes and the influence of their parents for long daily periods and brought them under the authority of the state. Laws prohibiting child labor, promoted by the newly organized labor unions, were ineffective at first, but gradually resulted in a substantial reduction in the number of children used in factories and mines, reaffirming the notion that childhood should be devoted to activities different from those of adult life.

1.5 Origins of the Juvenile Court

Although the creation of orphan asylums and Houses of Refuge resulted in the removal of many homeless and uncontrolled children from the public eye, these institutions were incapable of handling the growing number of youths in the crowded cities who, in the eyes of the middle class, presented a serious threat to the public welfare by their idleness, poverty, and criminal activity.

> The low level of "morality" of the new occupants of the burgeoning cities was a matter of frequent comment. Drinking, sexual immorality, vagrancy, and crime were not only intrinsically threatening to orderliness, but were also particularly distressing influences on the young. The rapid breeding, the continuing threat of "street Arabs," evoked a cry that the state intercede in restraining and training the young. (Bakan, 1982, p. 29)

At the same time, social forces were set in motion to separate and differentiate juvenile offenders from adults. The concept of a "juvenile delinquent" as a distinct entity began to emerge.

We noted earlier that in Europe and Colonial America children who broke laws could be treated in the same manner as adult offenders. Under English law, which formed the basis for treatment of juveniles by the courts in America, children under the age of 7 were regarded as incapable of forming criminal intent (*legally mens rea,* "a guilty mind"). A child between the ages of 7 and 14 could be charged with crimes and tried in criminal courts like an adult of it was demonstrated that the child could distinguish between right and wrong. Youths over 14 were considered adults and subject to the criminal law as such. If a child tried as an adult was found guilty, the judge was required to impose the penalty set by law without taking into account the age of the offender (Johnson, 1975, pp. 1-2).

Certain devices were frequently used, however, to save children from the severest penalties of the criminal law. One of these was the chancery court that was developed in the thirteenth and fourteenth centuries. This court operated under the doctrine of *parens patriae* (literally "father of his country"), which was applied to mean that the king, acting through his representative, the chancellor of the court, could depart from the due process of law and, as a benevolent parent, not only exempt children from the penalties set for various criminal offenses but also take control over children who had not committed crimes but were involved in vagrancy, idleness, incorrigibility, or association with undesirable persons. Under the concept of *parens patriae*, all children are regarded as subject to the benevolent protections of the courts. The viability of the principle of *parens patriae* was confirmed in 1838 by a Pennsylvania Supreme Court decision in the case *Ex parte Crouse*. When Mary Ann Crouse was committed to a House of Refuge as unmanageable by her mother, her father appealed the decision on the ground that she had been sent there by decision of a justice of the peace, without a jury trial. The Pennsylvania Supreme Court upheld the commitment, stating that no trial was necessary because the court applying the *parens patriae* principle, was acting in the best interests of the child.

> The object of the charity is reformation, by training its inmates to industry; by imbuing their minds with principles of morality and religion; by furnishing them with means to earn a living, and, above all, by separating them from the corrupting influence of improper associates. To this

end may not the natural parents, when unequal to the task of education, or unworthy of it, be superseded by the *parens patriae* or common guardian of the community? It is to be remembered that the public has a paramount interest in the virtue and knowledge of its members, and that of strict right, the business of education belongs to it (Ex parte Crouse, 1838, p. 9).

In England, the chancery court, with its *parens patriae* orientation, was used chiefly as a vehicle for disposing of or safeguarding the estates of children whose wealthy parents had died before the children reached the age of majority. In the late nineteenth century, certain social philosophers in the United State seized upon the idea as the basis for the development of a new kind of court that would consider only the cases and behavior of juveniles.

1.5.1 The Child Savers

A group of reformers, characterized as the "child savers," was instrumental in pressuring various state legislatures to provide separate detention facilities and hearings for juveniles, and eventually to establish juvenile courts. The child savers, among whom Jane Addams and Louise DeKoven Bowen are the best known, were upper- and middle-class women who were dedicated to improving the lot of the less fortunate and to bringing the poverty-stricken children they encountered closer to middle class standards of morality and conduct. They viewed juvenile delinquency as the outgrowth of slum living and the horrible conditions under which youths labored in the factories and mines (Platt, 1969, p. 4). Although many of these women were persons of high principles who were genuinely concerned about the needs and problems of the poor, the Child Saving Movement was also motivated by the desire to control the lower classes and preserve the privileged position of its middle-class advocates. Some viewed these troublesome juveniles as a genuine present and future threat to society and sought to gain influence over their lives as a means of self-protection and preservation. The prevailing notion among the child savers was that these children just be brought under proper influences as soon as possible so that they could be exposed to middle class morality and work habits and brought into conformity with accepted lifestyles. They reasoned that such intervention in the lives of children could be made without regard for legal procedures or the rights of children, since they were acting in the children's best interest.

> The unique character of the Child Saving Movement was its concern for predelinquent offenders… and its claim that it could transform potential criminals into respectable citizens by training them in "habits of industry, self-control, and obedience to law." This policy justified the diminishing of traditional procedures and allowed police, judges, probation officers, and truant officers to work together without legal hindrance. If children were to be rescued, it was important that the rescuers be free to pursue their mission without the interference of defense lawyers and due process. Delinquents had to be saved, transformed, and reconstituted. (Platt in Rojek and Jensen, 1982, p. 41)

The efforts of the reformers soon bore fruit. In 1870, separate hearings were required for juveniles brought to trial in Boston. Seven years later, the New York Society for the Prevention of Cruelty to Children was successful in gaining a prohibition on housing youths under the age of 16 in any prison, jail, or courtroom, where adult offenders were kept or tried, unless officers were present at all times (Lou, 1927, p. 14).

1.5.2   Creation of the First Juvenile Court

Legislation that is generally credited with creating the first juvenile court in the United States was enacted on July 1, 1899 by the Illinois legislature. An Act to Regulate the Treatment and Control of Dependent, Neglected, and Delinquent Children provided that in any jurisdiction with a population of 500,000 or over, one circuit judge should be designated to hear all juvenile cases in a separate courtroom, with its own records. Since Cook County (Chicago) was the only jurisdiction with a population this size, it became the site of the first juvenile court. The jurisdiction of this court extended to delinquent, neglected, and dependent children. The Act stated that:

> The words "dependent child" and "neglected child" shall mean any child who for any reason is destitute or homeless or abandoned; or dependent upon the public for support; or has not proper parental care or guardianship; or who habitually begs or receives alms; or who is found living in any house of ill fame or with any vicious or disreputable person; or whose home, by reason of neglect, cruelty, or depravity on the part of its parents, guardian, or other person in whose care it may be, is an unfit place for such a child; and any child under the age of 8 years who is found peddling or selling any article or singing or playing any musical instrument upon the streets or giving any public entertainment.

The Act specified appropriate dispositions for youths found to be dependent, neglected, or delinquent (Laws, 1899, pp. 131–137, Sections 1, 7, 9).

In the same years, the Colorado School Laws provided that youthful offenders would be charged with improper conduct, rather than with crimes, and that truant officers or teachers would supervise their activities (Robinson, 1964, pp. 250–251). The idea of juvenile courts caught on rapidly. By 1932, there were more than 600 juvenile courts and over 2000 juvenile sessions of other courts. Wyoming was the last state to establish a juvenile court system, in 1945 (U. S. Children's Bureau 1970, p. 67).

1.6   Extent of Delinquency

Behavior by a society's young people that deviates from accepted standards will often be tolerated or even encouraged it does not appear to threaten the well-being of the society as a whole. When those in authority decide that certain actions by some youths are threatening to the common good, however, the behavior is no longer tolerated and attempts are made to suppress it and punish the violators. If "normal" behavior is behavior that is considered acceptable at a particular time in a particular society, then a juvenile delinquent is, in a sociological sense, "any child who deviates from normal behavior so as to endanger him/herself or the community."

Deviant behavior of a youth can be defined as any type of behavior committed by a person in a specified age category that violates the norms (standards of proper behavior) of the controlling group. If one accepts this broad definition, juveniles could be considered deviant if they adopted modes of hairstyle, dress, or actions opposed to the standards set by those in authority. For example, if the policies of the administration of a school may state that boys are not allowed to wear their hair long, or girls are not allowed to wear short skirts to school. Those who defy these rules are subject to the penalties, including a possible suspension, that are given to those who deviate from the rules. Thus the types of behavior by youth that are defined as unacceptable may range from extremely antisocial actions or only minor nonconformity; and the society's response to this youthful behavior may range from strong condemnation to mild disapproval. In a highly urbanized, mobile, industrial society, the degree of conformity to standards and values held by the society is not absolute. Children are not expected to be perfect in their behavior and deviation is tolerated if the behavior is not viewed by adults as particularly threatening. In fact, children who conform exactly to the expectations set up for them tend to be viewed by adults and their peers as somewhat abnormal. Occasional disobedience, mischief, violating parents' or the city's curfew, or fighting when provoked generally do not lead to an official response and punishment. However, as the degree of nonconforming behavior moves farther away from accepted standards the tolerance of such behavior declines. Even though a youth may not be subject to official action at this stage, he or she may be characterized by adults as "a bad influence," or "looking for trouble." The less serious misbehavior of a youth may be handled by the parents, the school administration, or even by the police. The more serious misbehavior will general result in formal involvement with the juvenile justice system. When youthful misbehavior reaches the point of frequent dishonesty, deceitful or destructive activity, theft, or serious assault, the violator will begin to feel the full weight of public disapproval. Parents and school officials may feel inadequate to handle the problems and the youth is likely to become involved with the juvenile justice system. The involvement may be the result of a complaint made by a parent, victim of the offender, or by a law enforcement official.

An additional consideration is the fact that the acceptable standards of behavior for youths vary from society to society and even within the same society. The deviant behavior of children of different social-economic groups, races, and gender may be handled differently. In a narrower sense, a juvenile (Black, 1991, p. 599, 560) is defined as "A young person who has not yet attained the age at which he or she should be treated as an adult for purposes of criminal law," and a juvenile delinquent is, "a minor involved in illegal behavior who falls under a statutory age limit." Neither one of these definitions eliminates all of the confusion regarding who is a juvenile delinquent. A wide variety of acts committed by a juvenile may violate the norms of a person who has authority over the juvenile, such as a parent, For example, a 15-year-old girl who sneaks out at night to meet with an older man, even though her parents have forbidden her to meet with the man, violates the norms of the parent, but her behavior does not constitute delinquency, since she has not broken a criminal law. Nevertheless, she can be subject to the authority of a juvenile court if her parents decide to file a charge of disobedience, Another problem with defining juvenile delinquency centers on the fact that the large majority of youths who commit an act that is defined as criminal are never detected and even many of those who are detected are never processed through the juvenile justice system. Should the term "juvenile delinquent" be limited to those who are caught, arrested, and found to be delinquent in a court, or should the term be extended to any youth who has committed a criminal act?

Mature adults, when reflecting on their childhood and particularly on their adolescence years, may recall behavior they engaged in that would constitute some type of violation of the law. In some instances they probably were not even aware that their actions were law violations. In addition, some of the delinquent behavior they engaged in, such as minor property destruction, trespassing and theft, shoplifting, and simple assault were not motivated by any particular reason. If questioned about the incident, they might rationalize and attribute the incident to being a prank, they were bored, or they were just following the behavior of others in the group who were the leaders.

The following list of activities shown in Box 1.1 denotes some of the activities that an offense if committed by a person in the age group designed juvenile. Some of these actions would not be considered criminal if committed by an adult.

Box 1.1 Criminal and Juvenile Offenses
Truant from school
Making harassing or threatening telephone or Internet messages
Staying out past curfew
Running away from home
Purchasing or drinking wine, beer, or liquor
Buying, using, or selling illicit drugs
Setting fire to buildings, or other types of property
Driving a car without a license
Driving recklessly
Using threat of force to get something from someone else
Drag racing
Taking or riding in a person's car without permission
Shoplifting an item from a store
Sneaking into a movie theater without paying the admission charge
Carrying a weapon without having a permit to carry the weapon
Bringing a weapon, illicit drugs into a facility in which the item is prohibited
Taking part in a gang fight
Hitting another person with one's fists
Accepting something from another person, knowing that the item was stolen
Trespassing
Sending in a false fire alarm
Deliberately disobeying parents
Forcing another person to engage in a sexual act
Killing another person with a deadly weapon
Breaking into or forcibly entering a residence or place of business

As shown above, the severity of the acts for which a juvenile could be sanctioned ranges from one extreme, for example murder, to the other extreme, such as being disobedient to one's parents. Box 1.2 illustrates several cases of juvenile behavior exemplifying these extremes:

Box 1.2
Case 1: Teens held in deadly shooting
"Two teen age boys were arrested in Canton in the fatal shooting of a man during a South Akron home invasion June 26 that wounded three other occupants." ……. Both were placed into the custody of the Summit County Juvenile Detention Center. "The two were wanted on warrants of aggravated burglary and murder." (Akron Beacon Journal, Wednesday, July 3, 2019-B1)
Case 2: Hangout turns deadly
"After sundown Wednesday, a group of seven or eight teenagers escaped the cold in the basement of a two-story red-brick duplex on Grand Avenue, goofing around an old television in the laundry room.

On Thursday, the smell of iron clung to the cold floor where the blood of two boys shot in the head, one dead and the other hospitalized, had dried in the thick streaks on the cement.

Hysterical, angry and distraught, witnesses-including the mother of two girls who live in the duplex-said Thursday that none of the kids should have been there, especially not a boy suspected of entering through a side door and bringing a gun into the Highland Square Home. The boy's mother could not be reached.

Witnesses, who heard the story from the two girls who live there, said the boys were not welcome in the home, and they and two other girls there were not supposed to be hanging out with them in the basement. But the adults said, they could not control kids they described as "acting the fool." Kendrick lashed the gun, which went off, striking the 14-year-old boy in the head. Then, from the other end of the basement, he shot himself in the head. Kendrick was enrolled in Akron Public Schools' YMCA-operated Phoenix program for juveniles with behavioral, criminal and disciplinary issues. (Doug Livingston, Akron Beacon Journal, November 30, 2018, A1, A4)
Case 3: Boy Bullied is Not Allowed to Go to School
"The juvenile court was notified by the school administration that Steven, a 10h grade student, had been truant from school for 20 days. Steven's mother claimed that she was aware of the truancy and in fact would not allow Steven to attend school because he was the constant target of bullies who threatened him, stole his money, and beat him. Steven's mother stated that she informed their school principal about what was happening, but was told they could not do anything to the boys who were bullying Steve unless they were caught in the act."
(Kratcoski, 2012, p. 4)

1.7 The Concept Juvenile

Although any of the actions listed above, as well as numerous others, may result in action by a legal authority, the person committing the act is not normally considered a juvenile delinquent, unless the act is detected and some response is taken by a court having jurisdiction. The court having jurisdiction is determined by the age of the offender and the specific statute of the state code that defines the concept "juvenile."

The statutes of the 50 states and the District of Columbia use age as a defining characteristic of what categories of youth are subject to the original jurisdiction of the juvenile court if they had committed an offense. Sickmund and Puzzanchera (2014, p. 93) found that "In most states, the juvenile court has original jurisdiction over all youth charged with a law violation who were younger than age 18 at the time of the offense, arrest, or referral to court. Since 1975, five states have changed their age criteria. Alabama raised its upper age limit from 15 to 16 in 1976 and to 17 in 1977; Wyoming lowered its upper age limit from 18 to 17 in 1993; New Hampshire and Wisconsin lowered their upper age limit from 17 to 16 in 1996; and in 2007 passed a law that gradually raised its upper age from 15 to 17 by July 1, 2012." Currently, two states have 15 as the upper age limit, 11 states have 16 as the upper age limit and the remaining states, 37, and the District of Columbia have 17 as the upper age limit for youths who have committed an offense that would be criminal if committed by an adult.

Sickmund and Puzzanchera (2014) note that some states have original jurisdiction over youths who commit a status offense (an act that would not be defined as criminal if committed by an adult), or who are found to be abused or dependent that exceeds the upper age of jurisdiction for youth who commit a delinquent offense. In those states where the age of the juvenile court's original jurisdiction differs from that of the age of delinquency, the most common upper age is 20.

Typically, if a youth is under the jurisdiction of the juvenile court for an offense committed before the age of 18 and is under supervision of the court or a designated agency, the court has the authority to extend its jurisdiction until the youth reaches the age of 21. This jurisdiction can be extended beyond the age of 21 in certain cases, and in several states the jurisdiction can be transferred to agencies of the adult criminal system.

In regard to the lower age for holding a youth responsible for an illegal act, Sickmund and Puzzanchera (2014, p. 93) note that only 16 states have set a lower limit for presuming that a child is incapable of criminal intent and thus should not be held responsible for his/her behavior. Two states have established the age of 6, four states the age of 7 and 11 states use the age of 10 as the lower age for exempting a youth from prosecution and punishment for an illegal act. The remaining states rely on case law and common law to make a determination if a youth is capable of criminal intent.

1.7.1   Status Offenders

Many young people are arrested, referred to juvenile court, and even institutional-ized for activities that would not be considered criminal for adults, such as truancy, incorrigibility, running away from home, violations of curfew laws, purchasing and drinking of alcoholic beverages, or engaging in various sexual acts. In the sections of the penal codes pertaining to juveniles, a distinction is made between status and delinquent offenders.

According to Sickmund and Puzzanchera (2014, p. 179), "Some states have decriminalized some of these behaviors. In these states, the behaviors are no longer violations. Juveniles who engage in the behaviors may be classified as dependent children, which gives child protective service agencies rather than juvenile courts the primary responsibility for responding to this population."

Some states have developed such categories as Minors in Need of Supervision (MINS, Children in Need of Supervision (CHINS) or Juveniles in Need of Supervision (JINS) to differentiate status offenders from delinquent offenders. Even though the states may make a distinction between delinquent and status offenders, the status offenders are still subject to juvenile court jurisdiction unless the state has decriminalized these offenses.

Status offending can have more serious repercussions for a child if that child has violated an order of the court by committing a new offense or failed to adhere to the sanctions given by the court. Such actions could lead to the court declaring the child a delinquent offender and, depending on the circumstances, even lead to an out of home placement.

Despite the changes in the laws governing status offenders and the trend toward diversion of such offenders from juvenile justice processing, the number of status offenders referred to the juvenile court has increased in recent years. Sickmund and Puzzanchera (2014, p. 179) report that the juvenile court's formal status caseload increased by 6% between 1995 and 2010. In 2010, the largest numbers of referrals and formal processing for status offenders was for truancy, followed by liquor law violations, ungovernable behavior, runaway cases, curfew violations, and other offenses such as smoking tobacco and violation of a court order.

The 137,000 cases of status offenders formally processed by the juvenile courts represent a very small portion of the actual number of offenses. As will be shown in later chapters, almost every child will commit at least one offense designated a sta-tus offense at some time during their childhood. The large majority of offenders are never detected and those who are detected are handled by their parents, school authorities, or diverted from the juvenile justice system.

1.8   Measuring Juvenile Delinquency

The total number of offenses by juveniles in any given period of time is impossible to ascertain. Although the Federal Bureau of Investigation (FBI) records and statisti-cally analyzes the number of juveniles arrested for various offenses each year, the illegal behavior by juveniles that is not detected or reported to the police is not accounted for in any statistical report. Information about the amount and nature of juvenile misbehavior comes from three major sources. Official statistical information is provided by police departments to the FBI and reports by other agencies that deal with juvenile offenders are summarized by the Department of Justice. Another way of obtaining information on juvenile delinquency is through surveys that ask the young respondents whether they have committed acts that resulted in or could have resulted in an arrest or a referral to the juvenile court. The findings of such surveys are called "self-reported delinquency" data. Research of this type has certain shortcomings, including the difficulty of knowing whether youths are over-reporting or under-reporting the amount and types of deviant behavior in which they have engaged. Often the respondents may forget the number and types of illegal behavior they have engaged in and thus their responses may not be an accurate accounting of their behavior. Some researchers who have conducted self-reported delinquency research have sought to verify their results by comparing their findings with official statistics collected by the courts or by the police. However, this technique has its limitations because it does not allow for the anonymity that respondents need if they are to reply to surveys truthfully, without fear of punishment if identified by an authority. Crime victimization surveys provide another source of information about offenses committed by juveniles. These surveys, usually conducted by telephone, solicit information from a random sample of people about their experiences as victims of crime Those surveyed are asked to provide information on the types and numbers of offenses committed against them and to estimate the ages of the offenders. Again, the possibility of ascertaining the actual amount and nature of juvenile illegal activity is limited, since the victim must be willing to discuss the crime and must be able to identify the perpetrator, or at least be able to estimate the age of the offender in the case of stranger to stranger victimization.

1.9 Officially Recorded Delinquency

In its Uniform Crime Report, *Crime in the United States*, the FBI provides information on the arrests made by law enforcement agencies in the United States during a year. These annual arrest figures do not reflect the actual number of persons arrested during the year, since a person could be arrested several times during that year for a number of different offenses occurring at different time periods.

The Uniform Crime Report provides information on the ages of those arrested. In regard to juveniles, the number of arrests of youth under age 18 is provided in the table pertaining to the age of the person arrested. As mentioned earlier in the chapter, the upper age limit for the large majority of the states, including the federal law is seventeen. Table 1.1 compares the proportion of the total arrests of juvenile for the year 2001 with the proportion of total arrests of juveniles for the year 2016.

When the two time periods are compared, is it evident that there has been a substantial reduction in the proportion of arrests for juveniles for all types of offenses. This change may be a reflection of the smaller number of youths in the under 18 age

Table 1.1   Arrests of youth age 17 and under

Juvenile arrests, 2001	Juvenile arrests 2016	Change
17%	8%	−9.0%
Juvenile arrests violent crimes	**Juvenile arrests violent crimes**	**Change**
15%	11.1	−3.9
Juvenile arrests property crimes	**Juvenile arrests property crimes**	**Change**
30%	13.6	−16.4
Juvenile arrests for drug abuse	**Juvenile arrests for drug abuse**	**Change**
13%	6.3%	−6.7%

The 2001 figures have been rounded to the nearest percentage

category in 2016 compared to 2001, or a change in the way the juvenile authorities, including the police, respond to young offenders. The use of diversion and informal sanctions by the police in their response to juveniles who commit crimes, particularly those pertaining to drug, alcohol related violations and minor property offenses might be reflected in the reduction of arrests for some offenses. For example, the proportion of all arrests in 2002 for disorderly conduct for juveniles was 28% and in 2016 the proportion was 17.8%. The proportion of all arrests for motor vehicle theft for juveniles in 2001 was 33% and the proportion of arrests of juveniles in 2016 for this offense was 19.8%, a 13.2 decrease. Other serious crimes such as murder and nonnegligent manslaughter, rape, robbery, and aggravated assault also showed a significant decrease in the proportion of arrests for juveniles when the figures for 2001 and 2016 are compared. Of course, the proportion of arrests for status offenses did not change when 2001 is compared with 2016. For example, 100% of arrests for curfew and loitering law violations and for running away in 2001 were juveniles under the age of 18 and in 2016 there was the same proportion of juvenile arrests for these offenses.

1.9.1   Comparison of Arrests of Female and Male Juveniles

The statistics on arrests of youths under 18 years of age collected in the Uniform Crime Report—*Crime in America*, as well as information collected in self-report studies of delinquency reveal that, with the exception of running away and prostitution/commercialized vice, females commit fewer offenses than males in every juvenile offense category. However, the differences in the amount of delinquency by gender appears to be narrowing. For example, the ratio of male to female arrests of juveniles was 6 to 1 in 1960 and remained approximately 3.5 to 1 in the 1970s, 1980s, and 1990s and the ratio dropped to 2.5 males under 18 arrested in 2001 to 1 female under 18 arrested. In 2012 (Uniform Crime Report, 2012, Table 33) males under 18 accounted for 10.3% of all arrests and females under 18 accounted for 4.0% of all arrests. Thus the ratio of arrests for males and females remained approximately the same as in the year 2001. The trend toward females engaging in violent crimes, such as assaults, as well as property crimes and public order crimes that became apparent in the late early twentieth century has continued. For example, in 2012, 7% of males under 18 were arrested for aggravated assault and 3% of females under 18 were arrested for aggravated assault, a 2.1 to 1 ratio. The arrests of males under 18 for the property crime of larceny-theft was 24.2% of total arrests, while the arrests for females under 18 for larceny-theft in 2012 was 17.2%. The arrests for drug abuse violations of males under 18 in 2012 was 11.3% and the arrests for drug abuse violations was for females in 2012 was 2.0%.

Loeber et al. (2016, pp, 38, 39) completed a study of the offending patterns of a large sample of females who were in the transition from child to young adulthood. They focused on the prevalence, frequency, and duration of the offenses by individuals in the study. In regard to prevalence, they found that the large majority of the females in the study reported that they did not offend. The typical age-crime curve for those who did engage in violent crimes increased from age 11 to a peak at ages 14-15 and then declined, while the prevalence of drug dealing increased linearly from age 12 to age 19. The frequency of self-reported offending by active offenders increased in an almost linear fashion from age 11 to 18, and the duration of delinquent offending for many of the female offenders was very short. One fifth of the females reported that they have committed only one offense. The average career length of those who started offending between the ages of 11 and 14 was 2.7 years, compared to less than 1 year for those who started offending between ages 15 and 19. In addition, the researchers found that those females that started their criminal career at an early age (11-14) tended to have more offenses, higher recidivism and a longer career in crime and delinquency.

1.10   Referrals to the Juvenile Courts

Another source of officially recorded statistics on juvenile offenders is Juvenile Court Statistics, compiled by the National Center for Juvenile Justice for the Office of Juvenile Justice and Delinquency Prevention within the U.S. Department of Justice. According to Snyder and Sickmund (1999, p. 166), nearly two million cases of persons under the age 18 were referred to the juvenile courts in that year. Ninety-two percent of these cases were for delinquency and 8% for status offenses. More than three-fourths of the referrals for delinquency were males and more than one-half of the referrals for status offenses were males. For 2010, Sickmund and Puzzanchera (2014, p. 151) reported that the juvenile courts handled 1.4 million delinquency cases, a decrease of almost 30%. The number of status offenses handled by the juvenile courts also declined. Sickmund and Puzzanchera (2014, p. 179) note, "Between 1995 and 2002, the formally handled status offense caseload increased considerably (5%) and then declined 33% through 2010." The most frequent referrals of youth to the juvenile courts for status offenses are for truancy and for liquor law violations.

Even if youths come to the attention of the police, there is a good chance that they will escape processing by the juvenile court and thus avoid the "juvenile delinquent" label. The majority of police contacts with youths are handled informally, with the youths being given warnings, ordered to leave the area if the complaint is related to disturbing the peace, trespassing, or disorderly conduct, or, if the youths are is taken into custody, they are released to their parents after being given a warning.

Although in any given year the likelihood of a youth being referred to a juvenile court for an offense is relatively small (1 in 25), if the behavior of the youth is followed through the age period of 10 through 17, the likelihood for a youth to have some contact with the juvenile court increases significantly. Two longitudinal studies (Tracy, et al., 1985, p. 5) of boys in the city of Philadelphia, involving a sample of youths born in 1945 and another sample of youths born in 1958, found that 33% of the first group and 35% of the second group had at least one police contact before reaching their 18th birthday.

In more recent research, Loeber, Farrington, Stouthamer-Loeber, and White (2008) found in their research on youth in the Pittsburgh Youth Study that the percentage of the youths who claimed to have committed a serious violent crime on the self-report survey was much higher than the percentage of youth arrested and or convicted on the official reports. Jennings, Loeber, Pardini, Piquero, and Farrington (2018), using the data from the longitudinal study of youth in the Pittsburgh, Pennsylvania area (PYS), compared the number of offenses and the types of offenses of the youth in the sample were compared on official report (arrests) with the number and types of offenses found in the self-report data.

Jennings et al. (2018, p. 27) found a dramatic difference between the number youth who reported that they had committed crimes with the number of youths convicted for crimes during the ages of 10-14. For example, the average number of self-reports for such crimes as moderate theft, serious theft, moderate violence and serious violence was much higher than the average for the number found in the official statistics. They concluded (Jennings et al., 2018, p. 520) that these findings revealed that there are many more self-reported offenders relative to those that are documented. For every one officially recorded offense the PYS cohort participants self-reported committing approximately 15-23 offenses.

1.11   Juveniles Tried as Adult Criminals

Almost all of the states allow juveniles to be tried as adults in criminal courts under certain circumstances. In several states, if the offense is a very serious felony, such as homicide, the juvenile court does not have *original* jurisdiction. Sickmund and Puzzanchera (2014, p. 103) note, "Legislatures transfer large numbers of young offenders to criminal court by enacting statutes that exclude certain cases from original juvenile court jurisdiction. As of the end of the 2011 legislative session, 29 states have statutory exclusion provisions." Sickmund and Puzzanchera (2014, p. 101) state, "As of the end of the 2011 legislative session, a total of 45 states have laws designating some category of cases in which waiver of jurisdiction by juvenile court judges transferred cases to criminal court. Such action is usually in response to a request by the prosecutor. In several states, however, juveniles or their parents may request judicial waiver. In most states, waiver is limited by age and offense boundaries." Sickmund and Puzzanchera (2014, p. 104) after completing a search of the state statutes on this matter, found that 22 states did not have a minimum age for transfer if the youth was being charged with a very serious offenses. For example, for murder the large majority of the states established the age of 14 as the minimum age for transfer. Several states established the ages of 10, 12, and 13 as the minimum age for transfer.

A juvenile may also be tried in an adult court in a case of *concurrent* jurisdiction. In such instances, which usually involve serious, violent, or repeated offenses, the prosecutor has the choice of filing charges against a youth in either the juvenile court or the adult criminal court. The predominant means by which cases involving juveniles come to adult criminal courts is through *judicial waiver*, or transfer from the juvenile court that has original jurisdiction.

In some instances, the criminal court may elect to transfer a case to the juvenile court. For example, a very young child charged with a serious offense would be a candidate for transfer. This process is sometimes termed *reverse waiver*.

In an appendix to the Kent v. U.S. decision, the U.S. Supreme Court set the criteria to be used by states in deciding on transfers of juveniles to criminal court for trial. These criteria include the seriousness of the alleged offense and the need to protect the community, whether the alleged offense was against persons or against property, with greater weight given to offenses against persons, the likelihood that prosecuting the case will yield a conviction whether adults involved in the alleged offense will be charged in criminal court, the sophistication and maturity of the juvenile, and the previous history and record of the juvenile (Kent v. U.S., 1966).

The number of juveniles tried in the criminal courts is difficult to ascertain. One estimate (Sickmund & Puzzanchera, 2014, p. 103) shows that the number of juvenile offenders held in jails and correctional facilities for adults is not a good basis for determining the number of juveniles tried in the criminal courts, since many of the juveniles may have been found not guilty and others, no doubt the majority, were given probation or some other community sanction. In 2010, juveniles below the age of 18 constituted 1% of the jail population and 1% of the adult correctional institutional population (Sickmund & Puzzanchera, 2014, p. 220).

1.11.1   Self-Reported Delinquency

Self-report studies of delinquency are usually conducted by asking groups of youths to respond anonymously to a check list of acts they may have performed that could, if discovered, have resulted in referral to juvenile authorities. The respondents are asked to indicate if they have engaged in any of these types of behavior and, if so, how often the participants are assured that the information will not be revealed in such a way that they could be identified. Interviews of selected respondents are used at times in the self-report delinquency research for the purpose of illustrating some of the types of delinquent acts admitted to and to explore the youth's motivation for committing the act. Some interviewing most often is used with youths who have already been identified by juvenile justice agencies and are under a justice agency's supervision.

Self-report studies consistently reveal that the amount of juvenile illegal activity is much greater than officially recorded. The Institute of Social Research, located at the University of Michigan, has been collecting data on self-report delinquency over several decade period. In an attempt to record trends in delinquent behavior, using the findings of self-report research projects, Johnston, O' Malley, and Bachman (2002) made an extensive attempt to collect and compare the research on self-reported delinquency, beginning in 1975. Since 1975, annual self-report surveys of high school seniors' behavior have been conducted using a random sample of high school seniors attending public and private schools throughout the United States. The respondents were asked to report their involvement in specific activities during the past 12 months. A comparison of the seniors' responses from 1989 to 2001 reveals only small variations in behavior from year to year. The most frequent offenses committed related to alcohol and drug use (more than three-fourths of the respondents) followed by traffic offenses (almost one-third of the respondents), followed by minor theft and shoplifting (almost one-third of the respondents), with less than 25% of the respondents indicating that they had broken into a house or other dwelling, or engaged in a fight at school or in the community.

Another source of self-report delinquency comes from the National Youth Survey Project. The research by this organization began in 1976, and the first report was printed in 1983. The respondents were contacted for a reassessment of their behavior in succeeding years, when their ages were 18 to 24. Over the years their highest levels of illegal involvement were in alcohol use, public drunkenness, marijuana use, disorderly conduct, truancy, and vandalism. Few of the respondents reported involvement in serious violent crime (murder, rape, aggravated assault, armed robbery) (Elliot, 1983a, pp. 413–422).

The notion that the undetected or unrecorded delinquent behavior by youths generally only pertains to minor offenses was challenged by a self-report study involving high school students and youth incarcerated in a juvenile correctional facility (Kratcoski & Kratcoski, 1977). The mean number of offenses the high school students admitted having committed was almost nine. As expected, the institutionalized youth admitted to a much higher number of offenses, the mean being 15.

There has always been a debate over the worth of self-report delinquency data compared to official data on delinquency. The argument that self-report data can capture information on the deviant behavior of youths that never comes to the attention of the authorities, and that self-report research can record trends to juvenile delinquency, particularly in the case of longitudinal studies, is counteracted by arguments that point out the limitations of self-report research, including the fact that respondents forget behavior, they may not be honest in their responses, they may be too ashamed to report some behavior, or they may fear that their identity will be disclosed. Sickmund and Puzzanchera (2014, p. 60) contend that the use of both self-report and official statistics can be very useful in providing insight into trends in crime and victimization. Using the work of Delbert Elliot to bolster they position, they state that Elliot has argued that to abandon either self-report or official statistics in favor of the other is, "rather shortsighted, to systematically ignore the findings of either is dangerous, particularly when the two measures provide apparently contradictory findings." Elliot stated that "a full understanding of the etiology and development of delinquent behavior is enhanced by using and integrating both self-report and official record research."

1.12 Summary

Juvenile delinquency may be defined as any action by a person considered a juvenile that would make him or her subject to action by the juvenile court. Most young people are involved in some unlawful behavior during the adolescent years, but escape detection, apprehension, or court involvement. Only those who have been officially adjudicated as such by a juvenile court are normally designated "juvenile delinquents."

The definition of the juvenile age status differs in various states. A lower age limit has been set in 16 states; in the others, the age of 7, the common-law minimum for criminal responsibility, is normally applied. The upper age limit of juvenile court jurisdiction is 17 in 37 states and the District of Columbia, 16 in 10 states, and 15 in 3 states. Juveniles guilty of certain serious crimes may be tried in adult criminal courts in every state. This may occur when state statutes give juvenile courts no jurisdiction over certain offenses; when concurrent jurisdiction of the adult and juvenile courts exists and the prosecutor decides to try the case in the adult court; or by judicial waiver, in which the case is transferred from the juvenile court to an adult criminal court.

Juvenile deviation from societal norms has existed throughout history, and it is usually tolerated unless the behavior becomes so extreme that the common good is threatened. As behavior becomes more seriously antisocial, sanctions may be applied by parents or the school, or by police in an unofficial manner. But if such methods fail, arrest and referral to court may follow.

Juveniles may be referred courts for two broad types of offenses. Acts that would also be illegal for adults are termed "delinquent" offenses, violations of regulations that apply only to juveniles are variously known as "status," "unruly," or beyond control" offenses. Both types of offenses can lead to court involvement, adjudication as a delinquent, and even institutionalization. The question of whether status offenses should be removed from juvenile court jurisdiction is a hotly debated issue in juvenile justice. Several states have decriminalized many of the status offenses, including incorrigibility and running away from home, and these problems are referred to children's services agencies.

The actual amount of delinquent activity by juveniles each year is impossible to estimate, since so much of it is not reported to police or made known to the courts.

Self-reported delinquency surveys have shown that delinquent behavior exists in all social environments, and is committed by both males and females. Victimization surveys have revealed that victims of crimes of violence perceived many of the offenders who acted against them either alone or in multiple offender incidents to be juveniles

Official measurements of delinquency have identified crimes of violence in and near schools, gang-related violence, and substance abuse as presenting significant problems. Violent behavior by female juveniles has increased substantially, and minority group members are overrepresented in arrests for both violent and property crimes in relation to their proportion in the population.

Self-report surveys reveal that a large proportion of offenders may have only one contact with justice agencies. Longitudinal research that follows the careers of delinquents finds that, at early age of first offense and first contact with a justice agency are good predictors of further contact with justice agencies. Generally, the younger the age at first offense, the more likely it is that the youth will have a long career in delinquency. Often, the deviant behavior extends into adulthood. This is true for both males and females.

1.13   Discussion Questions

1. Why are officially recorded statistics, such as those found in the FBI's Uniform Crime Report, *Crime in the United States*, misleading when one is trying to determine the amount of juvenile delinquency in the United States?
2. Identify several factors that might account for the increase in violent crime by young females in the United States.
3. Discuss the reasons why the various state legislatures have enacted statutes that have resulted in an increase in the number of juvenile offenders being transferred to the criminal courts.
4. Identify self-report delinquency surveys. How do the results from these surveys help us to understand the extent and types of offenses committed by juveniles and the characteristics of these offenders?
5. Discuss the status of the child during the Middle Ages. How did the status of children change after the industrial revolution?
6. Discuss the role of religion in the moral development of children during the Colonial period of the development of America.
7. Virtually every person in the United States could have been or could be labeled a juvenile offender if his or her behavior history as a juvenile were known to authorities. Discuss.
8. In your opinion, which method of gathering information about delinquent behavior, arrest and juvenile court statistics, victimization surveys, or self-reported delinquency studies most accurately reflects the true amount of juvenile misbehavior that is occurring?

9. What conclusions can be reached regarding the regarding early age at first offense and the continuation of deviant behavior, even into adulthood? Does this apply to both males and females?

10. What are the factors that may explain why the number of youths arrested for delinquent behavior has significantly declined in recent years? Is this true for all types of offenses?

References

Akron Beacon Journal, (2019). *Teens held in deadly shooting,* July 3, 2019, B1

Bakan, D. (1982). Adolescence in American society. In D. Rojek & G. Jensen (Eds.), *Readings in juvenile delinquency* (pp. 30–31). Lexington, MA: D.C. Heath.

Black, H. (1991). *Black's law dictionary* (6th ed.). St. Paul, Minn: West Publishing Co.

Cole, L. (1974). *Our children's keepers*. Greenwick, CT: Fawcett.

Elliot, D. (1983a). *The prevalence and incidence of delinquent behavior:1976-1980*. Boulder, CO: Behavior Research Institute.

Empey, L. (1982). *American delinquency*. Homewood, IL: Dorsey Press.

Ex parte Crouse, 4. (1838). Philadelphia, PA, Warton School of Business. 9

Feld, B. (Ed.). (1999). *Readings in juvenile justice administration*. New York: Oxford University Press.

Jennings, W., Loeber, R., Pardini, D., Piquero, A., & Farrington, D. (2018). *Offending from childhood to young adulthood: Recent results from the Pittsburgh Youth Study*. Cham, Switzerland, Springer.

Johnson, T. (1975). *Introduction to the juvenile justice system*. St. Paul, MN: West Publishing Co.

Johnston, L. D,, O' Malley, P.M., and Bachman, J.G., (2002) *National survey results on drug use from the Monitoring the future study, 975-2001, reported in U. S. Department of Justice, TTTTSourcebook of criminal justice statistics 2001*, (p. 251).

Kent v. U.S. (1966), 383 U.S. 541.

Kratcoski, P. (2012). *Juvenile justice administration*. Boca Raton, FL: CRC Press/Taylor & Franc Group.

Kratcoski, P. & Kratcoski, J. (1977). The balance of social status groupings within schools as an influencing variable on the frequency and character of delinquent behavior, in Friday, P. & Stewart, V. *Youth crime and juvenile justice. New York: Praeger*.

Lawrence, R., & Hemmens, C. (2008). *Juvenile justice: A text/reader*. Los Angeles: Sage.

Laws, I. (1899). (pp. 131-137), Sections 1, 7, 9.

Lerman, P. (1970). *Delinquency and social policy* (pp. 12–14). New York: Praeger.

Livingston, D. (2018). *Hangout turns deadly* (p. Ai, A4). Ohio: Akron Beacon Journal, November 30.

Loeber, R., Farrington, D., Stouthamer-Loeber, M., & White, H. (2008). *Violence and serious theft: Development and prediction from childhood to adulthood*. NY: Routledge.

Loeber, R., Jennings, W., Ahonen, L., Piquero, A., & Farrington, D. (2016). *Female delinquency from childhood to young adult: Recent results from the Pittsburgh Girls Study*. Cham: Springer.

Lou, H. (1927). *Juvenile courts in the United States*. Chapel Hill, NC: University of North Carolina Press.

Platt, A. (1969). *The child savers: The invention of delinquency*. Chicago, ILL: University of Chicago Press.

Platt, A. (1982). The triumph of benevolence: The origins of the juvenile justice system in the United States. In D. Rojek & G. Jenson (Eds.), *Readings in juvenile delinquency*. Lexington, MA: D.C. Heath.

Porman, N. (1982). *The disappearance of children*. New York: Delacorte Press.

Robertson, P. (1974). Home as a nest: Middle-class childhood in nineteenth-century Europe. In L. Mause (Ed.), *The history of childhood* (p. 411). NY: Psychohistory Press.

Robinson, S. M. (1964). *Juvenile delinquency* (pp. 250–251). New York: Holt, Rinehart & Winston.

Rojek, D., & Jenson, G. (1982). The social history of delinquency. In D. Rojek & G. Jensen (Eds.), *Readings in juvenile delinquency*. Lexington, MA: D.C. Heath.

Rothman, D. (1971). *Discovery of the asylum*. Boston: Little, Brown.

Shoemaker, D. (2009). *Juvenile delinquency*. New York: Rowman & Littlefield Publishers, Inc.

Sickmund, M., & Puzzanchera, C. (Eds.). (2014). *Juvenile offenders and victims: 2014 National Report*. Pittsburgh: National Center for Juvenile Justice.

Snyder, H., & Sickmund, M. (1999). *Juvenile offenders and victims 1999: National report*. Pittsburgh: National Center for Juvenile Justice.

Thornton, W., James, J., & Doerner, W. (1982). *Delinquency and justice Glenview*. Scott Foresman: ILL.

Tracy, P., Wolfgang, M., & Figlio, R. (1985). *Delinquency in two birth cohorts*. Washington, D.C: U.S. Department of Justice.

United States Children's Bureau, (1970). *Report to the United States Congress on juvenile delinquency*. Cited in the Lincoln Law Review, 6,1 (Dec. 1970) (p. 67).

Chapter 2
Past and Current Bio-Social Perspectives on Delinquency Causation

2.1 Introduction

Those who have control of youths, including parents, school officials, and law enforcement officials in every society have been concerned about behavior by youths that deviates from society's norms to such an extent that it causes problems of social control. Such behavior is labeled undesirable, and sanctions are imposed in the hope of reducing its incidence and severity. Explanations for youthful deviance have varied according to the characteristics of the society in question, the period of history, the philosophical and social backgrounds of the theorists, and the degree of sophistication reached in sampling and data analysis methods at the time the research was conducted. Low intelligence was hypothesized to be a cause of delinquency. The notion that some individuals were destined to become criminals, insane, or feeble-minded as a result of their heredity was an accepted theory during the late nineteenth and early twentieth centuries. The theory that delinquency was caused by low intelligence could not be empirically tested until delinquents and nondelinquents could be meaningfully compared after the development of intelligence tests. The theory of Lombroso (Wolfgang, 1961, pp. 361–391) that a "criminal type" existed with such physical characteristics as protruding ears, abundant body hair, and broad cheekbones, was later put to a scientific test by Goring (1913),who found no significant anatomical differences in the physical measurements of 3000 English prisoners and a comparison group of Cambridge and Oxford graduates (Schafer & Knudten, 1970, pp. 60–61). Other early theories, which seemed in their time to have made important progress in discovering the causes of delinquency, were disproved or displaced by later researchers who used more sophisticated research methods, For example, the research of Sheldon and Eleanor Glueck (Glueck & Glueck, 1950, 1956), which employed a number of scientific controls in the selection of samples of delinquent and nondelinquent youths used in the research, has been criticized as not being broad enough in scope to substantiate the conclusions drawn. Similarly, more recent theories, such as the XYY chromosome theory (Shah & Roth, 1974, p. 137) which sought

© Springer Nature Switzerland AG 2020
P. C. Kratcoski et al., *Juvenile Delinquency*,
https://doi.org/10.1007/978-3-030-31452-1_2

to link the existence of an extra Y chromosome in some males to their involvement in aggressive and violent behavior, and theories that the diet of an offender, particularly a high amount of sugar ingestion, could be related to inappropriate behavior (Milich & Pelham, 1986), were not substantiated when more extensive controlled research examined the subjects.

According to Shoemaker (1984, p. 8), when one considers the later standards of measurement and research, many of the earlier theories would be considered naïve. He observes that, "A hundred years ago this kind of research led to many conclusions that crime and delinquency were inherited." The development of any theory is an elaborate process, involving the gathering and analysis of data to discover the interrelationships of certain variables and their degree of importance in producing the observed condition. The end product of this activity, the theory, is a scientifically acceptable general principle or group of principles. Theories, then, provide explanations for the relation between two or more variables. For example, if we assume that delinquency is caused by a lack of recreational opportunities, this assumption might be tested by locating a group of adolescents who have ample recreational facilities and opportunities and comparing the amount and nature of their delinquent behavior with those of a group of adolescence who have little or no opportunity for recreational activities. In order to scientifically test the theory that a lack of having sufficient recreational facilities and opportunities causes delinquency, the researcher would have to standardize or match every possible factor other than the recreational variable that could conceivably contribute to delinquent behavior. If, after an observation period and careful recording of the behavior of both groups, the non-recreational group was shown to have a level of delinquency significantly higher than that of the other group, then lack of recreational opportunities could be advanced as the explanation for the delinquency of this particular sample.

Box 2.1 Breaking into the School Gym to Practice Basketball
Source: Personal Observation of P. C. Kratcoski.

The residents of a small working class town located in Eastern Pennsylvania took great pride in their school. The recently built brick school replaced the old school that had to be abandoned because it was a fire hazard. The new school served all of the students in the community, including both grade school students and high school students. There was sufficient land surrounding the school for a playground (swings, slides) for the smaller children, a baseball field that could be converted into a football field, and a few outdoor basketball hoops. The school did not compete with other schools in the area in football, but was very competitive in baseball and basketball. The school was centrally located in the town and the children in the community, especially the older boys, would use the outside area for various sports, depending on the season and the sport. However, during the months when the weather was nasty with rain or snow, the opportunities for the youths to engage in any time of team sports there were limited.

Since basketball was the main competitive school sport in the community, having a large sized gym that included bleachers, lockers rooms, and a hardwood floor for basketball was a high priority when the new school was built. The gym also served as a theater and was used for band concerts, plays, school assemblies, and the senior graduation ceremony. It had a fairly large stage, and behind the stage were two dressing rooms and a large room used to store the large band equipment, such as the tubas and drums. The entire school was locked from the closing of the school day on Friday and not opened again until early Monday morning. During the times of vacations, such as Christmas, the school would not be open until the semester resumed at the end of the vacation period. The school did not have a night watchman, but there were houses close to the school and a few of the owners would keep their eyes of the school, especially during times such as Halloween when some of the boys might try to wax the windows or vandalize the school in some other way.

A number of the older boys in the community wanted to get into the gym during the weekends to practice basketball. Several of the boys were on either the varsity or junior varsity teams, and these teams were very competitive with the basketball teams from the other communities in the area. Others just wanted something to do on the weekend and also liked to play any kind of competitive sports. One day, during a gym class, one of the boys noticed that the windows in the gym could be opened if one used a short ladder or step stool. The windows would often be opened during the months of May and early June when there was a large crowd of people in the gym and it became stuffy. When the boy was sure that no one was looking he had another boy get on his shoulders and undo the latch of one of the windows. The boys than spread the word that the gym would be open on Saturday in the afternoon.

On Saturday afternoon, a tall boy lifted a smaller boy on his shoulders to push open the unlatched window and crawl through it into the gym. He proceeded to the front door of the school, opened it, and allowed the tall boy to enter. They then closed the window, making sure that it remained unlatched. For the next hour or so, the neighborhood boys entered the school through the unlocked front door. They knew that they were trespassing and should not be in the building, but tended to rationalize with one excuse or another.

The Saturday and Sunday break-ins continued for several weeks without any major interruptions. The school janitor would notice that the gym floor was rather dirty (some of the boys wore their street shoes when playing), and suspected that someone was using the gym, but did not report it the school principal, since he was friendly with some of the boys who often helped with the janitorial work such as taking out the ashes from the coal furnace that serviced the school. In exchange for their help, the janitor would allow them to take a quick cigarette behind the furnace. He never observed them smoking, in case the principal inquired about their behavior during the time they were absent from class. No doubt some of the town residents who lived near the school also figured out that the boys were entering the school, but did not report it to anyone, either because they did not want to have the boys get into trouble or just wanted to "mind their own business."

The breaking into the school ended abruptly when the music teacher, who also served as band director, discovered that the skins of the bass drum and two of the snare drums were broken. It was obvious that someone had kicked the skins with a foot. The teacher reported it to the school principal and he indicated that he would investigate. The following Saturday, the boys climbed in the window as usual, turned the lights on in the gym and began to play. A few minutes later, the boys were surprised when the principal and the coach entered the gym. The boys were reminded that they were trespassing and breaking the law and they were questioned on how they were able to get into the school and who was responsible for breaking the skins of the drums. None of the boys admitted to the vandalism and suggested that perhaps one or a few of the younger boys who was not present might be responsible. They indicated that they were just trying to get as much practice in as possible to be ready for the season. One boy rationalized the break-in by noting that some of the other schools were practicing at their schools during the week-ends. The coach, not wanting to see his players get into trouble and perhaps be suspended, tended to offer support to the boys, indicated that they are "good kids" and probably were not responsible for the destruction of the drums. The principal decided to not take any immediate punitive action. He informed the boys that the investigation into the destruction of the drums would continue and as long as the boys "kept their noses clean" and did not break into the school again they would not be punished. It is difficult to isolate those factors that produce a specific result in this case, delinquency. In fact, it is customary to think of a delinquent as the end product of a whole variety of causes or factors that independently might not have a drastic influence but that in a specific combination produce the observed undesirable behavior. A search for cause is essentially a search for those things that make something happen. In the case described above, the boys were aware that they were committing a deviant act by breaking into the school and were aware that, if caught, they could be punished. However, their immediate interest of having a place to play basketball was more important than the more remote concern that they might be caught and punished. The incident actually ended with some positive effects for the boys, and other students in the school and even the residents of the community. The incident was discussed at a teachers' meeting and a few of the younger teachers suggested that since the gym was the only facility in the community that was available for any type of community activity, it should be more accessible to the residents and to the students during the evenings and weekends.

One teacher informed the group that the school she had attended schools that held record dances for the junior and high school students on Saturday afternoons. These dances provided an opportunity for the girls and boys to mix while being under supervision. A few of the teachers volunteered to be supervisors at the dance. The dance idea was implemented and turned out to be a huge success. Eventually the gym became open for other affairs involving the parents.

2.2   The Theory Development Process

A very rigid definition of theory would accept only those explanations that have been empirically tested, with the causative variables being isolated and all other possible explanations being eliminated. This view would exclude most of the explanations of delinquency causation. In this book, theory will be considered in a more general sense as encompassing any attempt to understand and/or explain why something happens. Shoemaker's (1984, p. 8) broad definition, in which an explanation of delinquency is regarded as a theory "if it attempts to explain or understand delinquency, regardless of the level of its causal assumptions and irrespective of the sophistication of its concepts and propositions," is relevant to this approach.

Much of the research on delinquency causation does not venture beyond finding correlations, that is, showing that two or more variables are associated with each other and that a change in the independent variable (the cause) is likely to result in a change in the dependent variable (the effect). Even when a factor has been defined as statistically significant as a cause of some type of juvenile misbehavior, its importance in proportion to other causes must be taken into account. As Nettler (1978, pp. 119–120) observed, rather than viewing certain behavior correlations as "the cause," we should consider them "candidates nominated to be causes. Correlation is a necessary sign of causation, but it is not a sufficient sign. It is not even a clear sign, for we do not know from the correlations that social scientists compute. "how much *power* is demonstrated by the finding of a significant association."

Cohen (1955, p. 21) noted that many explanations of delinquency that were accepted at one time were eventually discarded because they failed to respect the truth that, "if one wants to explain something that has a number of distinct parts, his explanation must fit all the parts and not just some facet of the thing which happens, for some reason, to intrigue him....... If one fails to keep in mind the whole, he is not likely to find a satisfactory explanation of the part. Vold et al. (1998, p. 37) contends that the development of new research tools that has resulted in the collection of empirical data has allowed researchers to dwell more deeply into the complexities of human behavior. In reference to the relationship between positivist and classical theories of criminal behavior, they state that although classical theories and positivist theories contend that the classical and positivist theories are in opposition, they are not necessarily different. Vold et al. (1998, p. 37) state, "Classical criminologists therefore could expand their theoretical frame of reference and examine how crime rates are influenced by a wide range of factors outside the criminal justice system, including biological, psychological, and social fact.

Dambazau (2007, p. 6) states, " Every criminological theory contains a set of assumptions which are the theoretical issues that involve debates such as those of human nature and free will, conflict and consensus, a description of the phenomenon to be explained, which provides the statistical profile representing the patterns, trends, and correlates of crime; and an explanation in terms of the variable arranged in causal order in order to create a statistical significance." Dambazau claims theories of crime and delinquency can be found in six broad different categories, or schools of thought. They are classical, neoclassical, positivist, sociological, psychological, and radical or critical. Many of these categories can be broken down into subcategories, such as bio-social, social-psychological, strain, control, learning, functionalism, and many others subcategories.

A theorist, whether a psychologist, social psychologist, social worker, or sociologist, will draw upon those concepts and methods of investigation that are the basic foundation stones of his or her particular discipline. These will tend to provide the perspectives that guide the scientist in developing theories of causation. For example, researchers who have sought explanations of delinquent and criminal behavior have formulated their hypotheses and conducted studies according to their areas of interest (philosophical, biological, psychological, or sociological). Their methods and conclusions have been influenced by the eras in which they lived, the earlier research or theories with which they were familiar, and their access to various delinquent or criminal populations for testing and comparison. The theories touched on in this chapter will be treated under the general headings of the classical school, the biological school, heredity-based theories, and current biological and psychological explanations. Many of the studies were not confined to examining the influence of one set of factors. Rather, they took into account ideas from other schools of thought and their relation to the hypotheses under investigation. Theorists from the biological and psychological schools tended to seek the causes of delinquency within the individual, while the classical school, rather than focusing on the causes of delinquent behavior, examined the nature of the act and explored measures that might be taken to persuade the individual not to repeat it.

2.2.1   The Classical School

During the sixteenth and seventeenth centuries, European criminal justice was geared toward punishment and deterrence. Severe penalties were provided even for trivial offenses. Capital punishment was dictated for over 200 offenses in seventeenth-century England, with lesser offenses punished by such horrors as burning a hole in the tongue or ears, cutting out the tongue, or severing a limb (Reid, 1976). Prisons were used to detain political prisoners and those awaiting trial, rather than as places of incarceration for those convicted of crimes.

Against this background, the thinking of Cesare Beccaria (1738–1794), an Italian university professor, seemed revolutionary indeed. Beccaria developed the "pleasure–pain" principle—the idea that each human behavior choice involves a decision between the amount of pleasure that would accompany an act and the pain (physical or psychological) that could result. He maintained that the punishments for various crimes should be just severe enough to deter people from the criminal act and that punishments should be applied equally to all citizens, regardless of their social status. Those who knew in advance exactly what the consequences of their behavior would be could then exercise their free will (a concept popular in that era) to decide on the proper course of action. Theorists analyzing the decision would focus on traits and characteristics that are internal to the individual (feelings of inferiority, negative self-concept, emotional stress, peculiar personality traits) and attempt to associate them with the presence or absence of delinquency. By contrast, a sociologist may look at factors external to the individual (poverty, slums, peer-group influences, broken family, effects of the mass media) and their relation to delinquency.

Researchers investigating the problems of delinquency generally agree that it is a complex subject and that no single theory is going to offer plausible explanations for all varieties of deviant behavior. Each pattern of delinquency may be result of a host of inter-related factors. For example, in self-reported delinquency studies virtually every youth involved admitted having performed one or more acts violating the law as it applies to juveniles. The vast majority of these youthful offenses were ignored or considered too trivial to warrant official action. Some were never detected, and others that did come to the attention of law enforcement officials were not officially processed. The reasons why some offenders are brought into the juvenile justice system, labeled delinquent, and officially handled, while others who commit comparable offenses are not will be considered in later chapters. Chance, luck, or extenuating circumstances may well enter into the matter; therefore, it would be unwarranted to attribute the behavior of an apprehended youth to an intricately related set of causative factors while ignoring the fact that youths not labeled delinquent have engaged in exactly the same behavior. Youths may engage in a deviant act on impulse, because of the influence of peers, or in a fit of anger, and later may be unable to give a logical explanation for their action. In some cases, a reasonable causative explanation simply does not exist, and such behavior must be regarded as an impulsive response. Theorists and researchers have learned from experience that to understand delinquency causation, several different perspectives can be followed. These include the following:

- A personality perspective, that is, focusing on the characteristic and traits of a youth that have an effect on the youth's behavior.
- A sociological perspective, that is, focusing on the social factors that have an effect on the youth's behavior.
- A social-psychological perspective, that is, focusing on the social and psychological factors relating to the youth's current situation, such as peer groups, family matters, and the environment have an effect on the youth's behavior.

These perspectives will be addressed in the theories on causes of crime and delinquency presented in this chapter and the chapters that follow.

2.3 The Classical and Neoclassical Theories

The classical and neoclassical theorists such as Beccaria, often referred to as "free-will" advocates, believed that the human is rational and can make a rational decision on what acts are proper and what are wrong. Those who decide to engage in criminal behavior know in advance what the consequences of their illegal behavior will be if they decide to engage in an improper course of action. These theorists did recognize that there were exceptions in that the insane and children under the age of seven could not be considered responsible for their behavior, since they have either lost the ability to make a rational decision or have not yet developed the intellectual capacity to reason. Children under the age of seven and the insane were to be excluded from these punishments as incapable *of* making rational choices of pleasure or pain (Sutherland & Cressey, 1974, p. 50). The "right to punishment" concept in juvenile justice follows many *of* Beccaria's ideas regarding the need for a set punishment for each offense to be impartially administered to all offenders. (Vold et al., 1998, p. 23) Beccaria is regarded by some as the founder *of* modem penology. He saw imprisonment as a deterrent to criminal activity, and he believed it would be most effective if it were applied impartially, without exception, and in a degree appropriate for the severity of the offense.

While Beccaria was writing in Italy, in England Jeremy Bentham (1748–1832) was developing a theory of "utilitarianism" that was in virtual agreement with Beccaria's idea. He also emphasized the setting *of* specific punishments applicable to all, which would serve as deterrents. He assumed that a rational man, through exercise *of* free will, would be disposed to choose pleasure over pain. Bentham expanded his concept to include "the greatest good for the greatest number," noting that behavior must be controlled by a set system of punishments for the good of the larger society. In an era when most convicts were assigned to galley ships, transported to penal colonies, or punished by some form *of* physical mutilation or flogging, Bentham developed the concept of the prison as a "correctional" institution. He urged that the prison be located near the center of the city, so that citizens would observe it in their daily activities and ponder their own behavior according to the "pleasure–pain" ratio. He also advocated that prisoners be kept busy during their incarceration, taught trades, and classified according to their offenses (Reid, 1976, pp. 111–112).

2.3.1 Neoclassical Thought

The neoclassical thinkers believe that the justice system should focus on the act and not the offender. They maintain that it is not the concern of the justice system to change the offender, only to assure that the offender receives his or her "just deserts." The utilitarian theorists also assert that punishment deters potential criminal behavior. They believe that most people would commit crimes if they dared. For them, society is held together by an implied social contract. Humans are social beings who must follow the rules and regulations set by law if order is to be maintained. Conduct prohibited by law must be punished, because each violation threatens the welfare *of* the whole society.

Fogel (1975) put these ideas into a theoretical concept known as the "justice model," in which justice and compliance with the law are the standards by which both offenders and law enforcement and correctional personnel should be judged. The justice model suggests that offenders, in addition to being punished, should make restitution or compensation to the victim. Just punishment quickly applied and harsh enough to deter future illegal activity is the central focus of the justice mode Wilson (1975) reiterated the idea of just punishment, noting that serious offenders should receive a punishment that would remove them from the community and put a stop to their criminal careers for a substantial period of time. Bailey et.al. (1974, p. 140) found that certainty of punishment and the potential offender's perceptions of the probability of detection and punishment were the keys to deterrence. For example, signs in department stores beside television surveillance cameras or mirrors stating that all shoplifters will be prosecuted should deter shoplifting by youths, even if the cameras are not in operation.

The ideas of the neoclassical theorists are reflected in certain revisions of the juvenile code. For example, requiring mandatory institutionalization of youths charged with serious offenses and "career criminals" (those with an extensive history of delinquent offenses), or setting exact penalties (determinate dispositions) for certain offenses, that cannot be shortened or lifted, are consistent with neoclassic theory. The movement to remove from juvenile court jurisdiction status offenses that pose no threat to public safety or order and handle them instead through social agencies is another reflection of the application of the neoclassic theory.

2.3.2 The Biological School

Classical and neoclassical thought on criminal behavior emphasizes that since people "choose" to commit criminal acts, their "free-will" decisions must be directed toward choices of noncriminal behavior through the setting of specific standards of punishment for certain offenses. The biological school, in contrast, holds that in most cases criminals are predetermined, or at least predisposed, toward criminal behavior.

Although biological theories of criminality have been advanced for hundreds of years, no one has definitively identified the causative links or internal biological factors that bring about unacceptable behavior. Many theorists do not distinguish between biological and psychological traits or discuss the degree to which the characteristics may intertwine to produce criminality. The early biological theorists believed that certain physical characteristics, such as the shape of the head or hands, body type, or chemical imbalances in the system, were indicators of a predisposition toward criminal behavior. The current biological theorists also see a cause-and-effect relationship between certain biological factors and the onset of criminal and delinquent behavior, although they recognize that the destructive potential of these factors can be affected by environmental conditions. For example, hyperactivity in children, which can result in impulsive deviant acts such as vandalism or assault, can be controlled by behavior modification therapy or by medication.

Lombroso, a physician, formulated his theory by observing the physical characteristics of criminals with whom he came in contact. After the death of a particularly notorious prisoner, he performed an autopsy and observed that the interior of the skull was abnormal, with a depression where there should have been a protrusion. This finding led Lombroso to believe that in criminals the evolutionary process had somehow been arrested, and that the brains of criminals were biological throwbacks to the savage man, or atavist.

Lombroso stated,

> "At the sight of that skull, I seemed to see all of a sudden, lighted as a vast plain under a flaming sky, the problem of the nature of the criminal—an atavistic being who reproduces in his person the ferocious instincts of primitive humanity and the inferior animals. Thus were explained anatomically the enormous jaws, high cheekbones, prominent superciliary arches, lines in the palms, extreme size of the orbits, handle-shaped or sessile ears found in criminals, savages and apes, insensibility to pain, extremely acute sight, tattooing, excessive idleness, love of orgies, and the irresistible craving for evil for its own sake, the desire not only to extinguish life in the victim, but to mutilate the corpse, tear its flesh and drink its blood." (Ferrero, 1911, p. 10)

The abnormalities or "stigmata" that Lombroso thought were characteristics of criminals were not the causes of the criminal behavior but rather identification marks of those born with the atavistic condition. He declared that female atavists could also be differentiated by such characteristics as excessive body hair, moles, and masculine traits. The first attempt to relate body traits systematically to juvenile delinquency came from the work of William Sheldon in the 1940s. He differentiated three body types, or "somatotypes," and associated each with certain personality traits. The first type, endomorphic, is characterized by a fat, soft, round body; this type of person is extroverted and a lover of comfort. The second body type, mesomorphic, is muscular and hard; persons of the type Sheldon considered assertive and aggressive. Ectomorphic types are frail, thin, and weak and shy, sensitive, and introverted.

Sheldon rated juvenile offenders on a scale of 1–7 on each body type. Then, after comparing 200 delinquent boys in a rehabilitation home with 4000 college students, he concluded that the large majority of the delinquents were "decidedly mesomorphic." (Sheldon, 1949, p. 726). In contrast, his nondelinquent comparison group was more evenly distributed among the somatotypes Sheldon viewed body types as inborn and stated that there is a very strong correlation between physique and temperament. The assertive-aggressive temperament he associated with the mesomorphic body type explained the violent offenses of the delinquents, and their assertiveaggressive temperaments helped these youths survive in the unfavorable sociocultural environment in which many of them lived.

The Gluecks (1950. p. 193) also employed body-type designations in their research on delinquents. Like Sheldon, they found that the majority of the 500 institutionalized delinquent boys they studied were mesomorphic. When they compared these boys with a sample of 500 boys believed to be nondelinquent, almost two-thirds of the delinquents were categorized as mesomorphic, compared to less than one-third of the nondelinquents. A later analysis of the same samples of delinquents and nondelinquents led the Gluecks to conclude that personality and family characteristics must be considered along with body type when attempting to explain the causes of delinquency. For example, they found that mesomorphic delinquents tended to come from homes that were disorganized. These delinquents were also characterized as emotionally unstable. Thus, the mesomorphic delinquents exhibited severe psychological and social problems, while the nondelinquent mesomorphs did not. For a boy growing up in a harsh sociocultural environment such as the inner city, the aggressiveness and muscular build of the mesomorph could be a key to survival. The specific physiological connection between body type and delinquent behavior has never been empirically established. When social and psychological factors are taken into consideration, the importance of body type appears insignificant.

2.4 Heredity-Based Theories

Theorists who claim a basis in heredity for delinquent behavior believe that the tendency to delinquency and other aberrations, such as mental illness and alcoholism, is genetically transmitted from parents to children. When various researchers began to challenge the conclusions reached by Lombroso, the emphasis of those who continued to support the biological explanations shifted to inherited lack of mental capacity as a possible cause of criminality. The most colorful of these studies, Dugdale's (1877) tracing of the descendants of the Jukes family and Henry Goddard's (1914) examination of the foibles of the Kallikak family, sought to document long histories of illegitimacy, idiocy, prostitution, alcoholism, and other social aberrations in certain families. Goddard maintained that feeblemindedness is inherited and causes crime because those who are mentally inferior are unable to assess the consequences of their behavior. He developed the following summary of the Kallikak family:

> Martin Kallikak, Sr., A Revolutionary soldier, and a man of good stock, became the father of an illegitimate son, Martin Kallikak, Jr. The mother was a feeble-minded girl. To 1912 the known descendants from this source were 480. Thirty-six of these illegitimate; 33 sexually immoral; 24 alcoholics; 3 epileptics; 3 were criminal. There is conclusive proof that 143 (29.7%) of these were feeble-minded while only 46 were certainly known to be normal. The rest are doubtful.—(Goddard, 1914, pp. 8–9)

Goddard also tested the intelligence of delinquents and concluded that at least 25% of them, and perhaps as many as 70%, were of inferior intelligence, using the mental age of 12 or under as a standard for feeblemindedness. When Zeleny (Empey, 1982, p. 166) applied the same standards to thousands of draftees for military service, however, he found that more than 30% of them were also feebleminded according to Goddard's standards. Goddard retreated from his original position and decided that only about 5% of all delinquents could be considered feebleminded (Empey, 1982, p. 166).

McGloin et al. (2004, p. 624), in their research on the relationship of the IQ to delinquent behavior, concluded that there is no direct effect of IQ on the level of youths' deviant behavior. They concluded that, "IQ is an important criminogenic risk factor only to the extent that it inhibits youths' school performance, increases the likelihood of experiencing pressure from deviant peers, and affects the development of self-control."

In the 1930s, Harvard anthropologist Hooton (1931, pp. 376–378) renewed the notion first promoted by Lombroso that criminals could be identified by certain physical characteristics. On the basis of a comparison of 13,000 inmates of reformatories and jails with a sample of more than 3000 non-criminals, he defined a list of physical characteristics, quite similar to those of Lombroso, which were indicative of criminals. He even related the criminal's particular physical characteristics to the type of crime committed. For example, tall, heavy men are most inclined to be killers, while men with small, undersized builds are likely to be thieves.

The theories that related delinquent and criminal behavior to heredity were attacked by sociologists and psychologists as being defective in their research methods, the reasoning employed to develop their conclusions, and the lack of consideration given to personality and environment. Nevertheless, they had profound effects on juvenile court and correctional practices. Because intelligence tests were used as the basis for determining mental deficiency or defectiveness, the courts and correctional administrators tended to go along with the results obtained. The IQ test had an aura of scientific reliability in their eyes, and conclusions that youths were mentally deficient or defective that were based on this test were given considerable weight. Consequently, those tested and found to be "defective" were isolated from their families and placed in institutions, where it was felt that the inferior intelligence they possessed could be used to develop some skills. Early testing of children who showed delinquent tendencies was encouraged so that these children could be isolated before they had an opportunity to become deeply involved in unacceptable behavior.

Sterilization was used to prevent the procreation of new generations of these "feeble minded" and "inferior" children. More than 30 states passed laws allowing sterilization of the feebleminded, the mentally ill, epileptics, and certain categories of criminal and delinquent offenders. Although these laws were eventually declared unconstitutional, as late as 1970 more than 20 states still retained them in their statutory laws (McCaghy, 1976, p. 20).

2.4.1   Current Biological Explanations of Delinquency

Interest in biological and heredity linked explanations of deviant behavior has increased in recent years, as methods of genetic research and machinery for observing brain waves and other types of biological functioning have become increasingly sophisticated. Researchers have abandoned the earlier assumptions of direct causal links between biological traits and deviance, and instead are exploring the interaction of genetic and environmental factors on the functioning of the nervous system.

The findings of official statistical reports on delinquency as well as the findings of self-report surveys on delinquency as well as self-report surveys find that males are much more likely than females to engage in delinquent behavior, and they do so at an earlier age. However, for both male and female misbehavior peaks at age 16 or 17, and from this point on their behavior generally begins to conform more and more to accepted norms. Both biological and sociological explanations have been developed to explain these variations. Male hormonal changes during puberty have been used to explain the fact that males become more aggressive and less subject to control at that time. Physical and mental development (maturation) may also help to explain why behavior changes for the better during the late teens. However, many social factors, including the family structure, physical and cultural environment, peer group influence, and unique personality factors may also be related with gender and age to produce these results.

2.5   Biochemical Explanations

The "biochemical" or "orthomolecular" explanation of delinquency, which has gained popularity in recent years, suggests that chemical deficiencies or abnormalities in the body can affect the entire nervous system and directly or indirectly lessen a youth's ability to perform in a socially acceptable manner. Brain damage caused by injury or disease can alter brain patterns. Vitamin deficiencies or the effects of certain foods or food additives may also be related to aggressive or out of control behavior. Hypoglycemia (a low blood count) has also been associated with violent behavior. Philpott (1978, pp. 116–137)

Deviant behavior in youth has also been associated with (Gonzalez-Cossio et al., 1997, pp. 856–862) exposure to high levels of lead, asbestos, complicated births, water fluoridation, smoking and use of alcohol during pregnancy, and other forms of drug use. For example, a study conducted in Mexico revealed that children born to mothers with a history of exposure to lead were at risk for low birth weight, a powerful predictor of child behavior problems and learning disabilities.

Kosofsky (1998, p. 121) reviewed the research studies on the effects of children being exposed to cocaine in the uterus. The "crack babies" were found to have language and behavioral deficits, short attention spans and impulsivity. The extent of these problems was found to be related to the amount and length of cocaine use by the mothers. Kosofsky concluded that the prenatal cocaine exposure may have a significant effect on the socialization of the child, as well as on the educability, and ability of the child to develop the adaptive skills needed for individuals to be productive in school, the community and society.

2.6   Hyperactivity and Learning Disabilities

Hyperactivity or hyperkinesis has also been advanced as a biological explanation for some delinquent activity. This type of minimal brain dysfunction has been observed in many children who are discipline problems in school because of their highly impulsive behavior. Research has found a link between learning disabilities and delinquency.

The National Advisory Committee on Handicapped Children (Murray, 1976, p. 12) describes children with learning disabilities in the following way:

Children with special learning disabilities exhibit a disorder in one or more of the basic psychological processes involved in understanding or using spoken language. These may be manifested in disorders of listening, thinking, talking, reading, writing, spelling, or arithmetic. They include conditions which have been referred to as perceptual handicaps. Brain injury, minimal brain dysfunction, dyslexia, developmental aphasia, etc. They do not include learning problems which are primarily to visual, hearing, or motor handicaps, to mental retardation, emotional disturbance, or to environmental disadvantage.

Three types of learning disabilities have been broadly recognized and defined. *Dyslexia,* sometimes termed "word blindness," refers in a broad sense to defective language achievement in reading writing, and spelling (Mulligan, 1972). It may include such problems as poor ability to discriminate between words in which only one letter differs (some, same), writing or perceiving words or letters backward or upside down (b for d, saw for was, w for m), and spelling words with letters out of sequence (Mulligan, 1972). *Aphasia i*nvolves hearing and speaking difficulties in ascertaining and pronouncing words. *Hyperkinesis* refers to excessive muscular movement in the performance of activities (Murray, 1976). Males have been estimated to outnumber females four to one in the incidence of learning disabilities. Experts have estimated that from 5 to 10% of all children under 10 years of age have such disabilities (Murray, 1976).

The effects of learning disabilities on school behavior may begin when teachers perceive these physically awkward youths as discipline problems, or when a child who has normal or above-average intelligence is placed in the slow-learning group because of a disability and experiences the frustration of falling behind classmates, in spite of his or her best efforts. A child's reaction may be despair, frustration acted out in disruptive behavior, avoidance of school by feigning sickness, deliberate truancy, or eventual involvement in delinquent activity as a method of gaining acceptance or recognition. Certain other personality characteristics of learning-disabled children may also make them prone to delinquent behavior, such as their poor ability to learn from experience and their tendency to act on impulse (Murray, 1976).

Pratt and Cullen (2000), in their analysis of hyperactivity of children, found that low cognitive ability may be related to the youth's inability to resist the desire for immediate gratification, as well as the young person being less able to appreciate the long term consequences of their behavior. Pratt, Cullen, Blevins, Daigle, and Unnever (2002) found that individual biological factors, such as attention deficit disorders and hyperactivity disorders, as well as psychopathic tendencies, are linked to self-control.

A number of researchers have identified a high proportion of learning disabled youngsters among populations already defined as delinquent, and have attempted to establish a causal relationship between learning disabilities and delinquency. Bohman (1972), who tested 100 juveniles referred to the Norfolk (Virginia) Juvenile Court for incorrigibility, truancy, and runaway behavior, found that 57% of the 100 youth had a general learning disability. Mulligan (1972) tested 60 juveniles placed with the Sonoma County (California) Special Supervision Unit, designed to supervise the more severely delinquent children on probation, found that 80% of them were reading below grade level, even though they were typically of average or superior intelligence. As a result of the research, the Special Supervision Unit now refers children with truancy or school related problems for a screening test for learning disabilities, and it also interviews the child's mother to attempt to uncover any condition in the child's early life that may have been responsible for minimal brain damage or neurological handicaps that may contribute to such disabilities. When a problem is recognized, referrals are then made to appropriate remedial programs.

2.6.1   Twin Research

Other attempts to isolate the relative effects of heredity and environment on deviant behavior have been made through studies of twins. Research has compared twins developed from the same egg (monozygotic) with twins developed from two eggs (dizygotic) and discovered that the monozygotic twins, who have the identical genetic makeup, are more similar in their criminal or delinquent behavior than the dizygotic twins. Studies of this type conducted by Dalgard and Kringler in Norway (1978) found that rates of involvement in such criminal acts as violence, theft, and sexual assault were more similar for pairs of monozygotic twins that for dizygotic twins. Further research into the environmental factors of their childhoods revealed that the monozygotic twins generally felt that they were reared and treated alike and experienced closeness and common identity much more than the dizygotic twins, indicating that both their genetic and environmental backgrounds were more similar than those of the dizygotic twins. Studies of alcoholism among twins have revealed similar patterns. Monozygotic twins were more likely to both be alcoholic than dizygotic twins (Miller & Toft, 1990).

2.7   Studies of Adopted Children

The question of the relative influence of heredity and environment on deviant behavior has also been explored through studies of youths adopted shortly after birth. Their degree of criminality in later years was compared to that of their genetic parents and their adoptive parents to determine which they more closely resembled. It must be noted that at the time of adoption, most agencies make efforts to match children as closely as possible with their adoptive parents in terms of race, socioeconomic background, and physical appearance. For this reason, the results of adoptee studies may not be as valid as if the children had been randomly placed in homes other than their own. Nevertheless, such controlled experiments have yielded interesting results. Bohman (1972), for example, found that adoptees whose natural mother or father (or both) had a criminal record were more likely to be involved in criminal behavior than adoptees whose genetic parents had no criminal record. He related much of the criminality of the adoptees to alcohol abuse, a trait he found more often among the adoptees' genetic parents than among their adoptive parents. Genetic factors might contribute to alcohol abuse and thus may have influenced the adoptees' criminality.

Hutchings and Mednick (1977), comparing the genetic and adoptive fathers of adopted males with criminal records, found that 31% of the genetic fathers also had criminal records, compared to only 11% of the adoptive fathers. The fathers of a comparison group of un-adopted offspring in the general population were found to have the same percentage of criminal convictions (11%) as the adoptive fathers of adoptees with criminal convictions. This study's findings support the idea that genetics have some significant relationship to criminal behavior. With regard to the onset of alcoholism, studies have shown a biological link between adopted children and their birth parents. Studies in several countries followed adopted children separated from their birth parents before the children were 6 months old. Alcoholism occurred much more frequently in the children whose biological parents were alcoholics, while alcoholism in the adoptive parents was not strongly related to alcoholism in the adopted children (Miller & Toft, 1990).

A 4-year study of nearly 900 adopted adolescents and their families, funded by the National Institute of Mental Health (Benson, Sharma, & Roehkepartain, 1994) found that birthparents' problems with alcohol and drugs, or psychological difficulties, were not significantly linked to the psychological health of the adopted children in the study. However, in the component of the study that dealt with self-reported behaviors it was discovered that adopted adolescents were slightly more prone to delinquent and aggressive behavior than the non-adopted youths in the study.

2.8 Summary

In this chapter, we have examined the process by which a theory of delinquency develops, taking note of the difficulties inherent in assigning causal properties to various factors in the production of delinquency. Even when correlations between or among various factors have been established to indicate that a certain factor has causal properties, the strength or power of its impact on the behavior of the juvenile has yet to be assessed.

The theories of delinquency causation discussed in this chapter include those of the classical and neoclassical schools, the biological school, heredity-based theories, and the current biological theories.

Beccaria and Bentham, the classical theorists, believed that the decision to become involved in delinquent or criminal behavior is a rational one, and that criminality can be deterred by establishing a system of sure and quickly administered punishments severe enough to outweigh any pleasure or gain received from committing an illegal act.

This "pleasure–pain" principle is also embraced by the neoclassical thinkers, who support the notion of "just desserts." Those who are found guilty of delinquent or criminal acts, according to this idea, must receive exact punishments set by law, which may include mandatory institutionalization for certain offenses. The certainty and severity of punishment are regarded as deterrents to future crime.

In contrast to the freedom of choice stressed by the classical and neoclassical theorists, the biological theorists believe that offenders are predetermined, or at least predisposed, toward criminality by features of their biological makeup, and that certain physical characteristics can be noted in individuals who have this predisposition. The early biological theorists focused on particular physical features, while later ones developed "body types" characteristics of criminals or delinquents.

Those who promote heredity-based theories follow a similar line of reasoning, claiming that the tendency toward delinquency and other aberrations such as mental illness and alcoholism is genetically transmitted from parents to children. Through the use of comparison studies, researchers have disproved the conclusions reached by the early biological theorists. But current genetic research has focused on new theories of delinquency causation. These include the influence of brain damage, vitamin deficiencies, chemical imbalances in the body, hyperactivity, and learning disabilities. Controlled experiments with twins and adopted children have been used to attempt to establish the relative influences of heredity and environment. Searches for biological explanations of delinquency continue at more sophisticated levels today, bolstered by new genetic research techniques and more detailed methods. To date, however, no specific biological or physiological trait has been found to be a definite predisposing or influencing factor for delinquency and criminal behavior.

2.9 Discussion Questions

1. Describe how a theory of delinquency is developed. How did early theories of delinquency, which seemed logical and sound at the time they were developed, come to be disproved or rejected?
2. What types of current biological research are exploring the relative influences of heredity and environment on delinquency? Do you believe that a tendency to delinquency and criminality is inherited?
3. Some researchers have suggested that many children are mistakenly diagnosed as hyperactive when their behavior problems have other explanations. Discuss.
4. Several studies have found that identical twins separated early in life who have grown up in widely different economic and cultural circumstances still exhibit similar behavior patterns. Do these findings strongly support the idea that a

tendency to delinquency or criminality is inherited, or are there other possible explanations?

5. Discuss how the theories of the classical and the biological schools were related to the concepts of free will and determinism, which were widely debated at the time these theories were advanced.

6. Researchers have found that while there is not a direct relationship between learning disabilities and delinquency, the disabilities may have some indirect effects. What are some of the possible indirect effects that learning disabilities might have on delinquent behavior?

7. Define and outline the major components of a theory. What are the major categories of theories pertaining to criminology and delinquency?

8. Compare the basic components of the classical school of thought with those of the biological school of thought on the causes of crime.

9. Many of the biological theories of crime and delinquency were discarded after researchers were not able to establish a link between such factors as intelligence or mental illness and delinquency causation. However, there has been a resurgence of research on the possible relation of learning disorders to delinquency. Why?

10. There have been several studies of identical twins that were separated at birth and raised in widely different family and cultural situations. Discuss the conclusions reached by this research.

References

Bailey, W. C., Martin, J. D., & Gray, L. N. (1974). Crime and delinquency: A correlation analysis. *Journal of Research on Crime and Delinquency, 11*(July), 140.

Benson, P., Sharma, A., & Roehkepartain. (1994). *Growing up adopted*. Minneapolis, MN: Serach Institute.

Bohman, M. (1972). A study of adopted children, their background, environment, and adjustment. *Acta Paediatrica Scandinavia, 61*, 997.

Cohen, D. (1955). *The culture of the gang*. New York: Free Press.

Dalgard, O. S., & Kringler. (1978). Criminal behavior in twins. In L. D. Savitz & Johnston (Eds.), *Crime in society* (pp. 292–307). New York: Wiley.

Dambazau, A. (2007). *Criminology and criminal justice* (2nd ed.). Ibadan: Spectrum Books Limited.

Dugdale, R. (1877). *The jukes: A study in crime, pauperism, and heredity*. New York: Putnam.

Empey, L. T. (1982). *American delinquency*. Homewood, IL: Dorsey Press.

Ferrero, G. (1911). *Lombroso's criminal man*. New York: Putnam.

Fogel, D. (1975). *We are the living proof*. Cincinnati, OH: Anderson Publishing Company.

Glueck, S., & Glueck, E. (1950). *Unraveling juvenile delinquency*. New York: Common Wealth Fund.

Glueck, S., & Glueck, E. (1956). *Physique and delinquency*. New York: Harper and Row.

Goddard, H. (1914). *Febblemindness*. New York: Macmillan.

Gonzalez-Cossio, T., Peterson, K. E., Sanin, L. H., Fishbein, E., Palazuelos, E., Aro, A., et al. (1997). *Pediatrics, 100*(5 (Nov.)), 856–862.

Goring, C. (1913). *The English convict*. London: His Majesty's Stationery Office.

Hooton, E. A. (1931). *Crime and the man*. Cambridge, MA: Harvard University Press.

Hutchings, B., & Mednick, S. A. (1977). Criminality in adoptees and their adoptive and biological parents: A pilot study. In S. A. Mednick & K. O. Christiansen (Eds.), *Biosocia basis of criminal behavior* (pp. 127–141). New York: Gardner.

Kosofsky, B. (1998). Cocaine-induced alterations in neuro-development. *Seminars in Speech and Language, 19*(2), 21.

McCaghy, C. H. (1976). *Deviant behavior*. New York: Macmillan.

McGloin, J., Pratt, T., & Maahs, J. (2004). Rethinking the I.O. delinquency relationship: A longitudinal analysis of multiple theoretical models. *Justice Quarterly, 21*(3), 603–631.

Milich, R., & Pelham, W. (1986). Effects of sugar ingestion on the classroom and playground behavior of attention deficit disordered boys. *Journal of Counseling and Clinical Psychology, 54.*

Miller, N., & Toft, D. (1990). *The disease concept of alcoholism and other drug addiction*. Center City, MN: Hazeldon.

Mulligan, W. (1972). Dyslexia, specific learning disability and delinquency. *Juvenile Justice, 32*(3 (Nov.)), 21.

Murray, C. (1976). *The link between learning disabilities and juvenile delinquency*. Washington, D.C: U.S. Government Printing Office.

Nettler, G. (1978). *Explaining crime*. New York: McGraw-Hill.

Philpott, W. H. (1978). Ecological aspects of anti-social behavior. In L. J. Hippchen (Ed.), *Ecologic-biochemical approaches to treatment of delinquents and criminals* (pp. 116–137). New York: Van Nostrand Reinhold.

Pratt, T., & Cullen, F. (2000). The empirical status of Gottfrecdson and Hirschi's general theory of crime: A meta-analysis. *Criminology, 38*, 931–964.

Pratt, T., Cullen, F., Blevins, K., Daigle, L., & Unnever, J. (2002). The relationship of attention deficit hyperactivity disorder to crime and delinquency: A meta-analysis. *International Journal of Police Science and Management, 4*, 344–360.

Reid, S. T. (1976). *Crime and criminology*. Hinsdale, IL: Dryden Press.

Schafer, S., & Knudten, R. D. (1970). *Juvenile delinquency: An introduction*. New York: Random House.

Shah, S., & Roth, L. (1974). Biological and psychological factors in criminology. In D. Glazer (Ed.), *Handbook of criminality* (p. 137). Chicago: Rand Mc Nally p.

Sheldon, W. H. (1949). *The varieties of delinquency*. New York: Harper & Row.

Shoemaker, D. (1984). *Theories of delinquency*. New York: Oxford University Press.

Vold, G., Bernard, T., & Snipes, J. (1998). *Theoretical criminology* (4th ed.). New York: Oxford University Press.

Wilson, J. Q. (1975). *Thinking about crime* (pp. 210–243). New York: Basic Books.

Wolfgang, M. E. (1961). Pioneers in criminology: Cesare Lombroso (1835–1909). *Journal of Criminal Law, Criminology, and Police Sciences, 5*(6), 361–391.

Chapter 3
Social-Psychological Theories of Delinquency

3.1 Introduction

A 13-year-old pleaded no contest Wednesday to a homicide charge in the... death of a 7 year old playmate who was shot while riding a snowmobile.... The boy pleaded no contest to a charge of criminal homicide, a felony charge similar to murder in the shooting death of Jessica Ann Carr Jessica was killed as she rode a snowmobile in a field next to the boy's home.... At the time, Cameron {the offender} was a couple of months shy of his 10th birthday.... The boy had an argument with Jessica, went home, unlocked his father's gun cabinet, removed a high-powered rifle that his father had taught him to shoot. He loaded it, rested his weapon on a window sill, and fired at the girl 100 yards away. She was struck in the back and the bullet pierced her spine and right lung.

After the shooting, according to testimony.... Cameron cleaned the weapon and put it back into the gun cabinet.

(Source: Daily Kent Stater, September 3, 1992, p. 3)

The suicide rate in Ohio increased by 24% from 2008 to 2017, according to a study analyzing vital statistics.... Rates also increased 80% among children 14 and younger and 57% for Ohioans 60 and older... (Source: JoAnne Viviano, Ohio suicide rate jumps 24% from 2008 to 2017, Akron Beacon Journal, May 15, 2019, p. A1.

...A dozen teens living in Perry, Plain, Jackson, Northwest, and Canton Local school districts (Ohio) died by suicide between August 2017 and March 2018.... A survey conducted last spring of 15,083 area students in grades 7 through 12 found that more than 5% of the surveyed students had attempted suicide at least once during the last school year, and 22.8% of them were at an elevated risk of suicide. Female students thought about suicide more often, and suicide attempts during the past school year were highest among freshmen.... The report... identified Stark County's unusual constellation of suicide risk facts for youths as adverse childhood experiences, opioid misuse, death of a loved one by suicide in the past year, posting on social media about the suicide cluster deaths, and having a strong emotional reaction to the... suicide cluster.... A traumatic event at one school could easily affect another school.

(Kelly Weir, Akron Beacon Journal, April 26, 2019, pp. A1, 6.)

The taking of the life of another person and taking one's own life often have the same root causes. There are several motives for committing the act. Some are well planned and directed toward a definite goal, while others are spontaneous and may

© Springer Nature Switzerland AG 2020
P. C. Kratcoski et al., *Juvenile Delinquency*,
https://doi.org/10.1007/978-3-030-31452-1_3

be the result of anger, a perceived danger, or "just for fun." In some cases, the person is suffering from an extreme psychological disturbance and in other cases the person does not have the mental capacity to distinguish what behavior is morally and legally acceptable and that behavior violates the norms and laws of the society.

Some of the assertions made about those who commit homicide can also be made for those who attempt suicide, or are successful. The motives range from an attempt to get attention, being in a state of deep depression, failure in school, feelings of hopelessness about the future, to get revenge on someone who has hurt the person, perhaps a parent, boyfriend, or teacher, or even because of a feeling of failure, as in the case of the star member of a sports team who does not win a letter in sports, or does not live up to the expectations of his or her parents.

Perhaps the main factor to consider when comparing those who are children or those in their adolescent years with adults who commit homicide, suicide, or other crimes, is that the child or adolescent has not reached the peak of maturity. Even those in their teen years who are strong enough to beat another human to death, or can learn to use the latest technological devices with ease still may not fully comprehend the importance and consequences of their actions in taking another's or his or her own life or causing harm to others in some other manner.

In this chapter, we will explore some of the psychological and social psychological theories pertaining to the mental development of children and their personality development. The human personality has been exhaustively examined by psychologists and psychiatrists, who claim to have traced the various stages of its development, defined its component parts, outlined its functioning, sought the causes of the development of various personality traits, and related certain patterns of deviant behavior to the malfunctioning of the personality.

According to Shoemaker (2009), explanations of behavior that can be broadly categorized as psychological theories are numerous and diverse, but they generally share some common assumptions. First, they view delinquent behavior as caused by some disturbance or trauma in the youth's development. Second, they regard this psychological disturbance as beginning not later than early childhood and continuing during the maturation process. Third, they see delinquency as a problem within the individual that must be approached through direct treatment of this person rather than modification of external environmental factors.

3.2   Psychoanalytic Theories of Crime and Delinquency

A great deal of the personality development theory that is applied to explaining juvenile delinquency is based on the psychoanalytic theories of Sigmund Freud (1856–1939). Freud defined the personality as having three structural components—the id, the ego, and the superego. Brenner (1955, p. 45) described them in the following way:

> The id comprises the psychic representatives of the drives, the ego consists of those functions which have to do with the individual's relations to his environment, and the superego comprises the moral precepts of our minds as well as our ideal aspirations.

In the 1950s and 1960s, many of the agencies working with disturber and delinquent children, including the juvenile courts, employed social workers who had
been trained to apply Freudian and Neo-Freudian therapy in their work. However,
in the 1970s and afterward, the emphasis moved to reality therapy and cognitive-
based approaches in the counseling and programming of the agencies working with
disturbed and delinquent youths.

Psychoanalytic theory places great emphasis on early childhood as the critical
period in personality formation and defines various stages of psychological development that correspond to the child's mastery of certain bodily functions and drives
(e.g., oral, anal, and genital phases of development). The parents are viewed as critical factors in the child's personality formation, and conduct disorders and neuroses
are regarded as reflections of the effects of inadequate parenting. Critical parent–
child relationships deficiencies that may result in personality and conduct disorders,
according to psychoanalysts, are the absence of the mother or her rejection of the
child during infancy and very early childhood, lack of affection, and discipline by
both parents during the first 5 years of life, and for boys, lack of the influence of a
father figure during the preadolescent years (Schoenfeld, 1975, pp. 24–26).

The parents are also regarded as important influences in the formation of the
superego (somewhat similar to the conscience). Schoenfeld (1975, p. 23) describes
the relation of the superego formation to delinquency in the following way:

> The vast majority of delinquent acts reflect the presence not of an unduly strict superego or
> of a superego with criminal tendencies but rather of a superego that is somehow so weak,
> defective, or incomplete that it proves unable to control properly the primitive and powerful
> urges of early childhood that are resurrected just before puberty, with the result that some
> of these antisocial urges … are expressed in delinquent behavior.

Freud tested and modified his theories during his lifetime, and his co-researchers
and followers, including Anna Freud, Heinz Hartman, and Eric Erikson, continued
to examine and apply Freud theories after his death. Erikson (1959) defined eight
ages of the life of a human being that require adjustment and adaptation, and maintained that failure to progress successfully from one stage to the next can set off
unacceptable behavioral activity. These eight stages are as follows:

1. The development of trust by an infant in his or her caretakers.
2. Gaining control over the bodily functions.
3. Experimentation by the child with various behavioral roles in his or her
   environment.
4. Attempts to master physical, social, and cognitive skills.
5. Development by an adolescent of an identity and sense of purpose.
6. Development by an adult of intimacy with others.
7. Acceptance of adult caretaking activities in which the family and external relations are the absorbing preoccupations.
8. Development of the personal integrity needed to face life's final crisis, that is,
   illness and death.

The Freudians and Neo-Freudians based their theories on the assumption that interpretation of this sequential order of development, or the inability to proceed past a given stage, can trigger unacceptable behavior. Erikson postulated the development of a "negative identity" by some youths, who deliberately embrace the roles or lifestyles that parents and significant others in their lives characterized as unacceptable, (Erikson, 1968). According to White (1989, p. 367), this negative identity is a defense mechanism, a method of coping with self-doubt and fear of not being able to live up to expectations. Such youths tend to seek each other out, developing relationships based on their mutual rejection of society's norms, and they become involved in a delinquent subculture.

3.3 Moral Development Theories

Researchers since the Neo-Freudians have concentrated on the concept of the superego, or the moral judgment-developmental stage of the personality. Piaget (1948) viewed the internalization of moral values as involving two stages, which he termed *"moral realism"* and *"moral relativism."* At the stage of moral realism, a child realizes that he or she is required to obey rules set by some authority (in most cases, the parents or the caregiver). With the development of moral relativism, the child becomes cognizant of the reasons behind certain requirements and begins to develop an internalized set of moral precepts. Piaget believed that a child begins to develop moral relativism at about the age of eight. Concurrent with moral development is the intellectual growth of the child, which moves from sensory-motor responses to the world in which Piaget terms concrete operations, or reality-based, logical efforts to understand the world, beginning at about the age of seven. The child's experiences in the family and in society obviously have strong influences on both moral and intellectual development.

Kohlberg (1963) believed the internalization of moral judgment occurs later, during adolescence. He characterized the various stages as the *moral-development period*, normally completed by the age of seven, in which avoiding punishment is the motivation for conformity and a child is completely caught up in a search for self-gratification; the period of *conventional conformity,* beginning in the preadolescent and continuing into the adolescent period, when deviant behavior is avoided because there are rules against it and a child comes to respect the authorities who enforce the rules; and a period of *autonomy*, when a young person conforms to a specific set of norms or moral principles that have been internalized. If this theory of moral development is considered valid, juvenile misbehavior may be attributed to the failure of the young person to progress beyond, or in some cases even reach, the pre-moral level of conformity, where conformity is motivated by fear of punishment. The reasons for this failure may be related to negative life experiences, a lack of interaction with persons who subscribe to conventional conformity, or even conscious decisions to pursue self-gratification and thrills rather than conform.

Perhaps the major contribution of the psychoanalytic and moral-development theorists is the notion that personality and moral-judgment are gradually developed conditions, influenced by many factors in the child's life, and that internalization of moral values rather than exposure to moral influences (religion, social programs, parents' concepts of morality) is the key to the development of the child's moral values that are in conformity with values that are accepted in the general community.

3.4 Cognitive Development Theories

Cognitive development applies to decision making and judgment. Psychological researchers have defined these as developmental processes and discovered that children, preadolescents, and younger teenage youths differ substantially in their capacities to make appropriate decisions and judgments. They have found that many children may be quite deviant in their preteens and early teen years, but are not deviant or delinquent in their later teens. The theory explaining these variations targets potential costs and rewards associated with engaging in deviant behavior. In early adolescence, children may be rebellious and destructive because they perceive their behavior as a way of gaining independence from adults. They do not perceive their unacceptable behavior as having long-range negative effects on their goals or lifestyles. As they develop cognitively and are capable of making better judgments and decisions, and as they come closer to the goals they have established for themselves (graduating from high school, going to college, getting a good job), they begin to realize the potential costs associated with delinquency and misbehavior in general. The following case in Box 3.1 illustrates the cognitive developmental process.

Box 3.1 Jake's Story
Jake, a 14-year-old boy and two other boys were cited to the_____ Juvenile Court on a charge of property destruction. He and two other 16-year-old boys threw some eggs on the front of a house inhabited by an elderly couple. The owner of the house had yelled at the boys for riding their bicycles across his lawn. Jake was asked during the Intake interview why he engaged in the delinquent act. Jake responded, "I don't know. I have done some bad things in the past, and afterwards I asked myself, "Why did I do it." After some probing by the intake officer about these "bad things," Jake started to recall some of the events. In some cases, it appeared as if Jake was influenced by older boys who were involved in the delinquent behavior. Jake stated, "One time, on Halloween, we broke into the school and threw papers all around, and wrote some bad things on the board about a few of the teachers. Everyone, including me, thought it was great fun. We were not worried about getting caught. Another time, Tom and me went to a store where they sold ice cream and candy and we stole some candy bars. We were caught and had to give back the candy. The

owner of the store told our teacher and she gave a big speech to the class about obeying the commandants and not to steal. She didn't tell our names, but I think the other students knew we were the ones caught stealing. I did not go back to that store. On another occasion, I was waiting for the math teacher to come into the classroom. I was bored and took out my compass and started carving my name on the wooden desk. After a few minutes, I realized that I would get into a lot of trouble for carving up the desk, so I changed my seat before the teacher came into the room. The teacher noticed the desk and tried to get the other class members to squeal and tell him who was carving the desk, but all of them said they didn't know. "Why did I do bad things?" Somethings it seemed like fun, sometimes because I wanted something and the only way to get it was to steal, sometimes I was bored and did not thing about what I was doing and other times I just went along with the gang. We really did not think much about getting caught and being punished until afterwards.

(Abstracted from interviews by the author.)

Scott and Grisso (1997, p. 137) contend that it is necessary to understand the youth's cognitive developmental process to gain insight into the choices that children make. They note,

> …Youthful antisocial risk-taking acts are personal statements of independence by individuals who are precluded from yet assuming legitimate adult roles. Desistance in young adulthood is explained under the theory as the adequate response to changed contingencies, as more legitimate adult roles become available. Delinquent behavior becomes costly rather than rewarding, as many young adults perceive that it threatens now-available conventional opportunities and may foreclose future goals. In short, they come to realize that they have something to lose.

3.5   Coping Mechanisms Used by Adolescents

The developmental process involves repeated testing of self and of the limits set by parents and the larger society. In adolescence, young people are constantly questioning the values and standards presented to them and making their own judgments as to whether they wish to adhere to them or deviate from them. Internal conflict and conflicts with others, including parents, peers, teachers, employers, and others who have power over them, are inevitable parts of growing up. However, if adolescents deal with the pressures and conflicts in their lives in inappropriate ways, the results may be psychological disturbances and/or delinquent behavior.

Just as a person under physical attack will ordinarily defend himself, a youth experiencing conflicts may use psychological defense mechanisms to deal with stress and conflicts being experienced, as shown in Fig. 3.1 (White, 1989, p. 31).

Facing and dealing with stress is a normal problem almost every adolescent must encounter during their preadult life. Most adolescents are resilient and able to make

- repression - The automatic or unconscious screening out of unacceptable wishes, drives, images, and impulses. Repression begins in childhood and is one of the basic defense mechanisms;

- Suppression - Consciously tuning out unpleasant feelings, ideas, or emotions by trying not to work it out. Suppression is conscious, whereas repression is unconscious;

- Denial - Denial usually refers to the screening out of unpleasant external values or feelings generated by unpleasant external realities. Repression usually refers to intrapsychic feelings. All defenses involve some degree of repression or denial;

- Displacement - A shift of feelings from one object to another. The second object becomes a more acceptable target of such feelings as anger and hostility;

- Rationalization - The assessment of a socially acceptable explanation for our behavior so we appear to be acting rationally or logically;

- Intellectualization - Dealing with the anxiety and stress-provoking problems as if they were intellectually interesting, emotionally neural events;

- Projection - Attributing one's own anxiety arousal, or unacceptable motives to someone else;

- Sublimation - Channeling unacceptable aggressive and sexual energies into socially approved behaviors such as athletics, school, or performing arts;

- Acting out - Poorly controlled release of sexual, aggressive, or angry impulses to reduce tension; and

- Regression - Retreating to earlier ways of behaving when one is under stress.

Fig. 3.1 Commonly used defense mechanisms

the adjustments needed to solve their problems without having any long-lasting psychological difficulties.

However, some are not able to make the cognitive decisions, or to control their emotions needed to make an acceptable adjustment. White (1989, pp. 30–31), in Fig. 3.2, describes some maladaptive behavior sometimes used by those who have difficulty adjusting to the emotional and psychological problems they face during their adolescent years.

- Depression - Conflicts which are preventing the emergence of self-worth, hope, confidence, and feelings of being capable, powerful and loved;

- Suicide - Suicide in adolescence represents the ultimate loss of hope. Case conflicts involve deficits in connectedness to others, unconditional love, and a sense of belonging;

- Anorexia and eating disorders - Conflicts around body image and nurturance;

- Schizophrenia - Core conflicts involve difficulties in perceptual, cognitive, and emotional organization which may be caused by a combination of biochemical and psychological vulnerabilities and predispositions. Schizophrenia can also be a defense against further hurt by withdrawing from reality;

- Excessive use of drugs and alcohol - Core conflict involves the inability or unwillingness to cope with the demands of adolescent life and feel good about one's self without using substances; and

- Delinquency and conduct disturbances - Conflicts between the adolescent and the rules of society. If delinquent behavior persists, society has the power to create adverse-consequences by restricting personal freedom and punishment.

Fig. 3.2 Maladaptive coping behavior

As a young person seeks to understand, accept, or deal with a stressful situation, employment of one or several of these defense mechanisms may be a positive response. The repression or suppression of painful feelings may help a youth get through the immediate situation and, as time goes by, their ways of coping may be used. For example, trying out for a sports team and not being chosen can be a stressful occurrence, but if the young person tries not to think about it (suppression), or decides that it would not have been that exciting anyway (rationalization), the lack of acceptance may be less traumatic. In contrast, acting out through aggressive or angry behavior toward those who were selected as team members would be unacceptable use of a defense mechanism.

3.6 Personality Trait Explanations of Delinquency

Psychologists have devoted considerable attention to discovering the configuration of personality traits that are characteristic of persons involved in deviant behavior. The personality-trait approach assumes that delinquents are different from "normal" youths and that the differences can be found in their personality makeup. Although personality theorists do not consider delinquents mentally ill, they regard them as having personality disturbances that interfere with their normal functioning in the family, school, and community.

Among the early personality trait theorists were Jenkins and Hewitt (1946). On the basis of their experience with young people in a child-guidance clinic, they defined three distinct maladapted personality types among their clients. These included the *unsocialized aggressive,* who displayed assaultive, malicious tendencies and openly defied authority figures, the *socialized delinquents,* whose misbehavior was peer related, and the *over inhibited* delinquents, who were shy, apathetic children that came from repressive family situations. In the Glueck and Glueck (1950) study of 500 delinquent youths and 500 nondelinquent youths, they found that the most common personality traits of delinquent youths were that they were extroverted, suspicious and hostile toward authority figures, defiant, resentful, and afraid of failing more often than non-delinquent youth.

Persons involved in the classification and handling of delinquents incorporated the ideas of the early theorists into testing and classification systems that came to be widely used in the diagnosis and treatment of delinquent youths. Gerard (1970), in his analysis of the Quay system, identified four dimensions of delinquent behavior that frequently occurred. Those delinquents who were *unsocialized aggressives* displayed constant conflict with parents, peers, and authority figures in the school and the community. *The neurotic-conflicted* youths, in contrast, expressed strong feelings of unhappiness, anxiety, and distress and had many complaints of being physically ill. Those who were inadequate-*immature* were victimized by aggressive behavior and ridicule from other children and other delinquents. They withdrew from stressful situations through daydreaming and apathy. The *socialized* delinquents committed their offenses in the company of peers and were drawn to delinquency by social rather than psychological pressures. These personality theories were incorporated into a system for classifying and treating juvenile offenders that came to be used in youth correctional facilities.

3.7 Personality Measurement Methods to Ascertain Behavior Disorders

Psychologists, social workers, and counselors who worked with both delinquent and non-delinquent youths in juvenile justice agencies, schools, and group homes have viewed some youths with delinquency tendencies, or who have been adjudicated delinquent in the juvenile court, as having personal emotional problems of some type. They have observed that delinquents frequently have difficulty establishing close relationships with peers and adults, and that they tend to be insecure and experience feelings of inferiority, inadequacy, or rejection, coupled with strong resentment of authority figures. Another characteristic of many delinquents is a sole concern for the present, with unrealistic ideas of what the future will bring for them, or a lack of interest in making future plans.

Much time and energy has been devoted to the development of various types of tests used to measure facets of the personality (self-image, aspirations, values, ego strength, interests) and uncover precisely how young people with difficulties differ from "normal" youths. Inherent in the development of such tests are the problems of whether specific test items really measure what they are designed to measure (validity) and whether the items are interpreted and applied in the same way by all young people taking the tests (reliability).

The Minnesota Multiphasic Personality Inventory (MMPI) has been widely used as a diagnostic tool for older adolescents in juvenile court services and institutions. This self-rating schedule contains 550 statements designed to uncover the possible existence of depression, paranoia, a psychopathic personality, and various other behavioral ills. Once the major difficulty of the young person has been disclosed by the diagnostic tool, programs are applied that are designed to overcome or reduce the emotional difficulty.

Another instrument used to identify personality traits is the Jesness Inventory (Jesness, 1966). It contains a series of written statements that are checked as "true" if the respondent agrees or "false" if the respondent disagrees with the statement. One section of the inventory, referred to as the *asocial index,* attempts to measure potential or susceptibility for delinquent behavior. The 155 items pertain to control of anger, response to authority figures, and the mechanisms used in problem-solving. The *asocial index* is structured in such a way that affirmative answers to answers indicate the possession of deviant personality traits. Thus the higher the score of "true" responses on the asocial index, the more likely it is that the youths being tested would use unacceptable ways to solve problems (Jesness, 1984).

Van Ness (1987) used a modified version of the Jesness Inventory in a study of more than 1500 institutionalized delinquents who had been involved in predatory violence. She defined predatory delinquents as those with clear descriptions in their case files of having committed five or more non-defensive, non-accidental physical attacks on others or attempted to use force that could lead to the physical injury to a human victim. She found that these youths scored much higher on the Inventory than did the nonviolent delinquents who were included in the study. Her findings suggest that the Jesness Inventory is not only useful in identifying personality traits that may be predictive of delinquent behavior, but also helpful in differentiating potential violent, predatory delinquents from those who, while engaging in a deviant act, are not likely to persist with their unlawful behavior through their later adolescence and adulthood.

3.8   The Criminal Personality

Publication of the books *The Criminal Personality: A Profile for Change (*Yochelson & Samenow, 1976*)* and Samenow's *Inside the Criminal Mind* (Samenow, 1984) brought about a renewed interest in the personality theories of crime and delinquency. The authors, Yochelson and Samenow, were a neuropsychiatrist and a psychologist at the St. Elizabeth Hospital in Washington, D.C. Their research spanned 16 years of work with patients who had committed serious criminal offenses.

The authors contended that certain deviant thinking patterns were present to an extreme degree in all of the criminals they studied and they identified 52 "errors of thinking" present in all of these offenders. The criminals the y studied regarded everyday interaction with family. Friends, or coworkers as dull and they sought excitement in doing everything forbidden. For them, crime was the ultimate excitement. They appeared to enjoy thinking about crime, talking about crime, planning crime, carrying it out, and even getting caught engaging in a criminal act.

The researchers focused on the notion that the erroneous thinking patterns of criminals, which are different from those of "normal" persons, show up in early childhood. Although the exact cause of the development of the criminal mind has not been established, the authors concluded that it is futile to search for causes of delinquency and crime outside the individual (in poverty, the environment, the family, or the school).

In the book written by Samenow (1984, pp. 26, 39, 42), titled *Inside the Criminal Mind*, he describes the criminal personality in the following way:

> Beginning during the preschool years, patterns evolve that become part of a criminal life style. As a child, the criminal is a dynamo of energy, a being with an iron will, insistent upon taking charge, expecting others to indulge his every whim.... He takes risks, becomes embroiled in difficulties, and demands to be bailed out and forgiven...
>
> As a child, the criminal has contempt not only for his parents' advice and authority but also for the way they live, no matter what their social and economic circumstances.... To him, having a good time is what life is all about...
>
> As the personality of the criminally inclined child unfolds, his parents are gripped by a gnawing fear that something terrible is going to happen.... Every time the phone rings, their hearts sink.... As their concerns mount, parents try new ways to cope with the youngster's misbehavior. They restrict his movement and privileges, but end up suffering more than the child, who blatantly and sneakily circumvents the restrictions or flouts them.

Samenow (1984, p. 35) also noted that lawbreakers frequently claim to have been rejected by their parents, school teachers, or other authority figures in their lives, but see no link between their behavior and this purported rejection.

The premise that a specific "criminal personality" type can be identified has come under criticism from other researchers. Most of the research maintains that aggression and violence are learned responses rather than innate personality traits. Aggression, violence, and deviance are learned from a variety of sources, including the family, peers, and through the mass media, the internet and particularly television. Biskup and Cozic (1992) contend that many children who kill have learned about violence by watching their parents, aunts, uncles, and siblings.

An inmate serving a life sentence in a California prison after being convicted of murder, reflecting on his feelings about his first gang fight involving an ambush of a rival gang in which several youths were killed, noted that he looked forward to the fight and the possibility of killing members of the rival gang, but later experienced feelings of guilt. He described his feelings in the following way:

> The seriousness of what I had done that evening did not dawn on me until I was alone at home that night. My heart had slowed to its normal pace and the alcohol and pot had worn

off. I was left then with just myself and the awesome flashes of light that lit up my mind to reveal bodies in abnormal positions and grotesque shapes, twisting and bending in arcs that defied bone structure. The actual impact was on my return back past the bodies of the first fallen, my first real look bodies torn to shreds. It did little to me then, because it was all about survival. But as I lay awake in my bed, safe, a live, I felt guilty and ashamed of myself. Upon further contemplation, I felt that they were too easy to kill. Why had they been out there! I tried every conceivable alibi within the realm of reason to justify my actions. There were none. I slept very little that night. (Shakur, 1993, p. 13)

3.9   The Development of Self-Control, Introspection, and Resilience

The term self-control, that is, self-restraint in the way a person responds to others or situations, can be viewed as being basically fixed and thus fairly predictable in humans or viewed as something that is learned through one's socialization and experiences and often changes during one's lifetime. Hirschi (2004) contends that the social bonds with parents, friends, and teachers that a child has made during their life's experience and the impressions these figures have made on the child serve as the basis for the development of self-control.

Steinberg et al. (2015, p. 1) stating the conventional view of psychologists for the reasons why youths who were involved in delinquency, but who have desisted because they have reached a certain level of maturity and now have the ability to control their impulses, have learned to consider the implications of their actions, and know how to delay immediate gratification in the pursuance of long term goals and how to resist the influence of peers. They state, "Thus, psychologists see that much juvenile offending reflects psychological immaturity and, accordingly, they view desistance from antisocial behavior as a natural consequence of growing up-emotionally, socially, and intellectually. As individuals, become better able to regulate their behavior, they become less likely to engage in impulsive, ill-considered acts." Their longitudinal study included more than 6000 respondents whose behavior was recorded from the age of 14 to age 21. The enrollment in the research project began in 2000, and the research team ended the collection of data in 2010. A youth had to be at least 14 years of age to participate. The participants were interviewed for 4 h to establish the baseline information, and every 6 months for 3 years and annually until the end of the research. Approximately 90% of those who enrolled in the research completed the study. The psycho-social maturity of the participants was measured in three areas, temperance, (impulse control), perspective (consideration of others), and responsibility (personality responsibility). Through the use of self-report questions, the participants' antisocial behavior was measured and recorded, as well as changes in their psychosocial maturity. The authors concluded (p. 8), "As hypothesized, individuals in different antisocial trajectory groups differed in their absolute levels of psychosocial maturity and the extent to which their psychosocial maturity increased with age."

In addition, they found that even those in the serious juvenile offender group showed a significant increase in psychosocial maturity at age 16, continuing into early adulthood. Also, they concluded that variability in psychosocial maturity is linked to patterns of antisocial behavior. Less mature individuals are more likely to be persistent offenders, and high frequency offenders who desist from antisocial activity are likely to become more mature psychosocially than those who continue to commit crimes as adults.

Researchers Hay (2001) and Perrone, Sullivan, Pratt, and Margaryan (2009) have shown a relationship between adolescents who exhibit low self-control and delinquent behavior. Pratt (2016, p. 130) proposed that the individual's way of responding to one's life experiences is not fundamentally fixed, but contends, "Self-control is viewed as dynamic and subject to considerable change both situationally and over time, and self-control is seen as an important cause of selection into the kinds of significant life events, both positive and negative (turning points), that are assumed to, in turn, influence offending." In regard to the dynamics of self-control, Pratt (2016, p. 131) emphasizes the dynamics of self-control. He states "First, self-control can change within the individual at any given time and is subject to depletion at all points in the life course. Second, individuals vary with respect to how susceptible they are to self-control depletion throughout the life course. Of particular importance are the criminogenic social contexts and stressful life events that can drain one's level of self-control at any given time (Pratt, 2009). And third, young people are more vulnerable to self-control depletion than older people are. The notion that young people, those in their adolescent years, are more vulnerable to self-control depletion at any given time, and especially during the times of being confronted with serious emotional problems, might explain why an adolescent boy or girl who was always thought of as being "so normal" might commit suicide as a result of breaking up with a friend, or even kill another person.

Zemel, Ronel, and Einat (2016) interviewed three groups of individuals (normal adolescents with neither current or past involvement in criminal behavior; adolescents limited to temporary delinquent behavior with a criminal past, but not currently involved in delinquent behavior; and adolescents who had a persistent criminal past and were currently involved in criminal behavior). The authors found that through introspection, a process used by individuals to explore their "internal world" by examining motives for behavior, reflecting on the outcomes of past and reflecting on the people who have had a major influence in their lives, can be used to "identify the risk factors and consider them as emotional, emotional, and challenges to judge themselves more accurately, and improve their ability to change" (Zemel et al., 2016, p. 113).

They concluded that, through introspection, those individuals in the group who had some delinquent behavior in the past, but were not involved in delinquency at the present time, developed resilience to abstain from delinquent behavior through introspection. Generally, those in this group had had a devastating emotional experience, such as the death of a parent. Through assistance and influence provided by a significant person (parent, teacher, foster parent) they were motivated to engage in introspection and develop the resilience to avoid those risk situations that might result in a resumption of deviant behavior. On the other hand, the group who had histories of delinquency and were currently involved in delinquent behavior did not engage in the introspection process. Zemel et al. (2016. p. 116) concluded, "As to the persistent criminal participants, the interviews reveal that they did not experience any processes of introspection and, as a result, did not try to examine and discover the factors causing them to continue with their criminal conduct."

3.10 The Psychopathic, Sociopathic, and Conduct Disorder Personalities

Psychologists have identified a type of disturbed individual quite similar to Yochelson and Samenow's "criminal personality," labeling this personality type a *psychopath*. The *psychopath* is an aggressive, impulsive person who has developed no bond of affection with others and experiences no feelings of guilt for committing delinquent or criminal acts. For example, Reid and Lee (2018, p. 267) in their analysis of the confession of a person they identify as a psychopath, who may have killed up to 50 individuals before being convicted and sentenced to prison, state, "Notably, Pickton does not show signs of remorse for his crimes. In fact, the only indication of regret comes from having messed up, or having 'been sloppy' near the end of his murder series. Pickton did not regret the murders, but rather, he regretted his inability to have killed more. Additionally, Pickton's narcissism surfaces when he begins to discuss himself in relation to serial killers in the USA. For example, Pickton brags that his record has surpassed the record of the most prolific serial killers in the country." The search for pleasure or personal gratification, frequently at the expense of others, is a hallmark of this personality type. Mc Cord and McCord (1964), who did extensive research on the psychopathic personality, noted that the two traits of guiltlessness and lovelessness make the psychopath different from other people.

Kielhl and Hoffman (2011) contend that as much as one-fifth of the adult prison population may have psychopathic personalities, and their criminal acts before being caught probably caused a considerable amount of grief and cost to the victims of their crimes. Research on juveniles who express traits and behavior characteristic of the typical psychopath, except for clinical case studies, is somewhat limited. Yablonsky (1966) described the behavior of the "core leaders" in his research on violent gangs as being "psychopathic," but generally, research on children and adolescent individuals tend to use other labels such as "sociopath" or "character disorder" when describing behaviors that are similar to those attributed to the psychopath.

The term *sociopath* is often used in lieu of *psychopath* by social scientists to emphasize the notion that the characteristics of this type of personality are more likely to be a product of the person's environment and experiences rather than being hereditary. Cleckley (1954, pp. 567–588) defines sociopaths as "Chronically antisocial individuals who are always in trouble, profiting neither from experiences nor punishment and maintaining no real loyalties to any person, group, or code. They are frequently callous and hedonistic, showing marked emotional immaturity, with lack of responsibility, lack of judgment, and an ability to rationalize their behaviors so that it appears warranted, reasonable, and justified." The terms *anti-social personality*, *conduct disorder* or *oppositional defiant disorder* are now used by the Diagnostic and Statistical Manual of Mental Illness in place of psychopath or sociopath to describe youths who have many of the characteristics of the typical psychopath or sociopath.

The more current term *oppositional defiant* is used to describe a person who is deliberately defiant, easily loses his/her temper, is constantly angry or vindictive, and does not take responsibility for the mistakes he or she made but instead blames others for mistakes.

While Yokelson and Samenow advanced no explanation for the existence of a criminal personality in a given individual, Mc Cord and McCord (1964) suggested that the *psychopathic personality* has its origins in brain damage or other physical trauma, or most commonly, extreme emotional deprivation in childhood. Whereas the research on psychopathic behavior has identified its presence in a relatively small percentage of the total population of delinquents and criminal offenders, Yochelson and Samenow declared that the criminal personality existed in all of the offenders they treated and included in their research at the Saint Elizabeth Hospital. Although they were counseling adults who were in the hospital as a result of having been convicted of a criminal offense and were declared to be mentally ill by the courts, Samenow and Yochelson did not consider them to be psychotic, but their illness was the result of their "thinking errors" and the characteristics of the residents they studied were very similar to those of the profile of a psychopath. Based on their analysis of the detailed case records of the criminal offenders they studied, they concluded the "thinking errors" developed in early childhood. Frick, Kimonis, Dandreaux, and Farrell (2003) appear to confirm that the psychopathic behaviors were evident in the preteens and persisted throughout their adolescence and into adulthood. Forth and Book (2007) found that offenders with psychopathy are likely to have become involved in criminal behavior at a very early age. However, Robbins (1966) contends that a child is not intellectually or morally developed enough to establish the traits typically associated with the psychopath, sociopath, or conduct disorder personality. Research on child development would tend to confirm this assertion, since it is often typical for children at the age of 12 or 13 to act rebellious, obnoxious, annoying, or disobedient, and by the time they reach ages 16 or 17, they personalities completely change.

3.11 Mental Illness and Delinquency

The notion that misbehaving young people are "ill" and in need of "diagnosis and treatment for their mental illness" has been popular in the past with social agencies working with juvenile offenders. Sometimes termed the "medical model," such an approach presupposes that some problem within the individual rather than in the external environment is the cause of misbehavior and that once this condition is uncovered, it can be treated in some manner to make the person "healthy" again. The medical model has been challenged in recent years by those who believe that environmental influences or situational factors play a more important role in delinquency than the mental illness, or emotional disturbances of the typical juvenile offender.

Studies of homicide suggest that most juvenile murders are not extremely psychotic. Biskup and Cozic. (1992, p. 62) studied 72 Michigan youths charged with murder and concluded that only five (7%) were psychotic when they committed their crimes. Rather than mental illness, extensive participation in delinquent activities or involvement in violent peer groups, rather than mental illness, were advanced as alternative explanations for juvenile homicides. Other possible motives for a juvenile to commit homicide include, revenge, the victim was killed while in the he process of committing another offense, such as robbery, self-defense, or in the case of a boy who was killed during a school shooting, the boy was killed as he was trying to protect another person who was being victimized. This story is given in Box 3.2:

Box 3.2 Teen Who Charged Attackers Killed in School Shooting

"Highlands Ranch, Colorado: The lone fatality in the Colorado high school shooting was Kendrick Castillo, a friendly 18-year-old who witnesses said, leaped from his desk in a literature class and charged the two attackers, sacrificing his life to but classmates time to escape."

"Another 18-year-old who was preparing to enter the Marines also tackled at least one of the shooters, and an armed security guard then confronted and detained one of the gunmen, officials said."

"Authorities said these acts of bravery helped minimize the bloodshed from the attack, which also wounded eight people."

"The attackers were identified by law enforcement officials as 18-year-old Devon Erickson and a younger student who is a juvenile and was not named. They allegedly walked into the STEM School Highlands Ranch through an entrance without metal detectors and opened fire in the two classrooms."

"Both suspects were students at the school, and they were not previously known to authorities…." (Foody, Bands, and Riccard (2019) Akron Beacon Journal, May 9, p. A4)

The deviant behavior of delinquents who suffer from some form of mental illness is generally so bizarre, extreme, or unpredictable that it can readily be differentiated from general delinquency. Acts of torture, brutality, murder, sadistic rape, and arson may be the signal of the presence of mental illness. A study by Sorrells Jr. (1980), of juvenile murders led him to classify

youths who kill into three personality types: the *non-emphatic*, who have no feelings of sympathy toward or identification with others; the *pre-psychotic*, who are trapped in painful and conflict-ridden interpersonal situations, usually in their families, and see no possibility of escaping; and the *neurotically fearful*, who are so insecure that they overreact to threatening circumstances as though they were potentially lethal.

The causes of mental illness in children are varied. They include inadequate diet, neurological injury, excessive drug or alcohol use, physical or emotional deprivation, emotional traumas (sexual abuse, death of a parent) or physical or emotional abuse. Other factors related to juvenile mental illness include a violent, chaotic family, and emotionally disturbed, alcoholic, or incompetent parents (Sorrells Jr., 1980).

The matter of holding the juvenile offender responsible for a delinquent act arises if there is a question of the juvenile being mentally ill. It is routine practice to hold a competency hearing in any case in which there is some evidence of a juvenile offender being mentally ill. Dr. Thomas Webb, psychologist for the Summit County Juvenile Court, Ohio, responded to a question regarding the matter of a youth's competency in the following way. "If there is some question whether or not the juvenile charged with a serious crime does not have the mental capacity to relay information to his attorney or appreciate the nature of court proceedings, an extensive assessment would be required using standardized test instruments and personal interviews. The question of competence will come up more often with younger juveniles, but can be an important consideration for a youth of any age, that is, whenever issues of a child's mental capacity or developmental health are raised." (Kratcoski, 2012, p. 256).

If the assessments of a youth charged with an serious offense confirm that the child is not mentally competent, and if the child is very young, the case may be heard in a domestic relations court, or the child may be sent to a hospital for treatment for the mental illness. In some instances with older offenders, the case may be transferred to the adult criminal court to assure that the youth will have all of the legal rights (including the right to make an insanity plea) afforded adults charged with a crime.

3.12 Summary

In this chapter, the social-psychological theories of delinquency causation, which have sought the explanations for delinquency within the personality of youths and have related to the problems in the youth's mental or emotional development are presented.

The psychoanalytic theories of delinquency place great emphasis on early childhood and relate delinquency to deficiencies in parent–child relationships or a young person's progress through specific emotional-development stages.

Those who advance moral-development theories of delinquency emphasize the importance of the internalization of moral values in a gradual, developmental sequence.

Cognitive development theories maintain that the ability to make appropriate choices and judgments is a gradual maturation process, related to perceived costs and rewards. Adolescents use psychological defense coping mechanisms to deal with the stresses in their lives.

Personality-trait theorists, including Jenkins and Hewitt and Sheldon and Eleanor Glueck, have identified certain personality traits as characteristics of delinquents. The classification system used in juvenile and adult corrections institutions is specifically based on the separation and treatment of offenders according to the specific personality characteristics they display. Personality tests are widely used to identify the existence of undesirable personality traits. In their book, *The Criminal Personality*, Yochelson and Samenow maintained that criminals display erroneous thinking patterns and the criminal personality characteristics are present in delinquent youth at a very early age. Although the criminal personality theory has strong appeal as an explanation of criminal behavior in youths who have suffered no apparent psychological deprivation, it cannot be accepted uncritically. There is evidence that even those who display many of the traits of a criminal personality have had negative influences in their lives that could have triggered their deviant behavior.

Psychopathic individuals, who apparently experience no guilt feelings for their delinquent acts and display no bonds of affection with others, are regarded as having experienced extreme emotional deprivation or physical trauma in childhood. This personality has been identified in a small percentage of the total delinquent population. The terms *sociopath*, *anti-social personality*, and *oppositional defiant disorder* have been applied to youths who exhibit some of the traits of the classic psychopath. However, the reasons given for the cause for the development of the personality are generally attributed to social, environmental influences rather than the traits of the individual.

Some youths who commit very serious offenses, even murder, do not have the capacity to distinguish the difference between behavior that is morally and legally acceptable and behavior that is wrong. If such youths are found to be incompetent (mentally ill), as discovered by a battery of psychological tests, they typically will be given treatment in a hospital rather than processed in the juvenile justice system.

3.13   Discussion Questions

1. Define personality. Discuss whether a person is born with a specific personality or if the personality is developed. If developed, what are some of the factors that contribute to its development?
2. Many psychologists believe that anyone who commits a deviant act has a character disorder, and thus should be considered abnormal. Do you agree?
3. Discuss the theories of criminality as set forth in Yochelson and Samenow's books on the criminal personality. Why does the theory have a strong appeal?
4. Define psychopathic personality. How does the psychopath differ from the sociopath? Should those youths who are labeled as having an antisocial personalities or having a conduct disorder, or oppositional defiant disorder be considered to be in the same category as the psychopath and sociopath?
5. How is it determined if a youth who has committed a serious offense is competent to be held legally responsible for the act?
6. Discuss the reasons why adolescent youths commit acts of homicide.
7. What are some of the traits that can be found in children and adolescent youths who have been diagnosed as having character disorders?

8. Researchers have found that juveniles with low levels of self-control are high risks for engaging in delinquency. How is self-control measured? Discuss the reasons why low self-control is likely to increase the risk of engaging in deviant behavior.
9. Should juveniles diagnosed as having psychopathic or sociopathic personalities be considered mentally ill? Discuss.
10. Discuss the differences between the moral development theories of child development and the cognitive development theories of child development.

References

Biskup, M., & Cozic, C. (Eds.). (1992). *Youth violence*. San Diego, CA: Green Haven Press.

Brenner, C. (1955). *An elementary textbook of psychoanalysis*. New York: Oxford University Press.

Cleckley, H. M. (1954). Psychopathic states. In S. Arieri (Ed.), *American handbook of psychiatry*. New York: Basic Books.

Daily Kent Stater. (1992). *Boy shoots 7- year-old playmate,* September 3, (p. 1).

Erikson, E. (1959). *Identity and the life cycle* (pp. 35–46). New York: International Universities Press.

Erikson, E. (1968). *Identity youth and crisis*. New York: Norton.

Foody, K., Bands, P., & Riccard, N. (2019). *Teen who charged attackers killed in school shooting* (p. A 4). Ohio: Akron Beacon Journal.

Forth, A., & Book, A. (2007). Psychopathy and youth: A valid construction. In H. Harve & J. Yuille (Eds.), *The psychopath: Theory, research and practice* (pp. 369–387). Mahwah: Erlbuim.

Frick, P., Kimonis, E., Dandreaux, D., & Farrell, J. (2003). The four- year stability of psychopathic traits in non-referred youth. *Behavioral Sciences & the Law, 21*, 713–736.

Gerard, R. (1970). Institutional innovations in juvenile corrections. *Federal Probation, 34*, 4.

Glueck, S., & Glueck, E. (1950). *Unraveling delinquency* (pp. 281–282). New York: Commonwealth fund.

Hay, C. (2001). Parenting, self-control, and delinquency. A test of self-control theory. *Criminology, 39*, 707–736.

Hirschi, T. (2004). Self control and crime. In R. Baumeister & K. Vohs (Eds.), *Handbook of self regulation: Research, t, and application*. NY: Guildford Press.

Jesness, C. (1966). *The Jesness inventory*. Palo Alto, CA: Consulting Psychologists Press.

Jesness, C. (1984). An empirical approach to offender classification. *Contemporary Psychology, 29*, 709–720.

Kielhl, K., & Hoffman, M. (2011). The criminal psychopath: History, neuroscience, treatment and economics. *Jurismetrics, 51*, 355–397.

Kohlberg, L. (1963). Moral development and identification. In *Child psychology: A yearbook of the national society for the study of education* (pp. 277–333). Chicago: University of Chicago Press.

Kratcoski, P. (2012). *Juvenile justice administration*. Boca Raton, FL: CRC Press/Taylor & Francis Group.

Mc Cord, W., & McCord, J. (1964). *The psychopath*. Princeton, NJ: D. Van Nostrand.

Perrone, D., Sullivan, C., Pratt, T., & Margaryan, S. (2009). Parental efficiency, self-control, and delinquency: A test of the general theory of crime on a nationally representative sample of youth. *International Journal of Offender Therapy and Comparative Criminology, 48*, 298–312.

Piaget, J. (1948). *The moral development of the child*. NY: Free Press.

Pratt, T. (2016). A self-control/life-course theory of criminal behavior. *European Journal of Social-Psychological Theories of Delinquency and Criminology, 13*(1), 129–145.

Reid, S., & Lee, J. (2018). Confessions of a criminal psychopath: An analysis of the Robert Pickton cell-plant. *Journal of Police and Criminal Psychology, 33*(3), 257–270.

Robbins, L. (1966). *Deviant children grow up*. Baltimore: Williams and Wilkins.

Samenow, S. (1984). *Inside the criminal mind*. New York: Times Books.

Schoenfeld, C. (1975). A psychoanalytic theory of juvenile delinquency. In Peoples, E (Ed.), *Readings in correctional casework and counseling*. N.Y. Pacific Palisades: CA GoodYear.

Scott, E. S., & Grisso, T. (1997). The evolution of adolescence: A developmental perspective on juvenile justice reform. *Journal of Criminal Law and Criminology, 88*(1), 137–145.

Shakur, S. (1993). *Monster: The autobiography of a L.A. gang member*. New York: Penguin Books.

Shoemaker, D. (2009). *Theories of delinquency*. Lanham, MD: Rowman & Littlefield Publishers Inc.

Sorrells Jr., J. (1980). What can be done about juvenile homicide? *Crime and Delinquency, 2*(April), 423–427.

Steinberg, L., Cauffman, E., & Monahan, K. (2015). *Psychosocial maturity and desistance from crime in a sample of serious juvenile offenders*. Laurel, MD: Office of Juvenile Justice and Delinquency Prevention, U.S. Department of Justice.

Van Ness, S. (1987). *Theoretical origins of predatory violent phenomenon: A study of juvenile offenders in Ohio*. Unpublished doctoral dissertation, Kent State University.

Viviano, J. (2019). *Ohio suicide rate jumps 24% from 2008 to 2017* (p. A1). Ohio: Akron Beacon Journal.

Weir, K. (2019). *Teen suicides* (pp. A1–A6). Ohio: Akron Beacon Journal.

White, J. (1989). *The troubled adolescent*. New York: Pergamon Press.

Yablonsky, L. (1966). *The violent gang*. Baltimore: Penguin Books.

Yochelson, S., & Samenow, S. (1976). *The criminal personality* (Vol. 1). New York: Jason Aronson.

Zemel, O., Ronel, N., & Einat, T. (2016). The impact of introspection and resilience on abstention and desistance from delinquent behavior among adolescents at risk. *European Journal of Criminology, 13*(1), 111–128.

Chapter 4
Social Organization Perspectives on Delinquency Causation

4.1 Introduction

We noted in Chap. 3 that psychological theories of delinquency locate the problem within the individual or in the developmental phase of human life. In contrast, the sociological theories of delinquency presented in this chapter suggest that external factors or combinations of factors act to heighten the possibility of delinquency. These factors include inadequate family functioning, poverty, school problems, environmental factors, and the influence of delinquent peers.

4.2 Social Strain Theory

Contemporary American families vary in structure, economic status, racial and ethnic group membership, family customs, traditions, and styles of life. Children are less likely to live in a two-parent family than in the past. From 1970 to 1997, the proportion of children in the United States living in two-parent homes declined from 85 to 68%. In 1997, 85% of the children in single-parent households lived with their mother, but the percentage living with only their father increased from 9% in 1970 to 15% in 1997. In 1997, 38% of the children in one-parent families were living with a never-married parent (U.S. Bureau of the Census, 1999, p. 8). The problems that face the young, never-married female heads of one-parent families often include dropping out of school, inability to work outside the home, and an environment of poverty and social deprivation for the children.

Children who live in poverty present a compelling social problem in American society. In 1997, 14.1 million children (approximately one fifth of the juvenile population lived in poverty (U.S. Bureau of the Census, 1999, p. 5). The National Center for Children in Poverty (2019, p. 1) reported that "About 15 million children in the United States—21% of all children—live in families with incomes below the federal poverty

© Springer Nature Switzerland AG 2020
P. C. Kratcoski et al., *Juvenile Delinquency*,
https://doi.org/10.1007/978-3-030-31452-1_4

threshold, a measure that has been shown to underestimate the needs of families." Children International (2019, p. 1) noted that the Department reported, "The Department of Health and Human Services issues poverty guidelines for each household size. For example, the poverty level for a household of four is an annual income of $25,750. To get the poverty level for larger families, add $4,420 for each additional person in the household. For smaller families, subtract $ 4,420 per person." Other estimates of the number of children who live in poverty are much higher, based on a calculation that the federal guidelines on income used to determine poverty are much too low. Regardless of the measure used, the fact remains that the proportion of children living in poverty in the United States has remained essentially the same (20%) in the two time periods. The Urban Institute (2019, p.2) indicated, "Almost 40% of American kids spend at least 1 year in poverty before they turn 18." This higher figure on children in poverty is based on a consideration of the factors that affect the annual income of the families that fall into the poverty level. For example, persons who are employed in seasonal jobs, or who have contract employment, such as constructional workers, or who hold part time employment, may have incomes for a period of time that brings them above the poverty level, but may find a significant drop in their incomes if they become unemployed for various reasons. The U.S. Bureau of the Census (1999) reported that poverty rates were highest for children of black families (34% in poverty) and Hispanic families (24% in poverty). During a 2-year period starting in 2000, the United States experienced an economic decline, resulting in significant increases in unemployment, homelessness, and poverty. At the end of 2002, the unemployment rate in the United States was 6%, the highest in 8 years, and the number of people living in poverty increased, compared to 2000.

In contrast, in 2019, the unemployment rate was below 4%. Despite the strong economic situation, the proportion of families and children living in poverty has not changed.

4.2.1 Homelessness

A report on homelessness completed by the U.S. Department of Housing and Urban Development (Williams, 2002, p. A9) revealed that homelessness was increasing in the United States and that minorities and children are the most affected segments of the population. It was reported that Blacks constituted 40% of the homeless, but only 11% of the population; Hispanics made up 11% of the homeless, but only 9% of the population in that year; and 8% of the homeless were American Indians, although they represent less than 1% of the population. The report also revealed that 15% of all the homeless were part of a family, with the family head being a woman in 84% of the families. The average number of children attached to the homeless families was 2.2. The U.S. Department of Housing and Urban Development (2018) found that a half million people living in the U.S. are homeless. While there were significant decreases in the number of homeless and people with disabling health and behavior conditions, there was only a slight decrease (5.1%) in the number of children who are homeless. The number of single adults experiencing homelessness had increased from 2017 to 2018. The report draws attention to the high proportion of those who are homeless who are minorities, with 40% of the people counted as experiencing homelessness being African American, while African Americans make up 13% of the general population. Although it is difficult to compare the figures on homelessness for the two time periods, since many factors that contributed to changes in the economy may have a direct bearing on the amount and distribution of people who are homeless, the trend seems to indicate that homelessness is still a major concern for children living in single parent households and for racial and ethnic minority groups.

4.2.2   Effects of Poverty

Changes in the structure of the American family and the economic deprivation that many families are experiencing have resulted in the creation of a permanent segment of the American population that can be characterized as an *underclass*. Living on welfare or Aid for Dependent Children (AFDC), residing in substandard housing or homeless, being poorly educated, lacking job skills or the desire to obtain them, or seeking employment without success, a large segment of this population is clustered in the large cities of the United States. Children International (2019, p. 3) quoting from Feeding America, noted, "Poor kids are more likely to experience hunger. And food insecurity has a lifelong effect; lower reading and math scores, more physical and mental health problems, more emotional and behavioral problems and a greater chance of obesity."

Children living in poverty are vulnerable to a wide variety of problems, including poor nutrition, inadequate housing, substandard medical attention, lack of proper supervision, and physical or emotional abuse. Adolescents from these backgrounds become part of a cycle of low income or unemployment. Black and Hispanic teenagers have particularly acute problems obtaining employment.

Criminal and delinquent activity may also be an accepted part of the total picture for deprived children. It is difficult to emerge from such surroundings unscarred. Just how strong is the influence of these experiences on the production of delinquency? Many researchers have sought to locate the causes of delinquency in the environment and the effects poverty and social disorganization can have on young people.

4.3   Environmental Influences on Delinquency

Much of the early sociological research on delinquency focused on the environment within which individuals act and on the factors in social organization and social processes that they develop to adapt to the environment. Researchers concentrated on adaptation to slums, deteriorated housing, high population density, areas with heterogeneous populations and cultural conflicts because of uprooting, effects of urbanization, unemployment, poverty, broken families, and other factors.

The theoretical assumptions of many sociological studies were borrowed from ecology, which is concerned with the distribution of certain organisms and their relationship to their environment. Human ecology is the sociological evaluation of relations between the social and institutional distribution of human beings and their geographical environment (Taft, 1956, p. 204).

The influence of the physical and social environment on the physical and social development of children has been recognized by scholars for hundreds of years. In the United States, during the early part of the twentieth century, a number of researchers studied social disorganization, industrialization, population movements, and changes in neighborhoods to determine their influence on delinquency and crime in cities. In their study, *The Polish Peasant,* Thomas and Znaniecki examined social disorganization in a Polish neighborhood of Chicago. They noted the failure of existing social rules and norms to control behavior, and they documented the fact that the home, neighborhood, church, and friendship patterns lost their influence when rapid social change occurred (Thomas & Znaniecki, 1918).

The term "social disorganization" is used to denote a breakdown in conventional institutional controls within a community and the inability of organizations, groups, or individuals within the community to solve common problems (Shoemaker, 1984). Several approaches to studying social disorganization and its effects were developed by the "Chicago School," a group of sociologists who used the city of Chicago as a natural laboratory for their research on all facets of social organization within the communities of the city. Dambazau (2007, pp. 77–78) noted, "The environment is said to play a significant role in determining criminal behavior of both the juvenile and adult offender Factors within the environment considered to be crucial in contributing to criminal behavior include drug trafficking and abuse, urbanization, poverty, unemployment, corruption, moral decadence, poor education, family, technology, child abuse, architectural or environment designs, and so on.

4.4   Social Organizational Perspectives

4.4.1   Delinquency Areas

Burgess (Park, Burgress, & Kenzie, 1925) showed the uses and activities of various parts of a large city in a pattern moving from the center of the city outward. His "concentric zone" concept divided the city into different zones. Zone I, the inner city, contained the downtown area, where business and government buildings were located. Zone II, the zone in transition, was characterized by factories, tenement buildings, transportation lines, and ghettos. Zone III, the area of working-class homes, was a residential area of multiple-family dwellings. Zone IV, also a residential area, was made up of single-family dwellings for the middle class. Zone

V was a suburban commuter area. Delinquency was most likely to occur in Zone II, the least stable area in terms of permanent residents, strong community feeling or control, and church or neighborhood involvement.

The term "delinquency area" is used to designate a geographical part of a city that has delinquency rates higher than average for that city. It frequently is separated from other sections by a physical boundary such as a railroad track or highway. The values and traditions of the persons who live in a delinquency area have been found to support or even encourage delinquent and criminal behavior in many instances.

Shaw (1929) attempted a geographic analysis of the distribution of juvenile court petitions filed in the city of Chicago, according to the areas of residence of the alleged delinquents, as part of the Chicago Area Project, a joint effort during the 1930s by the University of Chicago and residents of high-delinquency neighborhoods to control delinquent behavior and discover its causes. On the basis of his analysis, he developed a theory that juvenile delinquency occurs most frequently in the center of the city, decreasing as one moves out toward the peripheral suburban areas. He also asserted that the high-delinquency areas were those in which the population was declining and that were deteriorating physically, with a consequent movement from residential to business zoning. Shaw termed such an area "interstitial."

Shaw was later joined in his research by McKay. The two sought to apply the same approach of analysis of the distribution of delinquency in other major American cities. The findings of these studies appeared to be consistent with Shaw's analysis of Chicago, although later researchers questioned their validity on the basis of the omission of certain important variables from the research design, including whether the delinquency petitions were found to be true, and whether agencies for diversion of juveniles were more likely to exist in the fringe areas than in the central city. Shaw and McKay's analysis of the Chicago delinquency areas continued periodically for 35 years (1927–1962). Data from various time periods within this 35-year span showed remarkable consistency in the characteristics and delinquency rates of those "interstitial" areas of the city initially identified by Shaw and McKay. These areas tended to maintain the characteristics of mobility, high population density, and slum conditions, regardless of the ethnic or racial makeup of the population. (McKay, 1967). In Shaw and McKay's (1969) work in which they commented on the importance of race and ethnicity in delinquency causation, they concluded that no racial, national native born or ethnic group exhibited an overall uniform rate of delinquency, but rather the rates varied for each group, between high rates and low rates depending on the type of area surveyed. Shaw and McKay concluded that the significantly higher rates of delinquency found among racial and ethnic groups can be attributed more to the economic and social conditions of the neighborhoods, rather than the racial and ethnic origins of the youths.

A number of more recent researchers have also sought to locate the delinquency areas of large cities. A comparison of data from Indianapolis, Baltimore, and Detroit revealed that despite other dissimilarities, the cities all tended to have zones with high levels of delinquency and that these were characterized by a transient population residing in overcrowded, substandard housing. The residents of these homes were chiefly those with low incomes and minimal occupational skills (Chilton, 1972).

Bloom (1968), in a survey of delinquent behavior in an American city, found that the areas in which family, marital, economic, environmental, and educational disruption were most prevalent were those that had the highest delinquency rates. Tracy, Wolfgang, and Figlio (1985) analyzed the police contacts of nearly 10,000 buys born in Philadelphia in 1945 and 14,000 males born in Philadelphia in 1958. They discovered that for both cohorts, delinquency was more prevalent among nonwhites and that residential instability, poor school achievement, and failure to graduate from high school were related to involvement in delinquency.

In summary, environmental conditions have been identified as contributing to the delinquency of some youths, regardless of the specific settings in which they live. Urban, suburban, and rural youths are at risk. Researchers have continued to try to explain why some neighborhoods continue to have high rates of crime and delinquency despite the fact that the residency of these neighborhoods has changed, perhaps several times during a period of years. In pursuing an answer to what conditions in the neighborhoods are related to the high crime in some neighborhoods, Several structural factors of the neighborhoods with high crime rates were identified as being contributors to the amount of crime. These factors were high density of population, a constant movement of people in and out of the neighborhoods, a high proportion of the residents having low incomes (poverty), a mixed usage of the same area, that is, resident homes, industry, retail stores, entertainment establishments (theaters, bars, dance halls) intermixed in the same area, and a number of dilapidated and vacant buildings located in a small geographic area.

Sampson (1995) focused on the social structure and values of the residents in neighborhoods in which there were high levels of crime and delinquency. Sampson concluded that the contributing factors of poverty, high proportion of residents renting their residences, high density of people living in a congested area, and other factors led to social disorganization, a lack of cohesion, and leadership in the community. Those permanent residents, such as home owners, who have a stake in the community would like to rid the neighborhoods of crime and delinquency, but do not have the "social capital," the network of people who have the ability and resources to initiate actions directed toward eliminating the law breakers.

4.4.2 Delinquency and Drift

Environmental conditions that contribute to delinquency are not confined to urban settings. Suburban and rural youths also may become caught up in delinquent behavior as a result of their surroundings. Matza (1964), who developed the theory of delinquency and drift, theorized that many juveniles are not committed to a delinquent lifestyle but become involved in situations and circumstances that lead to delinquent behavior. Rural youths may break into summer homes when the owners are away, vandalize school buildings, drag race on deserted highways late at night, or steal from unsecured garages or warehouses; suburban youths may shoplift from mall stores; and urban youngsters may vandalize or hang out in vacant apartments.

All become caught up in activities that seem to be profitable or fun at a particular moment. In most cases, the juvenile offenders are not caught unless their deviant behavior becomes a frequent activity pertaining to their lives. According to Sykes and Matza (1957), the youths *neutralize* or *rationalize* their behavior by contending that they didn't really mean any harm, that the person from whom they stole deserved it, that school officials "had it coming" because they treated the youths badly, or that they got caught up in the excitement.

4.5 Routine Activities

The theory of routine activities, closely allied to delinquency and drift, would help explain why youths living in various environments engage in different types of delinquent activities. Felson and Boba (2017), in explaining the application of routine activities theory to crime, claim that there are three conditions that must be met for crime to occur. They are a motivated offender, an opportunity to victimize a suitable target, and the absence of a capable or moral guardian. Gottschalk (2018, p. 46) contends, "The existence or absence of a likely guardian represents an inhibitor or facilitator for crime. The premise of routine activity theory is that crime is to a minor extent affected by social causes such as poverty, inequality, and unemployment. Motivated offenders are individuals who are not only capable of committing criminal activity, but are willing to do so. Suitable targets can be someone that is seen by offenders as particularly attractive."

According to Gottschalk (2018, p. 47), "The premise of routine activity theory is that crime to a minor extent is affected by social causes such as poverty, inequality, and unemployment."

Thus, according to this theory, delinquent behavior occurs when opportunities for the activities are available, there is a lack supervision of the youths or of the targets of the activities, and youths who would consider becoming involved in unlawful behavior are present. Thus, inner city youths are drawn to form gangs or engage in unlawful activities that they observe adults performing in their neighborhoods, while rural youths resort to underage drinking, theft, or vandalism. Studies of delinquencies committed by rural youths have shown that their offenses are generally less serious than those committed by urban youths (Roche, 1985).

4.5.1 Intergenerational Conflict Theory

Several of the earlier studies of delinquency and gangs in the cities Thomas and Znaniecki (1918) and Whyte (1955) drew attention to the conflict that often emerged between parents who were recent immigrants for various European countries and the first generation of American born children. The conflict was especially acute with male children who identified with the American way of life. Khondaker (2005) completed a study of deviant behavior among youths in an immigrant community in New York City in which he used control theory and intergenerational conflict theory to guide his research. The qualitative research relied on formal and informal interviews of community residents as well as news items as sources of data. The focus of the interviews consisted of what the residents considered deviant behavior of youth and what traits characterize "good" kids from "bad" kids. According to the majority of the respondents (predominately immigrants from Bangladesh) "bad kids" Khondaker (2005, pp. 328–329) are those youths who not only defy the traditional values of the community, but also seem to possess a type of hatred toward these values" A "bad kid" does not show respect for adults, does not obey parents or other adults, smokes, drinks and sometimes takes drugs, hangs around the street corner, fights with other kids, does not adhere to Bangladeshi culture, used vulgar words, prick their bodies/or has tattoos, and have dates with boyfriends and girlfriends in the community in front of parents and other adults, "On the other hand a "good kid" is one who obeys and respects parents and adults, who goes to the mosque and prays, reads the Holy Book, does not smoke or drink or take drugs, follows the traditional culture, does not hang around with bad kids, home most of the time unless he/she has other things to do outside the home and wears decent clothes."

The distinctions between "good and bad kids" made by the residents of the community were based on their subjective notions of what constitutes appropriate behavior. Very few of the youths in the community had any official contact with law enforcement or the juvenile court.

4.6   Anomie and Delinquency

The term *anomie* was used by the French sociologist Emile Durkheim to describe a way of life in which many of the old customs, values, and beliefs have been discarded, and a new value or belief system has not yet been ingrained (Durkheim, 1951). Individuals exist in a state of "normlessness," lacking moral convictions and not responding to social controls such as the influence of neighbors, community leaders, church representatives, or teachers.

Merton (1938) identified such conditions as existing among disadvantaged persons. He maintained that members of all social classes seek success, defined in terms of economic affluence and manifested by possession of material status symbols. Those living in areas characterized by rapid changes in the population, lack of interpersonal interaction, poverty, and family disruption have limited opportunities to achieve through legitimate means, so they react by seeking success through illegitimate means. The social disorganization that exists around them reduces their response to social controls and in many instances causes them to seek success or pleasure without regard for the rules of society.

Social strain theory implies that there are circumstances arising within both the physical and the social environment of an individual or group that create confusion, disruption, breakdown of norms and values, or lack of direction. Changes in family structure, economic situation, or opportunities can produce these problems. In his studies of the relation of economic factors to rates of crime and delinquency for black males, Sampson concluded that their commitments to family life and marital commitment are affected by their lack of opportunities for steady, good paying jobs (Sampson, 1987).

Chilton (1991) also suggested that urban life and the isolation of poor families in disadvantaged areas of the cities limit the types of socialization that serve as positive influences for children living in suburban areas and small towns.

Agnew (2002) broadened the scope of social strain theory by introducing the concepts of vicarious and anticipated strain. He contended that vicarious experiences (interacting with persons who describe being treated in a negative manner, especially if they are close family members, friends, or neighbors) may have a significant impact on an individual, even though that person has not actually witnessed the incidents or been treated in this manner. Anticipated strain refers to a person's expectation that the strain he or she is currently experiencing will continue or intensify in the future. Agnew's study of adolescent boys concluded that both actual physical victimization and experiencing certain types of vicarious and anticipated physical victimization (assaults on family members or friends, presence of drug addicts or dealers or other undesirables in the neighborhood, violence in the schools, or fear of physical attacks) were associated with delinquent behavior.

Vold, Bernard, and Snipes (1998, p. 126) state that "Durkheim argued that to the extent a society remains mechanical crime is 'normal' in the sense that a society without crime would be pathologically over controlled. As the society develops toward the organic form, it is possible for a pathological state, which he called 'anomie' to occur, and such a state would produce a variety of social maladies, including crime." Durkheim considered crime to be normal, because in a society the notions of what is criminal behavior and what is not are not clearly defined. Unless behaviors are codified into law, the behavior that is considered criminal is based on the moral standards of the community.

4.6.1 Reaction Formation Defense Mechanisms

In his book, *Delinquent Boys,* Cohen (1955) noted that youths who realize they cannot achieve their goals develop various behavior characteristics in reaction to their failure. They not only defy conventional norms but deliberately seek to oppose them. This "reaction formation" behavior may involve engaging in delinquent behavior that seems to have no purpose other than to express rebellion and display disregard for conventional norms. It may include involvement in activities that are deliberately undertaken to shock or outrage those in authority or take the form of self-destructive behavior.

4.6.2 Lack of Opportunity and Delinquency

Cloward and Ohlin (1961) also noted that youths may seek gratification through illegitimate methods without regard for the social acceptability of their activities. Their "opportunity theory" stressed the importance of the social environment in determining which of the opportunities open to them youths will follow. When opportunities for success by following conventional norms appear to be blocked, they may engage in an apparently normless lifestyle that includes violence, con games, drug or alcohol abuse, or prostitution, without regard for the conventional values of society, which define such activities as improper.

Today, anomic behavior is not restricted to youths living in poverty areas or those lacking educational or social advantages. Changes in American life, notably in the stability of family life, have caused young people of all social classes to experience a lack of structure, continuity, and goal orientation in their day-to-day existence. Parents chiefly concerned with their own professional or personal development frequently lack the motivation or time to provide strong control and guidance. The youth culture offers the appeal of drug and alcohol use as a means of coping with personal problems. The emphasis on personal gratification and immediate pleasure, which can be sought without concern for the needs, wishes, and rights of others, promotes normlessness as a way of life.

4.6.3 Stress Factors Relating to Delinquency

Stress theorists view violent behavior as a means of coping with intolerable stress, which may occur when youths are faced with pressure from a single trauma or when pressure has gradually accumulated from several sources. The ensuing violence may be directed against intimates or toward strangers. Such violent incidents tend to be unplanned and unintended. Mawson (1981) theorized that aggressive violent behavior may be directed toward family members or peer-group members when an aggressor experiencing stress wishes to maintain intense physical and emotional contact with the victim. This may be true even when the person toward whom the violence is directed is the source of the stress.

In his study of the impact of community violence on African-American children and families, Isaacs (1992) found that African-American children were more likely than non-African-American children to experience or witness violence, and that the family and the school are no longer safe havens for a large number of African-American children. As a result, they expressed feelings of fatalism and acceptance of death, felt powerless to prevent being victimized, and experienced psychological problems. The possible factors identified as helping children who experienced these stresses were their own personal resources, positive role models, support from family and peers, and internalization of positive community values and beliefs.

4.7 Social Learning Theory

Social learning explanations of violent behavior hold that early childhood experiences are related to behavior patterns later in life. Physical abuse of children by parents or violence of spouses toward each other is internalized by the children as the appropriate reaction to problems. A study that followed the offense careers of nearly 1600 persons from childhood until they became adults found that being abused or neglected as a child increased the likelihood of being arrested as a juvenile by 53% and being arrested as an adult by 38%. It also discovered that such mistreatment increased the likelihood of being arrested for a violent crime by 38% (Widon, 1992). Kratcoski's (1983) study of institutionalized delinquents revealed that 26% of the youths in his sample had experienced physical abuse and that the abused delinquents tended to direct their violence toward members of their immediate families or significant others in their lives (teachers, youth counselors, friends. In another study by Kratcoski (1984) of self-reported violent behavior by high school students and youths referred to a juvenile court, he found that those who had experienced violence from their parents and who lived in families characterized by low levels of family functioning were more likely to have committed violent acts than those who had not had such experiences,

Researchers who have examined the family situations of youths who threatened to kill or actually killed their parents found that the youths' family environment was characterized by physical abuse of children, heavy drinking by parents, and constant verbal and physical fighting between parents (Duncan & Duncan, 1971; Sorrells, 1977; Tanay, 1973).

A history of drug abuse has also been identified as being related to violent delinquency. When drug use histories of incarcerated youths were explored according to the types of offenses they had committed, it was found that those who had abused drugs were more likely to have been involved in violent offenses against persons than in property offenses. (Beck, Kline, & Greenfield, 1988).

Katz, Webb, and Decker (2005) used a large sample of juvenile arrestees from the Arizona Arrestee Drug Abuse Monitoring (ADAM) program to study the relationship between gang membership and drug use. They used both self-report data and official arrest data in their analysis. They found (Katz, et al. (2005, p. 81) that a high proportion of those arrested claimed to be gang members; drug use included soft (marijuana) and hard drugs (crack cocaine, cocaine) was quite common among the gang members; gang members were more involved in drug use than non-gang members; and the level of drug use tended to decline for those youths who belonged to a gang in the past, but were no longer associated with a gang.

Bellau and McNulty (2009) used the 1997 National Longitudinal Survey of Youth to research the relationship of gang membership, selling drugs, and violence. They found (p. 661), "Drug selling to be a major facilitator of violence. Gang members who report selling drugs, engage in violence at a significantly higher rate than non-selling drug sellers." In addition, Ballaw et al. (p.661) stated, "Gang members who sell drugs are by far most violent when they reside in highly disadvantaged locales."

The authors concluded that selling drugs by gang members was a means for these youths to have an opportunity to obtain material things within their disadvantaged neighborhood, an opportunity that did not exist for them in the mainstream society.

All of these explanations of youth violence involve causative influences throughout a youth's lifetime. They emphasize the difficulties encountered by the courts in making decisions on the appropriate dispositions and treatment for these offenders, using the limited options and resources at their disposal. The following incident observed by one of the authors (Peter C. Kratcoski) illustrates the difficulties justice officials, particularly, judges, must make in their decisions that can have an effect on the juveniles for the remainder of their lives (Box 4.1).

Box 4.1 Juvenile Appearing Before a Judge for a Detention Hearing

In the juvenile court of a large metropolitan county, the judge was holding a detention hearing for a 17-year-old male charged with robbery and attempted rape. After listening to some of the particulars of the alleged offense, presented by an assistant prosecutor, the judge asked if a judicial waiver would be requested by the Prosecutor's Office. The assistant prosecutor noted that the boy had a previous conviction for rape and several other delinquency convictions and that he was currently on probation.

The judge then asked the public defender, who represented the boy, if he had any recommendations concerning the need for detention while the boy was awaiting a hearing on the current charge. The defense counsel tried to convince the judge that the youth respected his mother and would listen to her if he was released to her custody. The judge then consulted the boy's probation officer. He stated that the youth had not adhered to probation rules and wanted to do as he pleased. The probation officer recommended that the youth be held in detention until the hearing.

The judge informed the boy that he would be detained until the hearing and transferred to the county jail because of the aggressive nature of his behavior, an option allowed by state law if the youth in question is age 16 or older and appears to be too difficult to control in the juvenile detention facility. As the youth was being led away by a sheriff's deputy, the boy broke free and began pounding a wall with his fists. He then ran toward the probation officer wildly swinging his fists. The deputies needed the assistance of several others in the court room to bring the youth under control.

When the youth had left the room, the judge commented that he recognized in this boy had a potential for out-of-control behavior and that by keeping him in secure detention he was both protecting the community and preventing the boy from lashing out at others and further complicating his own problems.

4.7.1   Differential Association Theory

Edwin Sutherland (1975) developed a broad, general theory of crime and delinquency grounded in the learning process. According to this theory, criminal behavior is learned through association with persons who are law violators, or through observing the mechanisms of criminal activity. This learning involves both internalization of attitudes that are favorable toward criminal behavior and specific techniques for performing criminal actions.

According to Sutherland, a person may have many associations, some of them having a pro-criminal-behavior influence and others having essentially a noncriminal behavior influence. A young person may thus experience internal conflict in trying to decide which set of values, attitudes, and codes of behavior to accept and internalize. For example, to a youth living in a neighborhood that has many criminal types, these people may be symbols of economic and social success because they have money, expensive clothes, flashy automobiles, attractive woman companions, and other material possessions that inspire respect and envy.

The young may be drawn to the criminal lifestyle of these people because they want the same symbols of success for themselves. At the same time, a number of youths in the neighborhood may have good relationships with parents or other adults who are noncriminal in their lifestyles and who try to instill non-delinquent values in them. A young person exposed to both types of influences must balance out their merits and decide whether to accept the values of one set of associates or those of the other.

Although Sutherland originally developed this *differential-association* theory to apply within the context of a single disorganized community in which normative values and attitudes and societal controls were weak, the theory was later applied to explain the learning process for white-collar crime. The theory of differential association has received a good deal of criticism. It has been faulted as being too broad and vague, not taking into consideration personality factors as causes of crime, failing to explain the exact process by which criminal behavior is learned, and ignoring crimes that result from mental illness or compulsive behavior. Why do some youths exposed to criminal influences succumb to them while others do not? And why do some who have no criminal associations in their social background turn to crime? The answer to the first question may lie in defining the strength of influences that operate on some youngsters to counteract criminal associations; the answer to the second may be that the results or "rewards" of some types of criminal activity serve as powerful reinforcement, comparable to the praise or approval of criminal associates. For example, being able to use loot from a burglary to improve one's lifestyle may serve as a stimulant to further criminal behavior.

Leader (1964) believed that personality factors and need satisfaction were the basic causal elements in the production of acceptable or unacceptable behavior. If a person's needs are not met by acceptable behavior, that person turns to alternative forms of behavior that do meet those needs and conform to the person's value system.

4.7.2   Differential Reinforcement Theory

Jeffery (1975) argued that Sutherland overemphasized the role of intimate association in the learning of criminal techniques and internalization of values that justify
criminal behavior. Jeffery maintained that criminal behavior can be learned without
ever associating with those who commit crimes (e.g., through the influence of television portrayals of crime). Jeffery advanced his own theory of *differential reinforcement.* He emphasized the notion that criminal behavior is maintained by its
consequences, both material and social. Such social variables as age, sex, social
class, ethnic membership, and residential area influence the manner in which criminal behavior is conditioned. Punishment decreases a response rate only if it is used
in a consistent manner and is applied near the time of the occurrence of the forbidden act. As it is used to control criminal behavior, punishment is likely to create
avoidance and escape behaviors rather than law-abiding behaviors.

   In summary, differential association serves as the cornerstone for learning and
crime and delinquency causation theories. Sutherland's work produced a good deal
of interest and research. The application of differential association principles in
forms of peer group associations, such as delinquent gangs is found in much of the
research related to the influence of peer groups on delinquency causation. Reiss
(1986) emphasized the relevance of differential association theory to the study of
the causes of juvenile delinquency since the data available shows that the large
majority of delinquent acts are committed within a group context.

4.7.3   Risky Life Styles and Delinquency

Engstrom (2018) uses a lifestyle exposure theory in researching the relationship of
the lifestyles of a sample of adolescent and their involvement in violent crime, as
well as their being victims of crime. The lifestyle exposure theory is grounded in the
routine activities theory (Cohen & Felson, 1979), but with the additional consideration that it includes the more recent versions of the theory, such as how the presence of peers creates an audience that the offender may wish to impress or frighten,
while handlers may hinder offenders from carrying out their actions (Felson &
Boba, 2017). Engstrom (2018) used a self-report questionnaire in asking the sample
of adolescent boys and girls questions pertaining to their involvement in risky
behavior, and the consequences of their involvement, both as an offender and as a
victim of violence. The findings confirmed those of other studies. For example, the
adolescent boys in which their routine activities involved risky behavior with members of their peer group had higher amounts of delinquent behavior and higher
amounts of victimization than the boys in the study who did not engage in "risky"
behavior. As in other studies, it was found that the deviant behavior was predominately committed in the presence of other members of their peer group that were
also involved in the deviant acts. Engstrom (2018, p. 26) noted, "There were actually

more victim-offenders than offenders only in the present sample, indicating that a large proportion of violent offenders were also victims." The girls in the study who admitted being involved in risky behavior were much less likely to be violent offenders than the boys, but were as likely to be victims of violence as were the boys.

4.7.4   The Influence of Mass Media and Internet Violence on Adolescent Behavior

Although a cause-and-effect relationship between exposure to violence and aggression on television, video games, and on-line media outlets and aggressive delinquencies by juveniles has not been confirmed by research studies, many people are convinced that such a relationship exists.

Various explanations have been advanced for the appeal television violence, the violence that is the theme of many video games, and on-line productions holds for children. One is the so-called "catharsis theory"-the belief that by observing characters working out their aggressions on television, children are able to discharge their own aggressive impulses in ways that are socially acceptable. Lopiparo (1977, p. 346), discussing the effects of television, believed that violence and aggression as shown on television had a positive effect on children; he stated, "It helps [them] cope with [their] feelings of powerlessness.... If they want to do something, they must ask an adult; if they want something changed, they have to hope adults feel the same way.... It is for this reason that children are drawn to TV violence. Many of the frustrations they feel can be very effectively worked out via the screen. It is safe the person you're attacking cannot retaliate, you can be a hero or a villain with just a flip of the dial, and, most important, you can experience that elusive feeling of power."

While noting that for a small minority of children viewing television violence may trigger an unacceptable level of aggression, Lopiparo (1977, p. 346) observed that, "with all of us, child and adult alike, there reposes a potential for violence, TV or no TV. Once this is accepted, we may then be more receptive of the notion that the expression this aggression, whether via fantasy or outright overt behavior, is not only normal, but, in many respects, quite beneficial."

Another explanation of the appeal of television violence and video games for young people is that it makes the brutality and violence that may be present in their own lives seem less terrible. By observing television violence, which in most cases is far worse than the aggression they experience in their own lives, they begin to feel that what they are going through is not so unusual. Life in an urban ghetto may seem less terrible after television heroes are viewed in more difficult situations and have shown that they can overcome their problems through aggression.

A third explanation of the attraction of young people to violent portrayals is that watching these "adventure stories" provides the excitement and danger that is missing in their own day-to-day existence. In much the same way that youths of an earlier era poured over Western adventure stories or mysteries, the contemporary youth "escapes" into the world of television violence, lives vicariously, and apparently emerges and returns to his own world without being seriously affected. However, Atkinson and Rodger (2015, p. 1) hold a different view. They contend, "New media formats and technologies raise questions about new-found abilities to indulge apparently limitless violence and sadistic curiosity within our culture. In this context, the mainstreaming of sex and violence via mobile and screen media systems opens important questions about the degree to which these influences are harmful or indicative of deeper social problems." The authors continue, "We suggest that a key implication of these zones of cultural exception in which social rules can be more or less abandoned, is their role in further assisting denials of harm from the perspective of hyper-masculinist and militaristic social value systems." Atkinson and Rodgers (2015, p. 6) contend, "Today's media architecture enables a range of deviant acts to be engaged in or viewed at a moment's notice, providing access to a wave of material detailing and allowing us to interact with a phantasmagoria of pain, suffering and humiliation-extreme pornography, videos of beheading and animal torture, rapes, fights, archives of (falls) involving human injury, game worlds based around the bodily destruction or murder of simulated victims and so on. In short, the rending of flesh and fascination with death, injury and violence have become major sources of entertainment." For those who are fascinated with such media, the effect is a loss of the ability of the person to empathize with those who experience pain and suffering, as well as giving those engaging in the presentation, either as a viewer or a player of a game, a false sense of power, of being invincible. Atkinson & Rodgers (2015, p. 6) "For some who play games compulsively, it may be just a form of escapism, while for others it provides a way of articulating the perverse core of their personalities which because of ethico-social constraints they are not able to act out in real life." Atkinson and Rogers (2015, p. 9) offer their perspective on the harm to some individuals for the excessive devotion to violent games, videos, and television shows, but do not have any empirical data to support their perspective on the harmful effects. Urbanik and Haggerty (2018) conducted a field study in a neighborhood in the city of Toronto that was being revitalized (rebuilt) to serve as a "mixed-income, mixed-use community." Using several methods of data collection (field notes, observation, interviews) the researchers were able to gain considerable insight and make conclusions on the interplay of the social media, the Internet, online identity management, the street code, violence and risk management of the various groups, including the residents of the community, a mixed usage area that was notorious as one of the city's high crime areas, with a city park that was used by both permanent residents and transients. Beginning in 2014, Urbanik focused on how the revitalization was altering the structures of local groups involved in street crime and drug dealing. For 3 months in the summers of 2015 and 2016, she spent 5–8 h a day, 5–6 days a week in Regent Park, where she "hung out" with the neighborhoods' major criminal players to gain a richer perspective on the local street-level criminal structures. Many of the contacts she made during that period of field work were maintained in the following years of the study. Urbanik and Haggerty (2018, p. 7) note that all of those who participated in their research used their smartphones to communicate about drug sales and coordinate violence against their rivals. Most regularly used social media to connect with friends and family, but also with unknown strangers who followed their accounts. They stated, "The rappers in Regent Park were particularly eager to capitalize on the cultural capital that they could accrue from being (or associating with) violent criminals. Consequently, their association with crime and violence is prominently displayed in their lyrics, social media messaging, photographs, and videos. The themes in their lyrics and music videos often revolve around guns, women, drug dealing, violence, stacks of cash, shooting rivals and generally rapping in "their neighborhood."" In conclusion, Urbanik & Haggerty, 2018, p. 19) stated, "What the research made clear, however, is that our participants reside in the fluid interstitial spaces that demarcate the physical street from the street as manifest on social media." They concluded that gang members use both the streets and the internet to carry on and coordinate their violent activities, and attract new customers for their drug dealing and other delinquent activities. A number of research studies have explained the effects of viewing violence and aggressive behavior on television and other media formats. Several factors are important, in the effect of viewing such acts, including the person's ability to distinguish between what is real and what is make-believe as well as the extent the viewer identifies with the person or groups engaging in the violence. One widely quoted study was completed by Bandura (1965). Four groups of nursery-school-age children observed an adult performing acts of aggression toward a large doll. One group observed the adult kick and punch the doll, a second group saw a movie of the adult doing exactly the same thing, and the third group watched a movie on television in which the adult, costumed as a cartoon cat, performed the same aggressive acts toward the doll. A fourth (control) group did not observe any presentation. Bandura discovered that during a 20-min period after observing various forms of the aggressive behavior, the children who had seen the in-person performance and those who had seen the movie used toys that were available in the observation room to imitate the adult's actions more frequently than did those who had observed the cartoon character. The children in the control group, who had not witnessed any form of aggressive behavior in the experiment, displayed the least aggression. In another experiment, the adult who performed aggressive acts was shown to one group of children receiving candy and soda immediately after the aggressive behavior and to another group receiving a spanking and scolding after the aggression; a third group was shown only the aggressive behavior. The play activity of the children immediately afterward was observed. Aggressive behavior by the children was most frequent in the group that had seen the aggressive adult rewarded, and least frequent among the group that had seen him punished.

Viewing aggressive behavior on television influences some children more strongly than it does others. Bandura (1965) found that boys were more likely than girls to imitate aggressive behavior seen on television. Chafee and McLeod (1971) found that the family backgrounds of children who viewed aggression on television influenced its effects. They discovered only a slight relationship between viewing violence on television and aggressive behavior in children from families that stressed nonaggressive behavior, but a strong relationship between them among children from families that did not. Additional research is needed to clarify the true role of television violence in producing delinquent behavior. There is agreement that viewing aggression on television can result in delinquent behavior by certain youths who are stimulated by such portrayals to commit aggressive acts. Television programs that show actual violent events and police responses to them; emergency service responses to gory shootings, stabbings, automobile accidents, or other calamities; and reenactments of murders, robberies, or abductions, under the guise of informing the public about at-large criminals or catching "most wanted" fugitives are a popular trend on television and may also affect juveniles in negative ways. Will they come to view such events and behaviors as commonplace occurrences in most people's lives! Will they become de sensitized to suffering and tragedy! ls it possible that some youths will imitate offenses they see performed.

4.7.5 The Culture of Violence

Ferracuti and Wolfgang (1970, p. 71) hypothesized that expressions of violence are part of the norms of the lower socioeconomic classes and are a learned response to pressures of survival. According to this theory, young males, particularly those in female-headed households in socially deprived areas, frustrated in their search for self-esteem and material goods, turn to violence as a means of achieving status. These researchers made a distinction between "idiopathic" v "prescribed" violent crimes (committed by members of a subculture of violence who are goal-oriented).

In their study of child abuse and aggressive behavior within the family, Glasser and Galvin (1981) hypothesized that children who have weak affectional family bonds are prime candidates for gang delinquency and peer-oriented violent delinquent behavior. The relationship of being abused within the family, physically abused within one's community or in the school and that person later become an offender involved in school bullying or becoming a member of a violent street gang has been documented. It is important to point out that engaging in violent acts is not always associated with a particular socio-economic group or culture.

Raymen and Smith (2016), theorized that at some times the norms of the society are relaxed and during these times people engaging in "routine activities" are given the opportunity to engage in forms of aggression and even violence without having to assume responsibility for their actions. Incidents of spectators at sporting events becoming upset about a particular ruling by the officials, throwing missiles at the officials, and even occasionally rushing onto the playing area are common. Aggressive actions during political rallies, or protests against government policies, if not extreme, are often tolerated by the law enforcement officials. Also, the practice of "hazing" new members of fraternities by inflicting pain with a paddle or strap or forcing them to drink excessive amounts of alcoholic beverages was generally accepted, until tragic incidents created pressures for its elimination. Rayman and Smith (2016, p.8) use the aggressive behavior used by shoppers during "Black Friday Sales" to illustrate how some behavior that is normally defined as deviant by society is tolerated during these days. The authors contend that shopping has become a leisure activity that offers opportunities for self-gratification. In a summary of their research on "Black Friday Sales" at stores located in a large metropolitan city, the authors observed various forms of disorder, aggression and even violent behavior by some stoppers toward other shoppers, or store personnel. Rayman & Smith (2016, p. 3) concluded, "The perpetrators of the disorder we witnessed were not the criminalized 'other' or a specific population resolutely rejecting the social norms and values of 'law-abiding society.' This raises important questions for criminologists around the nature of what constitutes 'crime' in both starkly legal terms as well as more tolerable forms of socially defined deviance."

In regard to juveniles, as previously discussed, much of the routine activity of many youths is just "hanging around." It is unstructured and not supervised by adults. While engaging in violence is not a regularly activity, some of the youths will engage in violent behavior, if persuaded by a leader, threatened by another group, or determine the selected victim will be an "easy target." This will be discussed in more detail in the following chapter.

4.8 Social-Psychological Explanations of Delinquency

A number of delinquency theorists have regarded sociological and psychological factors as contributing in combination to the occurrence of delinquency.

4.8.1 The Gluecks' Multiple-Factor Approach

One of the first major efforts to develop a multiple-factor approach to explanations of delinquency causation was that of Sheldon and Eleanor Glueck (Glueck & Glueck, 1950). In their comparison of 500 chronic delinquents with 500 non-delinquents of matched age, intelligence, ethnic and racial origin, and residence neighborhoods, they emphasized physique-specifically the mesomorphic body type (muscular, athletic, bony) as an indication of delinquency proneness. They also stressed the bearing and interaction of other factors in violent delinquency production. Their extensive research led them to conclude that delinquents can be distinguished from non-delinquents in the following ways:

1. Physically, in being essentially mesomorphic.
2. Temperamentally, in being restless, impulsive, aggressive, destructive.
3. Emotionally, in being hostile, defiant, resentful, assertive, non-submissive.
4. Psychologically, in being direct, concrete learners.
5. Socio-culturally, in being reared by unfit parents.

Reckless (1969, p. 169) termed the Gluecks' schema the "4 to 1 Causal Law," since they saw four individual factors and one situational factor (number 5) combining to produce delinquency. It is difficult to apply this law to the general population, since the sample was limited to lower class youths so delinquent that they had been institutionalized. The Gluecks' characterization nevertheless offers an example of an early effort to develop a multiple-factor approach to juvenile delinquency causation.

4.8.2 Containment Theory

Reckless (1969, pp. 164–174) proposed another multi-factor theory, which he termed containment theory. To "contain" or prevent delinquency activity, certain factors must be present in a child's life. They may take the form of "inner containment" (a positive self-concept, well-developed superego, strong sense of responsibility, positive goal orientations) within the child or "outer containment" (factors in the child's social environment that resist delinquency). Outer-containment factors could include strong parental supervision and support of non-delinquent activities, reinforcement of the youngster's positive self-concept by the school and other social institutions, opportunities to interact with other non-delinquents who share the youth's goals and ambitions, and a sense of personal identity and belonging within the social circle. Reckless believed that both inner and outer containment could serve as buffers against what he termed the "pulls" toward delinquency-the delinquent subculture, acquaintance with patterns of deviance, temptations, and other pro-delinquency environment influences. He maintained that the existence of both inner- and outercontainment elements in a youth's life would be the most effective anti-delinquency factors, but that the presence of strong inner containment could compensate for poor or defective outer containment, and vice versa. He believed that this theory of containment could be used effectively to explain the non-delinquency of some youths who were exposed to strong delinquent influences in their environments and that those who were noted at an early age to be delinquency endangered because of a lack of either inner- or outer-containment factors in their lives could be identified and helped.

4.8.3 Social Control/Bonding Theory

Hirschi (1969) used social control/bonding theory as an explanation of why some youths become delinquent and others do not. He contended that those young people who have established strong social bonds with their families and in the community will be more likely to accept the norms and values of the community and abide by the rules and laws of society, while youths with weak social bonds become prime candidates for delinquency.

Hirschi (1969, pp. 20–22) described four elements of social bonding: attachment (based on an emotional feeling of respect and caring for others, particularly parents and family members, including the development of a conscience and the ability to differentiate between right and wrong); commitment (acceptance of conventional goals, including wanting to succeed in school and developing career aspirations and a personal reputation for being honest and crimes (virtuous); involvement (the investment of time and effort in pursuit of conventional goals); and belief in the moral worth of the values, norms, and laws of society. In his research, Hirschi explored the social bonding and delinquency involvement of more than 4000 students. His comparison of delinquent and non-delinquent youths revealed that the delinquent youths were less attached to parents, peers, and teachers; less involved in conventional behavior; and less conforming to community norms. Other researchers replicated Hirschi's research and their findings generally supported his conclusions. Junger and Marshall (1997), and Waitrowski, Griswald, and Roberts (1981) tested social control theory in a study of youths in four countries, and they found that the propositions of social bonding advanced by Hirsch were applicable and virtually interrelated in the same matter for youth of his research.

In a research effort to test the hypothesis that a positive self-concept serves as an insulator against delinquency whereas a poor self-concept may enhance the chances for delinquency to occur, Reckless et al. (1970, p. 317) conducted an experiment involving sixth grade boys, their teachers, and their parents. Thirty teachers who taught sixth grade in schools in the highest delinquency areas of a medium-sized western city were asked to name male, white students in their classes who, in their opinion, would not ever have contact with the police and the juvenile courts, and to give the reasons why they considered their choices "good boys." A sample of those named by the teachers was selected for study. All youths who actually had police or juvenile court records were eliminated. The sample of "good boys" was given a battery of tests measuring delinquency proneness; social responsibility; occupational preference; and the boys' conceptions of self, family, and other interpersonal relationships. Also, the boys' mothers were interviewed to check the information received from teachers and from the standardized tests.

In response to self-evaluation items, the boys reported themselves to be law abiding and obedient. They felt they had moral standards about principles of right and wrong, did not feel they would ever become delinquents, had not participated in delinquent activities to any appreciable extent, and chose friends who had similar orientations. Their homes were characterized as economically stable and their parents were found to offer careful supervision. The researchers concluded that the youths' positive self-concepts and the stability and control offered by their family situations enabled them to remain law-abiding in spite of the strong pro-delinquency influences in their neighborhood.

A follow-up study (Reckless et al., 1970, pp. 0.318–319) of the "good boys" 4 years later found that teachers and parents still considered the vast majority of them to be "good boys," and that they continued to have positive self-images and stable families.

At the time the "good boys" were originally selected, the researchers (Reckless et al., 1970, p.238) also selected a sample of "bad boys" who were regarded by their teachers and parents as likely to have police contacts or become involved with the juvenile courts. One fourth of this sample was found to have had police or juvenile court contacts by the age of 12. Testing revealed that the "bad boys" had less positive self-concepts and less stable family backgrounds than the "good boys" Four years later, a follow-up study of the "bad boys" found that 39% of those who were located had had serious and frequent police and court contacts by the age of 16, and interviews with the boys, their teachers, and their parents revealed that they were considered likely to experience further problems.

It can also be argued that a negative self-concept is the product of social interaction. In his description of a "developmental" theory of delinquency, Hackler (1971) argues that children in a recognizable status, such as "lower class," are expected by significant persons in their lives, particularly their teachers, to behave in a certain way. The youths perceive these expectations, and they influence their developing selfconcepts. He cites an example from his own experience of a girl with a Spanish accent, the daughter of a migrant worker, who transferred to a new school without records from her previous school. The school counselor placed the girl in a slow learner section, automatically assuming that she must be academically deficient because of her parent's occupation. Subsequently, it was discovered that she was very bright and had no academic problems. When teachers and other important members of society anticipate that certain children will be failures or behavior problems and communicate these expectations to the youth they interact with, either through direct verbal Labeling Theory.

Those who adhere to the "labeling theory" concentrate on the consequences of a delinquent act in an offender's life rather than on the act itself or the social and psychological characteristics of the offender. Thus, the processing of the youth through the juvenile justice system and the labeling as delinquent are the primary focuses of their attention.

Schur (1973, p. 19) refers to this as the "patterned-reaction" approach to the study of delinquency. There is considerable evidence that most adolescents commit acts that could lead to involvement with the police and other juvenile justice officials. Most youths escape the delinquent label, however, since they are not formally processed. The labeling theorists argue that there is no great difference between the characteristics of those youths who are labeled delinquent and those who commit delinquent acts but are not caught, or who escape official handling for various other reasons. The labeling theorists are interested in studying why some offender, are selected for official processing by juvenile justice agencies and others are not. They seek to measure the effects of official processing on self-image; on relationships with peers, family, the school, and other individuals in the community; and on the character and amount of subsequent delinquent behavior. They try to discover how much involvement with the justice system must occur before a young person accepts the "deviant" label and regards himself or herself as a "delinquent" rather than a "non-delinquent" person. Sociological research has tended to emphasize the negative consequence of being labeled. However, some research (Thorsell & Klemke, 1972, p. 403) has noted that the labeling process can have positive effects in leading youths to recognize the seriousness of their deviant behavior and turn away from it.

4.9 Summary

Those who advance sociological explanations for delinquency locate them in the youth's environment and social relationships. Social disorganization, which is a breakdown in conventional institutional controls within a community and the inability of organizations, groups, or individuals there to solve common problems, is an important influence on delinquency. Radical changes in the American family, including a huge increase in the number of children living in one-parent families; the emergence of an underclass of poorly educated, inadequately housed, and unemployed persons living in poverty and depending on the government for support; and a lack of personal commitment on the part of many parents to care for and supervise their children, are evidence of such disorganization. Environmental theorists, including Burgess, Shaw and McKay, Bloom, and Wolfgang, all regarded the conditions of poverty, deteriorated and crowded housing, family disorganization, educational disruption and deprivation, and lack of opportunity as important factors contributing to the occurrence of delinquency.

Other theorists, including Merton, Cohen, and Cloward and Ohlin, noted that youths who live in highly disruptive environments, with few stabilizing influences, are likely to develop a "normless" attitude toward their social interactions and engage in activities that are illegal, provided they produce some short-run feelings of status or well-being.

Other researchers maintain that delinquent activity is a learned process and results from association with persons involved in delinquent or criminal activity and who display symbols of economic and social success that appear to have been gained by illegal means. Sutherland described the delinquent and non-delinquent values present in youths' lives as "differential associations. Ferracuti and Wolfgang described expressions of violence as part of the norms of the lower socioeconomic classes and termed this behavior a "culture of violence."

Social psychologists have viewed juvenile delinquency as a result of multiple influences in the child's life and have advanced containment theory and social control/bonding theory to support the idea that both the inner strength of the child and the positive or negative supportive influences of the environment make the difference between opting for or against delinquency. If a child becomes involved with the juvenile justice system, the effects of this contact on the self-image and future behavior of the youth are examined by labeling theorists.

4.10 Discussion Questions

1. Anomie denotes a state of normlessness with a lack of direction and no definitive values or goals. Can you think of examples in present-day society that would illustrate such a state?

2. Although poverty cannot be considered the only cause of delinquency, many believe it is a major cause. Discuss the ways in which poverty affects the lives of youths to turn them toward delinquent behavior.
3. Why is it important to have a positive self-concept? Do you think delinquents generally have a positive or a negative self-concept?
4. Discuss the major assumptions underlying labeling theory. What are some criticisms of this theory?
5. Discuss the arguments for and against the theory that viewing television violence produces aggressive behavior by children. What are some practical ways in which the amount of aggressive violence viewed by children can be controlled?
6. Researchers have found a relationship between being a member of a gang and drug trafficking and drug use. Discuss this research.
7. What are the key components of routine activity theory? How does this theory differ from drift theory?
8. Researchers have found that youths who are members of a gang engage in more violent activity towards others, as well as become victims of violent behavior more often than non-gang members. Discuss the reasons why membership in a gang is related to violent behavior.
9. Discuss the findings of research on the relationship between low self-concept and deviant behavior. What are the factors related to self-concept that can make a youth more prone to engage in delinquent behavior and what factors related to a positive self-concept are likely to serve as a barrier to delinquency?
10. Discuss the negative consequences that labeling can have on a young person. Do you agree with Thorsell and Kemke's contention that labeling can sometimes have positive consequences.

References

Agnew, R. (2002). Experienced, vicarious, and anticipated strain: An exploratory study on physical victimization and delinquency. *Justice Quarterly, 19*(40), 603–632.

Atkinson, R., & Rodgers, T. (2015). Pleasure zones and murder boxes: Online pornography and violent video games as cultural zones of exception. *The British Journal of Criminology, 56*(6), 1291–1307. https://academic.oup.com/bcj/article/56/6//1291/2415118. Accessed 10 Mar 2019.

Bandura, A. (1965). Influence of model's reinforcement contingencies on the acquisition of imitative responses. *Journal of Personality and Social Psychology, I*, 589–595.

Beck, A., Kline, S., & Greenfield, L. (1988). *Survey of youth in custody, 1987* (p. 8). Washington D.C.: U.S. Department of Justice Statistics.

Bellau, P., & McNulty, T. (2009). Gang membership, drug selling, and violence in neighborhood context. *Justice Quarterly, 26*(4), 664–669.

Bloom, B. (1968). A census tract analysis of socially deviant behaviors. *Multivariate Behavioral Research I*, 307–320.

Chafee, S. & McLeod (1971). *Adolescents, parents, and television violence*, paper presented at the annual meeting of the American Psychological Association, Washington, D.C.

Children International. (2019). *Child poverty in the U.S.* https:www.children.org/globalpoverty/global-poverty-facts/facts-about-poverty-in-usa. Accessed 24 Jul 2019.

Chilton, R. (1972). Delinquent area research in Baltimore, Detroit, and Indianapolis. *American Sociological Review, 37,* 93–99.

Chilton, R. (1991). Urban crime trends and criminological theory. *Criminal Justice Research Bulletin, 29,* 6.3.

Cloward, R., & Ohlin, L. (1961). Illegitimate means, differential opportunity and delinquent subculture. In R. Cloward & L. Ohlin (Eds.), *Delinquency and opportunity: A theory of delinquent gangs.* New York, NY: Free Press.

Cohen, L., & Felson , M., (1979). Social change and crime rate trends: Aroutine activities approach. American sociological review *44,* pp. 588–608.

Cohen, A. (1955). *Delinquent boys.* New York: The Free Press.

Dambazau, A. (2007). *Criminology and criminal justice* (2nd ed.). Abadan: Spectrum Books Limited.

Duncan, J., & Duncan, G. (1971). Murder in the family: A study of some homicidal adolescents. *American Journal of Psychiatry, 127,* 1498–1502.

Durkheim, E. (1951). *Suicide.* Translated by J. Spaulding & G. Simpson (19??) (pp. 348–382) By the Free Press, a division of Simon & Schuster. 987.

Engstrom, A. (2018). Associations between risky lifestyles and involvement in violent crime during adolescence. Victim & Offenders: An International Journal of Evidence-Based Research, Policy, and Practice. 139. https://www.tandfonline.com/doi/full/10.1080/15564886.2018.1503984?utm_medium+email&utm_source+EmailStudio_JB&utm_campaign+JME0076. Accessed 10 Mar 2019.

Felson, M., & Boba, R. L. (2017). Chapter 12: White collar crime. In *Crime and everyday life.* Thousand Oaks, CA: Sage.

Ferracuti, F., & Wolfgang, M. (1970). *Violence in Sardinia* (p. 21). Rome: Bulzoni, Social Organization Perspective.

Glasser, P., & Galvin, C. (1981). A framework for family analysis relevant to child abuse, neglect and juvenile delinquency. In R. Munner & Y. Walker (Eds.), *Exploring the relationship between child abuse and delinquency* (pp. 101–109). Montclair, NJ: Allanheld, Osmun.

Glueck, S., & Glueck, E. (1950). *Unraveling juvenile delinquency.* New York: Commonwealth Fund.

Gottschalk, P. (2018). Convenience theory on crime in the corporate sector. In P. Kratcoski & M. Edelbacher (Eds.), *Fraud and corruption: Major types, prevention and control* (pp. 43–60). Cham: Springer Natural.

Hackler, J. (1971). A developmental theory of delinquency. *Canadian Review of Sociology and Anthropology,* 61–75.

Hirschi, T. (1969). *Causes of delinquency.* Berkeley, CA: University of California Press.

Isaacs, M. (1992). *Violence: The impact of community violence on African-American children and their families.* Arlington, VA: National Center for Education in Material and Child Health.

Jeffery, C. (1975). Criminal behavior and learning theory. In E. Peoples (Ed.), *Readings in correctional casework and counseling.* Pacific palisades, CA: Goodyear.

Junger, M., & Marshall, I. (1997). The inter-ethnic generalizability of social control theory: An empirical test. *Journal of Research in Crime and Delinquency, 34,* 79–112.

Katz, C., Webb, V., & Decker, S. (2005). Using the arrestee drug abuse monitoring (ADAM) program to further understand the relationship between drug use and gang membership. *Justice Quarterly, 22*(1), 58–88.

Khondaker, M. (2005). Deviant behavior among youths of an immigrant Bangladeshi community in New York City. *Criminal Justice Studies, 18*(4), 321–333.

Kratcoski, P. (1983). The relationship of victimization through child abuse to aggressive delinquent behavior. *Victimology, 7,* 199–203.

Kratcoski, P. (1984). Perspectives on intra-family violence. *Human Relations, 37*(8), 443–454.

Leader, A. (1964). The role of intervention in family group treatment. *Social Casework, 45*(4), 327–333.

Lopiparo, J. (1977). Aggression on TV could be helping our children. *Intellect, 105*, 238–246.

Matza, D. (1964). *Delinquency and drift*. NY: Wiley.

Mawson, R. (1981). Aggression, attachment behavior, and crimes of violence. In T. Hirschi & M. Gottfrededson (Eds.), *Understanding crime* (p. 12). Beverly Hills, CA: Sage.

McKay, H. D. (1967). A note on trends in rates of delinquency in certain areas in Chicago. In *Appendix F in task force report: Juvenile delinquency and youth crime* (pp. 114–118). Washington, D.C: U.S. Government Printing Office.

Merton, R. (1938). Social structure and anomie. *American Sociological Review, 3*, 672–682.

National Center for Children in Poverty. (2019). *Child poverty*. National Center for Children in Poverty. Hll: l. www.nccp.org/topics/chuldpoverty.html. Accessed 3 2019.

Park, R., Burgress, E., & Kenzie, M. (1925). *The city*. Chicago: University of Chicago Press.

Raymen, T., & Smith, O. (2016). *What's deviance got to do with it? Black Friday sales, violence.* https://academic.oup.com/bjc/article/56/2/389/2462334. Accessed 10 Mar 2019.

Reckless, W. C. (1969). A new theory of delinquency and crime. In R. S. Cavan (Ed.), *Readings in juvenile delinquency* (3rd ed.). Philadelphia: J. B. Lippincott.

Reckless, W. C., Dinitz, S., & Murray, E. (1970). Self-concept as an insulator against delinquency. In J. E. Tesle (Ed.), *Juvenile delinquency: a reader*. Ithica, IL: F.E. Peacock.

Reiss, A. (1986). Co-offenders on criminal careers. In J. Blimstein, J. Cohen, J. Roth, & C. Visher (Eds.), *Criminal careers and career criminals* (Vol. 2, pp. 145–152). Washington, D.C.: National Academy Press.

Roche, M. (1985). *Rural police and rural youth*. Charlottesville, VA: University Press of Virginia.

Sampson, R. (1987). Urban black violence: The effect of male nobleness among family disruption. *American Journal of Sociology, 93*, 348–382.

Sampson, R. (1995). The community. In J. Wilson & J. Petersilia (Eds.), *Crime* (pp. 193–216). San Francisco: ICS Press.

Schur, E. M. (1973). Radical non-intervention: rethinking the delinquency problem. Englewood Cliffs, NJ: Prentice Hall.

Shaw, C. (1929). *Delinquency areas*. Chicago: University of Chicago Press.

Shaw, C., & McKay, H. (1969). *Juvenile delinquency and urban areas*. Chicago: University of Chicago Press.

Shoemaker, D. (1984). *Theories of delinquency*. NY: Oxford University Press.

Sorrells, J. (1977). Kids who kill. *Crime and Delinquency, 23*(2), 312–320.

Sykes, P., & Matza, D. (1957). Techniques of neutralization: A theory of delinquency. *American Journal of Sociology, 22*, 664–670.

Taft, D. R. (1956). *Criminology* (3rd ed.). New York: Macmillan.

Tanay, E. (1973). Adolescents who kill parents: Reactive parricide. *Australian and New Zealand Journal of Psychiatry, 7*, 263–277.

The Urban Institute (2019) Child poverty and adult success. http:www.urban.org/sites/default/files/alfresco/publicationpdfs/2000369-Child-Poverty-and-Adult-Success.pdf. Accessed 24 Jul 2019.

Thomas, W., & Znaniecki, F. (1918). *The Polish Peasant in Europe and America*. New York: Alfred A Knopf.

Thorsell, B. A., & Klemke, L. W. (1972). The labeling process: Reinforcement and deterrent? *Law and Society Review, 6.2*, 403.

Tracy, P., Wolfgang, M., & Figlio, R. (1985). *Delinquency in two birth cohorts*. Washington, DC: U.S. Department of Justice.

U.S. Bureau of the Census. (1999). *Population characteristics: Marital status and living arrangements. Current population reports*.. Washington, D.C.: U.S. Government Printing Office cited in H. Snyder & M. Sickmund, *Juvenile offenders and victims: 1998 National report*. Washington, D.C.: Office of Juvenile Justice and Delinquency Prevention.

Urbanik, M. & Haggerty, K. (2018). 'It's dangerous': The online world of drug dealers, rappers and the street code. The British Journal of Criminology. https://academic-oup.com/bjc/advance-article/doi/10.1093/bjc/azx083/4797365. Accessed 17 Mar 2019.

Vold, G., Bernard, T., & Snipes, J. (1998). *Theoretical criminology*. New York: Oxford University Press.

Waitrowski, M., Griswald, D., & Roberts, M. (1981). Social control theory and delinquency. *American Sociological Review, 46*, 525–541.

Whyte, W. F. (1955). *Street corner society* (2nd ed.). Chicago, IL: University of Chicago Press.

Widon, C. (1992). *The cycle of violence*. Washington, D.C: U.S. Department of Justice.

Williams, T. (2002). Homelessness breaking NYC. Akron Beacon Journal OH, A9.

Chapter 5
Perspectives on Interpersonal Relationships in the Family

5.1 Introduction

Studies of delinquency causation conducted by psychological and sociological researchers have invariably touched in some way on the influence of the family, and particularly on the parents' influence on the development or prevention of delinquency. Recognizing the importance of parents in the care and protection of children, and in their moral development, the juvenile court was developed around the principle of *parens patriae*, meaning the court adopts the posture of a "benevolent parent" towards youths whose natural parents have been unable or unwilling to assume responsibility for providing for the care and supervision of their children. In those cases in which the training and supervision by their natural parents has been apparently inadequate to prevent the occurrence of unacceptable behavior, the juvenile court has assumed these responsibilities.

Psychologists, in their studies of the relationship of family life to delinquency development, have concentrated on testing the effects of early childhood influences on delinquent behavior in adolescence, the effects of family size and ordinal position of a child within the family on juvenile misbehavior patterns, and the role of various child-rearing practices in character formation. Sociologists have tended to concentrate their research on such matters as the influence of broken and dysfunctional homes, mothers working outside the home, poverty, social class position of the family, educational levels of the parents, living arrangements, the occupation of the primary breadwinner, and, parental problems such as criminal behavior, substance abuse, and mental illness as factors that might relate to the delinquent behavior of the children.

Much of the earlier research on the family used an idealized standard of the typical American family as being composed of two parents, with the father being the chief breadwinner and authority figure, the mother the major source of emotional support for the children, and the children as the objects of the parents' efforts to prepare them

© Springer Nature Switzerland AG 2020
P. C. Kratcoski et al., *Juvenile Delinquency*,
https://doi.org/10.1007/978-3-030-31452-1_5

for an adulthood not radically different from their own. Economic and geographic stability were also regarded as indicative of family integration and stability.

It is now apparent that the "typical American family" no longer exists. The majority of mothers with young children hold employment outside the home, and many children live in one parent households as a result of the parents being divorced, never married, or separated.

Obviously, modifications in the family structure and lifestyles are necessary to deal with these situations. Even the most traditional families find they have to make adjustments in such routine matters as having a standard time for meals, and times set aside for family interaction. Children who are involved in extracurricular activities in the school, sports programs, and other activities conduced outside the family environs often dictate the schedules and activities of the parents. Weekends are no longer days of rest for many contemporary families. In spite of all this, a contemporary family can offer stability and emotional support to its members when they cooperate in adhering to a common set of values, work toward common goals, and receive satisfaction from interacting with each other. This remains true even though the family must constantly adjust to the demands and pressures of modern life. The family can best adapt when it functions as a system.

The notion that the family constitutes a system is developed from a comparison of the family with a living body having a structure and interrelated parts that support and complement each other's functions. Just as a malfunction of one body part affects the entire physical system and may require compensation by the other parts to keep the system functioning, or may eventually lead to morbidity or death, difficulties within the family regarded as a system may have analogous results. The common values and goals of the family make it possible for it to function as a system and meet the challenges that confront the individual members of the entire unit. The specific structure and mechanisms a family adopts to meet these challenges and problems may vary widely from one family to another.

If family members are comfortable in the roles they play and perform them in a routine manner, with all of the members adhering to the norms and values of the family, it is likely to be functioning in a manner that is in accordance with the goals either explicitly or implicitly established for the family. The family members provide emotional support to each other, especially at times when a member is experiencing a problem. For adolescent children, it could be something that may seem trivial to an adult, such as not being chosen to be a member of a sports team, or the break-up with a boy or girlfriend, but to the adolescent it may be appear to be a very serious problem and even lead to depression. There may be occasional more serious setbacks, such as serious illness in one or several members of the family, the loss of employment by the chief breadwinner, or failure in school of a child, but when the family members work as a unit, and are able to express their problems and concerns to each other, these problems are overcome.

The early involvement of a child within a family provides the framework in which the child learns about the culture, develops personality traits, and forms a character and a sense of morality. Not only does the child depend upon its parents for food, clothing, and shelter, but the child's self-image and feelings of worth and of being loved or rejected are developed within the family. Parents are responsible for the behavior of their children, with the widest possible application of the word "responsible." This implies not only their acceptance of responsibility for the children's supervision, but also their realization that they contribute to their moral and education development in a manner that external agencies cannot duplicate.

The teaching process between parent and child is most often not a formal instructional exercise, but a day-to-day exchange of cues as to what is appropriate and what is not for a member of their particular family. From observation of their parents, children internalize notions about how a husband should treat a wife and a wife should treat a husband, what the place of a child is in a family setting; how to respond to crisis situations; how to regard and relate to neighbors, acquaintances, and strangers; and many other complex lessons in human interaction.

5.2   Historical Development of the Role of Children in the Family

Rojek and Jensen (1982, p. 25) noted that the division of the human life cycle by age into childhood, adolescence, young adulthood, middle-age adulthood, and old age is a relatively recent phenomenon that developed in the latter part of the nineteenth century. Up until that time, children, with the exception of the children of the nobility who might someday inherit property or wealth, were treated as property. They had no rights except those they received through being members of a family.

Gradually, as the societies became industrialized and urbanized, the traditional laws and norms governing the relationship between parents and children changed. Large numbers of children were freed from the immediate control of the head of the family household, and children were separated from their families because of the death of parents, abandonment, or becoming apprentices. New compulsory education and immigration laws and legal tribunals had to be established to address matters that had always been handled through more tradition means, such as customs, but many of the customary ways of settling matters were codified and became law.

Some legal historians claim that the origins of the present day juvenile court, as structured in the United States and in other countries, can be traced to the Chancery Court of England, established in the seventeenth century. This high court of equity, administered by the Lord Chancellor, had jurisdiction in all common law matters relating to equity cases. In matters involving children in which the child was not represented by a parent or guardian, the court assumed the role of *parens patriae* or substitute parent (Kratcoski & Kratcoski, 1986, p. 75).

The establishment of the first juvenile court in the United States, in 1899, in Chicago, with its commitment to the *parens-patriae* philosophy and its jurisdiction over a wide variety of children, including those with needs for care and supervision as well as those who violated the law, set the framework for all of the other states to develop separate courts for children. Although these courts adopted the *parens patriae* philosophy, the structure and jurisdiction of the courts varied. This also held true for the state statutes pertaining to child-related matters, as well as the state interpretations of the laws pertaining to children. Even within the same state, courts were often structured and administered differently. The courts designated as juvenile courts had a narrow jurisdiction and handled matters pertaining to delinquency, abuse, neglect, and traffic offenses committed by juveniles. They were not empowered to hear matters relating to divorce, childcare payments, and establishing parentage. Courts with these powers were generally designated as family courts.

5.2.1   Development of the Legal Concept "Child"

Until the thirteenth and fourteenth centuries, a large number of newborns scarcely lived beyond infancy, since they were wiped out by disease, lack of proper shelter, starvation, or accidents. In some cases, children were deliberately abandoned because they were not considered to be of any benefit to the family. For the larger portion of the population, work was grounded in agriculture and children's work contributed to the family's economic status. Large families were the rule, with parents anticipating that some of their children might die before they reached adulthood. By tradition and law, children were considered to be the property of the head of the household. If the head of the family was a landowner, the father had the authority and right to control and discipline the other members of the household, including his spouse, children, and servants. If the family did not own the land on which they worked, but were tenants, the family was not allowed to own property and was subject to the control of the landlord (lord of the manor). In the middle ages, by tradition, serfs were bound to reside on the land on which they worked.

In the agricultural family, the authority of the head of the family over the children often extended well into adulthood. If a child continued to live in the same household as the parents, that child was expected to obey the commands of the father. If the head of a family were to die or become so ill as to be unable to function and provide for the family, close relatives were expected to look after the children and provide them with the food, clothing, and shelter needed to survive. If a young child were to commit an act that would be considered a crime if committed by an adult, the child's father or the head of the household generally would be held responsible for providing the proper discipline. There were exceptions to this rule. The child might be brought before the authorities and charged with a crime if the offense was considered a threat to the welfare of the society. In such cases, once it was established that the child could distinguish between right and wrong (*mens rea*), the accused was given the rights of an adult and, if convicted, was subject to the penalties an adult might receive.

The growth of industry throughout Europe, which began during the fourteenth and fifteenth centuries and continued throughout the nineteenth and twentieth centuries, led to the decline of the traditionally based agricultural social system. Land that had been farmed by a family line for hundreds of years was turned into pasture land, and families who knew nothing but farming were forced off the land. They moved to the cities in search of employment. During the transition from rural to urban areas, the traditional family structure and values were disrupted and often destroyed. The lives of children were affected by these changes. Because they were not able to contribute to the household by doing farm work, they were contracted out to serve as apprentices to large landholders, merchants, and tradesmen. In these cases, the master became a parent substitute and assumed responsibility for providing food, clothing, and shelter for the apprentice. The master also assumed the right to discipline the child, just as a parent would have if the child were still living in the family household. Some children were abandoned, became orphaned on the death of their parents, or ran away from their masters. Such children were forced to fend by themselves, either through begging, engaging in criminal behavior such as stealing and prostitution, or depending on some type of charitable organization. As the number of children who lacked parental or guardianship supervision increased in the cities, these children began to be defined as a threat to the welfare of the community and thus they were likely to be brought before the authorities, particularly if it could be shown that they were involved in illegal behavior.

The Industrial Revolution in England and other countries in Europe wrought a great deal of havoc in family life. When the economy was primarily based on agriculture, children worked alongside their parents in the fields and were constantly under their care and supervision. With the coming of the Industrial Revolution, children were employed in factories and mines, aboard fishing and merchant ships, and as apprentices to various types of tradesmen. Their workdays were long, and while at work, they were under the control of their supervisors. Even for families that remained intact, the almost absolute control of the head of the household over the other members of the family began to weaken.

5.2.2 Children in the United States

The early American colonists were able to maintain the traditions, values, and laws pertaining to family life that they brought with them from England and other European countries, as long as the colonies remained predominately agricultural. As in pre-Industrial England, the head of the family had almost absolute power over its members. For example, the Connecticut Blue Laws of 1650 stated that a stubborn and rebellious child who had reached the age of reason could be brought before the magistrate, charged, and, if the charges were found to be true, severely punished by the court (Cole, 1974, p. 13).

After the American Revolution and throughout the nineteenth century, there was a tremendous growth of industry in the United States. The country experienced the same types of population shifts from the rural areas to the urban areas that were occurring in Europe. In addition to the migration of the U.S. population from rural to urban areas, millions of immigrants came from countries throughout the world to find employment. The majority of these immigrants settled in the cities, and this tremendous growth of the urban population led to overcrowding, the creation of slums, poverty for those unable to work, and often a breakup of the primary family unit. Children who were unsupervised, not attending school, and often living on the streets engaged in mischief and criminal behavior. Such children, who apparently were not under any parental control, were feared by the citizenry, and there was a clamor to do something about controlling these wayward children.

5.2.3 Houses of Refuge

In 1824, the New York State legislature granted a charter to the Society for the Reformation of Juvenile Delinquents to maintain a House of Refuge for wayward, homeless, and delinquent children. Soon after this, the legislation needed to establish such "houses of refuge" was passed in a number of states, and such facilities, some under private auspices and others under public auspices, were opened in a number of U.S. cities. The specific goals and legal jurisdiction of the houses of refuge varied, depending on the city and state in which they were established. Generally, their goals were to rescue poor children, particularly those who were homeless, wayward, or vagabonds, and protect them from associating with adult criminals or engaging in criminal behavior by placing them in institutions that provided a program grounded in discipline, moral training, and hard work. The houses of refuge set the groundwork for separating incarcerated youths from adults who were convicted of crimes and held in secure facilities (Rothman, 1971, p. 207).

The legislation that provided a foundation for the selection of youths who were eligible for commitment was often vague in wording and could be interpreted to include those who were merely in danger of becoming delinquent as well as those who had committed offenses. According to Bernard (1949), the committed youths often were not convicted of criminal offenses. Children could be picked up off the streets for loitering, and some parents routinely committed children on the basis of the children being disobedient. In addition, a child could be removed from the home on the premise that the parents were not providing the proper care, control, and discipline. Children committed to houses of refuge were eligible to be held there until the age of their majority. When this occurred, the children's relationships with their own families virtually ended.

The benefits the house of refuge movement gave to society are debatable. Many scholars argue that these facilities represented the first phase of a movement to establish a separate justice system for youths, one that would be more concerned with the needs of youths than with the punishment that should be given to those who committed offenses. Others argue that the low standard of living provided in the houses, in terms of food, clothing, recreation, and general care, in conjunction with the harsh discipline given to those who violated rules, offset the benefits received from their stay. Many children ran away from the houses of refuge if the opportunity presented itself. Still other scholars contend that the movement had a detrimental effect, because the legislation governing such houses extended the control of the state over children as well as over parents. In addition, the legislation stripped the children accused of crimes of their legal rights. It appears that the movement represented another phase in the gradual erosion of parental powers and rights. The power given to the houses of refuge to serve in the role of *parens patriae* or parent substitute by the state legislatures was reaffirmed by the Pennsylvania Supreme Court decision (*Ex parte Crouse* 1838). The court ruled that a mother had a right to send her daughter to the Philadelphia House of Refuge for being incorrigible. The writ of habeas corpus filed by Mary Crouse's father, asking that she be released from the house of refuge, was dismissed by the Pennsylvania Supreme Court on the ground that

> The House of Refuge is not a prison, but a school, where reformation and not punishment is the end…. The object of the charity is reformation, by training its inmates to industry; by imbuing their minds with principles of morality and religion; by furnishing them with means to earn a living; and above all by separating them from the corrupting influence of improper associates…. To this end may not the natural parents, when unequal to the task, or unworthy, be superseded by the parens patriae, or common guardian.

5.2.4 Compulsory Education

Legislation requiring compulsory attendance at school was enacted in New York and Massachusetts in the early part of the nineteenth century. This legislation not only required children between the ages of 6 and 16 to attend school, but also granted school officials the right of in loco parentis, allowing them to serve as parent substitutes during the time the children were in school (Bokan, 1982). School officials had the right to discipline children at school, using methods to administer the discipline that were often used by parents, such as spanking or slapping, and hitting them with an object like a paddle or strap. The fact that children were now out of the home for a major part of the day tended to weaken the control that parents had over their children.

5.2.5 Origins of the Legal Status of Children

The early settlers of the American colonies at first maintained the traditions, laws, and forms of government they had known in their countries of origin. These were predominately based on the English heritage. Gradually, particularly after the colonies received their independence and the U.S. Constitution became the law of the land, the individual rights of citizens were expanded. Because the Constitution does not specifically make reference to children and the age at which a child becomes an adult, these matters were left to the states to determine. In some states, the age of majority—that is, the age at which a person is guaranteed all of the rights and privileges of citizens of that state, including the right to marry, own property, vote for local or state officials, and enter into contracts—was defined as 21, whereas in other states, the age was set at 18. Generally, the lowest age set for being held responsible for behavior defined as criminal was seven. For children between the ages of 7 and 14, the state had to show that the accused knew the difference between right and wrong.

During the course of the history of the United States, numerous state laws and laws passed by the U.S. Congress affected the relationship between parents and children. In addition, various courts, including the U.S. Supreme Court, made decisions that defined parental rights over their children as well as the rights of children in regard to their status as citizens of a state and of the country. In these matters, federal laws supersede state law.

5.3 Significant Cases Pertaining to Parent–Child Relations

As has been noted, the laws of most countries pertaining to children were based on the assumption that parents have the natural right to provide the care and discipline of their children. This parental right is almost absolute during the period the child is residing in the household of the parent. The parents may have been required to temporarily relinquish their rights to control and discipline children during times they were out of the family environs, such as when a child was in school and under the supervision of school authorities, or contracted out as an apprentice. When the apprenticed youth was no longer living at home, the master to whom the youth was apprenticed assumed the responsibilities of the parents in regard to care and control. With a few exceptions, the parent–child relationship was generally considered sacred and not to be tampered with unless the circumstances were such that outside intervention seemed necessary. Legislation pertaining to houses of refuge allowed the state to intervene in family affairs and to remove a child from the home. The state could place the child in a house of refuge if it could be shown that the parents were unable or unwilling to provide the standard care and discipline considered necessary. In addition, a parent could voluntarily ask for assistance from the state by asking that the child be placed in a house of refuge because of an inability to control the child within the family household.

Over the years, the rights of parents to control and discipline their children were tested in the courts. The courts have consistently affirmed the rights of parents to care for and discipline their children, but the courts have been somewhat vague in defining what constitutes reasonable punishment. As a result, cases that came before the courts pertaining to parents being accused of being excessively harsh or physical in the disciplining of their children were decided on a case-by-case basis. In one state, harsh physical methods of discipline, such as the use of a leather strap or belt, might be considered appropriate by the courts, whereas in another state, the same form of punishment might be defined as unreasonable and thus exceeding the rights given to the parent to discipline their children.

For example, in Stanley v. Illinois (1972), the U.S. Supreme Court reiterated the rights of parents to provide care, companionship, and management of their children. The Court noted that the Constitutional rights of the parents must be considered in any efforts to temporarily or permanently remove children from the home because of instances of excessive or inappropriate discipline. In the Santosky v. Kramer (1982) case, the Court again reaffirmed the fundamental rights of the parents in regard to disciplining children and questioned the procedure followed by a New York court for terminating the rights of the parents of the Santosky children. In this case, the Santosky children were removed from their home by a county social services agency. The family court judge declared the children "permanently neglected" and terminated the rights of their parents to provide care and discipline. The case eventually was appealed to the U.S. Supreme Court. In a split decision, the Court ruled in favor of the Santosky parents' appeal to have their parental rights restored and have the children returned to their natural home. Justice Blackmun, rendering the majority opinion, reiterated the position that the parents' interest in the family is protected by the liberty clause of the Fourteenth Amendment and is not nullified when they neglect their children or lose temporary custody over them. Consequently, all parents are entitled to "fundamentally fair procedures when facing the abolition of their parental rights" (Mezey, 1996, p, 112). The Court acknowledged that there are circumstances in which punishment or discipline administered by parents is not reasonable and is likely to be harmful to the best interests of the child being punished. In these cases, the state should take action to protect the child and may require the termination of parental rights. The burden of proof required to show that the parents have been neglectful is "a clear and convincing standard," a level of proof above that used in deciding most civil cases (Santosky v. Kramer, 1982).

5.3.1   State Obligations to Protect a Child Under State Supervision

Child protective agencies can make mistakes. They may place children in group homes or with foster parents in situations that turn out to be more harmful to the children than the setting from which they were removed. Caseworkers often have huge caseloads and do not have the time required to properly investigate the potential foster parents and the environment recommended for placement.

Some children are placed in group homes or with foster parents and are more or less forgotten by the child protective agency. In such cases, should the child protective agency be held legally responsible for problems that arise? This question was addressed in *DeShaney v. Winnebago County Department of Social Services* (1989). The issue was whether the state had failed to take the necessary action needed to provide for the care and security of a child who needed *parens patriae* protection. The U.S. Supreme Court was asked to decide whether a state or county child protective agency that had assumed the protective care of a child, acting in accordance with the *parens patriae* doctrine, had failed to protect that child and should be held legally responsible.

The case involved Joshua, a four-year-old boy who was so savagely beaten by his father that he became permanently disabled. The issue centered on the fact that the Department of Social Services was aware that Joshua had been beaten by the father in the past and had been hospitalized as a result of the wounds received from the beating. The social services agency investigated the alleged abuse incident and decided that there was not sufficient evidence for the court to take any official action, such as removing Joshua from the custody of his father. Joshua's father, although not admitting to abusing Joshua, did agree to several unofficial recommendations made by the agency, including counseling.

When Joshua was discharged from the hospital, he was returned to his home to live with his father. A social worker was assigned to the case and made regular visits to the home. In her reports, she recorded several signs that the child possibly was being abused. Shortly after the social worker's last visit, Joshua was so severely beaten by his father that he went into a coma. He was operated on for brain damage. Although he survived the operation, the damage to his brain was so irreversible that permanent institutionalization was required. Joshua's father was convicted of child abuse and sentenced to prison.

The Winnebago Department of Social Services was sued by Joshua's mother on the grounds that the state has deprived Joshua of his rights by failing to protect him from his father's violence. The U.S. District Court for the Eastern District of Wisconsin ruled against Joshua and his mother and the Seventh Circuit Court of Appeals affirmed the district court decision (Mezey, 1996, p, 114). When the case was appealed to the U.S. Supreme Court, the plaintiff argued that "Wisconsin law charged the state with the responsibility for protecting children from abuse," and because the state was aware of abuse to Joshua on the part of his father and did not take the appropriate action to protect him, the state was liable for its failure to act (Mezey, 1996, p. 114). The majority opinion of the Supreme Court was that Joshua was under his father's care, not the state's care, at the time that he was physically abused and thus a special relationship between.

Joshua and the state did not exist. In short, the state did not have a constitutional obligation to protect Joshua. In the Court's summary of the case, it was noted that if the agency had removed Joshua from his father's supervision and had placed him in a foster home, the due process clause of the Fourteenth Amendment might have applied, because in a sense, Joshua would have been deprived of his liberty (Mezey, 1996, p. 114).

The findings in these cases guide the legislators of the various states in establishing criteria to be followed by social service agencies when investigating and processing cases of parental abuse and neglect. The new legislation pertains to parents' rights to control and discipline their children as well as to children's rights to be protected and secure from being harmed, regardless of the source of the danger, be it parents or others.

5.3.2 Juvenile Rights Pertaining to the Family

Implicit in the legal precedents that parents have the natural rights to protect their children and to ensure that they will be cared for in terms of food, clothing, shelter, safety, and supervision is the assumption that children are entitled to receive these necessities, as well as care, affection, discipline, and guidance, from parents or caretakers.

Several of the areas in which the rights of the parent, child, and the state may be in dispute include matters relating to support and maintenance, education, medical care, termination of parental rights, child custody, adoption, visitation rights, and disputes between parents and nonparents.

Traditionally, as well as in statutory law, fathers were primarily responsible for providing their minor children with the basic necessities of life. In cases in which the father was not capable of doing this or refused to provide support, the responsibility fell to the mother. Current state statutory laws place these obligations on both parents. The amount of "necessary support" in regard to shelter, food, clothing, medical attention, and education to which children are entitled will vary, depending on the financial resources of each family and assessment of the child's needs. In regard to education, the state becomes involved because of compulsory education laws. Typically, the duty of parents to ensure that their children receive schooling extends to the upper age limit of compulsory education law or ends when the child reaches the age of majority, which is 18 years of age in most states. If parents do not assume this responsibility, the state may intervene under the *parens-patriae* doctrine. Children do not have the right to postsecondary education, and parents are not required to provide it. With regard to medical care, the courts have allowed parents discretion regarding the provision and type of medical care, but the state may intervene in situations in which the health and welfare of the child are seriously threatened, even though this action may be against the wishes of the parents.

5.4 The Family and Delinquency

The results of research on strain and social control explanations of delinquency pertaining to the family (Thaxton & Agnew (2004, p. 785) suggest that "It is the presence or absence of negative attachments that is most consequential for delinquency. Individuals who are negatively attached to parents and teachers are much higher in delinquency than neutral and positively attached individuals. The difference in delinquency between neutral and positively attached individuals, however, is slight." A study by Higgins, Ricketts, Marceem, and Mahoney (2010) found that ".... The delinquency group becomes more severe in their offending, attachment to parents becomes less important."

Kjeldal (2004, p. 268) reports that the bonding process between mother and child is complex, and a mother might engage in irrational behavior, even infanticide, to protect a child from what is perceived as extreme danger. In attempting to explain the rationalization of Susan Smith, who drove her automobile into a lake and allowed her children to drown, Kjeldal used decisions theories to develop a model of human decision making that may be useful in explaining Susan Smith's actions. She notes (p. 281), "Researchers are not really able to offer explanations for behavior that is so far beyond the realms of typical human actions.... It has been demonstrated that contemporary decisions theory supports the conclusion of non-rational factors that assist in understanding the actions of Susan Smith."

5.4.1   *Delinquency and Disrupted Family Structure*

Families may be physically disrupted by the loss of either parent through death, desertion, separation, or divorce. Although youths from broken homes tend to be referred to juvenile courts more often than youths from intact ones, this fact cannot be taken at face value as an indicator that broken homes foster delinquent activity. Instead, it may be a reflection of differential treatment of young people by the police and the courts. When interacting with youths from broken homes, police officers and court officials may decide to handle a case officially rather than informally because they believe that a single parent needs more support in controlling a child's behavior. Some research has substantiated this hypothesis. A self-reported delinquency study of high school students (Van Voorhis, Cullen, Mathers, & Chenoweth Garner, 1988) found that a broken home was less important in determining delinquency than was the quality of family life.

Thijs et al. (2015, p. 601) note that both social stress theory and strain theory emphasize the frustrations that can be caused in the family by children and parents being economically deprived or when young people have insufficient means to achieve their goals. Barrett and Turner (2006) found that economic deprivation within the family household can be stressful for children and may be related to delinquent behavior. Levin, Kirby, and Carrie (2012) found that children living in single parent and divorced families are more likely to engage in deviant behavior than children living in two-parent households. Thijs et al. (2015, pp. 599, 610) used the 2010 European Union Kids On Line Survey that included the responses from more than 18,000 youths from 24 European countries to determine if boys and girls reacted differently to the stresses and strains within the family that are associated with delinquent behavior. They found that the gender gap is largely explained by personality traits such as self-control. They stated, "Adolescents from single parent families were more likely to engage in problem behavior, as we expected. We found no direct effect of parental social economic status (SES) on adolescent problem behavior. In addition, we found no evidence that boys and girls react differently to family factors; growing up in a single parent family and parental socio-economic background affect boys' and girls' problem behavior similarly." Getting and Donnermeyer (1998) suggest that delinquent norms and behavior patterned may actually be transmitted to the children in the socialization process. When the parents engage in stealing, excessive drinking, are violent, and engage in other forms of deviant behavior, the children may imitate these forms of behavior during their routine relations in the family.

When parents separate or divorce, decisions must be made regarding the custody of children. Under the Uniform Marriage and Divorce Act (National Conference of Commissioners on Uniform State Laws, 1970, 1973, 1998), factors to be considered in custody decisions include the wishes of the parent or parents as to the child's custody; the wishes of the child as to his or her placement; the quality of the relationship of the child with his or her parents, siblings, and other persons involved in the child's life; the child's social and psychological adjustment at home, in school and in the community; and the mental stability and physical health of all those involved in the custody arrangement. The best interest of the child is the primary consideration. One parent may voluntarily relinquish custody to the other parent because of relocation, remarriage, or inability to provide for the child.

In custody disputes, the courts, when making the decision on which parent should be designated as the primary caretaker, have considered such factors as the age of the child and the past performance of each parent in such matters as the day-to-day care of the child, including providing for physical needs, supervision, and discipline, and assuming responsibilities related to medical care, education, and social activities. The physical and mental health of each person requesting custody is also considered. When the custody is worked out amicably between the parents, shared joint custody is frequently an option. Legal custody is shared by both parents, and the child spends a specified amount of time with each parent, even though the primary residence may be with one of the parents.

The courts have generally determined the rights of visitation of children by the parent who did not obtain custody of the child on the basis of the best interests of the child. There may be one or more compelling reasons why the noncustodial parent should not be given visitation rights. These may include the fact that the noncustodial parent victimized the children in the past, has a substance abuse addiction, engages in criminal behavior, or does not provide proper supervision and care of the children during the hours of the visitation. If none of these factors exist, the parent who did not obtain custody will be granted some visitation privileges. The visitation rights of other persons, including grandparents and other relatives, are determined by the individual state statutes. Most states have enacted legislation that grants nonparental visitation rights, again on the basis of the "best interests of the child." In the U.S. Supreme Court case of Troxel v. Granville (2000), however, a case in which the custodial parents objected to the grandparents visiting their children, the Court ruled that grandparents do not have a constitutional right to visit their grandchildren, and the custodial parents can legally prevent the grandparents from making such visitations.

5.4.2   Child Emancipation

Child emancipation, an idea derived from Roman law, occurs when parental support duties and rights to control the life of the child are terminated. Parents lose common law entitlements to the services and earnings of the child. Juvenile courts and family courts have the authority to address matters related to emancipation of children, and a decree of emancipation may be granted if such a separation of parents and child is considered to be in the best interest of the persons involved. A request for emancipation from parental rights over the child may occur as a result of extreme conflict within the family, or when a child below the age of 18 enlists in the military or marries. In instances in which the child requests to move out of the parents' home, the minimum age for emancipation is normally 16. The child must be financially able to live independently, and the parents must agree to the request.

5.4.3 *Socialization in the Family and Delinquency*

Analysis of the socialization of children within families can offer insight into the causes and motivations for delinquent behavior. Parents' attitudes, behavior, communication or lack of communication with their children, and manner and consistency of disciplining are all factors associated with developing self-control, respect for authority, responses to stressful events, acceptance of responsibility, and realization of consequences for behavior (Lamb, 1995). Attachment to parents helps explain the process through which norms are internalized by a child.

Hope (2003) gathered data from more than 1000 middle school and high school students from a semi-rural university town. She explored the relationship of family characteristics of students and their membership or lack of membership in gangs. Hope found that parental deviance had a direct effect on gang members. She concluded that "Those who live in violent homes are at a greater risk for gang membership" (Hope, 2003, p. 180). Gang members, however, did not differ significantly from non-gang members on measures of attachment to their parents or being poorly supervised.

5.4.4 *Family Violence and Delinquency*

Physical violence directed by children toward parents has also been found to be closely related to high levels of emotional tension within the family and physical abuse of children by parents.

A study by Straus (1994, p. 32) found that despite the fact that almost all American children have been hit, there are large differences between families in the frequency of hitting, the severity of the hitting, and the duration of the attacks (the number of years parents continue to hit, Some stop when the child is about school age, others continue to hit for many years.

Straus found that mothers hit both younger and older children more often than fathers did, possibly because they spend so much more time with the children, their early age of marriage, the birth of unwanted children, lack of parenting skills, and social isolation. Parents who were hit by their own parents tended to hit their own children at a higher rate (Straus, 1994, p. 54, 58). Parents who were violent toward each other were more likely than other parents to hit their children, and marital violence also increased the probability that holder children (ages 16 and older) would be hit by their parents. Almost all parent hit toddlers, although the spanking tended to be very mild. He also found that there was no relationship between socioeconomic status and the use of corporal punishment. Straus concluded that, while the majority of children who are spanked no not become delinquent, and for most children mild spanking may be harmless, receiving corporal punishment as a child is significantly related to marital violence as an adult (Straus, 1994, p. 119).

Mann (1996 p. 71) who researched the murder of pre-school-age children by their mothers, discovered that children under age six accounted for 61% of the children murdered by their mothers.

Children who have been the subjects of abusive treatment frequently become child abusers when they become parents because they have internalized the notion that severe physical punishment is an acceptable part of child rearing. In the same way, delinquent behavior by children, while not necessarily imitative of the conduct of parents, may be a direct result of adaptations to life learned or experienced at home. For example, drug or alcohol abuse by children may be an imitation of the methods they have seen their parents use to deal with or escape from pressures, even though the parental conduct is far less extreme in degree or style than that of the children.

The relation of family functioning to violent behavior of family members toward each other was the topic of a national study of family violence conducted by the URSA Institute (1981), based on victims' accounts, concluded that exposure to domestic violence during childlood, as either victim or witness, is the strongest predictor of future violence toward other family members. A study of homicides in which the assailant and the victim were members of the same family revealed that 19% of the killings were performed by persons under 24 years of age, usually young males. The incidents tended to occur in the home, during or after a quarrel, in a spontaneous manner. The assailants tended to have previous delinquency records that included violent behavior, and in many instances they had experienced disruptive family lives (Kratcoski, 1987).

5.4.5   Delinquency and Parental Rejection

A father can play a role in preventing delinquency by establishing strong and meaningful contacts with his children. If the father accepts his role of parent with all of the responsibilities attached, his children are likely to imitate his roles and values. This is particularly important during a young person's adolescent years, when many forces in the social environment and the mass media could have negative influences on the young person.

Lurie (1993) described the Responsive Fathers Program, a national demonstration project that explored ways to help young unwed fathers take legal, financial, and emotional responsibility for their children. Since many of those involved were inner-city men with limited education and little work experience they were encouraged to complete Graduate Equivalency Diplomas (GEDs) from high school and become involved in job training programs. They were also provided opportunities to interact with and care for their children. Many of these men received little or no attention from their own fathers and needed assistance in learning how to relate to their children.

5.4.6   *Relationship of Parental Discipline to Delinquency*

The mechanisms used within families for controlling youthful behavior can have a significant bearing on the activities of children. The trend for unmarried adolescent mothers to keep their babies rather than give them up for adoption has created a new type if family situation in many areas. Single girls with one or more small children are leaving home and setting up independent households with male companions or other unmarried young women. The children of these women, who are frequently supported by welfare payments, are reared in environments of poverty and unstructured family life. Sometimes termed the "underclass," this population of child mothers—school dropouts with minimal education and skills—and their children presents problems for education and social institutions that are unique. The mothers lack the personal resources or commitment to discipline their children adequately. The children become streetwise at an early age and are endangered for involvement in delinquent activity. Juvenile courts and family courts that become involved in such cases are severely limited in their options for handling these children, as illustrated by the following case.

> Two brothers—ages 11 and 12—appeared yesterday in _____ _____ Juvenile Court to face charges in connection with a stolen car.
>
>   They appeared alone…. They had no attorney. None of their relatives had come to court to be with them.
>
>   "We've had no inquiries from their family about their whereabouts," _____ said after the hearing. "We've been unable to contact a parent or guardian."
>
>   The boys and their 8-year-old brother were all picked up by_____ police in a [car] that had been reported stolen about an hour earlier…
>
>   All three boys—and two other siblings—have been in the custody of their grandmother. The boys' mother has eight children and does not have custody of any of them, said their aunt. (Akron Beacon Journal, 1994, p. B1)

Studies have concluded that the level of parental control is related to delinquent behavior. Wells and Rankin (1988) found that direct controls of adolescents' behavior, in the form of setting rules, monitoring the youths' activities, and punishing them for violating rules, were related to involvement in delinquency. However, very strong or very weak parental involvement led to greater frequency of delinquency and was less effective in obtaining desired behaviors from children than were moderately strict parental rules.

5.5   Counseling Families and Juvenile Offenders

Family counseling with juvenile offenders is often directed at crisis intervention. Clark (1996, pp. 58-60) describes the guiding principles of *brief solution-focused* work, noting that "All offenders and families have some resources such as skills, capabilities, interests, and positive character traits, even perseverance and hope, which can be brought to bear for exiting our system…. Problem-solving abilities are called from the past to be utilized in the present.... Although teaching and skill building will always have a place in our field, consider that it is far easier to utilize what is already present or what has been successful than to import vocabulary, methods, or strategies foreign to those we work with." Clark further observed, "A Solution-Focused approach does not belabor the past, nor does it fully need to understand the problem before solution work can begin." Clark gives two basic criteria to follow when a counselor ii working with a juvenile offender and family on setting up the goals. First, the goals must be meaningful to the youth and parents and be realistic in terms of the youth's problem/s with the family school, police, juvenile court, of the community.... A second principle to be followed when the counselor and client are engaged in goal setting is that goals must be small and interactional. Clark states, "The brief solution therapist does not ignore long-range goals but is most concerned with short-range goals, that is, what behavioral changes can be made now, immediately."

In many communities, juvenile and family courts and community social service agencies, as well as volunteer agencies, collaborate to provide counseling and treatment services for families. For example, the Family Resource Center of the Summit County Juvenile Court was established to offer case management, referral and follow-up for appropriate community services and resources. The Center assists pregnant female youths or those who are mothers and male youths who are fathers. Others served are chronic truants, and youths involved in domestic violence or school performance problems. Other problems addressed are violence and conflict at home, youths returning home from treatment or the Department of Youth Services, and job readiness and search.

In the Court's Responder Program, case managers provide services to students in several of the county's middle schools who have behavior, mental health or attendance problems. Truancy is also addressed. The goal is to improve school attendance and performance to avoid official referral to the Court (Summit County Juvenile Court, The Family Resource Center, 2019, pp. 1–2).

5.6 Summary

In this chapter, we noted the changing nature of the American family and the stresses that contemporary living places on parental efforts to achieve stability in the family unit. The dynamic balance in the interaction of family members, known as homeostasis, may be achieved by widely varied homeostatic mechanisms, depending upon the lifestyle and role ascriptions or acceptances in that particular household. Loss of this balance caused by rapid or unforeseen changes may contribute to the development of juvenile misbehavior. Parents have been identified as the first and most influential educators of their children in cultural, personality, and moral development. Such teaching may include the inculcation of undesirable as well as desirable attitudes and values. Delinquent behavior may result from youths; internalization of attitudes or behavior patterns that are at variance with accepted community norms.

A number of changes in contemporary society have been identified as affecting American family structures and practices. These include urbanization, industrialization, mobility complex communication networks, and changing value systems. Most notable among observed changing values are the greater relaxation of sexual standards, the acceptance of divorce and varied marriage styles, a turning away from child-centered family life, and new views on the appropriate roles for women in the family unit and in the larger society.

Research studies of the influence of the family on delinquent behavior have documented the relation between the development of delinquency and the physical or psychological disruption of the family structure. Psychological disruption of the family through alcoholism, mental illness, emotional disturbances of parents, or home atmospheres characterized by internal conflict and constant tension have been identified as factors in delinquency production. Conversely, a number of studies have shown that a happy and well-structured family life is related to lack of delinquency and successful adjustment to society. Socialization was also identified as an important factor. Attachment to parents was found to be closely related to a lack of deviance, and children who observed and/or experienced family violence and excessive corporal punishment were found to be more prone to violent acts.

A number of researchers have established a relation between parental rejection and aggressive delinquent behavior. The important role of the father in delinquency prevention has also been stressed. Lack of consistent and adequate discipline has been documented in many cases of delinquent behavior. Finally, the extensive use of physical punishment is a recognized factor in the production of aggressive delinquent activity.

Although some testing and rejection of parental values is recognized as a normal part of the maturation process, excessive hostility toward parents and rejection of their values has been noted as a characteristic of certain types of delinquents, while the desire for approval by parents and school authorities has been documented as a delinquency-inhibiting factor. The "costs-and-rewards" theory of delinquency holds youths to be inhibited from delinquent behavior by their recognition of the potential costs of such activity. Researchers have discovered, however, that the costs-and-rewards factor was a more potent delinquency-reducing variable for white youths than for blacks, and suggested that socialization factors might be responsible for this variation. Successful family adjustment was also found to be related to lack of involvement in the drug subculture.

On the basis of these observations, it can be seen that the contemporary family, regardless of its style and structure, continues to be a potent force in delinquency prevention or generation. In combination with the influence of the school, the community, and the economic and social structure, it contributes greatly to the milieu in which each child is socialized and prepared for adult life.

5.7 Discussion Questions

1. Compare the family as a system to the operation of a living body. What are some of the homeostatic mechanisms that might be part of the activities of a family with very small children?
2. Discuss how changing values and economic necessities in American life have altered the conception of the "typical American family."
3. How has the increase in the number of very young single mothers and their children created special problems for juvenile courts and social agencies? How can these problems be addressed?
4. Discuss how a strong family unit can serve as a buffer against delinquency.
5. Is it ever appropriate for parents to use physical punishment (spanking) as a means of controlling their misbehaving children?
6. There has been a movement toward involving the parents of delinquent youths in the treatment programs used by the courts and children service agencies for delinquent youths. Discuss the reasons for taking this broad approach.
7. What are the effects on children who experience or observe a considerable among of violence in the family unit?
8. Why is the family so important in the socialization process of a child?
9. Discuss some of the findings of research on parental disciplining of their children.
10. . Discuss some of the reasons why a parent or parents might reject or mistreat one of the children in the household and not the other children in the family.

Court Cases *DeShaney v. Winnebago County Department of Social Services*, 489 U.S. 189 (1989).

Ex parte Crouse, 4 Wharton 9 (Pa. 1838).
Santosky v. Kramer, 455 U.S. 745, 753 (1982).
Stanley v. Illinois, 405 U.S. 645, 651 (1972).
Troxel v. Granville, 530 U.S. 57 (2000).

References

Akron Beacon Journal. (1994). (p. B1).
Barrett, M., & Turner, V. (2006). Family structure and substance use with problems in adolescence and early childhood. *Addiction, 101*(1), 109–120.
Bernard, W. (1949). *Jail bait.* New York: Breenberg.
Bokan, D. (1982). Adolescence in America: From idea to social fact. In D. Rojek & G. Jensen (Eds.), *Readings in juvenile delinquency.* Lexington, MA: D.C. Heath.
Clark, M. (1996). Brief-solution-focused work: A strength-based method for juvenile justice practice. *Juvenile and Family Court Journal, 47*(1), 57–65.
Cole, L. (1974). *Our children's keepers.* Greenwich, CT: Fawcett.
Getting, E., & Donnermeyer, J. (1998). Primary socialization theory; the etiology of drug use and deviance. *Substance Use and Misuse, 33*, 999–1026.

Higgins, G., Ricketts, M., Marceem, C., & Mahoney, M. (2010). Primary socialization theory: An exploratory study of delinquent trajectories. *Criminal Justice Studies, 23*(2), 133–146.

Hope, T. (2003). Do families matter. In T. Calhoun & C. Chapple (Eds.), *Readings in juvenile delinquency and juvenile justice* (pp. 180–196). Upper Saddle River, NJ: Prentice Hall.

Kjeldal, S. (2004). Susan Smith and her children: A reasoning dialectic. *Critical Criminology, 12*(30), 265–228.

Kratcoski, P. (1987). Families who kill, Marriage and Family Review, 12. ½. Pp. 47–70.

Kratcoski, P., & Kratcoski, L. D. (1986). *Juvenile delinquency* (2nd ed.). Englewood, NJ: Prentice Hall.

Lamb, K. (1995). The causal factors of crime: Understanding the subculture of violence. *The Mankind Quarterly, 36*, 105–116.

Levin, K., Kirby, J., & Carrie, C. (2012). Adolescent risk behaviors and mealtime routines: Does family meal frequency alter the association between family structure and risk behavior? *Health Education Research, 27*(1), 24–35.

Lurie, T. (1993). Fathers and families; forging ties that bind. *USA Today, 121*(257), 30–33.

Mann, C. R. (1996). *When women kill.* Albany, NY: State University of New York Press.

Mezey, S. (1996). *Children in court.* Albany, NY: State University of New York Press.

National Conference Commissioner on Uniform State Law (1970, 1973, 1998). Washington, D.C.: U.S Department of Justice.

Rojek, D., & Jensen, G. (1982). The social history of delinquency. In D. Rojek & G. jenson (Eds.), *Readings in juvenile delinquency* (pp. 25–37). Lexington, MA: D.C. Heath.

Rothman, D. (1971). *The discovery of the asylum.* Boston: Little Brown.

Straus, M. A. (1994). *Beating the devil out of them.* New York: Lexington Books.

Summit County Juvenile Court (2019). *The family resource center* (pp. 1–2). www.co.summit.oh.us/JuvenileCourt/Index. Accessed 13 July 2019.

Thaxton, S., & Agnew, R. (2004). The nonlinear effect of parental and teacher attachment on delinquency: Disentangling strain from social control explanations. *Justice Quarterly, 21*(4), 763–789.

Thijs, P., VanDyk, I., Stoof, R., & Natascha, N. (2015). Adolescent problem behavior: The gender gap in European perspective. *European Journal of Criminology, 2*(5), 598–615.

URSA Institute. (1981). *Characteristics of successful programs for the serious juvenile offender, issues and strategies / special report.* San Francisco, CA: URSA Institute.

Van Voorhis, P., Cullen, F., Mathers, R., & Chenoweth Garner, C. (1988). The impact of family structure and quality on delinquency: A comparative assessment of structural and functional factors. *Criminology, 26*(2), 235–262.

Wells, L. E., & Rankin, J. H. (1988). Direct parental controls and delinquency. *Criminology, 26*(2 (May)), 263–286.

Chapter 6
Perspectives on Gangs and Peer Group Influences Pertaining to Delinquency Causation

6.1 Introduction

When I was 8 years old I did my first job in the racket… That day I was hanging around with the oldest brother and his gang… The big guys got to talking about stealing, and my brother said he had a good place spotted where we would get some easy "dough" (money)… My brother had been in the place a few days before to see how to get in and where the cash register was… We all went up to the back door, and then my brother got a box and stood on it and tried the transom—and it opened. It was too little for my brother or the other guys to get through. I was thrilled when they said I'd have to crawl though the transom…

My brother lifted me up on his shoulders and I crawled through… The door was locked with a padlock and chain, but I was able to unlock the window and let the big guys in that way… I felt like a "big-shot" after that night and the big guys said I could go with them every time they went robbin'… many times I had to crawl through transoms and one time through an ice-box hole. That's why the big guys called me the "baby bandit" (Shaw, 1968, pp. 86–87).

Officers found Robert Sandifer in a pool of blood beneath a railroad overpass yesterday. He was 11.

Robert's body—not yet 5 ft., not quite 70 pounds—lay about seven blocks from where police believe he opened fire Sunday at two groups of boys, fatally hitting a 14-year-old girl…

Robert was suspected of having gang ties and two gun-shot wounds—one to the back of the head, one to the top—led police to suggest that fellow gang members had killed him (Baltimore Sun, 1994, p. 3A).

These two descriptions of very young boys involved in gang activity, one in the 1930s and the other in the 1990s, reveal that gang formation and loyalties, and the appeal of gang membership, have long existed. Gang formation has been a consistent element in juvenile reaction to urban life and gangs have also been found to exist in suburban and rural areas. Currently, youth gangs pose a serious threat in

© Springer Nature Switzerland AG 2020
P. C. Kratcoski et al., *Juvenile Delinquency*,
https://doi.org/10.1007/978-3-030-31452-1_6

urban areas and suburban and rural gang membership is on the increase. Although gang members still come predominantly from the "underclass" and lower and working classes, certain types of gangs have strong appeal for middle-class youths.

> The signs are everywhere: kids bringing guns onto junior high and high school campuses and shooting each other; teenagers forming sex posses and racking up "body counts" of the number of girls they have "scored with" or "sacked"; mall rats rampaging through suburban shopping arcades, "streaming," as it is called, through aisles of department stores and grabbing stacks of clothing before making a quick getaway; tagger crews "mapping the heavens," spray painting their three-letter monikers on overhead freeway signs. The "cry for help" of punk rockers and their offshoots, ignored as they were by families and society that do not take time to listen. And these are just the good kids!

> And what about the others? Racist teenage skinheads plot revenge on unsuspecting fellow students at suburban high schools for no other reason than that they dislike them because of their skin color, nationality, or presumed sexual orientation. White, youthful, stoner gang members adrift, wander aimlessly with the suburban "homies," or homeboys, looking for the next high, surviving on dope and booze. Juvenile Satanists, participating in a fad, find themselves caught up in a cult. (The Times Leader, 1994, p. B1)

There are certain factors that make contemporary gangs more threatening to the common good than gangs of the past. The use of firearms by gang members has greatly increased, and there has been a sharp rise in the levels of gang violence. While gang fights and violent interactions have been documented throughout the history of gangs in the USA, gang activity now frequently involves random attacks against persons or places that have little or no connection to the gang itself, and gang-related drive-by shootings carried out without concern for innocent bystanders have become everyday occurrences in major cities.

> Authorities responded to a report of three people shot after 10 p.m. in the 400 block of Noah Avenue in the city's West Akron neighborhood.The victims were a 15-year old boy, a 16-year old boy, and a 20-year old man…

> According to witnesses, the victims were standing at a party on Noah Avenue when a black four-door car drove by and an unknown man fired shots toward them. A house at the 400 block of Noah Avenue was also struck by stray bullets.

> Shortly after 1 a.m. Thursday, officers responded to the 800 block of Raymond Street in the Sherbondy Hill neighborhood for a shooting. A 57-year old man was found lying in the kitchen floor with a gunshot wound to his leg.…

> The shooting appeared to be related as an ongoing feud between the victims on Noah Avenue and relatives of the residents on Raymond Street, police said in a news release (Akron Beacon Journal, 2019, pp. B1–B4).

In this chapter, we discuss in detail the magnitude and seriousness of gang behavior; the reasons for gang formation; various theories explaining gang development and behavior; and methods for preventing, controlling, or refocusing gang activities.

6.2 Definition of Gangs and Scope of the Problem

The definitions of "gang" vary, depending upon who is doing the defining. The term "gang" has been used to denote a neighborhood street corner group or highly organized criminals who are oriented toward profit-making through their criminal activity. According to Moore (1988, p. 5), a gang is,

A friendship group of adolescent who share common interests, with a more or less clearly defined territory, in which most of the members live. They are committed to defending one another, the territory, and the gang name in the status-seeking fights that occur on school and on the streets.

The Chicago Police Department, concerned with the controlling illegal behavior by gang members, defines a "street gang" as

An Association of individuals who exhibit the following characteristics in varying degrees:

- A gang name and recognizable symbols
- A geographic territory
- A regular meeting pattern
- An organized, continuous course of criminality (Block & Block, 1993, p. 3).

Beyond the basic fact that a gang is a group of persons who have joined together for mutual benefit, other characteristics of gangs are readily apparent. There is some type of organizational structure and leadership, a name and some type of insignia or "colors" to identify gang members, a specific "turf" or area where the gang meets and seeks to be in control, and involvement in some type of illegal or undesirable behavior that is frowned upon by the larger society.

From the perspective of gang members, the name and "colors" of the group may be the most significant characteristic.

Each street gang in Chicago has its own distinct symbols and emblems. These are used to distinguish rival gangs and to decorate territorial objects. Signs, signals, sweaters, colors, jewelry, and forms of dress are used to promote gang recognition and solidarity. (Bensinger, 1984, p. 3)

The development of many of today's gangs appears to be almost identical to the process described in research on gangs on Chicago in the 1920s. That is, a group of adolescent friends gathered on the street corner, having nothing to do, perhaps skipping or excluded from school, drinking or getting high, and occasionally fighting with other groups. At first, spontaneous, the groups later become identified as gangs once they adopt names and some identifiable insignias. When asked how his gang got started, a member gave this description:

You know we were just standing on the corner, then we got to just getting together every day, and then we came up with something called the 34th Street Players. And as we kept going north, the gangs got to coming around and they got to have gang fights and they got to robbing and just carrying on. (Hagedorn & Macon, 1988, p. 60)

6.2.1 Number of Youth Gangs and Gang Membership

The National Youth Gangs and Gang Center conducts surveys on youth gang activity in the US cities with populations of 25,000 or more, all suburban counties, and a randomly selected sample of smaller cities and rural counties. The information is

Table 6.1 Distribution of
gangs by area type

Area	Percent
Rural counties	5.5%
Suburban counties	25.8%
Smaller cities	27.1%
Large cities	41.6%

Source: National Youth Gang
Analysis, 2012, pp. 2–3

obtained from police and sheriff's departments. The 2012 survey estimated that there were more than 30,000 gangs with 850,000 members in the USA. This was an 8.6% increase in the number of gangs over the previous year and a 15% increase in the number of gangs since 2006. The estimated number of gangs increased and steadily from 2005 to 2012.

As shown in Table 6.1, the larger cities and suburban counties are the primary locations of gangs with more than 2/3 of the gangs located in either the larger cities or suburban counties. The larger cities and suburban counties accounted for more than 80% of the 85,000 members of youth gangs in the USA in 2012.

6.3   The History of Gang Development

The existence of gangs in New York City and Boston in the early nineteenth century, and the bitter feuds that took place between gangs from various sections of the cities, have been documented. In *The Gangs of New York* (1928, p. 7), Asbury described how, during the draft riots in New York City in 1863, the gangs joined forces against the police in efforts to pillage the city. In the Bowery section of New York, where gang membership was principally Irish, battles between rival gangs sometimes raged for 2 or 3 days, streets were barricaded, and both hand-to-hand combat and gun battles took place.

Of particular interest in the accounts of early gang battles is the presence of girls. In this early era, the girls carried the weapons and reserve ammunition, a service that, as we shall see, became an ascribed activity of girl members and persists today. However, some of the girls also took part in the fighting, as documents by this graphic account:

> Often these Amazons fought in the ranks, and many of them achieved great renown as ferocious battlers. They were particularly gifted in the art of mayhem, and during the Draft Riots it was the women who inflicted the most fiendish tortures upon Negroes, soldiers, and policemen captured by the mob, slicing their flesh with butcher knives, ripping out eyes and tongues and applying the torch after the victims has been sprayed with oil and hanged to trees. (Asbury, 1928, p. 29)

Thrasher (1927, pp. 23–24) was one of the first sociologists to conduct extensive research on gang formation and behavior. His book, *The Gang,* focused on 1313 cases of gang activity in the Chicago area during the early decades of the twentieth century. Thrasher maintained that gangs tended to develop in the slums of the city, where a large number of youths were forced to live in crowded conditions, and that the majority of gangs developed from conflicts between spontaneous play groups over territory, play space, and privileges to exploit or claim new territory.

Whyte (1955) identified other factors in his book *Street Corner Society,* which examined gang behavior in an Italian neighborhood in Boston during the Depression years of the 1930s. He found that the gang members (the "corner boys") provided each other with protection, status, and material assistance within the neighborhood community.

In the 1950s, gang organization and activity seemed to center around defense of territory and proof of strength through fighting. In the book *Manny* (Rettig, Torres, & Garrett, 1977, p. 19), Manny describes the test of personal valor that won him the position of "warlord" (arranger of fights with other gangs) at the tender age of 13:

I walk into this movie; I'm with this girl and we buy some popcorn and stuff and walk up into the balcony to watch the flick. And there's a bunch of Italian dudes sittin' up there. They say, "Hey guys, look at the goddam Spic."

I thought there would be some of my gang at the movie. I take off my jacket so the Italians can see my sweater, and I holler, "Young Star here!"

They say, "Yeah, Young Star!"

Only one problem. I jump up, but I'm the only Young Star in the place. I was the only one standing, the only Spic in the balcony, and they just pick me up and heave me over. Wow! I woke up in the hospital. Had several broken bones and a bad concussion. They almost killed me.

... When I woke up in that hospital I thought I was a big deal. Guys and debs would come up to see Manny, the kid that defended the honor of the Young Stars against all odds. I was a big hero. It got me elected warlord.

The social concerns among the general population during the 1960s found echoes in gang activity. Members of gangs developed an intensified spirit of brotherhood and camaraderie and were more conscious of the ethnic or racial qualities enhanced by gang membership. In his study of a black Chicago gang called the Vice Lords, Keiser, R. (1969), identified the elements of the gang's culture as heart ideology, soul ideology, brotherhood ideology, and game ideology. "Heart" has reference to the total devotion of individuals to the gang, in which they are willing to follow the leadership and suggestion of the chieftains, regardless of the personal risk involved. "Soul" refers to both the black experience and the stripping away of pretense to bare one's most intense feelings and emotions. "Brotherhood" involves the concept of mutual help and is frequently reinforced through ritualistic behavior. "Game" has reference to the ability to manipulate others through craftiness.

In the late 1960s, the energies of the Vice Lords were channeled toward improving the lot of the black community. Dawley (1973, pp. 109, 110–113) documented these efforts in the book, *A Nation of Lords*:

In 1964 the Lords vowed to see that our community and children get a chance, and 3 years later, as spokesman for the Nation, Bobby said:

'We could not turn our backs on them. We were and are the last resort for many, and if we didn't listen, who would?'

'As black people, we gotta start worryin' bout what's happening, where our real humbug is and the what to humbug with it.'

'... In the three years from 1964 to 1967 we stopped gang wars and started to build a new kind of Vice Lord Nation... Between 1967 and 1969 we opened several businesses and community programs. The police never thought they would see the day when we'd put our minds to do something like that... Not even the younger fellas thought we could change.'

Gang activity in the 1960s gained little public attention, since other forms of youth protest and rebellion had captured the headlines and the interest of social researchers. Some crime analysts took the position that the wide use of drugs by gang members had weakened gang cohesion and diminished members' fighting spirit (Miller, 1975, pp. 1–2). Others felt that involvement in policy in policy protests and social programs did in fact lead to a decline in gang activity. Miller contended that gang activity did not decrease significantly during the 1960s but simply received less public attention because of the overwhelming social problems facing the nation. The "resurgence" of gang activity that seemed to occur in the 1970s, he said, was merely a return to the spotlight of a form of youthful deviance that had never really declined.

6.3.1 Gang Behavior in the 1970s

Whether gang activity increased in the 1970s or merely captured renewed public interest is a matter open to debate. The gangs of the 1970s, however, had distinctive characteristics that set them apart from their predecessors of earlier decades. A study of street gangs operating in New York City in the period 1971–1976 revealed that this "new" gang had "bigger and better organizations, more sophisticated weapons, and a greater propensity for crime and violence than its ancestor, the "fighting gang" of the 1950s (Collins, 1977, pp. 5, 10–11).

Miller researched the youth-gang activities of the 1970s to ascertain what proportion of crime in the cities could be attributed to gangs and how effective the police and service agencies were i controlling their activities. His study extended to 12 major cities in the USA. Information was obtained from a variety of sources, including representatives of police departments, Youth Gang Divisions of Youth Service Bureaus, criminal justice planning agencies, outreach workers, judicial representatives, probation officers, youth-aftercare departments, juvenile courts, and public schools. The following definition of "gang" was used in the research:

A gang is a group of recurrently associating individuals with identifiable leadership an internal organization, identifying with or claiming control over territory in the community, and engaging either individually or collectively in violent or other forms of illegal behavior. (Miller, 1975, p. 9)

Miller's research defined the age range of gang members as from 12 to about 21. Reports that many gang members were in their late 20s or early 30s did not seem to be substantiated by the research. In fact, the gang age distribution appeared to be quite similar to the age range traditionally associated with gang members, with the largest concentration in the 16–17-year-old age group (Miller, 1975, p. 26).

Miller found that urban youth gangs were predominantly male (90% or more of the membership). Autonomous female gangs were not identified, although female "auxiliaries" or "branches" of male gangs were quite evident (Miller, 1975, p. 26). When the racial and ethnic compositions of the gang membership were compares, more than 80% of gang members were found to be of black or Hispanic background.

The primary locus of serious gang activity was found to be in the slum areas of cities. These areas were not necessarily concentrated in the central city, however; they were found to exist also in formerly middle-class and working-class neighborhoods that had deteriorated.

Gang violence was identified as assuming four forms:

1. "Normal" gang violence (attacks in which both assailants and victims are gang members);
2. Victimization of non-gang members with social characteristics similar to those of gang members;
3. Crimes against the general public;
4. Victimization of young children, the elderly, females, or those who are not community members (Miller, 1975, p. 39).

An increased tendency of gang members to victimize innocent children and adults appeared to be on important aspect of gang behavior in the 1970s that was different from the behavior of gangs of earlier eras. Non-gang members (teenagers, children, adults) were the victims of nearly 40% of gang activity (Miller, 1975, p. 39).

In the late 1970s, Miller (1982) expanded his research into a nationwide study of youth gangs. He concluded that by 1980 there were more gang members in the USA than at any time in the past and that gangs were active in more cities than at any earlier time. He also found that in the 1970s more people were the victims of gang-related killings than in any previous 10-year period and that property destruction by gangs in the 1970s was more extensive than in any earlier decade.

6.3.2   Gang Behavior in the 1980s, 1990s, and 2000s

The trend toward increased violence and use of more sophisticated weapons by certain types of gangs continued in the 1980s, 1990s, and 2000s. A study of gang activity in seven large Ohio cities identified three typologies: informal, *hedonistic gangs,* concerned with having a good time and getting high on drugs and alcohol; *instrumentally oriented gangs,* focused on property crimes for economic gain; and *predatory gangs,* which commit robberies and other crimes of opportunity, and whose members' use of highly addictive drugs contributes to their violent, assaultive behavior (Huff, 1988, p. 8).

Although members of these gangs and those identified in other large cities have been found to be predominantly blacks or Hispanics, other distinct types have also emerged. These included gangs of Asians (Vietnamese, Chinese) involved in crimes against property, extortion for protection, and kidnapping, with members of their own ethnic group usually the targets of their activity. Other new gang variations are the heavy metal, punk rockers, and Satanic groups. Their members are predominantly white youths devoted to heavy metal rock music and behavior chosen for its shock value. Their gang activities have included drug trafficking, parent abuse, grave robbing, and desecration of animal and human remains. Their potential for violence is recognized by those who must deal with them (Final Report; State Task Force on Youth Gang Violence, 1986, p. 11).

> Punk rock and heavy metal youngsters come from all socio-economic classes. They're of average intelligence and they're capable youngsters. They have very little parental authority. They're angry youngsters. Their dance is violent. Their behavior is violent. They enjoy shock value. They're into anarchy.The escalating violence of gang activity has been of great concern in many large cities. The situation in Chicago parallels that in many other cities. (Bensinger, 1984. p. 7)

> The type of crime committed by today's gangs includes the sale of narcotics, running guns, rapes, murder,... robbery, burglary, theft, harassment, intimidation and extortion.

> Some of the gangs' activities have become so sophisticated that they are thought by law enforcement officials to be linked to organized crime...

Homicides committed by gang members have distinctive characteristics. They are more likely than non-gang homicides to take place in public areas, with consequent danger to innocent bystanders, and to involve automobiles and firearms. An example of such activity is the drive-by shooting, when one gang seeks out the home, automobile, or hangout of a rival gang member, and sprays it with bullets from assorted weapons in the gangland style of the 1920s. Victims and assailants in these criminal events, although they are not likely to be personally known to each other, are of the same racial or ethnic background, with the relationship between offenders and victim likely to be based on gang affiliations (Klein et al., 1986, pp. 495–496).

Since 2000, gang-related homicides, involving gang members killing each other or killing persons caught in the crossfire of gang violence, have increased sharply in several large cities. Declines in the number of homicides in large cities in the late 1990s were attributed in part to police pressure on gangs, the strong economy, and a decline in trafficking in crack cocaine. Many large cities reduced the size of their gang units or abolished them because the gang problem seemed to be under control.

Drug involvement and trafficking have been identified as factors in the violence of gangs, but researchers differ in their assessments of the strength of the connection. In a survey conducted by the National Youth Gang Center, law enforcement officials estimated that 43% of drug sales in their jurisdictions involved gang members (Howell & Gleason, 1999, p. 3), but several researchers have concluded that gang violence is more closely related to the intergang interpersonal conflict than to "drug wars" (Decker & Van Winkle, 1994, pp. 583–604).

Peterson et al. (2004, pp. 8, 12, and 13) examined the relationship between gang membership and violent victimization in a sample of adolescents. They found that the majority of gang members reported being members for only 1 year. Youths move in and out of gangs quickly. The membership of most gangs they studied did not have stability. Adolescents who were members of gangs had higher involvement in violent crimes before, during, and after their gang membership than did adolescents who were not members of gangs. The researchers found that being a member of a gang did not offer protection from violence from other gangs. Violent delinquents were often victims of violence, whether they were gang members or not.

The ability of juveniles to easily acquire firearms has also been recognized as a factor in the deadliness of gang violence. In a recent study, which included serious offenders who were incarcerated in juvenile correctional facilities in in four states and male students from ten inner-city high schools located near the correctional facilities, it was found that most of those surveyed from either group stated it would be "easy to acquire a gun." Fifty-five percent of the incarcerated juveniles had carried guns "all or most of the time" in the year or 2 before being incarcerated, 12% of the high school students routinely carried a gun, and another 13% carried them "now and then" (Sheley & Wright, 1993, p. 9). While this study did not specifically focus on gangs and gang behavior, it was determined that 68% of the institutionalized juveniles and 22% of the students were affiliated with a gang or quasi-gang. More than 80% of the incarcerated gang members reported that they owned a revolver, automatic weapon, or semiautomatic handgun. The researchers concluded that

> For the inmates, and to a lesser extent the students as well, movement from non-gang member to member of a gang was associated with increased in possessing and carrying guns (Sheley & Wright, 1993, p. 9).

Changes in the focus of gang activity have been observed. Large-scale gang fights for turf are rarely reported, partly because blighted inner-city area formerly used as gang hangouts have been razed in many cities to make way for redevelopment projects or parking lots. The sites of gang warfare appear to have shifted in some instances to the schools. With the consolidation of middle school and high schools, members of gangs from diverse sections of large cities are thrown together in a common school location, where they victimize other students and teachers and challenge each other for control.

The types of gang activity reported within the schools include attacks upon members of other gangs, non-gang members, and teachers; intimidation of teachers; charging protection money from non-gang members or extorting money from them for use of school facilities; school vandalism; and general classroom disruption. Gang fighting in schoolyards and adjoining areas and attacks upon youths going to and from school also occur. The increase in gang activity in or close to schools has been attributed in part to the greater holding power of schools, which now (as a result of various legal decisions related to students' rights) cannot legally exclude many youths who formerly would have been expelled.

Outside the schools, street hustling appears to be a major activity of youth-gang members. It is undertaken for economic survival, support of drug habits, or status. Hustling involves a broad range of illegal income-generating activities such as burglary, disposal of stolen property, shoplifting, prostitution, con games, and drug sales. Interviews with gang leaders reveal that they take pride in their hustling skills.

Gang members regard their activities as necessary for survival, and may view the victimization of others as just "part of a day's work" (Krisberg, 1978, p. 244).

Is the appeal of gang membership today based on the same factors that led youths to become involved in gangs in the past? To explore this question, we now turn to the theories formulated over the years to explain gang development.

6.4   Theories of Gang Formation

6.4.1   Thrasher's Theory of Gang Development

The pioneer of gang-formation research, Thrasher (1927, pp. 31–33), contended that gangs develop from spontaneous play groups, when threats from youthful enemies lead them to protect their territory through mutual support. Groups that evolve into gangs develop a formalized structure, complete with defined leadership status, division of labor, distinctive styles of dress, and well-defined goals. Threats from others were found to be a unifying force. Thrasher identified marriage as the most potent cause of attrition from gangs.

Thrasher maintained that those play groups that eventually become gangs go through an evolutionary process, in which a loosely organized group develops into a closely knit gang with strong group loyalty, ready to present a united front against enemies. He characterized gangs as either *diffuse* or *solidified*. Diffuse gangs are loosely organized; those that are solidified have developed a strong internal structure and *esprit de corps*. Solidified gangs were identified as being "conventional," "criminal," or "secret societies."

Thrasher (1927, pp. 47–48) described the movement of one group from a diffuse to a solidified status:

> A crowd of about fifteen Polish lads from fourteen to sixteen years old were accustomed to meet on a street corner in front of a store. From loafing, smoking, and "rag-chewing," they turned to shooting craps, which excited hostility toward them.
>
> "Jigs, de bulls!" someone would shout, and they would scatter. As the group grew, business men and residents regarded as a nuisance the crowd which blocked the way on the sidewalk, interfered with traffic on the street, and hang about at night, keeping people awake with their noise. The crowd had now become a rudimentary gang.
>
> The next step in their development was to organize a ball team to which they gave the name "Pershing Tigers." With a name, group-consciousness increased, for they could say proudly, "We belong to the Pershings!"
>
> One night the Altons, a gang from another neighborhood, swooped down for a raid and attempted to "clean out" their corner. Bitter enmity developed, and the Pershings cleaned out the Altons' alley with rocks, guns, and daggers. With about six months of fighting the gang became fully solidified.

6.4.2 Research of the Chicago School

A number of early research projects on gang behavior were undertaken by the members of the Chicago School of sociological theorists, Shaw (1929) developed a geographical analysis of the distribution of juvenile court petitions filed in Chicago, which showed that delinquency occurred most often in the areas of the city that were deteriorating physically and decreased in proportion to one's distance from the center of the city. Shaw, later joined in his research by McKay (1967), sought to apply the same approach to analysis of the distribution of delinquency in other American cities. The findings of these studies appeared to be consistent with Shaw's analysis of Chicago, although later researchers questioned their validity on the basis of the omission of certain important variables from the research design, including whether the delinquency petitions (charges) were found to be true and whether agencies for diversion were more likely to exist or be used in suburban areas than in the cities (McKay, 1967, pp. 114–118).

Tannenbaum (1939, pp. 9–13), another member of the Chicago School, regarded the gang as fulfilling a need for primary-group involvement that was missing in the lives of youths from physically or psychologically broken homes who resided in high delinquency areas. For such youths, group solidarity is attained by identifying enemies of the group and acting against them. These enemies may be individuals from other gangs, the police, the adult establishment, or merely the broad rules and regulations of society that seem too restrictive and confining to the youthful gang members.

In *Street Corner Society* (Whyte, 1955, another classic study of gang formation, Whyte documented the activities of a group he called the Norton gang, unemployed young Italian men who used gang activity as a method of survival. Whyte's contribution to the mutual-assistance aspects of gang development was his identification of the brotherhood or mutual-assistance aspects of gang development. The "corner boys" from the Norton gang were poor and underprivileged in comparison to young men in the community who could afford to go to college; they received their status, recognition, and economic assistance within the gang and the local community, whereas college bound youths developed broader reference groups and values A number of the college bound youths eventually became doctors, lawyers, and politicians, while some gang members exercised the type of upward mobility open to them by moving into the rackets.

6.4.3 Lower-Class Culture

In his book, *Delinquent Boys,* Cohen (1955, pp. 24–31), contended that working-class youths who have failed to win status through achieving goals set by the middle class turn to delinquent behavior to gain some measure of status and recognition from their peers, engender respect by being feared, or receive public attention. Cohen believed that the middle class lifestyle is held in high esteem and desired by members of all social classes and that when youths realize that they cannot achieve the approved middle-class goals, they develop various behavior characteristics as a reaction to their failures.

In Cohen's "reaction-formation" behavior, a youth tries to turn the middleclass value system upside down by engaging in activity that displays its antithesis. For example, the middle-class value of academic success is flouted by engaging in truancy and respect for property is defied by vandalism.

Miller (1958, p. 10), on the other hand, did not view juvenile delinquency as predominantly a reaction to the inability to achieve middle-class standards, but saw it instead as the natural outgrowth of being socialized with a lower-class culture. He theorized,

> A large body or systematically interrelated attitudes, practices, behaviors, and values characteristic of lower-class culture are designed to support and maintain the basic features of the lower-class way of life... Action oriented to the achievement and maintenance of the lower-class system may violate norms of middle-class culture and be perceived as deliberately nonconforming.

In other words, delinquency occurs not because youths are trying to topple middle-class values, but because they are following a *different* value system, one that conflicts with that of the middle class on any points. Miller believed that the predominant concerns of the lower-class youths include trouble, toughness, smartness, excitement, fate, and autonomy. These concerns permeate the working-class and lower-class way of life, and people in these social strata, both adults and juveniles, develop means of adapting to situations related to these concerns as part of their socialization process. Some of the concerns (such as trouble) are met through avoidance, while others (toughness, smartness, and autonomy) require the development of skills and style in dealing with the problems of life.

The cultural practices followed in dealing with these basic concerns may violate the law, but since they appear to be appropriate to the situations encountered, they are frequently practiced anyway. Miller (1958, p. 10) maintained that not all youths adapt to their cultural situations in the same way. He delineated three forms of adaptation: (1) acceptance to the lower-class culture as a reference to and internalization of lower-class norms; (2) aspiration to middle class lifestyle and values, and embracing opportunities to achieve the goals set by the middleclass; or (3) aspiration to the middle-class system of material rewards and values, then failure to achieve them owing to lack of opportunities or lack of needed skills and personal characteristics, followed by reversion to the lower-class lifestyle.

Lewis (1970) disagreed with some of Miller's assumptions; he formulated a modified gang theory, based on acceptance or rejection of a number of Miller's premises. Lewis maintained that lower-class culture is not so completely distinct from middle-class culture that following the norms of the lower class automatically violates the laws set up in support of the middle-class culture. Rather, he took the position that lower-class gang members were in fact following the norms set by the middle class but were using deviant ways to achieve these norms:

> The gang ... is not delinquent in response to deviant norms; but it is delinquent to the extent that its members are socialized to mainstream norms while at the same time they find themselves impeded from expressing their commitments in the manner of the middle class. (Lewis, 1970, p. 189)

6.4.4   Delinquency and Opportunity

Cloward and Ohlin's theory (1961) of delinquency, sometimes termed "opportunity theory," combines and expands elements of Shaw and McKay's theory of delinquency areas and Cohen's conception of the universal acceptance of middle-class values. According to Cloward and Ohlin, youths who experience frustration of their efforts to achieve the middle-class goals delineated by society may resort to various illegitimate methods of achieving them. The form their reaction to blockages of their aspirations will take is dependent upon the opportunities open to them in their environment.

Cloward and Ohlin held that delinquent behavior is a search for solutions to the problem of adjustment that arises when lower-class youths must face and recognize a discrepancy between their aspirations and the opportunities open to them for achieving their goals. In exploring the reasons why different types of delinquent subcultures or gangs develop in lower-class urban areas, these researchers identified three types that may emerge, depending on the opportunity, or lack of opportunity, to engage in illegitimate means of obtaining material rewards. The three types of gangs delineated by Cloward and Ohlin are the criminal gang, the conflict gang, and the retreatist gang.

The *criminal* gang is apt to develop in neighborhoods where there is a tradition of organized crime; where organized crime operates fairly openly, is accepted by the residents, and is protected by the political structure; and where there is close communication among the various age groups in the population. According to Cloward and Ohlin,

> The "big shots"—conspicuous successes in the criminal world—become role-models for youth, much more important as such than successful figures in the conventional world, who are usually socially and geographically remote from the slum area... structural connections between delinquents, semi-mature criminals, and the adult criminal world, where they exist, provide opportunities for upward mobility... (Cloward & Ohlin, 1961, p. 23)

The *conflict* subculture may emerge when it is difficult for youths to succeed through either legitimate or criminal channels. The ensuing frustration and discontent are manifested in violent behavior as a means of achieving status by being feared or by showing independence of social control by the larger community. The conflict gang's behavior includes violent confrontations with other groups, unpredictable and destructive assaults on persons and property, freedom from conventional societal norms, and in-group solidarity, with the immediate motive a reputation of toughness—as a group to be feared.

Those who do not have the criminal contacts or the strength to become part of either a criminal or a conflict subgroup may abandon efforts to achieve status through either legitimate or illegitimate means and become involved in a *retreatist* subculture or gang, which relies on alcohol or drugs to escape from the awareness of aspirational failures. Others may join retreatist gangs after growing weary of the violence and danger associated with other types of gang activity. Such youths try to develop a sophisticated lifestyle in the world of alcohol and drug use or through other unusual ("cool") experiences. They may engage in criminal behavior such as con games, drug sales, or pimping to support their lifestyle, but their distinctive characteristic is an apparent desire to withdraw from conventional activities and norms valued by the larger society (Cloward & Ohlin, 1961, pp. 24–25).

6.4.5   Research Findings on Criminal Gangs

The attempts to empirically document the existence of criminal, conflict, and retreatist gangs, as delineated by Cloward and Ohlin, have met with limited success. However, in some cases the close links between gangs and organized crime described by Cloward and Ohlin as part of their criminal gang structure have been demonstrated.

There has been research that suggests some gangs focus their activities predominantly on crimes for profit. In a study of street gang crime in Chicago, Block and Block found that 40 major street gangs were active in the city (Block & Block, 1993, pp. 2–3). Many of the members of the four "super gangs" (Black Gangster Disciples Nation, Latin Disciples, Latin Kings, and Vice Lords) began their gang careers as adolescents, continued on into their late teens and 20s, and are now adult criminals. Since many of the gangs operate out of the large public housing projects, they have opportunities to organize and control drug sales there.

The degree to which the illegal activities of the gangs were drug related varied. Block and Block found that

> ... More incidents of cocaine possession (the most common offense) were attributed to the Vice Lords or to the Black Gangster Disciples Nation than to all other street gangs combines. The Vice Lords were also active in heroin possession offense, with twice as many incidents attributed to them than to all other street gangs combined. (Block & Block, 1993, pp. 2–3)

In his study of Detroit Gangs, Taylor (1990, p. 105) used the term "corporate gang" to describe gang structure that closely resembles the "criminal gang" of Cloward and Ohlin. Taylor categorized the Detroit gangs as "scavenger," "territorial," and "corporate." While scavenger gangs were loosely organized thrill seekers who chose petty and spontaneous crimes, and territorial gangs were committed to turf defense, the corporate gangs went far beyond these activated and boundaries. Describing the corporate gangs (Taylor 1990, p. 108) stated:

> These well-organized groups have very strong leaders and managers. The main focus of their organization is participation in illegal money-making ventures. Membership is based on the worth of the individual to the organization... Different divisions handle sales, marketing, distribution, enforcement, and so on... Criminal actions are motivated by profit... Crimes are committed for a purpose, not for fun.

Organized criminal activity among gangs has been documented in other large cities in the USA. Apparently, crack cocaine is the most readily available drug, and the search for markers has led to the expansion of corporate gangs into other cities and smaller communities.

> When young Detroiters invade the state of Ohio, they are in pursuit of the American dream. The dream may appear distorted to middle-class or working-class America, yet it is truly business, the spirit of American entrepreneurship. Cocaine rocks in Detroit sell for $5.00, while in Cleveland, Toledo, or Cincinnati the same rocks will bring $20.00—supply and demand (Taylor, 1990, p. 115).

The gangs that are profit-oriented and migratory expand their operations into new areas where they believe they can gain control because the law enforcement presence there is perceived as ineffective or inadequate to control them.

Another characteristic of the well-organized, profit-oriented gangs is their total lack of fear for law enforcement and the juvenile system. Discussions with the Cleveland, Ohio, Caribbean Gang Task Force revealed that they felt that the juvenile gang members involved in drug dealing have no regard for the legal system, and, in fact, can be very threatening to police officers. Even if they are arrested, they know that if they remain under the jurisdiction of the juvenile court, the likelihood of remaining incarcerated for any significant period of time is slim. These gang members have ties with the "headpins" of the drug traffickers, and they are provided with attorneys that are assured that, even If convicted, they will soon be out on the streets again. If sent to a juvenile institution, they have friends who will look after them. They do not "rat" on each other (Kratcoski, 1995).

Although gangs in certain cities fit Cloward and Ohlin's description of criminal gangs, in other instances the gangs' criminal activities do not seem to be highly organized. In Milwaukee, it was found that the Vice Lords, for a short period of time, focused on shoplifting, purse snatching, and other activities for profit, but this stopped after the police began to seriously monitor the Vice Lords' activities. The researchers concluded that the Vice Lords had gone through a phase of criminal activity that was only one facet of the gang's behavior (Hagedorn & Macon, 1988, p. 100).

6.4.6 Research Findings on Youth Gangs

Conflict or violence is the single defining characteristic of youth gangs, and there is considerable evidence that conflict is a theme of much of youth gang activity. However, contrary to the message communicated by the mass media and by the police officials in large cities concerned about controlling youth gangs, the major activity of most gangs is not violent confrontations. In addition, even for those gangs that have been identified as involved in violence, the actual violent activity may only be carried on by core leaders.

Jackson and McBride (1990, pp. 90–91) note that gathering accurate information on the violent activity of gangs is a difficult task.

> Identification of the various gangs and their members is an on-going process. The very nature of gang membership is transitory. As members gravitate away from gang involvement or are sent to jail, new, younger members join who must be identified.

In regard to determining the amount of gang violence, they state:

> Drive-by attacks, five to ten suspects robbing one or two victims, ambushes and snipings do not lend themselves easily to inclusion within gang crime statistics inasmuch as such crimes can be, and are, committed by individuals other than gang members.

Gang violence tends to involve homicide and aggravated assault, and is not equally distributed throughout the cities, but concentrated in certain neighborhoods. While this violence may be directly connected to disputes related to other types of criminal activity, such as drug distribution, studies seem to confirm that in instances turf battles are its focus.

Shown in Box 6.1 is the story of Eridito Musse Jr., for many it was the daily life of an adolescent growing up in a high crime neighborhood in the 1990s.

Box 6.1

Erodito Musse Jr., 19, is a big fellow, with a neat mustache and short brown hair. He lives in Brooklyn, in a neighborhood in 4which drugs and guns are more plentiful than fresh air…

"My primary concern," said Eroditio, "is just staying alive. I didn't think, when I was growing up, that it could get this bad. I've lost 19 friends.

"I was 12 when I witnessed my first murder. It was right in front of me, right on the sidewalk. We lived in East Flatbush then. I knew the guy who killed the person. He came right up to him and shot him in the back of the head. I just ran up the stairs. I was shocked. I told the cops I didn't know nothing.

"I was 14 the first time a friend of mine got killed. We called him Tazz. He moved to New Jersey, but he came back to Brooklyn and he got shot up. He died, and then suddenly people just started dying, to tell you the truth…"

Mariano Esquilin it tall and thin and a bearer of hair-raising stories delivered in a matter-of-fact tone. "Crime happens every other minute," he said.

"You could just be coming out of the grocery store and just catch a stray bullet. Last year I got shot myself. May 4. A young kid on a bicycle, no older than 15 or 16, pulled a .380 automatic from his waist and began shooting. I don't know why. Nobody said nothing to him. Maybe somebody stared at him (Herbert, Akron Beacon Journal, 1994, p. A9)

Researchers sought to differentiate violent gangs from other types and determine why they focus on violence. Yablonsky (1966, pp. 141–147) developed a three-pronged classification of gangs, characterizing them as social, delinquent, or violent. *Social* gangs are composed of youths who seek to realize their individual social goals in a gang atmosphere, *delinquent* gangs have as their primary objective material profit as a result of delinquent activity, and *violent* gangs are those that seek emotional gratification through violent behavior. Even in such a classification scheme, it becomes difficult to characterize a particular gang as purely social, delinquent, or violent, since elements of all three types of activity may be present during various stages of the gang's activity or development. Retreatist characteristics are also found at various stages of the development and activity of delinquent and violent gangs.

Lewis highlighted the importance of making distinctions between "amorphously structured" peer groups (youths who hang around together for fun, excitement, and companionship) and "organized" gangs, which have structures, rules, defined goals, and distinctive concerns. Lewis maintained that the organized gangs behave as they do not in an irrational effort to get back at society, but to pursue very definite purposes and goals. Their delinquency occurs when, in this pursuit, they4 violate laws formulated in the basis of middle-class standards. As Lewis noted:

> The organized gang is a far cry from the rebellious congeries of individuals implied in Cohen's treatment and also in Miller's lower-class street corner group, depicted as pursuing distinctive normative concerns into certain conflict with middle-class morality and legality. The gangs of which I write are organizationally sophisticated in a manner not unlike middle-class collectives. T4hey emphasize universalistic task rationality in their allocation of roles, the necessity for rational planning, and obedience to rules of collective action and individual demeanor. (Lewis, 1970, pp. 194–195)

The major goal of the organized juvenile gang is to maintain sovereignty or control over its turf. To this end, rules and norms must be developed, and a division of labor takes place. The concept of sovereignty, according to Lewis (1970, pp. 194–195) implies control over a physical territory established as the gang's turf. Those who live within the boundaries of the territory fall within an age category established by the gang are candidates for gang membership (in-group) or subjection to the power of the gang (out-group). Organized gangs, according to Lewis, normally do not try to subject all residents of the turf but concentrate on gaining the respect and fear of members of their peer group. Although rules for the activities of the gang members are well defined, dealings with the out-group are relatively normless, and may involve violence, property destruction, extortion, intimidation—virtually any means that the gang can conceive of as useful. Thus, the organized gang is in essence a miniature society establishing its own rules, regulations, and value system, which apply only to its members and serve the gang's needs.

Well aware of the differences in handling and penalties for juvenile and adult offenders, gangs frequently use very young members for tasks that pose a strong possibility for arrest, if the offender is detected.

Although the potential for conflict and violence is always present in the youth-gang setting, much of the gang members' activity is not violent and in many ways resembles the behavior of other adolescents. Moore (1988, pp. 12–13), in her study of gangs in Los Angeles, discovered that the frequency and severity of violent behavior varied tremendously from gang to gang. Even for the gangs considered the most violent by the police and the mass media, less time was spent in violent pursuits than in such activities as hanging around and getting high. Hagedorn and Macon (1988, p. 142) noted that Puerto Rican gangs in Milwaukee went to great lengths to avoid large-scale gang warfare and that several Hispanic gang-related homicides reports in Milwaukee were the result of intra-gang conflicts rather than intergang warfare.

Jackson and McBride (1990, p. 90) analyzed how conflict becomes enmeshed with the routine activities of gang members.

"Partying" and "getting down with the home boys" is an integral part of gang life and offers members social contracts not previously available. Loyalty outweighs personal interests. An individual cannot merely assimilate into the gang without proving his toughness and worth to the group. He must see himself as a soldier protecting his turf in an ongoing was with rival gangs. H4e is expected to prove himself in battle. It is not uncommon for a gang member to seek out situations where he can build his reputation. Often these incidents follow a party or other gang function. When the member is accepted by the gang, he is expected to share with fellow members. This includes narcotics, alcohol, and money. The gang is the first and most important part of his life.

6.4.7 Drug and Alcohol Use by Gang Members

Most accounts of youth gang activities reveal that the use of various kinds of drugs by members is quite common. However, the contention that this drug use is a way of retreating or withdrawing from society does not seem to be true. Rather, the drug use is part of the day-to-day activity, along with the other socially unacceptable practices, in which members indulge.

Huff (1989, pp. 528–529) found alcohol, marijuana, and crack cocaine use to be frequent among the members of all three different types of gangs he identified (hedonistic, instrumental, and predatory) as operating in Cleveland and Columbus, Ohio.

In a study of youth gang in Milwaukee; it was found that (Hagedorn & Macon, 1988, p. 142)

Sixty percent of the gang members interviewed admitted they used drugs (mainly marijuana) most or all of the time, meaning at least every other day. Nearly one third said they used drugs every day. Less than 5 percent of those interviewed said that at this time they "never used drugs."

Research has also discovered that the gang drug users are involved in the sale of drugs, particularly crack cocaine. In the Milwaukee study, nearly half of the gang members interviewed said that they sold drugs "now and then," and drug sales were seen as ventures for profit.

A Miami study revealed that youth's involvement in drug sales was highly correlated with drug use. The majority of the youths who were involved in robberies were also frequent drug users. When asked, "Of the money you make illegally, how much goes to buying drugs?", nearly two-thirds of the youths in the study said that 90% or more of their profits went for drugs. A 17-year-old robber described how he acquired money for drugs:

To get enough money for whatever we wanted to do (whatever drugs), sometimes me and a friend would go downtown, maybe down the street from some nice restaurants, and wait for them (potential victims) to go to their cars. We'd know what cars they'd be goin' to. It was the rental cars—Hertz, Alamo, you know, those cars—for the tourists. When the guy would bend down to unlock the door, we'd run across from the street real fast, knock him with a club an' kick him a few times, take his wallet, jewelry. And the guy would always have a lady with him, and she would stand there in shock, so I'd run around the car an' take her bag, a chain from the neck if she had it. (Inciardi, Horowitz, & Pottieger, 1993, p. 105)

It seems, on the basis of recent research, that retreatist gangs, who use drugs to withdraw from society and establish a drug-centered way of life, are uncommon today, particularly in the inner cities. Some suburban youth gangs may still fit this pattern, but even there the drug involvement is only part of their lifestyle and not their chief reason for existence.

In summary, the work of Thrasher (1927), in which he stated that many gangs develop out of neighborhood play groups, with some evolving into more formalized structures with defined leadership and concerned with turf protection, and others becoming more oriented toward criminal behavior as the members mature and become more sophisticated, may be an adequate description of the larger majority of contemporary gang formation activities in the inner cities. Much of the research considered here points out that the activities of gang members usually involve an intermeshing of social interactions, such as hanging around, partying, and drug use, with delinquent behavior that initially is recreational in nature.

Sullivan (1992, p. 93), researched street gangs in Brooklyn. He pointed out that the gangs did not start out as groups oriented toward economic crime. When youths first became involved in gang activities, their primary motivation was the excitement of committing the acts, and only later did the profit motive emerge.

> Many stole initially in order to enjoy direct use of stolen objects. Stealing that took place in adolescent street fights, for example, usually involved the appropriation of youth culture consumer items—radios, bicycles, sneakers, coats—which were then as likely to be used directly as to be sold… Some youths who snatched gold jewelry on the streets and subways did so initially in order to wear it themselves… After the first few experiences with economic crime, however, their motivations began to change… Crime proved a viable way to make money at the same time that they were beginning to perceive a need for more regular income… Stealing for direct use gave way to conversion of stolen goods into cash… The risks and rewards associated with specific criminal opportunities were weighed against those associated with opportunities for other types of crime or for legitimate work.

6.4.8   The Underclass as a Generating Milieu for Gang Formation

The emergence of an underclass, particularly in the eastern and mid-western cities of the USA referred to as the "rust belt," is related to a drastic decline in employment opportunities in the large cities, primarily through the loss of the types of factory jobs that provided employment for the unskilled, poorly educated children of the immigrants who came to these cities at the height of the industrial revolution. Hagedorn and Macon (1988) contend that the black and Hispanic gangs of Milwaukee resemble the immigrant gangs of the past who lived in the inner-city, deteriorated neighborhoods, but the one major difference from the gangs of the past is that those youths who had job opportunities gradually matured out of gang behavior. With the industrial jobs greatly reduced or eliminated, the present gang members do not have the education or skills to find employment in the highly skilled professional or service occupations, and are destined to remain in the underclass. As a result of the welfare reforms of the late 1990s, millions of single mothers who formerly qualified for welfare benefits are now working in low paying jobs that do not provide health benefits. Sheldon et al. (2001, p. 191) termed this the "feminization of poverty" and noted that these women find it very difficult to find affordable child care and provide supervision for their children while they are at work.

In the past, adolescents who dropped out of school might take up street life for a while, but it was possible for them to find factory jobs and eventually become self-supporting.

A study (Baron, Kennedy, & Forde, 2001) of 125 homeless male street youths who were runaways or throwaways found that most of these youths were unemployed or underemployed. They spent considerable amounts of time without shelter, hung out in public places (streets, parks, or shopping malls), and experienced poverty and hunger as daily conditions. The researchers discovered that these youths developed subcultural rules that favored violence as a way to meet their daily needs or settle conflicts that occurred in their lives. Interviews with these youths revealed that they generally came from family backgrounds where violence was frequently used as a disciplining strategy and had developed the outlook that intimidation and violence were appropriate methods of self-protection. Their continuous interaction with other homeless, angry youths and their perceptions of threats to their security increased the likelihood that they would use violence. When their violence produced a successful outcome, it reinforced the likelihood that they would use it again in similar situations.

It is recognized that adolescents in all social classes may be susceptible to the lure of gang membership, in terms of the expected excitement, status, and camaraderie. However, as they mature, youths who have family support and other opportunities open to them may disengage from the gang and turn away from the types of deviant activity they pursued as gang members. However, many youths having few options or opportunities are more likely to remain within the gang structure. In these families, younger brothers follow older ones into the gang and remain with the gang after they have reached adulthood.

For many youths, the gang becomes a "family," as well as an avenue for economic survival. The money made from selling drugs or robberies, activities that gang members participate in, helps provide for some basic needs, and the companionship, recognition, and status enhancement from gang membership fulfill other needs of the youth that are not met at home, at school, or in a job situation.

6.4.9 Motivation for Joining a Gang

Maslow (1989, pp. 81–82) believed that a person's behavior can be explained in terms of that individual's response to five basic human needs. These include physiological needs (basic items required for physical survival such as food and water), things needed for safety and security (environmental factors, such as a place to live and protection from harm), belonging needs (membership in family, friendship, or other groups), self-esteem needs (recognition or approval from others), and self-actualization needs (desires to achieve and excel).

Maslow placed these needs in a pyramidal hierarchy, with the needs of physiological survival and safety and security being the most basic, and needs of belonging, self-esteem, and self-actualization met or gratified in successive order after the basic needs are satisfied. Thus, a person's motives for engaging in a specific behavior at any given time can be interpreted as an attempt by that person to use the behavior to satisfy his or her strongest need at that moment.

It should not be concluded that lower level needs must be completely satisfied before one becomes motivated to attempt to fill a higher level need. In general, most people are partially satisfied at all levels, but not completely satisfied at any need level. At times, individuals may defer gratification of a lower level need in order to focus on fulfilling the higher level needs of self-esteem and self-actualization.

Jackson and McBride (1990, p. 6) developed a theory of gang formation that employed Maslow's hierarchy of needs levels. They stated that what they termed Level I needs (physiological needs for survival, such as food and clothing) are often obtained by future gang members' parents through illegal acts, and the young people, at an early age, begin to develop mindsets that approve antisocial behavior. For level II (safety and security), these youths initially look to family members, but, finding what is provided inadequate, may see the gang as the way to obtain security in a hostile environment. Thus, when they reach Level III (belonging needs), they gravitate toward gang membership as a way of "socializing with others who have also learned to use unacceptable means to satisfy their needs for survival and security. As the group becomes more cohesive, the levels of criminal activity rise. Jackson and McBride theorized that a lack of parental guidance and a lack of love from family members drives youths to seek friendship and respect in a gang setting. Once involved with a gang, youth seeks Level IV needs (the desire for self-esteem, the need to attain recognition by displaying skills and talents) through turf fights, displays of "colors," graffiti writing, and criminal activities. These lead to Leve V (self-actualization), in the form of efforts to be the toughest, most violent, most feared gang member, with the goal of winning the admiration of fellow members (Jackson & McBride, 1990, p. 8).

Short and Strodtbeck (1965, pp. 25–46) in their study of Chicago gangs, also discovered that the gang members had needs and aspirations that they hoped to fulfill. For example, many gang boys revealed their desired for good jobs, material rewards, stable family life, and opportunities for their children. There was ambivalence in their value system, however, since they also enjoyed the activities of the lower-class way of life (excitement, freedom, concentration on fun) and their acceptance of middle-class standards was rather superficial. They did not perceive that their delinquent behavior would have an effect on their future opportunities. Their aspirations tended to be rather unrealistic in light of the amount preparation they were making to achieve them; few were studying to achieve in school or working at a part-time job to have enough money to buy some of the things they desired.

6.4.10   Development of the Gang

We have already noted the development of gangs from small groups that interact and come to recognize their common interests. While the gang theorists have emphasized the importance of neighborhood groups in the evolution of gang activity, Huff observed that the word "neighbor" now has an expanded definition.

> Forerunners of the current gangs in Cleveland and Columbus (Ohio) were neighborhood street corner groups and "turf"-oriented gangs who fought against one another over turf issues, ethnic and racial conflict, and other issues… "Neighborhood" no longer conveys the same kind of meaning… If still in school, they (gang members) attend schools whose pupils come from various neighborhoods. Gang membership is no longer confined to the neighborhood, but involves confederates recruited at school, at skating rinks, and elsewhere throughout the city. (Huff, 1988, p. 11)

Thrasher (1927, p. 20), made the observation that a gang does not become one until it "begins to excited disapproval and opposition, and thus acquires a more definite group consciousness."

Various levels of involvement in gang activity have been identified. Yablonsky, presented evidence that the average gang is composed of a number of "hard-core" members (estimated to be 10–15% of the gang) who lead, plan, and manage the day-to-day activities of the gang and a much larger group of "marginal" members who are their followers. A study by Esbensen and Huizinga (1993, pp. 565–590)) supported Yablonsky's theory (1966, p. 227) of impermanence of commitment on the part of many gang members. In their survey of urban gang members, more than half of the youths indicated that they did not want to be or did not expect to be gang members in the near future.

Retention of the top leadership position in the gang may depend upon meeting the physical challenges presented by other candidates, demonstrating "heart" by fearlessly leading the gang into battle, or show in the ability to "look out for" the other gang members through cunning and manipulations. The other leadership positions are frequently conferred as a result of extraordinary performance in the gang's behalf.

Entrance into the gang frequently involves an elaborate initiation rite, which may include demonstrations of personal valor.

Symbolic efforts to heighten group solidarity center on names of gangs and distinctive patterns of dress. A gang's name may refer to the turf the gang claims as its own (West Side Devils) or to claims of superior strength (Invincibles). A gang emblem may be developed and used to indicate the group's presence or domination, by being spray-painted or written on walls. Distinctive styles of dress are also characteristic of well-developed gang structures.

The primary appeal of social or violent gangs is status enhancement. Social gangs offer opportunities for developing a sense of belonging to youths who may never have experienced such a feeling in their family or school situations. The existence of rules and taboos also has an appeal to those who have known little control at home or in the community. Brotherhood, protection from neighborhood toughs, opportunities to "get even" with members of other gangs or adults who are perceived as threatening are all part of the gang appeal. Self-preservations is a strong motive in violent-gang membership.

The gang members protect each other from being victimized by other gangs and authority figures. Gang solidarity and a sense of security are enhanced for delinquent or violent gangs by the amassing of a large collection of weapons, which are handled, concealed, and made ready for use. The stockpile of weaponry for the gang is obtained in various ways. Guns taken in burglaries form an important part of the collection, and others are purchased with the proceeds from drug sale and robberies. Many of the gang members carry guns with them as part of their daily routines and even try to bring them into the schools.

The meeting place of the gang is another important feature in its development of group cohesion. It serves as the location for planning and setting gang activities in motion; concealing loot; and taking part in sexual activities, drinking, drug use, and general socialization. Abandoned buildings, public places, or apartments of older members of the gang may serve this function.

6.5   Variations in Gang Membership and Structures

6.5.1   Female Gangs

Although involvement of females in gang activity has long been documents, their attachments to gangs have usually been in the roles of weapons carriers or girlfriends of gang members. Often, they were part of female auxiliaries of male gangs.

Over the years, gang behavior researchers have given female gangs only cursory analysis. Thrasher's (1927, p. 161) study located several gangs whose membership was entirely female, but only one of these was oriented toward delinquent behavior.

In the 1950s and 1960s, Miller (1958, p. 23) studied two female gangs—an all-white gang of Catholic girls called the Molls and a black female gang known as the Queens. Each was affiliated with a male gang but also performed delinquent acts on its own.

Miller's (1975, pp. 32–35) survey of youth-gang activities in major cities reported the same pattern. The activities of the female gangs were described as complementing the male gang members by serving as weapon carriers or decoys. Only occasionally were they found to be involved in gang fights or organized criminal activities.

Campbell (1984, p. 28) summarized the research on female gangs that had taken place. She notes that girls were found to have a "marginal status" and that "sexual objectification" is a second major theme.

> Girls join gangs to meet boys. Innocent girls are corrupted by sex and as "fallen women" slip into the underworld of gang life. Girls in gangs perform sexual roles (lures, spies) are "passive, property, and promiscuous," are sexually and physically abused by men, want to excel as females by having sex with as many members as possible, get pregnant, and work as prostitutes.

In 2000, the National Youth Gang Survey reported that only 2% of gangs were identified as predominantly female and 82% of the police agencies that provided the data reported no predominantly female gangs in their jurisdictions (Egley & Arjunana, 2000, p. 2).

Miller (1982, p. 2) classified female gangs into three types—mixed gender gangs, female gangs affiliated with male gangs (auxiliary gangs), and independent female gangs. Jody Miller (2001, p. 2) found that females' attachment to the gang lifestyle and other gang members and involvement in drug use and violence varied by gang type. Females affiliated with male gangs had a low status. In the mixed gender gangs their status varied with the number of girls in the gang. Females still had a lower status than the males, but they were treated with more respect than those affiliated with all male gangs. The females in the mixed gender gangs were rarely directly involved in violence or even in serious criminal acts. The independent female gangs appeared to be less criminal and violent than the other types, but members of these gangs associated with members of other types of gangs.

6.5.2   Suburban, and Small-Town Gangs

Traditionally, gangs have been regarded as a large city phenomenon. Although ganging did occur in suburban areas and in small towns, the behavior of these youths was more antisocial than criminal, and the delinquent behavior in which they were involved was mostly nonviolent. In recent years, however, the presence of violent and criminal gangs has been reported in suburban and smaller communities, particularly those that are adjacent to large urban centers.)

We noted earlier in this chapter that street gangs from large cities have migrated to smaller ones, motivated chiefly by the possibilities of high profits from drug sales. In addition, members of big-city gangs may be commuting from the cities to suburban malls and small towns to commit crimes, then returning to their home base. Alexander (1994, p. 2), a member of the Columbus, Ohio gang control unit, remarked that when he recognized a gang member he had worked with in Columbus at a shopping center in a middle-class, suburban town, he approached the boy and said, "You shouldn't be here, this isn't your turf." The gang member responded, "Our house is where we want it to be."

The National Youth Gang Survey Analysis (Office of Juvenile Justice and Delinquency Prevention, 2012, p. 2) reveals the rural estimates in the USA included in the survey reported having 5.5% of all the rural gangs and the suburban countries reported 25.8% of the known gangs in regard to the member of gang members. The report indicated that the rural counties had only 2.7% of the total estimated 850,000 gang members. Approximately one-fourth of the rural counties reported fewer than 25 gang members in the county (NYGSAM, p. 5). The smaller cities had 15.6% of the total of estimated gang members, and the suburban counties 24.4% of the total.

Although some migration of gangs from large cities to small towns and rural areas occurs, chiefly in the form of gangs engaged in the drug trafficking that are expanding their operations. However, it appears as if rural and small town youths form their own gangs, hang out in malls and parks, display distinctive garb and "colors," vandalize, and engage in other delinquent activity.

Loosely structured gangs that develop in suburbs, small towns, or rural areas may take various forms. Wooden (1995, pp. 2–3) divided the suburban gang members he studied into "renegade kids" or "suburban outlaws." The "renegade kids," whom he regarded as "identity seekers," engaged in relatively harmless behaviors, while the "suburban outlaws" were nonconformists, rebellious, and had developed defiant and delinquent identities and behavior. The types of suburban outlaws he differentiated included tagger crews (graffiti painters competing to identify their turf); stoners (drug users also involved with heavy metal music); Satanists (devil worshippers and cult members); and skinheads (white supremacists, racists). Of the youths who purport to be members of such gangs, some are deeply committed to them and others are only marginal members.

6.6 Control of Youth Gangs

Typically, the control of gang activity has been defined as a police matter. However, those who have observed, and researched gang behavior conclude that its prevention and control is a complex task and must involve the entire community.

Measures used to reduce and control gang activities may be proactive or reactive. Proactive control focuses on preventing gangs from forming. The appeal of gang membership is strong, particularly for inner-city youngsters who have few other options to channel their energy and meet their needs. If young people are to resist the gangs' appeal, positive alternative must be provided. These may include sports, youth clubs, afterschool programs at churches or civic centers, or extension of the hours that schools are open. Since the school is the point of contact with the community for all children, provision of late afternoon and evening athletic, fine arts, tutoring, computer training, and life-skill programs, well organized and supervised, can help meet the needs of children who have empty hours to fill. In addition, neighborhood residents may be organized to observe and report suspected drug sale or use or identify places where gangs gather.

Reactive gang control, which occurs when gangs are recognized as present in a community, may include formation of special police gang control units, gang streetworker programs, and implementation of firm justice system responses to unlawful gang activity.

Spergel and Curry (1992, p. 175), in a major research project titled, "National Youth Gang Suppression and Intervention Research Development," identified the strategy for gang suppression and control as community organization, social intervention, opportunities provision, and suppression. Activity in all of these areas is needed.

The Office of Juvenile Justice and Delinquency Prevention (2019, p. 6) has developed a comprehensive gang suppression model and solicits proposals for state, city, or local governments to work toward the suppression of gangs in their jurisdictions. The model has five core strategies: community mobilization, involving local citizens, former gang members, community groups and agencies, providing opportunities to develop a variety of education, training, and employment programs targeting gang involved youths, social intervention, involving youth serving agencies such as schools, grass-root groups, faith based organizations, law enforcement and other criminal justice organization to reach out to gang-endangered youths to provide needed services, suppression through formal and informal social control procedures that supervise or monitor gang youths, and organizational change and development, that is focused on developing and implementing policies and procedures directed toward using available resources to address gang problems.

6.6.1 Community Organization for Gang Control

Until the mid-1980s, most communities, and even some large cities, did not have serious gang problems, at least in terms of random violence, set off with little or no warning provocation. Although gangs existed, and they were regarded as troublesome and at times destructive, through their vandalism and graffiti writing, they did not pose a major threat to the physical well-being of most common community residents. With the sudden upsurge in violent behavior by gangs in the late 1980s, 1990s, and the twenty-first century, and the spread of gangs from large cities to medium-sized and even smaller cities, a whole new situation was recognized.

Youths who had few opportunities—who were not succeeding in school or were out of school and unemployed—found role models in the charismatic gang leaders and were eager to be identified with notorious gangs. Television programs and rap music brought gang activities to the attention of these youths and endowed them with a certain glamor. The communities and neighborhoods in which these young people resided provided no activities or opportunities to match the appeal of the gangs.

Now that the peril posed by gangs has aroused community awareness, quick action must be taken to combat the gangs' appeal. There are no "quick fix" solutions, and the problems faced are formidable. As Block and Block (1993, p. 9) observed,

> Street gang patterns and trends reflect not only chronic problems, such as racial and class discrimination and adjustment of immigrants, but also acute, often rapidly changing problems stemming from the existing economic situation, weapon availability, drug markets, and spatial arrangement of street gang territories across a city.

6.6.2 Social Intervention

Mentoring programs, in which children from disadvantaged neighborhoods are introduced to lifestyles and role models that would otherwise be unavailable to them, can be used. Successful professionals, businessmen and women, or college students are paired one-on-one with youths. The mentors may take the youths to their places of employment or may interact with them at social or athletic events. Such activities give the youths visions of life beyond their everyday experiences and may motivate them to work hard to achieve new goals.

6.6.3   Opportunities Provision

Most social scientists agree that opportunities are the key to resisting gang influence. Government, community organizations, schools, and businesses must work
together to make meaningful opportunities available to at-risk youths, and the
potential for misuse or ineffective use of funds that are provided for such programs
is very great. Apprenticeship programs, in which employers and the schools cooperate in training youths for jobs that hold real opportunities, would be one solution.
Unfortunately, very few placements of this type exist, and many high school students are too poorly prepared academically to succeed in those that are available.
Providing youths with quality education is the best possible solution, but there are
many obstacles to their academic success, including lack of student or parent interest, lack of knowledge about what employment in jobs other than service occupations actually involves, poor preparation for school entry, no quiet places or
resources in the home for study, peer influences that pull youths towards "easy
money" and downplay deferred gratification, lack of positive adult role models, and
poorly financed and administered schools.

6.6.4   Special Police Gang Units

One approach to reducing and controlling gang activity is the development of
"gang-intelligence" units that work out of the police departments of large cities and
seek to discover who the core leaders of various gangs are, what their plans and
habits may be, and how their influence on other youths and propensity toward violence can best be counteracted.

An important facet of intelligence gathering is identifying the type of gang activity that is taking place in specific areas, so that programs to reduce or eliminate the
activity can be implemented. As Block and Block (1993, p. 9) pointed out in their
research on gangs in Chicago, instituting a program to reduce gang involvement in
drug sales would not be warranted in an area where it is discovered that the violence
is predominantly related to turf defense. Because gang activities may change quickly
or may shift to new neighborhoods without warning, gang intelligence units are vital.

Archbold and Meyer (1999) cautioned against overestimating gang problems.
When groups of adolescents are observed gathering in certain areas and episodes of
violence or property destruction occurs, a gang problem may be defined when one
does not actually exist. They researched the development of a gang suppression unit
in a small mid-western community and found that the police department's failure to
accurately distinguish between crimes committed by individual youths and those
that were gang related led to erroneous conclusions about the extent of gang problems in their community. After a gang suppression unit was established, the police
realized that there was little evidence that organized gangs existed or presented a
serious threat to the community.

Making weapons less easily available is another method of suppressing gang violence. Although such legislation as the Brady Law, which mandated a 5-day waiting period between the application for and purchase of firearms and a criminal background check for the applicant, and other legislation, which banned the sale of certain semiautomatic weapons, is a tangible move toward reducing the availability of weapons to youths, it cannot prevent such purchases from occurring.

Others believe that punishing the hard-core leaders of gangs and isolating them from the other youths through institutionalization is needed for effective control of violent gangs. This view is likely to be received enthusiastically by the public, particularly residents of communities that have been harassed, terrorized, or vandalized by gangs.

On the basis of his findings from a study of youth gangs in seven Ohio cities, Huff (1989, pp. 11–14) developed a number of policy recommendations for gang membership reduction and control of gang activities. These included identification of at-risk areas of cities and development of prevention programs to reach youths before they become involved in gangs; development of school curriculum that presents situational ethics to students in relation to the problems they face in everyday life, stressing teacher and principal assertiveness and the need to hold students accountable for their behavior; establishment of a statewide intergovernmental task force on gangs, organized crime, and narcotics as a preventive measure; aggressive but professional police behavior in dealing with gangs; intensive probations, supplemented by telephone or electronic monitoring for gang members who have been found delinquent but who do not pose a threat to public safety; development of school board policies that clearly forbid all types of weapons in school; close cooperation of schools with local police to assure that the school is a safe environment; and implementation of programs that will offer young people who live in inner-city poverty areas opportunities to become involved in positive experiences that will help counter the appeal of gang membership.

6.6.5 Legislation for Youth Gang Prevention and Control

States legislation enacted to deal with the gang problem varies by state in purpose, scope, and definition, but generally includes one or more of the following provisions:

- Makes it a crime to belong to a gang organization that is known to be involved in random crimes of violence, terrorism, or intimidation or takes part in criminal activity for economic gain.
- Allows for increased bail figure or preventive detention if an accused offender is charged with gang-related crime.
- Supports civil courses of action against gang leaders and members, so that individuals or the state can pursue civil actions to seize proceeds and instrumentalities accumulated by or used by street gangs and allows the government to recover compensatory damages and all court costs of filing these suits.

- Allows juveniles accused of gang-related crimes to be fingerprinted and photographed, and requires gang members and leaders convicted of gang-related offenses to register with local law enforcement officials when they are released back into the community.
- Provides for curfew laws as gang control mechanism.
- Provides funds to local law enforcement agencies that can be used to protect victims and witnesses who are aiding in the prosecution of those involved in gang crimes.
- Provides for creation of law enforcement and violent crime task forces that focus on gang-related drug trafficking, terrorism, and violence.
- Prohibits youths under 18 from exhibiting tattoos that have gang symbols or markings without parental consent.
- Provides funds for antiaging counseling programs and prevention activities in schools and the community (Kratcoski, 2003, pp. 1–27).

The descriptions of gang behavior and the characteristics of gang members presented in this chapter testify to the difficulty of generalizing about the nature, motivations, and extent of gang activity. Various types of gangs have defined their goals as status, companionship, protection, recognition, or material gain. Any attempt to discover the most effective method of preventing or controlling gang behavior must take into account not only the wide range of gang types and who are seeking to reduce or eliminate gang behavior. Opinions on the most proper or effective methods will vary with the professional status of those involved, such as police officers, social workers, ministers, poverty workers, or politicians. Extreme gang control measures could range from attempts at destruction of the gangs and institutionalization of all core members to rechanneling gang activities through socially acceptable behavior. Another view is that gang behavior will become less appealing and destructive in nature when its social and economic causes, including poverty, slum living, and lack of educational and employment opportunities, are attacked. There are no easy solutions.

6.7 Summary

A review of the history of gang development reveals that gangs have existed in the urban areas of this country virtually from the time cities became large enough to develop slim areas. Conflict over control of territory was the chief concern of the earliest gangs and is still important. Contemporary gangs, however, may be competing for control over a particular area for the purpose of profiting from the drug sales there. The levels of gang violence escalated markedly in the late 1980s and 1990s, and gang problems, especially in the large cities continue to exist. The gangs' increased use of firearms created threats to innocent bystanders.

Involvement of Asians and white youths in gangs is also apparent. The age range of gang members is expanding, with preteen youngsters now becoming gang members and youths in their 20s remaining active in gangs. Violent crimes and drug trafficking by gangs are of great concern. Gang activity has been reported in the schools in many large cities, and in-school robberies and assaults on teachers and students frequently involve youths acting in groups. Street crime is also a major activity of youth-gang members. Gang theorists include the members of the Chicago School (Thrasher, Shaw, McKay, and Tannenbaum); Whyte, Cohen, Miller, Lewis, Cloward and Ohlin, Yablonsky, Jackson and McBride (applying Maslow's "need theory" to gang formation); and Short and Strodtbeck. They developed contrasting or complementary theories of gang-behavior causation. The emergence of an under-class of impoverished, poorly educated, unemployed persons who seem to have few options for breaking out of a cycle of welfare dependency and hopelessness has also been recognized as contributing to gang formation.

Gang structure most frequently involves an inner circle of leaders who plan strategy and control the gang's decision-making, a group of regular members, and other youths who remain on the fringes of gang activity and participate only occasionally. Leaders must frequently justify their positions by demonstrations of strength or courage. Gang solidarity is developed by use of initiation rites; distinctive patterns of dress, emblems, and names; and collection of a large cache of weapons.

Although gang activity is most frequently associated with inner-city males, females are involved in male-dominated gangs in various roles and sometimes form independent female gangs. Gang activity occurs in suburbs, small cities, and rural areas as well as in urban settings, and middle-class youths who do not fit the gang member profile of "disadvantaged youths" also create gangs.

Approaches to gang control may be proactive or reactive. Proactive efforts focus on preventing gang formation by developing community and school activities and programs to meet the needs of youths who might fall prey to the gangs' appeal. Reactive control occurs when gangs are recognized as present in the community. Reactive approaches may take the form of collection of intelligence and attempts to destroy the gang, isolation of the leaders through arrest and institutionalization, and debunking the romanticized versions of gang behavior in the mass media. Because of the violent nature of a good deal of current gang activity, legislation for transfer of gang members' cases to adult criminal courts, development of special units of prosecutors to work on gang cases, and to determinate sentences for certain violent crimes have been implemented. The schools are regarded as the best avenue for reaching youths who may be in danger of gang involvement and seek to influence them in a positive way by providing educational and employment opportunities. Although control programs may have limited success, real solutions to the problem of gang delinquency depend on a broad, sweeping attack on the social problems that breed it.

6.8 Discussion Questions

1. Describe the levels of membership and leadership in typical gang. What are the methods used by leaders to inspire loyalty and produce feelings of group solidarity?

2. Discuss the possible explanations for the strong pull toward gang involvement for certain youths in disadvantaged neighborhoods, while other youths who live in the same area do not seek such attachments.

3. Describe the three types of gangs identified by Cloward and Ohlin in their studies of delinquency and opportunity. Why do different types of gangs develop?

4. How have the activities and interests of gangs in the inner cities of large metropolitan areas changed in the last several decades?

5. What mechanisms are used by police and the courts to control gangs? How effective do you think these are?

6. Identify the types of legislation enacted by various states to suppress youth gangs.

7. Discuss the ways youth gangs of the 1950s and 1960s differ from the youth gangs at the present time.

8. The results of the Surveys of Youth Gangs completed by the National Youth Gang Center reveal that there has been a steady increase in the number of youth gangs and gang members in the USA since 1995. Discuss the reasons (motivation) for a youth to become a member of a youth gang,

9. What are some of the alternatives to joining a gang that a community can offer a youth who may be considering becoming a member of a youth gang?

10. Frederick Thrasher's classic work, *The Gang*, published in 1927 has relevance to the understanding of the formation and structure of youth gangs existing at the present time. Discuss the key elements of his research that can be applied to the origins and development of youth gangs at the present time. What characteristics of youth groups and gangs are different from those described by Thrasher?

References

Akron Beacon Journal. (2019, May 31). *Four wounded in Akron shootings*. pp. B1, B4.

Alexander, T. Panelist. (1994, October 21). Violence in the schools seminar, Columbus, OH.

Archbold, C. A., & Meyer, M. (1999, June). Anatomy of a gang suppression unit: The social construction of an organizational response to gang problems. *Police Quarterly, 2*(2), 201–224.

Asbury, H. (1928). *The gangs of New York*. New York: Capricorn Books.

Baltimore Sun. (1994, September 2). p. 3A.

Baron, S., Kennedy, L., & Forde, D. (2001). Male street youths' conflict: The role of background, subcultural, and situational factors. *Justice Quarterly, 18*(4), 759–790.

Bensinger, G. J. (1984). Chicago youth gangs: A new old problem. *Journal of Crime and Justice, 7*, 3–17.

Block, R., & Block, R. (1993). *Street gang crime in Chicago*. Washington, DC: U.S. Department of Justice.

Campbell, A. (1984). *The girls in the gang*. New York: Basil Blackwell.

Cloward, R., & Ohlin, L. (1961). Illegitimate means, differential opportunity and delinquent subcultures. In *Delinquency and opportunity: A theory of delinquent gangs*. New York: Free Press.

Cohen, A. (1955). *Delinquent boys*. New York: Free Press.

Collins, H. (1977). Street gangs in New York: A prototype of organized youth crime. *Law and Order, 25*(5), 5–10.

David Curry, G., Decker, S. H., & Pyrooz, D. C. (2014). *Confronting gangs: Crime and community* (3rd ed.). New York: Oxford University Press.

Dawley, D. (1973). *A nation of lords*. New York: Anchor Books.

Decker, S., & Van Winkle, B. (1994). Slinging dope: The role of gangs and gang members. In drug sales. *Justice Quarterly, 11*(4), 583–604.

Egley & Arjunana. (2000). *Highlights of the 2000 National Young Gang Survey*. Washington, DC: Office of Juvenile Justice and Delinquency Prevention.

Esbensen, F., & Huizinga, D. (1993). Gangs, drugs, and delinquency in a survey of urban youth. *Criminology, 31*(4), 565–590.

Final Report. (1986). *State task force on youth violence*. Sacramento, CA: California Council on Criminal Justice.

Hagedorn, J., & Macon, P. (1988). *People & folks*. Chicago, IL: Lakeview Press.

Herbert, B. (1994, August 26). A river of blood links the street to the Capitol. *Akron Beacon Journal*, p. A9

Howell, J., & Gleason, D. (1999). *Youth gang drug trafficking, OJJDP juvenile justice bulletin* (pp. 1–6). Washington, DC: Department of Justice.

Huff, R., (1988, May 25). *Youth gangs and public policy in Ohio: Findings and recommendations.* Paper presented at the Ohio Conference on Youth Gangs and the Urban Underclass, Ohio State University, Columbus.

Huff, R. (1989, October). Youth gangs and public policy in Ohio: Findings and recommendations. *Crime and Delinquency, 35*, 528–529.

Inciardi, J., Horowitz, R., & Pottieger, A. (1993). *Street kids, street drugs, street crime: An examination of drug use and serious delinquency in Miami*. Belmont, CA: Wadsworth.

Jackson, R., & McBride, W. (1990). *Understanding street gangs*. Placerville, CA: Custom.

Keiser, R., (1969). The vice lords; Garden City, NY: Holt, Rinehart & Winston.

Klein, M.W., Gordon, M.A., and Maxson, C.L. (1986). The impact of police investigations on police-reported rates of gang and nongang homicides. *Criminology 24*(3), 495–496

Kratcoski, P. (1995, February 8). Interview with members of the Caribbean Gang Task Force, Cleveland, OH.

Kratcoski, P. (2003). Summary of gang related legislation. Retrieved February 16, 2003, from www.iir.com/nyge/ganglegis/Miscellaneous%20gang%20Legislation.htm

Krisberg, B. (1978). Gang youth and hustling: The psychology of survival. In B. Krisberg & J. Uarin (Eds.), *The children of Ishmael*. Palo Alton, CA: Mayfield.

Lewis, M. (1970). Structured deviance and normative conformity: The "hustle" and the gang.

Maslow, A. H. (1989). Motivation and personality. In J. Klofas, S. Stojkovic, & D. Kalinich (Eds.), *Criminal justice organizations: Administration and management*. Pacific Grove, CA: Brooks/Cole.

McKay, H. (1967). *A note on trends in rates of delinquency in certain areas of Chicago, Appendix F. Task force report: Juvenile delinquency and youth crime* (pp. 114–118). Washington, DC: U.S. Government Printing Office.

Miller, J. (2001). *One of the guys*. New York: Oxford University Press.

Miller, W. (1958). Lower class culture as a generating milieu of gang delinquency. *Journal of Social Issues, 14*(3), 10.

Miller, W. (1975). *Violence by youth gangs and youth groups as a crime problem in major American cities*. Washington, DC: Government Printing Office.

Miller, W. (1982). *Crimes by youth gangs and groups in the United States*. Washington, DC: Office of Juvenile Justice and Delinquency Prevention.

Moore, J. (1988). Gangs and the underclass: A comparative perspective. In J. Hagedorn & P. Macon (Eds.), *People and folks*. Chicago, IL: Lakeview Press.

Office of Juvenile Justice and Delinquency Prevention. (2019). *Gang Suppression Implementation Grants Program FY 2019 Competitive Grant Solicitation*. Washington, DC: U. S. Department of Justice.

Office of Juvenile Justice and Delinquency Prevention, National Youth Gang Survey: Trends from 2005 to 2012. (2012). *OJJDP fact sheet*. Washington, DC: Office of Juvenile Justice and Delinquency Prevention.

Rettig, R., Torres, M. J., & Garrett, G. R. (1977). *Manny: A criminal addict's story*. Boston, MA: Houghton Mifflin.

Shaw, C. (1929). *Delinquency areas*. Chicago, IL: University of Chicago Press.

Shaw, C. (1968). Juvenile delinquency: A group tradition. In J. Short Jr. (Ed.), *Gang delinquency and delinquent subcultures* (pp. 86–87). New York: Harper & Row.

Sheldon, R., Tracy, S., & Brown, W. (2001). *Youth gangs in American society*. Belmont, CA: Wadsworth.

Sheley, J. F., & Wright, J. D. (1993). *Gun acquisitions and possession in selected juvenile samples*. Washington, DC: U.S. Department of Justice.

Short Jr., J. F., & Strodtbeck, F. L. (1965). *Group process and gang delinquency* (pp. 25–46). Chicago, IL: University of Chicago Press.

Spergel, I. A., & Curry, G. D. (1992). Reducing gang violence: an overview. In M. D. Biskup (Ed.), *Youth violence*. San Diego, CA: Greenhaven Press.

Sullivan, M. L. (1992). Greed causes youth violence. In M. D. Biskus (Ed.), *Youth violence*. San Diego, CA: Greenhaven Press.

Tannenbaum, F. (1939). *Crime and the community*. New York: Columbia University Press.

Taylor, C. (1990). Gang imperialism. In R. Huff (Ed.), *Gangs in America* (p. 105). Newbury Park, CA: Sage.

The Times Leader. (1994, September 2). p. 3A.

Thrasher, F. (1927). *The gang*. Chicago: Chicago University Press.

Whyte, W. (1955). *Street corner society* (2nd ed.). Chicago: University of Chicago Press.

Wooden, W. S. (1995). *Renegade kids, suburban outlaws*. New York: Wadsworth.

Yablonsky, L. (1966). *The violent gang*. Baltimore: Penguin Books.

Chapter 7
Perspectives on Delinquency and Violence in the Schools

7.1 Introduction

The experiences of millions of students who pass through the schools each year are remembered by them as either "good times" or "bad times." For some the "good times" predominated, while for others what happened to them constituted "bad times." The school years of many students were a combination of good times and bad times.

Take, for example, the experiences of Tiffany, who had many good times.

Tiffany checked her cell phone for the second time. She hoped the graduation ceremony speaker would finish soon, so the principal could start giving out the diplomas. She began to think about her high school experiences and her plans for the future. She would be sad about leaving the school and her many friends, but she was already looking forward to attending the University in the fall.

She was feeling very good about herself. She had accomplished the goals she had set for herself when she first entered high school. She was graduating with honors, had played leading roles in several of the productions put on by the drama department, and was selected as the head of the cheerleading squad. The speaker finished his speech and the students began to line up to receive their diplomas. Source: Information from personal conversations conducted by P. C. Kratcoski (2019).

In contrast to Tiffany's experiences, what happened to an 8-year-old boy at school that led to his suicide illustrate the bad times for one student.

School officials never told the mother of an 8-year-old Ohio boy who killed himself that another student had thrown him against the wall two days earlier and knocked him unconscious in an attack recorded by a surveillance video, attorneys for the boy's mother said Thursday.

The 8-year-old hanged himself with a necktie in the bedroom of his Cincinnati home on Jan. 26. School officials called the boy's mother the day her son was bullied and said he had fainted, attorney Carla Leader told the Associated Press.... The mother learned of the bullying and the surveillance video after her attorneys obtained a Cincinnati police investigative file of her son's death. Other students stepped over the boy while others poked him with their feet as he lay unconscious for 7 1/2 minutes before an assistant principal and then a school nurse came to his aid. (Gillispie, 2017. *Akron Beacon Journal*, May 12, 2017, p. B3)

© Springer Nature Switzerland AG 2020
P. C. Kratcoski et al., *Juvenile Delinquency*,
https://doi.org/10.1007/978-3-030-31452-1_7

The school experience produces lifelong memories. For some it was pleasant, exciting, and rewarding, and the goal of becoming educated was accomplished. For others it was miserable, boring, uneventful, and unrewarding. Very little learning occurred. Most youths pass through their school years without experiencing trauma on a daily basis. Researchers believe that the combined efforts of school administrators, teachers, parents, students, and community groups can make attending school a rewarding experience. The end result of their efforts can be an improvement in the school climate and reductions in school disruption.

In this chapter, we examine the role of education in American society, particularly its function as a means to advance economically, socially, and culturally. The problems that inhibit the achievement of these goals for some children are considered in detail. Although school violence has captured media attention in recent years, the school is one of the safest places for many students. They are less likely to be victims of violent crime at school than in their homes or in their communities. The major problems facing a number of school systems include lack of adequate financial support, overcrowded classrooms, dilapidated buildings, and lack of equipment for special needs students. The threat of extreme violence still exists, but, as we will demonstrate, measures have been taken to assure the safety of students. However, the day-to-day problems of victimization faced by the more than one million students who attend public schools (bullying by peers, fist fights, physical abuse by peers, character assassination, sexual harassment, or fear of being victimized going to and returning from school) are also of great concern for students, as well as for the school administrators who are charged with providing safety and security for those under their care.

The American dream, as forged and promulgated from the beginning of our national experience, has always included reference to education as the "great equalizer," the ladder by which the poorest immigrant, ghetto dweller, or deprived rural child could climb to the pinnacle of success, as measured by occupational status, cultural attainment, or conspicuous consumption. Public schools, designed to assist in their realization of this dream, even in Colonial times, and the child-saving reforms at the turn of the twentieth century included pressures for the enactment of compulsory school attendance laws, regulations against child labor that would encourage young people to remain in school, and community pride in their educational system (Platt, 1969).

Currently, while the goals of most of the schools in the United States are still being fulfilled, and the large majority of the students have the opportunity to achieve and fulfill their goals, for some the dreams and visions of earlier eras are taking on the trappings of a national nightmare. Financial crises force many school districts to operate in an atmosphere of uncertainty, constantly appealing to taxpayers for levies that would provide funds to prevent teachers' strikes or pay for badly needed physical plant repairs. New technological equipment, such as computers, is not purchased for the schools and the students are not given the opportunity to develop the skills needed to be competitive when seeking employment after leaving school. Financial crises in some school districts have led to the elimination of "nonessential" programs such as classical and foreign languages, music, and art. Many experienced teachers as well as new teachers are pressured to take on larger classes, or to teach classes out of their specialized areas of knowledge. Teachers with many years of experience are encouraged to take early retirement and reduce the financial burden their salaries place on the district, resulting in the hiring of inexperienced new teachers whose entry-level salaries will fit more comfortable into the school budget. Often these new teachers, who lack the experience to handle large classes, have problems with discipline and quickly become disillusioned with the teaching profession.

Although a child is less likely to be physically assaulted in the schools than in other places where children spend considerable time, such as in the family or the neighborhood, the amount of victimizations in the schools is sufficient to be a cause of alarm. Property theft and personal assaults on children in schools is not evenly distributed. In some schools, the amount of victimization of any type, including theft of property, is very small, while in other schools the amount is quite high.

The amount of criminal victimization of children is increasing at an alarming rate. This victimization comes from a number of sources and in a variety of forms. These sources are local, such as "bullying" in the schools, and mass murders and gang violence in the schools and the community, and also take on national and international implications through Internet sexual exploitation of children. Police programs operated in the schools and in the community are designed to prevent victimization of children and youth deviance. Community policing programs with youths, School Resource Officer programs, school security programs, and police cooperation with schools and communities in the United States and in other countries are part of the effort to contain or limit this victimization.

Kratcoski, Edelbacher, Graff, and Norden (2012, p. 197) note, "During the latter part of the 20th century and up to the present time, the problems of crime and disorder in the schools and the effects crime and violence have on the entire school body, in terms of being victimized, but also in terms of fear, have been brought to public awareness through mass media reports." The mass murders of students and teachers in schools attended by children of high-income families made people realize that school violence and crime are not limited to school districts in low income neighborhoods. Bulling has emerged as a serious problem occurring in schools today. Although bulling has always existed in schools, school administrators have often ignored it, rationalizing that being a victim of bullying was a problem that some students had to accept as a normal experience.

7.2   The Socialization Process: Rewards and Punishments

The indictment of many schools as delinquency producing institutions seems to center on two types of accusations: (1) that the schools have failed as socialization institutions; that is, delinquency is produced because young people have not been taught the social skills that enable them to interact appropriately with peers and adults; or (2) that failure in academic subjects leads to situations in which youths are shamed or downgraded by peers and teachers or in which they develop such a negative self-image that they undertake delinquent behavior as a defense mechanism or a method of gaining attention or status. Each of these charges will be examined in detail in the following sections.

Outside of the family, the school is the scene of most youthful activity from childhood through adolescence. The school provides a much more complex socialization setting than the family unit does. Since more varied forces interact and pull against each other, there is a competition for a youth's attention and loyalty.

Although schools are established and administered by adults and their organizational goals are set by adults, they are also the focal point of interaction for the peer culture, which in many instances has goals different from, or at least not in total accord with, the goals set by the school administration and pursued by the faculty.

The school provides the first location of socialization away from the family unit, where a child can be exposed to ideas at variance with those learned at home, and where choices of behavior and companions must be made without dependence on parents.

The criticism of the American school system as an agent of socialization has centered on its apparent inability in many instances to meld the divergent elements presented to it by the family and the community, to serve as the location of peer culture formation, and to produce a socially acceptable citizen. It appears that somewhere in the process, the tendency toward deviance promoted by forces brought into the school from the family, the neighborhood, or peers overcomes the efforts exerted by the school toward positive socialization, and delinquent behavior results. Within the school environment, enforcement of discipline is recognized as a pressing school interaction problem. Explanations for the perceived breakdown in discipline include a lessening of respect by youths for adults in general; development of sophistication and disillusionment at increasingly earlier ages; parents' failure to support school personnel in their attempts to maintain discipline; students' increasing demands for their "rights" without concomitant realization of their responsibility to conform to the school rules and regulations; home environments that are lacking in supervision and discipline; the need to be entertained, brought on by constant exposure to the mass media, and related to decreased attention spans; and the inability to sit still or concentrate for extended periods of time.

Another cause of discipline problems in school is student apathy. School is viewed by many young people as a necessary evil that must be endured, but in which they are not bound to take an active interest. They are there to pass the time, and they lack the motivation to achieve or even to actively participate. Somewhere in the process of socialization within the school experience, they have ceased to view themselves as a vital part of the activity within the school setting. They come to function as spectators rather than participants in the social interaction of the school.

The problems of socialization faced by school systems in some areas go far beyond basic educational activities. In disadvantaged urban settings in particular, the schools may be regarded by parents as free babysitters and expected to assume responsibility for many types of training that should have been accomplished long before the child enters school. Children may enter school without having experienced or mastered the basic skills needed to succeed there, including the ability to listen, to answer a direct question, or to go through elementary problem-solving processes. In extreme cases children may not even know their own names.

Parents with serious financial problems may turn to the school as the obvious source of some kinds of help for their children, particularly in cases where the lack of shoes or new clothes is keeping the child from wanting to attend school. Just one experience of having several students make fun of a child's clothing may be a sufficient motive for that child to want to stay away from school. Although some schools have well organized programs to assist such children, others do not. Rebuffs received when requests of this type are made known to insensitive or uncaring school personnel may serve to alienate parents and children from close involvement with the schools.

In spite of what may seem at times to be insurmountable odds, schools must continue to provide a social milieu that supplies many experiences and benefits not available in the home, if they are to function as delinquency preventing rather than delinquency producing institutions. The examples of schools based programs that include the community as well as community service agencies are numerous. For example, having an opportunity to participate in extra-curricular programs, both during school hours and after school provides an outlet for children to develop talents as well as to engage in social activities. Many school systems have developed in-school sports programs for those youths who enjoy playing, but are not likely to make any of the teams that compete with others schools. Other outlets for students to develop their talents, as well as their social skills, include music, theater, drama, and crafts. In some school districts where there is a high concentration of poverty level families with school age children, the school administrators have made it one of their primary goals to assure that every child attending that school will have the opportunity to receive food nourishment, either breakfast, lunch or both, as needed.

7.3   School Environment and Delinquency

Although almost every school will experience some deviant behavior from its students, but in some cases a school where an extreme act of violence, such as a mass killing of students, occurs is one where such violence is least expected. The impersonal, oppressive atmosphere of some school systems may be conducive to delinquent behavior. This type of atmosphere may have been created by the consolidation of many small schools into large systems, particularly those on the junior and senior high school levels. Styles of building construction, consolidation of districts into huge central schools, budget crunches that have forced the creation of large classes and formalized student-teacher contacts, and even computerization of scheduling and grading have reduced the opportunities for positive social interaction between school personnel and students.

Two major factors determine the climate or environment of a school. These are the characteristics of the students, parents, and community from which the students are drawn and the manner in which the school is administered. Pigott, Sterns, and Khey (2018, pp. 128–131) found that the likelihood for students to be removed from school, as in the case of expulsions, were related to school location, with schools in a rural setting being the least likely to expel students for offenses, compared with those schools located in suburban areas and those schools located in urban areas. The researchers also found that the principal's perception of the amount of crime existing in the neighborhood of the students who were disciplined for deviant acts, either crimes or violations of school rules, had an effect on their disciplinary decisions. The higher the perception of the amount of crime in the student's neighborhood, the more likelihood the student would be removed from the school. Students attending schools with a larger student population were more likely to be removed for offenses than students from schools with a smaller population (Under 300) for similar offenses. They also found "... the percentage of the student body that is male, is associated with an increase in student removals, ... an increase in the percentage of the student body that has a limited English proficiency is associated with an increase in student removals, ... an increase in the level of racial tensions equates to an increase in the level of school removals, and ... an increase in the percentage of students considered special education is associated with an increase in school removals" (Pigott et al., 2018, pp. 128–131).

The safety of their children in the schools they attend, as well as other factors are sources of great concern for parents with school-age children. Funding for school systems in the United States is a major venture between the states and the local communities. Therefore, the physical plant of a school, the equipment, and the quality of the instruction are highly dependent on the wealth of the community in which the school is located. Other than the core curriculum and programs required by the state boards of education, the variety of courses, special programs offered, and often the quality of the teacher staff of a school will often be a reflection of the priorities of the citizens within the community, particularly the value they place on education.

Generally, the wealthier a community is, the more likely it is that an enriched educational program will exist. Some schools in upper middle-class communities will have indoor swimming pools, gyms with state of the art equipment, and science labs comparable to those found in universities, as well as programs for gifted children that may even include semesters in foreign countries. In contrast, other schools have the atmosphere of prisons. Although this is also becoming more frequent in all schools, including those in upper income communities, students may have to pass through metal detectors as they enter the school buildings, drug-sniffing dogs are periodically called in to check student' lockers, and security guards or uniformed police officers are present in the schools during operating hours. If these conditions of control are not utilized in the school, the alternative may be a climate of apprehension that makes the school experience one of daily fear of being physically harmed. These are the schools that are likely to be located in communities with high rates of crime, poverty, and unemployment, many single-parent households, and poorly educated parents. The communities where these schools are located are often not stable communities the residents not owning their housing units, and there is a high transient population in these communities. The home owners may resist increases in school taxes, either because they no longer have children in the schools, send their children to private schools, or are on fixed. Limited incomes and barely staying above the poverty level. The students attending such schools bring with them the values, norms, expectations, and attitudes about the value of education that they have learned through interaction with parents, peers, and others in the community.

The communities in which the large majority of school systems in the United States operate fall between the extremes of wealth or socio-economic deprivation. The problems related to physical plants, educational resources, quality of teachers, and student deviancy and disruptive behavior, including violence within the schools exist in varying degrees.

7.3.1 School Climate and School Disorder

The concept "school climate" (Welsh, 2001) includes communication patterns, norms about what are appropriate behavior patterns of influence, role relationships between students and staff, friendship patterns between student peers, protection from victimization, and discipline measures within the school. Welsh conducted a study of the relationship between school climate and school disruption in Philadelphia, PA middle schools. More than 5000 students, the majority of whom were minority group members, were involved in the research. The school climate measurement scale consisted of items related to student characteristics, including involvement in school activities, positive peer associations, belief in school rules, respect for students, efforts in school, and school rewards given. The psychosocial climate measurement item included perception of school safety, clarity of the rules, fairness of the rules, respect for students, student influence in school affairs, and administration planning and action. It was found that students' perceptions of respect for students, fairness of the rules, clarity of the rules, and planning and action were associated with low levels of student victimization. Even though the youths in the sample came from very similar backgrounds, the researchers found considerable variation within the schools in the amount of disorder and misconduct that occurred. The author concluded that a positive social climate can reduce social disorder within schools and this positive climate can be created by cooperative and coordinated efforts of administrators, teachers, parents, and other community members.

Several recent studies relating to the concept of school climate, used the concepts found in the parenting literature to conceptualize different organizational structures and administrative approach to schools. The *authoritarian* approach requires obedience to the rules and the authority figures that enforce the rules, and a rigid response of punishment to those who violence the rules and commands of the authority figures. On the other extreme, the *permissive school* administration is overly accepting of violations and nonpunitive in its response to violations by students. In the middle of these two extremes (Fisher, Viano, Curran, Pearman, & Gardella, 2018, p. 8) identify *authoritative* schools by stating, "Schools that demonstrate high levels of both support and structure are conceptualized as having a more authoritative school climate." The authoritative structure requires that students take responsibility for their behavior and that they be disciplined in a strict, fair, and consistent manner. The discipline occurs in a milieu where students know behavior expectations and consequences and agree that the consequences are fair. The students also feel that the teachers and administrators are supportive, fair, and are willing to accept input from the students on matters of importance. Research on the relationship between school climate and students' feeling of security in the schools tend to confirm that school climate is related to positive feelings of security and safety by the students attending those schools. A study (Steinberg, Allensworth, & Johnson, 2018) of public school children attending schools in Chicago found that the quality of relationships between student and school staff, between parents and school staff, and between the school staff members themselves was a predictor of greater feelings of safety among the students. Fisher et al. (2018, p. 21) concluded from the results of their research that used the database from the Education Longitudinal Study (2011 version) "The findings from this study suggest that school climate may be one malleable school-level factor that can help students feel safer at school. Enhancing students' supportive relationships with adults in schools and crafting discipline policies that are perceived by students as fair and consistently enforced is a promising direction for both reducing violence and victimization in schools, but also for increasing students' feelings of safety."

7.3.2 Use of Medication as a Control Mechanism

The use of medication to alter the behavior of students who are disruptive is a control technique that has a great potential for abuse. One of the most frequently diagnosed disorders handled with drug therapy in the schools is attention deficit disorder (ADD). The attention deficit disorder appears to be much more frequent in boys than girls. According to McBurnett, Llahe, and Pfiffner (1993), ADD is characterized by a combination of inattentive, impulsive, and hyperactive behavior. The most frequently used drug to handle the impulsive and hyperactive behavior of children diagnosed as being ADD is Ritalin. Not all members of the medical profession as well as those in the academic profession are in agreement on the use of drugs as a means to solve the classroom problems created by those children who do not seem to be concerned about their behavior and the likelihood of being punished for their disruptive behavior. They contend that children being treated for ADD only disorder may be bored, not being challenged, not understanding the subject matter being addressed, or just seeking attention. Often, children who did not experience any structured activity or discipline in the home will exhibit behavior in the school that is in conformity to that used in their home. Of course, this is inappropriate for the school. However, instead of attributing the behavior to the early socialization of the children, the behavior is attributed to some form of physical or mental disorder. The use of medication for such students labeled as having ADD is often more for the benefit of the teachers who are trying to find a way to maintain order in their classes than for the benefit of the children given the medication. Often, the disruptive students have one or several problems that in some way interfere with ability to maintain proper control of their behavior in the classroom or to develop social relationships with adults and their peers. Pigott et al. (2018) found that the level of student removals (expulsions) from the schools in their study was higher for those students who had limited proficiency in the English language, were in special education classes, or who were known to live in neighborhoods perceived as having high amounts of crime. The child may have been labeled as a potential troublemaker and at the first indication of any form of deviance and disciplined harshly. The dangers of indiscriminate referrals for drug therapy have the potential for introducing the child to a life- long dependency or addiction and thus it is recommended that the ADD diagnosis of children be given with more caution.

7.3.3   Aspirations of Students, Fear of Failure and Delinquency

In past decades graduating from high school was seen as the ticket for finding employment that would lead to a secure, comfortable life style. Students with high school diplomas were confident that they would find work in high paid manufacturing plants or in service occupations that may require some training beyond a high school diploma. Those students not college bound did not expect that anything they learned in high school, except for some of the math, would ever be used in their lives after graduation. High school for some was viewed as either a passing phase in their lives that had to be endured, but of no real significance, or a fun time, free of responsibility and worry. Regardless of their long range aspirations, most students have a desire to graduate from high school. For some students, who do not share in the goal of being college bound, the engagement in deviant behavior, such as property destruction, bullying of students, or engaging in behaviors such as drinking alcohol, staying out beyond curfew, drug usage and disobeying the rules and regulations of the school are ways to show their disregard for the rewards and punishments associated with the role of student. The continued emphasis on "going to college" as a definition of high school success may serve as a stimulus to deviant behavior for those who have little hope or desire to achieve the status of a college graduate.

The path to a college education is much more open in present times than it was in the past. Most students, even those who received slightly better than an average grade point averages, can find admittance in some higher education institution. However, the cost of a college education has increased so much that it has become difficult for parents with average incomes to be able to finance the higher education costs of their children. Those determined to continue their education either finance the costs through loans or by holding either full or part time employment during the time they attend college. Many high school students have jobs and are able to save enough money to partially pay for their education after graduating from high school. For these students, the responsibilities of adulthood come quickly, and they have few problems making the transition to adulthood after high school graduation. Others, especially those from affluent families, have already achieved a number of symbols of adulthood, even though there is a prolongation of their childhood during the years in college. In high school, they were given many of the material things associated with adulthood, such as an automobile, money to spend exclusively on themselves, or nice clothes. With the exception of being a successful student, they do not have the responsibilities of an adult. In addition, they still must assume a posture of submission and respect while in school as the price of their "ticket of admission" to college. Placed in such a situation, young people who are outwardly conforming, may at times explode in paradoxical behavior—vandalism, sexual promiscuity, or drug and alcohol abuse—as a means of expressing their adulthood and a desire for independence which seems to be denied them.

Young people who are not planning to go to college, on the other hand, may not feel the same constraints to maintain an outward demeanor of conforming behavior. They may anticipate the full status of adulthood that will be theirs upon high school graduation and may regard many of the activities and regulations of high school as meaningless and having little relationship to their future plans.

7.4   Learning Disabilities and Delinquency in the Schools

It has been suggested that children with learning disabilities are more prone to be disruptive in schools, as well as more prone to be aggressive and destroy property, but the causative link has not been established. In spite of the apparent lack of definitive data to make a connection between learning disabilities and delinquency, some juvenile court administrators, as well as school personnel have been sufficiently convinced that there is a causative link and thus they have established special programs for such children. Their perceptions that a child with a learning disability is likely to be disruptive is generally based more on observation than on any scientific evidence. For example, Kratcoski (2012) a teacher who observes a student in the classroom who does not respond to directions or commands may interpret the behavior as being belligerent, when in reality the student just does not understand what the expectations of the teacher are. The same may be the case for outbursts of laughter for no apparent reason or the failure to sit quietly in one's seat as instructed. In some cases, teachers, rather than trying to address the problem, will take the easy way out and request that the student be removed from the class. For example, Pigott et al. (2018, p. 131) found, "an increase in the number of students considered special education is associated with an increase in student removals,"

It is likely that the more severe cases of children with learning disabilities will be recognized at the time that a child entering school is given a battery of tests to determine if there are mental or physical disabilities that may interfere with the child's learning. If the existence of a learning disability is uncovered, referrals may be made to developmental optometrists, audiologists, ophthalmologists, clinical psychiatrists, or occupational therapists. However, it is the borderline students that are not likely to be recognized as having special needs. The National Council of Juvenile and Family Court Judges (1987), published a book titled *Learning Disabilities and the Juvenile Justice System*. In this publication, it was noted that learning disabilities contribute to academic under-achievement, poor impulse control, low frustration tolerance, inability to understand social cues, and aggressive behavior. The difficulties that may inhibit children's ability to learn and succeed academically may also include various types of health problems. Inadequate prenatal care or post-natal diet can result in retardation or poor health.

The most important matter needed to be addressed by the school administrators is the early recognition of children who have one or several disabilities and to combat these problems by having the proper placement and remedial programs. In some cases, the child may have to be referred to another community agency that is better equipped to provide for the special needs of children with learning disabilities.

7.5 School Drop Out and Delinquency

Although compulsory school attendance laws in the various states set-school attendance requirements at ages 6 through 18 (or through graduation), not only do students drop out before the upper age of compulsory attendance, or before graduation, but a surprisingly high number never "drop in." These may include handicapped children who have never been identified and thus never received the services needed to facilitate their learning. Many illegal immigrant children never are enrolled in a school system because their parents are afraid it would lead to a discovery of their illegal status. In 1996 (National Center for Education Statistics, 1998, p. 12), 86% of school children had completed high school by the age of 21. Ten percent of these had finished their studies by passing a high school equivalence exam such as the GED. More recent statistics (National Center for Education Statistics, 2018, p. 1) using the status drop-out rate as a measure reported, "The status dropout rate represents the percentage of 16-to-24 years-olds (referred to as youths in this indicator who are not enrolled in school and have not earned a high school credential, either a diploma or an equivalency credential such as a GED certificate.) Reported that "The overall status drop-out rate decreased from 10.9% in 2000 to 6.1% in 2016. During this time, the Hispanic status drop-out rate decreased by 19.2 points, while the Black and White status dropout rates decreased by 6.9% and 1.7 percentage points." It was found that the dropout rate was 2% higher for males than for females. The NCES report (2018, p. 2) revealed that, "From 2000 to 2016, the status dropout rate declined from 6.9 to 5.2 percent for White youth, from 13.1 to 6.2 percentage points for Black youth, and 27.8 to 8.6 percent for Hispanic youth."

There are two major categories of students who do not complete high school. The first are those who are those who voluntarily drop out for a variety of reasons, some being beyond the control of the student, and for others the decision is made after the student has carefully thought out the advantages and disadvantages of staying in school until graduation. The second category involves students who were forced out of school, predominantly by suspension and expulsion. The reasons for those who voluntarily leave school at the first opportunity are varied. They consist of:

- Alienation from the school. The decision to drop out is the final step in a progressive discontent with the school experience starting with failure or having difficulty with subjects in the elementary grades, becoming apathetic or disruptive in junior high school, having periods of absenteeism that became progressively longer, and culminating in dropping out when allowed by the law;
- Failure in subjects. Some students drop out as a result of failing to make the passing grades to be promoted to the next level. They become embarrassed and do not want

to face the ridicule of their peers. These students will often rationalize their decision by saying they dropped out because they were bored, or had better things to do;

- Drop out because of family situation, ethnic origins, poverty, language barriers, or customs of family
- Drop out as a result of physical or mental conditions. These include students who become pregnant, have severe physical or mental handicaps and feel they cannot cope with the demands of school;
- Students drop out to seek employment. Some may leave school to join the military, or to accept a job. At times their decision is based on the need to assist their families who are experiencing an economic crisis;
- Some drop out as a result of having poor social relations with teachers, fellow student; and
- Students drop out to avoid being bullied, ridiculed. Isolated and victimized by other students and school staff.

7.6 Removal from School—Suspension and Expulsion

A major conclusion reached in a study by Hirschfield (2008) was that the traditional foundation for dispensing discipline and punishment to students for violations of school rules, and even some minor criminal acts, such as trespassing, unauthorized entrance into the school building and even minor property damage, are more and more being assumed by the criminal justice system. Changes in the structure of the school systems, with students having more legal opportunities to challenge the decisions made by school officials, as well as changes in school policies, including "zero tolerance" policies have led to a decline in the discretion school administrators have in making decisions pertaining to what penalties to give for student violations. A decision to expel a student from school, if not carefully documented by evidence pertaining to the reasons for the expulsion, may result in a lawsuit being filed and extensive litigation. For example, the sections of the Michigan Complied Laws pertaining to the Revised School Code, Michigan Department of Education (2019, p. 2) allows each school board the authority to establish a local discipline policy pertaining to suspensions and expulsions. These policies must be in accordance with the sections of the Revised School Code in the Michigan Compiled Laws. In addition, to assure that the conduct rules and procedures are known by the students, the Code states, "Fairness dictates that students be given notice of the types of conduct which are prohibited and the potential consequences of the misconduct. A school's rules and procedures for suspending or expelling a student should be outlined in the handbook adopted by the local board of education." Various sections of the Code pertain to the number of days allowed for suspensions for violation of the rules, depending on the severity of the offense. For example, "If the student's presence poses a danger to persons or property or threatens to disrupt the academic process, a suspension of ten days or less is appropriate." More severe punishment, such as expulsion, is allowed for more serious offenses. For example, "A student in grade 6 or above who commits a physical assault against an employee or a volunteer of the district, at school or on school grounds, shall be expelled permanently, subject to possible reinstatement provided by the law." The Revised School Code has provisions for allowing students expelled to enter an alternative education school.

A study by Pigott et al. (2018) while not having access to information on individuals who were removed from school on disciplinary matters, but having access to aggregate data from school systems, found that the students attending larger schools located in urban areas with high amounts of crime in the neighborhoods were associated with the amount of students being removed (expelled) from the schools. In addition, the proportion of students attending the schools who had limited proficiency in the English language, and the frequency of racial tensions in the communities resulted in an increase in the level of student removals.

Baggett (2018, p. 1) referring to a study, conducted by Pamela Orpinas and colleagues, professors at the College of Public Health, University of Georgia, found that, "Although the factors that may lead to a student's decision to leave school are complex … two behaviors—aggression and weak study skills—contribute to the problem." The researchers selected students from the sixth grade attending schools in Georgia and had the teachers periodically rate the students on aggression and study skills from the sixth grade to the time of their graduation, or the time they dropped out of school. The researchers found that students in the high aggression/low study group had a 50% dropout rate, compared to the students in a low aggression/high study group. They concluded "The key to helping a student stay in school is spotting the signs and behaviors that put students at risk of dropping out early in their academic careers. Students exhibit both aggression and study skills early in school, and both behaviors have been independently associated with learning and success, or lack of it." Another study on reasons for students to drop out of school found that being bullied is a good predictor of students dropping out of school (Cornell, Gregory, Huang, & Fan, 2013). The research, completed in schools located in Virginia, obtained input from students and their teachers for a 4-year period. Data was collected on incidences of being teased and bullied in school and student decisions to drop out. They found that schools with high levels of bullying had dropout rates close to one-third above the national average for dropouts and schools with low levels of bullying had dropout rates close to one-third below the national average.

Despite the "zero tolerance" rules adopted by many school districts throughout the United States that limit the discretion of school administrator when making determinations on matters pertaining to the suspension and expulsion of students, some research would seem to indicate that school administrators still use considerable discretion when applying the rules to specific cases. Lowe (2015, p. 2), citing a report titled *Disproportionate Impact of k-12 School Suspension and Expulsion on Black Students in Southern States* completed by the University of Pennsylvania Graduate School of Education Center for the Study of Race and Equity and Education, notes, "Nationally, 1.2 million black students were suspended from k-12 public schools in a single academic year, and 55% of the suspensions occurred in 13 Southern states." Lowe (2015, p. 3) reported that "black students were most often suspended for being disrespectful and threatening, loitering, or excessive noise. However, their white classmates were likely to be referred to school discipline officers for less subjective offenses, such as smoking, leaving school classrooms or school grounds without permission, vandalism and using obscene language."

Peguero, Popp, and Shekarkhar (2015), in their research on the relationship between school officials stereotyping of minority students and punishment, focus on whether stereotypes of minority students influence the punishment of racial and ethnic minority students. The sample of students was drawn from the Education Longitudinal Study of 2002 conducted by the National Center for Educational Statistics of the U.S. Department of Education. The data used in the study included information on experiences and backgrounds of more than 10,000 students from 580 public schools. Students were asked if they ever received one of four forms of school punishment that included teacher referral, in school suspension, suspension or probation, or transfer to another school for disciplinary reasons and if they did, how many times did this occur. They found that Latino American adolescents in particular are receiving biased treatment within the schools that could include a disproportionate number of punishments. Their research found that, for Latino American adolescents, being from higher levels of family economic status and engaged in academic extracurricular activities could increase the odds and severity of school punishment, compared to other groups. Peguero et al. (2015, p. 77) stated that, "Tentative findings from this study suggest that racial and ethnic minorities who do not adhere to the stereotypes imposed on them are more vulnerable to being punished at school. In some instances, family, socioeconomic status, test scores, and academic extracurricular and interscholastic sports activity participation, which are factors that typically facilitate students' education progress and success, may be linked to racial and ethnic minorities being at increased risk of experiencing school punishment."

7.7   Alternative School Programs

Alternative programming is used by most school districts for a variety of students. These include those with special needs who not have the ability to learn or adjust in the regular classroom setting, as well as students who have been suspended from school for a long period of time, or expelled. Typically, those with special needs (no fault) and those who have been removed from the regular school (fault) will not be assigned to the same alternative school program. However, discretion must be used when making decisions on the appropriate alternative school for those students suspended or expelled for disciplinary reasons, if their exclusion from school might be related to their learning disabilities.

Alternative programming usually involves small class sizes and testing to determine the student's entering level of competency and potential. Individual attention, behavioral contracting, and assistance may be given with special problems students may face, such as providing day care for small children, so that their teenage mothers can attend classes.

Fantini (1976) noted that alternative schools were developed in the United States during the early 1970s as options to the conventional school experience in the hope that the high risk student dropout population would have its needs better served. More than 2500 alternative school programs developed in the 1970s. Many of them funded through grants, but many of these eventually closed once the grant money was terminated. The alternative schools currently in operation throughout the United States generally have common goals and have similar structures and programming. They operate to meet various types of student needs, including security (offering a safe and orderly learning environment), social needs (through development of new peer and adult networks), self-esteem (by encouraging both academic and social achievement), and self-actualization needs (increasing the students' motivation toward becoming socially integrated individual). These needs, important for all students, are given intensive attention in alternative programs, with the goal of helping at risk adolescents succeed and remain in school.

The alternative school described in Box 7.1, the Phoenix Program, was first established in 1972. The buildings in which it was housed and the teaching personnel changed several times, but the goals of the program have remained essentially the same as they were at its inception.

Box 7.1 YMCA Phoenix Alternative Program/Barrett Alternative Program

Dezolt and Kratcoski (1992) examined this program, an alternative project for delinquent youths in Summit County, Ohio, that has demonstrated success in attacking the drop out problem. The program involves an academic program that stresses basic reading, writing and math skills; a behavior change component which includes a point-accumulation system for acceptable behavior and rule compliance in school and at home; and individual and group counseling. On its website, The Phoenix School is described in this way:

"Since 1972, the YMCA Phoenix Alternative School is recognized throughout the country as a pioneer in providing education and behavioral modification management services for special needs students referred by local public school districts or the Summit County Juvenile Court. This school serves nearly 200 youths per year, in grades 4-12, who are unable to maintain proper behavior in a traditional school setting..... The East Akron YMCA also sponsors the Minority Achievers Program, which is funded by the Akron Community Foundation, City of Akron, and Ranstad USA.... The YMCA Phoenix Alternative School creates a positive change in the student's attitude and view of life. The program challenges the student to take responsibility for his or her actions. With a strong emphasis on discipline and character development, the program provides the student with the behavioral management tools needed to achieve their goals." (Source: East Akron YMCA Phoenix Program, 2019, p. 1).

7.8　The Amount of Crime in Schools

In the FBI Report, *Crimes in Schools and Colleges* (2016, p. 4), an overview of the trends of crimes reported in the schools for the years 2000 through 2004 is given. Of the 17,065,074 incidences reported for that 5-year period, the total for all locations for each year and the total of crimes reported for all schools tended to increase. There were 558,219 (3.3% of the total) crimes reported that occurred in schools or on school grounds. While this may seem to be a low percentage, one must keep in mind that the population of the schools and colleges is a small proportion of the total population of the United States. The number of arrests for crimes committed in the school totaled 181,468. This constitutes 32.5% of the total. It should also be pointed out that the percentage of arrests for crimes reported in the schools tended to increase each year from 2000 through 2004. For example, in 2000, 29.1% of the crimes reported resulted in arrests, in 2001, 33.3% of reported crimes resulted in arrests, in 2002, 27.8% of reported crimes ended in arrests, in 2003, 31% of reported crimes ended arrests, and in 2004, 32.6% of reported crimes ended in arrests (FBI, Crimes in Schools and Colleges, 2016, p. 4). For the 5-year period, the average for the crimes reported that ended with an arrest was slightly less than one-third.

7.8.1　Characteristics of Offenders

The predominate age category for known offenders was ages 13–15 (38%), followed by the ages 16–18 age category (30.7%). The gender of the known offenders was predominately male (76.6%). The race for the known offenders was 71.1% white, 27.4% black, and all other races less than 2% (FBI, Crimes in Schools and Colleges, 2016, p. 5). The relationship of the offender and the victim for those known offenders consisted predominately of "acquaintance" and otherwise known. The number of victim-stranger incidences was very small compared to the total. The offenders who were known to the victim consisted of friends, classmates, neighbors, and siblings (FBI, Crimes in Schools and Colleges, 2016, p. 6). The peak months of the year for crimes to occur in the schools were October, March, and September. The time of the crime is often difficult to ascertain, since some crimes, in particular vandalism, may have occurred on the weekends, but were not detected until Monday morning. The most common type of weapons used were personal weapons (the offenders' hands, fists, feet). Handguns and other types of firearms such as shotguns and rifles made up the next largest category of weapons, but use of personal weapons was reported 3.4 more often than all other weapons combined (FBI, Crimes in Schools and Colleges, 2016, p. 7).

7.8.2   Types of Offenses Reported

For offenses against persons, simple assault constituted the largest category (more than ¾ of the total). This was followed by intimidation, aggravated assault, and forcible fondling. Only 2.7% of the total consisted of murder and nonnegligent manslaughter. Other crimes against persons reported consisted of forcible rape, kidnapping and abduction, negligent *manslaughter, and statutory rape.* When comparing the crimes against persons in the schools for 2000 with those of 2004, the statistics reveal that the number of crimes against persons reported increased by more than 73% (FBI, Crimes in Schools and Colleges, p. 8). This large increase does not necessarily mean that the student populations had become more violent. Several factors might explain the increase, including a larger student population, as well the fact that a larger proportion of crimes against persons were detected and reported. The antibullying programs and improved security programs instituted in the schools no doubt had an effect on the reporting and detection of crimes against persons in the schools.

7.8.3   Property Crimes in the Schools

Property crime frequently committed in the schools include:

- Destruction of property/vandalism;
- Larceny, burglary;
- Breaking and entering;
- Stolen property offenses;
- Arson; and
- Theft from motor vehicle.

Most of the other property crimes, such as credit card fraud or bribery, were very infrequently reported, probably because of the lack of opportunity for the offender to commit such crimes in the schools. Destruction/damage/vandalism of property constituted 24% of all property crimes for the 5-year period. When property crimes for the year 2000 were compared with those of 2004, the total number of property crimes increased by 60.3%.

The most frequently reported crimes against society were drug/narcotic violations, weapon law violations, drug equipment violations and disorderly conduct. Other crimes, such as trespass, liquor law violations, and drunkenness, constituted a small proportion of the total number of crimes against society that occurred in the schools (FBI, Crimes in Schools and Colleges, p. 8).

7.8.4 Arrestees of Crimes in Schools

The characteristics of those arrested for crimes in schools followed the same patterns as the crimes reported in which the offender/s was known. In regard to age, almost 75% were in the age categories 13–18 years old, more than 75% were male, almost 75% were white, and 25% were black (FBI, Crimes in Schools and Colleges, p. 8). The residency of those arrested consisted of 37% being a resident of the community in which the crime occurred and the others were either nonresidents or the residency was unknown (FBI, Crimes in Schools and Colleges, 2016, p. 9).

A report by the National Institute of Justice on victimization in primary and secondary school for the year 2012 revealed that theft, violent crime and student homicides declined over the past decade (National Institute of Justice, 2012 modified 2016, p. 1). In the report, it is stated that, "A growing body of evidence shows that violence prevention programs can help to reduce opportunities for criminal behaviors and effectively instruct young people on other ways to resolve conflict and express their feelings safely. Schools and communities can work together to make these programs available and prevent violence before it occurs." However, Robers, Zhang, Morgan, and Musu-Gillette (2015) found that in 2013 almost one-fourth of the students in the schools in the United States reported that they had been offered drugs, sold drugs, or were given drugs on school property. In addition, 22% indicated that they were bullied, and 75 claimed to have been threatened or injured with a weapon. These statistics and those given above might be construed to mean that schools are, if not dangerous places for children, at least places where the children attending the schools are likely to become victims of either personal or property crime. However, when one compares the number of children victimized in any given year with the number of children who have attended schools in that year, it becomes apparent that the proportion of students victimized is quite low. However, when a school experiences a shooting, and especially a mass killing, the citizenry, with the help of the mass media, perceive the schools as being dangerous places and they often react with concern for the safety of the children and demand that measures be taken to improve the safety of the children attending the schools.

7.9 School Shootings

Zhang, Musu-Gillette, and Qudekerk (2016, p. 2) report that "In 2014, there were about 486,400 nonfatal violent victimizations at school among students 12 to 18 years of age in U.S. schools." During the academic year 2012–2013, there were 31 homicides of school-age youths that occurred in the schools or on school grounds. While schools may be considered dangerous places, and the large number of nonfatal violent victimizations would tend to confirm that they are dangerous, in regard to homicides, the 31 homicides that occurred in the schools during the 2012–2013 academic year represented only 2.6% of the total number of homicides among youth homicides that occurred during the same time period (Zhang et al., 2016).

The report of Everytown for Gun Safety (2016, p. 1) notes that "Since 2013, there have been at least 199 school shooting in America—an average of nearly one a week." The same report (2016, p. 2) defines a school shooting as "anytime a firearm is discharged inside a school building or on a school campus or grounds, as documented by the press and confirmed through further inquiries with law enforcement.

Incidents in which guns were brought into the schools but not fired, or were fired off school grounds after having been possessed in schools, are not included." Information Please (2016) constructed a timetable of worldwide school and other mass shootings starting with the year 1996 and ending with Oct.18, 2016. During that period, there were 92 incidents of school shootings, many of these involving mass shootings. Of these, 76 (84%) occurred in U.S. schools and 24 (16%) occurred in the schools of other countries, including countries from Europe, Africa, Asia, Australia, Central America, and South America. The number of victims involved in each school shooting incident ranged from 1 to more than 25. Not all incidents involved a victim other than the shooter, who in some cases took his own life. In 2012, at the Sandy Hook Elementary School, Newtown, Connecticut, a gunman killed 26 students, teachers, and staff before killing himself.

7.9.1   Victims of School Violence

The National Center for Injury Prevention and Control (2016, p. 2) suggests that a number of factors are conducive to increasing the risk of a student being a perpetrator of violence. These include:

- Having a prior history of violence;
- Being involved with drug, alcohol, or tobacco use;
- Having delinquent associations;
- Being a member of a disorganized family; and
- Having poor grades in school; and living in a poverty stricken community.

The factors listed above do not necessarily mean that students having one or several of these characteristics will become involved in school violence. Other factors may be involved that motivate those who commit violence and kill others. In some of the worst shootings in terms of the number killed, none of the items above seemed to be factors relating to the perpetuator/s of the murders.

7.9.1.1   Terrorist Attacks on Schools

Bradford and Wilson (2013) completed a comprehensive chronology of all terrorist armed assaults on educational institutions throughout the world. They used the Global Terrorism Database and several other sources of information, such as government documents, academic journals, and the Mickolus edited reference series as a database (Bradford & Wilson, 2013, p. 129). In order to be included as a terrorist

incident in their database, an incident had to have had two of the following characteristics. The act had to be aimed at attaining a political, economic, religious, or
social goal, there had to be evidence of an intention to coerce, intimidate, or convey
some other message to a wider audience than the victims directly targeted by the
attack, or the act occurred outside the context of legitimate warfare. Between 1980
and 2010, there were 146 incidents (terrorist attacks on educational institutions) that
were recorded. None of the terrorist attacks that fit the definition used occurred in the
United States. After analyzing the terrorist attacks on the schools included in their
study, Bradford and Wilson (2013, p. 137) concluded, "Although terrorist attacks on
schools are rare, they can cause severe emotional, psychological, and financial damage. Being prepared for such an event reduces their destructive potential." They suggest that school systems should develop the types of emergency messages that were
adopted in the United States to respond to emergencies and school shootings.

Bradford and Wilson may have been somewhat optimistic with their assessment
of the effectiveness of the models used in the school systems developed in the
United States for school security and the prevention of school shootings and terrorist attacks. Mass shootings such as Columbine and others did lead to the development and implementation of security systems in the many schools throughout the
United States, but as noted by Kratcoski et al. (2012, p. 198), given the governing
and jurisdictional models used by the administration of schools in the United States,
"A nationwide strategy for the prevention of school violence and security has never
been developed. Elementary and high school education systems are locally controlled and supported by local taxes, with some support from state and federal governments. School board members of a local system tend to be concerned only with
the problems of their schools."

7.9.1.2 Bullying in Schools, in the Community and on the Internet

Although bullying, aggressive behavior of one or more persons toward a person or
persons perceived as weaker, has been a common practice in schools throughout
history, it has not gained considerable attention until recently. No doubt, the majority of former and current students can remember at least one incident of being bullied. Acts that fall under a broad definition of "bullying" include any form of
physical or verbal abuse, including threats and insults. With the advent of electronic
communications, much of the current bullying is conducted by way of "cyberbully-
ing," that is, by e-mail, cell phones, social media, and chat rooms.

7.9.2 Approaches to Prevention of Bullying in the Schools

Choi, Cronin, and Correia (2016, p. 150) discuss the use of Routine Activity Theory
(RAT) as a way police can work with the school administration and school personnel to reduce the amount of bullying in the schools. The authors suggest that,

"through application of community based policing practices, officers may also be able to foster trust between students and law enforcement to facilitate open communications about bullying and other crime concerns with the school." The authors employed a qualitative approach, using interviews of police officers to collect data on how officers view their role in promoting safety within the schools. In addition, officers were asked to provide recommendations on ways to improve security.

Choi et al. (2016, p. 154) noted, "Officers viewed their highly visible position and unique authority (over the school administration in criminal related matters) as an asset to collecting information and intervening in developing situations that had the potential to becoming criminal." Officers suggested that their mere presence on school grounds and engaging with students on school grounds by taking part in extra-curriculum activity and making a connection with the students is important in building the trust between the students and the police that is needed to build a preventive atmosphere in the schools. Choi et al. (2016, p. 155) stated, "Most young people could report instances where they felt bullied in the school, but bullying victimization experiences vary considerably by a variety of risk factors, according to risk surveys."

Policing literature has long recognized that building connections to and developing trust between groups differentially impacted by particular crime problems is an important step to effective prevention and response. Individuals that are reluctant to report victimization experiences to capable guardians (police, school officials) for a variety of reasons (lack of trust, concerns about the responses, fear of future victimization) could be a higher risk for victimization. The police in the schools following a community police approach can establish good communications with the students and this can place them in a position to prevent developing bullying situations before they materialize. The respondents also indicated that the police assigned to schools (School resource officers) must be careful in their eagerness to protect the students and to assure a safe environment that they do not become involved in responding to student misconduct matters that only pertain to violations of school policy and not criminal matters. In addition, they must not become overzealous by assisting the school administration in bullying and other student conduct situations in such a way that what started as a matter of violation of school rules does not turn into a criminal conduct matter.

Johnson, Burke, and Gielen (2011) surveyed students on the question of in what ways do the police and school personnel contribute to the development of a positive atmosphere in the school and in what ways do their actions contribute to a negative atmosphere, and encourage bullying in the schools. The student responses pertaining to the negatives associated with the police and school administration, included teachers being disrespectful toward students, and not providing security in those places in which bullying is likely to occur in the school building or on school grounds. Other factors mentioned by students were police and teachers not being interested in the welfare of the students and police not being friendly. On the positive side, the factors that the students surveyed mentioned that enhanced the school experience were related to police caring about the welfare of students, taking action when students are unruly, police being aware of what is happening in the school, police interacting with the students and police not being unnecessarily harsh with students. The authors concluded that when teachers, school administrators, and the police assigned to the school work together to develop an informal guardianship, based on trust and a willingness to share information, the students will become more supportive of the police in the schools and bullying as well as other problems relating to the safety and security of the schools will decline.

7.9.3 Security Programs to Prevent School Shootings and Violence

The initial response to the threat of violence, including mass killings by students and/or persons outside the school population (parents, former students, terrorist groups), by school administrators in the United States was somewhat disjointed and tended to concentrate on improving the electrical surveillance systems used to monitor the school building and the movement of persons entering the building. Sugal, Sprague, Horner, and Walker (2000) contend that the general reaction of school administrators after a violent incident occurred in their school was to institute new security measures such as technical devices and to restrict the movement and activities of the students.

Kratcoski et al. (2012) completed a survey of school administrators, teachers, and security personnel from 35 school districts representing middle schools and high schools in small towns, large and medium sized cities and suburban communities. They found that the school security systems could be categorized into one of three models. Several of the school districts employed a private security model. In these school districts, security staff, under the direct authority of the school district, developed the security system, implemented it, and were responsible for the day by day activities. The local police or federal law enforcement agents became involved in cases where violations of state or federal laws occurred.

A second model found in the research was the police in the schools model. Kratcoski et al. (2012, p. 203) state, "Districts using the police in the schools model had security policies and programs designed by the school administration and carried out by police officers employed by the local department who were assigned to work in the schools, generally as SROs." The roles of the Security Resource Officers (SROs) were similar to those of officers involved in community policing. The third security model found can be referred to as the school administration model. This model was found in small school districts where there were minimal problems with school violence and the threat of an outside attack on the school seemed unlikely. The school security plans were developed and implemented by the school administrator. These school districts generally had one small high school, one middle school, and one or two elementary schools. The major changes in security were made in response to mass school shootings that were publicized and analyzed by law enforcement officials and the news media. The changes in school policies typically involved the implementation of a "zero tolerance" policy for violations of school policies, particularly in cases involving threats to the safety of students and school personnel. If a crime was suspected or observed by any member of the administration, the local police were called in. If a student committed even minor infractions of some rules, such as bringing a small knife into the school building, the student was suspended from school. The school administrators who followed the school administration model contended that the effectiveness of the school administration model can be attributed to the positive communications, cooperation and good working relationships between the community, the local law enforcement agencies, and the school administrators. The school administrators who followed this model were quick to admit that the school administration security model would probably not be effective in large school systems where communications and cooperation of the school administrators with the police and the community would *not be as easy to establish*. In addition, several of the administrators stated that they had to back off somewhat on the "zero tolerance" policies. This was accomplished by the school administrators using more discretion when reviewing noncriminal acts of students and by taking the circumstances into consideration before making decisions.

A study on delinquency prevention in schools in the United States (Gottfredson et al., 2004) found that the typical school operates an average of 14 programs or activities related to crime prevention and school security. These programs run the gamut from inserting new security cameras or lighting to rather complex projects that involve the community. Their research on school security programs found that the typical program used private security or police in the school. School administrations tended to focus on assuring the safety and security of the students and school staff within the school building by preventing or controlling students who were disruptive or violent and providing safety measures that would prevent threats from external sources. As the treat of terrorist attacks on schools became a possibility, school emergency event training response plans that normally included fire drills, or exercises in responding to natural disasters, such as a tornados or floods, began to include drills on responding to terrorist attacks and mass shootings. State governments began to require each school district to have a plan and periodic training for teachers and students in place for such possibilities.

Cech (2016, p. 1) completed a literature review of books, journal articles, training guides, and government documents pertaining to how to conduct school drills for cases involving "school shooters." He concluded, "Active-shooter training is about practicing response mechanisms to remain calm and safe while following a protocol. The mechanisms are to run away and bring nothing along with you. Second, it is to hide in an area out of the shooter's view. Block the entry to your hiding place, block the doors and silence the cell phones. Third, is to fight as the last resort and only when your life is in danger. Attempt to incapacitate the shooter and throw items at the shooter. The reasoning behind the protocol is that an active-shooter is running wild without any direction, only desiring to kill as many people in a short period of time that he can." Cech (2016, p. 2) came to the conclusion that there is not enough research available to provide answers as to what approach in responding to active shooters in schools is the most likely to be effective in securing the safety of those students, teachers, and staff who are involved in the situation.

The research on school shooters, including terrorist groups who attack schools, reveals that they have a variety of characteristics, different motives, and goals and thus are difficult to fit in one neat category. Cech states that schools that have only one lockdown procedure for responding to all types of disasters, natural and man-made, and provide training for the school personnel in this one procedure are likely to fail in their response to school shooter situations. He states (2016, p. 4), "There are a variety of codes used in school and under pressure they can be misconstrued." It is apparent that matters relating to what protocol should be followed in an active shooter lockdown situation as opposed to a tornado code or fire code must be clarified in the training. Also, there must be a protocol for the most effective communication pattern, including who is in command and has the authority to call a lockdown of the school if the person who normally has the authority to do this is not available at the time the lockdown is required.

7.9.3.1 The Use of School Resource Officers: A School, Police, Community Team Approach

The report, *To Protect and Educate: The School Resource Officer and the Prevention of Violence in Schools,* produced by The National Association of School Resource Officers (NASRO) was published in 2012 (Canady, James, & Nease, 2012). The goal of the report was to provide information about the role of SROs in the schools in terms of the assistance they provide to school policymakers when developing policies and implementing programs pertaining to school safety. In the report (Canady et al., 2012, p. 7), the role of the SRO working in public schools is described as assisting school policy makers in merging information and resources, helping to eliminate disruptions in normal school operations, reducing victimization in the schools, increasing pupil attendance, and improving the learning environment. The report also addresses some of the criticisms of the SRO programs, in particular the notion that the SRO is "ill-suited to the education environment, a source of confusion and intimidation on campus, and responsible for an increase in the number of referrals from schools to the juvenile justice system" (Canady et al., 2012, p. 8). In addition, the report provides evidence that there is no correlation between the presence of SRO on the school campus and an increase in crime on that campus. In fact, evidence is offered in the report that indicates exactly the opposite. (Canady et al., 2012, p. 11)

The report (Canady et al., 2012, p. 17) notes that the failure of the schools, child welfare agencies, and the police to cooperate and share information before and after 9/11 has resulted in wasted opportunities to enhance school security, to prevent victimization in the schools, and to create a school environment more conducive to learning. The child welfare team approach reduces the barriers that create agency isolation (Canady et al., 2012, p. 17). This collaborative model uses the numerous statutory provisions relating to the welfare of children. These laws authorize or require some aspects of interagency teamwork in providing services to children and their families. While each public or private agency on the "team" remains distinct as to statutory obligations, the agencies work together to produce the best possible outcomes for the children. In the report (Canady et al., 2012, pp. 18–19), it is stated that, "School resource officers assist educators in protecting the students and the education mission by being an active part of at least three education-initiated strategies. These include safe school training, purposeful use of technology, and effective use of inter-agency partnerships." The major portion of the report is devoted to offering empirical evidence grounded in research to show that these strategies are actually working.

Sneed (2015, p. 3), referring to figures from a Congressional Research Report, stated that in 1997 there were approximately 12,500 full time school resource officers employed by local law enforcement agencies. The number increased to almost 20,000 in 2003, but declined to approximately 18,000 in 2007.

7.9.3.2 Potential for Role Conflict for Police in Schools

Coon and Travis (2012) completed research to determine if the role expectations of School Resource Officers are compatible with the role expectations of police officers in general. Since the onset of having police officers assigned to schools on a regular basis, there has been debate over the appropriate part they should play in regard to school security, such as when it is appropriate for SROs to discipline students who violate school rules and policies and what is the authority relationship between school administrators and police officers in such matters.

Although much of the earlier resistance to having police in the schools that came from students and school administrators has dissipated, there still are some differences of opinion as to what should be their role, that is, what tasks should they perform. To address these questions, Coon and Travis (2012) selected a sample of public schools that represented the various characteristics of public schools throughout the United States. A questionnaire developed from a previously used instrument that was used in the school Survey of Crime and Safety was pretested and disturbed to the school administrators included in the sample. A question in the instrument asked the principals to identify the policing agencies that had police officers assigned to their school/s on a regular basis. Most of the principals mentioned only one police agency. Some principals indicated that there was no need for police on their campus, and several others indicated that they used private security agencies or had implemented their own system. The chiefs of police of those agencies that were specifically identified by the school principals (1508 police agencies) were sent a questionnaire that included questions about the role of the police officers that were assigned to the schools. The police chiefs and the principals were asked how involved SROs were in 60 functions and activities that pertained to the school. Coon and Travis (2012, p. 21) stated, "These activities included traditional law enforcement-related matters (patrolling school grounds, advising/mentoring staff on avoiding violence/victimization, advising/mentoring groups (e.g., police athletic leagues), advising/mentoring students and families (e.g., helping students with court involvement or intervention), presence at school events (e.g., presence for athletic events), teaching (e.g., anti-drug classes), and involvement in safety plans or meeting with schools (e.g., helping the school develop written plans for crisis situations))."

The analysis of the responses revealed that the police chiefs and school principals were in the highest level of agreement on the SROs participation in those activities that pertained to law enforcement. In regard to other activities, the principals and the police chiefs were in agreement that the SROs participated to some extent in the activities mentioned, but the level of participation estimated by the police chiefs was much higher than that of the principals, with the one exception of writing disciplinary reports. There was common agreement that advising and mentoring of students and their families was an activity in which the SROs frequently participated. School principals reported that the officers assigned to their schools assisted in creating a written plan to deal with bomb scares or other schoolwide threats at a significantly higher frequency than the police chiefs reported. In trying to explain the reasons for the differences in perception of SROs' participation in school-related activities, the authors suggest that both school principals and police chiefs may not be aware of all of the activities the SROs engage in on a fairly regular basis. The police chiefs may be more aware than the school principals of the law enforcement proactive prevention activities of the SRO officers, since some of these activities may not come to the attention of the principals unless there is some type of major incident. For example, SROs tend to follow a community policing approach, and as a result some incidents of student misbehavior detected by the police are diverted from any formal action. On the other hand, the school principals are likely to be aware of SROs' participation in meetings directed toward the improvement of security in the school or development of a plan for responding to crises.

In summary, it would appear that this study confirms the NASRO Report on the range and types of tasks School Resource Officers perform. The matter of how frequently they engage in some acts, such as teaching, advising, and assisting in the development of school security plans, is a matter that might differ in each school, depending on the working agreement between the school administration and the police.

The individual characteristics of the officers, as well as the officers' enjoyment of the work, may have an effect on the day-to-day activities of the officers. Finn (2006, p. 17) concluded that, "The main benefits of the STO programs have been defined as reducing the frequency of patrol officers visiting the schools, improving the image of police officers among juveniles, and fostering better relationships between the police and the schools."

7.10   Summary

In this chapter the problems of school-related delinquency have been examined. The dramatic amounts of violent behavior, vandalism, and drug and alcohol use by high school students were highlighted, as well as the financial difficulties, failing achievement levels, truancy, absenteeism, and dropout problems encountered by the schools.

When delinquency is school-related, it may be the result of socialization difficulties experienced there by some children. Those from disadvantaged backgrounds may come to school without mastery of the basic skills needed to succeed, and perhaps without needed clothing and food. The inability of the schools to provide resources that are not their responsibility may handicap efforts to teach these children. Insensitivity of some teachers to the backgrounds and problems of such children is also destructive of school progress. In many instances, parents identify the school as the nearest and most accessible source of assistance with their problems and rely on the social and counseling services provided there, even though they may be minimal.

The impersonal, bureaucratic atmosphere in some schools is also blamed for student socialization problems. Large classes, strict regulations regarding movement within the school, and lack of opportunity for interaction with teachers on a one-to-one basis all contribute to truancy, absenteeism, or a climate that makes both teaching and learning difficult. Fear of physical violence either going to or coming from school or within the school building may contribute to truancy and absenteeism. A lack of social standing in the school is another variable in the production of delinquent behavior. While socially successful students must be careful to preserve their reputations and maintain their images, those who are not so defined have little to lose by not conforming. Young people who do not see a relationship between school programs and their future status, or who are not involved in school activities, have been found to have higher rates of delinquency. Those who are defined as "college-bound" are less likely to engage in delinquent acts that jeopardize their futures. Academic failure has also been correlated with delinquency. Such factors as having a learning disability or a mental or physical handicap have been shown to be associated with delinquency. Some children with normal or above-average intelligence who have reading disabilities experience frustration and defeat, and they may act out their frustrations through aggressive or other forms of disruptive behavior. The relation between dropping out of school and delinquency is a complex one. Dropping out emerges as another progressive step in a delinquency-endangered youth's alienation and isolation from society. Violations of school rules and policies such as truancy or showing defiance toward a teacher can have serious consequences for the student and may result in being suspended or expelled.

Although the large majority of students who are victimized in the schools are victimized by other students, attacks on students and staff that occurred in several schools resulted in students, teachers and school officials being murdered, or physically harmed. The mass murders of students and school staff in which the offender/s were often not students of the schools have vividly shown how vulnerable the schools are to becoming victims and highlight the need for developing new and better security programs in the schools. One response to such incidents in the United States was to increase cooperation between the schools, police, and the communities they serve. The police have been involved in many schools for a number of years, beginning with the community policing efforts of the 1970s and the School Resource Officer (SRO) programs. SROs are trained in community policing and emphasize the type of cooperation, coordination and communications required to be effective in crime prevention in the schools and in reducing the amount of victimization. SROs perform many other roles in the schools in addition to law enforcement, including teaching, security planning, and counseling of students. Research on the effectiveness of SROs reveals that they may be particularly effective in the prevention of crimes against persons, particularly those related to bullying in the schools, and they have been effective in working with community child protection agencies and police departments in detecting various forms of child abuse.

7.11 Discussion Questions

1. What are the changes in American society that have forced the schools to assume a number of the socialization functions that were formerly performed by the family?
2. How does fear of physical violence affect student attendance and involvement in school activities? Describe some programs that have been initiated to make schools safer for teachers and students.
3. What are the most important factors that influence youths to drop out of school? What should schools do to reduce the influence of these factors?
4. Several experts on education have recommended that compulsory school attendance laws be changed so that a young person could drop out of school around the age of 14 or 15. Do you agree? What are the possible negative consequences of such a policy?
5. Define school environment. What are some of the factors that contribute to making the school environment conducive to learning? What are some of the factors that make the school environment an oppressive environment for students?
6. Discuss some the measures school administrators have taken to make the school building and grounds safe and secure for students.
7. Discuss the relationship between learning disabilities of students and delinquent behavior in the schools.
8. What are alternative schools? Discuss the characteristics of the students who enrolled in alternative schools.
9. Discuss the reasons for the increase of violence in the schools. What are the characteristics of the victims of crimes in the schools?
10. What are some of the findings of the research on the characteristics of students who engage in mass shootings in the schools?

References

Baggett, L. (2018). *Two behaviors linked to high school dropout rates*. Accessed 3/8/2019 from, http://www.phys.org/news/2018-03-behaviors-linked-high-school-dropout.htmi.

Bradford, E., & Wilson, M. (2013). When terrorists target schools: An exploratory analysis of attacks on educational institutions. *Journal of Police and Criminal Psychology, 28*, 127–138.

Canady, M., James, B., & Nease, J. (2012). *To protect and educate: The school resource officer and the prevention of violence in schools*. Washington, DC: National Association of School Resource Officers.

Cech, P. (2016). *Police psychology/active school shooter drills: A reflection; A request in inside police psychology.* pp. 1–3. Accessed 10/6/2016 from http://www.policepsychologyblog.com/?p=4269.

Choi, K., Cronin, S., & Correia, H. (2016). The assessment of capable guardianship measures against bullying victimization in the school environment. *Police Practice and Research, 17*(2), 149–159.

Coon, J., & Travis, L. (2012). The role of police in public schools: A comparison of principal and police reports of activities in schools. *Police Practice and Research, 13*(1), 15–30.

Cornell, D., Gregory, A., Huang, F., & Fan, X. (2013). Perceived prevalence of teasing and bullying predicts high school dropout rates. *Journal of Educational Psychology, 105*(1), 138–149.

DeZolt, E., & Kratcoski, P. (1992, March). Alternative education: Another change for delinquents. Unpublished paper presented at the annual meeting of the Academy of Criminal Justices Sciences, Pittsburgh, PA, pp. 1–23.

East Akron YMCA. (2019). *YMCA Phoenix Alternative Program/Barrett Alternative Program.* Retrieved July 6, 2019, from https://www.kronymca.org/EastAkron/PhoenixSchool/

Everytown for Gun Safety. (2016). *199 school shootings in America since 2013.* pp. 1–61. Retrieved October 23, 2016, from http://www.everytownresearch.org/school-shootings

Fantini, M. (1976). *Alternative education: A source book for parents, teachers, students, and administrators.* Garden City, NY: Anchor Books.

Federal Bureau of Investigation. (2016). *Crimes in schools and colleges.* Washington, DC: U.S. Department of Justice.

Finn, P. (2006). School resource officer programs: Finding the funding, reaping the benefits. *FBI Law Enforcement Bulletin, 8*(August), 1–17.

Fisher, B., Viano, S., Curran, E., Pearman, F., & Gardella, J. (2018). Students' feelings of safety, exposure to violence, and victimization, and authoritative school climate. *American Journal of Criminal Justice, 43*, 6–25.

Gillispie, M. (2017, May 12). Boy, 8, assaulted at school before killing self. *Akron Beacon Journal,* p. B5.

Gottfredson, G., Gottfredson, E., Czeh, E., Cantor, S., Crosse, B., & Hantman, I. (2004). In National Institute of Justice in Brief (Ed.), *Toward safe schools: The national study of delinquency prevention in schools.* Washington, DC: U.S. Department of Justice.

Hirschfield, P. (2008). Preparing for prison? The criminalization of the school discipline in the U.S.A. *Theoretical Criminology, 12*(79), 79–113.

Information Please. (2016). Time line of worldwide school and mass shootings. Retrieved November 1, 2016, from http:www.infoplease.com/ipa/A0777958./html.

Johnson, S., Burke, J., & Gielen, A. (2011). Prioritizing the school environment in school violence prevention efforts. *Journal of School Health, 81*, 331–340.

Kratcoski, P., Edelbacher, M., Graff, D., & Norden, G. (2012). School security: A comparison between Austria and the United States. In P. Kratcoski (Ed.), *Juvenile justice administration* (pp. 197–216). Boca Raton, FL: CRC Press.

Kratcoski, P. C. (2012). Law enforcement administration of juvenile justice in the United States. In P. C. Kratcoski (Ed.), *Juvenile justice administration* (pp. 131–156). Boca Raton, FL: CRC Press/Taylor & Francis Group.

Kratcoski, P. C. (2019). Personal conversation with student.

Lowe, F. (2015). Schools of suspensions and expulsions. *Blackmans Street.Today,* pp. 1–7. Retrieved March 8, 2015, from http://www.northstarnewstoday.com/news/schools-of-suspensions-and-expulsions/

McBurnett, K., Llahe, B. B., & Pfiffner, L. J. (1993). Diagnosis of attention deficit disorders in DSM-IV: Scientific basis and implications for education. *Exceptional Children, 60*(2), 108–117.

Michigan Department of Education. (2019). *Suspensions and expulsions.* Retrieved March 9, 2019, from http://www.michigan.gov/studentissues.

National Center for Education Statistics. (1998). *Status dropout rates.* Retrieved March 8, 2019, from http://www.nces.ed.gov/programs/coe/indicator_coj.asp

National Center for Education Statistics. (2018). *Status dropout rates*. Retrieved March 8, 2019, from http://www.nces.ed.gov/programs/coe/indicator_coj.asp

National Center for Injury Prevention and Control division of Violence Prevention (2016). *Understanding school violence*, pp. 1–3. Retrieved October 25, 2016, from http://www.cdc. gov/violenceprevention/pdf/School_Violence_Fact-Sheet-apdf

National Council of Juvenile and Family Court Judges. (1987). *Learning disabilities and the juvenile justice system*. Reno, NV: National Council of Juvenile and Family Court Judges.

National Institute of Justice. (2012, modified 5/14/2016). *School crime and safety*. Washington, DC: U.S. Department of Justice, Office of Justice Programs. Accessed 10/19/2016 from http:// www.nij.gov/topics/crime/schoolcrime/Pages/welcome.aspx

NCED Report (2018) - The citation in the text should be NCES report (2018) instead of NCED Report (2018) The reference is National Center for Education Statistics (2018). Status dropout rates. https://nces.ed.gov/programs/coe/indicator_coj.asp. Accessed 3/8/2019/

Peguero, A., Popp, A., & Shekarkhar, Z. (2015). Breaking stereotypes and school punishment: Family socioeconomic status, test scores, academic and sport activities, backlash, and racial and ethnic discipline disparities. *Journal of Ethnicity in Criminal Justice, 13*(1), 59–86.

Pigott, C., Sterns, A., & Khey, D. (2018). School resource officers and the school to prison pipeline: Discovering trends of expulsion in public schools. *American Journal of Criminal Justice, 43*, 120–138.

Platt, A., (1969). *The child savers: The invention of delinquency*. Chicago: University of Chicago Press.

Robers, S., Zhang, A., Morgan, R., & Musu-Gillette, L. (2015). *Indicators of school crime and safety-2014. (NCES2015-072NCJ248036)*. Washington, DC: National Center for Education Statistics; U.S. Department of Education, and Bureau of Justice Statistics, Office of Justice Programs, U.S. Department of Justice.

Sneed, T. (2015). School resource officers: Safety priority or part of the problem? News(//www/ USNEWS.COM/NEWS).

Steinberg, M., Allensworth, E., & Johnson, D. (2018). *Student and teacher safety in Chicago Public Schools: The roles of community context and school social organization*. Retrieved from http://files.eric.ed.gov/fulltext/EDS519414.pdf

Sugal, G., Sprague, H., Horner, H., & Walker, H. (2000). Preventing school violence: The use of office discipline referrals to assess and monitor school-wide discipline interventions. *Journal of Emotional and Behavioral Disorders, 8*(3), 94–101.

Welsh, W. (2001). Effects of student and school factors on five measures of school disorder. *Justice Quarterly, 18*(4), 911–947.

Zhang, A., Musu-Gillette, L., & Qudekerk, B. (2016). *Indicators of school crime and safety: 2015 (NCES 2016-079/NCJ 249758)*. Washington, DC: Office of Justice Programs, U.S. Department of Justice.

Part II
Youth in the Juvenile Justice System

In this part , Chap. 8 presents a broad overview of the legislation enacted by the states and the federal government related to the rights of children who have been victimized through physical and psychological abuse and neglect and also presents the significant court decisions on these matters. Juveniles as either serious or minor offenders are described. A short history of the juvenile justice system provides information on its development as a legal system to address the special needs of juveniles.

Chapter 9 focuses on the difficulties in estimating the amount of physical and psychological abuse of children that occurs each year, which most professionals who work in juvenile justice believe is much more frequent than official statistics indicate. Sexual abuse of children is also believed to be vastly underreported.

Children who have been identified as high risk for child abuse include those who for some reason need a great deal more attention than usually required or whose parents do not have the experience or maturity to properly care for a child. Those at risk include babies, children of very young parents, children with single mothers, premature children, those with physical deformities, and children of parents who are experiencing physical or psychological problems and may abuse their children to relieve their own frustrations.

Child welfare agencies and the courts become involved when investigation of a complaint reveals that claims of abuse or neglect can be substantiated. The majority of cases are handled informally, but in some cases the courts will take official action and have the children removed from the custody of the parents. In the most extreme cases, the abuser will be criminally prosecuted.

Chapter 10 focuses on the role of the police in the prevention and control of delinquency. Police work with juveniles involves the investigation of complaints initiated by citizens or of the behavior of juveniles observed by officers. This chapter provides the reasons for taking a youth into custody (arrest, as well as police use of discretion in determining when a juvenile offender can be diverted from the juvenile justice system by informal handling) and when it is required to refer juvenile offenders to the juvenile court. Examples of police involvement in delinquency prevention programs are given.

Chapter 11 describes the informal processing of juvenile offenders. Examples of diversion programs used for the juvenile court and administered internally and programs administered by a community child service agency are given to illustrate the informal process.

The use of special courts (dockets), such as traffic, drug abuse, and family, in the diversion of offenders from the formal juvenile justice process is discussed.

Chapter 12 presents the formal processing of juveniles by the juvenile court who allegedly have committed delinquency. The process, from the initial appearance, detention, intake, formal hearing, and disposition, is explained.

The juvenile court process begins when a petition (complaint that specifies the law that the youth has allegedly violated) is made to the court. If the case is scheduled for a formal hearing, an initial hearing is scheduled, the rights of the juvenile are read, and the youth has an opportunity to make a plea. If the plea is "not true" to the charges, a formal hearing is conducted. The juvenile has the right to an attorney at the hearing and is guaranteed other rights similar to those granted for adults being tried for crimes. Some youths, depending on the seriousness of the offenses, prior delinquent history, and other circumstances, are bound over to the criminal courts. If they are found guilty in the criminal court, they are subject to the same penalties as adults, with the exception of capital punishment and mandatory life imprisonment.

Many juvenile courts have established special divisions that focus on one type of deviant behavior such as drug abuse, family violence, or sex abuse. Youth adjudicated delinquent in these courts are subject to mandatory counseling and treatment for their problem. The large majority of adjudicated delinquents in the juvenile courts are given community-based sanction.

Chapter 13 focuses on the community dispositions used with juveniles who have been adjudicated delinquent. Probation is the most frequently used sanction. Those placed on probation are required to abide by general and specific rules, to report to their probation officers, and not to engage in any behavior that violates the laws. Probation can be revoked if the youth violates the conditions of probation. A revocation hearing must be held before a juvenile's probation can be revoked. If the charges are found to be true, the juvenile might be committed to a correctional facility, given additional special rules, or placed in a secure community residential facility. Juveniles with special needs, such as drug addiction, may be placed in a residential treatment center and provided with special treatment for their problem.

Chapter 14 describes juveniles incarcerated in secure correctional facilities. Correctional facilities for juveniles can be differentiated on the basis of the amount of security at the facility, the functions performed by the facility, the type of programs offered at the facility, and the typical length of time juveniles are likely to spend at the correctional facility. Some short-term facilities such as detention centers and diagnostic centers have specific functions. In the case of the detention center, it typically holds youths who are awaiting a hearing and those who have been adjudicated delinquent and are awaiting transfer to either a diagnostic center or a long-term correctional facility. Such facilities as forestry camps or farms house low-risk juvenile offenders. Those given a disposition to a long-term correctional facility are likely to be the more serious offenders, who are considered a high risk to the safety of the community. The effect being incarcerated in a correctional facility has on the youth is considered in this chapter as well as alternatives to secure facilities for adjudicated youths.

Chapter 15 focuses on the supervision and assistance given to juveniles who have been released from secure correctional facilities and placed under parole (aftercare) supervision or placed in a community residential facility.

Juveniles who are placed on parole (aftercare) supervision may present special needs and require considerable supervision. Often there is a problem finding a suitable placement if the family situation is disorganized. Returning to a former place of residence may result in re-association with an undesirable peer group the youth was involved with before being institutionalized. Those youths considered to be a serious threat to the community are often placed on intensive parole and those in need of treatment may be placed in a residential treatment center.

Chapter 16 presents the programs and methods used to counsel and treat juvenile offenders. The roles of counselors and other personnel, different types of programs such as individual counseling, reality therapy, group counseling (guided or positive peer group interaction), family counseling, or music, art and writing therapies, as well as special programs provided by volunteer groups are considered.

Chapter 8
Laws and Court Cases Pertaining to Children: Offenders and Victims

8.1 Introduction

Throughout most of history, the concept "adolescence" did not have a reference point. Children were either considered to be babies or adults. Most children, except for the children of the nobility, were expected to take on adult roles very early in their lives. Kratcoski (2012, p. 117) notes, "the concept adolescence is a relatively recent phenomenon that developed in Europe and the United States in the latter part of the 19th century." Children had no rights and were considered to be the property of the family, particularly the head of the household.

However, Kratcoski (2012, p. 117) states, "Gradually, as the societies became industrialized and urbanized, the traditional laws and norms governing the relationship between parents and children changed. Large numbers of children were freed from immediate control of the head of the household, and the children were separated from their families because of the death of parents, abandonment, or becoming apprentices." In the cities and industrial towns that needed cheap labor, boys as young as 10 years were often employed in factories, coal mines and lumber mills. Young girls were often sent to live with more affluent families and serve as maids. The testimony of a man who grew up in a small coal mining town in the early twentieth century illustrates the point.

> I really liked school. The teachers told me that I was smart, but when my father died when I was in the fifth grade, I had to quit and go to work in the coal breaker. I worked for 10 hours a day with other boys "picking slate" (separating the slate from the coal before it went into the coal breaker). I was the oldest boy in our family and we did not have any money except what I earned and what my younger brothers could make by doing jobs around the neighborhood. When they became old enough to go to work in the coal breaker, they quit school and worked with me and the other boys until they were old enough to go into the mine. None of us ever went back to school. (Interview conducted by Peter C. Kratcoski)

As compulsory education and new laws were enacted to curtail child labor, many of the traditional customs relating to the role of children in the family were abandoned and traditions and customs were codified into law. Kratcoski (2012, p. 119)

© Springer Nature Switzerland AG 2020
P. C. Kratcoski et al., *Juvenile Delinquency*,
https://doi.org/10.1007/978-3-030-31452-1_8

observes, "In the agricultural family, the authority of the head of the household over the children often extended well into adulthood. If the child continued to live in the same household as the parents, that child was expected to obey the demands of the father. If the head of the family were to die or become so ill as to be unable to function and provide for the family, close relatives were expected to look after the children and provide them with food, clothing and shelter needed to survive."

A young child who committed an act that constituted a crime, such as stealing some fruit from a neighbor or causing some damage to a neighbor's property was generally punished by the father, or if the father was absent for some reason, by the person who held the position of the head of the household. If a child committed a very serious crime, such as murder, arson, or felonious assault, Kratcoski (2012, p. 119) noted, "The child might be brought before the authorities and charged with a crime if the offense was considered a threat to the welfare of the society. In such cases, once it was established that the child could distinguish right and wrong (*mens rea*) the accused was given the rights of an adult and if convicted, was subject to the same penalties an adult might receive."

The passage of laws that provided assistance for "deserving mothers" and financial aid to support the children of poverty stricken families helped to reduce the demands made on the immediate family members, particularly the younger children of the family, as well as on close relatives. However, when these agencies assumed some responsibility for the well-being of children, they also assumed some control over children, resulting in the family head no longer having absolute control over the children and other members of the family.

The children who left their immediate families to serve as apprentices to farmers, tradesman, merchants, or to owners of merchant ships were now under the control of their masters, who had the responsibility to provide food, clothing, and shelter, as well as to assume the responsibility for the child's moral development and behavior. In essence, the master served as a parent substitute and had the right to administer punishment, just as the head of the household had when the child lived in the family home.

During the latter part of the nineteenth century, the United States experienced a huge increase in population due to the millions of immigrants who came from various countries throughout Europe. Although some of the immigrants migrated to rural areas, particularly to the mid-western states, and established family farms, the large majority of the immigrants settled in the cities and found work in various industries. Kratcoski (2012), said that the rapid growth, of the urban population "… led to overcrowding, the creation of slums, poverty for those who were unable to work and often a breakup of the primary family unit." Many of the older established residents of the cities began to feel that their safety and way of life was being threatened when they saw youths roaming the streets, apparently unsupervised, creating mischief, and engaging in criminal behavior. As a result, a concerted effort was made to do something about the situation by finding ways to control the deviant behavior of these wayward children.

In the early part of the nineteenth century, Houses of Refuge were established in several states for the sole purpose of finding a legal method to control children who were homeless, unsupervised, living by their wits on the streets, and suspected of being involved in criminal behavior. For example, the New York state legislature granted a charter to the Society for the Reformation of Juvenile Delinquents to establish a House of Refuge for wayward, homeless, and delinquent children. Other states soon followed the lead set by New York. Rothman (1971, p. 207) indicated that the goals set by the administration of the Houses of Refuge were often vague in wording. Generally they were lofty, such as recuing poor, homeless, and vagabond children, protecting them from adult criminals, and providing them with a routine that included hard work, discipline and moral training. The Houses of Refuge were granted the powers of *parens patriae* (substitute parent), and those youths who violated the rules and regulations were subject to harsh punishment. Bernard (1949) questioned the legality of the actions of the officials who had the power to commit children to a House of Refuge who were not accused of any crime except loitering, or a parent who could commit a child for being disobedient. Officials also had the power to remove a child from a home on the premise that the parents were not providing proper care and discipline. However, the authority of the House of Refuge to serve as *parens patriae* was confirmed by the Pennsylvania Supreme Court in the *Ex parte Crouse* decision, in which the Court ruled that a mother had the right to commit her daughter to the Philadelphia House of Refuge for being incorrigible (*Ex Parte Crouse*, 1838).

Other significant court cases, relating to the parental care and disciplining of their children by parents, and the powers of those agencies that assumed the parent substitute role over children who were removed from the care and supervision of their parents were heard in the courts in the years after Ex Parte Crouse.

Mezey (1996, p. 27) noted that "Children's rights claims have involved a mix of constitutional and statutory challenges to government policies relating to the distribution of public welfare benefits, autonomy in speech and reproductive decision making, conditions of confinement and sentencing in the juvenile justice system, treatment of children in mental health facilities and schools, and the ineffectiveness of the child welfare system." In this chapter, we will focus on the most important U.S. Supreme Court or U.S. District Court cases that resulted in providing rights to children in the areas of the family, child welfare and the juvenile justice system.

8.2 Supreme Court Decisions Relating to Parents and Their Children

Following *the Ex parte Crouse* case, Kratcoski (2012, p. 123) states, "The courts have consistently affirmed the rights of parents to care for and discipline their children, but the courts have been somewhat vague in defining what constitutes reasonable punishment. As a result, cases that came before the courts pertaining to parents being accused of being excessively harsh or physical in the disciplining of their children were decided on a case-by-case basis." A presentation of dates and outcomes of the cases that have had the most far reaching implications follows.

Box 8.1 Significant Cases Pertaining to Family and Child Welfare Agencies

Case	Year	Issue	Outcome
Ex Parte Crouse	1838	Commitment of a juvenile to a PA House of refuge without a trial	The Pennsylvania Supreme Court ruled that a trial was not necessary because the Court was acting as a benevolent parent to protect the child from harm
Stanley v. Illinois	1972	Parental use of excessive punishment, when disciplining their children	The Supreme Court reaffirmed the rights of parents to provide care, companionship, and management of their children
Santosky v. Kramer	1982	The interference in the fundamental right of parent to discipline their children	The Supreme Court reaffirmed the fundamental right of parents to discipline their children
De Shaney v. Winnebago County Department of Social Services	1989	Social Services Department's failure to provide protection of a child from physical abuse	U. S. Supreme Court ruled the agency did not take the action to protect the child from the abusing father

---

8.3   Summary of the Family Law Cases

A more detailed explanation of the legal issues and the Court's explanation of its decision for each case presented above are given on the following pages.

8.3.1   *Ex Parte Crouse (1838)*

Mary Ann Crouse was committed to a Pennsylvania House of Refuge by her mother on the grounds of being unmanageable. The Pennsylvania Supreme Court upheld the commitment, stating that no trial was necessary because the court, applying *the parens patriae* principle, was acting in the best interests of the child. Mary Ann's father appealed the decision on the grounds that Mary Ann was committed on a decision made by a justice of peace, without being given a jury trial. The Court stated, "The object of the charity is reformation, by training its inmates to industry; by imbuing their minds with principles of morality and religion; by furnishing them with means to earn a living; and above all, by separating them from the corrupting influence of improper associates. To this end may not the natural parents, when unequal to the task of education, or unworthy of it, be superseded by the *parens patriae* or common guardian of the community? It is to be remembered that the public has a paramount interest in the virtue and knowledge of its members, and that of strict right, the business of education belongs to it." (Ex parte Crouse, 4, Wharton (Pa.) 9, 1838).

8.3.2   Stanley v. Illinois (1973)

Joan Stanley lived with Peter Stanley intermittently for 18 years during which time the unmarried couple had three children. Joan Stanley died. Pursuant to Illinois law, the children of unwed fathers automatically became wards of the State upon the death of the mother. Peter Stanley's three children were placed in foster care without a hearing being held on the issue of the fitness of Peter as a father.

Peter Stanley appealed to the U.S. Supreme Court the decision of the Illinois Supreme Court that the removal of his children did not violate his rights to due process pursuant to the 14th Amendment. The U.S. Supreme Court held that as a matter of due process of law, Peter Stanley was entitled to a hearing on his fitness as a parent before his children could be taken from him by the State of Illinois. The Court further held that the State's interest in caring for Stanley's children is minimal if it is legally determined that an unwed father is a fit parent.

8.3.3   Santosky v. Kramer (1982)

A New York State court terminated the family right of the children of parents to have custody over their children The Santosky children were removed from their home by a county social service agency on the grounds that the children were neglected. A hearing on the matter resulted in a family court judge stating that the children were "permanently neglected" and thus the rights of the parents to provide care and discipline to their children were terminated.

The case was appealed to the U.S. Supreme Court and the Court ruled in favor of the Santosky parents' appeal. The rights of the Santoskys to provide care and discipline to their children were restored. In addition, the children were to be returned to the Santosky residence.

The Supreme Court decision on this case reaffirmed the fundamental right of parents to provide care and discipline to their children. In cases in which these rights are temporary removed for cause, the parents are entitled to "fundamentally fair procedures when facing the abolition of their parental rights."

8.3.4 DeShaney v. Winnebago County Department of Social Services (1989)

Petitioner Joshua DeShaney was born in 1979. In 1980, Joshua's parents divorced and a Wyoming Court awarded custody of Joshua to his father, Randy DeShaney. Randy DeShaney moved to Neenah, a city located in Winnebago County Wisconsin, taking his infant child with him.

After moving to Wisconsin, the father subjected his son to a series of physically abusive beatings over a course of the next 3 years. The Winnebago County Department of Social Services and its social workers received multiple complaints over the 3-year period that Randy DeShaney was abusing his son. The County Department investigated and took various steps to protect the child but never removed the child from the father's custody. The child's father ultimately beat the child so severely that Joshua De Shaney suffered permanent brain damage.

Petitioner Joshua DeShaney and his mother brought an action pursuant to 42 USC Section 1983 alleging that the Winnebago County DDS had deprived Joshua of his liberty without due process of law, in violation of his rights under the Fourteenth Amendment of the U.S. Constitution Specifically the petitioners alleged that the County Child Protective Services failed to intervene to protect the child against the father's violence. The District Court granted summary judgment in favor of the Winnebago County DDS. The U.S. Court of Appeals affirmed.

The U.S. Supreme Court held that the State's failure to protect an individual against private violence generally does not constitute a violation of the Due Process Clause. The Supreme Court determined that the Equal Protection Clause imposes no duty on the State to provide members of the general public with adequate protective services. The Court determined that the Equal Protection Clause forbids the State from depriving individuals of life, liberty and property without due process but the Clause does not impose affirmative duty on the State to ensure individuals of these rights.

8.3.5 Troxel v. Granville (2000)

Tommie Granville and Brad Troxel shared a relationship but were never married. The couple had two daughters, Isabelle and Natalie. Brad's parents, Jennifer and Gary Troxel, were the parental grandparents of Isabelle and Natalie. The children's parents Tommie and Brad separated. Brad subsequently lived with his parents and regularly brought his daughters to the parent's home for weekend visitation for a period of approximately 2 years until Brad committed suicide. After Bead's death, the children regularly visited their parental grandparents, but within 6 months of his death, Tammie Granville informed the Troxels that she wished to limit their visits with their granddaughters to one short visit per month. The Troxels petitioned the Washington Superior Court for the right to visit their grandchildren pursuant to Section 26,10, 160 (3) of the Revised Code of Washington which permitted "any person" to petition a Superior.

Court for visitation rights at any time and authorized the court to grant such rights whenever "visitation may serve the best interest of the children.)" The Washington Superior Court granted the grandparents petition and ordered visitation for the grandparents one weekend per month. The mother, Tommie Granville, appealed. The Washington Court of Appeals reversed the lower Court's visitation order. The Washington Supreme Court upheld the Court of Appeals ultimate conclusion that the parental grandparents could not obtain visitation of their grandchildren pursuant to Section 21.10.160 (30). The Court based its decision on the federal Constitution, holding that the Washington Statute infringed on the fundamental right of parents to raise their children.

The U.S. Supreme Court upheld the Washington Superior Court's Decision, claiming that the entry of a visitation order by the Lower Court violated the U.S. Constitution. Specifically, the Court found that the application of the Washington Statute to the mother violated her due process right to make decisions concerning the care, custody and control of her daughters. The U.S. Supreme Court determined that the Due Process Clause does not permit a State to infringe on the fundamental right of parents to make childrearing decisions simply because a State Judge believes that "better" parenting decisions could be made.

8.4 Interaction Between the Police and Juveniles

The large majority of the complaints filed to the juvenile court related to the misbehavior of children and adolescents are made by the police. The police become involved with juveniles by way of residents in the community calling the police regarding some delinquent behavior of neighborhood youths. The police investigate and, if warranted, take action against the youths. School administrators may call in the police if criminal behavior by students is suspected. Parents may call the police regarding the behavior of one or more of their children, and the police may observe delinquent behavior while on patrol. In addition, any adult who is a resident of the community in which an alleged offense occurs can file a complaint. In the majority of instances, the persons making a complaint with first contact the police, and after the police have made an investigation in the matter to determine if there is sufficient ground to take action on the complaint, the police will follow through and take whatever action is considered necessary. In some cases the complainant will go directly to the juvenile court with the complaint. More often than not, these complaints will be for minor offenses.

Until the mid-1950s, the police could use a number of methods in dealing with alleged juvenile offenders and not be concerned about the legality of their methods. The police had, and still have a considerable amount of discretion on how to handle juvenile matters and in many cases their response to a deviant act through diversion is beneficial to the child's welfare. However, during the late 1960s the State courts as well as the U.S. Supreme Court began to intervene when the methods used by the police in their investigations of crime and interaction with criminal suspects were questioned. Many of the early decisions on police methods, such as the *Miranda v.*

Box 8.2 Legal Rights of Juveniles Pertaining to the Police

Case	Year	Issue	Outcome
Haley v. Ohio	1948	Conditions under which a juvenile may be questioned	The Supreme Court ruled a confession by a juvenile is inadmissible as evidence because the circumstance surrounding the youth's questioning, including the absence of parents or counsel, the length of the questioning period, and the approach used by the officers
Miranda v. Arizona	1966	Advising an arrested person of rights	The Supreme Court ruled that a person must be advised at the time of arrest of the right to counsel and the right to remain silent, and be told that anything said may be held against him/her
Stovall v. Denno	1967	Face-to-face identification of suspects	The Supreme Court ruled that the principle of "fundamental fairness" was violated because the victim was violated because the suspect was taken to the victim in a one-on-one situation while in handcuffs
Wade v. U.S.	1968	Lineup identification	The Supreme Court set standards, including the requirement that others in the lineup must be similar in physical characteristics to those of the suspect
Simmons v. U.S.	1968	Photo identification of suspects	The Supreme Court ruled that the principle of "fundamental fairness" must be maintained by showing the witness a group photo of persons who are similar in physical characteristics rather than using a single photograph to have the witness identify the suspect
Fare v. Michael C.	1979	Interrogation of a youth in custody	The Supreme Court ruled that Michael's rights were violated when the police refused to call his probation officer during the time Michael was in custody and was being interrogated. Michael did not ask for an attorney
New Jersey v. T.L.O.	1984	Search of youth's personal property	The Supreme Court ruled that T.L.O.'s rights were not violated, even though the police did not have probable cause that a crime had been committed, since the search was completed on school grounds and with permission of a school official who acted in the role *in loco parentis*
Yarborough v. Alvarado	2004	Custodial interrogation of juveniles	The Supreme Court ruled that the juvenile came into station voluntarily and was allowed to leave. Thus, he was not in police custody during the interrogation
J.D.B v. North Carolina	2011	Custodial interrogation of a juvenile without informing the youth of Miranda rights	The Supreme Court ruled that the youth's age is a factor to consider in determining if a person is in "custody" during a questioning of a suspect

Arizona decision, involved adults, but the court decisions which tended to protect the rights were also extended to juveniles. Other cases pertained specifically to juveniles. Some of the police interact with juveniles requires a proactive response, as in cases in which the police observe as when they observe juveniles involved in delinquent behavior, and other situation require a reactive response, as when the police respond to a call related to a complaint about the behavior of a juvenile. In Box 8.2 the significant U.S. Supreme Court Cases that relate to juveniles' rights are listed;

A more detailed explanation of the critical cases listed above follows.

8.5   Juvenile Rights Pertaining to Questioning, Interrogation, and Custody by the Police

8.5.1   Haley v. Ohio (1948)

Haley, a 15-year-old boy was arrested as a suspect in the robbery of a confectionery store. Haley was continuously questioned for long period of time without being allowed to contact his parents or an attorney. He was convicted and Haley appealed to the U.S. Supreme Court. The Supreme Court ruled that his subsequent confession was inadmissible because of the "totality of circumstances," that is, the absence of parents or lawyer, the age of the youth, the length of the questioning period and the approach used by the officers.

8.5.2   Gallegos v. Colorado (1962)

On December 20, 1958, Gallegos, a 14-year-old boy, and another juvenile followed an elderly man into a hotel. They overpowered him, assaulted him, and stole $1300 from his pockets.

His parents asked to see him on January 2nd, but permission was denied because visiting hours were over. From January 1 through January 7, 1959, Gallegos was kept in Juvenile Hall under security.

On January 7, 1959, Gallegos signed a full and formal confession. On January 13th, a charge of assault to injure was filed against him. A trial took place on the charge on January 16th and Gallegos was convicted. Subsequently the assault victim died and Gallegos was charged with first degree murder. At his trial in State Court, a jury found him guilty. The criminal evidence against him in State Court was the formal confession which Gallegos had signed on January 7th, a confession that he provided after a confinement for 6 days without seeing a lawyer or parent.

Gallegos appealed his murder conviction to the U.S. Supreme Court. The Court held that the confession which was obtained against Gallegos was obtained in violation of the Due Process Clause of the U.S. Constitution. Specifically, The Court found that based on the totality of circumstances, such as the youth of the accused, the failure of the police to send for his parents, the failure of the State to immediately bring him before a Judge in the Juvenile Court and the failure to allow access to a lawyer all combined to make the formal confession void.

8.5.3   *Miranda v. Arizona (1966)*

Miranda was arrested by the police as a suspect in an alleged kidnapping and rape. He was interrogated by the police. He was never informed of due process rights guaranteed in the U.S. Constitution, such as the right to remain silent and to speak with an attorney. He eventually confessed to the crimes, and was convicted of the crimes, predominately as a result of his confession.

He made an appeal on the basis that his Constitutional rights were violated when the police interrogated him. And the case was heard by the U.S. Supreme Court. The Court found that his rights were violated, since he should have been told of the right to remain silent and to have an attorney before the police interrogation began. The Court also set forth guidelines on a suspect's due process rights, including the right to remain silent, right to counsel, and the right to terminate the questioning.

8.5.4   *Wade v. U.S. (1967)*

Billy Joe Wade, an adult male, was a suspect in a crime. The victim identified Wade as being the perpetrator of the crime during a police line-up. On the basis of the victim's identification, Wade was charged and convicted.

Wade appealed the case on the grounds that his Constitutional rights were violated, since he did not have an opportunity to have an attorney present during the police line-up. In addition, the line-up was not conducted in a fair and non-discriminatory manner.

The U.S. Supreme Court ruled in favor of Wade. It also set guidelines for the use of a line-up for the identification of a suspect of a crime. These included that the members of the line-up be similar in physical characteristics (gender, race, height, weight) to those of the suspect.

8.5.5   *Simmons v. U.S. (1968)*

Simmons, a male adolescent boy was brought to the victim of a crime for the purpose of asking the victim if Simmons could be identified as the perpetrator of the offense. The victim identified Simmons as the offender, and after a hearing in the juvenile court, he was adjudicated delinquent.

Simmons appealed to the U.S. Supreme Court, based on the premise that his Constitutional rights were violated, since the identification process followed by the police was unfair and discriminatory.

The Court ruled in favor of Simmons, stating that the principle of fundamental fairness was violated when a "one on one" identification procedure was used in the identification. In lieu of a line-up procedure, the Court offered other possible options that would meet the fundamental fairness principle, such as showing the witness a group photograph in which at least some of the other individuals had similar physical characteristics to those of the suspect.

8.5.6   Fare v. Michael C. (1979)

Michael C., age 16, was taken into custody by the Van Nuys, California police on a robbery charge. Prior to being questioned at the police station, he was fully advised of his Miranda Rights by the police officer who would eventually conduct his interrogation. At the time of his arrest, Michael C. was subject to probation supervision.

After receiving his Miranda Rights, Michael C. did not request to speak with an attorney. Instead, he requested to speak to his probation officer. Michael C. had previously been informed by his probation officer that in the event he should ever get into trouble, he should immediately contact him. The police officers conducting the investigation told Michael C. that he had a right to an attorney but not to talk with his probation officer.

After being denied the ability to contact his probation officer, Michael C. answered the police officer's questions by making statements that ultimately implicated him in the robbery for which he was eventually charged. He was adjudicated delinquent and sent to a juvenile correction facility. Shortly afterwards, the robbery victim died. Michael C. was fearful that he would be charged with murder, so he filed a petition with the Appellate Court to suppress the incriminating statements he made to the police officer on the grounds that his Fifth Amendment rights were violated when he was not granted the right to contact his probation officer.

The California Superior Court held that Michael C.'s request to contact his probation officer was a per se invocation of his fifth Amendment rights in the same manner as a request for an attorney. The U. S. Supreme Court reversed the California Superior Court's decision, holding that a probation officer is not in a position to offer the type of legal assistance necessary to protect the Fifth Amendment rights of an accused undergoing custodial interrogation that a lawyer can offer. The Court further held that a juvenile's request to speak with his probation officer did not constitute a per se right to remain silent, nor was it tantamount to requesting an attorney. The Court did indicate that there may be situations, depending on the circumstances, when it would be appropriate for the police to not question the youth unless a parent, guardian, or attorney were present. In Michael C.'s case, however, the circumstances did not warrant this consideration.

8.5.7 `New Jersey v. T.L.O. (1984)

T.L.O., a girl 14 years of age, and her companion were in the girls' lavatory, allegedly smoking a cigarette when a teacher walked in. The teacher did not see the girls engaged in the act but assumed that they were smoking, based on the smell of smoke in the air. She escorted the girls to the assistant vice principal's office and informed the principal of what she had observed and smelled.

When the girls denied smoking, the vice principal demanded that T.L.O. surrender her purse. On opening the purse, he found a package of cigarettes, and various types of paraphernalia, such as rolling papers, and a pipe of the type commonly used for taking drugs. In addition, a list of students who owed T.L.O money was found in the purse.

The State of New Jersey brought delinquency charges against the two girls in the juvenile court and they were adjudicated delinquent.

T.L.O. appealed on the grounds that the vice principal's search of T.L.O.'s purse was a violation of her Constitutional 4th Amendment right to be protected against illegal search and seizure. Since a delinquent act was not observed, there was not sufficient evidence to establish probable cause to justify a search of T.L.O.s purse.

The U.S. Supreme Court ruled that the vice principal was acting *in loco parentis* and thus did not need probable cause to conduct the search and that the contraband found was legally obtained. The Court stated that the role of in loco parentis *(substitute parent)* is given to school officials by parents who entrust their children to school officials during the time they are under the jurisdiction of the school. School officials have the authority to establish rules of conduct as well as take the necessary action to protect the safety and security of the students.

8.5.8 Yarborough v. Alvarado (2004)

Yarborough, a 17-year-old male, was requested by the Las Angeles Police to come to the station to determine if he had any information pertaining to a crime being investigated by the police. Yarborough came to the station with his parents and voluntarily answered questions. Since he was not suspected of a crime at that time, the police did not read him the required Miranda rights, given to all persons being questioned by the police who are considered suspects. During the questioning, Yarborough provided information that implicated him in the crime being investigated, a robbery in which the victim was beaten by the assailants. The victim died shortly after the robbery occurred.

Yarborough was allowed to leave the station and go home with his parents, even though the police had information connecting him to the robbery. He later was interrogated a second time by the police, but was read the Miranda Rights before the interrogation began.

He was arrested and found guilty of the crimes for which he was charged. The evidence presented during the adjudication hearing of the juvenile court was largely that which Yarborough had given during his first interrogation by the police. He was sent to a secure correctional facility.

The case was appealed to the California Supreme Court, and the conviction was overturned on the grounds that Yarborough's rights were violated when the police did not provide him with the Miranda Rights at the first questioning. The State of California appealed the decision of the California Supreme Court and the U.S. Supreme Court heard the case.

The U.S. Supreme Court upheld the I California Court's decision on the grounds that Yarborough came into the police station voluntarily and he was not a suspect at the time of the initial Questioning.

8.5.9   J.D.B. v. North Carolina (2011)

J.D. B., a special education student, age 13, was taken from his classroom by a police officer in uniform and taken to a conference room. He was questioned by the police officer, an assistant principal, and a school administrator about a burglary he was suspected of having committed. He was not read the Miranda rights, nor were his parents notified. It was not until after J.D.B incriminated himself during the questioning that he was informed that he was free to leave.

The case was appealed to the U.S. Supreme Court on the grounds that J.D.B. was in custody at the time he was questioned and incriminated himself and thus should have been given the Miranda rights. The Court concluded that age and other circumstances are factors that should have been considered when determining if J.D.B. was in custody at the time he was questioned on the burglaries. he Court ruled that a child's chronological age does not always determine if a youth can make a "reasonable judgment" on the matter of being in custody during the questioning by the police officer and school officials. However, it should be considered during the questioning of any child charged with a crime. Since children are less mature than adults and often lack the experience to recognize the possible outcomes resulting from their providing incriminating information.

8.6   Court Cases Pertaining to Release and Preventive Detention of Juveniles

The large majority of the referrals to the juvenile courts are made by the police. The police are generally the first responders to complaints on juvenile misbehavior and delinquency. These complaints may come from parents, neighborhood residents, school officials, and in many instances, the police observe the deviant behavior while on patrol, when responding to a call relating to a crime in progress or after an investigation of an alleged juvenile delinquent is completed and the juvenile is taken into custody. In cases in which the youth is taken into custody and transported to the juvenile court detention facility, Kratcoski (2012, p. 275) notes, "One function of detention centers is to hold a youth who is allegedly involved in a crime until the juvenile court can complete an arraignment hearing on the case and determine whether the child can be released to the parent or guardian or needs to be held in detention until an adjudication hearing is held and it is determined whether the charges are true." The U.S. Supreme Court made rulings on juveniles who were held in detention and denied bail and juveniles held in detention to prevent them from fleeing or from having an opportunity to committing other offenses. A summary of the most important U.S. Supreme Court cases that apply to juveniles held in detention while awaiting a hearing is presented in Box 8.3.

Box 8.3 Prehearing Detention and Right to a Jury Trial

Case	Year	Issue	Outcome
Mc Keiver v. PA	1971	Due process rights, including jury trial and right of bail for juveniles charged with delinquency	The Supreme Court ruled that a juvenile does not have a constitutional right to a jury trial or to be released on bail
Schall v. Martin	1984	Preventive detention of juveniles	The Supreme Court upheld a state court's decision that detention of juveniles before hearings on the charges if they present a serious risk of committing another offense

A more detailed explanation of these cases follows:

8.6.1 McKeiver v. Pennsylvania (1971)

Joseph McKeiver, at the age of 16, was charged with robbery, larceny and receiving stolen goods, which charges constituted felonies under Pennsylvania law as acts of juvenile delinquency. At the adjudication hearing, McKeiver was represented by counsel, who requested a jury trial. The jury trial request was denied and McKeiver was adjudicated delinquent.

The case was appealed to the U.S. Supreme Court, based upon the lower court's denial of his right to a jury trial and whether there is a constitutional right to a jury trial in Juvenile Court. The Court ruled that it is not a violation of the Fifth Amendment to the U.S. Constitution for a trial judge to deny a juvenile's request for a jury trial.

The Court's reasoning focused on the concept of judicial efficiency in Juvenile Court proceeding and that if a jury trial were required in all juvenile cases in which they were requested the operation of the entire juvenile system would be delayed. The Court further found that a jury trial in a juvenile adjudication hearing was not essential for a fair and impartial hearing.

8.6.2   *Schall v. Martin (1984)*

Martin, a New York City resident, was 14 years old at the time he was arrested and charged with first degree robbery, second degree assault and criminal possession of a weapon. The officers who arrested him transported Martin to the New York Family Court Detention Center.

He was not given a probable cause hearing until 5 days after being detained and 10 days had passed before he was adjudicated delinquent by the New York Family Court. He was granted probation and placed under the supervision of a New York Family Court probation officer.

Martin's attorney appealed the decision of the New York Family Court on the grounds that the evidence was not "clear and convincing" that he committed the crimes for which he was adjudicated delinquent, and there was not clear evidence presented that he was a serious risk to the community and therefore should not have been held in detention during the time he was awaiting a hearing on the charges.

An appeal to the U.S. Supreme Court resulted in a Court decision that in this case the preventive detention of Martin was justified because of the seriousness of the offenses Martin allegedly committed. However, the Court did not give a blanket endorsement of preventive detention for juvenile charged with serious crimes. The Court stated that the matter of preventive detention must be considered on a case by case basis and the 'fundamental fairness" required in the" Due Process Clause of the Fourteenth Amendment of the U.S. Constitution must be considered as well as the *parens patriae* power of the Family Court in making decisions on the use of preventive detention with youth charged with acts that are defined as crimes if committed by an adult.

8.7   Supreme Court Cases Pertaining to Petitioned Juvenile Court Cases

During the mid-1960s and up until the present time, the U.S. Supreme Court ruled on a number of cases pertaining to the rights of juveniles being tried for offenses that would constitute crimes if committed by adults. These cases related to the formal court process, from the initial appearance (arraignment) to the dispositional hearing. A summary of the cases follows in Box 8.4.

Box 8.4 The Juvenile Court Processing of Petitioned Cases

Case	Year	Issue	Outcome
Kent v. U.S.	1966	The due process rights of a juvenile whose case is being transferred to a criminal court for trial	The Supreme Court established the criteria to be used in a transfer hearing
In re Gault	1967	Due process rights of juveniles during the adjudication hearing	The Supreme Court ruled that juveniles eligible for commitment to a secure juvenile institution have *due process rights* during the entire proceedings of the court
In re Winship	1970	The standard of proof needed to convict a juvenile accused of an offense that would be criminal if committed by an adult	The Supreme Court ruled that the standard of proof required for conviction of juveniles who allegedly committed offenses defined as criminal is *beyond a reasonable doubt*
McKeiver v. PA	1971	The right of a juvenile to a jury trail	The Supreme Court ruled that a juvenile tried in the Juvenile court did not have a constitutional right to have the case tried before a jury
Breed v. Jones	1975	Double jeopardy	The Supreme Court ruled a hearing for a waiver for a juvenile case to an adult criminal court must be held prior to adjudication in the juvenile court

If a juvenile charged with an offense makes a plea of not true or deny (not guilty), at the arraignment (initial hearing), or if the case is not settled at a prehearing conference, an adjudication hearing (trial) is scheduled. The state's case is presented by an attorney from the prosecutor's office and the youth is entitled to be represented by an attorney. The following cases are applicable to the legal rights of juveniles during the judicial process.

8.7.1   Kent v. U.S. (1966)

Morris Kent, a 16-year-old male, was charged with forced entry into a Washington, D.C. apartment, where he alleged raped the occupant and stole her wallet. The juvenile court judge decided to transfer the case (voluntary waiver) to the jurisdiction of the adult criminal court, and Kent was tried as an adult. The judge made the decision to waive Kent's case without first holding a hearing in the juvenile court, or without discussing the matter with Kent's defense attorney. Kent was tried as an adult, convicted and given a sentence of 30–90 years in prison.

On the appeal of Kent's case to the U.S. Supreme Court in 1966, the Court declared that the issue with Kent was not that a judicial bind over was in violation of Kent's rights, but the process followed by the juvenile court was faulty. The Court set forth specific conditions for a valid waiver of jurisdiction by a juvenile court. The Court stated, "An opportunity for a hearing must be given prior to entry of a waiver order.... The child is entitled to counsel in connection with a waiver proceeding.... The hearing must measure up to the essentials of due process and fair treatment... the waiver order should be accompanied with a statement giving the reasons or consideration for the waiver order.... The statement should be sufficient to demonstrate that the statutory requirements of "full investigation" have been met; and it must set forth the basis for the order sufficient specificity to permit meaningful review." (Kent v. U.S., 383 U.S. 541, 1966)

8.7.2   Gault v. Arizona (1967)

Gerald Gault, age 15, was arrested for allegedly making an indecent phone call to a woman who was a neighbor. He was on probation with an Arizona Juvenile Court for being in the company of a boy who stole a wallet at the time of the new charge.

Gault was given an informal hearing by the Juvenile Court. He was not represented by an attorney at the hearing. The woman who made the complaint was not required to appear and testify at the hearing.

After a finding that the charges were true, Gault was committed to a state industrial school for a period of his minority (age 21 in Arizona) unless discharged sooner. If charged and tried and convicted in the criminal court, Gault would have been subject to pay a $50.00 fine and a maximum of 2 months imprisonment.

In 1967, almost 2 years after his institutionalization, Gault's case was heard by the U.S. Supreme Court. The Court ruled that Gault's due process rights, guaranteed in the U.S. Constitution, were violated. The Court ruled that in any case involving the possibility of imprisonment, the defendant must be provided with a written notice of the charges, the right to have counsel, the privilege against self-incrimination, and the right to confront witnesses (unless the defendant confessed).

8.7.3   In re Winship (1970)

Winship, a 12-year-old boy, was charged with larceny. He allegedly broke into a locker and stole more than $100 dollars from a woman's purse in the locker. He received an adjudication hearing in a New York family court and was found to be delinquent. He was given an indeterminate disposition and committed to a training school for juveniles for a period not to exceed 6 years.

"The case was appealed on the grounds that the judge used the civil court standard 'preponderance of evidence' to determine whether the charges against Winship were true, when the judge should have used the criminal court standard of proof 'beyond a reasonable doubt.' The decision of the U.S. Supreme Court judges stated that the Due Process Clause of the Fourteenth Amendment is applicable to juvenile court proceeding when the person is charged with an offense that would be defined as criminal if committed by an adult and in which incarceration may be the outcome if the charge is found to be true…. The Supreme Court acknowledged that the higher standard of proof need not apply for juveniles charged with status offenses or other offenses in which incarceration is not a possible outcome" (Kratcoski, 2012, p.279).

8.7.4   McKiever v. Pennsylvania (1971)

McKeiver, age 16, was charged with robbery, larceny, and receiving stolen property. McKeiver was represented by an attorney, who requested that McKeiver be released on bail and that he be given a jury trial. The request on both matters was denied by the judge. MCKiever was tried in the juvenile court and adjudicated delinquent.

The case was appealed and eventually heard by the U.S. Supreme Court. The Court ruled that states can pass legislation providing the right of a juvenile charged with a delinquent act to have a jury trial, but there is no violation of the Constitution if a state chooses not to provide the right to have a jury trial for an offender tried in the juvenile court.

The Court stated that if states guaranteed the right to a jury for all cases coming before the court, it would produce a drain of the courts time and resources and no doubt cause considerable delay and thus be disadvantageous to the youth being processed by the courts.

8.7.5   Breed v. Jones (1974)

Jones, a 17-year-old male was arrested on a charge of armed robbery. He was held in the juvenile detention center until his adjudication hearing (trial in the criminal court) in the juvenile court. He was adjudicated delinquent (guilty). The disposition (sentencing) hearing was postponed pending the completion of a predisposition (presentence report). He continued to be held in the detention center until the report was completed.

Jones's attorney appealed the case on the grounds that Jones should be released on grounds that the Jones was tried twice for the same crime and thus his Constitution right of protection against double jeopardy was violated.

The U.S. Supreme Court ruled that if a person is tried and adjudicated in the juvenile court and tried again in the criminal court and convicted on the same offense, it constitutes double jeopardy. The Court affirmed the right of juveniles to be treated fairly in the justice system.

Box 8.5 Cases Related to Juveniles' Dispositions

Case	Year	Issue	Outcome
Eddings v. OK	1982	The execution of a 16-year-old who committed a capital offense	The Supreme Court ruled that it is permissible to render the death penalty provided that the circumstances of the crime are considered
Thompson v. OK	1988	Execution of a person under 16 at the time the offense was committed	The Supreme Court ruled that the 8th and 14th Amendments to the U.S. Constitution prohibit the imposition of the death sentence in such cases because the penalty would not contribute to the either the retribution or deterrence goals of capital punishment
Stanford v. KY	1989	Death penalty for juveniles aged 16 and 17	The Supreme Court ruled that it is not cruel and unusual punichment to impose capital punishment on a 16- or 17-year-old person
Roper v. Simmons	2005	Capital punishment for youth who were under 18 when a capital offense was committed constitutes cruel and unusual punishment	The Supreme Court ruled that the execution of a juvenile who committed a capital offense at a age below 18 constituted cruel and unusual punishment and was a violation of the 8th and 14th Amendments to the U.S. Constitution
Graham v. FL	2010	Sentencing a juvenile to mandatory life in prison with no possibility of release on parole	The Supreme Court ruled that juveniles should have an opportunity to be released and thus a mandatory life prison sentence constitutes cruel and unusual punishment and a violation of the 8th and 14th Amendments of the U.S. Constitution
Miller v. AL	2012	Sentencing a juvenile under 18 years of age to mandatory life imprisonment	The Supreme Court ruled that a judge must take an offender's age into consideration before sentencing and it is unconstitutional to sentence a person under 18 to mandatory life imprisonment without opportunities for parole

8.8 Supreme Court Cases Related to Juvenile Dispositions

The U.S. Supreme Court has made decisions on the dispositions and sentencing of juveniles either adjudicated delinquent in the juvenile courts or convicted of crimes in the criminal courts. These decisions pertain to mandatory life sentences as well as the death sentence. Generally the youth's age, mental ability, maturity and circumstances surrounding the crime were considered in the Supreme Court's rulings.

The following cases are the most significant decisions of the Court on the matter of juvenile dispositions and sentences. A summary of the most important cases pertaining to the dispositions of juveniles is presented in Box 8.5.

A detailed summary of the more important cases is given below:

8.8.1   Eddings v. Oklahoma (1982)

Eddings, a 16-year-old male, was driving an automobile with several of his friends, while on the run from their homes. The automobile contained several stolen weapons. Upon being pulled over by a police officer, Eddings fired a loaded shotgun out of a window at the officer and killed him. Eddings was tried as an adult, convicted and given a death sentence.

At the sentencing hearing, Eddings' attorney argued that Eddings' life should be spared due to several mitigating circumstances including the fact that he suffered from a severe mental condition which was the result of being severely beaten by his father. After the sentencing hearing, Eddings was given a death sentence. Eddings appealed, and the case was eventually heard by the U.S. Supreme Court. The Supreme Court voided the death sentence on the ground that the trial Judge failed to consider all of the mitigating factors before sentencing. The Court found the failure to consider such factors violated the Eighth Amendment to the U.S. Constitution.

8.8.2   Thompson v. Oklahoma (1988)

Thompson, a 15-year-old boy, was involved in the murder of his brother-in-law. Thompson and his friends killed the brother-in-law in retaliation for beatings of Thompson's sister. At trial, Thompson was convicted of first degree murder and sentenced to death. Thompson's sentence was appealed and the case was eventually heard by the U.S. Supreme Court. The Supreme Court ruled that the execution of a person who committed a capital offense at the age of 15 constituted cruel and unusual punishment and was a violation of the Eighth and Fourteenth Amendments to the U.S. Constitution.

8.8.3   Roper v. Simmons (2005)

In this case, the U.S. Supreme Court ruled that it is unconstitutional for juveniles convicted of capital offenses who are below the age of 18 to be executed, because this is a violation of the Eighth Amendment that prohibits cruel and unusual punishment. As a result of this case, the state codes must adhere to the standard set by the Supreme Court.

8.8.4   Graham v. Florida (2010)

The U.S. Supreme Court ruled that it is unconstitutional to impose a sentence of life imprisonment without the possibility of being released at some time on a person below the age of 18. Although release on parole is not required, the State must provide a realistic opportunity for the person to be released The Court did not define what it meant by "realistic opportunity."

The U.S. Supreme Court ruled that, if a mandatory life sentence is the only option available for sentencing those defendants convicted of homicide crimes, the mitigating factors surrounding the homicide by a juvenile must be considered before a juvenile can be sentenced to a mandatory life sentence without the possibility of parole. The U.S. Supreme Court has also ruled on matters relevant to juveniles under the jurisdiction of the juvenile justice system. Although a convicted criminal offender and an adjudicated juvenile delinquent do not have a legal right to be placed on probation as a sentence, if placed on probation, the court cannot arbitrarily terminate the probation. There must be a hearing to show cause for the revocation (Morrissey v. Brewer, 1972). This also holds true for juveniles and adult who are under parole supervision (Mempa v. Rhay, 1967).

8.9   Juveniles' Right to Treatment When Under Juvenile Justice Supervision and Care

Since rehabilitation of the youthful offender is one of the primary goals of the juvenile court and the agencies providing the services and treatment programs needed to change the misbehavior of delinquent youths to that of law abiding behavior, the matter of a juvenile under the jurisdiction of a juvenile justice agency having a constitutional right to be provided with the treatment needed to accomplish this goal has come under consideration. The U.S. Supreme Court has not ruled on this matter. A federal district court decision (Morales v. Turman 1979) and other court cases would suggest that the provision of treatment must be provided by those agencies (the juvenile court, correctional facilities, community corrections facilities). Hemmens et al. (2004, p. 104) noted that juvenile courts, under the *parens patriae* philosophy, determined that juvenile delinquents had a constitutional right to be rehabilitated. However, in Santana v. Collazo (1983) a federal district court ruled that a juvenile correctional facility is not required to provide the full range of treatment for juveniles incarcerated in the facility since the primary reason for their incarceration is to protect the community from harm. A short explanation of these cases is provided in Box 8.6.

Box 8.6 Cases Pertaining to Juveniles' Right to Treatment While Under Supervision of a Justice Agency

Case	Year	Issue	Outcome
Mempa v. Rhay	1967	Probation Revocation	The Supreme Court ruled that a probationer charged with violation of probation had a right to have an attorney at the hearing on the probation violation
Morrisey v. Brewer	1972	Probation Revocation	The Supreme Court granted the accused due process rights at a probation revocation hearing
Gagnon v. Scarapelli	1973	Right to have a hearing if accused of violating probation or parole	The Supreme Court granted the right of a hearing for probationers or parolees charged with violating probation or parole
Morales v. Turman	1974	Juveniles under supervision right to treatment	A U.S. Court of Appeals ruled that those in involuntary confinement have a statutory and constitutional right to treatment

8.10   The Interplay of State Legislation and Court Decisions

The legislatures of every state in the United States have enacted laws pertaining to criminal justice and juvenile justice. These laws are generally embodied in a penal code that defines what acts are in violation of the criminal law and what are the penalties to expect if convicted of a violation of a law in the code. Special sections of the code pertain to those persons defined as children and juvenile.

In regard to the rights of juveniles accused of violating the criminal law, many states had provided a number of the legal rights to juveniles long before the U.S. Supreme Court required changes in the procedures followed in the juvenile justice process. In other states, the Supreme Court rulings forced the states to change their codes to be in conformity of the rulings of the Supreme Court.

Feld (1999) noted that the Supreme Court's due process decisions pertaining to juvenile justice resulted in substantive as well as procedural, changes in the system. Feld (2004, p. 599) stated, "By adopting some procedural safeguards to determine delinquency and judicial waiver, the Court shifted the focus of the juvenile courts from the progressives' emphasis on the 'real needs' and 'best interests' of the offender to proof of criminal acts and formalized the connection between criminal conduct and coercive intervention."

Often it is less difficult to enact new legislation than it is to implement and enforce the requirements of the legislation. For example, the Supreme Court granted juveniles charged with offenses that could lead to incarceration due process rights if the juvenile is adjudicated delinquent, including the right to be represented by an attorney. The courts are responsible for appointing an attorney in cases where employing a private attorney is not feasible. Some research (American Bar Association, 1993; Bookser, 2004; Bortner, 1982; Feld & Schaefer, 2010) would suggest that often those youths who have court appointed attorneys are not provided with competent representation because the attorneys are not familiar with juvenile law, or do not make their best effort because of the time involved and the low compensation received for their work. Feld & Schaefer, (2010, p. 717) suggests that in some cases juveniles represented by attorneys fare worst in dispositions than those who are not represented by counsel. Sickmund and Puzzanchera (2014, p. 107) reported that there is a concern about the quality of the counsel provided to juveniles by public defenders and 'Both state and county based public defender offices offered professional and developmental services and training for attorneys who handled juvenile cases."

Both State and federal legislation require that correctional facilities must provide at least minimum standards of living, including food, clothing, recreation, and living space for juveniles incarcerated in state operated facilities and for those under private ownership. What constitutes minimum standards is not clearly defined. If more youths are committed to the correctional facilities than the population capacity of the facility, the minimum standards in regard to living space and other aspects of the daily lives of the youth incarcerated in the institutions are compromised.

Finally, it should be noted that often states change laws and implement new policies pertaining to juvenile justice for reasons other than those required by the courts. In some cases changes are made for political reasons (the politicians believe the changes are wanted by the voters), in other cases for economic reasons, as is the case of the revival of community corrections with the state paying local jurisdictions for not committing juveniles to state administrated juvenile correctional facilities, and in other cases because the politicians believe the changes will serve the best interests of the juvenile offenders, as well as the interests of the community.

8.11 Summary

During the several hundred years after the establishment of the United States, the role of children in society has changed dramatically. In the country's early history, children, with the exception of the eldest son, had no rights or privileges except those given by the head of the household. Children who were harshly punished by a parent, or forced to work long hours, or not properly fed, clothed or sheltered had no way to seek redress or protection since the parents, or caretakers had exclusive rights to provide the care and disciplining of their children.

In the late nineteenth century and throughout the twentieth century, the states and the federal governments enacted legislation that in some measure challenged exclusive position of parents regarding their rights to care for and discipline their children in a manner of their choice. These laws pertained to education, child labor and standards of care. When these laws were challenged in the courts, the U.S. Supreme Court generally upheld the legislation.

The creation of the Juvenile Court in Cook County, IL in 1899, followed by the establishment of juvenile courts in all other states, led to the development of a juvenile justice system in which children accused of committing crimes and offenses against parents and caretakers no longer were handled in the same courts as adults, but now came under the jurisdiction of the juvenile court. Although the juvenile courts allegedly operated under the principle of *parens patriae*, or benevolent parent, there were a sufficient number of instances of abusive practices, such as violations of civil rights protected under the Constitution and extreme physical punishment, failure to provide sufficient food, clothing and shelter, and lack of protection from harm by the juvenile justice agencies who were charged with protecting the" best interests of the child," to warrant court involvement in these questionable practices by both state and federal courts.

The significant U.S. Court cases having an effect on the processing of juvenile offenders in the criminal justice and juvenile justice systems include those pertaining to the police interaction with juveniles suspected of committing crimes, such as Haley v. Ohio (1948), Miranda v. Arizona (1967) Fare v. Michael (1979), In re Gault (1967), N.J. v. T.L.O., Schall v. Martin (1984), Yarborough v. Alvarado (2004), and J.D. B. v. North Carolina (2011), in which the Supreme Court ruled that juveniles accused of crimes have essentially the same constitutional rights as adults accused of crimes when questioned, interrogated, arrested, and taken into custody. As with adults, the principle of "fundamental fairness" must apply. In addition, the age and maturity level of the youth and totality of circumstances must be considered.

Other significant Supreme Court decisions pertained to the judicial process that must be adhered to in hearings pertaining to the detention of juveniles, judicial waiver to the criminal court, adjudication, and dispositions. Kent v. United States (1966) provides the guidelines to be followed in judicial waiver hearings, Schall v. Martin (1984) focused on the legality of the use of "preventive detention" of juveniles to assure that the youth would not commit additional offenses while awaiting a hearing, and McKeiver v. Pennsylvania (1971) addressed the matter of a juvenile held in detention's right to bail. Other important Supreme Court cases pertaining to the adjudication and dispositional hearings include In re Gault (1967), in which the Supreme Court affirmed the constitutional rights of juveniles accused of delinquency. In re Winship (1970), in which the Court ruled that the standard of proof needed to adjudicate a juvenile delinquent is *beyond a reasonable doubt, and* McKeiver v. Pennsylvania (1971) in which the Court ruled that a jury trial for juvenile adjudication hearings is not required under the Constitution.

A number of cases pertained to juvenile dispositions involving community sentences, such as probation, Institutional release, parole (aftercare) institutional sentencing. Other cases involved mandatory life sentences and the death penalty for youth convicted of capital offenses. In Morrisey v. Brewer (1972), the Court ruled that while probation is not a right guaranteed to a convicted criminal in the Constitution, if a person is placed on probation, that person has a right to have a fair hearing before the probation can be revoked. The decision of the court in Mempha v. Rhay (1967) pertained to those released on parole and established the right of the parolee to have a hearing on parole revocation. Although these two cases involved adults convicted of violating criminal laws, the same rights to a fair and impartial hearing were extended to juveniles either through state legislation or state court decisions.

In regard to the death penalty and the age which would apply for a person convicted of capital offenses, the Supreme Court, after several rulings, including Thompson v. Oklahoma (1988), Stanford v. Kentucky (1989), and Wilkins v. Missouri (1989), finally ruled in Roper v. Simmons that it would be unconstitutional to execute a person convicted of a capital crime who was below the age of 18.

The Supreme Court cases of Miller v. Alabama (1010) and Graham v. Florida (20110) pertain to the constitutionality of sentencing a youthful offender to mandatory life imprisonment without having any opportunity to be released. The court ruled that such sentences for juveniles were not constitutional.

The matter of a juvenile having the right to treatment while incarcerated has not been decided by the U.S. Supreme Court. However, a federal district court and various state court decisions as well as state legislation have essentially confirmed that the care and supervision of juveniles under state supervision must adhere to minimum standards, including housing, food, clothing and recreational opportunities.

8.12   Discussion Questions

1. Discuss the changes in the U.S. during the late 19th are early 20th centuries that tended to result in an infringement of the exclusive authority of parents to care for and discipline their children.
2. Discuss the meaning of the concept in loco parentis. Describe a situation in which this concept applies.
3. Many who have researched the development of the juvenile system believe the In re Gault Supreme Court decision has had the most lasting effect on juvenile justice. How has this decision affected the juvenile justice process?
4. What is the relationship between statutes pertaining to criminal and juvenile justice and federal court decisions on juvenile justice matters?
5. In Ex Parte Crouse (1838), the Pennsylvania Supreme Court ruled that the juvenile Crouse could be committed to a House of Refuge, even though she was not charged with a crime and did not have a hearing. Discuss the reasoning followed by the Pennsylvania court.
6. The DeShaney v. Winnebago County Department of Social Services (1989) is considered a landmark Supreme Court decision. Discuss the Supreme Court's

ruling on this case. What is the responsibility a service agency has to those under its jurisdiction?

7. Discuss the meaning of "fundamental fairness" in reference to police questioning of juveniles suspected of delinquent behavior. Cite a few cases in which the Supreme Court found the police violated this principle.

8. Discuss the meaning of "preventive detention." When is preventive detention appropriate for juveniles charged with committing a crime? What position has the Supreme Court taken in regard to a juvenile's right to be released on bail?

9. The U.S. Supreme Court provided a set of guidelines (procedures) for juvenile court judges to follow when considering a youth for judicial waiver to the adult criminal court. Discuss these guidelines.

10. How have state courts and federal courts reacted to the claim that juveniles under the jurisdiction of the juvenile justice system have a right to treatment? What is the basis for their right to treatment claim?

8.13   Court Cases

Breed v. Jones, 421, U.S.517 (1975).
Commonwealth v. Fisher, 62 A. 198 (PA, 1905).
Eddings v. Okahoma, 445 U.S.104 (1982).
Fare v. Michael C. 442, U.S.707 (1979).
Gagnon v. Scarapelli (1979).
Gallegos v. Colorado, 370 U.S. 49 (1962).
Haley v. Ohio, 332 U.S.,596 (1948).
In re Gault, 387, U.S.1 (1967).
In re Winshiip, 397. U.S.358 (1970).
J. D. B. v. North Carolina (2011).
Kent v. United States, 383 U.S. 541 (1966).
Mempa v. Rhay, 189 U.S. 128 (1967).
Mc Keiver v. Pennsylvania,403 U.S. 528 (1971).
Miller v. Alabama (2011).
Miranda v. Arizona, 884 U.S. 436,86, S.Ct 1602 (1966).
Morales v. Turman, 383 E F.Supp.53 (E.D. Tex. 1974).
New Jersey v. T.L.O., 468 U.S. 1214 (1984).
Morrisey v. Brewer 408 U.S. 471, 92 S. Cr. 2593,33 L.Ed. 2 d 484 (1972).
Roper v. Simmons, 543 U.S. 551 (2005).
Schall v. Martin, 467 U.S. 253 (1984).
Stanford v. Kentucky, 492 U.S. 253 (1989).
Thompson v. Oklahoma, 487 U.S. 815 (1988).
Wilkens v. Missouri,492 U.S. 361 (1989).
Yarborough v. Alvarado, 541 U.S. 652 (2004).

References

American Bar Association. (1993). *America's children at risk: A national agenda for legal action.* Washington, DC: American Bar Association Presidential Working Group on the Unmet Needs of Children and Their Families.

Bernard, W. (1949). Jail bait, NY: Breenberg.

Bookser, S. (2004). Making Gault meaningful: Access to counsel and quality of representation in delinquent proceedings for indigent youth. *Whittier Journal of Child and Family Advocacy, 3,* 298–328.

Bortner, M. (1982). *Inside a juvenile court: The tarnished ideal of individualized justice.* New York: New York University Press.

Feld, B. (1999). The right to counsel in juvenile court: An empirical study of when lawyers appear and the difference they make. *Journal of Criminal Law & Criminology, 79,* 1185–1346.

Feld, B. (2004). Juvenile transfer. *Criminology and Public Policy, 3*(4), 599–604.

Feld, B., & Schaefer, S. (2010). The right to counsel in juvenile court: The conundrum of attorneys as an aggravating factor at disposition. *Justice Quarterly, 27*(5), 713–741.

Hemmens, C., Steiner, B., & Mueller, D. (2004). *Significant cases in juvenile justice.* Los Angeles, CA: Roxbury Publishing.

Kratcoski, P. (2012). *Juvenile justice administration.* Boca Raton: CRC Press/Taylor & Francis Group.

Mezey, S. (1996).Children in court, Albany, NY: State University of New York Press.

Rothman, D. (1971). The discovery of the asylum , Boston: Little Brown.

Sickmund, M., & Puzzanchera, C. (2014). *Juvenile offenders and victims: 2014 national report (editors).* Pittsburgh, PA: National Center for Juvenile Justice.

Chapter 9
Perspectives on Children as Victims of Abuse and Neglect

9.1 Introduction

The following cases illustrate the types of offenses of which a child may be the victim. These offenses include neglect, physical and/or sexual abuse, and in extreme cases murder. The person or persons know to have victimized children include, parents, caretakers, relatives, siblings, acquaintances, and strangers. The most frequent perpetrators are members of the immediate family.

Case 1 A 62 year-old _____ man was indicted Thursday on 36 counts of rape for allegedly having sex with two of his step-granddaughters and their cousin. An investigator for the _____. County prosecutor's office said police are looking for the man, who allegedly had been having sex with the girls, ages 6, 10 and 13, for the past three years. The man, the stepfather of the two girls, gave them candy and money after he tied them to as bed with rope, performed oral sex on them, and forced them to perform oral sex on him, said an investigator with the prosecutor's office.

> The man also forced the girls to dance nude in his cottage and regularly showed them pornographic magazines. The girls told investigators during the month-long investigation where the man kept pornographic magazines, the rope he used to tie them up, and see-through night gowns he made them wear.
> "We uncovered everything the kids told us would be there, exactly where they told us it would be (the investigator) said."
> Source: Cleveland Plain Dealer (1988, September 18, p. B5)

Case 2 A foster father who disciplined a 2-year-old by leaving her in a sweltering attic, where she died, was given his punishment Tuesday; four years in prison. He punished Letia for misbehavior by putting her in the attic of his Orlando Avenue home and making her pick up small pieces of plaster. Lillard fell asleep and returned to the attic about five hours later to find Letia dead. He initially lied about what happened to the girl, saying the girl died of hyperthermia from prolonged heat exposure.

© Springer Nature Switzerland AG 2020
P. C. Kratcoski et al., *Juvenile Delinquency*,
https://doi.org/10.1007/978-3-030-31452-1_9

Source: Andale Cross (2003). Girl's family sees man get 4 years for death, *Akron Beacon Journal*, February 19, pp. A1, A5)

Case 3 Crystal Lake, IL.

Missing boy's body found; parents charged
Authorities searching for a missing 5-year-old boy dug up his body Wednesday and charged his parents with murder.
The body, believed to be that of Andrew "AJ" Freund, was covered in plastic and buried in a shallow grave in a rural area of McHenry County, Crystal Lake Police Chief James Black said.
Source: Akron Beacon Journal (2019) April 25, p. A5.

Case 4 A 35-year-old …. woman was sentenced to six months in prison yesterday for leaving her three young daughters to fend for themselves while she spent a weekend with her boyfriend.

When … walked out of her apartment on a Friday morning in January, she left her 12-year-old daughter to look after 3-year-old and 4-year-old girls. When she had not returned by Sunday night, the 12-year-old called the police… .
Police found the apartment in disarray, smelling of urine, with beer cans strewn about, according to the charging document. _____, the father of the 3-year-old, said the apartment had trash on the kitchen floor, clothes piled in various rooms, no food in the refrigerator. He said the children slept on the floor.
Source: Baltimore Sun (1994) August 31, p. 3B.

9.2   Primary Victimizers

During the developmental years, a child interacts with several primary groups, including members of the immediate family and other relatives such as aunts, uncles, grandparents, and cousins. The profound influence a functioning family unit has in shaping the behavior of young people in regard to the development of morals and values, developing social interaction skills, and behaving in a manner acceptable to the community are parts the family plays in the child's maturation process. Several factors have an effect on family relationships and standards of living. Physically, economically, and emotionally broken families can have an important impact on the behavior of children. The strains and conflicts resulting from alcoholism, drug abuse, or mental illness of a parent can have a particularly detrimental effect on family relationships. Some family members, particularly parents, in response to the many pressures associated with being a caretaker of children, engage in behavior toward their children that is often inappropriate, if not criminal. At times, they believe their behavior is acceptable. A parent who is accused of using harsh discipline on a child might retort, "God gave me my children and I have a right to discipline them the way I see fit." In other cases, children may be neglected because the parent is not capable of providing proper care due to alcoholism, drug abuse, or mental illness.

Another aspect of family–child relations that has been given increased attention is child abuse. Shocking cases such as those described above have aroused public concern and indignation when they are detailed in the news media, but many other instances of child abuse and neglect impact the lives of children daily without ever being officially reported or investigated. However, revelations that child abuse occurs more frequently and more savagely than the general public ever imaged has led to the enactment of legislation requiring physicians, social agency personnel, teachers, and others who have direct contact with children in some official capacity to report known or suspected cases. Neglect of the physical and emotional needs of youngsters also has a high incidence, and occurs not only in a family setting, but also in foster homes and institutions where youths are removed from homes judged "unfit" have been placed. The physical, emotional, and sexual abuse of children occurs in all social classes, and is not limited to any educational level, ethnic or racial group, or family type.

In this chapter, we will explore the legal definitions of abuse and neglect, the characteristics of abused children, the types of parents and caretakers most likely to be abusers, methods for handling child abuse and neglect, and the possible resolutions of these situations that hold the most hope for both parents and the children involved.

9.3   What Are Child Abuse and Neglect?

Broad definitions of child abuse include not only physical injuries inflicted upon children by those who are in charge of them, but also psychological abuse. Physical abuse that results in reports or referrals to hospitals, social service agencies, or the police is the type of abuse most clearly documented and included in various regional and national statistical tabulations. In the U.S. Department of Health and Human Services, Children's Bureau Report titled *Child Maltreatment 2017* (2018, p. 1), child abuse and neglect are defined as, "Any recent act or failure to act on the part of a parent or caretaker which results in death, serious physical or emotional harm, sexual abuse or exploitation, or an act or failure to act, which presents an imminent risk of serious harm." In the Report it is noted that "Most states recognize four major types of maltreatment; neglect, physical abuse, psychological maltreatment, and sexual abuse. Although any of the forms of child maltreatment may be found separately, they can occur in combination" (U.S. Department of Health and Human Services, Children's Bureau, p. viii). A legal definition of neglected child can be found in the Ohio Penal Code, Juvenile Law, (RC 2151>03 (A) The Code defines neglected child as a child:

- Who is abandoned by the child's parents, guardian, or custodian
- Who lacks adequate parental care because of the faults or habits of the child's parents, guardian, or custodian;
- Whose parents, guardian, or custodian neglects the child or refuses to provide proper or necessary subsistence, education, medical or surgical care or treatment, or other care necessary for the child's health, morals, or well-being;

- Whose parents, guardian, or custodian neglects the child or refuses to provide the special care made necessary by the child's mental condition;
- Whose parents, legal guardian, or custodian have placed or attempted to place the child in violation of sections 5103.16 and 5103.17 of the Revised Code;
- Who, because of the omission of the child's parents, guardian, or custodian, suffers physical or mental injury that harms or threatens to harm the child's health or welfare; and
- Who is subjected to out-of-home care child neglect. (Abstracted from Giannelli & McCloud-Yeomans, 2004) Ohio Juvenile Law (p. 71), St Paul, MN, Thomson, West

As indicated in the legal definition of neglect, there are specific behaviors or failure to act on the part of parents, caretakers, or guardians that fall under the umbrella term "neglect." It is difficult to define the term exactly, since it may involve the disregard of physical. Emotional, or moral needs of children, such as the essentials of adequate food, clothing or shelter, as well as not providing proper supervision. Neglect may also be emotional, when the parents, caretakers, or guardian fail to express sufficient approval and affection to the child, as well as neglectful behavior by exposing the child to such situations within the home as engaging in drug abuse, alcohol use, or sexual behavior that is at variance with the moral standards of the society. It may also include failure to train or discipline a child. Although the laws are specific, determining whether the activity or lack of activity by parents or caretakers in specific situations constitutes neglect is difficult.

According to the legal definition of Abused-Child-Child Endangerment found in sections RC 2151.031 (B) of the Ohio Revised Code, an abused child is defined as any child who:

- Is the victim of "sexual activity" as defined under Chapter 2907 of the Revised Code,
- Is endangered as defined in section 2919.22 of the Revised Code,
- Exhibits evidence of any physical or mental injury or death, inflicted other than by accidental means, or an injury or death which is at variance with the history given of it. Except as provided in division (D) of this section, a child exhibiting evidence of corporal punishment or other physical disciplinary measure by a parent, guardian, custodian, person having custody or control, or person in loco parentis of a child...;
- Because of the acts of his parents, guardians, or custodian, suffers physical or mental injury that harms or threatens the child's health or welfare; and
- Is subjected to out-of-home care child abuse. (Abstracted from Giannelli & McCloud-Yeomans, 2004) Ohio Juvenile Law (p. 80).

When reviewing the various common usage definitions of abuse and neglect, it becomes apparent that the distinction between "abuse" and "neglect" may be a matter of semantics, since there is considerable overlap of the two concepts. However, the distinction can be all-important in terms of the types of measures that can be undertaken for the protection of the child. The amount and nature of the unacceptable parental behavior uncovered may depend on such factors as the identity and believability of the person making a complaint, the caseloads of the social worker assigned to investigate the complaint, the manipulative powers of the parents, or even the personality characteristics of the children who are allegedly being abused or neglected. The existence of abuse as opposed to accidental injury is difficult to prove in cases in which the child's injury could in fact have been accidental, but the demeanor or behavior of the adults involved arouses suspicion that it may have been deliberately inflicted. Parents are sometimes unable to give a logical explanation of how an injury occurred. In such instances, hospital personnel are hard pressed to decide whether this is because the parents are distraught or feel guilty that the child was accidentally injured, or whether it indicates abusive behavior.

In a report of the Task Force on Juvenile Justice and Delinquency Prevention, National Advisory Committee on Criminal Justice Standards and Goals (1977, pp. 335–336) proposed a new approach to the entire area of abuse and neglect. Labels such as "neglected" and "abused" would be discarded in favor of a new concept, the "endangered child." Under the Committee's standards, parents would not be found "at fault" if the family situation required intervention. But official intervention would occur when:

1. A child has no parent, guardian, or other adult to whom the child has substantial ties, available and willing to care for him or her;
2. A child has suffered or is likely to suffer physical injury imminently, inflicted non-accidentally by his or her parent, which causes or creates a substantial risk of disfigurement, impairment of bodily functioning, or severe bodily harm;
3. A child has suffered, or there is a substantial risk that the child will imminently suffer, disfigurement, impairment of bodily functioning or severe bodily harm as a result of conditions uncorrected by the parents or the failure of the parents to adequately supervise or protect the child;
4. A child is suffering serious emotional damage, evidenced by severe anxiety, depression, or withdrawal, or untoward aggressive behavior toward self or others, and the parents are unwilling to permit and cooperate with the necessary treatment for the child;
5. A child has been sexually abused by a member of the household;
6. A child is in need of medical treatment to cure, alleviate, or prevent serious physical harm that may result in death, disfigurement, substantial impairment of bodily functions, or severe bodily harm and the parents are unwilling to permit the medical treatment; and
7. A child is committing delinquent acts as a result of parental pressure, encouragement, or approval.

The recommendations given above are not laws and thus are not binding. Each state has a code that defines what acts or omissions constitute child abuse and neglect and the penalties given to those found liable for abuse or neglect. It is unlikely that anyone in the legal profession, including prosecutors and judges, as well as those in the children services agencies would disagree with any of the recommendations. Thus, one might ask why so many children are at risk, and why so many children are abused and neglected. The answers to these questions are not easy to come by. Despite the legislation requiring medical, educational, and social work personnel to report suspected abuse and to investigate, when warranted, a considerable amount of abuse is never detected. In addition, even when an investigation of the abuse is undertaken, it is often difficult, except in extreme cases, to make a determination if the behavior by the alleged abuser actually violated the law.

9.4   Process for Reporting and Investigating Child Abuse

All 50 states and the District of Columbia, Guam, and the Virgin Islands have enacted legislation requiring that suspected cases of abuse be reported (U.S. Department of Health and Human Services, Children's Bureau, 2018, p. viii). Under this legislation, medical and social work personnel must report instances of suspected abuse to the appropriate authorities, whereas others community members (neighbors, relatives) may report them. In the majority of states, child abuse reports are directed to the Child Welfare Services (Child Services) of the Department of Social Services at either the county or state level. In some states, reports are first filed with the local police department, or the prosecutor's office, before being sent to the child serves agency. The initial report is made, either by phone, electronically, or in writing within 24–48 h after the alleged abuse is known to the authorities. All of the states have provisions of immunity from legal retaliation for those making reports of suspected or confirmed abuse.

Mandatory reporting places a burden on professionals that is not always willingly assumed. Reporting suspected abuse means becoming involved in matters that are burdensome and time consuming and can raise the specter of false accusations, leading to embarrassment, retaliation from the alleged abuser and others who are involved in the case. Despite these concerns, the large majority of health care and child welfare professionals as well as teachers willingly assume their duty to report suspected abuse and adhere to the letter of the law even when the suspected abuse may be difficult to prove. The following quote (Koop, 1985, p. 23) from a member of the medical profession demonstrated what types of cases often are difficult to substantiate.

The most effective approaches to prevention in the area of interpersonal violence … could well spring from the disciplines of public health, medicine, nursing, and social service… .

We know the face of violence. We accept and care for the victims who are beaten, assaulted, raped and maimed. We in the health professions have tried to do this in a detached, even disinterested way. Some of us were mistakenly convinced that being detached and very "clinical" about these matters was also being very "professional." …

Health professionals don't have the luxury of choice any more. As citizens of a humane and compassionate society—and as physicians, nurses, psychologists all bound to the highest ethics of our professions and as human beings—we are obligated to provide the best possible care for the victims of violence and to contribute whenever we can to the prevention of violence standards.

In an interview with John Saros, retired Executive Director of Summit County, Ohio Children's Services Agency (Kratcoski, 2012, pp. 91–92), he was asked, "What is the jurisdiction of Summit County Children's Services," and asked to describe the types of events or incidents that result in referrals to children's services. He responded:

> Our jurisdiction covers the entire County of Summit. Children's Services has the responsibility of investigating all cases relating to abused, neglected, or dependent children and taking the appropriate action, if the facts appear to substantiate that the child or children need protection or service. We receive information on alleged child physical and sexual abuse, neglect, and lack of parental supervision from many sources. Some complaints come through our Child Abuse Hotline. They may be made by a parent, neighbor, and even the alleged victim. The majority of the referrals are made by the police, school teachers, and medical personnel. We also have working agreements with child protection agencies in other counties to handle cases in which we provide courtesy supervision or courtesy investigations when children have been placed out of county or conflicts of interests exist.

9.5   Extent and Nature of Child Maltreatment

The exact amount of child abuse is impossible to determine, since available statistical information includes only the reported cases and does not include those abused children who were never examined by a doctor or taken to a hospital for treatment, those who were treated by a physician who did not detect or suspect abuse, or those who were suspected of being abused but not reported as such. One major reason why it is difficult to even estimate the amount of physical abuse of children is that the practice of disciplining children through physical punishment has been and continues to be the right of parents. The line between acceptable and unacceptable physical punishment by parents and caretakers is often difficult to ascertain, except in the more extreme cases. Child welfare workers and the police assigned to investigate alleged abuse of a child or children by their parents, and who find it difficult to determine if the physical contact of the parent on a child is legitimate or constitutes abuse, will at times have to use their own judgment, based on their training and experience, to make a determination. For example, if a parent admits to 'spanking' a child because the child disobeyed the parent, the investigator with take notice of the total home situation as well as the circumstances pertaining to the current investigation. If the family situation appears to be normal, with no evidence of other violence or neglect, the police or child welfare workers may give the benefit of the doubt to the caretakers and not take legal action.

Corporal punishment, as it applies to parent-child interaction, is generally defined as, "the use of physical force with the intention of causing a child to experience physical pain, but not injury, for the purpose of correction or control of the child's behavior." (Straus, 1994, p. 4). Much activity in punishing a child may be related to the socialization, traditions, and values of the parents. In most cases, the parents use corporal punishment in disciplining their children in the same manner as they were disciplined during their childhood. Straus (1994, p. 32), in a study of the methods used by parents to discipline their children during a 10-year period of time, found that about two-thirds of the parents used corporal punishment as a primary method for providing discipline, and the proportion of parents using corporal punishment on their children did not change over the 10 years of the study. However, there was a decrease in the percentage of parents using the more extreme forms of punishment, such as throwing things at a child, or hitting them with an object. There was also a decrease in the frequency with which corporeal punishment was used, as well as the severity of the punishment. The most frequent forms used were mild slaps and using a belt or paddle.

Straus (1994, p. 32) found that spanking, slapping, grabbing or shoving children continued into the adolescent years. He noted that the common law and state statutes have a 'parental exemption" that protects parents from being charged with assault for physical disciplining their children. Straus concluded that adolescents who were corporally punished hive a higher probability of engaging in violent behavior, becoming depressed, and being alienated during their adolescent years and into adulthood than those who did not experience corporal punishment during their childhood and adolescent years.

9.6   Documentation of Child Maltreatment

The Children's Bureau, U.S. Department of Health and Human Services, collects data on child abuse, neglect and endangering from the 50 states, the Commonwealth of Puerto Rico and the District of Columbia provided by child protective service agencies each year. Although the states may use somewhat different definitions of abuse, neglect and child maltreatment, and have different rules and requirements for reporting suspected child maltreatment, there are enough similarities in the state systems for the Children's Bureau to compile a report (Sickmund & Puzzanchera, 2014, p. 27) provide the definitions of the terms pertaining to child abuse/and neglect that are commonly used by the personnel of the child protection agencies.

A referral is the "notification to the CPS agency of suspected child maltreatment." A report is, "a referral of child maltreatment that was accepted or 'assigned in' for an investigation or assessment by a CPS agency as being at risk of being maltreated and to determine the CPS agency's appropriate response." It generally results in a disposition as to whether or not the alleged abuse is substantiated. An assessment is, "The process by which CPS determines if a child or other persons involved in the report of alleged maltreatment needs services." Substantiated cases refer to "investigation dispositions that conclude that the allegation of maltreatment (or risk of maltreatment) was supported by or founded on state law or state policy. This is the highest level of finding by a CPS agency." The term unsubstantiated refers to an "Investigation disposition that determines that there is not sufficient evidence under state law to conclude or suspect that the child has been maltreated or is at risk of maltreatment." The term indicated is used for an "Investigation disposition that concludes that maltreatment cannot be substantiated under state law or policy, but there is reason to suspect that the child may have been maltreated or was at risk of maltreatment. Few states distinguish between substantiated and indicated dispositions." *Alternative response* refers to the "CPS response to a report that focuses on assessing the needs of the family and providing services. This approach may or may not include a determination regarding the alleged maltreatment." The concept *court action* refers to "Legal action initiated by the CPS agency on behalf of the child. This includes authorization to place the child in foster care, filing for temporary custody or dependency, or termination of parental rights. As used here, it does not include criminal proceedings against a perpetrator."

Box 9.1 provides some of the finding included in the U.S. Department of Health and Human Services' *Child Maltreatment 2017 Report.*

Box 9.1 Information Abstracted from Child Maltreatment 2017

- During 2017 Child Protective Services agencies received a national estimate of 4.1 referrals involving approximately 7.5 million children (p. ix)
- More than half (57.6%) of the cases were screened in (Initial investigation was warranted (p. ix)
- The percentage of child victims are similar for boys and girls. The victimization of girls was slightly higher (p. 21);
- Three-quarters of the child victims were neglected, 18.3% abused physically and 8.6% sexually abused. In addition, 7.1% of victims experienced some other type of maltreatment such as threatened abuse or neglect, drug/alcohol addiction, and lack of supervision (p. 22);
- More than one quarter of the child victims were younger than 3 years old. The victimization rates are the highest for children under 1 year of age (p. 21);
- In 2017, a national estimate of 1720 children died from abuse and neglect. The 2017 estimate is a rise of 11% from the 2013 national estimate. Seventy-two percent of all child fatalities were younger than 3 years of age and nearly one-half of child fatalities were younger than 1 year of age (pp. 55–56);
- More than 90% of child victims were maltreated by parents. The parents could have been acting alone (the mother being the abuser in more than 2/3 of the cases), acting together, or one or both parents being the perpetrators of the maltreatment with non-parent others (relative, non-parent partner, acquaintance) (pp. 25–26).

The 2017 Child Maltreatment Report revealed that more than half of the referrals were screened in, and 42.4% were screened out. "For FFY 2017, approximately 4.3 million children (duplicate count) are the subjects of reports (screened in referrals). A child may be a victim in one report and a non-victim in another report, and in this analysis, the child is counted both times. A total of 27% of children are classified as victims with dispositions of substantiated (18.3%) and indicated (6.7%). The remaining children are not determined to be victims or received an alternative response (83%) (Children's Bureau, 2018, p. 19). More children were classified as "neglected" than as "abused," but some children were classified as both neglected and abused. Maltreated children were victims of physical, emotional, or educational neglect or of physical, emotional, or sexual abuse. More than three-fourths of maltreated children were victimized by their parents, caretaker, or guardian.

9.7 Sexual Exploitation and Abuse of Children

Although the sexual abuse of children has historically been a concern, it has not been researched extensively until recent generations. The growth of mass communications and the development of the internet, have resulted in new opportunities for child molesters to obtain access to young children. While in the past the sexual abuse of children was predominately a matter of parents, relatives, and acquaintances having opportunities to exploit children, in the current society, the opportunities have broadened to include situations in which the victims and offenders are not complete strangers in the sense that they may have communicated via electronic communications, but have not had face to face communications until the time of the actual sexual encounter. In addition, the internet provides a lucrative market for pornographic pictures and films that depict sexual activity.

The internet is used by sexual predators to prey on children through chat room contacts that may result in exploitation of vulnerable and immature children. Advertising that lures young people into the pornography or prostitution market may offer them "modeling" career opportunities.

9.7.1 The Incidence of Sexual Abuse of Children

There is common agreement that the actual amount of sexual abuse of children is much greater than that officially reported. Some estimates place it as much as ten times as high as the officially reported statistics. The chances of an incident of child sexual abuse being reported vary with the following circumstances:

1. Whether the case involves acquaintances, family members, or strangers;
2. Whether the offender is arrested and charged with a crime, or if the situation is never made public and handled unofficially;
3. Whether the case came to the attention of officials through legal channels or through a social work or medical source; and
4. Whether the child came to the attention of social agency professionals as a specific referral for sexual abuse or for some other problem.

In an interview with Christa J. Cross, Former Forensic Interviewer, Stark County Job and Family Services (Kratcoski, 2012, pp. 104–105) she was asked, "How often do you cooperate and interact with public and private service agencies such as the police, family court, welfare agencies, or volunteer groups?" she responded, "In my current position, I work with child protective services, law enforcement agencies, Akron Children's Hospital, mental health private and public agencies, county prosecutors, and victims' advocates. In general, children services works hand in hand with the Stark County Family Court, drug and alcohol services providers, mental health agencies, sex offender treatment programs, parenting programs, rehab, public assistance, and various education programs for the parents. It takes a community to assist families in their struggles." Christa Cross was asked. "How much influence do you have in the decision to handle cases of physical and sexual abuse of children either formally or informally/" She replied, "That influence mainly comes from the social worker and detective who conduct the investigation and works with all of the parties involved in the case. We, as a multicounty MDT. We talk about the case and make a team decision. Although the multicounty MDT works together of the determination of the best solution for the interests of the child victim, the prosecutors decide if they want to charge the perpetrator of the abuse with a crime and prosecute" (Kratcoski, 2012, p. 105).

The forms of sexual abuse of children that may come under scrutiny by legal or social work agencies are rape. Gross sexual imposition, incest, sexual battery, or endangering children. If the incident involves a male victims or if the sexual battery was between family members, the matter is often not taken into court since the charge against the adult may be reduced to contributing to the delinquency of a minor or impairing the morals of a minor. Unless the case files are specifically read and released, the existence or extent of the sexual abuse remains hidden.

9.7.2 Sources of Referrals on Child Abuse

As shown below, in Table 9.1, professionals are the most frequent source of referrals for all types of abuse and neglect. Professionals included educators, social workers, law enforcement personnel, and medical personal. These groups are in the best position to detect abuse, neglect, and other types of child endangerment, since they are the people who have the responsible to investigate alleged cases of children at risk and to take the appropriate action. Teachers are also in a good position to detect possible abuse or neglect, since they have daily contact with the children and are in a position to notice such things as cuts, bruises, or broken bones, as well as the behavior of children who appears to be extremely emotionally upset, withdrawn, or disruptive. Of course, medical professionals are in a position to closely examine the physical abuse, committed by a parent, guardian, or caretaker. Doctors and members of the medical professions often are the first professionals who have contact with very young children, often those below the age of one, who were physically abused. The fact that the professional occupations mentioned above are required by law to report suspected cases of abuse is another reason for professionals being the major source of referrals.

Table 9.1 Sources of referrals on alleged child maltreatment

Sources of referral
Professionals
Education
Social service
Law enforcement
Medical
Family and community
Friends/neighbors
Relative (other than parents)
Parents
Other sources
Anonymous
Victims
Other[a]

[a]Includes child care providers, perpetrators, and sources not identified elsewhere

Source: U.S. Department of Health and Human Services (*Child maltreatment-2017*)

9.7.3   Victim-Precipitated Abuse

The theory of victim precipitation is often cited in the explanation of some cases of sexual abuse of children. It assumes or insinuates that the abused child either cooperated with the offender or sought the sexual involvement that developed between them. The relationship developed over a period of time, beginning with sexual touching and fondling and not progressing to intercourse until months, even years later. There is an absence of force and the sexual abuse is generally not viewed as threatening by the child. In fact, the abuser may be very affectionately involved with the child and show a strong interest in such aspects of the child's life as school or hobbies.

Rosenfeld (1979), who termed such sexual abuse "endogamous," suggested that the child becomes adjusted to this sexual activity because it is integrated with the other pleasurable experiences enjoyed with the adult. Rosenfeld characterized such an offender, often the child's father, as emotionally estranged from his wife and as a person who has experienced feelings of rejection or inadequacy. The child's mother is characterized as an insecure and needful woman, immature, incapable of managing, and searching for approval. The sexually abused girl may take over the housekeeping and child-rearing roles of the mother. The mother overtly supports the daughter's assumption of her social roles, and may covertly support the daughter's taking over her sexual role.

The characteristic of seductiveness is frequently attributed to the child who is the victim of sexual abuse. This may be particularly true in those cases in which the girl is in her adolescent years. Because of her seductive behavior, there is a tendency to imply that the child is to blame or at least some degree of fault is attributed to the child for instigating the sexual interaction. Rosenfeld (1979) believed that a child develops these seductive tendencies in an effort to obtain the attention and affection which were not given in a normal manner. The child learns to act in a charming and sexually arousing way as a means of gaining attention that would otherwise have been denied. The "seductive" behavior is another symptom of the child's abnormal personality and arrested psychological development. The victim-precipitated theory is also given some credence in the discussion of o the sexual abuse of boys.

The degree to which child sexual abuse of children is precipitated by the child-victim should be viewed with some caution. It is quite likely that those professionals (psychologists, social workers, or institutional staff) who treat sexually abused children overestimate the degree of compliance and cooperativeness on the part of the child. This may occur because they get information on abuse after the fact and they may be dealing with an atypical portion of the sexually abused child population. Even though the large majority of child sexual abuse occurs within the family or with close friends, force or the threat of force is frequently used by the perpetrator. This would indicate that the victim is not likely to be the instigator of the sexual activity.

9.7.4   The Generational Theory of Child Abuse

Another assumption that needs to be questioned is the notion that abuse of children occurs in families generation after generation and those who have been abused will later abuse their own children. It has been substantiated through research that some children who have been physically abused grow up to be abusers as adults, victimizing their own children as their parents victimized them. The concept has been applied to both physical and sexual abuse. A study by the American Humane Association (DeFrancis, 1977, pp. 6–8) found that mothers of sexually abused children had themselves been child victims of such abuse in 11% of the cases in the study. Nevertheless, it is difficult to establish a direct cause-and effect relationship between experiencing sexual abuse as a child and later deviance, emotional illness, or toleration of sexual abuse of one's own children. Case studies of delinquents, alcoholics, and mentally ill individuals reveal that, while physical or sexual abuse might have been a part of the life experiences of some of these persons, it was not experienced by the majority of them. Many cases of child sexual abuse occur in what might be termed a "permissive family setting." The family unit is characterized by disorganization, chaos antisocial personal behavior, violence, alcoholism, and various forms of deviance The physical or sexual abuse of the children is viewed as almost a minor part of this chaotic and unpredictable lifestyle. For example, Finkelhor (1979, pp. 88–89) found that a disproportionate number of those who were poly-victimized experienced the most serious types of victimization such as physical abuse or sexual abuse. In another study,

Finkelhor (2013) found that almost one-fourth of the victimized children in the study witnessed an act of violence in their homes, schools and communities within the past year. The Child Maltreatment 2017 Report (U.S. Department of Health and Human Services, 2018) provides data on how *risk factors* that exist in a household are likely to contribute to child maltreatment within that household. The Report (2018, pp. 23, 24) states, "Risk factors are characteristics of a child or caregiver that may increase the likelihood of child maltreatment." Four major risk factors considered in the Report pertaining to the caretaker of the family, or household are alcohol abuse, drug abuse, financial problems, and domestic violence. In the report, the percentage of caregivers with a high risk for child maltreatment was 12.1%, with a high risk for child maltreatment due to drug abuse was 30.8%, with a high risk as a result of financial problems was 14.9% and the percent of caretakers with domestic violence by the caretaker of a family was 27.2%.

The difficulty lies in determining how much adult deviant behavior can be attributed to experiencing physical or sexual abuse as a child and how much is the result of other forms of deviance and disorganization If a person who was physically or sexually abused as a child grows up to be a deviant or to have a distorted outlook, how much of this problem can be attributed to the person's prior experiences?

In regard to the generational hypothesis, it appears that the majority of those who were physical or sexual abusers were not abused themselves, and that even though a high correlation between being abused and becoming an abuser exists, there is also evidence that the large majority of those who were abused as children do not engage in abuse of their own children. In addition, a good proportion of the sexual abuse of adolescent girls within the family setting can be attributed to the increase in the number of families in which a stepfather or live in boyfriend, or stepbrother has entered into the family. The resulting sexual activity is not a result of an intricate family dysfunction, but rather a situational occurrence between non-relatives brought on by alcohol or drug abuse or a lack of moral conviction on the part of those involved. The socialization and value systems of these persons are such that they do not regard such behavior as being morally wrong.

9.8 Risk Factors of Children

Research findings, as well as other reports, have found that some children are at a higher risk for being neglected or abused as a result of their age, physical or mental handicaps, as well as their status within the family. The categories of children who have been identified as having a higher than normal risk of being abused or neglected include the following:

- Very young children; A larger portion of children under the age of one are abused than children falling into any other age group;
- Children born out of wedlock;
- Children who have a physical or mental handicap;

- Children with a personality disorder, such as sociopathy
- Children who are the off-spring of a previous spouse of either the mother or father; and
- Children in an out-of-home placement.

The identification of the categories of children who are more likely to be abused or neglected does not indicate that the large majority of these children will actually be endangered. In most instances the opposite is true. For example, the Health and Human Services Child Maltreatment Report 2017 (U.S. Department of Health and Human Services, 2018) reveals that less than one fourth of children under the age of two were maltreated. Those who are in out of home placements, such as foster care group homes or rehabilitation centers, while being in a situation in which being physically or psychologically abused by other residents or a staff member may occur, the large proportion of these children are not maltreated. Infants are vulnerable for several reasons. The helplessness of a very young child to escape from attack, coupled with the need for constant attention and its tendency to cry and to disrupt the social life or the other activities of parents, makes it particularly at risk. For example, the combination of an infant who is sickly and a mother who has a drug or alcohol problems presents a situation where the risks of abuse are elevated. In some cases of child abuse the baby is the offspring of a very young couple who are not financially secure or emotionally mature enough to accept the child. The child is seen as a physical symbol of their captivity and becomes a source of resentment. This attitude toward the child may persist throughout the child's life, helping to explain why in some families one of the children is the object of maltreatment, while the other children do not receive the abuse (usually psychological). A child who becomes the stepchild of a later marriage runs the risk of similar mistreatment by either the parent, stepparent or other children in the family. Premature, physically handicapped, or sickly babies also run the risk of being maltreated, since they require more than the amount of attention the parents are capable and willing to provide. There is no doubt that some children have personality and behavioral characteristics that make them particularly difficult to handle. Parents who might be perfectly capable of caring for and disciplining a normal child can be pushed over the brink by constantly having to put up with a hyperactive, nasty-tempered child who needs little sleep or who is constantly getting into mischief. Child abuse incidents involving such children tend to be isolated instances of too-severe reaction by the parent/s, rather than fitting into a pattern of abuse and neglect. When a single child is the object of maltreatment, it may not be related to any characteristic or trait of the child but more the problem of the abuser. For example, the abused child may bear a striking physical resemblance to a former husband or lover, a despised parent or other relative, or even to the abuser, who sees his or her worst characteristics personified in the child. Children who sense that they are disliked or resented may persist in angering and irritating their parents even though they are punished or abused because they perceive the activity as a method of gaining the parents' attention.

A homicide committed by most unusual means illustrates the potential for abuse present in such situations.

> When interrogated by the police (after the death of her three-and-a half year-old child) the mother stated that the child had developed the habit of taking the nursing bottle away from a 13-month-old sibling despite repeated attempts to discourage this practice. Following an additional instance of this activity, the mother unscrewed the top of a pepper shaker and poured the contents into the child's mouth. The child "swallowed" the material and immediately complained of burning in her throat and stomach. The mother said she gave her some sips of milk and some water, but the little girl started to gasp, turned blue, and collapsed. Screams for help aroused the neighbors who called the police. The child was rushed to a nearby hospital and was pronounced dead on arrival. (Adelson, 1964, pp. 393–394)

Although many cases of the physical abuse as well of sexual abuse of children consist of routine behavior on the part of the abuser, in other cases the abuse is the result of a spontaneous reaction to a frustrating or anger-producing circumstance of the abuser. Many youngsters become victims of abuse because they happen to be in the wrong place at the wrong time, as when a parent comes home in a drunken stupor or when a disagreement between the parents ends with one or the other directing the anger toward a child. Sometimes the frustrations of daily living reach a point where parents vent their anger on the nearest available object.

The ages of abused children cover the entire juvenile range. Premature infants and those who are overactive, demanding, and exhausting may wear down a parent's self-control temporarily and trigger a violent response. As indicated by statistics, various stages in the child's development, for example the first few years, including the "terrible twos" and the adolescent period have been identified as times when the child's behavior is such that it is more likely to trigger a violent response from a parent.

9.8.1 Identifying Child Abuse and Neglect

As previously indicated, the large majority of perpetrators of child maltreatment consist of caretakers of the children, including the parents and other members of the household. Child abuse occurs in all socioeconomic levels and is committed by members of every race, ethnic group and age group. However, according to the reports on those cases investigated, the highest levels of child maltreatment occur among the poor, those with lower levels of education, and among minority group members. Mothers are shown to be more involved in child maltreatment of very young children than are fathers, simply because mothers are with the child for much longer periods of time during the day and thus are the primary caretakers during that time. Fathers and stepfathers are more likely to be the perpetrators of physical and sexual abuse of older children. Males are identified as the perpetrators of sexual abuse of children in the large majority of cases reported, investigated, and substantiated.

Some abusers may be suffering from serious psychiatric disorders, alcoholism, and drug abuse. Others, may have been physically abused or neglected when they were children, and perhaps even brain damaged by blows to the head, or by malnutrition at critical periods of their developmental periods, but for the large majority of those who engage in the maltreatment of their children, the behavior is most likely learned during their socialization (this is particularly true with the use of physical punishment) or the result of personality traits.

The professionals, educators, social workers, physicians, who have the major responsibility for reporting suspected child maltreatment must be trained, in a sense like a detective to recognize the indicators of child maltreatment. In the Child Abuse and Neglect Report (U.S. Department of Health, Education and Welfare (2018, pp. 1, 4–5) and the Child Maltreatment Reports 2017 (Department of Health and Human Services, 2018) the following characteristics have been recognized as indicators of a child having been abused or neglected. Box 9.2 provides a list of these characteristics.

Of course, a child's behavior that corresponds to one or several of the indicators

---

Box 9.2 Indicators of Child Abuse and Neglect

1. They appear to be different from other children in physical or emotional make-up; or their parents inappropriately describe them as being "different" or "bad";
2. They seem unduly afraid of their parents;
3. They may often bear welts, bruises, untreated sores, or other skin injuries;
4. They show evidence of overall poor care;
5. They exhibit behavioral extremes, crying often, crying very little, being excessively fearful, or seeming fearless of adult authority; being unusually aggressive and destructive, or extremely passive and withdrawn;
6. Some are wary of physical contact, especially when it is initiated by an adult;
7. They may exhibit a sudden change in behavior; pants-wetting, thumb-sucking, frequent whining, becoming destructive, or becoming uncommonly shy and passive;
8. They have learning problems that cannot be diagnosed;
9. They are habitually truant or late for school. Frequent and prolonged absences sometimes result when a parent keeps an injured child at home until the evidence of abuse disappears;
10. In some cases, they frequently arrive at school too early and remain after class rather than going home;
11. They are always tired and often sleep in class; and
12. They are inappropriately dressed for the weather. Children who never have coats or shoes in cold weather are receiving below the normal amount of care. Those who regularly wear long sleeves or high necklines on hot days may be dressed to cover bruises, burns, or other marks of abuse.

---

listed above, may not be actually caused by the child being abused or neglected. As previously noted, almost half of the reports filed on child maltreatment are not substantiated, once an investigation is completed. Nevertheless, these indicators of possible maltreatment of a child can serve as clues for police officers, child services workers, teachers and others who interact with the child or who are conducting an investigation into alleged abuse or neglect.

Abused children are at risk for becoming delinquent because they may have developed ways of coping with the abuse or distorted views of life that lead them toward delinquent behavior. Mouzakitis (1984) identified two distinct groups of youths who had been abused or neglected since infancy and early childhood and those whose abuse began when they reached puberty. He concluded that those who had been abused for an extended period of time were more psychologically damaged and more likely to be involved in violent behavior, promiscuity, running away, or criminal behavior than those who had endured abuse for a shorter period of time. Abused children are at risk for involvement in delinquency because they cope with the abuse in ways that may lead toward unacceptable behavior. According to Moore (1991) these include aggressive behavior as a way of displacing the anger that they feel toward their victimizer, alienation from peers because they feel ashamed or fear that others will find out they have been sexually abused, distrust of adults and authority figures brought on by a sense of betrayal by adults, self-blame, created by feelings that they somehow brought about or encouraged the abuse; substance abuse, used to escape the feelings of hurt, anger and fear; or running away, which may remove the youth from the scene of the abuse but put him or her in jeopardy for committing offenses to survive on the street.

9.9   Legislation Directed Toward Protecting Maltreated Children

The U.S. Congress passed the Federal Child Abuse Protection and Treatment Act in 1974. This led to the establishment of a National Center on Child Abuse and Neglect and provided funds to states to establish the agencies needed to investigate and prevent child abuse. To be eligible for federal grants, the states had to demonstrate that they enacted mandatory child abuse report laws. Another provision in the Act was that a guardian ad litem had to be appointed by the court in every case of child maltreatment processed through the court. The guardian ad litem would represent the interests of the child. (42 U.S. C.A. Section 5103(b) (2) (G). The Victims of Child Abuse Act of 1990 (Sagatun & Edwards, 1995, p. 10) included the following:

- Provisions for improving techniques for investigating and prosecuting child abuse cases;
- Court-appointment of a special advocate for every child victim and use of guardian ad litem in more types of cases;
- Training of court personnel and staff in issues related to child abuse and neglect;
- Protection of victim's rights in testimony related to abuse, including use of closed-circuit television or videotaped depositions and grants for equipment to facilitate use of this type of testimony;

- Training for those conducting competency examinations and direct examinations involving children;
- Use of multidisciplinary child abuse teams; during investigations;
- Background checks for child care workers; and
- Treatment for juvenile offenders who were found to be neglectful of abuse victims.

Other legislation pertaining to child victimization and maltreatment enacted by the state legislatures encompassed the federal legislation and also have provisions for the individual state in which the legislation is enacted.

9.10   Juvenile Court Process in Neglect and Abuse Cases

Less than one fourth of all of the reports of child maltreatment that come before the child protection agencies, including those from the police, children service agencies and all others, will be brought before a juvenile or family court for a disposition. Sickmund and Puzzanhera (2014, pp. 24–25) provide a flow chart on the stages involved in a child maltreatment case that is reported and processed by child protective services and the juvenile/family court systems. The process is shown in Chart 9.1.

Abuse referrals to the juvenile court are generally made by the children services agencies or the police. In most jurisdictions, professionals such as teachers, physicians and children welfare workers will make the referrals to a child protective agency and, as shown in Chart 9.1, the children service agency will review the case and either determine that there is not sufficient evidence of child maltreatment to continue an investigation, or if the case should be processed. For example, the police may be called to a household where child abuse has alleged occurred or is in process. The responding officers must assess the situation. If the parents or caretakers refuse to allow officers entry into the home and the officers have reason to believe a child or children are in danger, the police may enter the home to investigate without permission. If there is evidence that the child has been beaten or molested, or is neglected, sexually molested and in immediate danger, the officers can remove the child from the home and take the appropriate action to assure that the health care needs are provided and that the child will be safe. Often, the police officers will transport a child directly to a hospital or call for emergency medical services to provide the transportation. If the child does not need medical care, but appears to be in immediate danger, the police can still make a decision to use emergency temporary custody and transport the youth to a temporary foster home. Regardless of the action taken by the police, the appropriate children's services agency is notified.

The processing of child abuse or neglect cases in the juvenile court involves preparation of a petition (written complaint) against the parent or the abuser that details the specific act of commission or omission with dates, times and frequency of their occurrences. A child service agency is the most frequent source of such a petition, but it may be filed by law enforcement officials. Often specific charges will not be filed until there is time to investigate the charges. This investigation is

Sources of Referral

Professionals	Law Enforcement	Others
Screen Out (Investigation)	Child Protective Services Intake Decision	Alternative Response
Case is Closed Services / Juvenile Court	Child Protective Services Investigated/Screened in Cases	Referred to Voluntary
Dismissed	Juvenile/Family Court Intake	Informal Processing
Dismissed	Juvenile/Family Court Formal Process	Adjudication Hearing
Dismissed or Closed to be returned to home/	Adjudication Hearing Outcome	Permanency planning/ not services provided/case closed
Permanency review	Permanency Determination Termination of Parental Rights Adoption	Dependency terminated; case Closed

Chart 9.1 Child maltreatment processing in the child protective services and juvenile/family court systems

generally completed by children's services, often with the assistance of the police officer who responded to the alleged report of child endangerment. If the case is not dismissed, or informally handled, the prosecutor's office, after reviewing the information available on the case, may decide not to refer it to the juvenile court because there are not sufficient grounds to prove that either physical or psychological abuse, neglect, or sexual abuse, as defined by law, actually occurred.

A protective custody hearing is generally held within 48–72 h of the initial referral. At the hearing, it is determined whether emergency protective custody of the child is warranted, and if warranted, whether it should be continued until the outcome of the case is decided.

During the intake, petition, and advisement stages, the accused are informed of their rights to private or court appointed counsel and if court appointed counsel is provided the attorney is selected. If the accused maintains that the charges are untrue, an adjournment is declared so that the defense attorney has some time to prepare the defense.

At the pretrial conference, the attorney for the complainant (generally a representative from a child services agency) provides a written statement in which the alleged offenses are described. Consultation between attorneys for the accused and those for the child protective agency may lead to a resolution of the issues. A common resolution takes the form of a consent decree agreement. Such an agreement is defined as "a judgement entered by consent of the parties whereby the defendant agrees to stop the alleged illegal activity without admitting guilt or wrong doing" (Black's Law Dictionary, 1991. p. 819). A consent decree agreement may be reached after there has been some bargaining on the specific charges in the complaint. For example, a charge of child neglect may be reduced to one of child dependency in exchange for the accused agreeing not to contest the action being proposed by the court to protect the interests of the child. In this way, no fault is attributed to the alleged offender, but the court has accomplished its primary goal of protecting the child from harm and assuring that the child's basic needs will be met.

If the case is not resolved at the pretrial conference, a trial, often referred to as a fact-finding hearing, takes place. In the hearing, the focus is not on proving the accused person or persons guilty of a crime, but on developing a solution to the problem. The juvenile court hearing is not a criminal procedure, where the offender must be proven guilty beyond a reasonable doubt, but a civil proceeding. The importance of the outcome in a civil proceeding determines the standard of proof to be applied. In child welfare cases that could result in placing the child for adoption because of the severity of the abuse or neglect on the part of person or persons (most often parents or other caretakers) a "clear and convincing" standard of proof is required. (This standard is considered to be a higher level than preponderance of the evidence but not as high la level as beyond a reasonable doubt, the standard used in criminal proceedings). Other child protective cases, in which the outcome could be placement of the child in temporary foster care, with the possibility of the family being reunited at a later date, use the "fair preponderance of evidence" standard of proof (more than 50% level of certainty).

At the trial (fact-finding hearing), the legal representative of the agency that brought the charges introduces the evidence, which may in the form of written documents such as medical reports, exhibits\ (x-rays of broken bones), evidence of sexual assault, and the oral testimony of witnesses, completed through direct examination. The attorney for the plaintiff may also cross-examine the witnesses for the defense. The attorney for the defendant has the right to confront all witnesses and cross-examine them, as well as contest the admissibility of the material evidence provided by the plaintiff. The child involved may be questioned in the judge's chambers, or be asked to testify before the court. To avoid having the child traumatized by appearing before the accused in court, in some cases, the victim may be allowed to provide testimony by way of closed circuit television. The accused are never required to take the stand and offer testimony, but may elect to do so to attempt to bolster their own defense. If the accused does take the stand, he or she must submit to a cross-examination.

9.10.1   *Special Consideration Giving to Victims of Abuse or Neglect*

In cases involving sexual abuse, testimony by children is a particularly difficult problem. Unless the abuse occurred in a single, violent instant, there may be no evidence, such as bruises or semen to substantiate the child's story. The court is faced with the dilemma of testing a child's word against that of an adult. The competency of a child as a witness is open to question, and the effect on the child being required to describe what has taken place in the presence of the accused can be particularly traumatic. In addition, the victim may recant the story or try to minimize what actually happened because he or she may feel that the family has been hurt by the revelations or that everyone may become angry if the perpetrator is a family member and the situation is brought out in court.

Certain innovations in court procedures have been used to try to minimize the possible traumatic effects on the child as a result of having to appear in court. These include using a single trained interviewer to conduct a joint investigation for law enforcement, the prosecutor, and social service agencies, rather than requiring that the child victim recount over and over again what happened to the various agencies involved. Christa Cross, former Child Forensic Interviewer for the Stark County, Ohio, Job and Family Service, who completes the interviewing of child victims and shares the information with the various legal and service agencies, described the process she used in the fact-finding interview. In response to a question "How do you set the stage and proceed with the interviewing of a child who allegedly was abused?" she responded, "A report comes through the Child Protective Services (CPS) hotline and is assigned to an intake social worker and detective of the jurisdiction in which the alleged abuse occurred. Contact is made with the caregiver of the alleged victim, and the interview is scheduled for the child to come to my office.... I then show the caretaker the interview room and where my cameras are located in the walls with the microphone, and I advise the caretaker that I do not inform the children that they are being videotaped during the interview. and give examples of why I do not want to let them know. The family advocate then takes the caretaker into her office and explains the entire process to him or her .... I then take the child into the room and as I go by I switch on the button that starts the video. During the interview, I first ask general questions about everything to do with the child's life ... and then go on to the more sensitive issues such as fears, worries, secrets and safe and unsafe body touches. I always advise the child that they are not in trouble, nor that they will get into trouble for anything that we talk about.... After the interview, depending on what the child discloses, they would next see my nurse practitioner. I advise the nurse of what the child disclosed and I move on to the next family, , , , , I have no further involvement with the child."

(Abstracted from Kratcoski (2012, pp. 100–101)

9.10.2 Dispositions in Child Abuse and Neglect Cases

If the court determines that abuse or neglect has taken place, the social agency that brought the information about the case to the court may be asked to make recommendations to the court or the court may determine the action to be taken. Dispositions might include supervision of the parents and child by a probation officer, medical or psychiatric examinations or treatment for members of the family; "orders of protection," which detail conditions that must be met by the parents or caretakers, temporary removal of the child from the home to foster care; or a permanent change of custody.

If removal of the child to foster care is indicated, a long history of displacement may begin. Parents with children who are in foster care are reluctant to release them for adoption, even though the chances of reestablishing a workable family unit may be remote. With every passing year, the child's chances of adoption diminish. The child may be placed in one foster home after another until reaching the upper limit to the juvenile status. Difficult foster children all too frequently return to the juvenile courts as truants, incorrigibles, or runaways, and eventually are placed in institutions simply because there is nowhere else to keep them. Here the cycle might begin all over again, in the form of abuse or neglect by institutional personnel. Patterns of unreasonable expectations and demands are all too familiar to these children enter in their lives.

9.11   Criminal Prosecution of Child Abusers

Although juvenile and family courts have some jurisdiction over adults in matters pertaining to criminal activity involving children, (e.g., contributing to the delinquency of a minor), the decision to file criminal charges against the perpetrators of child abuse and neglect is generally in the hands of the prosecutor. Most juvenile courts will have a prosecutor assigned to the court for the sole purpose of assisting the court in making decisions on matters pertaining to child abuse and neglect. The circumstances of each case are taken into consideration in the decision making process. For example, an adult who sexually molests a young child and is a stranger to the child will generally be criminally prosecuted. However, in cases in which the offender is a close family member, the circumstances might suggest that it would be in the best interests of the victim and the victim's family not to prosecute. Such factors as the offender being senile, suffering from dementia, the child having helped to instigate and facilitate the abuse, or the offender beating a child in a rare fit of anger and other factors will be considered. Also, if the offender provides the economic support for the family as is the situation for many cases of sexual abuse, if the offender were sent to prison the negative effect on the family might be so drastic that the entire family would suffer.

9.12   The Criminal Court Process

If an adult is charged with a crime pertaining to child abuse or neglect, the defendant is given all of the rights guaranteed by the U.S. Constitution and those provided as a result of Supreme Court decisions, including the right to have counsel and to request a jury trial. The case is under the jurisdiction of the criminal court. The charges against the defendant may have been found to be true in a civil hearing on child abuse or neglect completed in the juvenile court. However, the standard of proof for that hearing was either "a fair preponderance of evidence" or "clear and convincing evidence," while for a conviction in the criminal court the "beyond a reasonable doubt standard" must be met.

The pretrial process involves an informal fact investigation and planning on the part of the prosecutor, a legal investigation that includes the search for similar cases, collecting evidence, and planning a case strategy. The defendant will be informed of the charges and have an opportunity to make a plea during the arraignment. If the plea is "not guilty," a preliminary trial date as well as a trial date will be set, and the prosecuting and defense attorneys will have time to complete additional investigations, including a formal discovery, and to prepare motions to present to the trial judge. In addition, the prosecuting attorney and defense attorney will usually engage in a pretrial conference and if an agreement can be made, (generally some reduction of the severity of the charges in exchange for a guilty plea), the case will be settled without having a formal trial on the charges.

In those cases that are tried in court, a presentation on pretrial matters, including motions and stipulations, and a decision on these matters by the judge is followed by a reading of the charges, jury selection, if a jury is requested, opening statements by the prosecution and the defense, the direct examination of the witnesses by the prosecutor, and the cross examination of the witnesses for the prosecution by the defense attorney. After the prosecution has completed its case, the defense has the opportunity to directly examine witnesses and the prosecutor has the right to cross-examine the defense witnesses After the defense has completed its case, the prosecution and defense have the opportunity to give closing arguments. Mauer (2002, p. 401) contends, "Closing arguments are the chronological and psychological culmination of a jury trial. They are the last opportunity to communicate directly with the jury. For that reason, ,it is imperative that the arguments forcefully present your side's theory of the case, themes, and labels, position on the contested issues, and the reasons your party should get a favorable verdict."

After the closing arguments, the judge instructs the jury and it is sent to make a deliberation. The jury is only responsible for making a decision on the guilt or innocence of the defendant on the charges. For child abuse and neglect crimes, unless the charge is aggravated murder, the presiding judge will have the sole responsibility for sentencing the defendant found guilty of the charges. Usually for the more serious offenses pertaining to child maltreatment (rape, aggravated assault, manslaughter) the trial process will be bifurcated, that is, the adjudication hearing and the sentencing hearing are separated. Separating the two hearings gives the judge more time to determine the most appropriate sentence. There may be good reasons for the judge to give a convicted felon in child abuse a community based sentence rather than a sentence to a secure correctional institution. This is especially relevant if the offender is a close member of the family. If allowed to remain in the community, under strict supervision, and with specific conditions pertaining to the prevention of further abuse of the victim or victims, there may more opportunity for the offender to receive the appropriate counseling and for the family to eventually reunite.

9.13 Prevention Programs

Programs designed to protect children from molesters in the community or around the school are the easiest to implement. Everyone is in agreement that such programs are necessary, and community members are usually willing to take part in some way, even if it only involves putting a sign in a window indicating that the residence is a safe house.

Because the largest proportion of child abuse, including physical and sexual, as well as the neglect of children occurs within the family, many of the programs geared toward preventing abuse and neglect are directed toward strengthening the family unit and addressing the problems of individual members of the family. For some families, their problems are a reflection of the problems in the larger society. The increased incidence of violence, often promoted by the media, the relaxing of moral standards, the use of drugs and alcohol to relieve stress, and the desire for immediate gratification are factors in our present society that have been shown to be related in some way to crime causation in general and child maltreatment in particular.

Other influences on the increase in reported abuse and neglect include the pressure put on mothers who work outside the home and have to assume the responsibility for the children when they return home. The general preoccupation of personal fulfillment might lead to a mother resenting her children for their interference with her personal goals, as well as becoming depressed, or suffering from anxiety because of feelings of not being able to meet all of the expectations put on her. The abuse of alcohol and drugs by one or several members of the family has also been shown to be related to child maltreatment

For these reasons, many of the prevention programs emphasize either strengthening the individual family or improving the position of categories of people within the community. For example, for those under economic duress, expanded or revised welfare and family maintenance programs offer the best hope for relief, if coupled with job training and other activities to break the cycle of generation-to-generation welfare dependence.

Since a portion of abuse and neglect is directly related to alcohol and drug abuse or to mental illness, increased public awareness of the availability of help and expanded facilities to address these problems could offer some assistance. Abusive parents are difficult to counsel for a number of reasons. They are already on the defensive because of the exposure of the abusive activity and the threat of court action against them and they may not be willing to discuss other incidents that have occurred or other problems within the family because they fear that the information will later be used against them. In addition, abuse they experienced as a child may help them "con" others into thinking that they are behaving as expected. If abused as a child, the parent who is an abuser may not have ever experienced a trusting relationship with an adult, and a counselor may find it difficult to develop rapport or to even communicate. On the other hand, the abuser may be over cooperative and go along with anything suggested by the counselor while not thinking through the solutions to his or her problems.

Current efforts to uncover child abuse and neglect and to get help for the abusers should be expanded. The traditional manner of child rearing that has existed in some families from generation to generation that includes abusive and neglectful behavior must be broken, through individual or group counseling, therapy, and family training. Young mothers in particular need to be counseled in proper child care, family life activities, and awareness of the medical needs of children and of their responsibilities for meeting the needs of their children.

Removal from the home and placement in foster care should be the last resort, since it may prove to be as psychologically damaging to the child in the long run as parental mistreatment. The National Advisory Committee on Criminal Justice Standards and Goals (1977) recommended that after a child has been found by the courts to be endangered, every effort should be made to meet the needs of the child and the parents in the home setting. The Committee recommended court-ordered services to the family, day care, counseling and therapy, medical treatment, and provisions of services by professionals as alternatives to removal from the home.

When removal from the home is dictated by the seriousness of the danger, the Committee recommended that the status of each child placed outside the home should be reviewed every 6 months and if the changes in the home are substantial, the child should be reunited with the family. If it appears that reunification with the family is not a feasible goal, adoption should be pursued as a permanency goal. There is some evidence that many of these recommendations have been implemented. For example, Sickmund and Puzzanchera (2014, p. 35) report that "More than half of children who exit from foster care are reunited with their parents or primary caretakers. However, the frequency of this outcome has decreased in the past decade. In 1999, an estimated 58% of children exiting foster care were reunited with their parents, or primary caretakers; by 2010, the figure dropped to 51%. The second most common outcome for youth exiting foster care in 2010 was adoption (21%). Other outcomes for children include living with relatives, emancipation, guardianship, transfer to another agency, and running away, all of which accounted for less than one third of exits."

9.14 Summary

Child abuse and neglect are important concerns of the juvenile justice system and of the many community agencies that provide services to children. Abuse and neglect are defined in various jurisdictions as including physical mistreatment only or as extending to include emotional mistreatment or deprivation.

All states require medical, law enforcement, education, and social work personnel to report suspected abuse to appropriate authorities, and any other person may do so. Immunity from legal retaliation is assured to those who make such reports.

The exact amount of child abuse and neglect that occurs in the United States each year is not known. A large number of cases is never discovered, or reported. However, the proportion of abuse and neglect of children cases reported to the authorities has increased in recent years. No doubt this is due to the mandatory reporting for professionals and the growing public awareness of the problem.

Sexual abuse of children is believed to be vastly underreported. Although reported instances of sexual abuse of girls, is more frequent than those of boys, a large number of boys are also victims of sexual abuse. Explanations for the increases in the sexual abuse of children include changing life styles of the family, alcohol and drug abuse of the predators of the abuse, and a lack of socialization into the value system that regards sexual abuse of children as improper behavior.

Those identified as high risks for either physical abuse or sexual abuse include: babies, children of very young parents, stepchildren, children born out of wedlock, children with physical or mental handicaps, sickly children, hyperactive children, and children who are not living with their natural parents Child abuse occurs in all social-economic classes, racial and ethnic groups, although according to the reports it is more frequent in the lower social-economic groups, where there is a larger concentration of poor families, unemployment, and minority group members.

Researchers have discovered that many child abusers were physically or emotionally abused as children and as parents they consciously or unconsciously apply the treatment they received to their children Parents who have experienced life crises (death in the family, divorce, unemployment, sexual difficulties) and single parents have been found to be disproportionately represented among child abusers. Sexual abuse of children has also been found to occur in families where the abusers themselves observed abnormal sexual behavior within their families.

A large portion of child abuse and neglect is handled informally within neighborhoods and families through threats of exposure. Almost half of the cases reported to child service agencies are not substantiated. Of those that are reported to social agencies or the police and substantiated (alleged abuse confirmed), the large majority of the less serious cases are handled informally through counseling by social agencies. If cases are referred to the juvenile or family courts and the accused offender denies the charges, the court will conduct a hearing to determine if the alleged abuse or neglect can be proven. The accused has legal rights and can be defended by an attorney. The sole purpose of the hearing is to determine if the charges are true and if so, to determine what disposition would be in the best interests of the child. Dispositions may include keeping the child in the home but requiring the offender to receive counseling, medical or psychiatric treatment if there is evidence of a mental problem or drug and alcoholic abuse, issuing a protection order or in the more extreme cases removing the child from the home for placement in foster care. In some cases, the offender will be tried in the criminal court. In these cases, the offender, if found guilty, may be liable for imprisonment.

The recommendations related to current policies on out-of-home placements of children in foster homes or other residential placement centers is to attempt to reunite the child with the family as soon as possible. After a period of time, if the reunification goal does not appear to be feasible, the child should be put up for adoption. The longer the period of time the child is in foster care, the less likely the child will make a smooth transition into adulthood.

9.15   Discussion Questions

1. Is it possible for a parent who never physically abused a child to be guilty of emotional abuse or neglect? Could a parent be criminally prosecuted on such a charge?
2. Why must caution be used in investigation of any report of child abuse or neglect? What procedures might be followed by a physician on duty in an emergency room when he or she encounters a case that is suggestive of abusive nor neglectful behavior?
3. Why is it important for a child who allegedly has been abused or neglected to have a guardian ad litem present when the case is heard in court?
4. Discuss several types of children who are considered "high risks" for child abuse. How do you explain the finding that in many instances only one child in a family is singled out as the target of abuse?
5. Are abused children likely to grow up to be abusers? Discuss.
6. What professionals are required to report suspected abuse or neglect of a child? What proportion of alleged child abuse is substantiated?
7. Discuss the hearing process followed in the juvenile court to determine if a child has been abused or neglected.
8. A large majority of the abuse of children are committed by one or both parents of the child. Which parent is responsible for the largest proportion on abuse cases? Discuss the reasons why children's service agencies who handle these cases prefer to use informal means to resolve these matters.
9. Discuss the cases of abuse that will require the abused child or children to be removed from the home and placed in either a shelter care facility or a foster home.
10. Are cases of sexual abuse of children in terms of the characteristics of the abuser and the circumstances different from cases of physical abuse? Discuss.

References

Akron Beacon Journal (2019) April 25, p. A5.

Adelson, L. (1964). Homicide by pepper. *Journal of Forensic Science, 9*(3), 393–394.

Baltimore Sun (1994) August 31, p. 3B.

Black, H. (1991) Black's Law Dictionary, 6th edition; St.Paul, MN; West Publishing Co.

Cleveland Plain Dealer, (1988), September 18, B5

Cross, A. (2003, February 19). Girl's family fees man get 4 years for death. *Akron Beacon Journal,* pp. Al, A5.

DeFrancis, V. (1977). *American humane association publishes highlights of national study of child neglect and abuse reporting.* Washington, DC: U.S. Department of Health, Education and Welfare, National Center on Child Abuse and Neglect (February). Publication (OHD) 77-20086, pp. 6–8/.

Finkelhor, D. (1979). *Sexually victimized children.* New York: Free Press.

Finkelhor, D.(2013). Violence, crime and abuse exposure in a national sample of children and youth: An update. Pediatrics, 167 (7). 616. Retrieved May 6, 2019, from http:archpedi.jarnetwork.com/article.aspx?articleid=16869838resultClick=3

Giannelli, P., & McCloud-Yeomans, P. (2004). *Ohio juvenile law: 2004 edition.* St. Paul, MN: Thomson-West.

Koop, C. (1985). A challenge to the medical profession. *Justice for Children, 1*(3), 23.

Kratcoski, P. (2012). *Juvenile justice administration.* Boca Raton, FL: CRC Press/Taylor &Francis Group.

Mauer, T. (2002). *Trial techniques* (6th ed.). New York: Aspen Publishers.

Moore, J. (1991). What leads to sexually abused children to delinquency. *Corrections Today, 53*(2), 42.

Mouzakitis, C. (1984). Characteristics of abused adolescents and guidelines for intervention. *Child Welfare, 63*(2), 149–157.

National Advisory Committee on Criminal Justice Standards and Goals. (1977). *Juvenile justice and delinquency prevention.* Washington, DC: U.S. Government Printing Office.

Rosenfeld, A. A. (1979). Endogamic incest and the victim-perpetrator model. *American Journal of Diseases of Children, 133,* 406–410.

Sagatun, I., & Edwards, L. (1995). *Child abuse and the legal system.* Chicago: Nelson-Hall.

Sickmund, M., & Puzzanchera, C. (Eds.). (2014). *Juvenile offenders and victims: 2014 national report.* Pittsburgh, PA: National Center for Juvenile Justice.

Straus, M. A. (1994). *Beating the devil out of them.* New York: Lexington Books.

U.S. Department of Health and Human Services. (2018). Administration for children and families, administration on children, youth and families, Children's bureau. *Child maltreatment 2017.* Washington, DC: U.S. Government Printing Office.

U.S. Department of Health, Education, and Welfare. (2018). *Child abuse and neglect.* Washington, DC: U.S. Government Printing Office.

Chapter 10
The Police Role in Delinquency Prevention and Control

10.1 Introduction

Police officers play an important role in all communities in the prevention and control of delinquency. Their presence at public gatherings of juveniles, such as sporting events, dances, or rock concerts, is designed to serve as a deterrent to destructive or violent behavior. They have broad discretion in the handling of youths observed or reported committing unlawful acts. They also serve as the major source of referrals to the juvenile courts and frequently discover and report behavior by adults that is contributing to the delinquency of minors.

Officers who have frequent contact with juveniles, whether they are regular patrol officers or members of a specialized juvenile unit, have opportunities to observe them in situations that are reported to parents or members of social service agencies only "after the fact." Teachers, employers, and parents interact with youths in rather structured situations in the schools, on the job, and at home, but officers who observe young people with their peers in the community are aware of certain behaviors that are not displayed when these other adults are present. Parents frequently react to information about vandalism, violence, or other delinquent behavior with the response, "My son (or daughter) would never do such a thing!" But police are well aware that young people are capable of such behavior when under the influence of peer-group pressures.

The following case, Box 10.1, illustrates the way police officers may become involved in juvenile cases in the course of their patrol activities:

© Springer Nature Switzerland AG 2020
P. C. Kratcoski et al., *Juvenile Delinquency*,
https://doi.org/10.1007/978-3-030-31452-1_10

Box 10.1 Al Hollus Is Arrested for Speeding

(The following case is based on a juvenile court referral researched by Peter C. Kratcoski. The juvenile's name and several characteristics have been changed to protect the identity of the juvenile.)

Officers Mitchell and Lantano had just finished their dinner break and returned to the patrol car. As they waited to leave the restaurant's parking lot, a car sped by. Mitchell estimated that it was traveling at about 50 mph in a 35-mph zone. The officers gave chase and pulled over the auto. It was driven by a muscular white male who appeared to be 19 or 20. An attractive white woman was seated next to him. Both were neatly dressed. A clothing bag hanging in the rear of the car gave the officers the impression that they were a young couple traveling through town. Officer Mitchell told Lantano he would check them out. Lantano remained in the patrol car.

Mitchell asked the driver to produce his license and the auto's registration. The driver, who seemed very nervous and stammered as he spoke, told the officer that it was his father's car. He said he had forgotten to get the registration from him and that he had left his license at home on the dresser. He told the officer that his name was Al Hollus, that he was 18, and that his father's name was Frank Hollus.

Mitchell had not told Al the reason he had stopped him, but the young man's demeanor aroused the officer's suspicions. He returned to the patrol car for a moment and asked Lantano to check out the registration on the auto from the license plate number. The information that came back did not correspond to the name Al had given as his father's. A radio call to the station and a telephone call from the dispatcher to the person to whom the car was registered produced the information that the car had been parked in front of the owner's home and had disappeared. Office Lantano thereupon requested that the car be towed to the police station. During the time Lantano was checking the car's registration, Officer Mitchell remained with the couple. Finally, Lantano approached the car and informed the driver that he was under arrest for auto theft and that both he and his passenger would have to come to the police station. He read Al his rights. Al mumbled some feeble protest and slipped into the back seat of the cruiser. His female companion, now very frightened, kept pleading with Al to tell her what was going on. Finally, he began talking in a low voice. He informed the officers that he was really 16 years old and that he and his girlfriend were driving to a neighboring state to get married. Officer Lantano warned him that anything he said could be used against him, but he shrugged his shoulders and continued talking. When they reached the police station, Mitchell called the number listed in the local directory for Frank Hollus. Mrs. Hollus answered. She said that her husband had left town about an hour earlier on a long-distance run for his trucking company. She confirmed that her son Al was indeed only 16 years old. She agreed to come to the station as soon as she could find someone to stay with her other children. At this point, the boy was turned over to Officer Frank O'Neil, a member of the force's juvenile division.

When encountering juveniles, police officers must first consider the laws pertaining to the appropriate manner for responding to juvenile encounters, the policies established by the police organization in which they are employed, and their prior training and experiences. Police officers react to and deal with the various situations they encounter according to the seriousness of the offenses, the ages and attitudes of the offenders, and the possibilities for resolution open to them. Although most police departments have developed some type of specialized youth bureau or unit, the majority of initial contacts with young people involved in unacceptable behavior are still made by uniformed officers on patrol. Their handling of matters involving juveniles is a complex area of their overall responsibilities and an important facet of the police role.

10.2 Police Work with Juveniles

Kratcoski (2012, p. 132) notes, "Historically, the same types of concerns brought police attention to controlling juveniles. In the latter part of the 19th century and the early 20th century, there was a public outcry in the larger cities for the police to do something to protect the citizens from the large numbers of poor, vagrant children who congregated in the inner-city business and commercial areas. Their presence caused much concern for the property owners and merchants. The police were expected to keep the areas safe for 'decent people'. Action by the police toward juveniles was directed toward enforcing the law when children engaged in such crimes as pick-pocketing, shoplifting, begging, or robbery, rather than focused on providing for the needs and safety of the children living on the streets who were at great risk of being victimized." After the establishment of a separate juvenile justice system, starting in 1899 with the first juvenile court in Cook County, IL the formalization of the juvenile justice process was brought about by various U.S. Supreme Court decisions granting rights to juveniles charged with crimes. Before the formalization began, police, when encountering a youth engaged in an act that was a violation of the law, had the opportunity to use their own judgment on how to handle the situation. The less serious violations, such as vagrancy, disturbances of the peace, and minor theft, could be handled on the street, with the officers using their discretion regarding what was the best approach to follow. The factors that determined the course of action to take in cases involving the less serious offenses of juveniles were the same as those used by the police at the present day. If the situation allowed discretion, the officers relied on such factors as their knowledge of the youth and youth's family, prior contacts with the youth, the youth's cooperation, attitude, the victim's demand to take action, and, of course, the officers own approach to law enforcement.

With the professionalization of police work, and specialization, as well as the standardization of police policies pertaining to the processing of juvenile law violators, much of the discretion of the police has been eliminated.

The major areas of police efforts in dealing with juveniles include discovery and investigation of delinquency, disposition of cases, protection of juveniles, and delinquency prevention. Many situations that generate police contacts with juveniles are still resolved informally, and even when youths are taken into custody the police often make dispositions other than referral to juvenile courts. The offenses of juveniles that result in arrests range from the most serious (aggravated murder) to the least serious (loitering). Sickmund and Puzzanchera (2014, p. 118) reported that, "law enforcement agencies in the U.S. made 1.6 million arrests of persons under age 18 in 2010. The proportion of youth between the ages of 10–17 arrested during 2010 was less than 5%. Less than 5% of the arrests of juveniles were for violent index crimes (murder, nonnegligent manslaughter, forcible rape, robbery, aggravated assault) and 22% of the arrests were for Index property crimes (burglary, larceny-theft, motor vehicle theft, arson). The largest number of arrest for index violent crimes was aggravated assault (2.7% of the total arrests), and the largest number of arrests for index property crimes was for larceny-theft (17% of the total). For the non-index crimes, 12.9 of the arrests were for simple assault, 16.8% for drug abuse violations and liquor law violations, including drunkenness and 9.4% of the arrests were for disorderly conduct. The remaining number of youth arrested in 2010 were arrested for a range of offenses, some against persons, such as non-index sexual offenses, but the majority of arrests being for property or public order offenses, such as vagrancy, and curfew violations and loitering. Almost one fourth of the juveniles taken into custody are handled within the department and released, usually to their parents, other adult relatives, or friends of the families."

The attitudes of the community residents toward juvenile misbehavior will have an effect on how the police will respond to the encounters with juveniles in which they can use their discretionary judgment on how to proceed. If the community has taken a position in support of restorative justice, the police policies are likely to be more supportive of police using diversion of minor delinquent offenders than if the police are operating in a community in which the community leaders have embraced a "zero-tolerance" approach toward delinquent behavior. Often situational factors may determine the way the police respond to juvenile misbehavior. For example, communities that are vacation destinations for large numbers of adolescents may set policies that are very strict with regard to even minor instances of inappropriate behavior. The excerpt from an interview with Officer Joseph Weaver, of the Alliance, Ohio Police department (Kratcoski, 2012, pp. 137–138) helps to illustrate the type of insight an officer must develop to be effective in working with juveniles. In response to the question "You indicated that an officer needs to develop a special kind of insight when responding to juveniles involved in delinquency, please explain," Officer Weaver answered, "In our everyday life , we deal with lots of people of all ages and cultures, and we make hundreds of little judgments every second based on how someone is dressed, how they carry themselves, how they speak, and more importantly, their body language. We can add other factors to this like the time of day we see them, the location where we see them, and what they were doing when we see them. These are the very obvious insights we have into a person's life. All of us are exposed to these things countless times a day, but how much do we pay attention to them? When you are a police officer, honing these skills is very important; but when it comes to dealing with kids, it is even more so.

Being able to read into what a child is telling you and interpreting the words they use and even more important the words they don't use. All of this extra verbal and non-verbal information can tell you a lot about a situation that a child is in or what their home life is like. All of these things are essential to be able to detect when you are being lied to; then you have to put together what the purpose of the lie is." In response to the question "How does an officer obtain this insight? Officer Weaver said, "We need to train ourselves to people watch. Every person you come into contact with each day displays clues as to who they are. There is a difference between looking and seeing. World experiences are also very important, and these can be obtained not only through police work but through social work, probation, or parole work and a host of other disciplines. Getting out and dealing with people in their own environments, and seeing how differently people live from how you do can give you a huge leg up in building your insight."

10.2.1   Police Response to Misbehavior of Youth

Lawrence and Hemmens (2008) emphasize two points when examining the role of police officers in interaction with juveniles. They argue that young people's perceptions of the police are shaped to a great extent by their first encounter with the police, and believe that youths have less respect for authority than adults do. With regard to juveniles' encounters with patrol officers, the authors perceived that they viewed these officers as a challenge to avoid detection when engaging in many types of unacceptable behavior, ranging from petty mischief to serious offenses.

Research on police encounters with juveniles in Chicago found that police–juvenile contacts have two basic sources (Black & Reiss, 1976, p. 417). A citizen-initiated investigation occurs when a report is made to the police that unacceptable juvenile behavior is occurring. A police-initiated intervention takes place when an officer observes activity or a situation that is suspicious and investigates. The researchers found that most police attention to juveniles occurs as a result of citizen complaints. Almost three-fourths of the contacts were initiated by complaints from citizens. Thus, in a sense, the citizens of a jurisdiction set the parameters of delinquent behavior by defining through their complaints the types of juvenile activity they regard as unacceptable. The fact that, citizens often do not complain to the police when they are victimized by youth does not necessarily mean that the citizens condone the delinquency. The reasons for not complaining could include fear of retaliation when the youth discovers who initiated the complaint, or the delinquent may be a relative, child of a neighbor, or friend of the victim's own children. The research tended to confirm what was already know, that is a large number of deviant acts by juveniles, even when detected, is not reported and thus does not involve intervention by a juvenile justice agency.

A study of police–citizen encounters conducted in a large mid-western city (Lundman et al., 1978, pp. 158–168) demonstrates police use of discretion in their decision making. It was found that the vast majority of police–juvenile encounters could have ended in arrests, but the juvenile law violators were arrested in only 16% of the encounters. All instances of felony offenses ended in attempted or actual arrests, while few of the minor delinquency or status offenders were arrested by the police. If a complainant was present when the police arrived at the site of the delinquent behavior, the suspect was more likely to be arrested than if a complainant was not present. Black juveniles were arrested at a higher rate than white juveniles when a complainant was present. Although a higher rate of arrests occurred for blacks, it was concluded that this was not due to differential handling because of their race, but rather was related to the combined influences of the severity of their offenses, the more frequent presence of a complainant in black juvenile–police encounters, and the black juveniles' demeanor. Juveniles who were antagonistic toward the officers were more likely to be arrested than those who were not, regardless of their race. This was true even if the offense was minor.

Other factors such as specialization in the police organization, policy changes, and the introduction of new legislation pertaining to children can have an important effect on how police respond to youth who are either law violators or victims of criminal behavior.

Community policing has been introduced in many jurisdictions as a means of making officers more responsive to the needs of citizens in specific areas within larger jurisdictions. The question of whether police–juvenile encounters that involved community policing officers differed from encounters between juveniles and officers in traditional-style units was explored by Bazemore and Senjo (1997) through field observation of the first year that community policing was used in a highly urbanized city in South Florida. They concluded that officers in the neighborhoods where community policing was used were involved in activities designed to enhance prevention, create diversion possibilities, and increase youth advocacy and parental support. Although they did not cite arrest statistics, they noted that community policing may actually increase juvenile arrests because of the intense attention focused on the target areas.

10.2.2   Police Discretion in Responding to Youth Misbehavior

The police have a number of alternatives open to them in dealing with reported or observed instances of juvenile misbehavior. The seriousness of the offense; the youngster's age, appearance, and attitude; the neighborhood in which the behavior occurs; and the child's home situation all are factors in the decision as to how the young person will be handled. In addition, the local laws, the type of police department in which the officer is employed (whether it exercises strong, detailed control over officers' activities or is discretion-oriented), the type of training the officer has received, and the officer's own personal prejudices and opinions affect the way an officer will operate at each discretionary opportunity. An officer has a number of options in dealing with juvenile offenders. The officer may release the young person after questioning at the site of the misbehavior; admonish and then release the youth; divert the youth to a youth service agency; transport the youth to the police station for questioning and release; issue a citation for the youth to appear in juvenile court; or transport the youth to the juvenile detention center. If the police are unable to locate the parents of a juvenile, the chances of taking the child into custody increase. Formal handling is also more likely if the juvenile is known to the officers through earlier contacts or if he or she has a delinquency record. Police discretion is also limited by the laws of the particular state in which the police are employed as well as by the policies of the department in which they are employed.

The decision whether to use informal means to dispose of a case or to take formal action is more complex than it appears on the surface, although such objective factors as the seriousness of the offense, previous record, and availability of alternative means of handling the problem enter into the decision. Research has demonstrated that in many cases, the decision is grounded in less tangible factors. These include the attitude of the youth at the time of contact with the police; the officer's personal prejudices and biases; the race, sex, and social class of the youth; and the area in which the juvenile is apprehended.

Piliavin and Briar (1976, p. 45) observed the activities of a metropolitan police department for a 9-month period. They concluded that 90% of the youths with whom the police had contact were minor offenders and that the type of unacceptable behavior under investigation was not consequential in the police officers' decision on the course of action to be taken. They found the youths' attitudes to be the most important factor in determining the dispositions chosen by the police. Those youths who were uncooperative, cocky, or argumentative in their encounters with the police were more likely to be arrested than those who appeared to be sorry for their actions and acted fearful and respectful. Several later research studies on police–juvenile interaction confirm some of the conclusions made in the research of Piliavin and Briar, but question the importance of the youth's demeanor in the police's decision regarding the course of action to follow. Gray et al. (2019) completed exploratory research on young people's interactions with the police and how it related to their attitudes toward the police. They stated (Gray et al. 2019, p. 29), "Many of the young people we spoke to perceive the police behavior as unfair. They also expressed helplessness and dismay at the force used to undertake searches or make arrests. Aggressive behavior by either the young person or the police officer escalated situations, and increased the negative outcomes for that young person." They also stated, "Despite this, and witnessing or experiencing what they perceived as unfair police behavior, respondents also described positive encounters they had with the police, and how helpful these professionals had been. Such accounts indicate the ways in which young people discern between different police professionals, and distinguish between police 'just doing their job' and those who are abusing their power."

Other researchers (Hartstone & Richetti, 1995) found that minority youths are overrepresented among those arrested and held in detention and the decision making by the police was found to contribute to this overrepresentation. Hartstone and Richetti found that minority youths were held at the police station longer and placed in detention more often than nonminority youths. This differential treatment occurred for females as well as males. Kemp-Leonard et al. (1990) found that African-American juvenile females living in cities and urban areas were more likely than white juvenile females to be detained, while in rural settings white juvenile females were more likely to receive informal supervision than white males or African-American males and females with similar offense characteristics. Bridges et al. (1993) found that the degree of urbanization, levels of violent crime, concentration of minorities in the county, and chronic juvenile offending all were important in the decision-making process related to minority youths,

10.2.3   Police Juvenile Diversion Programs

Many police departments operate diversion programs. The goal of these programs is to keep youths from being formally involved with juvenile courts and being labeled as "delinquents" and to deter them from further unacceptable behavior. This is accomplished by assigning them to programs that provide supervision and counseling to address the particular problem behavior in which the youths have been involved

Kratcoski et al. (2004, pp. 160–161) studied the diversion programs of 16 police departments in five counties in Northeast Ohio. They analyzed the structures and administrative policies of the programs to determine if they were effective in curtailing further delinquency of the youth referred to the programs. During a 15-month period, several thousand juvenile offenders were referred to these programs. Ninety-five percent of the referrals were made by police officers and the others came from school systems, parents, and the juvenile courts. The diversion programs were placed into three distinct types of orientations. The orientations were:

1. Social service orientation, in which the dominant focus was to provide treatment intervention and services to the youth and their families;
2. Balanced (restorative justice) orientation, in which the dominate focus of the program was to equally emphasize the protection of the community, address the needs of the victim, and provide the services necessary for the needs of the youth referred to the program; and
3. Social control orientation, in which the dominant focus was to hold the child responsible for the deviant act, require strict compliance to the rules and regulations of the program, and terminate from the program any youth who did not adhere to the provisions of the contract

Of the youth referred to the programs approximately 15% were advised, counseled, and released at the intake interviews. The remaining were placed in the police diversion programs. Kratcoski (2012, p. 46) noted, "A check on the recidivism of the youths who completed the police diversion programs revealed that the average recidivism for the youths in the three programs was less than 15%. While the youth placed in the social service programs had the lowest recidivism, it was not significantly lower than that in the other programs. Of those who committed a new offense, 84% of the offenders committed either a status or misdemeanor offenses and 16% committed a felony offense.

The diversion program activities most frequently utilized were unofficial probation, community service, school-related disciplinary actions, referral to service agencies, and individual counseling. It was concluded that regardless of the way the police diversion programs were structured or the orientation of the programs. Certain factors worked toward making the diversion programs in the study succeed. First was the commitment of the youth who completed the programs. They had to assume responsibility for their delinquent acts (in most cases sign a form admitting to their guilt), second, they had to commit to the goals of the program, since they agreed to abide by the rules and regulations, and complete certain requirements, and third, regardless of the orientation of the program the participants had the opportunity to interact with adults who were concerned about their welfare and assisted them in achieving their goals. The majority of the programs were administered by lay people, either counselors or social workers and several of the programs were administered by police officers assigned to the programs. In a few cases, the diversion program was jointly administered by both a lay person and an officer of the department. However, regardless of the type of personnel assigned to the programs, there was a complete commitment to the children involved and the goals of the programs.

10.2.4 Factors Influencing Police Decisions to Take Youths into Custody

Under the Uniform Juvenile Court Act, (National Conference of Commissioners on Uniform State Laws, 1968), section 13 a child may be taken into custody:

1. Pursuant to an order of the court under this act;
2. Pursuant to an order of the court under the laws of arrest;
3. By a law enforcement officer (or duly authorized officer of the court), if there are reasonable grounds to believe that the child is suffering from illness or injury or is in immediate danger from his or her surroundings and that his or her removal is necessary; or by a law enforcement officer (or duly authorized officer of the court) if there are reasonable grounds to believe that the child has run away from his or her parents, guardian, or other custodian. It is apparent that juveniles may be taken into police custody for reasons unrelated to unlawful behavior on their part. The various state codes allow an officer to enter a private home and remove a youth if there is evidence present to indicate that the child is in danger or in need of immediate medical assistance. Such an action is termed "emergency temporary custody."

When used in reference to juveniles, the term "custody" is preferable to "arrest," even if the action is taken as a result of alleged illegal behavior on the part of the youth. Use of the term "custody" would eliminate the confusion that results when some departments record as an arrest any police–juvenile encounter in which a youth is brought to the police station; others record an arrest only if an official charge is made; and still other departments consider an arrest to be any recorded contact between an officer and a juvenile, even if the juvenile is not brought to the police station. Such variations in recording are the reason for the inexact nature of nationwide statistics on the number of youths arrested.

Juvenile court statutes have detailed provisions for the handling of juveniles once they have been taken into custody. For example, the *Legislative Guide for Drafting Family and Juvenile Court Acts* provides that a person taking a child into custody, "with all reasonable speed and without first taking the child elsewhere," shall release the child to parents, guardian, or other custodian upon their promise to bring the child before the court when requested by the court, unless detention or shelter care is warranted or required; or bring the child before the court to deliver him or her to a detention or shelter care facility designated by the court or to a medical facility if the child is believed to suffer from a serious physical condition or illness that requires prompt treatment. The person shall promptly give written notice, together with a statement of the reason for taking the child into custody, to a parent, guardian, or other custodian and to the court (Legislative Guide for Drafting family and Juvenile Court Acts, Sec. 15, 1968).

10.3   Police Procedures and Juvenile Rights

10.3.1   Questioning and Interrogation Procedures

If a youth is taken into custody for allegedly having committed a delinquent act by violating a criminal law, there are constitutional limitations to the custodial interrogation to which the youth may be subjected. In Miranda v. Arizona (1966), the Supreme Court found that any person accused of a crime must be advised of the right to remain silent and the right to have legal representation. The Supreme Court decision, in re Gault (1967), held that the constitutional privilege against self-incrimination is applicable in the case of juveniles just as it is with respect to adults. In the *Gault* decision, the Supreme Court specifically declined to address the issue of whether counsel is required in pre-adjudication stages of juvenile court proceedings. On the basis of the *Gault* decision, however, numerous lower courts have ruled that full *Miranda* warnings must be given to juveniles in custody during investigatory questionings. Several states have implemented legislation requiring that these *Miranda-type* warnings be given to juveniles.

The circumstances surrounding the interrogation of a juvenile have also been considered in court cases. In Haley v. Ohio (1948), a 15-year-old defendant was held by police and continuously questioned for a long period of time without being allowed to see his parents or an attorney. The Supreme Court ruled that his subsequent confession was inadmissible because of the principle of "totality of circumstances"; that is, the absence of parents or lawyer, the age of the youth, the length of the questioning period, and the approach used by the officers. In the case of Gallegos v. Colorado (1962), the Court reached a similar decision. As a result, great care must be taken by police in conducting interrogations, or a youth's confession may be ruled inadmissible in court, even though he or she was informed of the right to remain silent, if it can be shown that the circumstances surrounding the interrogation were improper.

The Yarborough v. Alvarado (2004) and J. D. B. v. North Carolina (2011) Supreme Court cases pertained to the police questioning of a juvenile while the juvenile is in police custody. In Yarborough v. Alvarado, Yarborough, age 17, at the request of the police voluntarily came to the police station to answer some questions pertaining to a robbery the police were investigating. He was not given the Miranda rights, nor were his parents or an attorney present during the questioning. During the questioning by the police, Yarborough provided some information that implicated him in the robbery. However, the police did not arrest him at that time and allowed him to return to his home. Later he was arrested, tried and convicted of the crime. The case was appealed to the Supreme Court on the grounds that his constitutional rights were violated during the first time he was questioned by the police. The U.S. Supreme Court upheld the conviction by a lower court on the grounds that Yarborough came to the station voluntarily, he was not a suspect, nor in police custody and at the initial questioning he could have stopped answering questions. However, in J.D.B. v. North Carolina (2011), the Supreme Court made the decision that J.D.B. was in police custody. J.D.B., age 13, a special education student was taken from his classroom and questioned by the police and a school administrator about a burglary in which he was a suspect. J.D.B. after a period of questioning implicated himself in the burglary. He was adjudicated delinquent as a result of his confession. The case was appealed and eventually heard by the Supreme Court. In this case the Court ruled that J.D.B. was in custody at the time he was questioned. The age and maturity of J.D.B. were major factors in the Supreme Court's decision.

10.3.2 Identification Procedures

In Wade v. U.S. (1967), the Supreme Court ruled that use of a line-up for the purpose of identifying a suspect is a critical stage of the criminal justice process, and therefore a suspect has a right to request that counsel be present to reduce the possibility that the lineup will be conducted in an unfair or discriminatory manner. Wade v. U.S. also set several standards as to how a lineup should be conducted, including the requirement that other members of the lineup be similar in physical characteristics to the suspect. While Wade v. U.S. involved an adult, it is assumed that the same constitutional guarantees that resulted from the case are also applicable to juveniles.

Arranging a lineup when a juvenile is a suspect is difficult. It requires that several other children who are similar in physical characteristics to the suspect must be found to serve as fill-ins. Because of the problems in arranging juvenile lineups, the one-to-one identification process tends to be more common in juvenile cases. In this procedure, there is either a face-to-face meeting between the suspect and the witness, or the witness is allowed to observe the suspect without any contact between the two individuals. In Stovall v. Denno (1967), the Supreme Court ruled that the principle of "fundamental fairness" was violated when a suspect was taken before the victim in a one-to-one situation while in handcuffs. In Simmons v. U.S. (1968), the Court ruled that this principle of "fundamental fairness" must also be maintained in photo identification. For example, an investigator may show the witness several photographs of persons who are similar in physical characteristics rather than a single photograph of a suspect, or the investigator could ask the witness to identify the suspect in a group photograph. The one-to-one and photograph identification procedures are particularly important in identifying juvenile suspects because the lineup is used infrequently in these cases.

10.3.3   Fingerprinting and Photographing Juveniles

The juvenile codes of various states have specific provisions regarding the fingerprinting or photographing of juveniles, publication of their names in the press, the question of where and with whom they may be detained, and the types and locations of their police records. The Uniform Juvenile Court Act (1968) and the Model Rules for Juvenile Courts of the National Council on Crime and Delinquency recommended that children not be photographed or fingerprinted unless such materials are necessary to prove the case, that the fingerprints of juveniles not be filed with those of adults or sent to central data banks, and that all fingerprint records of juveniles who are not found guilty be destroyed immediately. Many states require that for photographs to be taken, a court order must be obtained.

The report of the Task Force on Juvenile Justice and Delinquency Prevention (1977) included specific guidelines for fingerprinting, photographing, and otherwise identifying juveniles. It recommended that fingerprinting take place only when fingerprints have been found on or are expected to be found on evidence; if they are taken, they should be immediately destroyed if the comparison is negative. Also, fingerprints and photographs that are retained should be destroyed if no petition is filed, if the case is dismissed after a petition is filed, if the youth is not adjudicated delinquent, or when a youth reaches age 21 without additional recorded delinquency after the age of 16. The prohibitions against publication of the names of juvenile offenders are designed both to protect them and their families and to prevent the development of delinquent reputations that some offenders might feel required to live up to. Such idealistic motives are at times at odds with the harsh realities of the existence of hardened, violent juvenile offenders, particularly since some evidence has shown that treating such offenders severely reduces juvenile crime.

Even after an arrest has been made, in most states a juvenile has the opportunity to have the record expunged (destroyed or sealed from examination). Other states automatically destroy juvenile records after a specific number of years, but in some states, a youth must petition the court to have a record destroyed or sealed. Police departments may keep juvenile arrest records separate from those of adults and refuse to release information pertaining to juvenile arrests. In some cases, the police will provide names and information on juvenile offender if the age, (approaching adulthood) maturity, and seriousness of the offense seem to warrant giving this information to the community.

The degree of care and discretion with which juvenile arrests, arrest procedures, and arrest records are handled is dependent upon the philosophy of the police department. Those with a philosophy that juveniles should be given every opportunity to change their behavior will carry this over into their handling procedures, whereas departments less concerned with such matters will exercise less care.

10.4 Specialized Police Units

10.4.1 Investigating Offenses Against Children

There are numerous cases in which the police (either regular patrol officers or members of specialized units) become involved in situations in which a child is the victim of an offense rather than its perpetrator. For example, officers are frequently called upon to intervene in domestic situations that require a physically abused or sexually molested child to be removed from the home.

In most jurisdictions, the police have authority to act in the best interests of the child in emergency situations. An officer answering a domestic disturbance call in which children are involved must make a decision regarding the immediate danger to them or the need for medical attention. Transporting children to a hospital or shelter home may be necessary and agencies that will then assist the children, such as the juvenile court or Children's Services, must be notified of the emergency action taken.

Investigation of an offense against a juvenile may be undertaken by the officer initially involved in the complaint or by a special juvenile officer. This is a very delicate area, and skill is needed to collect needed facts without traumatizing the abused child further. If the person who has abused the child is criminally charged, it may be necessary for physicians, social workers, the prosecutor, or treatment specialists to question the child. For example, when Officer Weyer, attached to the Alliance, Ohio Police Juvenile Bureau (Kratcoski, 2012, pp. 140–141), was asked, "Are police relations with the courts, child welfare agencies, and the prosecutor generally positive cooperative or antagonistic?" Weyer responded, "This is a good question, because you can't afford for your relations to be anything but positive. You have to know what you are able to control and what you can't control when dealing with other agencies. You have to keep good relations with these people, and you have to let them do their part and assist them when you can. I know when I pick up the phone in need of support from these people, I will get it because I support them. There are times when I need to take emergency custody of a child in the middle of the night. The logistics behind this are not easy to say the least, but I know that if I pick up the phone CPS and the prosecutors will do everything they can to help me because they have confidence that I know my job, and they know I would help and have helped them during times they needed my service." To reduce the need for child victims to retell the story of their experiences many times, the interview process can be consolidated by conducting a joint interview by representatives of two or more agencies, or by videotaping the child's first statement, to possibly eliminate the need for the child to appear at formal proceedings, and by coordinating juvenile and criminal court proceedings. Regardless of the procedures followed, it is obvious that police officers involved in the investigation of offenses against children must be skilled and highly sensitive to their needs.

10.4.2   Juvenile Bureau

Today, virtually every police department has at least one officer whose primary function is to work with youth-related cases. In large departments, the juvenile bureau may be made up of **dozens of** officers and supporting personnel. They may operate out of the Special Investigations Unit or the Detective Bureau or be set up as an independent police bureau or unit. The prestige attached to juvenile-bureau assignments varies tremendously, depending on the department's goals and priorities. In some police departments, the officers in the juvenile bureau must have completed specialized education in dealing with juveniles and juvenile work is a sought-after assignment; in others, juvenile work has a low status.

A national survey of large police and sheriffs' departments (2007) revealed that special units were widely used. Sickmund and Puzzanchera (2014, p. 146) reported that, "90% of the local law enforcement agencies (county police departments and municipal police departments) had specific policies and procedures for dealing with juveniles, and 91.5% had provisions in place for responding to domestic disputes." In their summary of information from the national survey, Sickmund and Puzzanchera (2014, p. 46) note, "Many local police departments employ sworn officers as school resource officers. School resource officers not only provide law enforcement services but can also function as counselors."

If the procedures for dealing with youths are not specifically spelled out in department policies, such matters as providing assistance to juveniles, counseling, engaging in recreational and community activities, and the relationship between juvenile officers and patrol officers are handled according to the juvenile officers' own judgment.

The point at which officers from the juvenile bureau enter a case is determined according to the administrative policies of the police department. Some departments require that all children involved in police–juvenile encounters be referred immediately to the juvenile bureau, while others allow regular patrol officers to handle initial contacts and use their discretion in dealing with juveniles, calling in the juvenile bureau officers only in serious or unusual matters. Another method allows line officers to handle contacts with juveniles in the community, with juvenile unit officers taking over when youths are brought to the police station. Sometime the officers themselves are not sure of the department's policies because the juvenile unit operates as a seemingly independent entity. The activities of juvenile officers vary according to the size of the city or community served and the size of the juvenile unit. The duties of such officers may include investigating crimes in which juveniles are suspects; processing adults charged with contributing to the delinquency of a minor, child neglect or abuse, investigating school-related incidents reported to the police, investigating reports of missing or runaway children, supervising school and community social events involving juveniles, presenting delinquency control and prevention programs to community groups, and counseling parents and children. In large cities, there may be areas of specialization even within the juvenile bureau or unit. For example, a team of officers specially trained in gang control may operate out of the bureau and others may be assigned to a drug task force, or missing persons unit.

10.4.3 Police Youth Gang Control Units

Many large cities in the United States have established specialized units within their police departments to combat the problems posed by youth gangs. A survey of police departments in the 79 largest cities in the United States (Curry & Decker, 1998) found that 72% of these departments had created specialized gang units.

The extent of the gang problem is evident from the National Youth Gang Survey (2019, pp. 1–7). It reported that more than 75% of police agencies in large cities, and more than half of the agencies in the suburbs, and one fourth of agencies in rural areas reported that gangs were active in their communities. Not all of the gangs are youth gangs. Wilson (2000) found that less than half of the gangs reported in the survey were youth gangs.

Gang activity is not equally intense throughout the cities. Some neighborhoods are problem-free, while others are constantly troubled by excessive noise, harassment, vandalism, theft, and violence resulting from gang activity. Reduction of these problems through minimization of the gangs' criminal conduct may be the focus of the police department's gang unit activity. In the past, the strategy police often used was designed primarily to reduce intergang violence, to prevent the extortion of neighborhood citizen and merchants by the gangs, and to minimize the seriousness of the crimes committed by gang members. It was not designed to eliminate the gangs, although some efforts were made to turn them to legitimate and constructive activities. It depended for its success on such activities as establishing liaison with the gangs to communicate police expectations and aggressive police action against gang members, their clubhouses, and their activities when the gang stepped out of line.

While these tactics may still be effective in dealing with youth gangs that are developed predominantly to provide security, protection, and status for their members, they are not likely to be effective in curtailing the activity of criminal gangs that are organized for profit making through drug and weapons sales. Police work with such gangs is likely to include the development of informants through criminal prosecutions, payments, and witness protection programs; reliance on electronic surveillance and long-term undercover investigations; and the enactment of legislation by the states of special statutes that create criminal liabilities for conspiracy, extortion, or engaging in criminal enterprises (National Advisory Committee on Juvenile Justice (1980, p. 217).

Curry and Decker (1998, p. 151) noted that "gang [unit] responses must take into account variations in the structure and dynamics of gang crime problems that have been observed to exist across municipalities, communities, gender, and ethnicity." Some regular patrol officers in a major Midwestern city with a police gang unit that had more than 60 officers in its administrative, enforcement, investigative, intelligence, and surveillance components revealed to researchers that they felt the regular street patrol officers were the heart of gang control efforts and that gang units were created more for show and to appease the public than to actually deal with gang problems.

Suppression has been the dominant approach to gang problems. This has occurred because of increases in violent crime by young offenders, disillusionment with attempts at rehabilitation, and public demands that the police take some type of action that will produce visible results.

In Los Angeles County, California, the Sheriff's Department developed the Operation Safe Streets Program, a unit of 70 non-uniformed department personnel, to investigate gang activities and assist law enforcement agencies and the courts in their efforts to prosecute gang members for criminal acts. One of the unit's tools is GREAT (Gang Reporting, Evaluation, and Tracking), a computer system that helps investigators identify gang members and monitor their activities (Street Gangs, 1995, p. 70).

Legislation has also been used to strengthen police powers. For example, the California Street Terrorism Informant Protection Act (Street Gangs, 1995, p. 71) includes a provision that makes it a crime to participate in a "criminal" street gang for the purpose of promoting or assisting felonious criminal conduct.

It is difficult to ascertain how effective gang units are in curtailing illegal activities and particularly the violence attributed to gangs. Typically, the units' effectiveness would be assessed in terms of arrests of known gang members, reduction of violent crimes attributed to gangs, and confiscation of weapons or drugs from persons identified as gang-associated. It is often difficult for the police to determine if criminal violence and other illegal behavior is gang related or an individual act that it was committed by one or several members of a gang without involvement from the other members. For example, drive-by shootings, while often attributed to gangs by the police or the mass media, may be totally unrelated to gangs in some instances, and it is virtually impossible to determine this if the perpetrators are not identified. Some of the success stories about gang unit effectiveness have been viewed with skepticism, while others have been accepted as reliable.

Some gangs, particularly those associated with organized crime, are migratory and have branches in many American cities. Exchange of information between the police gang units of major cities is now occurring, enabling police to identify and respond effectively to the threats posed by gang members who have migrated from other cities to establish new bases of operation. Thus, such groups as the Caribbean Gang Task Force—which includes representatives of local law enforcement agencies, as well as federal, state, and county representatives—function for the expressed purpose of gaining the evidence needed to arrest and prosecute offenders who are gang members. Agents from the Federal Bureau of Investigation; Bureau of Alcohol, Tobacco, and Firearms; the Internal Revenue Service; and prosecutors from the U.S. Attorney's Office, as well as city police officials, are involved. The Middle-Atlantic Great Lakes Organized Crime Law Enforcement Network (MAGLOCLEN) is another example of such cooperation.

Local police departments are very helpful to those involved in this interagency approach to dealing with gangs since their officers, through working in the cities' neighborhoods, have gained knowledge about the community and can find persons who may serve as informants.

The question of whether today's gangs are developing locally or are part of broader gang organizations is still being researched. The National Youth Gang Survey (2019) reported that, although some exceptionally well-organized gangs are believed to be involved in interstate drug trafficking and to be expanding their operations through member relocation, most law enforcement agencies still regard gang problems as "home grown" rather than imported from other cities.

10.5   Police Role in Community and School Programs for Delinquency Prevention

Police-sponsored delinquency prevention activities can be traced back to the early years of the twentieth century. The early programs tended to focus on recreational or sports activities. The **best known** example is the Police Athletic League (PAL), which originated in Philadelphia in 1942 as a **boxing** program. Gradually, officers were given specific assignments to coach or supervise various **types** of sports teams, and the PAL program was adopted in many American cities. Officers also took part in other delinquency prevention measures through such activities as rigorous supervision of parks and recreation areas; establishing curfews; and forming cooperative relations with the schools, such as DARE and the School Resource Officer programs, the courts, and social agencies.

There are also youth programs developed and directed by the police that focus on improving the quality of life for juveniles through opportunity provision. COPY Kids, implemented in 1992 by the Spokane, Washington, Police Department, enables children from the city's economically disadvantaged areas to earn money through work for the community (Thurman et al., 1993).

Police delinquency prevention programs can also target specific endangered youth populations. A school based in-school program designed to address the problem of violence and victimization in the schools is GREAT, which originated in Phoenix in 1991. Local school administrators, in cooperation with local and federal law enforcement agencies, designed a school-based program for elementary grade children that would provide instruction and experiences to help them resist gang involvement (National Institute of Justice, 1994). Other GREAT programs following this model were quickly adopted throughout the United States. Typically, the local police department and the school system form a cooperative agreement in which police officers trained in the GREAT curriculum offer instruction and the schools provide personal development and cultural enrichment activities to show the students that there are alternatives to gang involvement.

10.6 Community Policing

Community policing involves the orientation of the police toward the creation of programs designed to establish close cooperative relations between the police and residents of the community. Community policing involves close, person-to-person contacts between officers and community residents, accomplished by assignment of an officer to a specific section of the community for an extended period of time. It stresses high visibility of the officer and use of various patrol methods, including a return to foot patrol. The goals of community policing include crime prevention and control, involving citizens in problem solving, increasing the satisfaction of all citizens with police services, and improving the quality of life for all community residents.

The focus of this type of police work is service. The officers must know how to get in touch with social and governmental agencies in the community, so that appropriate referrals can be made, and must follow up on referrals to be sure that services have been requested and received.

The emphasis given to certain community policing activities, such as focusing on sporting events and working with the young persons in the community in developing recreational programs draws criticism from some of the residents and political figures who believe such activities are distracting the police from their "real" work. While such criticism is valid in certain instances, community policing, if properly implemented, can produce very positive crime prevention and control results, as illustrated by the following case:

A study that examined community policing in seven Ohio cities (Kratcoski, 1994) summarized the conditions needed for effective police work of this type. He stated, if community policing is to work, the officers must believe they have such a stake in the neighborhoods in which they work that if something negatively affects the residents it also negatively affects them. When the neighborhood hurts, the police hurt. This type of commitment to the job is not easily developed. If achieved, it is generally after years of continuous personal interaction with numerous individuals and groups in the community. Much of the interaction will be focused on working with the young people. They are the ones who are perceived as being the must subject to the negative influences in the community and also the ones most likely to be influenced by positive forces.

In the absence of any national operating guidelines or even state standards, the functions and goals of police work with juveniles have developed according to local needs. Some juvenile units have concentrated on the law enforcement facet of police work with juveniles and have largely restricted their roles to investigative work. Others have deemphasized the law enforcement facet and expanded the role to include various forms of social and recreational services. Indeed, some have made the organization and supervision of recreational activities a part of juvenile bureau duties. The degree of which this detracts from the other police work facets is a point of contention.

If officers devote a great deal of time to organizing recreational activities, speaking in the community to various public and civic groups on teenage crime and problems, counseling youth, and visiting schools, what time is left for such activities as crime prevention and law enforcement involving juveniles? Have police officers received any training in recreational organization that qualifies them to develop such programs, and if not, must such training be included in police academy programs? Does acquaintance with these officers as recreation directors blur their images as police officers in the community? Is there strong evidence that involvement in recreational activities by a limited number of youngsters is as effective a deterrent to delinquency as other activities in which these officers might engage?

The same types of questions can be asked about the kind of police involvement with juveniles that really amounts to social work and counseling. Are they adequately prepared for this work? Does it duplicate services already available from specialists within the community? When a police department focuses heavily on programs of counseling and "social work," does this cause suspicion that the officers have little confidence in the juvenile court of that jurisdiction and are attempting to take over some of its functions because they believe they can do a better job?

The most important consideration is that a police officer, whether assigned to regular patrol, a specialized juvenile bureau, or community policing, should be primarily engaged in police work. Involvement in other activities should be carried out in conjunction with persons who hold expertise in the specific area. For example, many police departments have established juvenile diversion bureaus that operate directly from the departments. Minor delinquent offenders or status offenders who come into contact with the police are handled by these bureaus rather than referred to the juvenile courts. While these bureaus are set up under the auspices of the police departments, those who provide counseling and assistance there are generally not sworn police officers, but social workers or counselors. When police are directly assigned to schools, it is predominantly to maintain security for students and teachers. Through community policing or drug prevention programs, some specialized officers have taken the role of educators in very limited subject areas, and, in an unofficial way, many officers assigned to schools do counsel or assist students or serve as role models, but their primary function is police work.

10.7 Summary

Police work with juveniles involves the investigation of complaints initiated by citizens or of suspicious behavior observed by the officers themselves. Once a youth has been contacted by the police, officers must make immediate decisions as to whether to question and release the youth, release him or her after an admonition, take the young person to the police station for additional questioning, lodge a charge against the juvenile and release him or her in the custody of parents, or request secure detention. The majority of juvenile–police contacts do not lead to arrests or juvenile court referrals, but are disposed of in other ways.

When the officers do make a decision to take a juvenile into custody, they must have "probable cause" (sufficient evidence to substantiate the accusation) if the charged delinquency is a felony. A youth may be arrested for a misdemeanor or status offense when the behavior occurred in the officer's presence or when a complainant files a written petition. Specific safeguards of juveniles have been developed with regard to photographing, fingerprinting, publication of names, places of detention, and police records.

The decision as to the type of disposition made in each police–juvenile encounter is based on the seriousness of the offense; the offender's age, appearance, and attitude; the area in which the offense occurs; and facts the officer can discover about the child's home situation and previous juvenile record. In cases of minor delinquency, the youth's attitude has been found to be the most important factor determining the choice of disposition, with cooperative youths tending to be admonished and released far more often than uncooperative ones. Other researchers have found that sex, age, prior record, family status, and race, as well as the background and training of the officers themselves, are related to the types of police dispositions received.

Although officers on routine patrol are most likely to have initial contacts with juvenile offenders, most police departments also employ officers with special training to work with juveniles. These officers familiarize themselves with community centers of juvenile activity, are well-versed in juvenile court procedures, and develop communication and cooperation with the schools and with public and private social welfare agencies. They frequently operate out of a special police juvenile unit and they may become involved in investigation of all juvenile cases, all those in which youths are brought to the police station, or only those of a serious or unusual nature, depending upon the orientation of the particular police department. Juvenile officers' activities frequently include counseling parents and children and speaking engagements in the schools and community, in addition to investigative work. Many large cities have established specialized youth gang units to gain intelligence on the activities of gangs and aid in the apprehension of gang members who have violated the law. Gang control units frequently share information with units from other cities and with special task forces developed to monitor and inhibit gang activities.

Through community policing, many officers play important roles in delinquency prevention by their presence in places or situations where juvenile misbehavior might occur or through providing special programs or positive experiences for young people.

10.8   Discussion Questions

1. What are some of the guidelines set forth pertaining to the fingerprinting and photographing of juvenile offenders by police?
2. What position has the courts taken in regard to the publication of the names, addresses, and other identifying information of juvenile offenders in the news media? What are some of the circumstances under which it would be appropriate for the police to provide identifying information on an alleged offender to the public?
3. Discuss the circumstances surrounding a police–juvenile encounter that may require that an officer make an arrest of a juvenile. What are some of the situations that allow an officer to use discretion in deciding the appropriate action to take with a juvenile offender?
4. When is it appropriate for police officers to divert youths out of the juvenile justice system?
5. Discuss the concept of community policing. How does community policing relate to delinquency prevention and control?
6. What are the major tasks of police officers assigned to the juvenile bureau of a police department? Do juvenile bureau officers need special training to be effective in working with children and adolescents?
7. Discuss the findings on the effectiveness of police diversion programs for youths. Should such diversion programs be staffed and administered by sworn police officers or civilians?
8. Discuss the findings of the research that pertains to police relations with juveniles from various racial and ethnic minority groups. Give some of the reasons why juveniles from minority and facial groups are over-represented in the statistics on arrests of juveniles by the police.
9. Discuss the approaches the police of various cities have taken to suppress, control, or redirect juvenile gangs.
10. Discuss the delinquency prevention programs in which the police are involved.

References

Bazemore, G., & Senjo, S. (1997). Police encounters with juveniles revisited: An exploratory study of styles and themes in community policing. *Policing: An International Journal of Police Strategies And Management, 20*(1), 60–82.

Black, D., & Reiss, A. (1976). Police control of juveniles. In R. Moore Jr. & R. Barrows (Eds.), *Readings in criminal justice* (pp. 417–429). Indianapolis, IN: Bobbs-Merrill.

Bridges, G., Conley, D., Beretta, G., & Engen, R. (1993). *Racial disproportionality in the juvenile justice system. Report to the African-American Affairs and management Services Division/ Department of Social and Health Services.* Olympia ,WA: State of Washington Press.

Curry, G., & Decker, S. (1998). *Confronting gangs.* Los Angeles, CA: Roxberry Publishing Co.

Gallegos v. Colorado. (1962). 370, U.S. 596, 68, Cr. 1209.

Gray, R., Green, R., Bryant, J., Rance, J., & MacLean, S. (2019). Now vulnerable young people describe their interactions with police: Building pathways to drug diversion and treatment in Sydney and Melbourne, Australia. *Police Practice and Research, 20*(1), 18–33.

Haley v. Ohio. (1948). 332 U.S. 596, 68 S, Cr.302.

Hartstone, E., & Richetti, D. (1995). *An assessment of minority overrepresentation in Connecticut's juvenile justice system; Office of Policy and Management, Policy and Development Division.* Hartford, CT: Spectrum Associates.

In re Gault. (1967). 397, U.S. 1.

J.D.B. v. North Carolina. (2011).

Kempf-Leonard, K., Decker, S., & Bing, R. (1990). *An analysis of apparent disparities in handling black youth within Missouri's juvenile justice system.* St. Louis, MO: University of Missouri-Saint Louis.

Kratcoski, P. (1994). *Evaluation of Cleveland Police mini-station program.* Final research report for the Governor's Office of criminal Justice services, Columbus, OH.

Kratcoski, P. (2004). Al Hollis is arrested for speeding (personal notes).

Kratcoski, P. (2012). *Juvenile justice administration.* Boca Raton, FL: CRC/Taylor & Francis Group.

Lawrence, R., & Hemmens, C. (2008). *Juvenile justice: A text/reader.* Los Angeles, CA: Sage.

Legislative Bridge for Drafting Family & Juvenile Court Act. (1968). *Legislative guide for drafting family and juvenile court acts section 15*

Lundman, R., Sykes, R., & Clark, J. (1978). Police control of juveniles: A replication. In H. Rubin (Ed.), *Juvenile justice: A book of readings.* Beverly Hills, CA: Sage.

Miranda v. Arizona. (1966). 384 US. 436,448.

National Advisory Committee for Juvenile Justice and Delinquency Prevention. (1980). *Standards for the administration of juvenile justice.* Washington, DC: U.S. Government Printing Office.

National Conference of Commissions on Uniform State Laws. (1968). Section 13.

National Gang Center. (2019). National youth gang survey analysis, pp. 1–7. Retrieved July 7, 2019, from https://nationalgangcenter.gov/Survey-Ahalysis/Measuringthe-Extent-of-Gang-Problem s#estimatednumbergangs.

National Institute of Justice. (1994). *Solicitation for an evaluation of GREAT—Gang Resistance Education and Training.* Washington, DC: U.S. Department of Justice.

Piliavin, I., & Briar, S. (1976). Police encounters with juveniles. In W. Sanders & H. Daudistel (Eds.), *The criminal justice process.* Beverly Hills, CA: Glencoe.

Sickmund, M., & Puzzanchera, C. (2014). *Juvenile offenders and victims: 2014 national report.* Pittsburgh, PA: National Center for Juvenile Justice.

Simmons v. U.S. (1968). 390 U.S.377.

Stoval v. Denno. (1967). 388 U.S.293,302.

Street Gangs. (1995). *Street gangs: The law enforcement guide to today's urban violence.* Boulder, CO: Paladin Press.

Task Force on Juvenile Justice. (1977). *Delinquency prevention and control.* Washington, DC: U.S. Government Printing Office.

Thurman, Q., Giaconazzi, A., & Bogen, P. (1993). Research note: Cops, kids and community policing—An assessment of a community policing demonstration project. *Crime and Delinquency, 39*(4), 554–567.

Wade v. U.S. (1967). U.S.218.

Wilson, J. (2000). *National youth gang survey: Summary.* Washington, DC: U.S. Department of Justice.

Yarborough v. Alvarado. (2004). 541 U.S. 652.

Chapter 11
Processing the Juvenile Offender: Diversion, Informal Handling, and Special Dockets

11.1 Introduction

The Juvenile Court of Cook County, Illinois, established in 1899, assumed the responsibility of examining and regulating the behavior of young people. Eventually every state enacted legislation that resulted in the establishment of juvenile courts with specified jurisdictions. In addition, the states enacted legislation pertaining to the categories of children and the types of offenses that would be processed by the juvenile courts committed by youths defined as juveniles. During the years since the establishment of the first court, views of its appropriate role and procedures to follow by the juvenile courts have changed dramatically. In addition, the ways juveniles are processed in the courts have also changed. It was noted in an earlier chapter that the first juvenile courts were instituted to save children from the evils of being processed by adult criminal courts without any special consideration of their age or lack of experience. Today, because of the seriousness and violence of their offenses, certain juveniles' cases are being transferred (waived) from juvenile court jurisdiction to adult criminal courts and, in some states, prosecutors have the authority to file charges against juveniles in either the adult criminal court or the juvenile court. Many states have also lowered the upper age of juvenile court jurisdiction, resulting in some older adolescents being referred to the criminal courts. Many juveniles who would have been processed by the juvenile court no longer have their cases heard there.

Another characteristic of the early juvenile court was its informal atmosphere. Since the 1960s, however, juvenile courts have taken on many of the trappings of adult courts, including use of prosecutors and defense attorneys. U.S. Supreme Court decisions are largely responsible for this trend, but the changes have also been influenced by demands that the rights of children be safeguarded.

The scope of the juvenile court's authority has also been questioned. Because status offenders, those juveniles charged with offenses that only apply to juveniles, have been charged with acts that would not be illegal for adults, many feel that

© Springer Nature Switzerland AG 2020
P. C. Kratcoski et al., *Juvenile Delinquency*,
https://doi.org/10.1007/978-3-030-31452-1_11

these youths should be removed from juvenile court jurisdiction and handled by other agencies, or that such behavior does not require court involvement. This is a direct challenge to the purposes of the juvenile court, which was designed to intervene in and touch the lives of any youths believed to be disposed toward conduct defined as unacceptable or inappropriate for children, or children who are at risk. Finally, a huge increase in cases involving child abuse, neglect, and dependency has caused the juvenile court to devote a larger portion of its attention to such matters than it did in the past.

The State of Washington demonstrated its commitment to keeping status offenders out of the juvenile justice system by revising its juvenile code until, by the late 1970s, all status offenders had been removed from juvenile court jurisdiction. This process, termed *divestiture,* means that "the juvenile court cannot detain, petition, adjudicate, or place a youth on probation for the behaviors previously identified as status offenses (Schneider, 1984, p. 347). Counseling and other services are made available for status offenders through community health and human services agencies, but they are undertaken voluntarily. Although the divestiture actions successfully removed many young offenders from juvenile court involvement, an analysis of the effects of divestiture revealed that some youths who were basically status offenders were brought to the court and processed because some of their behavior could be construed as delinquent, while before divestiture, they would have been referred as status offenders. The result was that these youths tended to receive more severe sanctions from the court than they would have been given if supervision of status offenders had been retained by the juvenile courts (Schneider, 1984, p. 349).

Some states have retained jurisdiction of status offenders by the juvenile court, but have decriminalized some of the behaviors that were defined as law violations in the past. Sickmund and Puzzanchera (2014, p. 179) note, "The official processing of status offenders varies from state to state. In some states, for example, a runaway's entry into the official system may be through juvenile court intake, while in other states, the matter may enter through the child welfare agency."

In this chapter, several of the initial steps involved in the processing of a juvenile accused of an offense, either status or delinquent, will be examined. These steps include: the discovery of a juvenile in violation of the law, or in need of protection, a parent, caretaker, or official taking some action in response to the law violation, the filing of a complaint, referral to the juvenile court, the intake process, informal hearing, and programs used in the handling of youth who have been informally (unofficially) processed in the juvenile justice system The juvenile court process may vary, depending on a number of factors, but most important is the severity of the offense the youth is charged with and the prior history of the youth's involvement in the juvenile justice system. In Box 11.1, examples of youths charged with delinquency offenses and status offenses are given to illustrate the various options open to authority figures and law enforcement figures when responding to a youth who is in violation of the law.

The cases above illustrate the broad jurisdiction of the juvenile court as well as the courses of action the court can take in weighing the best interests of the child

Box 11.1 Examples of Juveniles in the Juvenile Justice System
Status Offender

Lisa, age 15, was referred to the juvenile court by her grandmother. At the intake hearing, the grandmother claimed that Lisa would no longer accept her authority, stayed out well beyond the curfew time, and often skipped school. The grandmother stated that she was just too old to handle Lisa and requested that the court do something to relieve her of her responsibility. The court decided to remove Lisa from her grandmother's residence and place her in a residential facility for girls. She would be on "unofficial probation," given a set of rules to follow, and if she did not become involved in any addition deviant behavior would not have a record of being adjudicated by the court.

Delinquent Offenders

Cid, age 16, and two of his friends were detected by the police driving up to mail boxes and hitting the boxes with a baseball bat. They completed destroyed a few boxes and damaged several others. The police officers took them into custody and held the boys at the police station until their parents came. They were released to the custody of their parents. A summons to appear in the juvenile court was issued for each of the boys and their parents. At the hearing, it was determined that Cid did not instigate the decision to destroy mail boxes. He indicated that he realized that his behavior was wrong, but he followed the other boys so he would not lose their friendship, He was placed in a court diversion program, given a set of rules to follow, and also required to pay restitution to the victims who had their mail boxes damaged.

and of the victims of the child's deviance, as well as the welfare of the community. Generally, the criminal codes of most states require that serious delinquent offenses such as murder, rape or aggravated assault, be handled formally by the court, and in some cases the juvenile court judge is mandated to commit the juvenile offender to a secure correctional facility, but in the large majority of cases that are referred to the juvenile courts the judge has the discretionary powers to divert the youth out of the system and handle the cases informally or formally, depending on the seriousness of the delinquent act and the circumstances. For example, in the case of Lisa, the youth was not adjudicated a status offender, but was placed in a controlled environment while her grandmother was relieved of a responsibility she felt incapable of fulfilling. In Cid case, the court determined that, while he used bad judgment by responding to the peer pressure and going along with the property destruction, it was his first recorded violation, he had strong family support, and it was unlikely that he would commit another offense. Unofficial supervision seemed to be a good option for the court to follow.

11.2 Sources of Juvenile Court Referrals

11.2.1 Types of Offenders

A youth may become involved in the juvenile court process as a result of having allegedly committed a law violation that would be a criminal offense if committed by an adult or having allegedly committed a law violation that applies only to youths and would not be a criminal offense for an adult. These "status offenses," as we have seen, include running away, incorrigibility, truancy, and underage drinking. Children may also come under the juvenile court's protection because they are considered to be dependent, neglected, or abused. Referrals to the juvenile court may come from parents, social agency personnel, school personnel, the police, or private individuals. If the alleged violation is a serious felony, it is very likely that the police will make the referral. Referrals for less serious delinquent offenses are also most likely to come from the police, while more than half of the referrals for status offenses come from other sources.

We noted in our discussion of the police processing of youths who violate the law that the police have broad discretionary powers in deciding the course of action to be taken in incidents involving juveniles and that the majority of contacts of juveniles with police result in diversion out of the juvenile justice system. Even when a case is referred to the juvenile court by the police, parents, social agencies, school, or other persons, opportunities exist for the youth to be diverted away from official handling and avoid being labeled a "juvenile delinquent."

11.2.2 Number of Cases Processed

The juvenile courts handled almost 1.4 million delinquency cases in 2010. Some youths are referred to the court several times during a given year, so it is likely that the 1.4 million cases represent a lower number of individuals (Sickmund & Puzzanchera, 2014, p. 151). In 2016, Hockenberry and Puzzanchera (2018, p. 63) reported that the juvenile courts handled an estimated 850,500 delinquency cases in 2016, a 40% reduction of delinquency cases since 2010. This is in line with the number of juvenile arrests between 2010 and 2018. Sickmund and Puzzanchera (2014, p. 118), using the statistics from the FBI report for 2010, *Crime in the United States*, they estimated that 1.6 million arrests of person under age of 18 were made by the police. Twenty-five percent of the arrests of persons under 18 involved offenses against persons, 37% dealt with offenses against property, 12% were related to drug law violations, and 26% involved public order offenses. In 2010, 72% of the referrals to the court were male and 28% of the referrals were female. Hockenberry and Puzzanchera (2018, p. 74) reported that in 2010, the juvenile courts formally processed an estimated 137,000 status offenders, while in 2016, the number of status offenses handled by the juvenile courts decreased to 94,700, a 31% decline.

The types of status offenses for which referrals were made were runaway cases, truancy cases, curfew cases, un-governability cases, status liquor law violations, and other status offense cases, such as smoking tobacco and violation of a valid court order. It is not possible to give accurate figures on the number of status offenders handled informally by the juvenile courts, but since the majority of status offenders are handled informally the number is likely to be much greater than the number of status offender referrals to the juvenile courts that were handled judicially.

Jurisdiction of most of the juvenile courts in the United States encompasses children who allegedly have violated the law as well as children who, although they are not at fault for the violation of any laws, nevertheless are in need of protection by the court. In some cases, the child may fit into both the *at fault* and *not at fault* categories, as in the case of a child who steals food, clothing or other material things after being instructed to do so by a parent. The categories of juveniles and adults that typically come under the legal jurisdiction of the juvenile or family courts include status offenses (acts that are not considered violations of the criminal law if committed by adults, delinquency offenses (acts that are violations of criminal law if committed by adults, violations of a court order, serious offenses by youths for which they could be waived to the criminal court for trial, youths for whom an arrest warrant has been issued by another jurisdiction.

In addition to the *at fault* categories of children who fall under the legal jurisdiction of the juvenile court, there are several categories of *no fault* children that typically are under the jurisdiction of the juvenile courts. These include (Kratcoski, 2012, pp. 222–223), dependent, neglected, or abused children, those removed from their homes for protection reasons, and other matters, including requests by minor for permission or marry without parent consent or to be emancipated from parental control.

In addition to the jurisdiction mentioned above, the juvenile courts also have some jurisdiction over adults who are *at fault* and can be liable for criminal sanctions. These include (Kratcoski, 2012, p. 223) parents or caretakers who are accused of neglecting or abusing their children and adults who are accused of contributing to the delinquency of minors.

Some adults may come under juvenile court jurisdiction, but may not be considered *at fault* for violation of a law, as in dependency cases in which the parent or guardian does not provide the child with proper food, clothing, shelter and supervision, due to physical, or mental problems or some other incapacity but is not *at fault* because the caretaker is not capable of providing these necessities.

11.3   The Juvenile Court Process and Diversion from Official Involvement

Diversion may be either total or partial. *Total* diversion involves turning a youth in trouble away from a course of action that is leading toward justice system involvement. This can be done by police or school officials through a warning that any further trouble will lead to court involvement or through referral to some agency other than the juvenile court for assistance. Such referrals offer an alternative to juvenile court involvement. When a youth has been brought to the attention of the juvenile court, total diversion may still occur if the intake officer releases him or her with only a reprimand, if the prosecuting attorney decides not to prosecute the case, or if the complainant drops the charges. In total diversion, the juvenile justice system has no claim on the diverted youth and the youth has no obligation to submit to any type of treatment.

It was noted earlier that police officers can take a child into custody for improper behavior that is serious, for minor delinquency, for status offenses, or for the youth's own protection because the officer decides that such action is in the best interests of the child. With the exception of serious offenses, most police have discretionary powers. In Cook County (Chicago), for example, police have the following options when they encounter status offenders, as reported by Fuller and Norton (1993, p. 30): "In the case of a child who is a runaway or beyond the control of parents, the Juvenile Court Act provides police officers and social agencies with various options to prevent the referral of such a child to the Juvenile Court. A police officer may take such a child into 'limited custody' (but only for up to 6 h) and, if the child agrees to return home, must transport and release the child to the parent and assist the family in contacting a social service agency if requested to do so. If the child refuses to return home or if the parents are unavailable, the officer must transport and release the child to a social agency offering crisis intervention services and shelter for the child."

11.3.1   Four Phases of Informal Handling by the Court

When police have diversionary discretion, the referral decision is based on such factors as the seriousness of the offense, the youth's physical condition (intoxicated, high on drugs), the child's or the parents' attitude, or the officers' belief that the child is in need of protective custody.

If persons other than the police (school officials, social service agencies, parents, neighbors, community members) are the source of the complaint, they will come to the juvenile court and sign a complaint and a summons will be issued for the child to appear.

The juvenile court process, once set in motion, has four distinct phases: (1) the filing of a petition, (2) referral to intake, (3) adjudication, and (4) disposition. The process may be halted at any of the three initial phases or proceed to the final step of disposition, depending upon decisions made by the person bringing the youth to the attention of the court, by intake officers, by the prosecuting attorney or the defense attorney, or by the juvenile court judge. At each stage of the juvenile court process, the juvenile's rights are safeguarded by various procedures that have been developed and refined in response to federal and state court decisions, including key United States Supreme Court decisions that have affected the juvenile justice process and juvenile court procedures. The procedures used in the juvenile court today gradually evolved as the rights granted to accused juvenile offenders and the procedures the courts must follow as mandated by these decisions were implemented.

11.3.2 The Petition

A petition may be defined as "a formal written application to a court requesting judicial action on a certain matter." In the juvenile court, a petition is not necessarily synonymous with a complaint. For example, parents or other persons may call the police or come to the juvenile court to "complain" about the actions of their children or others, but they may not seek formal action. The juvenile court petition is a legal document in which court action is sought as a result of the child's allegedly being delinquent; a status offender; or dependent, neglected, or abused. The petition is a formally stated complaint—a request for the court to become involved. To give an example of police initiation of juvenile court proceedings, the case of Al Hollus, presented in Box 11.2 is used to illustrate the first stage off the juvenile court process (Kratcoski, 2004).

> **Box 11.2 Al Hollus**
> At the time of his first contact with the police, Al had informed the officers that he was 16 years old. He had been taken to police headquarters and his mother had been contacted. Officer Frank O'Neil, a member of the police department's juvenile division, informed Al that a police complaint of delinquency by reason of auto theft had been filed against him by Officers Mitchell and Lantano and that his mother had been called. Questioning of Al's female companion in the auto, Rosemary Davis, convinced Mitchell and Lantano that she did not know the car was stolen, they also discovered that she was 23 years of age and had known Al for only a short time. She was not charged and she left the station. When Al's mother arrived, she was completely distraught and kept repeating that she could not believe Al would do such a thing to her and his father. She asked him over and over why he would take someone else's car and when she elicited the information that he had planned to run away and get married, she launched into a long, tearful tirade about that "no-good" girl who had gotten him into trouble. Officer O'Neil made no comment, except to inform both of them that Al's case had been referred to the juvenile court and that he would release Al in the custody of his mother until he was summoned to appear in juvenile court to answer the charges.

In the case of Al, the police officers decided that his case should be sent to the juvenile court for a decision. No doubt the seriousness of the offense, auto theft, as well as the indications that the mother was having difficulty in accepting the fact that "her son" was responsible for committing a criminal act were the major factors considered by the officers when the decision to refer to the court was made.

As noted in the introductory chapter, every state, as well as the U.S. Government, has enacted legislation and established codes pertaining to the acts that, when committed by a person defined as a juvenile, constitute delinquency. In addition, the procedures that must be followed when processing a juvenile charged with delinquency, and the legal rights of those youths charged with delinquency have been codified. The legislation enacted by the states relating to the matters of the ages that constitutes delinquency, offenses, and procedures juvenile justice officials must follow, with slight variations, tend to be rather uniform. Several U.S. Supreme Court decisions have resulted in some of the states being required to change their laws to make them in accordance with national standards.

11.3.3   Intake Functions

Generally, the first contact a youth has with a juvenile court official is with the intake division of the juvenile court. The exceptions are youths who are brought to the detention center during the late evenings or on the weekends, times when the court is closed. In these cases, the youth will be interviewed by an intake officer and placed on a schedule to appear before a judge or magistrate at the first opportunity, generally before 24 h have lapsed. The intake division receives all the complaints from the different sources (police, parents, school officials, service agencies, community residents, business establishments) that come into the court. The responsibilities of the intake division include reviewing the complaint to determine whether the court has jurisdiction, collecting information on the family, school, and prior delinquency record, completing risk and needs instruments, scheduling an intake hearing, making total or partial diversion decisions, filing a petition for a formal hearing, if needed, and supervising offenders placed in pretrial supervision and diversion programs.

When the youth first appears before an intake officer (generally with a parent or caretaker) the rights of the youth are read by the intake officer who first makes contact with the youth at the juvenile court. If the youth has been brought to the court by a police officer, the officer who took the child into custody is required to notify the child's parents of this action and the officer is also required to prepare a complaint that gives the name, age, and address of the child and the parents or guardians and specifies the law or ordinance that the youth is alleged to have violated. It may also include information on the attitude of the youth at the time of arrest and list accomplices, property recovered, or damage observed.

11.3.4   Custody of Parents or Temporary Detention

When a youth is arrested, (taken into custody) the first decision to be made is whether he or she may be released into the custody of his or her parents or some other responsible person and return at a later date to answer the charges or whether the youth will be detained until a court hearing takes place. The question of whether to detain or release a juvenile to the custody of a parent or guardian, pending court action on the case, is generally the responsibility of juvenile court personnel.

However, when law enforcement officers bring a juvenile to the court and request that he or she be detained, the court personnel will generally honor such requests.

Temporary detention consists of placing a youth in a restrictive facility between referral to the court's intake division and before having a hearing before a judge or magistrate to determine if continued detention is necessary to protect the interests of the community as well as the youth being held. Although a detention center (a secure holding facility) is normally used for those youths who are awaiting formal action, at times youths may be placed in detention centers after there has been formal action on their cases, but before permanent placement can be made. State statutes require that, dependent, abused, or neglected children who are in need of temporary emergency care or protection are not to be held in detention centers. Instead, they are placed in shelter care centers or foster homes. Most juvenile codes also prohibit holding status offenders in detention centers with delinquent offenders, but some are detained in these centers. Most of the juveniles who are referred to the juvenile courts are not detained. This is particularly true if the juvenile is likely to be diverted from formal processing. In the large majority of cases, juveniles brought to the juvenile detention center will be released to the custody of their parents or caretakers. However, in some cases the juvenile is held in detention as a way of protecting him/her from physical harm, as in a case where a parent might give a child a severe beating for "getting into trouble, or it is known that the home or family is so disrupted that it would be a danger to release The child to a parent. Also, in some cases the parent or caretaker refuses to take custody of the child, using physical illness, the argument that the child is a bad influence on the other children in the family or other reasons for not wanting the child in the home.

Even if a youth is initially held in detention, the youth may still be diverted from formal processing after he or she appears before a judge or magistrate and some of the circumstances of the offense become known. A youth will be detained if the juvenile court personnel believe that he or she presents a serious threat to the community or if the youth is not likely to appear for a future court hearing on the charges. The juvenile court judge has the final authority to decide whether detention is appropriate for a particular juvenile, but this power is usually delegated to a court intake official. A police officer's request for detention may be denied, but if it is approved, a formal hearing normally takes place within 24 h (72 h if the offense occurs on a weekend) to determine if detention should be continued the intake officer, who is also a probation officer of the court, has wide discretionary powers in handling referrals. Some cases may be dismissed because of the pettiness of the charges or because conflicting or questionable information has been presented. Other youths are "admonished and released," receiving nothing more than a stern lecture about the unacceptability of their conduct, perhaps with a warning that next time they will be dealt with more severely. Once these referrals leave the intake officer's presence, they are freed from the control of the juvenile justice system, unless another offense brings them to its attention. If the intake officer decides to handle a case judicially (officially), the case is placed on the court docket and scheduled for a hearing. However, in non-judicial (unofficial) handling parents and youths voluntarily agree to take certain action, often in the form of referral to programs of family or individual counseling con ducted by community agencies.

11.3.5 Diversion at Juvenile Court Intake

The court intake officer, in trying to determine whether the case should go to a formal process or be screened out and handled informally, must consider a number of factors. Certainly the seriousness of the offense will be of prime concern, but other matters that bear on the decision include whether the juvenile or family needs assistance or services but is not likely to seek them voluntarily, how much of an impact the case has on the community, whether the facts of the case are disputed, whether a "cooling-off period" appears to be necessary, and the degrees of cooperation likely to be received from the juvenile and the parents.

Generally, juveniles who are charged with status offenses (e.g., running away, truancy, or curfew violations) or minor delinquent offenses (e.g., shoplifting, trespassing, disorderly conduct, or minor assaults) are considered candidates for *nonjudicial* (informal) processing.

After a young person is referred to the juvenile court and becomes liable for juvenile court involvement, the court may seek to prevent the child from being officially handled or labeled as a delinquent. Such activity, termed *partial diversion,* amounts to an agreement between the intake officer of the juvenile court, the youth, and the parents that a certain course of action or program must be followed for the youth to be diverted out of formal (*judicial*) court processing. The informal programming is most often effected through referral to court-sponsored and court-supervised diversion programs, referral of the entire family to family counseling centers, remanding to receive medical or psychological or some other type of control, such as doing community service. The following Case provides an example of a youth diverted from official (judicial) processing.

Box 11.3 The Ice-Cream Bar Caper

Eleven-year-old Bobby and his nine-year-old brother Billy were walking home from a neighborhood grocery store when they were stopped by a police officer. The boys were each eating an ice cream bar when the officer pulled up in his squad car. He asked the boys if they got the ice cream bars from the neighborhood grocery store and they answered "yes." The officer next asked if they paid for the ice cream, and Billy answered "yes." The officer told them that the owner of the store called the police and said that two boys who fit their descriptions walked out of the store and did not pay for the ice-cream they took. He told the boys to go back to the store so the store owner could get a look at them and determine if they were they boys who allegedly stole the ice cream bars. After returning to the store and being identified as the boys who stole the ice-cream, the boys admitted that they were hungry for ice-cream and since they did not any money, they took the bars and walked out of the store, hoping that they would not be noticed stealing the ice cream.

Since the theft was of a small amount, the officer asked the store owner if she just wanted the officer to handle the matter informally by giving the boys a warning and notifying their parents about their delinquent act, or if she wanted to file a complaint. The owner indicated that she has had trouble with neighborhood boys stealing and suspected that Bobby and his brother stole some things before. Since she has to operate on a small profit margin, any theft from the store would hurt her business. If she filed complaint, it might cut down on the thefts from the store in the future.

The complaint was filed, and when the boys and their mother appeared before the court magistrate, and after having their rights explained, the boys were informed that they were eligible for the diversion program operated by the court. They were told that they would have to admit to the theft, and agree to accept the punishment given and to abide by the rules of the diversion program. The sanctions were explained (pay the store owner for the ice cream, do not go into the store unless accompanied by a parent or another adult) and avoid any behavior that constitutes delinquency. In addition, a court officer might check up on them from time to time. If the boys were successful in adhering to the rules and staying out of trouble for 1 year, the initial charge would be dropped and there will not be a record of the boys having been charged with delinquency.

If a youth is diverted, the youth is obligated to seek the treatment and sanctions indicated or the informal supervision terminated and the offender will be given an official court hearing. Partial diversion is most appropriate when some type of informal supervision is considered necessary; but even here the youth can avoid official processing and a record of being adjudicated delinquent. Youth diverted at intake are often referred to programs especially designed for certain types of offenders, such as drug or alcohol offenders or those with school related problems. The cost for a youth for having the option of being placed in a diversion program rather than being processed through the court with an official hearing may be the requirement to participate in a program designed to address the source of the problem that led to delinquent behavior. The programs might consist of alcohol or drug abuse counseling, attendance at a particular type counseling by a school counselor, Students who are not expected to finish school and will drop out at the time they are eligible, enrollment in a school program that combines a number of hours in the classroom with on-the-job experiences may be an option. Successful completion of the diversion program usually means avoidance of a juvenile court record for the offense that brought the youth to the attention of the court. In some instances, the entire family is referred to a family counseling center, and the preparation of the petition against the youth is suspended until attempts are made to work out the problems. When physical or mental health problems are suspected as the cause of the unlawful behavior, a referral for diagnostic testing may be made before a decision on filing is reached. The following diversion program as illustrated in the following Box 11.3, shows how the court, parents, and the community work together to reach a goal that is acceptable to the community as well as to the welfare of the youth involved.

11.4   Juvenile Court Diversion Programs

11.4.1   The Safe Harbor Program

"The Safe Harbor Diversion Program (Summit County Juvenile Court, 2019, p. 9) is a program that was launched in September 2014. The program is based largely on the direct provisions of the Safe Harbor statute, utilizing a human trafficking coordinator to organize the efforts between attorneys, court staff, guardians ad litem, and service providers. The program combines evidence-based practices, such as trauma informed treatment and substance abuse counseling, with services and activities that promote connection, healing and self-worth as a way of intervening and diverting youth from the path as early as possible. In addition to court-ordered diversion actions, the juveniles are permitted to contribute to the creation of their diversion plans, with mentoring as a central component. A specially trained case manager is assigned to each human trafficking case to make referrals, track progress and report to the court. Successful completion of the program results in immediate dismissal of the complaint and expungement of the record."

11.4.2   Truancy Mediation Diversion Program

The Truancy Mediation Diversion Program (Summit County Juvenile Court, 2019, p. 6) is "An alternative process to a traditional court hearing in which the youth or parent is given the opportunity to avoid prosecution by completing various program requirements. The diversion program youth, parents and school officials have an opportunity to work with an impartial party to generate solutions to truancy problems, all of which are then written into a mediation agreement. A mediator then closely monitors the youth's attendance and compliance have other requirements set forth in the agreement for a time period of 60 school days. Those who successfully complete this program will have their original complaint dismissed."

11.4.3   Diversion in Traffic Court

In Ohio, as well as in many other states, youths who fall within the jurisdiction of the juvenile or family court who are charged with non-criminal traffic offenses, are processed through the juvenile courts. Typically, in the larger counties, the administrative juvenile court judge will appoint one or several magistrates to hear cases on special dockets, often referred to as the traffic court. For example, Cody, (2019, p. 2) states; "The Ohio Revised Code section 2151.23 (A) (1) gives the juvenile court exclusive jurisdiction over a juvenile adjudicated as a juvenile traffic offender while the person is under the age of 18 until that person reaches the age of 21. The traffic offenses are generally found in Title 45 of the Ohio revised Code, or contained in local traffic ordinances. Also, the Ohio Traffic Rules and Juvenile Rules are applicable to juvenile traffic cases." Daniel Cody, a magistrate at the Summit County Juvenile Court, assigned to hear cases on the traffic docket was asked during an interview (Kratcoski & Kratcoski, 2019) if the court had a diversion program for traffic offenders and if so to describe the features of the program. Magistrate Cody responded, "Yes, Traffic Rule 13.1 provides that a Juvenile Traffic Violations Bureau may be established by Local Rule of Court. There are limitations on the juvenile traffic bureaus. Including accident cases, second or subsequent moving violations; or certain specified offenses found in Traffic Rule 13 (B0 (1) through (9). For example, leaving the scene of an accident, driving under suspension, failure to stop for a school bus, drag racing, and fleeing a police officer are offenses that are not eligible for diversion."

In Summit County, first time non-moving violations can be handled by having the juvenile and parent sign a waiver of hearing and paying a fine and court costs. These cases typically consist of a single offense such as failure to wear a seat belt, license plate violations, and improper vehicle equipment.

The Summit County traffic diversion program is titled *Staying Accident Free Through Education (SAFTE)*. First time offenders who have a speeding violation of 20 miles over the speed limit or less, and first time moving violations not involving an accident or prohibited by the Traffic Rules are eligible for the *SAFTE* diversion program. In Summit County, juvenile traffic offenders who qualify are eligible for the program one time. There is a fee to cover costs and program participation. The juvenile must donate an item of at least $ 10.00 in value. The donated items are given to needy families through the Court's Family Resource Center. The educational program that the traffic offenders are required to attend consists of a three and one half hour program on traffic safety taught by a retired police officer. Parents must attend the final 30 min of the program. The program focuses on the dangers commonly experienced by juvenile drivers as well as the parent's responsibility. If the program is successfully completed, the juvenile traffic record is sealed. A subsequent offense is treated as a first time offense, but the juvenile is not eligible for the diversion program regardless of the severity of the offense.

11.5   Juvenile Diversion Programs in the Community

Diversion programs for youthful offenders have been developed in communities throughout the United States. Some of these programs are administered in conjunction with the juvenile courts who have jurisdiction in the community, and others are independent of the courts and other justice agencies. These programs tend to follow a restorative justice model by addressing the needs of the offender, victims and the community in which the offender lives. For example, The Red Hook Community Justice Center, located in Brooklyn, NY (Lee et al., 2009, pp. 5 and 6) noted that a referral to the Center who had special needs, such as drug or alcohol abuse counseling, received individualized counseling. If applicable, those referred to the Center were expected to give back something to the victim, restitution, if possible, as well as something to the community (often some type of community service). Kratcoski (2017a, pp.105–106) noted, "In addition, the Justice Center was successful in diverting a large proportion of juvenile delinquency cases from prosecution, but still provided supervision and service to the diverted youths through the probation department."

11.5.1   Youth Courts

The Global Youth Justice Advocacy Organization (CYJO) reported that there were more than 1800 volunteers operated youth diversion programs in operation in the United States and other counties located on five continents (2019, p. 1). These organizations use several different titles such as Teen Courts, Youth Courts, Peer Courts, and Peer Jury Diversion Programs (Global Youth Advocacy Organization, 2019, p. 1). The American Bar Association (2019, p. 1) states, "Youth court is an intervention program and not a court within the judicial branch of government. It fits within the graduated, or accountability-based, sanctions approach to juvenile offenses" The American Bar Association publication (2019, p. 2) describes youth courts in this way, "All youth courts are diversion processes: These programs may handle crimes and offenses that would otherwise be eligible for prosecution in juvenile court, adult court, traffic court, or a school disciplinary process. Without a youth court, in some cases juvenile offenders would not be held accountable for their antisocial, delinquent and criminal behavior because of the backlog in the juvenile system. Youth courts provide a measured response for youths who violate the law." Youth court programs vary in name and structure. However, all programs have a common goal of diverting youths from the juvenile justice system. These specialty courts and programs are similar. Kratcoski (2017b, pp. 80–81) describes them as serving youths between the ages of 7 and 18 who have committed status offenses or minor delinquent offenses. Referrals can come from the police, school, officials, or parents or caregivers. Youths who are eligible for youth court can decide not to participate but have a formal juvenile hearing instead. If they choose to participate, the young people can either "true" to the charges and be sanctioned by a jury of their peers with a judge, prosecuting attorney, and defense attorney. A parent, guardian, or caretaker is required to be present. If the charges are found to be true they can be sanctioned by a peer jury. Sanctions imposed may include community service or participation in an alcohol and substance abuse, anger management, family counseling, truancy prevention, shoplifting or educational programs provided by community service agencies and supervised by an official of the court or the agency involved. If the youth completes the program successfully the charges will be dropped. If the youth does not successfully complete the program, the youth will be referred to the juvenile (family) court and formally processed.

Although the goals and structures of the youth courts are similar, since they all involve the use of volunteers and various community youth service agencies and tend to follow a restorative justice model, there are some major differences in the operations of the youth court programs. One major difference centers on the role of the juvenile court judge. In some programs, the youth court is completely independent of the juvenile court and the teen court members, under the guidance of a supervisor, function in the roles of prosecutor, defense attorney, and jury. All decisions are made by the teen court members, including if the charges are true and, if they are found to be true, the sanctioning of the youth. In other teen (youth courts) the juvenile court judge is a great deal more involved in the process. Generally, the judge will observe the sessions (hearings) of the teen court and, if there are any indications of the court acting improperly, as in violation of the alleged offenders' rights, or showing prejudice or bias, the process will be stopped. In some jurisdictions, the teen court members will determine if the charges are true, but the juvenile court judge will determine the appropriate sanction. Judge S. Watkins, who serves as director of two youth courts located in Independence, Missouri and Eastern Jackson County, Missouri, stated that, "the Independence Youth Court handles 400–600 juvenile cases per year. The two evening dockets each month are held in the Independence Municipal Court. The participants (teens in 8th–12th grades) fill all of the courtroom roles, which include bailiff, clerk, prosecuting attorney, defense attorney, and judge. The judge is typically a senior with experience in all of the roles. The teens are recruited from the local high schools, middle schools, and the home school association. Students in grades 8–12 must apply for admission, have good attendance, passing grades, and submit a letter of reference from a teacher. All new attorneys must complete a 3-month training program, successfully pass a written bar exam with a score of at least 75%, take an oath of confidentiality, and be sworn in to practice as youth court attorneys by a judge."

Judge Watkins indicated that the Teen Court process closely resembles the procedures followed in a criminal court. She indicated, "All juvenile offenders have an opportunity to enter a plea of not guilty after the charges are read at the arraignment. Less than 8% enter a plea of not guilty and go on for a full trial Some juveniles who pleaded not guilty change their minds when they come back for the trial and see that the witnesses are in court. The actual number of cases that have a trial is less than 5% .... The trial is supervised by an adult volunteer attorney, myself (to supervise the youth judge), and a police officer. The students spend a lot of time in preparation for any trial, and the actual trial process is very smooth and professional. The only issue during a trial is if someone is unhappy with the testimony or evidence that might be presented that points to their guilt or if they are unhappy with the verdict."

11.5.2   Diversion of Females

In addition to the conditions in American life that are conducive to delinquent behavior for both males and females, a number of factors are uniquely related to the occurrence of unacceptable behavior by adolescent girls. These include the special stresses adolescent girls undergo at the time of puberty, the double standard in American sexual definitions, the changing cultural position of women and convergence of the male and female roles, and the influence of family disorganization.

The Children's Advocacy Project (2019, p. 1) uses the Girls Circle Group Model for group therapy for adolescent girls. The Project describes this model in the following way: "The Girls Circle Model is a structured support group for girls from 9 to 18 years that does not aim to provide advice, but encourages girls to share experiences that are helpful to one another. Each week the group will talk and listen to one another about their concerns and interests. The girls will have opportunities to express themselves further through creative or focused activities, such as role playing, drama, journalism, poetry, dance, drawing, collage, clay, and anything else the girls can think of." Girls Circle groups such topics as what it means to be a girl, developing friendships, goals for life, and how to make decisions that affect their lives. The consequences of drug and alcohol use are also discussed.

The Portage Country Court of Common Pleas, Juvenile Division (2019, Girls Circle Program, p. 1) developed a specific program for female offenders that follows the Girls Circle Model. The participants in the group are selected by the court officers. "The Girls Circle Model consists of eight (8) structured weeks of groups designed to foster self-esteem, helps girls maintain a connection with peers and adult women in the community, works on self-doubt, and allows for self-expression through verbal sharing in group and participating in creative activities."

11.5.3   Critiques of Diversion

Diversion programs for status offenders and minor delinquents have not escaped criticism. The legality and propriety of treating minor delinquents who have not had a formal judicial hearing have been questioned. In addition, concerns have been raised regarding the "net widening" that may result from placing children in diversion programs for treatment when their behavior is not serious enough to warrant such intervention. At times, administrators have been criticized for choosing cases for diversion programs when a successful outcome is almost certain, thus assuring that evaluations of the programs will show that they should be continued. The potential harmful effects of being involved in a treatment program that stemmed from a court referral may be overlooked in these evaluations. These effects may be in the form of being labeled a deviant, leading to being ostracized by peers and adults in the community. In those instances where the diverted youth is provided with psychological counseling, the possibility of being bullied by schoolmates may increase. However, juvenile court judges, court administrators, and those juvenile justice personnel who have direct contact with the diverted youths are convinced that the diversion of youths out of the juvenile justice system and working with social service agencies and child protective agencies to deal with the causes of the delinquent youths' problems is the solution to preventing further delinquency. In answer to the "net widening" criticism of diversion programs, the reality is that most youths who commit delinquent acts that are not of a serious nature have already been diverted out of the system and only those who have caught the attention of a school or justice official are referred to the court. For example, a youth who vandalized a neighbor's property may escape involvement in the juvenile justice system when the youth's parents agree to pay for the damage, avoiding juvenile justice involvement. School officials will often handle offenses by students internally when the offenses are not of a serious nature. A police officers engage in the total diversion of youth may give the youth caught in some type of deviant act a warning to "not do it again" and not make out a contact report on the encounter. But in some cases involving minor acts of delinquency or status offenses, parents, school officials, or police officers recognize that a youth may be those who make in need of some counseling, supervision, or treatment and they refer the youth to the juvenile court in order for the youth to obtain the help needed rather than to have the child punished.

Summit County, OH, Juvenile Court Judge L. Teodosio is a firm believer in using diversion programs and is responsible for implementing several specialty programs with the court which she administers. When asked about the goals of the Summit County Juvenile Court (Kratcoski, 2012, p. 228), she responded, "I believe that we have adopted a philosophy that stresses the best interests of the child and community safety. We have been able to successfully collaborate with other agencies to provide the children and families the services they need." Former Stark County, OH Family Court Administrator, R. DeHeer, responded to the question, "What other agencies have the most influence or effect in determining what your agency does and how you do it" by stating, "The Stark Council Family Council has been a collaborating force in the community for over 20 years. This agency brings the major child-serving agencies in the community together with a common mission. Our court cannot operate successfully without the cooperation from Mental Health, Drug and Alcohol Recovery Services, and the Children Services Department" (Kratcoski, 2012, p. 240).

11.6 Summary

Views on the appropriate role and procedures for the juvenile court change somewhat from time to time, depending on the changes in thinking on the purpose of the court by legislators, who are responsible for creating new laws, or revising existing laws when it is thought that changes are needed. Often, these legislators are influenced by public opinion, that at one time may be emphasizing a "get tough" approach to juvenile offenders and at another time a "treatment" approach. On the local level, a change in the judge of a court may result in significant changes in the goals and focus of the court's operations.

Currently, the major focus of the juvenile justice system, particularly the juvenile court, is on restorative justice. This involves cooperating with community youth service agencies and other justice agencies to serve the best interests of the community as well as the youths who, while offenders, are still in need of services that can be provided by justice, educational, health, and social welfare agencies.

Youths may be referred to the juvenile court for offenses that are not illegal if committed by adults, such as running away from home, disobeying parents, being truant from school, and drinking alcohol when below the minimum age. If a youth is referred to the juvenile court for committing one or several of these status offenses, or for a less serious act that is defined as criminal for an adult, the youth is likely to be eligible for a diversion program.

Total diversion from court involvement can take place if the youth is counseled by the police and released or through referral to another agency. If this occurs, no juvenile court action is taken. Partial diversion occurs in those cases in which a petition is filed with the court, the intake officer reviews the charges, and the youth's situation, makes a decision to handle the case informally (non-judicially) and refers the youth to either a diversion program administered by the court or to a program administered by a community agency. The referral to a specific agency is determined by the youth's special needs as well as the resources available and the needs of the community in cases in which the youth might be a threat to the safety of the community.

Diversion programs vary in the functions they serve. Some are designed to focus on special problems of the youths in the program such as alcohol and drug abuse, mental health, or anger management, or for those youths involved in motor vehicle traffic violations. Other programs are broader in their goals. All youths referred to diversion programs are expected to abide by a set of rules and also are expected to give back something to the community, generally in the form of community service. Youth who are diverted through informal processing and who do not adhere to the rules and required behavior of the program are subject to being withdrawn from the diversion program for cause, such as non-participation, or as a result of having committed another offense, are then likely to be processed judicially. If the charges are found to be true at this judicial hearing, the juvenile will be adjudicated delinquent and is no longer eligible for a diversion program.

11.7   Discussion Questions

1. Discuss the differences between total diversion and partial diversion.
2. Discuss the role of a juvenile court intake officer in regard to decisions to divert juveniles from official handling. What are the criteria that the officer might use to make a determination on the avenue to follow?

3. When is it appropriate to place a juvenile charged with an offense who has not had any hearing before a court official in the court's detention center?

4. . What are youth courts? Explain how youth courts differ from juvenile courts.

5. Mediation is used in many juvenile courts as a way of diverting status offenders and misdemeanor offenders from formal court processing. Discuss the mediation process and give some examples of mediation programs.

6. .Describe how a behavior contract is used in a juvenile diversion program Give an example of the typical contents of a behavior contract.

7. Restitution and community service are often used in juvenile diversion programs. Discuss the differences between restitution and community service. What types of violations would be appropriate offenses for restitution dispositions?

8. Define "restorative justice" and explain how restorative justice is used in juvenile court diversion programs.

9. Several states have decriminalized some or all of the typical status offenses (running away, truancy, incorrigibility). Do you think this is an approach to the problem? What are the possible positive and negative effects of this legislation?

10. Discuss the benefits juveniles receive by having their cases diverted from formal court processing. What are the possible repercussions if a child violates a diversion agreement?

References

American Bar Association. (2019). *Youth cases for youth courts.* Retrieved June 26, 2019, from https://www.globalyouthjustice.org

Children's Advocacy Project, Inc. (2019). *Girls circle group—Group therapy for adolescent girls* (pp. 1–2). Retrieved August 1, 2019, from https://www.childrensadvocacyproject.org/girls_group.htm

Fuller, J., & Norton, W. (1993). Juvenile diversion: The impact of net widening on program philosophy on net widening. *Journal of Crime and Delinquency, 16*(1), 30–53.

Global Youth Justice Organization. (2019). *Youth/Teen/student/peer court and peer jury* (pp. 1–6). Retrieved June 26, 2019, from https://www.clobalyouthjustice.org

Hockenberry, S., & Puzzanchera, C. (2018). *Juvenile court statistics 2016.* Pittsburgh, PA: National Center for Juvenile Justice.

Kratcoski, P. (2004). *Al Hollus' story.* This story is based on a juvenile court referral, with the names and some of the circumstances altered to protect identities.

Kratcoski, P. (2012). *Juvenile justice administration.* Boca Raton: CRC Press/Taylor and Francis Group.

Kratcoski, P. (2017a). *Correctional counseling and treatment* (6th ed.). Cham, Switzerland: Springer.

Kratcoski, P. (2017b). Interview with Judge S. Watkins, July 3, 2016. In: P. Kratcoski (Ed.), *Correctional counseling and treatment* (6th ed., pp. 82–84). Cham: Springer.

Kratcoski, P., & Kratcoski, P. (2019). Interview of Dan Cody, Magistrate of Summit County, OH Juvenile Court. Interview completed April 1, 2019.

Lee, C., Chessman, F., Rottman, D., Swaner, R., Lambson, S., Rempel, M., et al. (2009). *A community court grows in Brooklyn: a comprehensive evaluation of the red hook community justice center (executive summary).* Williamsburg, VA: National Center for State Courts.

Portage County Court of Common Pleas, Juvenile Division. (2019). *Girls circle program.* Ravenna, OH: Portage County Juvenile Court.

Schneider, A. (1984). Divesting status offenses from juvenile court jurisdiction. *Crime and Delinquency, 30*(3), 149.

Sickmund, M., & Puzzanchera, C. (2014). *Juvenile offender sand victims: 2014 National Report.* Pittsburgh, PA: National Center for Juvenile Justice.

Summit County Juvenile Court. (2019). *A guide to programming and services.* Akron, OH: Summit County Juvenile Court.

Chapter 12
The Juvenile Court Process

12.1 Introduction

Although the jurisdiction of the juvenile and family courts of the United States are specified in the codes of the individual states, and there are some differences in the jurisdiction of the courts, generally the courts will have jurisdiction over children who are "at fault," that is they have violated a law and children who are "not at fault," that is, those who are in need of protection and service from the court. Those youths who fall into the "at fault" category (Kratcoski, 2012, pp. 222–223) include the following:

- Youths who are accused of committing status offenses (acts that are not considered violations of the law if committed by an adult);
- Youths who are accused of delinquent offenses (acts that would be a violation of the criminal law if committed by an adult);
- Youths who are under court supervision and have violated the rules and regulations established for them by the court and,
- Juveniles who are accused of serious offenses that make them eligible for waiver to the criminal court for trial; and youths who are wanted in another jurisdiction and a warrant has been issued for their arrest.

The jurisdiction of the juvenile court that applies to "not-at-fault" children includes the following:

- Children who are dependent, neglected, or abused
- Children who have been removed from their homes for emergency protection reasons; and
- Youths who petition the courts on special matters.

In this chapter, we will consider the formal processing of juveniles who are accused of committing serious offenses or who are habitual offenders. The offenses of these youths are so serious (murder, rape, aggravated assault) that they are not eligible for diversion or informal handling, and in fact in many cases they will be

© Springer Nature Switzerland AG 2020
P. C. Kratcoski et al., *Juvenile Delinquency*,
https://doi.org/10.1007/978-3-030-31452-1_12

bound over to adult the criminal court for processing. Sickmund and Puzzanchera (2014, p. 166) note that in 2010 more than 50% of the youths petitioned to the juvenile courts were handled formally (judicially). More than three-quarters of those accused of violent crimes (criminal homicide, forcible rape, robbery) were processed formally and more than two-thirds of those accused of aggravated assault were handled formally. In Box 12.1 Several examples of serious juvenile offenders are given.

Box 12.1 Examples of Serious Juvenile Offenders
Serious Delinquent Offender—Murder of a 14-year-old girl
   Source: E. Balint, *Akron Beacon Journal*, July 27, Balint, 2019, p. B4
   Second teen charged in death of 14-year-old.
   "A second teen has been charged in the shooting death of 14-year-old Sylvia McGee. _____, 14, of Canton, and faces juvenile counts of complicity to aggravated murder and obstructing justice. The indictment follows the previous arrest of 13-year-old _____, who faces juvenile counts of aggravated murder and obstructing justice. Lynch is accused of fatally shooting McGee in the head March 30 on Bieyl Court SW between 10th and 11th streets. A man walking his dog found her body about 4 a.m. ... The Juvenile Division of the Stark County Prosecutor's Office filed complaints and obtained indictments requesting that the two juveniles be tried as serious youthful offenders. If convicted, both defendants could receive what is known as a blended sentence, a combination of time in youth prison followed by a potential term in adult prison. State law prevents a juvenile defendant younger than 14 from being transferred to common pleas court and tried as an adult."
   Serious Delinquent Offender-Murder of an Elderly Woman
   Source: A. Garrett, *Akron Beacon Journal*, November 3, 2018, pp. A1, A6.
   Teen pleads no contest in killing of elderly neighbor
   "On Friday, after months of denying he killed his elderly neighbor, Ramsay pleaded no contest to nine charges against him, including multiple counts of murder, plus kidnapping, burglary. and abuse of a corpse.
   Medina County Common Pleas Judge Joyce Kimbler is scheduled to sentence Ramsay in January. The death penalty is not an option under Ohio law because Ramsay is under 18. Ramsay could, however, face life in prison without out the possibility of parole."

The cases above illustrate the courses of action the juvenile court can take when dealing with very serious juvenile offenses. In the first case, the murder of a young girl by 13- and 14-year-old boys, the options open to the court are limited by the State law relating to the ages of the defendants, and, if charges against the youths are determined to be true, the types of sentences they could receive. In the case of Ramsay, who pleaded "no contest" to nine very serious charges, he was bound over to the criminal court to be tried as an adult. At this point, the juvenile court no longer has jurisdiction. He can be sentenced to a state correctional facility for adult criminals, but the death penalty is not an option because of Ohio law stipulating that youths under 18 cannot receive the death penalty.

12.2 Sources of Juvenile Court Referrals

The police make the large majority of the referral of juvenile offenders to the juvenile courts. Hockenberry and Puzzanchera (2018, p. 31) reported that 81% of all delinquency cases were referred to the courts by law enforcement officials in the year 2016. Referrals for both serious delinquent offenses as well as minor delinquency are most likely to come from the police, while more than half of the referrals for status offenses come from other sources.

The police have broad powers when responding to youth who are allegedly involved in delinquency. The course of action taken by the police in incidents involving juveniles are either totally or partially diverted out of the juvenile justice system. Even when a case is referred to the juvenile court by the police, parents, social agencies, schools, or other persons, opportunities exist for the youth to be diverted away from official handling and avoid being labeled a "juvenile delinquent."

12.2.1 The Petition

A petition may be defined as "a formal written application to a court requesting judicial action on a certain matter." In the juvenile court, a petition is not necessarily synonymous with a complaint. For example, parents or other persons may call the police or come to the juvenile court to "complain" about the actions of their children or others, but they may not seek formal action. The Juvenile court petition is a legal document stating that court action is sought as a result of the child's allegedly being delinquent; a status offender; or dependent, neglected, or abused. The petition is a formally stated complaint-a request for the court to become involved. As noted in the introductory chapter, every state, as well as the U.S. Government, has enacted legislation and established codes pertaining to the acts that, when committed by a person defined as a juvenile, constitute delinquency. In addition, the procedures that must be followed when processing a juvenile charged with delinquency, and the legal rights of those youths charged with delinquency have been codified.

Relating to the matters of the age of responsibility and what that constitutes delinquency offenses, procedures juvenile justice officials must follow, with slight variations, tend to be rather uniform throughout the United States. Several U.S. Supreme Court decisions have resulted in some of the states being required to change their laws to be in accordance with national standards. The Supreme Court cases pertaining to police interaction with and processing of juveniles regarding questioning, interrogation, the identification process, police custody, and custodial interrogations were presented in Chap. 8. For example, if the police elect to arrest a juvenile rather than use some type of discretionary handling, the youth must be advised at the time of arrest of the right to counsel (either private or court-appointed), informed of the right to remain silent, and told that anything he or she says may be held against him or her. This information, known as the *"Miranda* warnings," because it was guaranteed to arrested persons by the *Miranda* v, *Arizona* Supreme Court decision (Miranda v. Arizona, 358 U.S. 436,448, 1966).

12.2.2   The Intake Functions

Generally, the first contact a youth has with a juvenile court official is with the intake division of the juvenile court. The exceptions are youths who are brought to the detention center during the late evenings or on the weekends, times when the court is closed. In these cases, the youth will be interviewed by an intake officer and placed on a schedule to appear before a judge or magistrate at the first opportunity, generally before 24 h has elapsed. The intake division receives all the complaints from the different sources (police, parents, school officials, service agencies, community residents, business establishments) that come into the court. As noted in Chap. 11, responsibilities of the intake division include reviewing the complaint to determine whether the court has jurisdiction, collecting information on the youth, completing risks and needs assessments, scheduling intake hearings, interviewing youths held in detention, making a determination of whether the youth should be informally or formally processed in the court, filing a petition to have a formal (judicial) hearing, and supervising youths who are placed in court pretrial supervision and diversion programs.

When the youth first appears before an intake officer (generally with a parent or caretaker), the rights of the youth are read by the intake officer who first makes contact with the youth at the juvenile court. If the youth has been brought to the court by a police officer, the officer who took a child into custody is required to notify the child's parents of this action, and the officer is also required to prepare a complaint that gives the name, age, and address of the child and the parents or guardians and specifies the law or ordinance that the youth is alleged to have violated.

12.2.3   Release or Temporary Detention

When a youth is arrested (taken into custody), the first decision to be made is whether he or she may be release into the custody of his or her parents or some other responsible person and return at a later date to answer the charges or whether the youth will be detained until a court hearing takes place. The question of whether to detain or release a juvenile to the custody of a parent or guardian, pending court action on the case, is generally the responsibility of juvenile court personnel. Normally, youth brought to the detention center for having allegedly committed serious offenses will be held in the facility until there is an opportunity to hold a detention hearing. Normally, this will occur within 24 h after being brought to the center. Hockenberry and Puzzanchera (2018, p. 32) note that the proportion of delinquency cases referred to the juvenile courts in 2016 held in detention was 27%.

Temporary detention consists of placing a youth in a restrictive facility between referral to the court's intake division and before having a hearing before a judge or magistrate to determine if continued detention is necessary to protect the interests of the community as well as the youth being held. Although a detention center (a secure holding facility) is normally used for those youths who are awaiting formal action, at times youths may be placed in detention centers after there has been formal action on their cases, but before permanent placement can be made. State statutes require that dependent, abused, or neglected children who are in need of temporary emergency care or protection are not to be held in detention centers. Instead, they are placed in shelter care centers or foster homes. Most juvenile codes also prohibit holding status offenders in detention centers with delinquent offenders, but some are detained in these centers.

Almost two-thirds of the juveniles who are referred to the juvenile courts are not detained. In the majority of cases, juveniles brought to the juvenile detention center will be released to the custody of their parents. A youth will be detained if the juvenile court personnel believe that he or she presents a serious threat to the community or if the youth is not likely to appear for a future court hearing on the charges.

A juvenile court judge has the final authority to decide whether temporary detention is appropriate for a particular juvenile, but this power is usually delegated to a court intake official. A formal hearing normally takes place within 24 h (72 h if the offense occurs on a weekend) to determine if detention should be continued.

With regard to the detention of juveniles, the National Advisory Committee for Juvenile Justice and Delinquency Prevention (1980, p. 279) recommended that juveniles subject to the jurisdiction of the court for delinquency should not be detained in a secure facility unless:

1. They are fugitives from another jurisdiction.
2. They request protection in writing in circumstances that present an immediate threat of serious physical injury.
3. They are charged with murder in the first or second degree.
4. They are charged with a serious property crime or a crime of violence other than first- or second-degree murder that, if committed by an adult would be a felony, and

   (a) They are already detained or on conditioned release in connection with another delinquency proceeding;
   (b) They have a demonstrable recent record of willful failures to appear at family court proceedings;
   (c) They have a demonstrable recent record of violent conduct resulting in physical injury to others; or
   (d) They have a demonstrable recent record of adjudications for serious property offenses.

5. There is no less restrictive alternative that will reduce the risk of flight or of serious harm to property or to the physical safety of the juvenile or others. Currently, most of the juvenile courts throughout the United States have a detention center to house juveniles, or have access to a center from a neighboring court. However, in a few jurisdictions, a section of the county jail in which the juveniles are separated from the adults, is used for detention of juveniles.

Another option is the use of home detention (house arrest). In addition to supervision by parents, this process involves behavior restrictions and monitoring by a court official who makes visits or telephones periodically, or through use of an electronic device that records and reports the youth's movements.

In *Schall* v. *Martin,* the U.S. Supreme Court upheld a New York State act that allowed detention of juveniles prior to their hearings if they presented a serious risk of committing another offense. Although juveniles do not have a right to bail (pretrial release with appearance at hearings secured by a specific amount of money that will be forfeited if the youth does not appear), some state juvenile codes have provisions for bail for juveniles. A judge may also require that parents or guardians sign a signature bond if the youth does not appear for hearings.

12.3   Official Processing of Juvenile Offenders

The juvenile court jurisdiction covers a variety of different types of cases, including delinquency, dependent and neglected children, and even in some cases adults, such as contributing to the delinquency of a minor. Adults can be charged and prosecuted in the juvenile court. In addition, many of the courts have established special dockets, referred to as drug courts, family courts, and traffic courts. These special dockets address specific problems and generally the larger courts will have a number of magistrates who reside over these special dockets.

12.3.1   Traffic Court

In Ohio, as well as many other states, youths who fall within the jurisdiction of the juvenile or family court who are charged with noncriminal traffic offenses are processed through the juvenile courts. Typically, in the larger counties, the chief juvenile court judge will appoint one or several magistrates to hear cases on special docket, often referred to as traffic court. For example, Cody (Kratcoski & Kratcoski, 2019a, p. 2) states, "The Ohio Revised Code section 2151.23 (A) (1) gives the juvenile court the exclusive jurisdiction over a juvenile adjudicated as a juvenile traffic offender while the person is under the age of 18 until that person reaches the age of 21. The traffic offenses are generally found in Title 45 of the Ohio revised Code, or contained in local traffic ordinances. Also the Ohio Traffic Rules and Juvenile Rules are applicable to juvenile traffic cases."

Box 12.2 Interview with Daniel Cody, Magistrate, Summit County Juvenile Court
Biography

Daniel Cody holds a B.A. degree in History, a B.S. degree in Secondary Social Studies Education and also attended graduate school at St. Meinrad School of Theology and at Kent State University. He taught courses in government, and psychology at Archbishop Hoban High School from 1973 to 1988. During that time, he also served as athletic director, soccer coach, and mock trial coordinator. He graduated from the University of Akron School of Law in 1990 and served as research assistant to Hon. Arthur Goldberg, Retired Justice of the United States Supreme Court, the Seiberling Professor of Constitutional Law in 1989. Before entering private practice in 1991, he was a judicial attorney at the Ohio Ninth District Court of Appeals. In private practice, he specialized in litigation of medical negligence and personal injury cases, as well as criminal and juvenile law cases, until his retirement in 2015. He became a magistrate at the Summit County Juvenile Court in 2011, where he is currently assigned to the traffic docket and dependency, neglect and abuse cases.

The Interview of Magistrate Cody was conducted by Dr. Peter C. Kratcoski and Attorney Peter Kratcoski on April 1, 2019.

Q: Mr. Cody, please explain the process followed for youths who have allegedly violated traffic law.

A: The uniform traffic citation serves as the complaint in a juvenile traffic case. The traffic ticket issued by the police, deputy sheriff or Highway Patrol officer is forwarded to the clerk at the Juvenile Court, who serves a copy of the ticket on the juvenile and parent by certified mail. A preliminary hearing is scheduled approximately 4 weeks after the citation arrives in the clerk's office. At the preliminary hearing, which must be done individually by the magistrate or judge, with the juvenile and parent being present, the juvenile is read the exact charge or traffic violation with the statutory or local ordinance identified in the charge against him or her. The juvenile is apprised of the possible penalties that may be imposed, including traffic essays or attendance at a safety school program.

The juvenile is then explained his/her rights, including the right to have an attorney, right to a trial, right to cross examine an accuser, right to remain silent, and the right to have the State prove the charge/s against the alleged offender. Unless the charge involves a potential sentence to the detention center, there is no right to a court appointed attorney.

After an explanation of the rights is given, the juvenile is given an explanation of the possible pleas that can be made. The juvenile may admit to the offense/s; or enter a plea of no contest if there was personal injury or property damage that would expose the juvenile to a civil law suit. The juvenile may also deny the charge/s. The nomenclature for the pleas is significant, since juveniles cannot be found guilty, but only found as a juvenile traffic offender.

If the juvenile admits or enters a plea of no contest, the court will sentence the juvenile after the juvenile is given an opportunity to explain what happened. If the juvenile denies the charge, a pretrial is immediately scheduled. At the pretrial, the juvenile and parent can choose to retain an attorney, as well as discuss the case with the prosecutor. Depending on the outcome of the discussion with the prosecutor, the juvenile may choose to enter a plea. If there is no resolution of the case at the pretrial, the case is set for a bench trial before a magistrate or the judge. Juveniles do not have a right to a jury trial in Ohio. If the juvenile now makes a plea of true or no contest to the charges, or if the charges are found to be true at the trial, the juvenile is given a penalty. The juvenile is informed of the right to file an objection with the juvenile court judge if the case was heard by a magistrate, or, after the judge reviews the case, an appeal can be made to the Court of Appeals.

Q: Please give a few examples of the typical cases you hear in traffic court.

A: The most common or typical offenses involve a failure to maintain an assured clear distance resulting in an accident or a speeding violation. Other common offenses are failure to stop at a traffic light or stop sign, and failing to yield to traffic at an intersection are also common. School zone violations and reckless operations as well as driving without a license occur, but not with the frequency of the speeding or rear end collision cases. The most serious offenses of operating a vehicle under the influence of alcohol, or drugs, or accidents involving a death are not that common.

Q: What are the most difficult cases you hear in traffic court?

A: I would say preadolescent, ages 11–14, youth taking a family vehicle and driving it off the roadway. Also, I have had accidents resulting from unsuccessful suicide attempts, and of course accidents that involved a loss of life.

Q: Do you know what proportion of traffic offenders, come back on a new offense?

A: Based on suspensions for second or third moving violation that are required to be imposed, the rate is 10–15% of all cases. The traffic court hears about 1500 cases in a year, and of these, approximately 125 have their licenses suspended.

Q: To what extent, if any, are parents/guardians held responsible for the traffic related violations of their children?

A: The Ohio law requires a parent/guardian to appear with the child in court, even if the child turns 18 before the hearing date. All vehicles must be insured under Ohio law. Ohio law limits the amount of financial recovery for a child's tort. Parents will often have to pay larger premiums for automobile insurance to have a juvenile continue to drive.

Q: What is the typical attitude/behavior you experience from the parents at juvenile traffic court hearings?

A: There is almost universal support for law enforcement. Some request an opportunity to plea bargain with the prosecutor at pretrial. Most of the parents are happy to see the court reinforce what they have been saying at home with their sons and daughters. Expressing hostility toward the court or trying to excuse the inappropriate behavior of their children is exceptionally rare. Few are willing to make frivolous challenges to the citations. A few do make challenges, but these are the exceptional cases.

Q: Mr. Cody, do you have any discretionary options to use when making decisions or penalties for juvenile traffic offenders?

A: No, with the exceptions of requiring participation in the diversion (SAFTE) program and several educational programs, the penalties are fairly fixed. Ohio has a fine schedule for the degree of the offense. Ninety-five percent of the traffic offences are classified as minor misdemeanors which have a limit of $50.00 plus court costs, that are determined locally. The fines and court costs (about $100 total), must be paid on the day of the hearing, or the youth's license will be held by the court until the amount is paid. Juvenile traffic offenders may be required to attend a remedial driving program offered by a commercial provider, but this penalty is rarely given. The juvenile traffic offenders generally behave quite differently than the juveniles appearing before the court on delinquent charges. The traffic offenders are usually well dressed, polite, and try to appear to be penitent. The court is aware that they may be trying to influence the court's decision and not allow either those whose attitude is very positive and behavior is supportive of the court, or those whose attitude and behavior are hostile to influence the decision making. Personally, I find that juveniles do not respond well to hostile and accusatory language from adults.

Q: Can you think of any other topics relating to the traffic court not covered in the interview?

A: Both parents and juveniles are the most concerned about losing their driving privileges. The suspension or restriction of their driving interferes with their school and work. The Court has the philosophy of wanting the youth to be involved in school and work and thus will generally allow some driving privileges to attend school activities or work, if not restricted by law. Parents want their children to have some type of part time work. As long as the employment does not involve the use of a car, such as having a job delivering pizza, driving to and from work privileges are given. However, if on suspension, no passengers, with the exception of the juvenile driving a younger sibling to and from school, are allowed. Driving to purely social activities is not permitted.

In Box 12.2, the Traffic Court process is explained by Daniel Cody, a magistrate for the Summit County Juvenile Court located in Ohio.

When a case is not dismissed at the intake level and diversion is not employed, the matter is handled judicially (formally). A formal case involves a petition in which it is requested that the court hold an adjudicatory hearing. In 2016, 52% of the approximately 850,000 delinquency cases were handled formally by the juvenile courts (Hockenberry & Puzzanchera, 2018, p. 52).

When a case is handled judicially (formally), an initial hearing is scheduled (analogous to the pretrial or preliminary hearing held in adult criminal court) at which the charges contained in the petition are read. The youth is again advised of his or her constitutional rights, including the right to have an attorney present and, depending on the specific provisions of the state's juvenile code and the seriousness of the charges, the youth could be given an opportunity to make a plea at this time. In some states, the youth's possible responses to the charges can be "guilty" or "not guilty," while others use "true" or "not true" or "admit" or "deny" or in some states "no contest." In states where juvenile traffic offenses are heard in the juvenile court rather than in a specialized traffic court, the plea of "no contest" is also available.

Although the majority of juveniles charged with offenses in juvenile courts eventually admit to the charges and enter pleas of "true" or "guilty," this normally does not occur at this phase of the process, but at later hearings. Analysis of the provisions of federal and state juvenile codes pertaining to the judge's obligations at the time a plea is entered reveal that some codes do not address the matter, but the majority of the codes spell out specific procedures that must be followed. These focus on the need for the judge to explain the charges to the defendant, to gain some assurance that the plea is voluntary, and, if the plea is the result of a plea bargain, to have this fact mentioned. It may also be required that a youth talk with parents or counsel before submitting a plea or that the youth be informed of the possible dispositions that may result from a guilty plea.

If a young person admits the truth of the allegations and the offenses are minor in nature, the adjudication and dispositional phases of the juvenile court process may be completed at this initial hearing. This can occur if state statutes permit a disposition to be made in minor offense cases without completion of a social investigation (report by a court probation officer on the child's background, school performance, and past offenses). Combination of the adjudication and dispositional phases is likely if enough information is contained in the intake officer's report or in already existing juvenile court records for the judge to make a disposition decision. If a plea of "guilty," "true," or "admit" is made, but the offense is rather serious in nature; if a social (predisposition) investigation is required by state statute; or if a social investigation is ordered by the judge, a youth may be returned to detention or released in the custody of his or her parents until a dispositional hearing takes place.

12.3.2 *Hearing to Transfer to Criminal Court*

Every state has some provision in its statutes for having juveniles' cases heard in the criminal justice system. However, the states use various methods to accomplish this. The most frequently used mechanism is "judicial waiver." Here, the juvenile court judges have considerable discretion in waiving or transferring cases to the criminal courts. A second method is termed "statutory exclusion." For specified offenses committed by juveniles, the criminal court has the original jurisdiction in the case and juvenile offenders are automatically excluded from consideration by the juvenile court. Normally, those who commit serious offenses, older juveniles, and those with prior offenses fall into the "statutory exclusion" category. A third option is exercised in states with "concurrent jurisdiction" provisions. Here both the juvenile court and the criminal court have jurisdiction over juveniles. The statutes give the prosecutor the discretion to file a case in either the criminal court or the juvenile court. While most states rely primarily on judicial waivers, some use a combination of the three systems. Sickmund and Puzzanchera (2014, p. 173) note that the number of delinquency cases waivered to criminal court climbed 132% from 1985 to 1994, from 5700 to 13,300. By 2010, the number of waived cases was 55% below the 1994 year total. In 2016, the number of juveniles waivered to the criminal courts was less than 3500, almost 75% less than those waived n 199 (Hockenberry & Puzzanchera, 2018, p. 36). The characteristics of the cases waivered in 1994, 2001, 2010, and 2016 were remarkably similar, with more than 90% of the cases being male in the four time periods, more than 50% of the cases being white, and more than 80% of the cases being 16 years old or older. When comparing the juvenile waivers by type of offense committed by those waived to criminal court, Sickmund and Puzzanchera (2014, p. 173) found, that between 1993 and 2010, person offenses outnumbered property offenses among waivered cases. In summary, less than 1% of all of the delinquent cases referred to the juvenile courts in 2016 were judicially waivered to the criminal courts.

12.3.3 The Waiver Hearing

In cases involving serious offenses, or those of youths who have shown a pattern of repeated delinquency and are at the minimum age or older that is required by statute for a youth to be waived to criminal court, the prosecuting attorney may request a waiver hearing.

The U.S. Supreme Court ruled in Kent v. U.S. (383 U.S.541, 1966) that a youth has a constitutional right to have counsel present at a waiver hearing and that the hearing must measure up to the essentials of due process and fair treatment. In addition to the criteria contained in the *Kent* decision, most state statutes require that the presiding judge at the waiver hearing consider two other factors-the likely threat to public safety or dangerousness by the youth and whether the youth is likely to be amenable to treatment under the juvenile system. Critics of these provisions cite the difficulty inherent in predicting a youth's future behavior or responses to treatment and believe that inclusion of these factors provides too much discretion to the judge. Feld (1987, p. 491) noted that, "judicial waiver statutes that are couched in terms of amenability to treatment or dangerousness are simply broad, standard-less grants of sentencing discretion characteristics of the individualized, offender-oriented dispositional statutes of the juvenile court."

Even when a very serious offense has been committed, factors such as the age or mental competence of the offender may stand in the way of judicial transfer. There may be an issue related to the youth being not able to function normally due to low intelligence or mental related disturbance. If prosecutors are unsure about just how to proceed with a juvenile being considered for prosecution as an adult, they would have to prove that the youth is "sophisticated and mature" enough to be considered adult in the eyes of the law. Also in a waiver hearing, the question of the mental competence of the youth must be addressed. Before a waiver can be ordered, the youth must undergo psychological testing. If the competence of the youth cannot be established, it is likely that the waiver request will be abandoned. If the alleged delinquent appears to be mentally ill, the court may hold a hearing to determine mental competency. If the court finds the defendant to be mentally ill, the original petition alleging delinquency may be dropped. The youth could then be admitted to a mental health institution for treatment.

Even though a case may qualify for waiver to an adult court because of the youth's age or the seriousness of the offense, it may not be transferred. The probability of waiver generally increases with the age of the offender for both violent and serious property offenses, and the juvenile court history of the offender is also an important consideration.

A study of South Carolina juvenile court waiver cases from 1985 through 1994 (Snyder, Sickmund, & Poe-Yamagata, 2000, pp. 11–15) revealed that 595 cases involved requests for waivers and 80% of these requests were approved. A profile of juveniles for whom the waiver requests were made showed that 95% were male, 80% were blacks, and 80% were age 16 or older. Juveniles with extensive court histories and those who had previous cases formally handed by the juvenile court were significantly more likely to have their cases waived than those without such histories. Those who had committed serious offenses against persons or property were significantly more likely to have their cases waived than youths who had committed less serious offenses, but juveniles with two or more prior adjudications who committed less serious offenses were more likely to have their cases waived than those with similar offenses who had fewer prior adjudications.

In an interview with Dr. Thomas Webb, Psychologist for the Summit County (OH) Juvenile Court (Kratcoski, 2012, pp. 259–260) the question was asked, "What were a few of the most difficult decisions you had to make during your work with the court?" The answer Dr. Webb gave was, "The most difficult decisions pertain to making recommendations on juveniles being considered for transfer to the adult system—the amenability proceedings. It is hard to determine whether a youth will indeed be responsive to treatments available in the juvenile system. Several years ago I had to recommend that a 15-year-old be sent to the adult system and it was not an easy decision. Just recently, there was a case in which a youth stole a truck and led police on a 50-mile chase, endangering the lives of many people and causing damage to cruisers and other cars. I am sure that many of the people in the community would have liked to have seen him bound over and tried as an adult, but his developmental and psychiatric history were such that the judge determined he should stay in the juvenile system, but with a blended sentence—one where, if he were to raise problems while incarcerated, he would be automatically sent to the adult system."

The increase in legal requirements, as well as the difficulty of showing that the youth is not amenable to treatment in the juvenile justice system, and the decline in the number of arrests of juveniles for serious offenses are several factors that may explain the decline in the number of juveniles transferred to the criminal courts. Another factor is the increase in the number of states that have enacted the blended sentence. Sickmund and Puzzanchera (2014, p. 105) state that, "As of the end of 2011 legislative session, 14 states have blended sentencing laws that enable juvenile courts to impose criminal sanctions on juvenile offenders." The specifics of these laws vary. Sickmund and Puzzanchera (2014, p. 105) observed, "The most common type of juvenile court blended sentencing provision allows juvenile court judges to order both a juvenile disposition and an adult criminal sentence. The adult sentence is suspended on the condition that the juvenile offender successfully completes the terms of the juvenile disposition and refrains from committing any new offenses."

The following example exemplifies the use of the blended sentence for a 14-year-old youth who murdered his brother, was tried in the juvenile court and given a blended sentence (Box 12.3).

Box 12.3 Portage County Murder Case
Streetsboro boy, 13, Won't Face Adult Prison Time by E. McClory, *Akron Beacon Journal*, Jan. 26, Mc Clory, 2019, p. B1.

"Teen who killed 11-year-old brother sentenced to juvenile facility until he's 21…(The judge) decided not to designate the boy, who will turn 14 next month, a *serious youthful offender*, which would have meant that breaking a set of conditions in youth prison could send him to an adult prison…The teen was found delinquent, a finding similar to guilty in adult court, in October of shooting and killing his 11-year-old brother. Police said the boy took a .357 Magnum from his grandparents' home by dismantling part of a locked cabinet…. He was found delinquent on two counts of aggravated murder with gun specifications."

During the waiver hearing, the prosecuting attorney argues for the transfer, and the defense attorney argues for retention of the case in the juvenile justice system. If a waiver is granted, the waiver order must be accompanied by a statement that shows the juvenile court has made an investigation of the matter and the reasons for the waiver must be listed.

The waiver hearing must take place early in the juvenile court process, before an adjudication has taken place. In *Breed* v. *Jones* (1975), a juvenile court waiver hearing was held *after* a youth had been adjudicated delinquent after it was determined that he was not amenable to treatment. The Supreme Court ruled that this action placed the youth in double jeopardy (subjected him to retrial for the same offense) and was unconstitutional. The court declared that a waiver hearing must be held *prior* to adjudication.

Once a juvenile's case is transferred to the adult criminal court, the youth is entitled to some rights that were not available in the juvenile court, including the right to bail and to a jury trial. If found guilty, the juvenile may also be subjected to the penalties that apply to adult offenders, although the U.S. Supreme Court ruled in Roper v Simmons (2005) that a person under 18 years of age cannot be sentenced to death. Some states provide other exceptions, such as not allowing juveniles to be housed with incarcerated adult offenders until they reach a specified age.

12.3.4   The Prehearing Conference

When a plea of "not guilty" or "not true" is made, and the case is to be heard by the juvenile court, an adjudicatory hearing is scheduled on the official court docket. If a youth makes a "not guilty" or "not true" plea, the option of a prehearing conference is available in many jurisdictions. Such a conference is generally held in the judge's chambers or in a conference room and is not an official court session. Court personnel who may participate include the judge, the prosecuting attorney, court workers assigned to the case, psychological personnel, and the juvenile's defense counsel, if one has been retained or appointed. Generally, the youth charged with the offense is excluded from the conference.

At the prehearing conference, the judge will request a report from a court worker and the various attorneys involved in the case. The conference centers on legal issues, that is, the amount and types of evidence that the prosecutor has available and the type of disposition that can reasonably be expected if the youth changes the plea to "guilty" or "true." In many ways, the conference is similar to the plea bargaining process in the adult criminal court. The majority of youths whose cases are given prehearing conferences will change their pleas to "guilty" or "true" at the adjudicatory hearing.

The complexity of the juvenile justice process today, even in its initial phases, highlights the fact that the roles of the judge, the prosecutor, and the defense counsel have developed and expanded with the evolution of juvenile court law.

12.3.5   Role of the Prosecutor

Until the 1960s, the charges against a juvenile were usually stated by the person filing the petition or by a court probation officer or were simply read aloud by the judge. This informal presentation conformed to the idea that what the child had done was not as important as what was to be done for the child. But the U.S. Supreme Court decision, *in re Gault* (1967), made apparent the need for representation of the complainant's side of the case by the prosecuting attorney. Gault had received a disposition of commitment to a juvenile institution at an informal court hearing at which he was not represented by counsel and for which the woman making accusations against him did not appear. The Supreme Court, in commenting on the case, declared that in all instances where commitment to an institution is a possible disposition, the child and the parents must be advised of the right to counsel, either their own or court-appointed. It also ruled that a juvenile has a right to have witnesses cross-examined.

The *Gault* decision's ruling with regard to the juvenile's rights in juvenile court proceedings made apparent the need for representation of the complainant by a prosecuting attorney. Juvenile court proceedings have thus moved away from informality toward an adversary (prosecutor versus defense attorney) style. In many states, statutes have been enacted that require the presence of a prosecutor at hearings for serious types of cases; in other states, court officials may request that a prosecutor be assigned.

A juvenile court prosecutor has broad powers. He or she can decline to prosecute a case, make plea bargains, release a youth from detention, or recommend to the judge a particular type of disposition. In an interview with Michelle Cordova, Chief Assistant Prosecutor, Juvenile Division, Stark County, Ohio Prosecutor's office (Kratcoski, 2012, p. 251), prosecutor Cordova was asked, "What are the duties or tasks that you are responsible for as chief of the juvenile division?" She responded, "We review complaints and reports generated by the approximately 23 law enforcement agencies in Stark County to insure that charges are appropriate and supported by the evidence. After review, we file the complaint(s) and make recommendations to the court about whether the charges should be handled informally or officially. We also consult with and advise law enforcement officers by phone or in the office regarding charging decisions. We represent the State of Ohio in all arraignments, pre-trials, motions, hearings, and trials in all juvenile delinquency matters. We provide discovery to all attorneys representing juveniles, respond to motions, and gather information for transfers. The statute governing transfers set forth specific factors, including the juvenile's age, the level and type of offense, and any enhancing factors, such as the use of a firearm or a prior youth prison commitment. If a case fulfills the factors in the statute, we can consider the juvenile's prior court involvement and rehabilitative efforts when deciding whether a mandatory transfer is necessary, or whether a discretionary transfer is appropriate or against the juvenile's best interest."

In the juvenile court process, the prosecutor may first enter the picture when a petition is written, checking to see that the officer or the private citizen filing it does so properly, or giving legal advice that another course of action might be more effective. The next step involves the decision whether to prosecute or drop any case in which a youth has responded "not guilty" or "not true" to a charge of delinquency. The prosecutor or a representative presents the state's case at the adjudicatory hearing and may recommend appropriate dispositions to the judge if a youth is adjudicated delinquent. Other matters of concern to a prosecutor include cases of dependency or neglect or of adults' contribution to the delinquency of minors. Prosecutors also serve as advocates for those who have allegedly been victimized by juveniles. They may assist them in making victim impact statements and help prepare them for court appearances.

12.3.6 Role of the Defense Attorney

The defense attorney may be active on a juvenile's behalf at intake and try to help the youth avoid a formal court hearing. This may be done by convincing the person making the complaint.

to drop the charges or by assuring court officials that the youth will be referred to another agency or a private source for treatment. If a petition is filed, the defense attorney examines it and advises the client to enter a plea of "admit," or "deny," or may enter a plea on his or her behalf. The attorney may present facts in favor of release in the custody of the parents rather than detention until the adjudicatory hearing. Before the adjudicatory hearing, the defense attorney may plea bargain with the prosecutor to drop the charges or may agree to have the client plead guilty to a reduced charge. This may occur at a prehearing conference, as described earlier in this chapter, or during an informal discussion between the prosecutor and the defense attorney.

As a result of the *in re Gault* decision (1967), a juvenile has a right to an attorney at every stage of the juvenile court process and an attorney must be provided for an indigent youth, if one is requested. In some courts, such counsel is made available at intake, but in most juvenile courts the attorney's services begin at the initial hearing.

One effect of the *Gault* decision was an increased formalization and use of defense attorneys in the juvenile court. In Box 12.4, information on the role of a defense attorney Troy Reeves, in juvenile proceeding is provided. Interview by P C. Kratcoski and Peter Christopher Kratcoski, June 11, 2019c.

Box 12.4 Interview of Troy Reeves, Defense Attorney
Biography

Attorney Reeves graduated from the Ohio State University in 1990 with a B.S. in Biology. He worked for the State of Ohio Emergency Management Agency in the radiology division from 1991 to 1995. He attended the Cleveland-Marshall College of Law from 1995 to 1998, passed the bar exam, and received his license in November, 1998. He worked as a lawyer at Aronson & Associates upon graduation, opened his own solo practice with Stephen Smith in September, 1999, and has been a solo practitioner ever since.

Q: Why did you decide to specialize in criminal law?

A: It is more interesting than environmental and civil law and I feel my work is more important than civil law. My cases drastically impact people's lives. Taking away one's freedom is a major consequence to a person and his family. Losing one of my cases means exactly that. One can lose a civil case and lose money, however, they can still see their family, go out to eat dinner, and visit friends. When I lose a case, not only does all that go away, but you end up spending time with a lot of unsavory people. You can always make more money, however you cannot make up lost time.

Q: Have you served as a defense attorney for youths charged with juvenile delinquency? If yes, how many times?

A: Yes, hundreds of times.

Q: Focusing on the juvenile cases, how did you happen to be selected?

A: Early on in my career, I was appointed to represent them. Over the past 15 years, their parents have retained me to represent them.

Q: What occurred the most frequently, court appointed or private counselor (assuming you served as court appointed)?

A: Early in my career, I was appointed. For the last 15 years, parents have retained me.

Q: Contrast your role when serving as defense for a juvenile with that of your role with an adult.

A: With juveniles, the goal is always rehabilitation and education. Most juveniles in the system lack parental guidance. However, there are also juveniles with excellent parental guidance that get into trouble as well. With adults, the goal is also rehabilitation; however, most times it is just to punish the offenders.

Q: What are the major sources of information you use in your preparation for the hearing (trial)?

A: Police reports and photographs. I have years of prior cross-exams and opening/closing statements that I use as a boiler plate; however, each case is different and each source of information is used differently.

Q: Do you ever plea bargain with the prosecutor on juvenile cases? If yes, when does this occur?

A: Constantly, with every case. It usually involves a reduction in charges in order to get the juvenile into a diversion program.

Q: Troy, have you ever served as a defense attorney for a juvenile bound over to the adult criminal court for trial? If yes, could you give a brief summary of the details of the case?

A: Yes, I represented a 17-year-old charged with the murder of a University student shot on Super Bowl Sunday about 3–4 years ago. It was over a drug deal gone bad. The court has an automatic bind over for youths 16 or 17 that are charged with homicide.

Q: Can you recall what was the most difficult case you had as defense for a juvenile offender? Why was the case so difficult?

A: I represented a 15-year-old who accidentally shot and killed his 11-year-old cousin when they were playing with a gun. The prosecutor treated it as a homicide, even though everyone knew it was an accident. It was so difficult because of the family connection. The two cousins spent a lot of time0 together and their mothers, who were sisters, were very close, but now do not talk to each other. It tore a close-knot family apart and my client has to live with the fact that he took his best friend's (cousin's) life.

Q: Are there rewards relating to defense work with juveniles that are not likely to be received when serving as defense for adults? If yes, explain.

A: The parents are extremely appreciative because they look out for their kids. As adults, the defendants knew what they did was wrong and did it anyway.

Q: Can you think of any important topics pertaining to the defense of juvenile offenders not covered in the previous question?

A: Most of these crimes committed are because of peer pressure. Kids rarely get into trouble by themselves. As kids, it is harder for them to say no and they get themselves into serious trouble without thinking. Also, it is important that these kids getting into trouble receive some type of counseling and/or mental health evaluation. Some of these kids just need to talk to someone and others have undiagnosed mental issues. Sadly, if either of these things could be detected earlier, then maybe it may prevent them from getting into trouble in the first place.

It should be noted here that the Task Force Report on Juvenile Justice and Delinquency Prevention (1977) included a recommendation that plea bargaining in all forms be eliminated from the delinquency adjudication process because of the pressures it places on the juvenile to submit to a bargain that may result in a disposition not in his or her best interests, because hardened juvenile offenders can use bargaining to receive less severe dispositions than they actually deserve, and because juveniles who need to receive treatment that would be required if the case proceeded through the adjudication process may not receive it if plea bargaining results in a dismissal or a too-mild disposition. At the adjudicatory hearing, the defense counsel represents the client's side of the case. He or she may introduce witnesses. If a client is adjudicated delinquent, the defense attorney may present information at the dispositional hearing that will aid the court in deciding upon an appropriate disposition.

A study by Feld (1988, p. 30) revealed that those youths who were charged with committing serious offenses, were held in detention prior to adjudication, and who had prior referrals to the court were more likely to be represented by counsel than youths who did not fit this description. However, when these factors were controlled and the youths who were represented by counsel were compared to those who were not, it was found that "represented youths received more severe dispositions in every category in the three large urban states included in the study and received more severe dispositions in the larger majority of categories in the three less populated, more rural states studied." The reasons for the more severe disposition could not be definitely ascertained, hut Feld offered plausible explanations. These included the possibility that defense attorneys may have antagonized the judges just by being present or that judges may tend to assume the "parent substitute" role and be more lenient with unrepresented youths than with those who have counsel present. Another hypothetical scenario raised was that the judges had studied the cases before the hearings and, in anticipation of guilty findings and subsequent institutionalization, had arranged for counsel for the youths so that questions about the proceedings would not be raised in the future.

12.3.7   Role of the Juvenile Court Judge

When juvenile courts were created, the judge was assigned the role of single-handedly deciding the course of action that would turn a child away from unacceptable behavior. Today, the juvenile court judge is still the sole decision maker as to whether a child is adjudicated delinquent. Although the courses of action a judge may follow have been modified somewhat by legal constraints set up as a result of various court decisions, the powers of juvenile court judges are still extensive. The dispositional decision, particularly when it involves institutionalization or removal from the parents' residence, cannot be made lightly. The following interview with a juvenile court judge, Box 12.5 will help illustrate the difficulties surrounding the judge's decision-making to assure that the interests of the child and the community are met.

Box 12.5 Interview with Judge Robert Berger, Portage County Juvenile Court (Interview by Dr. Peter C. Kratcoski and Peter Christopher Kratcoski, February 6, 2019a)

The organizational structure of the juvenile structure over which Judge Berger presides is given in Fig. 12.1.

Forty persons are employed by the court. This figure does not include the employees at the Portage Geauga Juvenile Detention Center, a facility serving the two counties of Portage and Geauga.

Biography

Judge Berger received his high school diploma from Theodore Roosevelt High School, Kent, and a BS degree in Education from Kent State University. He served in the U.S. Army from 1972–1974. He graduated from the University of Baltimore Law School in 1977. He was awarded the American Jurisprudence Award in Family Law-Trial Advocacy and voted the *Most Likely to Move Back to Ohio.* He moved to Ohio and began a solo practice until he became a partner in the Giulitto & Dickinson law firm in 1980 and Giulitto & Berger until 2007. Judger Berger served as a magistrate of the Portage County Court of Common Pleas, Ohio, under Judge Laurie Pittman from 2007 to 2015 and was elected Juvenile Court Judge of Portage County in 2015, a position he currently holds.

Being elected president of the Portage County Bar Association, recipient of the Norman Sandvoss Humanitarian Award, and serving as an adjunct professor at Kent State University are examples of the recognition he received for his service to the legal profession and to the community.

Q: Please tell us why you decided to pursue a career in the legal profession.

A: I was interested in government studies and particularly the Bill of Rights. Law seemed interesting and had a purpose in our daily affairs.

Q: Did your formal education have an effect on your career choice?

A: When I was a student at Kent State University, I had a constitutional law professor named Barclay McMillan whom I enjoyed. Two weeks before the May 4th shooting of students at Kent State, we were discussing the Amendment concerning the Freedom to Assemble. Temporary Restraining Orders (TROS) were placed on the doors of Bowman Hall, limiting the right to assemble. I thought, "This isn't right," and off I went studying law.

Q: What do you consider your most important professional experiences during your career to date?

A: Day-to-day cases affecting the rights of the normal citizen. Making our legal system accountable. The rights of parents and children. The most intense cases are jury trials. I have had seven murder cases and have tried a countless number of felony cases. All trial attorneys enjoy jury trials.

Q: What were the main factors that motivated you to run for the juvenile court judge?

A: I like children. I understood the "unique child" that is the Court. I also believe there is no more important right than the right to be a parent. Only the "best interest" of the child supersedes that right.

Q: When you first became a juvenile court judge, what were your impressions of the juvenile system compared with the adult system?

A: I love the Juvenile Court. It is the only court where true rehabilitation is practiced (for the child and the parent). We can never give up on an adolescent. You do not know who can succeed or at what point in time the child will mature and "get it." The adult system consequences are more about housing the convicted person.

Q. What are your specific duties?

A: As the only juvenile court judge in the county, I have both administrative and judicial duties. As an administrator, I am concerned with employment practices, having roughly 40 employees in the court, and I work with the courts of other counties (Our court detention center and its employees are separate entities that we share with Geauga County), work with county service agencies, and of course I must constantly be in contact with the county officials on matters pertaining to the funding of the court.

As a judicial official I conduct hearings in juvenile delinquency (including traffic), dependency, neglect and abuse cases, and private cases involving paternity, custody visitation, and child support. There are also other dockets that are filed less frequently than those mentioned, but they generally are more time consuming.

Q. Please describe your style of management (administration). How are decisions on policy matters, organizational changes, and hiring of new employees, made?

A: Delegation is made to the department head(s) on matters of hiring and terminating employees, pursuant to the Employee Handbook. However, I finalize all decisions. The court administrator, department heads and magistrates meet with me to go over policy and significant events.

Q: Since you became judge, have the goals of the Portage County Juvenile Court changed?

A: Yes, we have tried to become more transparent and user friendly. Also we have added outreach programs to that end.

Q: What is your personal philosophy regarding the judicial processing of the youth who appear before the court?

A: I follow the Juvenile Rules and the Ohio Revised Code. I always keep in mind that the goal of disposition is to hold youth accountable and to rehabilitate and act in the best interests of the youth and the families we serve.

Q: Are there any factors that prohibit or interfere with the efficiency and effectiveness of the administration of the juvenile court?

A: Yes, the budget and lack of resources.

Q: Has the use of modern technology had an effect on the effectiveness and efficiency of the administration of the juvenile court?

A: Yes, through networking we are able to obtain data more quickly and to share ideas and information with other courts and agencies.

Q: Have you noticed any changes in the legal response (laws) regarding juveniles who violate the law?

A: Not yet, the state legislative is slow to respond to the new philosophy of the juvenile court judges.

Q: Are the laws relating to the punishment of juvenile delinquents more punitive, less punitive, or about the same during the years you have been the juvenile court judge of Portage County?

A: It is hard to answer without being more specific. The idea in disposition is NOT to punish, but hold accountable and rehabilitate.

Q: Following up on the question. Are there offenses for which the law mandates a commitment to the Department of Youth Services for the adjudicated delinquent?

A: The Serious Youthful Offenders Act passed by the legislature in 2002 mandates that serious juvenile offenders (aggravated murder, murder, rape) be sentenced under the provisions of the new law. Depending on the age of the offender, they can be under the jurisdiction of either the juvenile justice system until age 21 or the criminal justice system, in certain specific cases, depending on the youth's age, offense, prior Department of Youth Services (DYS) commitment, use of a firearm, or gang affiliation and then after a hearing can be transferred to the criminal justice system until their sentences have been completed.

Q: Are there offenses for which the adjudicated youth is not eligible for community corrections (probation)?

A: Yes, aggravated murder, murder, rape, depending on the circumstances.

Q: Have you noticed any major changes in the characteristics of the youth brought into the court during your term of office?

A: No

Q: Has the type of offenses committed changed?

A: No. We see the whole range of offenses from the less serious to the most serious.

We have a few cases of bullying, but unless real serious, these are handled by the diversion program. Some schools like to cover up their bullying problems.

Q: Are there a greater number of chronic (habitual offenders)?

A: I do not believe so, although a lot of our youth are slow to progress in the rehabilitation process.

Q: Have you seen a greater number of youths with severe mental health problems?

A: Yes, drugs and mental illness are often linked and the diagnosis of the source of the youth's problem is often erroneous.

Q: Have you noticed a significant change in the number of female offenders?

A: Equality in numbers to the males is slowly marching forward. However, those held in detention are still predominately male.

Q: Has there been a significant change in the number of youth charged with a sexual offense?

A: No. Although we are identifying this population more readily. We try to distinguish reckless adolescent behavior from a sexual deviant behavior which is more permanent in nature.

Now we would like to have you focus on court jurisdiction and the processing of offenders.

Q: What is the jurisdiction of the Portage County Juvenile Court?

A: All children (under 18 years of age) who committed acts in Portage County or reside in Portage County (dispositions) and adults who are charged with contributing to delinquency.

If a Portage County youth commits an offense in another county, that county will complete the adjudication hearing and if found delinquent, the disposition hearing will be completed in Portage County.

Q: What types of juvenile crimes are the most difficult to handle in the juvenile court?

A: Those involving extreme violence, chronic child abuse or neglect cases, and sex offenses.

Q: Who makes the decision to have a juvenile offender bound over to the criminal court?

A: A distinction must be made between mandatory bind-over and discretionary bind over. Those offenders eligible for mandatory transfer are enumerated in the revised Ohio Code. In section 2152.10, For example, for a child who is 16 years of age at the time the offense was committed and committed a category one offense (aggravated murder, murder) a transfer is mandated. A child

14 or 15 who committed a category 1 or 2 (kidnapping) offense and had prior DYS commitment is eligible for a discretionary transfer. Any child who committed a felony offense who was 14 or older at the time of the offense is eligible for a discretionary transfer to the appropriate court for criminal prosecution.

For discretionary transfers, the juvenile court must follow the procedures specified in the revised Code.

Q: What are these procedures?

A: There are many criteria to be followed. In general, after a complaint has been filed and the alleged offense is one that is in the guidelines for transfer, a probable cause hearing will be held. If probable cause is established that the youth committed the act charged, the court, prior to the amenability hearing, must first order an investigation into the child's social history, education, family situation, and any other factor bearing on these factors. Also, a mental examination is required to determine competency. The decision to transfer or not is grounded in two major factors., "Is the child amenable to care or rehabilitation within the juvenile system, or whether the safety of the community may require that the child be subject to adult sanctions." A number of the characteristics of the child, such as age, prior offenses, emotional, physical and psychology maturity of the child are considered, as well as the circumstances surrounding the alleged offense, such as the age of the victim, amount of physical harm, use of a fire arm and others.

Q: Does the judge make the final decision on discretionary transfer?

A: Yes, but after considering all of the information from the parties involved (the prosecutor, defense counsel, psychologist, and others).

Q: To what extent does the court depend on service agencies in the County for assistance?

A: Quite a bit in Job and Family Services (JFS) cases, and as an additional resource in delinquency cases.

Q: Does the court have any programs that involve the parents of delinquent youth? Give an example.

A: Parents of delinquent youths are parties and thus must be involved. We have a few diversion programs requiring parental involvement. For example, some traffic offenders are given the option of attending a driving school class and if the youth does not commit another traffic offense for 6 months after completing the course, the original traffic offense is dropped. This involves the parents who have to drive the youth to the school and attend the class. We have several programs involving parents or caretakers in the abuse, neglect, and dependency cases.

Q: What do you see as the major problems and concerns that will confront the juvenile court judges in the future?

A: Drugs and mental illness, child abuse, lack of a belief or faith in the family

Q: Reflecting on your career as a juvenile court judge, what aspects of the position do you find to be the most rewarding? What aspects are the most distasteful?

A: REWARDING: Working with and aiding broken youth and/or their families. We have an excellent probation department that is creative and dedicated. We have added programs that touch our kids. DIFFICULT: Parents who do not care. Having sufficient budget to address these issues.

Judge

Chief Magistrate

Magistrate

| Director of Youth Rehabilitation | Court Fiscal Officer | Court Administrator |

| Chief Probation Officer | Psychology Department | Substance Abuse Services | Chief Deputy Clerk | Assignment Commissioner | Bailiffs |

Senior Probation Officer

Assistant Chief Deputy Clerk

| Probation/ EM Officers | Intensive Probation Officer | Community Services/Restitution Diversion Services | Deputy Clerks |

Administrative Assistant   Receptionist/ Traffic Clerk

Secretary/Receptionist

Fig. 12.1 Portage County Juvenile Court organizational structure

In contrast to the Portage County Juvenile Court, that serves a population of 160,000, over which Judge Berger presides, the Summit County Juvenile Court has a jurisdiction serving slightly more than 500,000. The court has one judge, Linda Teodosio and a number of magistrates. The interview, in Box 12.6 was completed on July 28, 2019 by Peter C. Kratcoski.

Box 12.6 Interview with Judge Teodosio
Biography

Judge Linda Tucci Teodosio was elected to the Cuyahoga Falls Municipal Court in 1997, where she served until her election to the Summit County Juvenile Court for the term beginning January 1, 2003.

Judge Teodosio's work on the Juvenile Court bench has been extensively recognized. In September 2016, she received the Thomas Moyer Award for Judicial Excellence from the Ohio State Bar Association. She has been honored by both the Ohio Juvenile Court Judges and Magistrate's Associations with their Judicial and Distinguished Services Awards, respectively. In late 2012, Judge Teodosio received the prestigious Award for Innovation from the Margaret Clark Morgan Foundation. In 2010, she received the MacArthur Foundation's "Champion for Change" Award for her work in the Models for Change Mental Health Juvenile Justice Action Network. Judge Teodosio was honored by the Dioceses of Cleveland with the St. Thomas More Award, which is awarded annually at the Red Mass in recognition of the virtues of integrity and public services that reflect those of Thomas More. Judge Teodosio has served as President of the Akron Bar Association, the Akron Bar Foundation, and the University of Akron School of Law Alumni Association. She has served as the District 11 Delegate to the Ohio State Bar Association and was elected President-Elect of the Association in May 2019.

Judge Teodosio is married to Judge Thomas Teodosio of the Ninth District Court of Appeals. Their son, Christopher, is a practicing attorney who makes his home in Summit County with his wife Katherine and two daughters. They remember their late daughter through the Andrea Rose Teodosio Foundation.

Q: What is the jurisdiction of the Summit County Juvenile Court?

A: The juvenile court has jurisdiction over cases where a youth commits an offense that would be either a misdemeanor or a felony if committed by an adult, as well as traffic offenses for those persons who are under the age of 18. We also handle all status offenses, where a person is alleged to have committed an act that is an offense solely because of his or her age. Our jurisdiction over the youth continues until the age of 21, so long as the offense occurred before the age of 18.

Q: Have you noticed any changes in the philosophy (legal response) to juveniles who violate the law since you became a juvenile court judge?

A: At the time I took the bench, Ohio, like many other states, had recently passed legislation to treat juvenile offenders more like adults by utilizing transfer of cases to adult courts and harsher sanctions for kids. In fact, several of the juvenile facilities that the state opened looked more like adult prisons. Since that time, after a great deal of research and study, it has been recognized that these harsh methods are often counterproductive for youth and can actually serve to increase the likelihood of recidivism. The result has been a shift to focus on community and home based programs that utilize evidence-based practice to address the needs of youth in our system, if that can be done without compromising community safety.

There has also been a tremendous rise in the use of mental health courts in Ohio and nationwide.

Q: Have you noticed any significant changes in the number of cases handled by the Summit County Juvenile Court in recent years:

A: We have seen a decrease in delinquency cases, due to reduced referrals and enhance of our diversion service. We have seen an increase in child welfare cases. I believe the increase in child welfare cases is due to the opiate crisis.

The Juvenile Court Process

Q: Have you noticed any major changes in the types of offenses committed?

A: The only notable thing that I have noticed is a significant increase in offenses involving firearms.

Q: Have you noticed any significant change in the number of female offenders?

Have the types of offenses for females changed?

A: We have started a specialized docket called "Restore Court" for youth either identified as human trafficking victims, or at high risk to become victims. These youths are primarily female. Their offenses vary, but all have a significant trauma history.

Q: What types of offenses are the most difficult to handle in the juvenile court?

A: From a human perspective, the most difficult are those where a death or severe injury has occurred to the victim. From the aspect of rehabilitation, the most difficult cases are those where the youth has become involved in gang activity and does not wish to lead a crime-free life.

Q: Judge Teodosio, has the state of Ohio made any recent changes in legislation relating to juveniles who violate the law that pertain to the juvenile court?

A: The state legislature has made some recent changes that relate to juveniles. The legislature amended the truancy law so that truancy is now considered an unruly offense as opposed to a delinquency offense. The law also defines "habitual truant" as a youth who is absent from the school he or she is supposed to attend for 30 or more consecutive hours, 42 or more hours in one school month, or 72 or more hours in one school year. Further, if the student meets these thresholds, the principal or superintendent must assign the student to an absence intervention team, which incorporates academic and nonacademic supports prior to the referral of the student to the juvenile court. Another change recently made by the Ohio legislature pertains to Ohio's "safe harbor" laws. This change allows a juvenile court to keep a human trafficking victim case open (active) in safe harbor diversion for a period of up to 360 days, as opposed to the prior period of 270 days, changes the requirement for treatment to engagement as opposed to the completion for dismissal of charges to occur and allows a court to place a youth in diversion for prostitution related charges without a hearing. It allows the state to request a hearing for non-prostitution changes.

Q: Were there any major Ohio Supreme Court or U.S. Supreme Court decisions recently that pertain to the juvenile court process?

A: The only thing I can think of is the requirement that the court appoint a Guardian ad Litem for every youth where it appears that they may be eligible for safe harbor diversion and, for youth in delinquency cases who do not have a parent or guardian.

Q: To what extent does the Summit County Juvenile Court utilize volunteers in the diversion or treatment programs provided for youths under the court's jurisdiction?

A: We use volunteers in our Court Appointed Special Advocate (CASA) Guardian ad Litem program. We also have a Women's Board that provides programming in detention and supports both our garden and greenhouse programs. Several faith-based agencies also provide support to our youth in detention.

The process by which a judge decides whether or not to deprive a child of his freedom is an intricate one. Although a background in social or justice work would seem to be ideal preparation for such decision making, few juvenile court judges are selected because they have demonstrated a concern for, or even an interest in, the social welfare of children. Instead, they are often chosen to run for these elective offices on the basis of political and social contacts.

After election, a juvenile court judge must continue to weigh the political consequences of his or her decisions. A judge who develops a reputation for leniency may become unpopular with local police, who may feel that their efforts at investigation and apprehension have borne little fruit. A judge who pushes for expansion of court services may alienate the county commissioners, who may fear that tax increases would jeopardize their positions. A judge who is strict and unbending may arouse the anger of child-advocacy groups. The result of miscalculating the electorate's reactions may well be defeat at the polls.

Revision of juvenile codes, increased use of prosecuting attorneys and defense counsel in the juvenile courts, and heightened community awareness of the problem of juvenile crime have caused many judges to adopt a policy of strict interpretation of the law in juvenile cases, even when such application seems to conflict with the needs of the community.

The alarming amount of violent juvenile crime, especially among youths in the early teens, as well as the growing number of families with needs that must be ascertained and provided for by the juvenile courts, underline the importance of the presence of well-qualified and experienced judges in these courts.

When the enormous responsibility, range, and implications of the juvenile court judge's decisions are considered, it becomes apparent that hopes for change through juvenile court action must extend far beyond the mere handing down of decisions in court proceedings. Rather than mediocre, mechanical decision makers, the juvenile court needs judges who are dynamic, progressive and even prophetic in their approaches.

12.3.8 Adjudication Hearing

If a youth makes a "not guilty" or "untrue" plea (sometimes stated as "affirm" or "deny") at the initial hearing, and the case is not later resolved in a prehearing conference, or if a youth makes no plea at the initial hearing, an adjudication hearing is held, presided over by a juvenile court judge. The state's case is presented by a prosecutor or a representative of the prosecutor's office. The youth may be, and frequently is, represented by a defense attorney.

In adjudication hearings, juveniles have been guaranteed the rights of due process and privilege against self-incrimination. As a result of the *In re Winship* decision (1970), the Supreme Court also established "proof beyond a reasonable doubt" as the standard required in any juvenile court case in which a finding of "true" could result in institutionalization. Prior to the *Winship* decision, the standard of proof required in the juvenile court was the same as that in civil law: a preponderance (majority) of the evidence, rather than proof beyond a reasonable doubt.

One right available in adult criminal courts that is not extended to youths having hearings in the juvenile court is that of a jury trial. In *McKeiver* v. *Pennsylvania* (1971) the Supreme court declared that juveniles do not have a constitutional right to a jury trial. Several state juvenile codes, however, do provide for the use of a jury in a juvenile proceeding if this is requested by defense counsel or if the state has a blended sentence provision.

We noted in our discussion of the role of the juvenile court judge that adjudication is a complex process. Some of the cases involve youths who have allegedly committed heinous crimes. For these, the court proceedings are formal and adversarial in nature. The role of the judge may be quite similar to that of a judge in a criminal trial—making sure that procedural rules are followed and that the evidence and witnesses are properly presented. Since the judge will be making the adjudication decision, he or she must also explore aggravating or mitigating circumstances surrounding the incidents. In cases involving children who have been abused or neglected, the demeanor of the judge toward the children must be quite different. Here the judge seeks to reassure the child and make the court appearance as nonthreatening as possible.

If a determination is made that the charge is not true, the case is dismissed by the judge. If a determination of "guilty" or "true" is reached and the charge is a minor one, disposition may be made at this point. Otherwise a date for the dispositional hearing is set.

12.3.9   Disposition Hearing

Many states require that the disposition or sentencing in a juvenile case be made at a hearing that is separated from the adjudication hearing. This separation has been termed the *bifurcated hearing* process. The reason for separating the adjudication and dispositional hearings is to afford the court an opportunity to obtain the information that will be needed to make an appropriate disposition. If considerable knowledge of the youth's background is already available to the court, as in instances where the young person has had a number of previous juvenile court appearances, an adjournment between the adjudication hearing and the dispositional hearing may not be necessary. In those cases in which the hearings are bifurcated, the major task to be completed during the interval between the two hearings (usually one to 2 weeks) is the preparation of a predisposition social investigation.

The social investigation is a key part of the juvenile court process. A probation officer assembles all the facts regarding the incident currently under consideration by the court, as well as the record of previous offenses; information about the offender gathered at the intake interview or by detention personnel if the youth was detained prior to the adjudication hearing about school progress and attitude; reports from any other social agencies in the community that have had contact with the youth or the family; and personal data on the child's abilities, interests, problems, and family situation. The probation officer may also suggest a dispositional alternative or treatment plan in the investigation. At the dispositional hearing, the judge has the social investigation report and may also hear information from the defense counsel, the prosecutor, or probation officers about possible treatment alternatives available to the youth. This hearing is considerably less adversarial than the adjudication hearing. The defense counsel may ask character witnesses (teachers, social workers, relatives) to speak on the youth's behalf and counsel may also examine the predisposition social investigation report to be sure that the information contained in it is accurate. If a plea bargain that included a suggested disposition was made, the defense counsel is present to assure that the terms of the plea bargain are carried out. If a prosecutor is present, he or she functions predominately to protect the interests of the community or of a specific victim. While, in general, prosecutors may argue for more severe dispositions than the defense counsel wishes they may be supportive of dispositions that involve treatment rather than punishment if the circumstances surrounding certain cases seem to warrant this.

In some states, juvenile codes *mandate* specific dispositions for certain offenses. For example, if a juvenile is adjudicated delinquent on a serious felony charge, commitment to a secure institution may be required by the code. In other cases, juvenile codes may *prohibit* certain dispositions. For example, many states prohibit secure institutionalization of status offenders. Generally, state codes allow juvenile court judges to make discretionary dispositions for the majority of delinquent offenses. The dispositions can range from those that are nominal, such as warnings nr reprimands, to those that are custodial and will result in the youth being placed in a secure correctional facility.

The dispositions a judge may make include (1) release of the youth to the supervision to his or her parents with a warning; (2) imposition of a fine or a requirement that restitution of some sort be made to an injured party; (3) referral to a community social agency for counseling or treatment; (4) assignment to official probation supervision by the court; (5) placement in a residential treatment center; (6) removal from the home and placement in a foster home; (7) making the child a ward of the court, who will receive needed medical or psychological treatment; or (8) commitment to a public or private institution, or to the state youth authority for placement. Hockenberry and Puzzanchera (2018, p. 50) stated that in 2016, formal probation was ordered in 62% of the cases in which the youth was adjudicated delinquent.

The dispositional hearing closes when the judge signs a decree of disposition, which is a written statement of the disposition chosen and the basis for it.

12.3.10   Sentencing of Juveniles Adjudicated in Criminal Court

Although juveniles tried and convicted in criminal courts can receive sentences similar to those adults convicted of identical offenses would receive, age is often used as a mitigating circumstance to justify a less severe sentence for a juvenile. Although, juveniles tried as adults in criminal courts may be eligible for probation, Hockenberry and Puzzanchera, 2018, p. 46) report that less than 25% receive probation or some other form of community based supervision, such as intensive probation or residential placement. The nature of their offenses, which were generally serious offenses against persons, usually results in sentencing to an adult correctional institution. The determining factors in the sentencing of juveniles to an adult correctional facility are related to the age of the offender, the type of crime committed, and the prior delinquent history of the youth, as well as the resources available in the community to provide the proper supervision and treatment needed. For example, a juvenile convicted in a criminal court for breaking and entering and grand theft, and it was determined that the criminal behavior was related to the youth's serious drug problem, might be given a sentence to a community residential drug treatment facility. At the other extreme, before the U.S. Supreme Court's Roper v Simmons (2005) decision, in which the Court ruled that the execution of a person below the age of 18 constituted cruel and unusual punishment, a majority of the states authorized the death penalty for juveniles. Between 1973 and July, 2002, 21 adults were executed for crimes they committed as juveniles (Strieb, 2003).

12.4 Summary

Views of the appropriate role and procedures for the juvenile court have changed over the years. Youths charged with serious offenses are being transferred to adult courts more frequently and some states allow prosecutors to choose to bring charges in either adult or juvenile court. During the "get tough" era of the late twentieth century, the upper age of juvenile court jurisdiction was lowered in several states and the propriety of including status offenders in the court's jurisdiction was debated. Hearings have become more formal, and there has been an increase in the number of abuse, neglect, and dependency cases handled. However, during the first part of the twenty-first century, the number of referrals to the juvenile courts has decreased dramatically, and there has been a change in the philosophy of the courts in regard to the mission of the courts. This change is demonstrated in the increase of community based dispositions for youths convicted of delinquency, the decline in commitments to juvenile correctional facilities, the decline in cases bound over to the adult criminal courts, and the emphasis placed on cooperation and collaboration with community agencies, such as mental health, drug and alcohol, and child welfare agencies.

Youths may be referred to the juvenile court for offenses that are also law violations for adults or for behavior that is unlawful only for juveniles (status offenses). The majority of juvenile court referrals are made by law enforcement agencies, but referrals may also come from parents, social agencies, schools, or private individuals.

The juvenile court process begins when the agency or person making the referral files a petition (complaint) that specifies the law or ordinance that the youth has violated. The offender may be arrested and brought to the court by police or may receive a summons to appear.

At the intake level, the intake officer of the juvenile court may decide to authorize detention, dismiss the case, or partially divert the youths from juvenile court action. Detention involves holding a youth in a center provided by the court or arrangement for home detention (house arrest) until action is taken on the case.

For those cases handled judicially (officially), an *initial hearing(arraignment)* is scheduled, at which the charges contained in the petition are read and the youth responds by answering "guilty" or "not guilty," "true" or "untrue," or "admit" or "deny." If a youth admits the truth of the allegations and the offenses are minor, the case may be disposed of at this hearing. If a plea of "guilty" or "true" is made to a serious offense, a social investigation is required to aid the judge in deciding upon an appropriate disposition. If a plea of "not guilty" or "untrue" is entered, an *adjudication hearing* is scheduled.

In cases involving serious offenses, the prosecuting attorney may request a *waiver hearing* to apply for transfer of the case to an adult criminal court for trial. Such hearings must be conducted according to the constitutional safeguards established in *Kent* v. *U.S.* and *Breed* v. *Jones*.

In some instances, a *prehearing conference* between the judge, court personnel, the prosecuting attorney, and the defense attorney may occur, in which the facts of the case are considered and the disposition that can be expected if a plea of "guilty" or "true" is made is outlined. The conference is analogous to the plea-bargaining process on the adult level.

At the *adjudication hearing,* the judge decides upon the truth of the charges and acts accordingly, basing the decision on the standard of "proof beyond a reasonable doubt." If the charges are found to be not true, they are dismissed. If a determination of "true" is reached and the offense is a minor one, a disposition may be given at this point. Otherwise a date for a dispositional hearing is set, with a social investigation conducted in the interim. The separation of adjudication and disposition into two separate hearings is termed the *bifurcated   hearing* process.

At the *dispositional hearing,* the judge reviews the social investigation report, informs the youth of the disposition decided upon, and signs a decree of disposition, which states the disposition chosen and its basis. Juvenile court dispositions may be appealed, and this occurs most frequently when the disposition involves institutionalization.

Although the majority of youths adjudicated delinquent do not recidivate, some offenders will have many appearances before the court before they reach the age of upper age of the juvenile court's jurisdiction. These youths often continue their criminal behavior into adulthood. If an offender is not referred again after a specific period of time, *expungement* (destruction or sealing) of the juvenile's record can be requested.

Youths whose cases are waived to adult criminal courts are liable to the same penalties adults can receive if they are found guilty, but the age of the waived youth may be a mitigating factor. However, juveniles can be sentenced to adult correctional institutions, but are no longer eligible for the death penalty if the capital offense was committed when they were below the age of 18.

12.5   Discussion Questions

1. Define total diversion and partial diversion. What are the primary goals of diversion?
2. Discuss the role of a juvenile court intake officer in decisions to divert juveniles from official handling. On what basis does an intake officer make these decisions?
3. How has the role of the defense attorney in the juvenile court expanded since the *Gault*, *Kent*, and *Winship* decisions?
4. When is it appropriate to place a juvenile charged with a delinquent act in a detention center? The U.S. Supreme Court ruled that preventive detention is acceptable for juveniles. Do you agree? Why?
5. Discuss the waiver process. When is it appropriate to have a juvenile case transferred to the criminal court?
6. Outline the juvenile court process, from the initial hearing through the dispositional hearing. Can the process be halted at any step in this process? Explain.
7. What occurs at the adjudication hearing in juvenile court? What safeguards must be followed to be sure that a juvenile receives all of the rights guaranteed to him or her by court decisions?

8. Why are jury trials not an option for juveniles in most states? Do you agree with this prohibition? Discuss.
9. What is a "blended sentence?" What happens to a juvenile given a blended sentence who does not abide by its stipulations?
10. What is a "bifurcated" hearing? What is the purpose of using this approach to the dispositional phase of the juvenile justice process?

References

Balint, E. (2019). Second teen charged in death of 14-year-old. *Akron Beacon Journal, 27*, B4.

Breed V. Jones. (1975). 421 U.S. 519.

Feld, B. (1987). The juvenile court meets the principle of the offense: Legislative changes in juvenile waiver statutes. *Journal of Criminal Law and Criminology, 78*(3), 49.

Feld, B. (1988). In re Gault revisited: A cross state comparison of the right to counsel in juvenile court. *Crime & delinquency 34 4,* Oct. 1988: 394widening. *Journal of Crime and Justice, 16*(1), 30.

Hockenberry, S., & Puzzanchera, C. (2018). *Juvenile Court Statistics 2016*. Pittsburgh, PA: National Center for Juvenile Justice.

In re Gault. (1967). 376, U.S. 1.

In re Winship. (1970). 397, U.S. 358.

Kratcoski, P. (2012). *Juvenile justice administration*. Boca Raton: CRC Press/Taylor &Francis Group.

Kratcoski, P. (2019, July 25). *Interview with Judge Linda Tucci Teodosio*. Akron, OH: Summit County Juvenile Court.

Kratcoski, P., & Kratcoski, P. (2019a, February 6). *Interview with Judge Robert Berger*. Portage County, OH: Juvenile Court Judge.

Kratcoski, P. & Kratcoski, P. (2019c, June 11). *Interview with Defense Attorney Troy Reeves.*

Mc Clory, E. (2019, January 26). Streetsboro boy, 13, won't face adult prison time. *Akron Beacon Journal*, B1, B4.

McKeiver v Pennsylvania. (1971). 403 U.S. 528.

Miranda v Arizona. (1966). 358 U.S. 436, 448.

National Advisory Committee for Juvenile Justice and Delinquency Prevention. (1980). *Standards for the administration of juvenile justice*. Washington, DC: U.S. Government Printing Office.

Roper v. Simmons. (2005). 543 U.S. 551.

Sickmund, M., & Puzzanchera, C. (Eds.). (2014). *Juvenile offenders & victims: 2014 National report*. Pittsburgh, PA: National Center for Juvenile Justice.

Snyder, H., Sickmund, M., & Poe-Yamagata, E. (2000). *Juvenile transfer to criminal court in the 1990s: Lessons learned from four studies*. Pittsburgh, PA: National Center for Juvenile Justice.

Strieb, V. L. (2003, January 15). *The juvenile death penalty today: Death sentences and executions for juvenile crimes. January 1973–June 30, 2002*. Retrieved from www.deathpenaltyinfo.org/juvchair.html

Task Force on Juvenile Justice and Delinquency Prevention. National Advisory Committee on Criminal Justice Standards and Goals. (1977). *Juvenile justice and delinquency prevention*. Washington, DC: U.S. Government Printing Office.

Chapter 13
Probation and Community-Based Programs

13.1 Introduction

Most of the youths who are brought into the courts are not too different from teenagers who have never had official contact with the law. Their unlawful acts are entangled with social, psychological, and cultural factors. Some young people faced with behavioral decisions receive little help or understanding from their parents and, being immature, select courses of action that lead to law violations and their apprehension. They may not recognize the seriousness of their behavior, and even if they do, their need for status, recognition or, money, or their desire to retaliate, seems more important at the time than the possible consequence of being caught.

The typical juvenile probation officer is expected to deal with complex situations in limited time and with strong pressure not to fail. The probation officer has many restraints regarding the courses of action he or she can follow and must constantly keep in mind the many publics being served. For example, a youthful offender is viewed by the members of the community in different ways, depending on their situations. As Sies (1965, p. 17). observed, "As an illustration take just one little vandal: call him 12 years old and you will see him as a baby who did not know what he was doing (according to his parents); as a kid who broke some 20 windows and was arrested (according to the police); as a little beast who should be locked up (according to the victim); as just another kid on the block (according to the neighbors); as one of 10,000 juveniles who are processed every year (according to the particular probation office); as one of 30 or more cases to decide on a given day (according to the Juvenile Court judge); as a fairly healthy physical specimen (according to the family doctor); as a reflection of the morality of the community (according to the social worker); as a child expressing frustration, aggression, and hostility (according to the psychiatrist); as a status seeker (according to the sociologist); as good copy for the newspaper; and as a project for a service club." Although this perspective on juveniles who are under the supervision of a justice agency was expressed more than 50 years ago, the same characteristics, with some modifications, is application at the present time. Those who work in the juvenile justice system and social services find some youths to be more violent, psychologically disturbed,

© Springer Nature Switzerland AG 2020
P. C. Kratcoski et al., *Juvenile Delinquency*,
https://doi.org/10.1007/978-3-030-31452-1_13

more defiant of authority, and more dependent on others than in the past, but nevertheless the characteristics of young people have not changed a great deal.

Just as youths who come to the attention of juvenile authorities are perceived in various ways by those who have an interest or stake in their behavior, they differ greatly in their attitudes, values, and amenability to counseling. Because of the wide range of backgrounds and personal attributes of probationers and the differences in the training and resources of probation officers, it is difficult to make generalizations about probation work and the people who complete the tasks related to providing supervision and assistance to those youths who have been convicted of violating the law and are being sanctioned by the courts. Generally, in the United States as well as many other countries throughout the world, juvenile probation officers serve under a specific court. Although their work is guided by the laws of the country and state in which they reside, the specific directions of the judicial body they serve can have a major effect on what aspect of their work, either supervision or service, is emphasized. Even though, an officer's personal preference, based on education and training, might lean toward the service aspect of the role, the major orientation of the probation department in which he or she is employed might be toward the supervision-surveillance aspect of the probation officer's role. In this regard, even the presiding juvenile court judge may feel pressure from the community to take a "get tough" position on the sentencing of juvenile delinquents and a "hard-nosed" position is required of the probation officers.

13.2 Historical Development of Probation

The roots of the practice of probation can be found in the Middle Ages, when certain types of offenders could be released to the custody of a member of the clergy, a peace-keeping officer, a relative, or a friend rather than given the harsh corporal or capital punishment prescribed by law. Such releases apparently were quite common with children who violated the law. They were given over to the custody of their parents or other supervisors with the stipulation that they be appropriately punished.

John Augustus (1774–1859) is credited with first using the term "probation" and initiating the practice as we know it today. He offered to supervise the activities of a man referred to the Police Court of Boston in 1841 to keep him from being sent to the House of Correction. When this case had a successful outcome, Augustus continued throughout his lifetime to supervise offenders and report their progress to the judges. By the time of his death he had supervised almost 2000 adults and several thousand children (Smyka, 1984, p. 67).

Following Augustus' lead, Massachusetts was the first state to institute a probation program for youths. In an act passed in 1869, a representative of the State Board of Charities was allowed to appear before the court in criminal cases involving juveniles. This agent could be given the responsibility of locating and placing youths in foster homes, if necessary, and was also empowered to supervise and assist the child after placement (Killinger, Kerper, & Cromwell, 1973, p. 45). By

1900, six states had enacted probation legislation for adults and juveniles. The Illinois Juvenile Court Act of 1899, which established the first juvenile court, provided for the appointment of juvenile probation officers and also specified their duties of the following way:

> The court shall have authority to appoint or designate one or more discreet persons of good character to serve as probation officers during the pleasure of the court; said probation officers to receive no compensation from the public treasury.... It shall be the duty of the said probation officer to make such investigation as may be required by the court; to be present in court in order to represent the interests of the child when the case is heard, to furnish to the court such information and assistance as the judge may require; and to take such charge of any child before and after trial as may be directed by the court. (Illinois Laws, 1899, pp. 131–137)

Gradually, as other states enacted legislation that created separate courts for juveniles, juvenile probation because an integral part of the juvenile justice process, and persons specifically trained in social work, psychology, or child welfare were hired as probation officers.

13.3   Definition on Probation

The term "probation" can refer to a disposition given to an adjudicated delinquent by a juvenile court judge or it may be used to describe a process. Under probation as a court disposition, the offender is allowed to remain in the community, subject to supervision by a court official. The youth must abide by certain rules and conditions established by the juvenile court. There are two ways in which a juvenile may be placed on probation. One method is termed "suspension of the imposition of the disposition." In this method, the juvenile is given a disposition of a commitment to a juvenile correctional institution, the commitment is suspended, and the youth is placed on probation. If the juvenile violates the terms of the probation, the suspension can be lifted and the juvenile may then be institutionalized. The second type of juvenile probation is an "order of probation" issued by a juvenile court judge. Conditions are set by the court and an agreement to meet them is signed by the juvenile and his or her parents. Violations are referred to the juvenile court. The judge can establish a specific period of probation (e.g., 1 year), or the probation may be for an indeterminate period, which would make the youth subject to court supervision until the upper age limit of the juvenile court's jurisdiction, unless the probation is terminated earlier by the court. Both methods of probation can be used within the same juvenile court jurisdiction, with the suspension of the imposition of the disposition used in more serious cases. For the year 2010, Sickmund and Puzzanchera (2014, p. 170) found that "In 61% of the (260,300) cases adjudicated delinquent, formal probation was the most severe sanction ordered by the court."

The penal codes of the states specify that a youth adjudicated delinquent can be under the supervision of a juvenile court until he or she reaches the age of majority, which is 21 in most states. However, the length of actual supervision by the courts is

Table 13.1 Case characteristics of adjudicated delinquents-2010

Case characteristic	Residential placement (%)	Formal probation (%)
All cases	26	54
Age		
15 and younger	26	66
16 and older	27	60
Gender		
Male	31	61
Female	21	68

Percent of adjudicated delinquency cases in 2010 given residential placement or probation dispositions

Other dispositions were given for 11% of the males and 16% of the females and for 8% of those 15 and younger and 9% for those 16 and older

Source: Table modified by Peter C. Kratcoski from information contained in Sickmund M. & Puzzanchera, C. eds. (2014). *Juvenile Offenders and* Victims. Pittsburgh: PA: Office of Juvenile Justice, p. 171)

generally a year or less. Youths would not necessarily he discharged at the end of this time period, but rather placed on inactive status, in which case there are no required contacts with the court or probation officer, but the youth is still technically on probation. Keeping a youth on inactive status expedites the handling of those who commit new offenses, since they are still under formal supervision of the juvenile court.

13.4   Adjudicated Delinquents on Probation

Most of the youths who are formally (judicially) processed by the juvenile courts and adjudicated delinquent receive as their disposition either an order of probation or a commitment to a secure juvenile correctional facility, with a suspension of the imposition of the commitment, and placed on probation.

For those serious offenders who are assessed to be a risk to the community, intensive supervision and other sanction may be imposed as part of the probation disposition. The possible sanctions given might be home detention, electronic monitoring, alcohol or drug abuse counseling, or placement in a residential treatment center.

For cases that are officially processed by the juvenile court, probation is the most frequent disposition. Sickmund and Puzzanchera (2014, p. 170) reported that, in 2010, for those cases that were brought before the juvenile courts but not *adjudicated delinquent* and informally processed, 42% of the cases were dismissed, 24% were given probation and 33% agreed to other sanctions, such as voluntary restitution, community service, or referral to another agency. Of those formally processed and adjudicated delinquent, 61% were given probation, 26% were given residential placement, and 13% were given other sanctions." As shown in Table 13.1, the proportion of adjudicated delinquents receiving either residential placement or formal probation varied by age, sex, and race. It should be noted that the criminal histories of the youths and the severity of the offenses they committed may account for some of the variations recorded. There are many other factors that may influence the decisions of juvenile court judges relating to the dispositions given to those youths adjudicated delinquent. These include, the judge's personal thoughts on the causes of delinquency and philosophy of the best methods to use on how to sanction those adjudicated delinquent. Other factors, include the resources available to handle the youth in the community and the laws of the state pertaining to juvenile justice. For example, the penal code of a state may actually prohibit sending minor offenders to the juvenile correctional facilities in the state administered by a state agency.

As shown in Table 13.1, the dispositions of juvenile adjudicated delinquent do not differ significantly by age and gender. However, the type of offense does determine the type of disposition given to a great extent. For example, Sickmund and Puzzanchera (2014, p. 171) found that 29% of those found delinquent of an offense against persons were given an institutional disposition, compared with 25% of a property offense, and 19% of those found delinquent of a drug offense.

Other factors that may determine the type of disposition given to a youth adjudicated delinquent include the number of youths found delinquent in a particular court and the size of the staff and resources available to handle the youths in the community. In courts serving large metropolitan areas, hundreds of officers may be involved in juvenile probation activities, while a small rural jurisdiction may have a single, part-time officer. Caseloads may be set at 40 or 50 or expanded to several hundred, depending on the number of youth being supervised and the number of probation officers who are available to supervise them. Since no nationally recognized qualifications or standards for probation officers have been established, their preparation and training may range from a college education and long experience as a specialist to no specific education or training at all for this type of work. In addition, the auxiliary court resources on which probation officers can draw are determined by the tone and philosophy set by the juvenile court judge, county or municipal budgets, the limitations of the court's physical plant, the degree of community knowledge of and involvement in the court's work, and the administrative and organizational abilities of court personnel.

13.5 The Probation Process

A probation officer wears many hats in the course of performing his or her duties. As a member of a specific probation department and a subordinate of a particular chief probation officer, the officer is committed to the defined goals of the department and satisfactory performance of specified duties within the department. In dealings with probationers, the officer must perform varied duties, including counseling, making referrals to service agencies, investigation of the probationers' activities, job or school placement assistance, mediation of family disputes, invocation of the court's authority, or reporting a youth's illegal behavior, which may result in probation being terminated.

The juvenile probation officer's role is broadly defined as providing supervision and assistance to adjudicated youths placed on probation. Role conflict can result when an officer who decides to become a probation officer with the expectation of helping youths change their lives around by offering guidance and assistance to them finds the job to be predominately related to the supervision of the youth's behavior, with the assistance facet being given held to a minimum. Often the officers become bogged down in report writing and completing the many administrative tasks and are forced to handle those under their supervision in an assembly line fashion.

Because of large caseloads and other pressures, probation officers in large jurisdictions may have to alter their role definitions. The following statements from an interview with Terry Walton, who was serving as the chief probation officer of a juvenile court located in an urban county in Ohio, illustrate how the role of an officer may have to change depending on the philosophy and orientation of the administration of the court under which the officer is employed. When asked why he pursued a career in juvenile justice, the officer answered "I got into it in a roundabout way. I initially wanted to be a police officer, but there were no openings. I accepted a job with the Summit County Sheriff's Office as a corrections officer in the jail. After I had a taste of working with adults, I decided that there was more opportunity to foster change in a person's behavior in the juvenile area. When a job opened up with the Juvenile Court, I accepted it" (Kratcoski, 2012a, p. 417). In response to the question, "Has the court changed its philosophy and mission during your years at the court?" Terry Walton answered, "The Summit County Juvenile Court was established in 1916. Since that time there were 10 judges and I have worked for five of the 10. When new judges are elected, they often bring their own agenda and mission. One judge may lean toward the law and order, protection of the community goals of the court, whereas another judge may emphasize rehabilitation more. The court is also controlled to some extent by legislation and court rulings. Thus, in answer to your question, I have seen shifts back and forth. Our current judge is oriented toward community corrections" (Kratcoski, 2012b, pp. 419–420).

The typical probation officer performs multiple number of tasks. These consist of obtaining information on the youth such as reviewing police report, reviewing prior delinquent history, completing predisposition investigations and risk and needs assessments, and conducting interviews; management of the probationers by providing counseling and assistance, and reporting on the performance of the youth under their supervision. The probation officer also serves as a resource broker by: maintaining contacts with children service agencies and making referrals to these agencies. Some of the youth may be in need of out of home placement and probation officers must be in contact with the available foster homes as well as residential group homes. Surveillance (law enforcement) is also a major task the probation officer performs. This is accomplished by making visits to the home, school, place of employment, if employed, and sometimes to places in the community where youths "hang out' to determine whether the youth is adhering to the rules of probation. The officer can make arrests if probation rules are violated. At times the probation officer will be required to testify in court if termination of the probation is being considered because of violations of the conditions of probation, or the commission of a new offense. Those probation officers who hold a supervisory position in the department, such as the chief probation officer, will be required to complete performance evaluations on the officers, maintain records, write reports, and provide assistance or special requests made by the court, such as completing research, implementing new programs, serving as bailiff, and serving on committees.

The duties of a juvenile probation officer can be broadly categorized as investigation and supervision. As an investigator, the probation officer is responsible for completing the predisposition social history report and for providing an assessment of the risks this youth poses to the community and the specific needs of the probationer. In a supervisory capacity, the probation officer provides counseling and guidance to the youth and monitors his or her activities. Probation officers' caseloads may include youths who are on official probation after adjudication, others who are on informal probation as part of a diversion arrangement, and youths involved in restitution or community service.

Rudes, Viglione, and Taxman (2011) completed research on the way juvenile probation officers perceived their role after they completed motivational training. The research was conducted with 12 randomly selected juvenile probation offices. The probation officers of each office were assigned to one of three training groups, enhanced motivational training, normal motivational training, and control motivational training. Officers were questioned on the predominant dimension of the role, law enforcement, social service, and resource broker they perceived as the most important and dominant in their work. Extensive interviews with the participants in the study lead to the researchers to conclude that (Rudes et al., 2011, p. 6), "Although POs at times display goals and perceptions related to a mixture of role orientations (as expected with juvenile POs) our data suggests the presence of two (rather than three) distinct roles, social service .... and resource broker.... dominate among juvenile POs, with a mixture of demographic and experience characteristics in each group."

13.6 Tasks Performed by Juvenile Probation Officers

When a disposition of probation is granted to a juvenile offender, the youth is ordered to report within a short period of time to the probation officer assigned to the case. Even before this post-disposition interview takes place, however, a youth who has been granted probation may have had some exposure to, or even numerous interactions with, the juvenile court's probation personnel.

The intake officer of a juvenile court is a probation officer who has been assigned to this specialty. Data on the juvenile gathered by this officer at the time of intake are available to the judge at the time the disposition decision is made. If the youth was previously involved in any sort of diversion program before official referral to the juvenile court, he or she may also have encountered probation officers who worked as diversion specialists. Such officers frequently serve as supervisors of volunteer, administer diversion programs, or may perform the tasks of the of the diversion program by working with the youths who were not adjudicated delinquent and were placed in the program with a requirement of informal court intervention. Probation personnel, under such titles as "street workers," "detached workers," "community workers," or "youth workers," make contact with and supervise youths who have been granted some type of diversion rather than official processing.

13.6.1 Investigator

Probationers may have had earlier contact with officers assigned to their cases if a predisposition investigation is completed on the juvenile offender. This report, frequently used in the past, has been replaced by most courts with risk- needs assessments, except in the more serious felony cases. A youth whose offense is serious enough that the disposition of a commitment to a juvenile correctional facility, or even being waivered to the criminal court is likely, a predisposition report must be completed. In some courts, probation officers are trained and assigned to specialize in predisposition investigations, in others, officers are assigned to investigation and supervision activities according to the current needs of the department. In courts serving a small population, it likely that the probation officers will be generalists, that is, performing both of the key roles of investigator and supervisor. In courts that serve a large population and have thousands of referrals to the court each year, it is most likely that the probation officers will be specialized and concentrate their time to one of the major tasks, either investigation or supervision. Often there will be specialization within the divisions. Some investigators will focus on minor delinquency cases and others on the serious cases. The supervision division might have officers who supervise the sex offenders, drug offenders, or violent offenders.

When a former chief probation officer of a juvenile court serving a population of almost one million was asked if the officers in the department specialized (Kratcoski, 2012a, p. 418), he reported that the officers were not divided into supervisors and investigators but instead were assigned to special offender categories. Some officers worked with serious offenders who had been given suspension of commitment to juvenile institutions. Others were assigned to work with youths who had mental health or substance abuse problems, because it was felt that these offenders needed a different type of supervision and treatment. The chief probation officer stated that he was currently supervision the sex offender unit, and also was the supervisor of the felony disposition unit, that conducts investigations from all sources for serious felony offenders (similar to a predisposition report) and gives a recommendation to the judge and magistrates at the dispositional hearing.

The predisposition investigation involves a detailed report on school situation, the youth's family record, social relationships, and previous offense record. The probation officer who prepares it may recommend a disposition in the report or may appear at the dispositional hearing to offer information and suggestions.

In those courts in which probation officers are trained and assigned to specialize in all facets of probation work, including investigation, supervision, and providing needed services to the youth assigned to the officer's caseload, there are advantages and disadvantages in having the same probation officer conduct the predisposition investigation and supervise the probationer. It is advantageous that the officer has been familiar with the case for a period of time and has more complete background information on the youth at the time the probation period begins; it is also advantageous because the juvenile realizes that this officer is aware of any past problems. Disadvantages include a possible transfer of the youth's negative feelings regarding the juvenile court experience to the probation officer who was a part of that experience, the juvenile may perceive the probation officer as a "law enforcement" officer rather than a "helping" person, and the lack of an opportunity for the youth to make a "new start" with new counselors. Specialization in case investigation or counseling may be a more efficient use of probation personnel, since officers may have special talents or training for one of these functions.

13.6.2 Case Management

Some large juvenile courts use standardized case management systems to classify probationers on the basis of the potential risk they pose to the community and the extent of need for services they present. The case management systems generally make use of risk instruments and, needs instruments through which a case management plan for the youth is developed.

The potential for the youth to be a serious danger to the community if placed on probation is assessed through use of a "risk" instrument (which weights the importance of such factors as prior felony convictions, substance abuse problems, and prior probation revocation) and the problems of the youth are assessed by a "needs" instrument (which weights the importance of peer associations, family situations, drug and alcohol abuse, and school problems). Based on the information gathered from these instruments, the youth is placed on a specific level of supervision, ranging from intensive to minimal supervision. In addition, the specific type of intervention needed to bring about the desired changes in behavior are also assessed.

According to Holsinger et al. (2018, p. 51), "In correctional settings (secure and/ or community based) the time investment that comprehensive risk and needs assessment requires is regarded as an essential component of an evidence-based decision making process. For example, those placed on probation are often given a sentence that can range from several months to several years, with the presumption that they will receive some interventions along the way that are designed to help them address some of the dynamic risk factors, such as substance abuse treatment or employment counseling." For juveniles, other problem areas that may need to be addressed include school related situations and family problems. Some youths might to be tested to determine if they need psychological counseling or if they have other special needs. There are several models employed by different probation agencies. One model widely used, referred to as the RNR (risk, needs, responsivity) is particularly useful for assessing juveniles, since it tends to assess not only static characteristics, such as age, gender, or prior delinquency, but also changeable factors. Holsinger et al. (2018) note that risk assessment models such as the RNR model have changed over the past several decades, and they no longer focus primarily on the static risk factors such as age at first offense, prior criminal history as the factors that are predictive of the potential for the offender to commit a new offense. There has been a change, to assessment instruments that can measure changeable factors empirically correlated with crime, such as the presence of pro-criminal attitudes, the manifestation of antisocial behavior patterns, living in a disruptive family situation, and struggling with substance abuse problems. The underlying components of an assessment model based on risk, needs and responsivity (RNR) are explained in Box 13.1.

Box 13.1 Risk-Needs Assessments
Risk factors are variables associated with problem behaviors (specifically, delinquent offending or violence). Some examples of risk factors are: early onset of aggressive behavior; patterns of high family conflict; school-related problems, such as truancy; gang involvement; and availability of drugs or firearms in the neighborhood.
   Protective factors are characteristic of the youth or the environment surrounding the youth that interact with risk factors to reduce the odds of involvement in delinquent or criminal activities. Some examples of protective factors are the presence of caring and supportive adults in the community and at school; having a stable family; and having a positive/ resilient temperament;
   Needs factors—These are characteristics of the youth or the environment of the youth that are associated with criminogenic factors; such as drug abuse, having a violent temper, engaging in violent acts and living in a dysfunctional family.
   Responsivity factors—They are factors that may affect a youth's ability to respond to treatment and programming, such as motivation to change, cognitive, functioning, and having the resources needed for a change of behavior (Office of Juvenile Justice Delinquency Prevention, 2015, pp. 3–4).

For a juvenile placed on probation, those factors that are associated with delinquent behavior are subject to change, depending on the success of the supervision and assistance given to the youth on probation. The typical risk-needs assessment models will have instruments that periodically reassess the changes in the probationer, on the risk factors as well as the needs factors.

Vincent, Guy, and Grisso (2012, p. 18) suggested, "New approaches to risk assessment are highly compatible with the most recent culture shift in juvenile justice because risk assessment tools, although not infallible, can contribute to public safety and promote youth potential in two ways. First, they offer validated input to inform the decision about whether youth are in need of secure custody or can be better served in the community. Second, modern risk assessment tools improve the ability of systems to help youth become productive members of the community when they leave the juvenile justice system, because many tools evaluate not only the degree of risk, but also the factors that are likely contributing to that risk." The Office of Juvenile Justice and Delinquency Prevention (OJJDP) (2014, p. 4) noted, "Risk/needs assessments generally consist of two components. The risk assessment component provides a way to predict the likelihood of recidivism of the youth. Recidivism is generally defined as future contact with the justice system—when a youth commits additional criminal or delinquent acts that come to the attention of law enforcement or other criminal justice personnel, such as a probation officer. The needs assessment component identifies factors about the youth that can be changed through individualized treatment or programming to reduce the likelihood that the youth will reoffend."

The earlier risk factor/needs assessment instruments were used in state and local probation and parole offices. Gradually, risk/needs instruments were developed and implemented for use with juvenile offenders by the juvenile courts. Although there are great similarities in the instruments used by various courts, there is some variations in the items selected for the instruments and in the way they are scored. Typically, the risk items that are used to assess the possibilities for recidivism for youths being considered for probation include age at first contact with a juvenile justice agency, seriousness of present offense (misdemeanor, felony, violent), number of prior adjudications in the juvenile court, past probation record, incarcerated in a juvenile correctional facility, performance at school; delinquent peers; abuse of alcohol or drugs, level of support from family, and attitude toward authority figures. Each item is given a weighted score in terms of the degree the item is a problem, with the scoring consisting of "not a problem," "somewhat of a problem," and "a significant problem." The scores of all of the items are added and, depending on the score, the juvenile is placed under minimum (low) supervision, medium (moderate) supervision or high (maximum) supervisions.

Once the youth's level of risk is determined, case assignments may be made to officers who are specifically trained or skilled in working with youngsters who require a certain level of supervision. Several risk instruments are designed to assess the risk of specific types of offenders, such as sex offenders and violent juvenile offenders. For example, Meyers and Schmidt (2008) describe the Structure Assessment of Violent Risk in Youth (SAVRY) as a tool used in the assessment of a youth to predict the potential (risk) for the manifestation of violence. It includes 24 items in three risk domains: historical risk factors, social/contextual risk factors, and individual factors. Items included pertain to prior acts of violence, school performance, delinquent peer groups, substance abuse and impulsiveness. SAVRY also includes items pertaining to "protective factors" such as family support.

In addition to the risk instrument, a needs assessment is often used to determine if the youth has special needs that should be addressed in the case management plan. The items on the needs assessment tend to more subjective than those found on the risk assessments. For example, such items as level of family support, extent of abuse of alcohol or drug use association with delinquent peer group, behavior problem in school, deviant sexual behavior, and emotional problems are often beyond the scope of knowledge of the person completing the assessment of the youth. There is also a potential for bias if the person completing the interview makes a judgment on the level of needs for a youth who comes from a cultural background that is quite different from that of the youth being assessed. The values and norms of the youth and youth's family, for example, the use of physical punishment, may not be in conformity with those of the person completing the assessment.

13.6.3   The Case Plan

The judge, with the assistance of the probation officer's risk and needs assessment as well as a predisposition report that is completed on the youth in some of the more difficult cases, can use great discretion in shaping an adjudicated youth's probation program. The judge may combine probation with other obligations, such as restitution to the offended party, involvement in a drug or alcohol rehabilitation program, or enrollment in a special school or work program. The judge may also make a disposition of probation contingent upon the juvenile's being placed in a halfway house or community residential facility, where the youth will be supervised by the staff provided with treatment if necessary and visited by court personnel.

In addition to combining probation with other requirements, juvenile court judges have a good deal of discretion in setting up the rules for each juvenile's probation period. If a youth adjudicated delinquent is placed on probation, the youth is required to obey a set of general conditions of probation, and specific conditions of probation. General conditions apply to all juveniles on probation. Following is an example of general probation conditions (Kratcoski & Kratcoski, 2004, p. 330).

1. The juvenile must obey all state, federal, and municipal laws.
2. The juvenile must obey all rules, regulations, and orders of the parents.
3. The juvenile must attend school, attend all classes, and obey all school rules and regulations until 18 years of age, unless the youth is granted a permit to leave school before reaching the 18th birthday.
4. Use of intoxicating beverages and drugs is prohibited.
5. The juvenile will develop and maintain a proper attitude and respect the rights and properties of others.
6. The juvenile is to report to the probation officer as scheduled or immediately upon notice to the juvenile or parents.
7. Permission must be given by the probation officer in order to leave the county under which is the jurisdiction of the court.
8. Parents, or caretakers must report any violations of the conditions to the probation officer.

In addition to the general rules of probation, specific regulations may be added. For example, association with a person who has been demonstrated to be a bad influence on the probationer may be forbidden, a youth who has been involved in car theft or joyriding may be prohibited from driving a car, or an exact curfew hour may be set. As a result of state court and federal court decisions, the constitutionality of some types of probation regulations used in the past, such as prohibitions on clothing styles or length of hair, may no longer be used.

Box 13.2 Interview of Rory Franks, Chief Probation Officer, Portage County, Ohio, Juvenile Court. Interview Conducted by P. C. Kratcoski, July 19, 2019

Biography

Rory Franks graduated from Kent State University in 1994 with a degree in criminal justice studies. He held several positions in criminal justice agencies and private corporations, including Harbor Light Correctional Halfway House, Sea World Security, Target Assets Protection, and the U.S. Bureau of Prisons, before assuming a position with the Portage County Juvenile Court in 1996.

Q: Mr. Franks, how long have you been employed at the Portage County Juvenile Court?

A: I have been employed with Portage County Juvenile Court since August 996. I started as an intensive supervision PO, handling only felony level offenders with suspended Ohio Department of Youth Services (ODYS) commitments. I was promoted to Assistant Chief Probation Officer in 2004 and Chief Probation Officer in 2018.

Q: Rory, why did you decide to pursue a career in juvenile justice?

A: I was very focused with the Federal Bureau of Prisons and worked in Colorado at the Federal Correctional Center that had just opened in the early 1990s. I already had past experiences with kids as a camp counselor for my high school and during college for the YMCA. I really enjoyed working with kids. Once I figured out the Federal Prison System was not satisfying my interests, I started focusing towards community based correction (probation and parole). My past experiences working with children, combined with my criminal justice experience directed me towards working with juveniles and I have enjoyed my work.

Q: How long have you been Chief Probation Officer?

A: One year

Q: As Chief Probation Officer, what are your specific responsibilities?

A: It involves a great deal of documentation of the entire probation department's work. I cover all Court related matters relating to the judge's schedule. I supervise and respond to all cases and staffing needs of the probation department.

Q: How many officers are in the probation department?

A: Seven

Q: What are the primary roles (tasks) of the officers?

A: We have two Intensive Officers for the risk level offenders and five regular POs, three females and four males, some of the regular officers are responsible for electric monitoring and house arrest, or they conduct evidence based cognitive behavioral programs in addition to their supervisory responsibilities in the community with the kids. They complete these tasks by conducting home visits, and office and school contacts. Officer roles can be summed up as to "Identify, Assess, and Refer," based on risk and needs of the youth and family, utilizing determined STRENGTHS found with the case. "Risk-Needs and Responsivity" principles of supervision are applied via our efforts with our interventions.

Q: Doe the probation department have any specialized programs for substance abuse offenders?

A: We use a substance abuse model called CBI-SA for some of our more advanced youths to assist them to overcome their addictions. It is a 39-week program administered by the POs. It is not a "drug court," but in many respects it is similar to a drug court program. For intensive supervision, all of our officers are trained and use E P.I.C.S. and Carey Guides as cognitive based interventions opposed to the" traditional" compliance-based supervision practices.

Q: How are policies and procedures in the probation department established? Do you have the authority to establish new procedures or rules?

A: In the Probation Department, I can implement some things with approval from the Director of the Portage County Juvenile Court, but realistically the Ohio Revised Code, 2152 will guide all Courts along with the presiding judge and his/her directives. Every county's administrative judge will guide and direct probation according to his/her orientation and of course in compliance with state and federal laws.

Q: In comparison with youth placed on probation when you first started as a probation officer, do you see any great changes in the characteristics and offenses of the juveniles who are coming to court and placed on probation at the present time?

A: Yes! So many more mentally ill kids than before. Also, the level of addiction these kids are in at a younger age. I also have watched the dramatic impact technology has had on the behavior of kids. This generation now has literally grown up with tech in their hands from infant onward. I sincerely believe we will see valid studies in the future on how tech has changed the development of their brains.

Q: How many judges have you served under?

A: Two, Judge Carnes and the current Judge Berger

Q: Has the court changed its philosophy or mission during your years at the court?

A: The system overall has changed dramatically. The population of Ohio Department of Youth Services (ODYS) correctional facilities decreased from 2500 in the late 90s to the current population of just over 400. ODYS closed most of its correctional facilities and now only operates three facilities. We are handling offenders in the community that in the past would have been sent to ODYS. The number of felony offenses as well as all other offenses committed by juveniles in our county has dramatically decreased during the past 20 years. This is in keeping with the national trend. There is now much more of a rehabilitative effort through evidence based practices in contrast to the emphasis on compliance and punitive measures taken in the past.

> **Q: Rory, what do you see as the major problems (concerns) pertaining to juvenile justice in general and the juvenile courts in particular that must be faced in the future?**
>
> A: Meeting all ends of the spectrum when cases are brought to our attention.... The community protection-the victims' restoration—providing quality assistance to families in need of services—not over servicing youth with probation and potentially creating delinquency by over supervision of minor matters.
>
> **Q: Rory, If you were just starting a career occupation, would you consider juvenile justice?**
>
> A: Yes. I found my niche by luck. You'll never work a day in your life if you enjoy what you do. I have fully enjoyed my experiences in juvenile justice and it prepared me to be a MUCH better father of my own kids than I would have otherwise if I did not have this experience.

A former chief probation officer of a juvenile court located in a large urban county was asked (Kratcoski, 2012a, p. 419) if there were any great changes in the characteristics of the juveniles who are now placed on probation, He stated that changes have occurred because of legislation and court decisions, and because the juvenile court and the probation department have developed new policies. For example, he noted that status offenders are now diverted from the court, and that misdemeanor offenders are not placed on official probation unless they are repeat offenders, so that now probation is generally reserved for felony offenders. In describing the changes in the personal characteristics of youths referred to probation, he stated that they see more emotionally disturbed youths than in the past, and more of the youths have been involved in weapons charges related to offenses against persons.

In Box 13.2, the interview with, the Chief Probation Officer Rory Franks of Portage County, Ohio, Juvenile Court, Ohio, illustrates the probation process that is followed in that county.

13.6.4   Service Provider and Research Broker

The initial interview with the probation officer is an important event in the probation process. It gives the officer an opportunity to review the juvenile court procedures with the child and the child's parents, explain the court's judgment, and spell out very clearly what the court's expectations are from that point on. Also at this time, the officer can define the role the officer will play in the probation process, noting that the responsibilities of the officer include both supervision and counseling. The officer may discuss the parents' responsibilities with them, and if family counseling has been recommended by the judge or is requested by the family, plans for implementing it should be formulated. If the judge's disposition included instructions that restitution of some type be made, the probation officer will draw up a payment schedule at this time or work out a system whereby the youth will provide services to the injured party. Another vital part of the initial interview is advising a youth of his or other responsibilities for reporting to the probation officer and for observing the general and specific rules set by the court. The officer may offer some encouragement that this period of supervision can be a helping experience, if the child cooperates. One function of the initial interview is to give the officer an opportunity to develop rapport with the youth.

The frequency of subsequent meetings between the probationer and the supervision officer depends upon the seriousness of the youth's problems and the size of the officer's caseload. At such meetings, goal setting is an effective device for allowing a juvenile to measure his or her progress and move toward release from probation. Goal setting is most effective if the goals set are attainable and are to be realized within a short period of time. Defining these goals should be the task of the probationer. They may be put in the form of a behavior contract, which sets certain specific rewards to be received when goals are achieved; for example, daily undisruptive attendance at school for several weeks may result in being released from home detention for an evening during the weekend. Parents play an important role in such contracting, for they must be firm enough to withhold the desired reward if the youth does not fulfill the obligation. The achievement of realistic short-term goals provides the probationer with feelings of success and is more helpful than working toward such abstract goals as "becoming a better person" or "changing my ways." The key to making the probation process a success is finding a way to motivate the youth to want to change.

Often there is a large difference between the ideal and the real in the expectations of how probation officers should interact with the youths on their caseloads. For example, a probation officer, when asked if the material taught in training sessions has had an effect on the way the probation officer role is performed, the replied, "In an ideal situation, I would love to use their JARPP program every single day. In reality, half the time we get literally two to five minutes to see our kids.... You don't have time to sit there and (use) ... open-ended questions galore, you just don't have time!" (Rudes et al., 2011, p. 8). This comment by the juvenile probation officer may reflect the feelings of a large number of officers who would like to do more in the way of providing assistance to those youths on their caseloads, but are stymied by having too many probationers and not enough time.

A youth's limitations must also be recognized in setting goals and promising rewards S young person whose academic ability would be reflected by a C level at maximum cannot be promised rewards for getting all B grades within the next school marking period, since this is obviously an unattainable goal. As part of the interaction between the probation officer and the probationer, the young person should be made aware of the positive consequences of conforming and also of the negative consequences of not conforming.

After considerable research and analysis of what works and what fails in the rehabilitation of delinquents, the specific method or technique applied has been found to be not as crucial in determining the outcome of the process as are the attributes of the people who occupy probation officer positions. Officers from a wide variety of educational, social, and philosophical backgrounds have demonstrated that they can successfully reach young people and assist them with their problems and needs. What works for one officer may not be viable for another. Some may be successful with group sessions in a structured setting, whereas the personalities, temperaments, and basic orientations of others would not be conducive to success using this method. Some officers may take a "buddy" position; others are more authoritarian; and some are successful in the role of rather formal, detached listeners. What seem to be the crucial ingredients are honesty and being oneself. in their dealings with clients. Probation officers who take a superior attitude or who try to impress their probationers with their knowledge of the "street culture" and use the "slang" terms used by the youth or try too hard to be a "buddy" often are using the probation meeting as a means to enhancing their own self-image and the meeting may not lead to any accomplishments, either in the supervision aspect of the role or the assistance facet of the probation officers role. For example, assuring a youth that certain rules do not have to be adhered to "to the letter" and then showing inconsistency by punishing the child for minor rule violations can quickly destroy the credibility of the officer. The officer who makes promises to the youth, such as "If you keep your nose clean for the next several months, I promise that the judge will take you off supervised probation" and not being able to live up to the promise could lead to a significant decline in the youth's trust of the probation officer. The meeting of a probationer with the officer, regardless of the environment where the meeting takes place, be it in the home, at the school or in the office, should provide the opportunity for both parties to give their honest expressions of the situation and what needs to be accomplished in order to make the probation process a success.

Of the variety of tools available to a probation officer in seeking to change the behavior of probationers or inhibit future misbehavior, the most powerful is the threat of institutionalization. A youth who is placed on probation is frequently returned to the same setting and associates with the same peer group that contributed to his or her problems with the juvenile court. But now the price to be paid for repeating the previous behavior is loss of freedom. The probation officer must impress upon the youth the necessity for sharing information that will make him or her "look bad," since taking over existing problems might be the best way to move toward better adjustment. Parents also may conceal information from the probation officer and the juvenile court, for fear that the child's probation will be revoked. The officer too may play upon the authoritarian aspects of his or her position in attempts to gain respect and control if "helping" efforts have proved ineffective. Thus, the probation officer, who ideally acts as a representative of the court with a mandate to provide assistance and support as well as supervision, may find that the supervision facet of the role taking precedence over other aspects or even interferes with his or her success in providing assistance and support.

13.7   Supervision of High Risk Probationers

A small proportion of the juveniles processed in the juvenile courts are assessed as being at a high risk for committing additional offenses and being a potential danger to the community. For these youths, the judges have a difficult decision when making a judgment either in favor of institutionalization or a community based disposition. If the judge decides on community corrections in these difficulty cases, it is likely that the youth will be placed under intensive supervision with a suspended commitment to a juvenile correctional facility. This will involve frequent contacts with the probation officer and possible assignment to some type of community correctional sanction. This could be home arrest, in which the youth is not allowed to leave home except for authorized activities, such as attendance at school, or restitution, drug counseling, electronic monitoring, or placement in a community based residential center.

In jurisdictions where the judge, police, school officials, or citizens exert considerable vocal pressure for control of juvenile offenders, a probation officer may find it necessary to devote a disproportionate amount of time to probationers who are "troublemakers," constantly keeping them under surveillance or checking on them while granting little attention to other youths who are not committing violations or creating disturbances but are badly in need of attention. In such dilemmas, the referral of such youths to other agencies may help to equalize the provision of services.

The influence of probation officers and their services to the community may extend far beyond the officer-probationer relationship. Effective probation work may help alleviate school problems and make the families of probationers more aware of the assistance available to them through community service agencies. Thomas Cerne, a probation supervisor in a juvenile court serving a metropolitan area, made this observation with regard to probation work: (Kratcoski & Kratcoski, 2004, p. 339) "I feel one of the most overlooked aspects of probation, and where I feel it is the most effective, is in the area of prevention. You may be helping other youths, younger siblings that are … in pre-delinquent status, or just helping the family resolve some other crises they have which they would otherwise not be able to handle to have assistance with if their child was not involved with the court. There is no way of measuring that success."

Tom Cerne had a number of years working in the Summit County Juvenile Court located in Ohio. Over the years he was involved in juvenile justice work, he experienced a wide range of approaches to dealing with juvenile offenders. At the beginning of his career, the "medical model" was in vogue. The emphasis was on individualized treatment for the juvenile offenders and on providing services to their families. At that time, delinquency was viewed as a social problem, and the youth's family situation, including the physical and social environment, was considered to be related to the youth's misbehavior. Later, he saw the court and the juvenile justice system move toward the "retribution model, with more emphasis on punishment and less concern about treatment." He stated that currently, "The court has taken a 'restorative justice' approach. There is much greater emphasis on the rights of the victims. The court works hand in hand with the victim assistance programs and the judge has appointed a court· liaison person who notifies the victims on all matters pertaining to their cases. By law, a victim has the right to complete a Victim Impact Statement if the offense committed by the juvenile is of a serious felony nature. If the offender is sent to a Department of Youth Services institution, the Victim Impact Statement is sent along and the victim must be notified when the youth is released from the institution" (Kratcoski & Kratcoski, 2004, pp. 339–340).

A juvenile probation officer who perceived the role of the probation officer in terms of being a resource broker (Rudes et al., 2011, p. 7) stated, "You follow the child, the child goes to intake and the decision is made whether to forward to court and if it goes to court, we follow the case through adjudication and then disposition, and then if placed on probation, we really try to help them complete all of the conditions of probation.... It seems to me (the role of probation officer) to be more about assessing the need and directing to the source to address that need."

Juvenile court administrators have come to realize that the amount of supervision and assistance needed by youths placed on probation differs from one client to another. Some probationers are able to make successful adjustments without much contact with the supervising officer. Experienced officers are able to assess the needs of various youths and adjust the intensity of their contacts with them accordingly, freeing additional time for contacts with multi-problem youths who most need their help.

Intensive probation is used in many courts as a substitute for institutionalization. It is grounded in the belief that, if juvenile offenders are closely supervised and given very strict rules and regulations to follow, the community can be protected. Probation officers who are assigned to intensive probation programs will generally have small caseloads, ranging from 10 to 25 probationers per officer. In addition to frequent supervision, intensive probation may involve home detention (house arrest) or requiring the youths to wear electronic devices that monitor their movements.

Many of the larger juvenile court systems, which process thousands of cases each year, have adopted standardized case classification procedures using "risk" and "needs" instruments similar to the measurements discussed earlier in this chapter. Probationers are placed into supervision categories (intensive, high, medium, and low), based on the probability of recidivism, as measured by standardized case classification instruments. Those identified as potential chronic offenders, who show a very high risk for recidivism, are generally placed in the intensive supervision category.

Those assigned to intensive supervision are given a significant amount of attention beyond that given to the high risk probationers. Often a team approach, consisting of a team leader, two surveillance officers, and a probation counselor, is used. The number of probationers serviced by an intensive probation team is usually much smaller than the normal caseload for the other probation officers working in the probation department. For example, an intensive supervision team might be assigned 25 or less probationers, compared with the number of probationers assigned to the other officers that often exceeds 50 or more. The surveillance officers assigned to the team usually devote a considerable amount of time in the early stages of the probation process to observing the youth's activities, often having daily contact with the probationer. The probation counselors, on the other hand, provide weekly counseling services to the client and the family. The frequency of contacts is reduced as progress is demonstrated. The team leader supervises, coordinates, and evaluates the progress made by the youth in regard to behavior change. If the probationer demonstrates significant changes in behavior and school performance and attitude, the team leader will general make an appeal to the court to have the youth's probation status changed from intensive probation to regular probation.

13.8   Probation Revocation

If a youth violates the conditions of probation or is involved in new illegal activity, probation can be revoked. Generally, the supervising probation officer will receive information that the juvenile has been arrested or will become aware of violations of conditions or probation while conducting routine supervision. The probation officer will then prepare a report of the violations, which includes a recommendation as to whether the juvenile should be brought into court to discuss the violations and whether revocation of probation should be sought. Minor violations usually do not result in revocation, but may bring about the assignment of additional conditions of probation. If the violations made known to the court are very serious, or if new offenses have occurred, a youth's probation may be revoked by the juvenile court judge. Institutionalization will probably be the result.

The decision to revoke probation is based on a substantial violation of the general or special rules of probation. For example, the commission of another delinquent act or violation of a court order to attend school could result in revocation. In *Mempa* v. *Rhay* (389 U.S. 128, 1967), the U.S. Supreme Court ruled that an adult probationer charged with a violation of his probation had a right to have an attorney present at the revocation hearing. In *Morrisey* v. *Brewer* (408 U.S. 471, 92 S. Ct. 2593, 33 L. Ed. 2d 484, 1972), the Court granted the accused due process rights at a probation hearing. The actual right to have a hearing, if revocation of probation is being considered, was established by the Court in *Gagnon* v. *Scarpelli* (411 U.S. 778, 1978). In that case, the Court decided that the accused had a right to both a preliminary and a final hearing on a violation of probation charge. Although none of these cases specifically involved juveniles, the courts have generally conceded that the rulings extend to juveniles and most juvenile courts have incorporated these rights into the juvenile justice process.

13.9   Community Residential Treatment for Delinquents

As research began to reveal that there are limitations in the probation approach, some courts and communities began combining probation with other rehabilitation programs. A youth might be assigned to probation coupled with a work program, a highly structured group counseling program, foster home placement, or placement in a community residential treatment center.

The first community-based programs for juveniles emphasized treatment using behavior modification, guided group interaction, or reality therapy The programs were operated under the auspices of the juvenile court or of the state's youth authority and the youths were under probation supervision. Community-based supervision followed the principle of "minimization of penetration," that is, the least restrictive alternative disposition was chosen for offenders to give them only the penetration into the juvenile justice system necessary to change their behavior and protect the community. Often the juvenile courts were given subsidies to develop treatment programs for youths in community settings as an alternative to placing them in institutions.

13.9.1   The Provo Experiment

One of the earliest programs that employed intensive community based treatment began in Provo, Utah, in 1959. Empey developed a system of group counseling in which the youths set the standards for all members of the group. The program, limited to 20 habitual delinquents, used the technique of guided group interaction. With staff guidance, the youths set group standards. They were permitted to participate in problem-solving interactions and involved in decisions regarding discipline, responsibilities of group members, and the readiness of group members for release from the program (Empey, 1977, p. 109).

13.9.2   Kentfields

Another program conducted in a community setting relied on the application of the theories and principles of the "behavior modification" treatment technique. The Kentfields Rehabilitation Program had the goals of increasing desirable behavior and drastically reducing deviant behavior through the use of behavior modification, of providing a less costly alternative to institutionalization, and of reintegrating the boys into the community as productive members. The Kentfields Program attacked the problem of delinquency through four tactics: *work projects*, *group sessions*, *monitoring of home behavior*, and *reintegration into the community*. The work projects involved 4 h of work, 4 days each week. The work was graded each hour by a supervisor, and the boys were given points according to the quality of their work performance. Monitoring of home behavior included contracts between the parents and the boy that were evaluated through the use of charts kept each day and collected weekly. The reintegration aspect of the Kentfields Program involved each boy's choosing a goal when he reached the highest level of the program and working toward its achievement. Goals included return to school, job placement, or vocational training (Davidson, 1970, p. 4).

The early halfway houses developed in the latter part of the twentieth century, such as Highfields and Kentfields, were designed to accommodate most types of adjudicated delinquents whose delinquent behavior was serious enough to warrant institutionalization. The treatment programs were designed to employ a specific approach to treatment, such as *guided group interaction* or *positive peer culture*. Research was completed on the outcomes of the youths who participated in the programs and the results were published. Since the primary orientation of the juvenile justice system was centered on providing treatment for deviant youths (the medical model) rather than punishment, the notion of community treatment facilities was readily accepted during the 1960s and early part of the 1970s. When the focus of the juvenile justice system moved more toward a "just deserts" model in the late 1970s, the notion of community residential treatment for juvenile offenders was not discarded, but there was a dramatic shift in the programs of these facilities. There was much more emphasis on rules, discipline and accepting responsibility for one's behavior. The "Boot Camp" approach that became a popular method for treating the more serious juvenile offender during the 1990s tried to combine the "medical model" and the "just deserts" methods. The camps were designed to provide sufficient punishment that hopefully would deter those youths housed in the camps from committing new offenses, but they also provided rehabilitation programs in the form of counseling and education (Peters, Thomas, & Zamberian, 1997).

As the title suggests, the underlying structure and process followed in the camps was based on a military model. The administrators of the camps as well as the staff were given military titles that designated their position in the hierarchy and wore military type uniforms appropriate for their positions. For example, the camp administrator was usually given a rank of colonel, commander, or above and other personnel, with the exception of the teachers and counselors, were given lower rank titles, such as drill squad corporal and other titles designating the functions they performed in the camp. Although the specific types of treatment provided by the camps varied, they were generally based on some type of behavior modification. The thing all of the boot camps programs had in common was their emphasis on regimentation. The programs stressed obeying rules, respect for superiors, physical fitness, and mental discipline.

Research completed on the effectiveness of "boot camps" revealed that the positive outcomes in terms of the re-offending of the boot camps participants, as well as the development of new social relationship skills, mental development, and attitudes were generally lower than expected. Hengesh (1991, p. 108) summed up the findings in this way, "Although they may be effective in instilling compliance in the short term, if boot camps fail to provide programs to address services and needs, such as education and employment, and if they do not provide intensive follow-up supervision, their value in reducing recidivism clearly seems to be limited."

There was a considerable decline in the use of "boot camps" as an alternative sanction for juveniles adjudicated delinquent during the latter part of the twentieth century. Several reasons for this decline in use include the fact that funding, both state and federal, was not available; many states developed and funded secure community based facilities that were administered at the local level and these were used in place of the boot camps for the offenders that needed to be placed in a secure setting; and the increase in the privatization of juvenile corrections and there was

increased support of "faith based" programs that were based on treatment orientations other than those of the typical boot camp program. However, there is still considerable support for using the boot camp approach as a viable tool for producing
positive change in the behavior of deviant youth. Meade and Steiner (2010) found
that there were 11 states in which boot camp style facilities were in operation, either
under government or private funding. As shown in Box 13.3, the current camps often
differ in philosophy, structure and program from those that were in operation during
the late twentieth century. In addition, the large majority of the centers are for-profit
privately owned programs, and while they generally offer excellent programs and a
highly qualified professional staff, the majority of the parents whose children could
benefit from their program do not have the resources to pay the cost of a stay at the
facilities. Generally, the courts cannot justify a decision to send a youth to one of
these facilities, particularly if the court is operating on a tight budget.

The New Philadelphia Girls Group Home is a public residential treatment facility for girls operated by the Multi County Juvenile Attention System. The program
is described in Box 13.3.

Box 13.3 The New Philadelphia Girls Group Home

The New Philadelphia Girls Group Home (NPGGH), located in New
Philadelphia, Ohio, is one of the seven facilities for youths operation under
the Multi-County Juvenile Attention System. The MCJAS serves five counties
in Ohio. The NPGGH is licensed by the Ohio Department of Job and Family
Services. Referrals to the Group Home can be made by the judges of the five
counties served by MCJAS, and by the children services agencies serving the
five counties. The New Philadelphia Group Home for Girls accepts youths
from counties not in the MCJAS, depending on available bed space.

The NPGGH is a ten-bed facility serving young women between the ages
of 12–17. Girls between 18 and 21 years of age who are either mentally or
physically handicapped, and are in temporary custody of the Department of
Jib and Family Services are also eligible to be housed in the Group Home. The
youths can be qualified for Title IV aid, but this is not a condition for admission.

The mission of NPGGH is to "meet the individual, physical, emotional,
and social needs of the young women, who reside at the Home and to reintegrate them into the community." The goals of the group home are addressed
by a comprehensive treatment program that includes: Education—the residents are to attend school and are enrolled in one of the several schools in the
community; Counseling—individual and family counseling are provided. A
treatment plan is created for the individual needs and history of every resident; Programming—includes group interaction related to the development of
life skills needed as an adult, such as securing employment, managing money,
and establishing priorities; and Group Interaction Programming—directed
toward developing positive interaction, including accountability, self-esteem,
and conflict resolution.

The NPGGH staff works very closely with other agencies in the community including the schools, employment agencies, child service agencies, and the various juvenile justice agencies, toward the ultimate goals of having the girls reunite with their families, be placed in a foster home, or set up for independent living.

Lisa Green, Administrator of the New Philadelphia Girls Group Home, was interviewed by P. C. Kratcoski on July 15, 2019.

Biography

Lisa Green married soon after high school. She raised a family of five children before attending and graduating from Stark State College. She interned at the New Philadelphia Girls Group Home and eventually was employed by the Multi-County Juvenile Attention System She worked at several of its facilities before assuming a position with the NPGGH. Her responses to the interview follows:

Q: How long have you been employed with MCJJA?

A: I have been Administrator since May, 2017.

Q: As Administrator, what are your duties?

A: I manage all of the direct care staff, monitor progress and activities to ensure that the group home operates in accordance with the standards set forth by federal, state, and local authorities. My job it to ensure the security of staff, youth, and all visitors. I assign tasks, provide direction, establish work priorities, and evaluate staff performance to be sure that we are in compliance with the policies and procedures. In addition, I conduct all of the intake and discharge summaries and write all other required reports.

Q: I would like to ask you a few questions about the residents. Who makes the referrals to the group home?

A: Referrals can come from any of our courts in the five counties, or any other agency that we have a contractwith. We cannot take a youth unless there is a contract in place.

Q: Are there any other criteria that must be met for a girl to be accepted into the home in addition to the age requirement?

A: We do not accept any youths that are on suicide watch or warning. Since we are an open setting, it would be too much of a risk. We look at each case individually to determine if they would be appropriate for the group home. We cannot accept a girl who is pregnant.

Q: Are there any other characteristics of a girl that would make her ineligible?

A: Yes, if it is evident that the girl has psychiatric problems or has a medical condition that requires skilled nursing care.

Q: Are there situations in which a girl has to be terminated from the group home?

A: Yes, if a girl continues to be disruptive and her program disrupts other girls' programs, I am able to issue a removal letter.

Q: Please give an example.

A: If a girl refuses to follow the program rules, or leaves the group home without proper permission, it might lead to a removal.

Q: What do you find to be the most difficult part of your job as administrator?

A: Being the administrator, I am not as directly involved with the kids as I was when I was a supervisor, and I miss that. Another difficult thing is when the staff members are struggling with problems or issues and I am not able to help them.

Q: Lisa, what do you find to be the most rewarding part of your job as administrator?

A: Seeing the great changes in the girls during the time they are in the program and when the girls call back after they have left the program to say "thank you," and tell me their success stories.

The community residential treatment programs used today tend to base their approaches on one or several treatment modalities. However, many current programs tend to focus on a specific type of offender (e.g., drug or sex offenders) rather than placing youths with varying problems together in the same treatment program. Another characteristic of current community supervision programs is an emphasis on accountability. Youths are required to show that they are abiding by the rules set for them, and in some instances must make reparation for their offenses by community service or other types of restitution.

13.9.3   Home Detention

In a number of courts, probation supervision is supplemented by home detention. Home detention programs are utilized in lieu of institutionalization for juvenile offenders who need more supervision than can normally be given under the conventional probation plan.

A youth placed in home detention is usually contacted on a daily basis. In exchange for being allowed to live at home, he or she is subjected to an extensive list of rules, which are rigidly enforced. A contract between the youth and the counselor is written up in some home detention programs. The rules include attending school, obeying a curfew, and keeping parents and the probation officer informed of his or her activities. Those under home detention, or house arrest are described as (Office of Juvenile Justice and Delinquency Prevention, 2015, p. 3), "closely monitored (electronically, or through frequent contacts with staff, or both) to ensure that they comply with the conditions that the court has set. Offenders must maintain this strict schedule, leaving their residences only for essential activities, for varying lengths of time depending on the case." Combination of home detention with probation, either regular supervision or intensive supervision, is a viable alternative for the case management of selected youths who have been adjudicated delinquent. For example, the youth is supervised by one officer throughout the progress in other areas, such as family relationships probation process. Also, since both male and female juveniles are eligible for this type of supervision plan, the entire unit can be administered by one director. Often some youths who are awaiting a formal hearing on charges relating to their offenses can be placed under home detention before their hearing in lieu of being held in the detention center. The home detention programs are designed to bring about behavior change and generally follow a behavior modification approach. The youths and their parents or caretakers are often required to sign behavior contracts that detail the conditions of probation and the behavior expected. The probation officers assigned to the youths placed under home detention are required to make frequent contacts with their probationers and provide counseling, when needed. Behavior at home and in school is carefully monitored and checks are made with the court to see if any new offenses had occurred during the time the youth was placed on probation and home detention.

The *home detention* program of the Superior Court, Tippecanoe County, Indiana offers an example of the typical *home detention* program. In this program juvenile probation officers may recommend *Home Detention* (intensive or electronic) to Superior Court IL. If the court mandates a juvenile to complete *Home Detention*, a court order is issued and the juvenile and parent/guardian complete an intake interview and sign a contract. The signed *Home Detention* contract is given to all parties. On average, a juvenile spends 30–60 days on *home detention*, however, the number of days a juvenile is ordered on the program varies" (juvenile Alternatives, 2019, p. 1).

It is difficult to complete comprehensive evaluation research on the effectiveness of home detention programs. A number of variables such as the size of the population being served, the criteria used by the courts to determine the eligibility for admission to home detention, and the differences in the characteristics of the youth placed under supervision. One study (Ball, Huff, & Lilly, 1988, p. 64) found that 82% of the youth placed o Home Detention in a large metropolitan county during a 5-year period were rated as successes, since they did not require placement in the detention center, were available for their court appearances, did not commit new offenses, and did not violate their behavior contracts.

13.9.4   Restitution and Community Service

In instances where the offenses committed by juveniles involve property damage, property loss, or personal injuries to victims, restitution programs are used as a method of holding the juvenile offenders responsible for their actions. In restitution programs, youths involved in offenses that have resulted in property damage or personal injury are required to work at job sites chosen by the court. They generally receive either no remuneration for their work, or just a small amount. The amount they earn, usually the minimum wage, is held until the figure set by the court as payment to the victim is reached. The victim then receives the restitution payment from the court.

Community service is another disposition available in conjunction with probation. Community service programs are closely related to restitution, since they hold a youth accountable for delinquent behavior by requiring work as compensation. In community service, however, the victim does not receive a direct cash payment. Instead, the offender is required to complete some type of public service. In most cases, however, the offender is required to work as a volunteer at a hospital or other type of health care facility or to engage in cleanup or maintenance work at public parks or buildings. No direct payment of the youth's wages is made to either the victim or the court. The judge can require the youth or parents to pay damages to the victim up to the amount allowed by law. Community-service programs do not require the amount of paperwork or the intensive levels of offender supervision needed for restitution programs. They provide some of the same benefits, including development personal Specialized Treatment Programs.

Many community-based programs focus on juveniles who have committed specific types of offenses, with criteria for involvement based on the exhibition of unacceptable behavior or symptoms. These programs are structured to provide specially developed treatment and counseling. For example, the evidence is quite clear that the majority of youths who are processed through the juvenile courts come from dysfunctional families. Those who work with probationers recognize the need to elicit the cooperation of parents, but they also recognize the difficulty in getting the cooperation of the parents. Many of the children are living with grandparents or other relatives and for others their caretakers are foster parents or the staff of a group home. Many of the youths brought before the courts have substance abuse problems, and others have problems controlling their anger and aggression toward others. Some youths have been referred to the juvenile courts as a result of having victimized a person on a sex abuse offense. Many of the youths may exhibit multiple problems that must be addressed by the courts or through referrals to service agencies.

Those who are involved in the management and administration of youth service agencies, including physical and mental health facilities, recreational programs, drug and alcohol treatment centers, family counseling services, welfare work, or juvenile justice agencies, are well aware of the fact that a sizable number of youths they serve are multi-problem adolescents.

If an agency follows the course of trying to address all of the problems identified as pertaining to a particular youth, the result may be to spread available personnel and resources so thin that little is actually accomplished. In addition, staff members may feel uncomfortable or inadequate when called upon to provide assistance in areas outside their professional expertise. If administrators caution personnel to provide services only in the areas in which the agency specializes, the staff may be prohibited from providing services or accepting clients for problems beyond these parameters. In such cases, other difficulties experienced by multi-problem youths may be identified, but ignored. The home situations of some delinquent or status offenders may be evaluated by the court as inadequate, inappropriate, or even dangerous. This may occur when parents lack the ability or inclination to care for or supervise their children or when situations in the home, such as alcohol or drug abuse, family conflicts, or sexual abuse, threaten the welfare of juveniles. Non-secure residential facilities operated or approved by the court meet the needs of such children. Foster homes and group homes are examples of such facilities. Some are designed to serve dependent, abused, or neglected children, while others may be used for status or delinquent offenders.

Foster care refers to the placement of a juvenile in a residential setting outside his or her own home where adults assume the role of parents. Foster parents may take children on a temporary, emergency basis for short periods of time or may assume long-term responsibility for them. Some foster parents will accept only one child at a time, while others have working arrangements with the court to house several children.

Adopt U.S. Kids (2019, p. 1), using government data, notes that there more than 400,000 children in foster care in the United States. It was found that "Children and youths enter foster care because they have been abused, neglected, or abandoned by their parents or guardians. All of these children have experienced loss and some form of trauma." The atmosphere and programs in such facilities should represent as closely as possible home life, to develop trust, respect, and affection toward those assuming the role of surrogate parents. Juvenile probation agencies use foster care for juveniles who have severe family problems. Children placed in foster homes generally have had negative experiences in their own homes and often have experienced rootless movement from relative to relative, or agency to agency, or even periods of institutional placement. Since the need for foster homes and foster parents exceeds the availability, many children who could benefit from such placement are denied the opportunity. A study by the Office of Juvenile Justice and Delinquency Prevention (Little, 1978, pp. 114–115) found that foster-home placements are most likely to be successful if the foster mother was from a family with several brothers and sisters and was an older sibling in the family; had experience caring for a child not her own; has and understanding in handling a number of specific behavior incidents typical of school age children and in understanding and handling the hypothetical behavior problems shown by a "defiant" and "withdrawn" child; and considers each of her own children as distinct individuals. The study also found that a successful foster father grew up in a family with a number of siblings; expresses warmth in talking about his own father and describes his father as affectionate toward him; indicates favorable attitudes toward having a social worker visit the home and make definite suggestions regarding the handling of the foster child; shows understanding and skill in responding to specific behavior incidents and in understanding and handling a "defiant" child and a child who is "careless with his clothes and the furniture in his foster home"; focuses on the foster child's problems, such as adjusting to a strange situation, in talking about what might be difficult in being a foster parent; reports that he and his wife together make major decisions in the family, rather than either of them having greater authority.

Additional factors that contribute to successful foster placement include circumstances in which the foster child becomes the youngest child in the family group; there are no preschool children in the home; and the foster child's natural family retains parental rights, rather than there being a transfer of custody to guardianship.

The social worker available to make and supervise the placement should have had at least several years of experience and is able to have several contacts with the prospective foster parents to prepare them for the placement (Little, Office of Juvenile Justice and Delinquency Prevention, Little, 1978, pp. 114–115.

Group home placement is another option available to the court for youths when removal from the home situation is indicated. Group homes are somewhat larger facilities than foster homes and feature round-the-clock availability of residential and treatment staff members who work in shifts and may not reside at the facility on a full-time basis. Such homes are used for adolescents who have difficulty adjusting to foster care because of behavior difficulties, who have experienced unsuccessful foster care placement in the past, who require more intensive supervision and treatment than foster parents can provide, and who seem to make a better adjustment to life with a group of peers than to a traditional family setting. Group homes in the community that receive delinquent offenders provide more extensive supervision of the youths and are termed "staff secure" facilities. Although the doors may not be locked from the inside and the facility does not normally have an outside fence, there is 24-h staff supervision of the residents, with the youths in someone's vision at all times. The Task Force on Juvenile Justice and Delinquency Prevention and Goals (Task Force on Juvenile Justice and Delinquency prevention, 1977, p. 706) recommended that group homes he limited in size to 4–12 beds and that they be located close to the community from which the residents come.

In group home settings, the development of constructive interpersonal relationships with adults and peers is stressed and decisions about daily life, conduct, discipline, and home activities are made in discussions between residents and staff members. Diagnostic and treatment services are provided by the staff members or through referrals to cooperating agencies. Participation of the group home residents in school and community events is stressed. The activities of the group home are carried out within the boundaries of the supporting agency's guidelines and the requirements for the residents' behavior set by the juvenile court.

13.10 Summary

It is obvious that probation is not the panacea or ideal disposition for all types of offenders. The concept of minimization of penetration entails involving a youth in the juvenile justice system to the least degree necessary to effect positive behavioral changes. Although institutionalization should he used only as a last resort according to this principle, it appears to be the only viable disposition for some youths. Between probation and institutionalization, various levels of structured supervision and treatment may be utilized. In keeping with the notion of individualized treatment, those responsible for developing case management plans for those youths placed on probation must develop a plan that is carefully tailored for the individual juvenile. The plan should consider the potential danger the youth presents to the community as well as the services the youth needs to make the types of changes needed in behavior to be accepted in the community. Various instruments have been developed to assess the potential risk of juvenile offenders to the community, as well as the needs of the juvenile offender in working on their problems. These assessments, as well as the experience of the supervisors are helpful in the development of a case management plan for the youth.

It is very difficult to determine the effects of supervision on probationers, because other factors in the youth's life may also have exerted influences on his or her behavior. Family members, peers, teachers, and other persons in the young person's life may have helped produce behavior changes. In addition, the likelihood that the youth will be able to avoid additional offenses is, to some extent, predictable at the time assignment to probation occurs. Therefore, the success of some probationers in specific programs may be related to their selection for inclusion to enhance the possibility of successful outcomes, so that grant money to continue the programs is assured.

Although some youths can be successfully supervised with few officer contacts, others require intensive surveillance and counseling. Many large juvenile court systems now classify probationers according to their risk fir recidivism and adjust the level of their supervision accordingly.

Probation can be revoked if a youth violates the conditions of probation or commits a new offense A revocation hearing must be held before a juvenile's probation can be terminated.

Many current community supervision programs emphasize accountability. In home detention programs, youths are carefully monitored and required to strictly follow all probation rules. In restitution programs, youths involved in offenses that have resulted in property damage or personal injuries to victims are required to work at job sits chose by the court. The victims receive the offenders' wages until a restitution amount set by the court is reached. Community-service programs require offenders to complete some type of work activity set by the court without pay. In addition, offenders may be required to make cash payments to victims.

The special needs of some youths require that they be placed in community residential treatment. These needs are met by foster and group homes. The activities of community residential treatment facilities are subject to requirements set for the residents' behavior by the court.

13.11 Discussion Questions

1. In some jurisdictions, the same probation officer who conducts the predisposition social investigation may also supervise the probationer after disposition, while in others separate officers are assigned to each of these activities. Discuss the advantages and disadvantages of both types of arrangements.
2. Since many juvenile probationers come from dysfunctional homes, should their parents be *required* to take part in family counseling or parent training? What can be done to assist probationers who are in need of parenting but receive little or no support or interest from their parents?

3. Should probation officers emphasize the surveillance and control of youths in their caseloads, or should they emphasize providing guidance and assistance?

4. Outline the components of a risk/needs assessment instrument used by juvenile courts. Should a standardized risk/needs assessment be required for all juvenile courts?

5. Juvenile court judges have an option of placing a youth on standard probation or imposing a disposition of a commitment to a juvenile correctional facility and then suspending the "imposition of the dis position." How do the two dispositions differ? Which of the two gives the court more control over the youth?

6. Outline the characteristics of community residential facilities. What are the general criteria used for admission to a residential facility? What are some of the factors that might exclude a juvenile male from being admitted? Why might a juvenile female be excluded?

7. Define "probation revocation." What are the reasons why a juvenile might have his/her probation revoked? What is the judicial process followed in a probation revocation?

8. Differentiate between general rules (conditions) of probation and special rules (conditions) of probation. Give an example of a general rule and a special rule.

9. Discuss some of the pressures related to the job faced by juvenile probation officers that might inhibit their effectiveness.

10. Discuss intensive supervision of juveniles placed on probation. Is intensive supervision a viable substitute for commitment to a juvenile correctional facility?

References

Adopt US Kids. (2019). *About the children* (pp. 1–4). Retrieved from https://www.adoptuskids. org/meet-the-children/children in-foster care/about-the-children

Ball, R., Huff, R., & Lilly, J. (1988). *A model house arrest program for juveniles: Doing time at home*. Newbury Park, CA: Sage Publication.

Davidson, W. (1970). *Kentfields rehabilitation program: An alternative to institutionalization*. Grand Rapids, MI: Kent County Juvenile Court.

Empey L. (1977). The Provo and Silverlake experiment. In E. Miller & M. Mintilla (Eds.), *Corrections in the community* (p. 109). Reston, VA: Reston Publishers.

Gagnon v. Scarpelli. (1978). 411 U.S. 778.

Hengesh, D. (1991). Think of boot camps as a foundation for change, not an instant cure. *Corrections Today, 53*, 6 (October), 106–108.

Holsinger, A., Lowenkamp, C., Latessa, E., Cohen, T., Robinson, C., Flores, A., et al. (2018). A rejoinder to Dressel and Farid: New study finds computer algorithm is more accurate than humans at predicting arrests and as good as a group of 20 experts. *Federal Probation, 82*(2), 50–55.

Illinois Laws. 1899. pp. 131–137. *Quoted in Paulsen, M. G. (1975)/The Problems of Juvenile Courts and the Rights of Children* (pp. 15–16). Philadelphia, PA: American Law Institute.

Juvenile Alternatives. (2019). *Home detention*. Tippecanoe County, IN. Retrieved February 2, 2019.

Killinger, G., Kerper, H., & Cromwell, P. (1973). *Probation and parole in the criminal justice system*. St. Paul, MN: West Publishing Co.

Kratcoski, P. (2012a). *Juvenile justice administration*. Boca Raton, FL: CRC Press/Taylor & Francis Group.

Kratcoski, P. (2012b). *Interview with Roy Franks*. Probation Officer, Portage County Juvenile Court.

Kratcoski, P. (2019). *Interview with Lisa Green*. Director New Philadelphia Group Home.

Kratcoski, P., & Kratcoski, L. (2004). *Juvenile delinquency* (5th ed.). Upper Saddle River, NJ: Prentice-Hall.

Little, A. D. (1978). *Foster parenting* (pp. 114–115). Washington, DC: Office of Juvenile Justice and Delinquency Prevention.

Meade, B., & Steiner, B. (2010). The total effects of boot camps that house juveniles: A systematic review of the evidence. *Journal of Criminal Justice, 38*, 841–853.

Mempa v. Rhay. (1967). 389 U.S.128.

Meyers, J., & Schmidt, F. (2008). Predictive validity of the structured assessment for violence risk in youth with juvenile offenders. *Criminal Justice and Behavior, 35*(30), 344–355.

Morrisey v. Brewer. (1972). 408, U.S., 471, 92, S.Cr. 2593, 331, ED. 2D 484.

New Philadelphia Group Home Brochure. (2019). Multi County Juvenile Attention System.

Office of Juvenile Justice and Delinquency Prevention. (2014). *Alternatives to detention and confinement* (pp. 1–8). Retrieved February 3, 2019, from www.ojjdp.gov

Office of Juvenile Justice and Delinquency Prevention. (2015). *Risk/needs assessments for youths* (pp. 1–8). Retrieved January 31, 2019, from www.ojjdp.gov/mpg

Peters, M., Thomas, D., & Zamberian, C. (1997). *Boot camps for juvenile offenders*. Washington, DC: Office of Juvenile Justice and Delinquency Prevention.

Rudes, D., Viglione, J., & Taxman, F. (2011). Juvenile probation officers: How the perception of roles affects training experiences for evidence-based practice implementation. *Federal Probation, 75*, 3–10.

Sickmund, M., & Puzzanchera, C. (Eds.). (2014). *Juvenile offenders and victims: 2014 national report*. Pittsburgh, PA: National Center for Juvenile Justice.

Sies, I. (1965). *From the probation officers desk*. New York: Exposition Press.

Smyka, K. (1984). *Probation and parole, crime control in the community*. New York: Macmillan.

Task Force on Juvenile Justice and Delinquency Prevention. (1977). *National Advisory Committee on Criminal Justice Standards and Goals, Juvenile Justice and Delinquency Prevention*. Washington, DC: U.S. Government Printing Office.

Vincent, G., Guy, L., & Grisso, T. (2012). *Risk assessment in juvenile justice: A guidebook for implementation*. New York, Models for Change. Retrieved January 31, 2019, from http://modelsforchange.net/publications/346

Chapter 14
Perspectives on Juveniles Incarcerated in Secure Facilities

14.1 Introduction

One option judges consider during their deliberation on an appropriate disposition for adjudicated delinquents in the juvenile court process is an out-of-home placement. Adjudicated offenders can be placed in nonsecure foster or group homes, secure residential treatment centers, or juvenile correctional facilities that have various levels of security. The juvenile codes of some states require placement in secure institutions for adjudicated delinquents who have committed certain serious or violent offenses, while other states continue to allow the judge discretion in the disposition choices for all offenses. If a youth receives a disposition of institutionalization, the length of time spent in the facility is dependent on the determinate or indeterminate disposition standards of the state. If indeterminate sentencing applies, the period of confinement is relatively open-ended, with the maximum stay generally being the age statutorily defined as the upper age of juvenile court jurisdiction in that state. Release of the youth occurs after a period decided by the youth's behavior in the institution and the institution staff's or committing judge's assessment of the youth's progress toward rehabilitation. In contrast, a determinate disposition is a specification of institutionalization for a narrowly defined length of time, set when the juvenile court disposition is made, with release occurring after completion of this time.

Although the majority of states still use indeterminate dispositions, a national survey revealed that a few states have implemented totally determinate dispositions for commitment or release of juvenile offenders and other states have adopted determinate sentencing for specific types of juvenile offender. Sickmund and Puzzanchera (2014, p. 186) report that the age limits of jurisdiction may be extended for juveniles who were convicted under provisions, called "serious delinquency" statutes, which "mandate that a subset of delinquents (usually statutorily labeled serious, violent, repeat or habitual) be adjudicated and committed in a specific manner different from other committed delinquents." They state, "Some states may keep a juvenile in placement for several years beyond the upper age limit of original jurisdiction, others can-

© Springer Nature Switzerland AG 2020
P. C. Kratcoski et al., *Juvenile Delinquency*,
https://doi.org/10.1007/978-3-030-31452-1_14

not. Laws that control the transfer of juveniles to criminal court also have an impact on juvenile placement rates." Those sentenced under a provision of a "serious offender" statute, as well as those juveniles bound over to the criminal courts will receive commitments that may vary significantly from the type given other adjudicated delinquents.

The statutes may require a minimum length of confinement or placement in a specific type of facility. On the basis of the trend toward statutorily required placement of serious and violent offenders in institutions, it is not surprising that many of those held in correctional facilities are juveniles who committed very serious offenses, or are repeat offenders. Sickmund and Puzzanchera (2014, p. 187) report that the number of youths held in residential placement decreased by almost one-third (116,701 in 1997 and 79,166 in 2010) from 1997 to 2010. However, the profiles of the youths held in residential facilities remained the same, with approximately 85% of the youths being held for delinquency offenses, almost one third of the offenses being against persons, and almost one-fourth of the delinquency offenses were violent offenses. From 1997 to 2010, the number of facilities holding juvenile offenders decreased by 21% (2842 in 1997 and 2259 in 2010). The major decline in residential facilities was in the private sector, with a decrease in the number by one-third. The number of public residential facilities for juveniles remained about the same during this time period. Sickmund and Puzzanchera (2014, p. 187) note, "In 2010, private facilities accounted for 51% of the facilities holding juvenile offenders, however, they held just 31% of juvenile offenders in residential placement." In addition, the characteristics of juvenile offenders in private facilities are often different from the characteristics and offenses of youth held in public facilities. An analysis of the profiles of youth houses in resident facilities, both private and public, and of the various types of structures and programs for these facilities will be given later in the chapter.

Commitment to a juvenile institution has been found to be strongly correlated with continued criminal behavior as an adult. In *The Young Criminal Years of the Violent Few,* Hamparian et al. (1985, p. 18) continued to follow the arrest and incarceration histories of a cohort of juveniles who had been arrested for at least one violent offense and followed through their juvenile years. As adults, more than three-fourths of those who had been committed to juvenile training schools were arrested after release from the training school and more than two-thirds of those arrested went to prison at least once.

The offenses committed by those youths held in residential placement ranges from the most serious felony offenses to minor misdemeanor offenses such as simple assault and vandalism. Sickmund and Puzzanchera (2014, p.188) provide the distribution of juvenile offenders in residential placement for the year 2010. Thirty-seven percent of these juveniles had committed one or more offenses against persons, 24% had committed property offenses, 7% drug related offenses, and 11% public order offenses. The most frequent person offenses was robbery (10% of the total), followed closely by aggravated assault (9% of the total). The most frequent property offense of the youth in residential placement was burglary (10% of the total) followed by theft (5%). Only 7% of the total number of youth in residential placement were committed on drug related crimes. These included trafficking, possession, and other drug related offenses. Of the 11% of the total who were in residential placement for public order offenses, 4% of the total were committed on weapons offenses and the remaining 7% on a variety of public order offenses such as disturbing the peace, creating a riot, and disobeying a lawful order.

Although the number of youth incarcerated in juvenile correctional facilities has been declining in recent years, the number of juveniles in secure institutions and the combination of serious, moderate, and minor severity offenders in the same facilities have resulted in a growing emphasis on control and impersonality, as evidenced by use of uniforms, regulation haircuts, regimentation of movement, and enforced silence. Threats of physical violence from other residents, assignment to demeaning tasks by institution staff, extortion, and physical and sexual assaults by stronger inmates occur. The endless, carefully programmed routine of institutional life offers little opportunity for developing personal skills or using creativity or imagination un less they are applied to schemes for obtaining or secreting contraband, planning criminal activities to be carried out after release, or fantasizing about the world outside and what life will be like after release.

As juvenile institutions become more and more like those for adult offenders, a look at the history and development of these institutions will place the problems they face today in perspective.

14.2   History of Juvenile Institutions in America

In the American colonies, children found guilty of repeated incorrigibility could be sentenced to death. Those who were regarded as having tendencies toward such behavior could be placed in adult houses of correction for indeterminate periods of time. The 1650 Connecticut Blue Laws made specific provisions to this effect:

> Whatsoever Childe or servant within these Lihherties, shall he convicted of any stuhhorne or rebellious carriage against their parents or governors, which is a forruner of the aformentioned evills, the Governor or any two Magistrates have lihberty and power from this Courte to committ such person or persons to the House of Corrections and there to remaine under hard labour and severe punishment so long as the Courte or the major parte of the Magistrates shall judge meete. (Cole, 1974, p. 13)

It should be noted that even though execution or imprisonment of children for committing various offenses, even minor ones, was allowed in the statutes, the most common court responses to youthful misbehavior were whippings or the release of the child to the custody of parents (Platt, 1974, p. 129).

Throughout the Colonial period and in the first years of the new republic, some children accused of crimes were sentenced in adult courts and remanded to adult prisons. The first institution specifically for juveniles was created in 1824 in New York City, financed by public funds and the Society for the Reformation of Juvenile Delinquents. This institution, dubbed a "House of Refuge" by its founders, James W. Gerard and Isaac Collins, separated juveniles from adults but did not offer them less severe treatment. Such devices as the ball and chain, handcuffs, leg irons, and whipping have been documented as being used there (Cole, 1974, pp. 14–15).

Children followed a regimented routine from sunrise to dark, without hope of release until they reached adulthood. The House of Refuge movement spread rapidly in the eastern United States and persisted until the close of the nineteenth century. In areas where such facilities were not constructed, children continued to be held in jails and prisons.

In 1857, a "cottage system" was implemented at a state reform school for boys in Lancaster, Ohio. Instead of housing the youths in one structure with cell blocks, the cottage system placed them in small groups in separate small buildings, under the supervision of cottage parents. This arrangement provided for more homelike surroundings and individualization of treatment. The cottage design is still widely used for many juvenile institutions (Caldwell & Black, 1971, p. 269). However, the more recently constructed juvenile correctional facilities tend to be modeled after the adult facilities holding medium security inmates. Rather than having a dormitory style sleeping area, they have separate rooms (cells) holding one or two residents and the doors to the rooms are locked during the bedtime hours.

The Child-Saving Movement not only led to the creation of the juvenile court system at the turn of the century, also had some influence on the design and treatment methods of institutions for juveniles. The fact that many juvenile institutions today are located in rural areas may have its origins in the "child savers" firm belief that urban life was conducive to delinquent behavior and that children would benefit from an acquaintance with rural life. A female advocate of the Movement expressed this notion in the following way:

> Children acquire a perverted taste for city life and crowded streets; but if introduced when young to country life, care of animals and plants, and rural pleasures, they are likely.... to be healthier in mind and body for such associations. (Leonard, 1879, p. 174)

14.2.1 Orphan Trains

From 1854 through 1929, New York's Children Aid Society operated "orphan trains" that transported homeless and deprived youngsters to the Midwest. These trains stopped at preselected towns and the local people, usually farm families, had opportunities to look over the passengers and, if they chose, select one or more to live with them. Children placed on the trains were either orphans or those whose parents had relinquished custody of them to the Society. One passenger on an "orphan train" described the experience in later years:

> The trip was a great adventure.... We couldn't get done gawking out the windows. Boys were in one compartment and girls in another. We had no idea where we were going. At Savannah [Missouri] they took us to the courthouse and lined us up, you know, like they was going to mow us down with a machine gun. People walked up to us and said a few words and moved on. My brothers were all picked the first day, but I wasn't taken 'till the second. People came up and felt our arms and legs, and mine were kind of spindly. I was hoping that whoever picked me would have plenty to eat, that was my main goal. (Cole, 1974, p. 13)

Some of the foster families treated the children well and eventually adopted them. Others kept them in an "indentured servant" status, overworking them and giving them little affection. Children who were separated from brothers and sisters sometimes lost contact with them or did not see them for many years (Jackson, 1984, p. 95).

Other ideas for juvenile institutionalization included school ships, which were anchored in the harbors of port cities and took the inmates on short voyages under the regulations of naval life, and military schools, which viewed strict martial discipline as beneficial. A wide variety of these were reserved for wayward children, orphans, or unwed mothers. They were generally under the auspices of religious groups, and often not available for the urban poor or for minority group members. Foster home placement was also introduced, but did not gain wide popularity (Cole, 1974, p. 13).

The development of the juvenile court, based on the idea that the state, acting as a benevolent substitute parent, would provide individualized attention to each child under its jurisdiction, ushered in the era of treatment and rehabilitation. In the early twentieth century, this took the form of inculcating what were viewed as desirable work habits, coupled with a liberal amount of religious training.

The techniques of placing youths on farms, using military or seamanship discipline, training them for specific trades, or using cottage arrangements were all fads of certain decades, but they persist in some manner in today's juvenile institutions The programs in these institutions appear to have run in cycles, with a certain form of program coming into existence, gaining wide acceptance, proliferating to other institutions, and then dying out in favor of some new strategy. There is a logical explanation for these changes to occur. During the 200 years or so juveniles have been institutionalized for one reason or another, and more specifically, during the more than 100 years since the establishment of a juvenile justice system, the philosophy and perspectives of those who had authority over youths who were defined as deviant has changed from time to time. At one period their perspective was predominately punishment orientated, at another period it was predominately orientated to "saving" the child by offering counseling and treatment. In addition, the types of programs offered in juvenile institutions, farms, and camps became obsolete and no longer a useful preparation for one's further occupation. For example, well into the latter part of the twentieth century delinquent youth were sent to forestry camps and farms. With the exception of developing good work habits, these types of programs are not likely to lead to any employment for the urban youths who are housed in the facilities. Even such vocational programs as auto mechanics and carpentry are not likely to be productive, because the facility does not have the resources to purchase the highly technical and expensive equipment needed to properly train the young people. In addition, the large majority of the youths do not have the educational background to succeed in such training programs. As will be shown in the following chapters, the main thrust of the programming in juvenile institutions at the present time is toward education and counseling.

14.3   Types of Correctional Facilities for Juveniles

Short-term facilities include detention centers, shelter homes, and reception and diagnostic centers. Juveniles may also be held for short periods of time in adult jails.

14.3.1   Detention Centers

Detention centers are secure facilities that hold youths for whom release prior to juvenile court hearings is judged too risky because of the nature of the offense (violent behavior or running away), the inadvisability or impossibility of return home (physically or emotionally threatening situations, or refusal of parents to accept responsibility), or the need for physical or mental examination or treatment. Youths held in detention centers or jails are guaranteed a hearing within an established time period. Detention centers also hold juveniles who have been adjudicated delinquent and are waiting residential or institutional placement or have been committed to the detention center as a disposition.

In the cases of habitual and violent juvenile offenders, placement in detention without possibilities for release prior to hearings has been upheld by the U.S. Supreme Court. The Court's support of such action, was given in *Schall* v. *Martin* (1984, 52 U.S.L.W. 4681). It was based on the need to promote the welfare of the community by barring the alleged offender the opportunity to commit new offenses while awaiting a hearing on the original offense.

The initial decision to place a child in detention is made by the juvenile court's intake officer or a member of the detention facility staff. Although most courts have guidelines as to the characteristics of youths who should be detained, research indicates that the detention decision is often based on several factors, including the severity of the offense, the number of prior offenses of the youth, the available alternatives, and the support of the parents or caretakers. Sickmund and Puzzanchera (2014, pp. 192–193) provide information on the characteristics of youths who are held in detention centers. Although the large majority were alleged juvenile offenders awaiting a hearing on a charge of delinquency, almost one-fourth were adjudicated offenders who were committed to the detention centers, or were given a community placement, such as probation, and had violated the conditions of probation, either by committing a new offense or through a technical violation. A survey of more than 100,000 youths held in residential placement (Sedlak & McPherson, 2010) found that 25% were held in a detention facility, 32% in correctional facilities, 10% in camps, 18% in community based residential facilities and 14% in residential treatment facilities.

The type of administration of detention facilities for youths, as well as the type of structure and programs offered for the youth housed in such facilities, vary, depending on the jurisdiction of the court, size of the population served, and the resources available. Kratcoski (2012) notes that, in its Standards and Goals for the Detention of Children and Youth report, the National Council on Crime and

Delinquency (1975, pp. 41–42) recommended that detention facilities should have administrative services, housekeeping services, arrangements for health services, access to psychiatric and psychological services, religious activities, educational programs, as well as individual and group counseling, as required by federal or state laws. State and federal minimum standards for detention centers require that the youth be given food, clothing and bedding, some recreation and opportunities to exercise, and the opportunity to participate in school (Kratcoski, 2012, p. 241).

Because the potential for a child to attempt suicide is the highest when first admitted to the detention center, those who exhibit any indication of suicidal or mental health symptoms should be tested by a psychologist or psychiatrist. Although state laws vary, many states prohibit children who are victims of abuse, neglect or were abandoned and have not been accused of a delinquent offense (no fault) from being housed in a youth detention center. If a state allows the housing of dependent, neglected and abused children in such facilities, they must be separated from those who are awaiting a hearing on delinquency charges and those youths who are serving a disposition (sentence) in the detention centers.

Since detention centers are short-term holding facilities, where a youth's stay may range from a few hours to 180 days, programs implemented in detention centers must be adaptable to a constantly changing resident population. Many of the youths are being held for relatively minor offenses, such as probation violations or property and public order offenses. Others have committed serious, violent offenses, and members of a third group may be experiencing detention as a disposition. Although the Juvenile Justice and Delinquency Act (JJDPA) enacted in 1974 (JJDPA, 1974, amended 1977, p. 310) stated that status offenders should not be placed in secure detention facilities, Sickmund and Puzzanchera (2014, p. 190) found that in 2010 5% of the youths committed to a secure juvenile facility were committed for status offenses. Many of these were youths who had violated a court order.

Several states permit placement of adjudicated delinquents in detention facilities for periods up to 180 days as a disposition. Rationales for such placements include the possibility that this will give a youth exposure to the deprivations of institutionalization without a long-term commitment and this experience may turn the youth away from activity that would lead in that direction. It also lets youths know that the juvenile court can deal with them in a more severe way than release on probation.

Programming in juvenile detention centers has two functions—maintaining control and providing some basic treatment. Well-developed programs in detention demonstrate to the youths involved that efforts to assist them and change their behavior have begun and they also keep the detainees occupied and reduce the possibilities for boredom and misbehavior.

The Responsible Behavior Program used by the Multi-County Juvenile Attention System in Ohio (Vanderwall, 2001, pp. 5–6) is grounded in behavior modification. A resident can progress from the lowest status (New Arrival) to the highest status (Youth Aide), depending on behavior and conformity to the rules and regulations of the Center. A higher status gives more privileges, freedom, and trust. Residents are evaluated daily on personal hygiene, room appearance, behavior at meals, job

Box 14.1 The Summer Learning Institute
Biographies of Directors: Dr. Kristine Pytash and Dr. Lisa Testa

Kristine E. Pytash is an Associate Professor in Teaching, Learning and Curriculum Studies at Kent State University's College of Education, Health, and Human Services (EHHS), where she directs the Secondary Integrated Language Arts Teacher Preparation Program. She is a former high school English teacher. Her research focuses on the literary practices of youths in detention facilities. The underlying theme across all her lines of inquiry is how technology significantly influences young adults' literacy practices and their literacy instruction. She recently published *Writing in the Margins: Exploring the Writing Practices of Youth in the Juvenile Justice System.*

Dr. Pytash and her colleague, Dr. Testa, were the recipients of the Directors Award for Programming in Juvenile Detention Centers from Ohio's Department of Youth Services and was the 2017 recipient of the Rewey Belle Inglis Award for Outstanding Service Relating to the Role and Image of Women in English Education sponsored by the National Council of Teachers of English Gender and Literacy Assembly.

Dr. Elizabeth "Lisa" Testa is an assistant professor in the School of Teaching, Learning and Curriculum Studies at Kent State University. She teaches under-graduate and graduate coursework on teaching and learning, as well as a course in English education and literacy. She works closely with many local K-12 partners, providing opportunities for preservice teachers to gain clinical field experiences in secondary schools. Her research interests include studying teacher education and preservice teachers' conceptions of teacher writing.

The Summer Learning Institute

The summer Learning Institute addresses two current issues in education. First, youth in juvenile detention centers often receive a basic skills education that does not adequately prepare them to return to their traditional school, nor is it culturally responsive, honoring their cultures and experiences, in ways that prompt student engagement and motivation. Second, teacher candidates need clinical experiences to learn how to develop and implement interdisciplinary learning units that are design-based and rooted in culturally relevant pedagogies. During the Summer Learning Institute, both of these issues are addressed, as teacher candidates from Kent State University's Masters in the Arts of teaching program, work closely with Dr. Pytash and Dr. Testa to design and implement engaging lessons to the youth housed at the Summit County Juvenile Detention Center.

The Summer Learning Institute is interdisciplinary, with a focus on topics that are relevant to the youths. The 2018 Institute focused on issues within the city of Akron, while the 2019 Institute focused on service learning by partnering with the non-profit organization, *Hands of Gratitude*.

The overall goal of the Summer Learning Institute is aligned to the belief that all students, especially our most disenfranchised and marginalized youths, deserve "access to a world class, intellectually challenging curriculum" and that teachers are prepared to meet this expectation. Thus, all lessons are rooted in culturally relevant pedagogies, and an emphasis is placed on showing how the students' lives and cultures are critically connected to their learning experiences.

Interview of Dr. Kristine Pytash (Conducted by Peter C. Kratcoski, August 3, 2019)

Q: Please describe how the idea for the program developed.

A: The idea grew from my research on investigating the literacy practices of youth in juvenile detention facilities. As I learned more about the authentic and meaningful ways that youth engage in reading and writing, I recognized disconnect between the education they receive and their personal literacy practices. While their personal literacy practices were highly relevant and meaningful, the educational opportunities they were receiving in detention centers were very much focused on remediation. As an educator, I knew that all youth had a right to an education and I wanted to work with teachers to make sure that the youth in detention centers had educational experiences that were highly motivating and engaging and drew on research-based literacy practices.

Q: Did either of you have experience working in juvenile justice, either as an employee or as a volunteer?

A: No, it was our first experience working with young people.

Q: Is the program open to youth who are not in the Summit County Juvenile Detention Center?

A: No our partnership exists with the Summit County Detention Center. It would be very difficult to have youth from the outside attend because of security reasons.

Q: How many participants were in the Summer Learning Institutes?

A: Typically, we serve approximately 40 youth. The number and the demographics (gender, age,) will vary depending on the number of youth in the Center and their demographics housed at the Detention Center.

Q: Did you have any major problems (obstacles) in implementing the program?

A: We have been incredibly thankful to work with the teachers and staff at Summit County. Their commitment to recognizing the need for this work has made it exciting to implement this program and so far we have not had any major obstacles.

Q: You mentioned that the first year of the Institute you focused on issues within the city of Akron. Please describe some of the activities the group engaged in during that summer.

A: Over the course of this project, students grew in their conceptions of public spaces and their understanding of the scope of purposes of these spaces and opportunities for citizens to share their interests with the city of Akron. The participants explored multimodal compositions and digital media; engaged in culturally responsive learning connecting students' lives' cultures, and communities to learning; designed "welcome to Akron" signs and sculptures; discussed the racial, political, and religious issues facing Akron; developed an understanding of special advantages and disadvantages; composed a photo essay centered around entertainment in Akron; and developed various skill sets, such as entrepreneurial, engineering and marketing.

Q: Have you thought about expanding the program to other juvenile courts?

A: Not at this time.

Q: What did you find the most gratifying from your experiences with the program?

A: Probably the most gratifying moments come when we are working directly with the youth- when they understand a concept or will talk about how much they liked an activity and we can see their passion for learning the material. Also, we have had teacher candidates decide to work in certain school settings because of this experience. To see their growth as teachers and their understanding that all students/youth deserve access to educational opportunities that are research based and engaging, is important. At the end of each session, youth present their work. To see their pride in their learning and the skills they developed makes us feel like we've accomplished our goals.

performance, participation in activities, performance in the educational classes, and respect for staff and other residents.

Youth held in detention centers for any length of time must be given at least the minimum standards of living as required by the laws of the state. These include decent living quarters, adequate food, and some opportunity to engage in some form of exercise. Some juvenile detention centers will have a gym and a weight room. In addition, the centers will have classrooms and employ certified teachers. The school year in many facilities extends throughout the entire year. Health needs must be met and nurses may be part of the staff or have been contracted to come to the facility when needed. Generally contracts are made with medical doctors, social workers and psychologists who provide their services when they are needed.

Generally, the administration of the detention center will allow various volunteer groups to come to the facility to provide some form of religious, educational or entertainment programs. For example, often students attending a local university will volunteer to provide assistance to the residence who are having difficulties in school, other groups may provide counseling in anger management and other provide faith-based services. Some volunteers do not have any planned program, they just interact with the residents or play board games with them during the time when the residents have free time in the early evening. Many of the programs are focused on having the participants express their feelings about themselves, and their feelings toward their parents, authority figures, and their community through art, poetry, music, and drama. For example, Dr. Kristine Pytash and Dr. Lisa Testa, after researching initiatives in alternative school settings, including juvenile detention centers, implemented a program, titled *Designing Identities* at the Summit County Juvenile Detention Center. Their programs runs through the school year, with the main focus in the summer, during the time the regular school held in the Detention Center is not in session The Summer Learning Institute is described in Box 14.1;

14.3.2   Juveniles in Adult Jails

In local jurisdictions that have no detention centers exclusively for juveniles, youths are held in detention by being placed in a separate section of the local jail. The 1974 Juvenile Justice and Delinquency Prevention Act required that to be eligible for federal funds for juvenile justice programs, jurisdictions must provide plans for separate, nonsecure detention facilities for status offenders and not house them with delinquent offenders (Correctional Council of the National Council on Crime and Delinquency, 1975, p. 6). The Act was amended in 1980 to prohibit confining any juveniles in adult jails (Dale, 1991, p. 30). In 1985, six conditions were set under which youths could be held up to 24 h in adult jails. These include being charged with a delinquent (criminal) offense; being held awaiting a court appearance; residing in a state that requires court appearance within 24 h, exclusive of holidays and weekends; being placed in a jail that is outside a major metropolitan area; no other acceptable alternative exists; and juveniles is separated by sight and sound from adult detainees. Youths who have been waived for trial in adult criminal court may be held in adult jails and a child may be held in jail up to 6 h for identification, processing, or transfer (Dale, 1991, p. 30). In 1996, these requirements were modified to provide that brief and inadvertent or accidental contact with adult offenders in nonresidential areas was not a violation, that the 6-h hold rule was expanded to include 6 h before and after court appearances, and that adjudicated delinquents held in juvenile facilities could be transferred to adult facilities in states where such transfers were authorized or required by law once they reached the state's age of full criminal responsibility.

Sickmund and Puzzanchera (2014, p. 220) reported that in 2010, 7600 inmates younger than 18 were housed in jails. This figure is approximately 1% of the total jail population for that year. Although there has been some variations in the percentage of youth held in adult jail facilities (the peak being 2%) the 1% of the jail population has remained relatively consistent over several decades. Sickmund and Puzzanchera (2014, p. 210) state, "The vast majority of jail inmates younger than 18 continue to be those held as adults. Youths younger than 18 may be held as adult inmates if they are convicted or awaiting trial as adult criminal offenders, either because they were transferred to criminal court or because they were in a state that considers all 17-year olds (or all 16 and 17 year-olds) as adults for purposes of criminal prosecution." There are several other reasons why a juvenile might be held in an adult jail facility. In some jurisdictions, there is no facility available to hold youths who allegedly committed a delinquency offense and if the youth is not released to the parents or caretaker, the youth is housed in the jail until there is a hearing. In such cases, youths adjudicated delinquent will either be given a community disposition, such as probation, or sent to a secure juvenile correctional facility. In other cases, juveniles may be held in the jail for a short period (no more than 24 h) until they can be transported to a juvenile detention facility located in another jurisdiction. In other cases, the juvenile may be housed in a lock-up cell in the jail for a few hours until the youth's parents are contacted or until arrangements can be made to house the youth in a community residential facility, such as a group home.

Incarceration in an adult jail can have devastating psychological effects on young people. The requirement that youths be held out of sight and sound of adult inmates has, in some instances, resulted in placement in solitary confinement. Kerle (1991, p. 3) states, "Compliance with this rule often meant that juveniles were placed in solitary confinement with all of the punitive consequences, such as curtailing the time a child could actually spend outside of his cell. Sight and sound separation in many instances has proved to be detrimental rather than beneficial. Although the practice of holding children in adult jails has been roundly condemned, it is apparent that efforts to remove juveniles from adult jails have not been successful. It is particularly important that strategies be implemented to inform and educate state and local elected officials, law enforcement personnel, and judges about the hazards and liabilities of jailing children. Jails lack adequate physical plant facilities; adequate numbers of appropriately trained staff members; as well as adequate health, recreational, and other programs to meet the minimum standards of juvenile confinement."

14.3.3 Shelter Homes

Shelter homes provide short-term care of youths in a nonsecure environment. These shelters are used primarily for juveniles referred to the courts as dependent or neglected children, although, as noted earlier, the Juvenile Justice Act of 1974 recommended that status offenders in need of temporary shelter be placed in such facilities rather than in detention centers with delinquents.

Public shelter homes are usually small facilities (housing 1–12 youths) and are most often administered at the local level. Private shelters are financed by contributions of public and private agencies, individual contributions, or support from the United Way or similar plans. Although youths placed in detention are almost always sent there by the police or the juvenile court, children placed in shelter facilities may be directly referred there by parents, children's service agencies, or other social agencies.

14.3.4 Reception or Diagnostic Centers

Some states have reception or diagnostic centers to which the youths given a disposition of institutionalization are referred for study and evaluation before placement in some type of long-term incarceration facility. In those states without reception or diagnostic centers, or in cases of referral to private institutions, the judge designates the specific facility in which the youth will be placed at the dispositional hearing.

A reception or diagnostic center generally operates under the administration of a state agency responsible for youth corrections. Youths are tested and evaluated for a period of 1–6 weeks after assignment to the center. The evaluation includes medical, psychological, and attitude testing to help the staff decide upon the most auspicious placement for each youth.

14.4 Long-Term Secure Facilities

Long-term incarceration facilities include training schools, ranches, forestry camps, farms, halfway houses, and group homes. Training schools (often termed "Youth Development Centers") are the more secure types of juvenile correctional facilities. Those known as ranches, forestry camps, or farms provide residential treatment for youths who are not regarded as needing secure confinement and separation from the community.

Sickmund and Puzzanchera (2014, p. 187) report that there were 2259 public and private facilities housing 79,166 juveniles in 2010. The large majority of these youth were adjudicated delinquent, but a small proportion were status offenders, or juveniles who had violated a court order. (VCO). Sickmund and Puzzanchera (2014, p. 187) note that although just over half of these facilities are private facilities, they house less than one-third of the juveniles in residential facilities. Public facilities are administered by the state. They comment that "State or local government agencies operate public facilities, those who work in these facilities are state or local government employees. Private facilities are operated by private non-profit or for-profit organizations; and those who work in these facilities are employees of the private corporation or organization." Private facilities tend to hold a smaller population than public juvenile residential facilities and many of them have a specialized program, such as drug abuse treatment.

Physical Structure. The type of structure used to house institutionalized delinquents may range from cell-like living quarters in an old facility resembling a fortress, with uniformed custody personnel who perform security functions, to the prep school or summer resort atmosphere of small cottages, which attempt to imitate a homelike setting, complete with house-parents. The majority have a relatively open architecture without a perimeter wall or fence, and include a number of dormitory-like buildings called cottages, a school building, an administration building, and a vocational (work) area. Generally, 15–40 or more youths may be assigned to each cottage. Often a special cottage that has more security will be used for those residents who present discipline problems. This cottage will have small rooms, and with the exception of having a door instead of bars at the entrance, tends to resemble the type of cell one would find in a jail or prison. Each room will have a toilet and sink to wash one's hands and face. Those held in the disciplinary cottage, will be isolated from the other residents in the juvenile institution. Examples of two facilities are given below in Box 14.2. The Red Wing Correctional Facility for Juveniles is an older structure and resembles a prison. In contrast, the Youth Correctional Center administered by the North Dakota Department of Corrections and Rehabilitation is structured along the cottage style and provides a secure environment for those juveniles who are held pending a court hearing and disposition of their case. It houses a variety of juvenile offenders, male and female, who are housed in different cottages, depending on security, safety concerns as well as their treatment needs.

Box 14.2 Minnesota Correctional Facility: Red Wing and North Dakota Youth Corrections Center

"The Minnesota Correctional Facility—Red Wing—was constructed in 1889. Red Wing provides treatment, education, and transitional services for serious and chronic male juvenile offenders placed at the facility either as a condition of court-ordered probationers as the result of having been committed to the commissioner of corrections. The facility also provides detention and predisposition evaluation services as requested by the courts." Minnesota Division of Juvenile Justice/Red Wing Facility (2019, p. 1).

"Juvenile residents participate in the facility's cognitive/behavior restructuring and skill development treatment program. Risk/needs assessments are completed for each resident, and outcomes are used to measure progress toward treatment plan completion. All residents are expected to develop an individualized relapse prevention plan and demonstrate its effectiveness during daily activities prior to their release."

"The Youth Correctional Center administered by the North Dakota Department of Corrections and Rehabilitation has the mission of providing professional care to troubled adolescents within a safe environment. The facility is structured to allow the residents to be housed in separate living quarters (cottages), depending on the type of offense committed and their personal characteristics…. The cottages are semi-independent in that all essential services pertaining to health, mental health, counseling, recreation, and education are provided for all residents, but in addition the staff of each cottage provides a variety of programs including assessment, detention, time out treatment and special management that are tailor-made to take into consideration the gender and special needs of the youths, designed on the evidence based principles of Motivational Interviewing and strengths-based approaches that target resiliency and protective factors, in additional to stimulating and critical thinking and moral reasoning through experiential activities and guided discussions" (Youth Correctional Center, 2019, p. 2). https://docr.nd/facilitiesoffice-locations-test/division-juvenile-services/youth-correctional-center Accessed 4/19/2019).

This description cannot be applied to all types of training schools, since many of the newer facilities, designed to house older, more hardcore types of delinquents, resemble prison structures, with individual rooms, an outer fence that may have sensing devices, and other means of closely controlling movement within the institution. There is a growing emphasis on control and an impersonal atmosphere, as evidenced by use of uniforms, regulation haircuts, regimentation of movement, and enforced silence.

Organizational Goals. It is difficult to generalize about the specific goals on which an institution has focused. Long-term institutions for youth have a general mandate to control those placed under their jurisdiction, protect the community, provide treatment, and rehabilitate inmates. The extent to which these goals are actually pursued depends in many ways upon the state youth authority under which the institution is operated, or upon the sponsoring organization in the case of private institutions. Some institutions are almost totally custody-oriented, some are strongly committed to treatment, and others attempt to balance custody and treatment in their programming. Street et al. (1966) characterized three types of organizational models found in juvenile institutions as *obedience/conformity, re-education/development*, and *treatment*. The *obedience/conformity* institutions were seen as focusing on close control, emphasis on rules, and enforcement of negative sanctions for inappropriate behavior. In contrast, they characterized the *re-education/development* institutions as emphasizing changing the youths through training, skill development, and rewards for appropriate behavior. *Treatment* institutions were committed to defining the sources of youths' misbehavior and addressing them through specific treatment techniques to help the youths to become better adjusted and prepare them for return to the community. They also noted the existence of "mixed goal" institutions, which focused on both custody and treatment (Street et al. 1966).

It is also possible for all of the organizational models described by Street et al. to exist within the same facility. In a study of ten cottages within a juvenile institution, Feld (1984) reported that some had programs similar to those of industrial training schools, while others concentrated on individual or group treatment. He also described a cottage that closely resembled the *obedience/conformity* type described by Street et al. (1966). The youths in this cottage had been runaways or discipline problems.

14.5   Unit Management (Functional Units) Organizational Model

The functional units organizational model was developed and used by the U.S. Bureau of Prisons at a facility for juvenile delinquents who were adjudicated by the federal judicial system for violation of federal law at a facility located in Morgan Town, West Virginia named the Robert F. Kennedy Facility. Gerard (1970, pp. 37–40) described the classification process. On arriving at the facility, the boys were initially housed in the classification cottage and given several tests based on the Quay Behavioral Classification Model. The housing (cottage) assignments were made based on the boys' behavioral traits revealed on the tests, observations by the staff, as well as interviews. For example "those considered to be "inadequate-immature" were housed in a unit in which the counselors were "instructive, patient, reassuring and supportive," in contrast to those youths who were "unsocialized aggressive" who were assigned to a cottage with counselors who were "tough minded, direct, and able to avoid being manipulated." Each cottage was self- contained. The unit managers and their staff could design programs that best fit the security needs and treatment needs for the youth housed in their cottages.

The Ohio Department of Youth Services Circleville Juvenile Correctional Facility comes close to filling the description of a "mixed goals" institution. It serves male youths. Units are designed to house and provide treatment based on the characteristics and needs of the residents. The Circleville Juvenile Correctional Facility (Ohio Department of Youth Services, 2019, p. 1) "provides a variety of services and treatment for youth including a fully accredited high school, behavioral health services, unit management, medical and dental care, recreation, religious services, community service opportunities and reentry services." The treatment programs are geared to assisting the youth who have problems relating to substance abuse, anger, aggression and violence, depression, anxiety, self-injury and others such as gang involvement. A number of programs either staffed by the Circleville JCF personnel or volunteers are offered in the areas of horticulture, victim awareness, graphic design, anger, aggression and violence management, music, and art. Students from several colleges and universities located near the facility provide tutoring (Ohio Department of Youth Services, 2019, p. 1).

Although most residents of juvenile institutions participate in school, work, or vocational programs and at times receive individual or group counseling, when matters of security arise, the overall concern tends to gravitate toward keeping down escapes and internal disturbances. The prevailing goal becomes maintaining order and security and treatment programs must conform to this reality. Institution administrators, as well as the directors of state agencies, are particularly sensitive to negative community reaction or political criticism. Smoothly running facilities tend to be equated with good facilities in the eyes of the public.

14.6 Classification of Residents: Based on Security Risks and Special Needs

When a youth is adjudicated delinquent and committed to a correctional facility, the committing judge will pronounce a commitment to a state agency but will not specify the specific correctional facility to which the youth should be sent. The exceptions to this procedure are those youths given dispositions to private facilities. In these cases, the youths are admitted directly to the private facility. The private facilities for juveniles usually offer specialized programs such as drug abuse treatment, or they are designed for offenders with specific problems such as being emotionally disturbed.

When a youth is admitted to long-term institutionalization, the facility to which he or she is committed and the specific assignment or type of treatment given are determined in a number of different ways. If there is a statewide reception and diagnostic system, the judge will remand the youth to the state youth authority at the time of disposition. The juvenile is then sent to a diagnostic center where a battery of physical psychological, personality, and vocational tests are administered. After a period of observation, a decision is made as to which institution would best serve the youth's needs. In the larger states, institutions may be differentiated on the basis of security needs, the sex and age levels of the inmates, and the seriousness of the offenses committed by the youths housed there.

Within a specific training school, the same types of categorizations are frequently made. The aggressive, older youths are assigned to one cottage or section and the younger, less mature ones are kept in another. Some states have incorporated classification treatment models that provide information to help make the initial placement. The models also furnish guidelines to the type of treatment that would most probably be beneficial to the youth. These models are grounded in the concept of differential treatment, which means tailoring the treatment program to the individual problems and psychological needs of the residents. The classification process involves several steps. First the youth's needs and problems are assessed. This step is achieved in several ways. The youth is interviewed, the file on the youth that was sent from the admitting court is reviewed, and the youth might be given several tests relating to personality, behavioral traits, and other related areas, including emotional and mental health matters. Next, a classification committee will develop a program for the youth, that includes the custodial level needed in terms of living quarters, and the type of treatment and programming that is best suited to the child's particular needs, and abilities. The next step is to follow through by implementing the plan, providing the guidance and treatment recommended, making observations on the progress of the child, and, if needed, modifying the program. The assessment s of the youth's behavior and progress while in the institution should be continuous up until the youth is discharged or released on parole.

14.7   Treatment Programs in Secure Institutions: Academic and Vocational Education, Individual and Group Counseling, Recreational Activities

As noted in an earlier chapter, the "medical model" of juvenile court intervention popular in the 1950s and 1960s regarded the problems that brought youths into the juvenile justice system as treatable once they were properly diagnosed. When treatment efforts appeared to produce little change in the behavior of the youths involved in a wide variety of programs, administrators became increasingly skeptical about the effectiveness of treatment. This was particularly true of institutional treatment programs. By the mid-1970s, a national survey of correctional administrators found that only about half of them viewed rehabilitation as the primary goal of juvenile institutions, while another quarter considered rehabilitation and public protection to be their major goal. The remainder regarded public protection, punishment, and other goals as most important. Skepticism over the effectiveness of institutional treatment continued to grow in the 1980s and 1990s, with resulting changes in the emphasis placed on treatment programs within institutions. As the inmate population becomes increasingly composed of more hardened and violent offenders, institutional treatment has focused on security, and less emphasis has been placed on resolving their personal difficulties or maladjustments.

The *right to treatment* for involuntarily confined juveniles was confirmed by the *Morales* v. *Turman* (1974) court decision. In this case a U.S. District Court ordered two Texas institutions closed because of the lack of treatment there and the harsh and cruel punishments given the inmates, including beatings, use of crowd-control chemicals, and long-term solitary confinement. It ordered the establishment of community-based treatment facilities for the youths involved and set up detailed procedures and standards for providing treatment. In *Nelson* v. *Heyne* (1974), the U.S. Court of Appeals declared that institutionalized juveniles have a constitutional as well as a statutory right to treatment under the 14th Amendment. The treatment techniques used in some institutions, including behavior modification and aversive conditioning, have been criticized as constituting control mechanisms rather than true treatment. Debates over the nature and types of treatment which should be offered in institutions continue.

Most long-term institutions provide some educational opportunities of an academic or vocational nature, work experiences, recreation, and some form of individual or group counseling. Which of these is given the highest priority depends upon the age, sex, and other characteristics of the residents. If the average age is approximately 13–15, the institutions tend to emphasize educational programs, supplemented by counseling, arts and crafts, and recreation.

Institutionalized youths do not differ from the general population in their intellectual ability, but they are usually functioning at several grade levels below their age group in academic achievement. This condition is frequently due to long absences from school or deprived home environments. In some institutions, students must attend school for the entire day, but half-day sessions with short classroom periods are more common. Small classes allow individualized instruction. The curriculum centers on the development of basic skills along with the internalization of good work habits and respect for authority. Juveniles who graduate from institutional school programs receive diplomas from the local school district, which do not contain the information that attendance took place within the institution. Some institutions (including many private ones) allow youths to attend the public schools in the community.

Vocational programs in institutions frequently stress skills that help maintain and serve the institutions' needs, such as cooking, gardening, or laundry service. Others incorporate training in computer skills, barbering, cosmetology, metalworking, woodshop, or auto mechanics. Such a program may be handicapped by a lack of modern equipment or well-trained instructors, but in some cases it has enough depth to prepare a youth for a work position after release.

In institutions for older offenders, those who will not be expected to return to school after release, the major focus of the treatment plan is centered on providing work experiences. In ranch, farm, or forestry-camp settings, work constitutes much of the daily activity of the resident. Some institutions allow youths to work in state facilities such as hospitals, parks, or forest reserves during the day and return to the institution at night. Because of the concern for security, however, the majority of the work activities tend to be concentrated on the grounds of the institutions.

Kratcoski (2012, p. 429) notes that the treatment programs generally found in use at juvenile correctional facilities combine cognitive and behavioral therapies. Regardless of the title given to the therapy, cognitive treatment strategies generally emphasis the principles that a youth should think before acting, consider the possible outcome of the behavior, consider alternative ways of responding, and the impact the action might have on others.:

Counseling is crucial to any treatment program for institutionalized youths. Much of the counseling is directed toward helping them adapt to the institutional setting and preparing them for return to the community after release. Group counseling is widely used because group techniques play upon the strong peer group influence present in adolescence, as well as upon the acknowledged importance of the inmate subculture in influencing institutional behavior. Some institutional group counseling focuses on specific offender needs. For example, after it was discovered that nearly 60% of those held in Kansas's only state institution for delinquent girls had been sexually abused (Moore, 1991), a counseling program was developed. In addition to helping the girls discuss the abuse they experienced in group sessions, the counseling focused on inappropriate feelings or behavior that may result from being sexually abused, including developing a negative self-image, distrust of adults, substance abuse, or running away. Participation is voluntary and, since dealing with sexual abuse is a long-term process, the group sessions continue through the girls' stay at the institution and the girls are encouraged to join support groups after release.

Guided group interaction is a group technique that has received favorable comment as a treatment method. In guided group interaction, there is an awareness of the dynamics of the peer group culture and the importance of the group in influencing the values, attitudes, and behavior of those incarcerated at the facility In guided group interaction, the professional staff (group leaders) are rather unintrusive; they only gets the group started and from time to time keeps the group directed. Each group member is considered responsible for all other members and each has an opportunity within the group setting to examine and evaluate his or her life experiences, personal deficiencies and handicaps, and strengths. Members of the group are expected to provide constructive support in helping each other achieve maturity and overcome their problems. If one member of the group fails, it is a reflection on the entire group.

Another method of group treatment that had aroused considerable public interest for a short period was the creation of "boot camps" designed to imitate the physically and emotionally challenging programs the armed services use for their new recruits. The appeal of boot camps is easy to understand. Offenders were given "no-nonsense" tough disciple in a no-frills atmosphere. They were held for relatively short periods of time (usually 90–120 days), thus making the programs less costly than long-term institutionalization. Those committed to boot camps were usually nonviolent, older adolescents incarcerated for the first time (Hengesh, 1991).

The majority of the state governments, and many local governments operated boot camps, but after several evaluation reports that concluded the outcomes of youths completing such programs were no different than those who were incarnated in the more traditional juvenile correctional facilities, the emphasis on boot camps faded for several reasons. Funding was not available; states started developing community based treatment facilities that served the same purpose as the boot camps; and the growth of private facilities that offered a different type of program and experience, including faith based programs became popular. The boot camp experience would seem to address many of the problems youthful offenders have, including low self-esteem and lack of self-discipline. Programming is designed to demonstrate to the youths that they can succeed in nondelinquent activity. It may be that the experience is too short to have a lasting effect. As Hengesh (1991, p. 108) observed, "Do not consider military boot camps as an instant cure. They are not intended to make a young person into a fully functional soldier. Rather, they provide a foundation of discipline, responsibility and self-esteem the military can build on during the advanced training that follows." Using this analogy, observers have concluded that boot camps will be much more effective if they are seen as the first step in a lengthier process of change. After the initial boot camp experience, the released youth should be given intensive supervision in the community in an aftercare status so that the habits of personal discipline and responsibility for one's actions can be monitored and reinforced in the environment to which the youth has returned.

14.8   Factors That Inhibit the Effectiveness of Institutional Programming

The power of juvenile institutional programs to provide treatment is often limited by pressures to maintain tight control and custody to present a good image to state officials and prevent adverse reactions from the citizenry. The quality or amount of education, vocational training, or even civilized interaction between confined juveniles is frequently reduced in the name of security. The outward appearance of a smoothly running, secure institution becomes the primary goal and other goals become subordinated to it. In addition, lengthy exposure to the deplorable conditions in many institutions for delinquent youths creates a kind of psychic numbness in the staff and they become indifferent.

Having observed numerous juvenile correctional facilities in several different states, as well as completed research, interviewed administrators and staff, during a period starting in the early 1960s to the present time, Kratcoski (2019) notes that the success or failure of an institution to achieve its goals depends on a variety of factors. Some of these are beyond the control of the administration and staff, because the philosophies and the goals change. Dedicated staff as well as administrators must go along with the changes ordered from officials. In some cases, the director of a facility just does not have the vision or experience to develop and implement a viable program. In other cases, the communications and cooperation between the treatment staff and custodial staff are flawed, and when a decision has to be made between placing an emphasis on security of treatment, the security emphasis usually takes priority.

There have been positive changes in the operations of juvenile correctional facilities. Evidence-based instruments for assessment of risk and needs have been implemented, new treatment modalities have been implemented, custodial staff are generally better trained, particularly in defusing potential conflict situations and disturbances. The use of classification systems helps to assure that the juveniles sent to institutions will be housed in the appropriate facilities. Many of the changes came about as a result of court decisions and legislation requiring minimum standards in regard to food, clothing and living quarters, restrictions on the use of solitary confinement and the use of physical punishment. Procedures that were acceptable during an earlier time, but are illegal at the present time.

14.9   The Juvenile's Response to Institutional Life

Juveniles placed in institutions find that they must adapt to two forces working upon them with conflicting goals and modes of operation—the staff and fellow residents. To achieve the goals of release, the juvenile resident must seem to be cooperating with the staff and progressing in the treatment program set up for him or her. At the same time there are pressures from fellow residents that must somehow be dealt with. The resident subculture may make demands upon the juvenile that are at odds with those made by the staff.

There is a great deal of evidence that correctional institutions have a negative impact on the residents. Even under optimal conditions, there are dangers that the youth might be physically or sexually assaulted by the staff or other residents, be victimized through extortion, be humiliated or confused, develop a negative self-image, and experience other forms of deprivation. Residents may be hostile to the staff and each other and react to the experience badly.

Research (Cellini, 1994; Poole & Regoli, 1983) revealed residents are not always treated equally or fairly. Deals are made between youth workers and strong juveniles in institutions to preserve the "peace." This may involve giving these youths special privileges that have not been merited through their behavior, smuggling in contraband for them, or looking the other way when the more aggressive residents use verbal abuse and threats to intimidate the weaker residents. In addition, some of the custodial staff were open to manipulation, because of being poorly trained, or because they just wanted to take the easiest way to "get through the day" without any major disruptions or conflicts. Underpaid youth workers struggling for advancement or older workers afraid of losing their positions may be particularly vulnerable to being manipulated by the residents.

14.10   Victimization and Violence in Institutions

Studies of violence and aggression by the inmates of secure institutions have attributed this behavior to either the *deprivation perspective* or the *cultural-importation perspective*. According to the deprivation perspective, aggressive behavior is a response to the harsh conditions, degradation, and deprivation the inmate experiences. The cultural-importation perspective, in contrast argues that violent and aggressive behavior is merely a manifestation of previously held values and behavior patterns that the inmate brings to the institution and uses to gain as many advantages and material rewards as possible.

Hamparian et al. (1985) conducted a study of aggressive behavior by youths in four juvenile correctional institutions that varied in organizational structure and programming from custodial to treatment-oriented. They found that a history of aggressive behavior was the most important variable in explaining inmate aggression within an institution, regardless of the type of institution in which the youth was held. A history of aggressive behavior, however, appeared to have a stronger influence on the aggressive behavior of individuals in treatment-oriented institutions than it did on those in institutions with a custodial emphasis. The researchers noted that the depersonalization and deprivation in this coercive environment may make the pains of imprisonment so acute, encompassing, and restrictive that the potential influences of pre-prison variables are largely blocked.

. To address the problem of institutional violence, security and treatment personnel are being trained in crisis intervention and management techniques and policies and procedures for handling disruptive incidents are being clearly defined. The physical environments in which youths with a history of violence are held must be designed to ensure the safety of the youths, other residents, and staff members. A staff team approach and staff education on how to deal with such emergency situations as resident assaults on staff, riot control, or hostage taking should be provided. The rural locations of many training schools also contribute to the isolation of residents from their families, since the majority of the incarcerated residents are urban youths.

14.11   Institutional Effectiveness

It is difficult to separate the effects of institutionalization from all the other factors in a youth's life that must be considered in attempting to ascertain if those effects are predominantly positive or negative. Most youths released from institutions return to their former environments, family situations, and peer-group influences, all of which may have contributed to the development of their delinquency.

Recidivism statistics for youths released from institutions are difficult to obtain. Once released, a youth may have no future contact with institutional personnel unless he or she is recommitted for a new offense. And since many youths leave institutions when they are close to the upper age limit of the juvenile status, future offenses are referred to the adult system and may not be brought to the attention of juvenile justice system personnel, since there is little communication and exchange of information between the two systems on such matters. These conditions, in addition to the geographic mobility of families, and particularly of young adults, make compilation of recidivism data a difficult task. There is a general perception that the failure rate for all types of institutionalized juveniles, measured in terms of new offenses, is quite substantial. This raises the question of how success and failure should be measured. If a child has learned to cope in a better matter with his or her environment, social situation, and family problems, and has developed ego strength and internalized a prosocial value system, should the institutionalization process by considered successful even if the young person engages in some future delinquencies? Or should a youth who stays within the law after release but emerges from the institution hostile, dependent, emotionally scarred, or fearful of authority be rated a success merely because of lack of recidivism. The contaminating effect of the association of less serious offenders with hardened delinquents is another harsh fact of institutional life. Even youths who do not learn specific modes of unacceptable behavior or criminal techniques from others are bound to be influenced by the barrenness of institutional life. For some youths the institutional experience provided a more secure and structured environment than they had before incarceration, nevertheless institutional life is not an experience that will prepare young people for the "real world" to which they will have to make an adjustment after being released from the juvenile correctional facility. Generally, there is little room for refinement, cultural development, or creativity in the experience, and most important, there is little opportunity for the youth to use their judgment to make decisions that will have an effect on their future lives.

14.12   Normalization

Normalization means providing those youths who are drawn into the justice system with experiences that approximate as nearly as possible those of normal community life. For example, the situation farthest from "normal" is removal of a child from home and community and placement in an artificial, structured environment that is far removed in activities and interactions from ordinary life. The situation closest to "normal" would be supervision within the home community, either in the youth's own home or in some type of community residential treatment. In the case of youths who need secure custody, the institutional experience should be made as nearly normal as possible, through placing them in small group units, allowing them to retain their individuality in dress and possessions, encouraging them to develop their talents, and providing opportunities for contact with the outside world.

In the 1970s, (U.S. Department of Justice (1977, pp. 5–7) the state of Massachusetts took a radical step toward normalization by closing almost all of its training schools and placing the formerly institutionalized youths in other types of programs. In an attempt to humanize treatment, therapeutic communities were developed within the existing institutions. Youths were allowed to wear their hair as they chose and wear street clothes rather than institutional garb. Marching in silent formation was discontinued. Several facilities for the most disturbed or rebellious youngsters were eventually closed. Attempts were made to develop programs for girls and boys in the same institution and even in the same cottage. The length of stay for youths was reduced from an average of 8 months to an average of 3 months.

Attempts were made to change the authority system in the institutions by emphasizing group processes within the cottages. The juveniles were given a good deal of decision-making responsibility for their individual units in the hope of counteracting the negative effects of the inmate subculture.

Although some of its juvenile institutions were reopened during the "just deserts/ get tough" era that followed, eventually the trend toward deinstitutionalization and normalization became a national movement, and continues today. The Massachusetts experiment must be regarded as a milestone in juvenile correctional reform. It advanced the goal of more humane treatment of youthful offenders and showed that community placement is a viable disposition that can safely and effectively be used in lieu of institutionalization for many juvenile offenders.

14.13   Summary

The youths institutionalized in the United States vary widely in their personal and behavioral characteristics. Populations of long-term, secure institutions are largely made up of hardcore offenders who have been placed there after repeated attempts to change their behavior or supervise their activities have been fruitless. These adjudicated delinquents receive determinate (set length) sentences or indeterminate (open-ended, possibly extending to the upper age of juvenile court jurisdiction) sentences, depending on the standards of their state. Other institutions, particularly private institutions, house youths who pose no threat to the community but have been placed in these facilities after options for their care or placement in other situations have been exhausted.

Juvenile correctional facilities include long-term facilities (training schools, ranches forestry camps, farms, halfway houses, and group homes) and short-term facilities (detention centers, shelter homes, and reception and diagnostic centers). Juveniles are also held in adult jails. Short-term facilities function as holding points for youths before their juvenile court hearings or after adjudication but prior to longer term placement, although in some states detention can be given as a disposition. Youths in adult jails may be held there because their cases have been transferred to adult criminal courts, or because there is no available detention facility for juveniles. Long-term facilities may be rather open or highly secure. The most secure type of juvenile facility, the training school, exists in all states. Training schools may vary in appearance from old fortress-style buildings to modern cottage settlements. Their programs and goal orientations also vary according to the attitudes and guidelines of the controlling state authority, the institution, and the staff. Youths are normally classified and treated according to their dangerousness, observed social or psychological problems, age, and sex. Educational and vocational programs are used, together with various types of individual or group therapy and counseling.

Institutions have not demonstrated their effectiveness in deterring youths from further criminal behavior. Punishment or control, rather than rehabilitation, is too often the most important consideration. Physical brutality and mentally debilitating cruelties have frequently been documented as occurring in juvenile institutions.

Young people respond to their institutional experiences in various ways, ranging from open rebellion, manipulation, or mindless conformity, to a genuine change of attitude and behavior. Harmful effects of institutionalization include isolation from family and community, exploitation by other inmates, acquaintance with more hardened delinquents and schooling in crime, and development of a general feeling of hopelessness and abandonment.

Experiments with removal of all but dangerous offenders from institutions and their placement in community-based treatment have been attempted, with the most radical approach being Massachusetts closing its juvenile institutions. The Massachusetts experiment revealed that community placement can be safely and effectively used instead of institutionalization for many juvenile offenders.

14.14 Discussion Questions

1. Why have some states passed serious delinquency statutes? Do you thing this trend is a reaction to the criticism that juvenile courts are "soft on serious delinquency offenders?"
2. Why is the decision to hold a juvenile in detention rather than release him or her such an important one? Do you agree that the factors presented on the risk assessment instruments used by juvenile detention centers are the appropriate ones to consider in making this decision?
3. Juveniles held in institutions for long periods of time tend to develop an informal social system, with the leaders having power and privileges over the other residents. What are the conditions in institutions that tend to bring about the formation of such informal groupings?
4. Why does the placement of juvenile offenders in "boot camps" have such appeal to the general public? Why do you think the boot camp experience does not seem to have long-term effects in changing behavior?
5. Are long-term juvenile correctional institutions effective in deterring delinquent behavior? Discuss.
6. What are the functions of classification (diagnostic) centers? Describe the process followed in the classification of a juvenile committed to a correctional facility.
7. What are the functions of juvenile detention centers? How do they differ from juvenile correctional facilities?
8. What factors account for the disturbances and violence that occasionally occur in long-term juvenile correctional facilities?

9. Discuss the difference between the importation theory and the cultural deprivation and the importation perspective with regard to institutional violence.
10. Administrators of juvenile correctional facilities must maintain a balance between
    their concern for the safety and security of the staff and the residents and providing
    treatment programs designed to make positive changes in the residents. Discuss
    the factors that can upset this delicate balance between security and treatment.

References

Caldwell, R., & Black, J. (1971). *Juvenile delinquency*. New York: Wiley.

Cellini, H. (1994). Management & treatment of violent institutionalized delinquents. *Corrections Today, 57*(40), 98–101.

Cole, L. (1974). *Our children's keepers*. Greenwich, CT: Fawcett.

Correctional Council of the National Council on Crime and Delinquency. (1975). *Status offenders and the juvenile court* NY: National Council on Crime and Delinquency.

Dale, M. (1991). Children in adult jails: A look at liability issues. *American Jails, 4*(5), 30–37.

Feld, B. C. (1984). A comparative analysis of organizational structure and inmate subculture in institutions for juvenile offenders. *Crime and Delinquency, 27*(3), 106–108.

Gerard, R. (1970). Institutional innovations in juvenile corrections. *Federal Probation, 34*(4), 37–44.

Hamparian, D., David, J., Jackson, J., & McGraw, R. (1985). *The young criminal years of the violent few*. Washington, DC: U.S. Department of Justice, Office of Juvenile Justice and Delinquency Prevention.

Hengesh, D. (1991). Think of boot camps as a foundation for change, not an instant cure. *Corrections Today, 53*(6), 106–108.

Jackson, D. (1984). *It took trains to put street kids on the right track out of the slums* (Vol. 15, p. 95). Washington, DC: Smithsonian.

Juvenile Justice and Delinquency Act. (1974, Amended 1977). *National Advisory Committee on Criminal Justice Standards and Goals, Juvenile justice and delinquency prevention* (p. 310). Washington, DC: U.S. Government Printing Office.

Kerle, K. (1991). Juveniles and jails. *American Jails, 4*(5), 30.

Kratcoski, P. (2012). *Juvenile justice administration*. Boca Raton, FL: CRC Press/Taylor & Francis Group.

Kratcoski, P. (2019). Unpublished research:1969–2019: Past and present.

Leonard, C. (1879). *Family homes for paupers and delinquent children*. Chicago; Proceedings: Annual Conference of Charities. Quoted in Platt, A. *The rise of the child saving movement* (p. 123).

Minnesoto Division of Juvenile Justice (2019). Red Wing Juvenile Facility https://mn.gov/doc/facilities/red-wing/juvenile/accessed7/6/2019

Moore, J. (1991). Overcoming the past. *Corrections Today, 53*(1), 43–47.

Morales v Turman. (1974). 383 F. Supp. 53 (Ed. Texas).

Nelson v. Heyne. (1974). 491 F.2.2d (7 Cir).

North Dakota Department of Corrections & Rehabilitation. (2019). Youth Correctional Center. Retrieved April 19, 2019, from https://docr.nd.gov/facilityoffice-locations-test/division-juvenile-services/youth-correctional-center

Ohio Department of Youth Services, (2019). Juvenile Correctional Facilities-Circleville. https//www.dys.ohio.gov/juvenile-correctionalfacilities/circlevilleJCF. Accessed 6 Jul 2019

Platt, A. (1974). The rise of the child-saving movement: A study of social policy and correctional reform. In F. Faust & P. Brantingham (Eds.), *Juvenile justice philosophy* (pp. 129–137). St. Paul, MN: West Publishing Company.

Poole, E., & Regoli, R. (1983). Violence in juvenile institutions. *Criminology, 21*(2), 213–232.

Schall v. Martin (1984). 52 U.S.L.W. 4681.

Sedlak, A., & McPherson, K. (2010). *Conditions of confinement: Findings from the survey of youth in residential placement. OJJDP Juvenile Justice Bulletin (May)*. Washington, DC: U.S. Department of Justice.

Sickmund, M., & Puzzanchera, C. (2014). *Juvenile offenders and victims: 2014 national report*. Pittsburgh, PA: National Center for Juvenile Justice.

Street, D., Vinter, R. D., & Perrow, C. (1966). *Organization for treatment*. New York: Free Press.

U.S. Department of Justice. (1977). *Juvenile correctional reform in Massachusetts*. Washington, DC: U.S. Government Printing Office.

Vanderwall, D. (2001). *Multi-county juvenile attention system responsibility behavior program*. Canton, OH: Multi-County Juvenile Attention System.

Chapter 15
Parole and Community Supervision

15.1 Introduction

The following cases illustrate the types and gravity of the offenses of juveniles adjudicated delinquent and committed to juvenile correctional institutions. After a period of time in the correctional facility, the majority of juvenile offenders are released before their 18th birthday and placed on parole (aftercare).

15.1.1 Case I: Teen Charged In Attack

A _____ High School student was charged in juvenile court Friday with the stabbing of an elderly couple in their home. [He] faces delinquency charges of two counts of attempted aggravated murder, one count of aggravated burglary, and one count of aggravated robbery.

The [elderly couple] were attacked when they answered the front door of their home. ... Police said Johnson, a tenth grader, came to the home after fleeing the school following a fight.... While handcuffed, (he) bolted from the principal's office and out of the school....

_____ spent 4 years in the custody of the Ohio Department of Youth Services after being convicted of rape in 1998. [He] was paroled in September (approximately 2 months before this incident), according to Kevin Miller of the youth services agency (*Akron Beacon Journal*, Teen charged in attack. November 2, 2002, B4).

© Springer Nature Switzerland AG 2020
P. C. Kratcoski et al., *Juvenile Delinquency*,
https://doi.org/10.1007/978-3-030-31452-1_15

15.1.2   Case II: Teen Suspected in Chapel Hill Robbery

A 16-year-old recently released from a youth prison was charged Saturday in connection with the kidnapping and robbery of two young women in the Chapel Hill
Mall parking lot... Police said _____ approached (the women) while they were
walking to their vehicle. (He) then allegedly pressed a handgun to the cheek of (one
of the women) and demanded money... forced the women into their car and made
them drive him to a cash machine... (He) got away with an undetermined amount of
cash from the victims. After being apprehended (he) told police that he was just
released from Indian River Juvenile Correctional Facility...where he had been serving time for an aggravated robbery charge (*Akron Beacon Journal*, teen suspected in
Chapel Hill robbery. January 20, 2003, B6).

   The trends in juvenile justice policy include longer dispositions (sentences) for
juvenile offenders, more juveniles being institutionalized, transfer of more and
more juvenile cases to adult criminal courts, and use of blended sentences. Even
though many serious juvenile offenders are held in institutions for long periods of
time, nearly all of them will be released and returned to the community at some
point. Most of these will still be under juvenile justice system supervision after their
release from the institution. In the large majority of cases, they will be returning to
the same situations they were involved in before incarceration. In spite of the best
efforts of institutional personnel to positively influence these youths, the institutional experience may have had detrimental effects on them and they may quickly
return to the same patterns of unacceptable behavior that led to their incarceration.
As a result, they may pose an immediate threat to the community. The aforemen-
tioned cases illustrate the importance of the release decision and the need for careful
supervision of youths after release.

15.2   The Juvenile Parole (Aftercare) Decision

There is no standard for determining when a youth should be released from an institution. In most states, commitments are indeterminate in length and can continue
until the juvenile is judged to be rehabilitated or teaches the age of majority, which
is 21 in some state and 18 in others. Most juveniles are not held to the age of majority but are released prior to that time under the supervision of parole (aftercare)
officers in the community. Although determinate dispositions, mandating a specific
length of institutionalization, are now the most widely used type, some states have
responded to the overcrowding problems caused by increased commitments by
releasing youths to aftercare after shorter periods of being housed in a secure juvenile correctional facility. Sickmund and Puzzanchera's (2014, p. 198) analysis of the
Office of Juvenile Justice and Delinquency Preventions Census of Juveniles in
Residential Placement for 2010 revealed that "Among committed juveniles, those
held as court-ordered dispositions 80% had been held for at least 30 days, and 58%

for at least 90 days. After a year, 12% of committed offenders remained in place-ment." Juvenile offenders committed for violent offenses were held for longer peri-ods than those committed for property offenses, boys were held for longer periods than girls, and those in public facilities were held an average of 1 month longer than those committed to private facilities Since the youths who were committed to the institutions for having committed serious (felony) and violent offenses tend to serve a longer period in the institution, and thus are separated from their families, schools and communities, it is expected that they will have a more difficult time reintegrat-ing than those who were institutionalized for shorter periods. In addition, they may be a greater threat to the community than those youths who had committed property types of offenses.

The process of releasing a juvenile from an institution varies, according to the organization of the juvenile justice system in the state from which the youth was originally committed. In those states with a state youth authority or youth commis-sion, the release decision is generally made by an institutional release committee composed of those staff members who have had opportunities to assess the juve-nile's progress in the institution, subject to the approval of a representative of the state youth authority or commission. In those states where commitment is made directly by a judge to a specific institution, the recommendation of the institutional release committee or board is subject to the approval of the committing judge. Even in states where the youth authority or commission makes the release decision, the committing judge may be informed of the youth's release as a matter of courtesy.

The institutional release committee is usually composed of such staff members as the unit (often referred to as pod, cottage, wing) supervisor, social workers, teachers, youth counselors, and a representative of the administrative staff. In cases where the offense for which the youth was committed was extremely serious (mur-der, rape), an examination by and a recommendation from a staff psychiatrist may be required by the committee making the decision.

The factors the committee generally considers in making its decision include the youth's adjustment within the institution, changes of attitude as perceived by test-ing, and observations by the staff members, and the offender's willingness and abil-ity to plan for the future by setting attainable goals. Risk and Needs Assessment Instruments are also employed. In Ohio, the Ohio Risk Assessment System (ORAS) and other assessment instructions, such as Structured Assessment of Violent Risk in Youth (SAVRY) are often used in the assessment of a youth's readiness to be released from a correctional facility to the community. Shepherd, Luebbers, and Ogloff (2016) found that youths incarcerated in a detention facility who scored high on the risk assessment and low on the protective items of SAVRY (pro-social involvement, strong social support, positive attitude toward intervention and author-ity, strong commitment to school, and resilient personality traits) were the most likely to commit another offense after being released from the detention facility. The results of this research suggest that such instruments are useful in helping to predict the youth's likelihood of committing another offense once in the community as well as what factors are likely to contribute to the youth making a successful reintegration in the community. Shepherd et al. (2016, p. 875) concluded that, although it has been established that association with deviant peers is a strong predictor of delinquency recidivism and if the association is discontinued the likelihood of recidivism will decline, the "desistance from criminal behavior may require more than simply a passive withdrawal from deviant peers but rather an active engagement with pro-social peers." In addition to having pro-social peers, Shepherd et al. (2016, p. 875) found, "Other strong predictors of non-recidivism included a positive attitude toward intervention and authority and a strong commitment to school." They conclude, "The findings of this study support the notion that protective factors/items play an important role in mitigating future re-offense. However, for high-risk individuals, these effects may be limited as evidenced in this analysis. Addressing criminogenic needs should be the primary focus for young offenders, particularly those with violent and/or chronic criminal histories."

When preparing a youth for release from a juvenile correctional facility, the officer preparing the report to be submitted to the release board should consider the youth's family situation, including how much support the youth is likely to receive from the parents, and other factors such as conflict, and drug use or excessive alcohol use by a member of the family, and if there is one or more members of the family involved in criminal activity. If the family situation does not seem to be conducive for the youth to make a successful reentry into the community, an alternative placement, such as a group home, will be arranged. Another consideration is the youth's school situation. If the young person had troubles in school such as poor academic performance, conflicts with teachers, violent and aggression behavior toward classmates, or was expelled from school before being committed to the institutions, a decision to send the youth to an alternative school might be considered.

The community and peer group situation must also be evaluated when preparing the youth for release. If there is a likelihood that the he or she will reestablish contacts with the same friends and try to reestablish the lifestyle that was followed before being incarcerated, a decision to place greater control over the youth after release may be included in the decision. More control can be established through intensive supervision or placement in a group home (halfway house). In some instances, the reaction of the community to having the youth return may be so negative that a decision may be made to have the youth released to a residency center located in another community. These extreme situations may occur if the youth committed a horrific crime such as raping a small child or seriously beating an old person. The decision to place the youth in another community may be for the youth's benefit, since living in the community in which the delinquent offense occurred would be difficult.

The Office of Juvenile Parole and Transitional Services in New Jersey (Department of Law & Public Safety 2019, p. 1) is a community oriented service agency. This office, "provides parole supervision to these juvenile offenders and assists them as they transition to home, their neighborhoods and schools through a gradual, planned and purposeful 'step-down' parole process. This process seeks to hold parolees accountable for their behavior while simultaneously maximizing opportunities to engage each parolee in a re-entry process that facilitates: family reunification; furthers the parolee's education; leads to the development of marketable skills; and the development of those normative skills, such as self-disciplined positive goal directed behavior, and moral values that will enable him or her to become a productive, contributing member of the community."

15.3   The Parole (Aftercare) Process

In keeping with the trend toward differentiating juvenile offenders from adults through the use of separate terminology, the release of juveniles from institutions under the supervision of officers in the community is commonly called *aftercare,* whereas release of adults under the same type of supervision is termed *parole.* However, in keeping with the movement toward more formalization of juvenile justice proceedings, several states now use the term *parole* rather than *aftercare* to describe supervision of juveniles returned to the community after institutionalization.

Youths released from institutions operated under the supervision of a state authority are supervised by aftercare officers employed by that body. Since there are no federal juvenile courts, children under 18 who violate federal laws are dealt with in the U.S. district courts or have their cases transferred to state juvenile or criminal courts and their aftercare is also supervised by state authorities (Federal Criminal Code and Rules, 1991, Section 501). In states where no central authority handles juvenile institutions, local jurisdictions employ juvenile parole officers. In some jurisdictions, the same people may serve as both probation and parole officers.

State juvenile codes provide for several different types of aftercare (parole), according to the determinate or indeterminate dispositions of specifications in the criminal law code of their state. The determinate types differ somewhat, since in some codes the length of parole (aftercare) is part of the specific length of commitment set by the court, while in other types of determinate sentencing the length is set by the supervising agency, based on offense and criminal history. State codes that follow an indeterminate sentencing (dispositions) plan have a set minimum period, but the maximum period, generally set at the age of the youth's 18th birthday, may be extended. Generally, the state codes give jurisdiction to their youth authorities over the youth until the 21st birthday, but the large majority of incarcerated youths will be released on or before their 18th birthday. If there is a need to have the youth incarcerated for a longer period, the youth would have either been bound-over to the criminal court or been given a blended sentence, which would allow the juvenile to be transferred to a correctional facility for adults after reaching a specified age.

The positive aspects of release to aftercare as opposed to continued institutionalization are readily discernible. The shorter the period of institutionalization, the smaller the chance that the youth will become deeply involved in the inmate subculture within the institution. Return to the community at the earliest opportune time allows the positive values, norms, and attitudes of the community to influence a youth's behavior. Return to regular school classes, as opposed to education in the artificial environment of the institution, can also aid the youth in the adjustment process. Aftercare officers' efforts to promote part- or full-time employment for the released juvenile may open doors for him or her and make the difference between continued delinquency and a turnaround in the young person's life. Finally, long periods of institutionalization, except in cases where they are dictated for the protection of the community, decrease the possibility of a successful adjustment after release.

Although the aftercare process is similar in some respects to the probation process, there are some differences. Youths under parole supervision may have had a number of probation supervisions before being sentenced to the correctional facility. Strategies of parole may call for different methods of supervision than those used in probation. Typically, the youth released from an institution will have committed more offenses and more serious offenses than those youths placed under probation supervision. Also, those youths released on parole normally will have been influenced by the institutional culture and will need some time to readjust to life on the "outside," as well as the new set of rules and regulations of the community. Assisting the youth in the readjustment to the family, school, and community is a task performed by the parole officer that is generally not related to a probation officer's role. For some youths, this involves helping them stay away from or resist influences toward misbehavior that are present in the peer culture to which they return. For others, institutionalization may have produced an unhealthy dependence upon others that must be reversed through aftercare activities.

15.4 Preparation for Release

Aftercare personnel deeply involved in the juvenile's treatment program should help the youth assess his or her strengths and weaknesses and make realistic plans for the future. If the juvenile is to return to his/her home on release, weekend visits to the home are often scheduled. In some cases, the youth will be sent to a halfway house before returning to live in the home. The family of the youth would have probably been in contact with him or her during the time of incarceration, and they no doubt had to keep the youth up to date on any new developments in the family. These might include, an older brother or sister getting married, leaving home for one reason or another, and even the mother giving birth to another child. Any major change in the family may have either a positive or negative effect on a young person who had spent months, even years, in a secure correctional facility. If returning to the home seems inadvisable because the environment seems to be unsuitable, or because the parents are unwilling to accept the responsibility for helping in the supervision of the behavior of the youth, or because they are not capable of performing the task, a placement in a resident treatment center, group home, or even a foster home may be an alternative to having the youth return to a family situation that is not likely to be supportive and to facilitate the readjustment process. The National Council of Juvenile and Family Court Judges (1984, p. 17) emphasized that aftercare supervision must be intensive, stating, "Attention should be directed toward gradual re-entry of youths into the community through a staging process, utilizing halfway houses, group homes, day treatment, and other appropriate aftercare programs."

The National Council (1984, p. 17) elaborated on its recommendation by noting that "Far too often serious offenders are returned to the community 'cold turkey,' straight from secure placement without adequate resources and without gradual reintegration into community living.... Failure to assist youths in the reintegration process often causes their gains in residential placement to 'wash out' upon the youth's return to the community."

Readjustment to the community can be more easily achieved if institutionalized juveniles have not been completely isolated during their commitment. Athletic contests, cultural events, field trips, and various types of recreational outings can keep juveniles in touch with community life. Preparation for employment after release should be stressed, in terms of teaching prereleased juveniles the techniques of applying for jobs or preparing them through development of specific skills, good work habits, and a positive attitude toward work. Educational programs in the institutional setting that focus on remedial work or vocational training may also be helpful in preparing juveniles for release. Returning released youths to public schools poses a dilemma for those involved in the transition. Normally, school officials are informed that the returning youth is being released from an institution, but are not given access to the youth's delinquency records, and they may not be informed about the past offenses committed by the youth because of confidentiality laws that are designed to protect the returning youth from being stigmatized or labeled as a deviant by teachers and fellow students. In the case described at the beginning of this chapter, a recently released juvenile who had been returned from the school he attended before being institutionalized fled from the school where he had been placed in detention for fighting, stabbed two elderly people when they answered the door the boy knocked on, and stole the elderly couple's car.

Investigation of the incident (Warsmith, 2002, p. A 9) led revelation of the information that from 45 to 75 juveniles from the state's youth prisons were directly returned to the public schools in the same city each year. As a result of this incident, two state legislators drafted a bill that would require all youths released from state juvenile facilities who have committed violent offenses to be sent to a special alternative school rather than returned to the regular school system.

15.5   The Parole (Aftercare) Treatment Plan

An aftercare treatment plan should be formulated for the juvenile before release. This may involve a return to public school or enrollment in a special type of educational program, registration in a school program that provides time for work release, or direct job placement for those older youths who will not return to school.

Aftercare is an important facet of the juvenile justice process. Most juveniles discharged from correctional facilities are placed under parole supervision. The parole (aftercare) officers are responsible for providing supervision for youths released from state corrections facilities. The major tasks of a parole officer are to assist the youths in making an adjustment to the family, school, and community. The duties of a parole officer that are similar to those of a probation officer include counseling, making referrals to community resources, and assisting the juveniles in developing a healthy adjustment within the community. Because those placed in aftercare are more likely than probationers to be hardcore, serious ex-offenders, the parole officer has extensive duties involving control, supervision, and surveillance. The officer must keep very close watch on the youth's behavior and associations, investigating matters that may indicate the need for a change in aftercare regulations or the desirability of a return to confinement. If the aftercare adjustment appears to be very successful (generally standardized assessment instruments are used to measure the youth's adjustment), the officer may recommend early termination of aftercare supervision.

15.5.1   General and Special Rules of Parole

The juvenile who is under aftercare supervision is expected to follow a set of general rules, including adhering to curfew regulations; attending school if still enrolled; abstaining from the use of drugs and alcohol; abiding by all local, state, and federal laws; and reporting regularly to the parole officer. As in probation supervision, the aftercare officer may request some specific conditions. These could involve forbidding associations with specific persons, attendance at Alcoholics Anonymous or drug-treatment programs, school attendance, or finding employment if the youth is no longer attending school.

The conditions of parole are similar to those given to youth placed under probation supervision. The general rules are applicable to all youths in parole. They include obeying laws, attendance at school, obeying parents and caretakers, and meeting with the parole officer as required. The special rules apply to an individual parolee and generally will pertain to forbidding specific associations, requiring counseling, forbidding the youth to frequent specific locations or places in the community, or paying restitution to a victim. In addition, youths on parole are not to travel to other communities or states without first obtaining the parole officer's permission.

The parole officer's effectiveness at supervising and assisting the youths assigned to him or her is determined by such factors as the number of cases, the resources available in the community, the cooperation and support received from the youth's family and significant others, and the juvenile's motivation to make a satisfactory adjustment in the community.

15.5.2   Discharge from Parole

When a juvenile is placed in aftercare status, the length of the period of supervision is indeterminate; that is, it extends to the age of majority in that state (18 or 21). Active aftercare supervision, however, is usually terminated earlier. A year of active supervision is generally considered adequate if there is evidence of a positive adjustment.

When the juvenile aftercare officer is satisfied that the juvenile has met parole rules and made an adequate adjustment in the community, the parole officer submits a written request to the youth authority from which the youth was released (also referred to as The Youth Commission). Complete discharge from supervision may be granted, or a youth may be transferred to inactive status, with very infrequent contacts or surveillance continuing until the youth authority is satisfied that the youth has adjusted and is no longer presents a threat to the community.

15.6   Parole Revocation

Youths on aftercare are in a precarious position because the possibility of return to the institution is always present. Although a standard revocation-of-aftercare process for juveniles has not been clearly established, several U.S. Supreme Court decisions relating to adult parole revocation have also been interpreted as applicable to juveniles. The cases of Mempa v. Rhay (1967), *Gagnon* v. *Scarpelli* (1973), and Morrisey v. Brewer (1972) all guaranteed a hearing and due process rights if parole revocation is threatened. The same safeguards are extended to a youth in aftercare status. Before these decisions, revocation of a juvenile's parole status was based on testimony of the parole officer, and the possibility existed that personality clashes or prejudice on the part of the officer could lead to unjust recommitment.

15.6.1   The Revocation Process

A number of jurisdictions have now developed formalized procedures for the parole revocation process. An alleged violation of aftercare regulations may be discovered by the parole officer or reported by parents, foster parents, halfway house personnel, or law enforcement officers. The aftercare officer will investigate the charge and may follow one of several courses of action, depending on the nature of the violation and other relevant circumstances. If the alleged violation is of a technical nature (violating the general or special rules of parole), the officer, after establishing that there is some evidence to support the allegations, may simply warn the youth that a violation has occurred and attempt to discover the reason for it. If it becomes apparent that certain factors in the youth's environment are contributing to violations, the officer may request that the juvenile's placement situation be changed. Perhaps, the problem may originate within the family and the youth may be transferred to a group home, or if the problems seems centered on adjustment in the school, the youth could be transferred to another school within the district or sent to an alternative school. Often the parolee gets into trouble by associating with friends who are involved in delinquent behavior. In such cases, rather than revoking the youth's parole, the judge, might decide to place more restrictions on the youth that could include wearing an electronic monitoring device or a very strict curfew.

If a youth under parole supervision is suspected of being involved in a delinquent offense, or has been taken into custody, the parole officer may request that he or she be held in detention while the police investigate the incident, or kept in detention if the police have already made an arrest. An adjudicatory hearing on the offense may result in recommitment to an institution, if the charges are found to be true.

15.6.2   Youth's Rights at a Revocation Hearing

At an aftercare-revocation hearing, a juvenile has the right to respond to and contest the allegations. While the U.S. Supreme Court has not specifically ruled on the rights of a delinquent during an aftercare revocation hearing, the majority of the states use the US Supreme Court ruling in *Morrissey* v. *Brewer* as a guideline. In that instance, the Court ruled that a defendant faced with parole revocation is entitled to the due process rights of a hearing, written notice of the charges, knowledge of evidence to be presented, and a written statement of the reasons that revocation is proposed. The parolee must also be given an opportunity to present witnesses in his or her behalf and to cross-examine other witnesses (Morrisey v. Brewer, 1972).

A revocation hearing is the culmination of a process that begins with a report of the parole violation by the parole officer to a supervisor. The supervisor may review the case and make the decision or a revocation committee may be formed to examine the problem. Generally, the parole officer is required to submit a written recommendation of revocation.

The parole officer assigned to the youth is not allowed to serve on the revocation committee, but usually will testify at the revocation hearing. The youth may also appear and speak in his or her own defense. The juvenile aftercare revocation is still relatively informal in nature; it has not yet been changed to the legalistic formulas now used in adult revocation hearings. If the juvenile's parole is revoked, the youth may be recommitted to the same institution from which he or she was released or may be sent to a different institution.

15.7   The Effectiveness of Parole (Aftercare)

The effectiveness of parole programs is difficult to assess, since many youths are close to the upper age limit of the juvenile status at the time they are released from institutions and may spend only a very short period under aftercare before becoming adults, when they are no longer carried in the juvenile offense statistics.

A study (Altschuler & Armstrong, 1994) that compared the offense patterns of offenders before institutionalization and after placement on parole found that youths who had committed certain types of offenses, particularly those involving violent gang delinquencies, had little success on parole in the community, and that many of these youths had to be returned to secure residential treatment. Parole appeared to be most successful when it was combined with some other type of assistance or involvement, such as living in a halfway house or being enrolled in job-training or educational programs.

15.8   Intensive Parole Supervision for High-Risk Juvenile Offenders

The backgrounds and delinquency histories of certain juvenile offenders cause them to be at high risk for reoffending, once they are released from institutions. These youths began their delinquent careers at early ages and the seriousness of their offenses progressively increases.

This high-risk group tends to exhibit a persistent pattern of intense and severe delinquent activity and is plagued by a multitude of other problems. Often, they have emotional and interpersonal problems that are sometimes accompanied by physical health problems; most come from family settings characterized by high levels of violence, chaos, and dysfunction; many are engaged in excessive alcohol and drug consumption and abuse; and a substantial proportion have become chronically truant or have dropped out of school (Altschuler & Armstrong, 1995).

The Office of Juvenile Justice and Delinquency Prevention funded several intensive community-based aftercare programs that it felt could be used as models for work with high-risk juveniles. As the programs developed, it became apparent that various organizational structures could be used and that the specific content of the programs would be affected by such factors as the level of resources available, the number of youths under supervision, the specific state statutes and laws governing juvenile parole (aftercare) in a particular state, whether the aftercare services would be provided by public or private agencies, and whether the population being served was predominantly urban or rural (Altschuler & Armstrong, 1994, p. 15).

Young (2004, p. 74) evaluated an Intensive Aftercare Programs (IAP). He noted that the key distinguishing elements of the IAP plan developed by the agency included:

- IAP participation was limited to youth identified to be a high risk of re-offending;
- Intensive aftercare began upon the youth's admission to a placement facility; the program stressed planning and preparing for life in the community while in the facility, and continuity of services and support in the institution and community;
- The program was designed around teams of three or four staff, each of whom played specialized roles while sharing responsibility for IAP youths;
- The teams had small caseload targets of 30 youth (representing a 1:10 or 1:7.5 staff to client ratio), permitting much more individual attention to youth and their families;

- Compared to standard aftercare, there were significantly more contacts made with the youth each week; and
- These contacts were to reflect the program's emphasis on services and support, in addition to supervision.

15.8.1   Developing Intensive Supervision Case Management Plans

Young (2004, p. 76) notes that in addition to having a mission, plan, strategy, and strong leadership, to achieve change in an organization, "transactional factors, such as structure, systems, line supervision, staff, and their everyday interactions and exchanges in the work setting must also be considered." In the assessments of the IPS programs that were implemented in several states, the situational factors mentioned above, particularly the inter-agency cooperation, tended to contribute to the success in some programs and inhibited the achievement of the goals in other programs.

Several states have developed programs by which those youths released from juvenile correctional facilities that are considered high risk for reoffending by committing violent crimes are placed on intensive supervision. For example, the Texas Juvenile Justice Department Parole Program (2019, p. 1) plays a significant role in the department's continuation of treatment and supervision after release. "The program is designed to increase accountability for youth returned to the community, include community service activities, and to enhance public, private, state, and local services for the young people and their families." Two tracks are available. Nonviolent offenders are generally placed in the "fast track" (medium surveillance) track. The "intensive surveillance" track is generally used for violent and repeat offenders.

The "intensive surveillance" program is designed to provide a high level of surveillance and supervision to most of the youths placed on parole. After a period of strong supervision, which includes monitoring the youth's overall progress, determining if the he or she is complying with the plan agreed upon when the youth was released, and after the youth's reintegration has been fully implemented and seems to be succeeding, the youth may be placed on the "fast track" (moderate or minimum supervision).

The Texas program uses a maximum level of surveillance for violent and repeat offenders initially, which involves the parole officer verifying the youth's location, daily schedule, and required activities. The program participant remains in that classification until it is determined that he or she has complied with the regulations set up. This may be the entire parole period. Parolees must report to their parole officers on a regular basis and may be visited by the officer at unscheduled times at home, school, or work sites.

Once a parole initially placed on "intensive surveillance," after evaluations, is changed to a "fast track" level, (moderate or minimum supervision) the intensity of supervision is reduced and the young person may become eligible for early release from parole.

To maximize aftercare effectiveness, the development of case management plans for high-risk offenders should begin while the youths are still institutionalized. The first step is an assessment of the risks the released offender will present to the community and the services or support the youth will need to succeed in aftercare. A standardized risk assessment approach is now being utilized in several states, using an instrument similar to the probation risk/classification instrument. Needs assessment focuses on the juvenile's problems and deficiencies and many of the identified needs are related to items in the risk assessment, such as substance abuse or a tendency toward violence. Risks and needs are usually interrelated. Once the risks and needs are assessed, a behavior or contingency contract may be developed. This specifies required behavior and/or treatment and spells out the positive or negative sanctions that will result from compliance or noncompliance. For high-risk offenders, surveillance and supervision may receive more emphasis in the case plan than intervention strategies that address the offenders' needs. Representatives of community or treatment agencies that will be involved are often consulted before the case plan is finalized. Specific provisions of the plan are made for assuring that the parole plan is followed once the offender returns to the community.

15.8.2   Implementing Intensive Supervision Case Management

A variety of methods or tools can be used to assure that the appropriate surveillance and supervision, as detailed in the case management plan, are carried out. These include frequent home or telephone contacts, house arrest, electronic monitoring, and drug or alcohol testing. During the intensive supervision, minor infractions or small technical violations of the behavior or contingency contract may be uncovered. Normally, these do not result in parole revocation, but if violations continue, harsher sanctions may be applied. To meet the offender's defined needs, the aftercare officer generally functions as a service broker, making the appropriate referrals to social service or treatment agencies and seeking support from schools, family members, or employers.

The key to success in intensive parole appears to be combining high levels of supervision with utilization of community resources.

15.8.3   Effectiveness of Intensive Parole

Intensive aftercare has demonstrated its effectiveness when researchers have compared it with other programs. Youths in the Violent Juvenile Offender Program (Fagan, 1990, p. 258) designed to provide intensive supervision for chronically violent juveniles placed under parole supervision from four institutions, were compared with the parole outcomes of juveniles randomly assigned to other programs. Those in the Violent Juvenile Offender Program showed significant reductions in the number and severity of arrests. The amount of time that had elapsed for those who were rearrested for additional crimes was significantly greater than that of the juveniles who were not under intensive parole. The researcher concluded that this carefully implemented and well-managed program helped protect the community and avert quick returns to delinquent behavior by the youths under parole after their release from juvenile correctional facilities. Chambers (2011, pp. 1–4), citing the Pathways to Desistance study published by the Office of Juvenile Justice, found that "only 8.5 % of the youth in the study persisted at high levels of offending; The factors that distinguish the high end *desisters* from *persisters* were lower levels of substance abuse and greater stability in their daily routine, as measured by stability in living arrangements, work and school attendance." The researchers found that "the youths who persisted in offending and those who reduced their offending behavior got about the same intensity of services; and youth who were given community based supervision were more likely to go to school, work, and avoid offending than were the youths who received institutional supervision; and treating youths with substance abuse problems for at least 90 days with their families involved in the treatment cut both their substance abuse and their offending, at least during the six months after treatment."

15.9   Parole and Residential Treatment

The use of residential treatment centers is an alternative for those who are "halfway out" in for youths being paroled from a juvenile correctional facility who may be a high risk to the residents of the community in which the youth lives. These centers may also be used to provide shelter and care for youths who must be removed from their homes for a "cooling-off period," but who will eventually be returned to supervision in their own homes. The function of halfway houses that we will consider in this chapter is their use for juveniles who are "halfway out" and "halfway in" of the correctional facility, but still under parole supervision and who are under obligation to abide by the conditions set at the time of their release.

When evidence mounted that parole (aftercare) alone was not an effective technique for preventing recidivism in many instances, a movement developed to combine parole with residential placement in nonsecure facilities. Placement of juveniles in residential treatment centers (halfway houses) for a period of time after release from a juvenile institution presents distinct advantages. It provides a less structured environment and more freedom than the institution but gives some direction and control to juveniles who may not be ready to completely regulate their own activities. It serves as an alternative to a disruptive home or neighborhood environment and returns the youth to the community without necessarily returning him or her to association with peers who were unhealthy influences. It provides friendship and counseling "on the spot" from the staff when a youth released from an institution needs immediate help to resist delinquent influences or to deal with their emotional needs. Res Residential treatment takes place in foster homes, group homes, and half-way houses. Foster and group homes are most concerned with providing a "homelike" environment to return the releasee to residence in the community; group homes and halfway houses, termed "residential treatment centers," incorporate a program of treatment into the day-to-day activities and employ professional staff who actively assist those placed on parole in arranging educational programs, job placements, and counseling.

15.9.1   History of the Halfway House Movement

The development of halfway houses in the United States came in two distinct eras. The halfway houses established before the 1950s were predominately concerned with meeting the ex-offenders' basic human needs and providing a place of residence during reentry into the community. These halfway houses, begun in the early nineteenth century in New York, Pennsylvania, and Massachusetts, were founded by private religious and volunteer groups, or even by individuals who sought to come to the aid of released prisoners. They operated independently of the correctional system and at times were open to critical attack from correction officials. The most frequently voiced objection was that in these houses the juveniles associated closely with other juvenile offenders and such interaction is forbidden by parole regulations.

Milestones in the development of the concept in this early period included the opening of a halfway house for women in Boston in 1864; and in 1896, the founding of the Isaac T. Hopper Home in New York by the Quakers and the opening of the first Hope Hall in New York City by the Volunteers of America. Hope Halls were subsequently established in six other large America cities (Solomon, 1976, pp. 241–242).

In the1950s, the interest in halfway houses was renewed, sparked by a growing awareness among correctional administrators that institutional treatment was not successful in preventing recidivism. The halfway houses established in the second era were more frequently funded by public agencies. They added the concept of treatment within the residential center itself to the already established goals of providing shelter, food, and companionship for those trying to reintegrate into society. The halfway house movement continued to expand and gain financial support from both private and government agencies in the 1960s and 1970s, but the community sentiment and federal as well as local government financial support tended to decline in the 1980s, and many of the halfway houses were forced to close their operations. However, in the 1990s, the pressure of overcrowding in the correctional facilities, both those for juveniles as well as those for adults, resulted in the establishment of many new community residential centers. The administration of these facilities usually have long term contracts with state, local or federal agencies and the problem of finding sufficient to operate each year has been reduced if not eliminated. Many of the community residential treatment centers house a specific type of offender such as those with drug abuse problems or mental health problems. This trend has continued well into the twenty-first century.

15.10   Community Corrections Centers

Adjudicated delinquents who are not eligible for probation may be placed in half-way houses instead of committing them to long term correctional institutions. These secure facilities are located in the community and administered by local officials. The youths committed to them are considered in need of supervision beyond that provided by probation. The advantages of community corrections centers include the smaller number of residents (usually 50 or less). They are easier to administer and less costly to operate than institutions. Face to face contact between the residents and treatment staff enhances the reintegration process.

15.10.1   Highfields

A strong impetus to the halfway house movement for juveniles was provided by the success of an experimental program begun in New Jersey in 1950. The idea of Highfields was conceived by F. Lovell Bixby and Lloyd W. McCorkle. They sought to establish a center where delinquent boys would be intensively treated with a type of group therapy termed *guided group interaction.* The plan called for residential treatment in small groups, with the boys supervised by house parents and a treatment director. The boys were given a work experience and hobby and craft activities were available. The heart of the program was the use of evening sessions, five times a week, of guided group interaction (Weeks, 1963, pp. 3 and 4).

One of the basic premises of this experiment was that the strong peer influence of adolescents, which might lead them into additional delinquency if they returned directly home, could be used in the residential-treatment-center setting to influence the youths toward rehabilitation.

Many of the youths released from juvenile institutions have reached the upper age limit of the juvenile status. Placement with their families may not be feasible or desirable for various reasons. The youths may not be returning to school, and an independent living status would be the most appropriate arrangement if they are not violent, hardcore offenders who require intensive supervision. In these cases, a community hostel may be the answer. This residential facility would function in a manner similar to a halfway house, except that there would be no treatment program or supervision within the house, although residents may be required to follow certain rules (no alcohol, sharing of housekeeping duties). In this type of setting, the released youths have opportunities to make educational, social services, or employment contacts, but this is their own responsibility.

15.10.2   *Volunteers*

The early development of delinquency control agencies at the local level involved actively involved volunteers, both in direct contact with youths and in groups that have worked for funding to support such programs. Through civic organizations and churches, many volunteers have become involved in efforts to establish halfway houses, refuges for runaways, and job-training programs.

As the handling of youths who are defined as "problems" is conducted more frequently in the community, people are becoming more knowledgeable about and interested in the fate of juveniles in trouble and a number seek to become involved in assisting them. This involvement may take the form of direct assistance through counseling, tutoring, friendship, companionship, or emotional support, or formation of organizations or committees within existing organizations to educate the general public on the causes and prevention of delinquency. Volunteer organizations also lobby or establish pressure groups to promote new legislation or work for passage of tax levies to increase funds for local community-based prevention and control programs. As a result of juvenile service agencies having limited funds to provide services beyond those mandated, they must depend on volunteers to staff programs that are innovative and additions to the basic services provided by the agency. In addition, volunteers often bring to their work a high level of motivation and commitment that cannot be duplicated.

College students have been found to be particularly effective in diversion programs for young people, because their closeness in age permits them to empathize with the problems of the youth they counsel.

15.11   Summary

In this chapter, we examined juvenile aftercare. In states with a state youth authority or commission, the release decision is made by an institutional release committee or board, subject to the approval of the authority or commission. In states where judges commit youths directly to specific institutions, the committing judge must approve the committee's decision. In making release decisions, release committees normally take into consideration the young person's adjustment within the institution, perceived changes of attitude, and ability to plan for the future. The decision to release may also be influenced by the nature of the offense prior to commitment and the juvenile's attitude.

To differentiate youthful offenders from adults, the process of supervision in the community after release some states refer the process of supervision of juveniles after release from an institution as "aftercare" instead of "parole." In states with a central youth authority, the officers are employed by that body. In states without a central youth authority, parole (aftercare) officers are employed by the local jurisdiction. The same people may serve as both probation and parole officers.

Juveniles in parole supervision present special problems, because their previous delinquent acts tend to include serious offenses. Often there is resistance to their return by members of the community and/ or the school administrations of the schools they were attending. In order to make the transition from institution to community work, there must be careful planning and an assessment of the youth's needs even before the youth is released from the correctional facility. Based on the scores of risk assessment instruments, intensive parole supervision is used for juveniles defined as high-risk for-reoffending. Case plans developed before they are released detail the behavior and treatment expected and state the positive and negative sanctions that will result from compliance or noncompliance. To protect the community, surveillance is coupled with addressing the offenders' needs.

For some youths, a return to the environment in which they were living before being institutionalized constitutes serious problems. Some youths can receive support from family and friends to resist unwholesome influences, but others have little chance of success on parole if they return home. For these youths, foster home placement or residential treatment centers offer the best hope.

Residential treatment combined with aftercare has been used in halfway houses in the United States since the early 1800s. Those that have been most successful have developed careful screening processes to discover which juveniles can best succeed in residential treatment and have fostered strong ties of communication and cooperation with the local law enforcement agencies, the juvenile court, and community agencies.

Violation of the general or special rules of aftercare or commission of a new offense may result in parole revocation. In some jurisdictions, recommitment is made on the basis of the recommendation of the parole officer or is ordered at an adjudication hearing at which a judge finds a new charge against the juvenile to be true. If a revocation hearing is held, a committee hears testimony concerning the parole rules violation or new offense and makes the decision to recommit or continue parole. A young person whose parole status has been revoked may be recommitted to the institution from which he or she was released, sent to a different institution, or given an extension of time to serve under parole supervision and new restrictions.

15.12 Discussion Questions

1. What are the factors that a release committee would consider in making the decision as to whether an institutionalized youth is ready to be recommended for parole?
2. Describe the process followed in preparing a youth for release to parole supervision. How are youth prepared for release?
3. What are the duties of a parole (aftercare) officer before and during the aftercare process? How do the duties of an aftercare officer differ from those of a probation officer?

4. How does intensive aftercare supervision of high-risk youths address the problem of protecting the community from released youths who present a serious risk of reoffending?
5. Discuss what is meant by the phrase "half-way-in and half-way-out" as it applies to juveniles under parole supervision.
6. What are community corrections centers? What are the benefits to a youth and to the community of committing a delinquent youth to a community corrections center rather than to a state administrated juvenile correctional facility?
7. Discuss the various roles volunteers play in work with juvenile offenders who are supervised in the community.
8. Describe the parole (aftercare) process. How might an officer deal with a parolee who has committed a technical violation, or minor delinquency offense if the offense does not appear to be serious enough to warrant a revocation of the youth's parole?
9. What is the difference between parole termination and parole revocation? Discuss the process followed in a parole revocation hearing. If the charges are found to be true, what are the options a judge can take in deciding on the action to take?
10. Several studies pertaining to juvenile delinquents who had been committed to juvenile correctional facilities and released on parole have found that there are several key factors that differentiate those youths who recidivate after release from the institution and those do not recidivate. What are these factors?

References

Akron Beacon Journal. (2002, November 2). *Teen charged in attack* (p. B4).
Akron Beacon Journal. (2003, January 10). *Teen suspected in Chapel Hill Robbery* (p. B6).
Altschuler, D., & Armstrong, T. (1994). *Intensive aftercare for high risk juveniles: Policies and procedures*. Washington, DC: Office of Juvenile Justice and Delinquency Prevention.
Altschuler, D., & Armstrong, T. (1995). Managing aftercare services for delinquents. In B. Glick & A. Goldstein (Eds.), *Managing delinquent programs that work* (pp. 137–170). Laurel, MD: American Correctional Association.
Chambers B. (2011). *What works with serious juvenile offender—Pathways to desistance study* (pp. 1–4). Retrieved June 14, 2019, from https://www.reclaimingfutures.org/news/what-works-serious-juvenile-offenders-pathways-desistance-study
Department of Law & Public Safety, Office of Juvenile Parole & Transitional Services. (n.d.) *Parole supervision*. Retrieved August 3, 2019, from https://www.nj.gov/oag/jjc/parole.hml
Fagan, J. A. (1990, June). Treatment and reintegration of violent juvenile offenders: Experimental results. *Justice Quarterly, 7*, 2.
Federal Criminal Codes and Rules, Section 5001 (1991). St. Paul, MN: West Publishing Company (p. 921).
Gagnon v. Scarpelli. (1973). 411 U.S. 778.
Mempa v. Rhay. (1967). 389 U.S. 128.
Morrisey v. Brewer. (1972). 408 U.S. 471,92 S.Cr. 2593, LEd. 2d 484.

National Council of Juvenile and Family Court Judges. (1984). The juvenile court and serious offenders: 38 recommendations. *Juvenile and Family Court Journal,* Special issue (Summer), 17.

Shepherd, S., Luebbers, S., & Ogloff, J. (2016). The role of protective factors and the relationship with recidivism for the high risk young people in detention. *Criminal Justice and Behavior, 43*(7), 863–878.

Sickmund, M., & Puzzanchera, C. (Eds.). (2014). *Juvenile offenders and victims: 2014 national report*. Pittsburgh, PA: National Center for Juvenile Justice.

Solomon, H. (1976). *Community corrections*. Boston, MA: Holbrook Press.

Texas Juvenile Justice Department. (2019). *Parole program overview* (pp. 1–2). Retrieved August 3, 2019, from www.tjjd.texas.govprograms/parole_overview.aspx

Warsmith, S. (2002). Akron stabbing may prompt reform. *Akron Beacon Journal, 4*, A1,9.

Weeks, H. A. (1963). *Youthful offenders at Highfields*. Ann Arbor, MI: University of Michigan Press.

Young, D. (2004). First count to ten: Innovation and implementation in juvenile reintegration programs. *Federal Probation, 68*(2), 70–77.

Chapter 16
Counseling and Treatment of Juvenile Offenders

16.1 Introduction

In the earlier chapters of this book, we noted that the state assumes responsibility for providing care and services for children in need of them at various levels of involvement in the juvenile justice system. Treatment is an important part of the handling of juvenile offenders referred to programs of diversion sponsored by either the juvenile court or community agencies, and it is also vital in probation and community-based services, institutionalization, aftercare, and community residential programs.

Theorists in delinquency causation have attempted to explain juvenile misbehavior in accordance with their own fields of interest and specialization. For example, psychoanalysts have advanced explanations that are heavily weighted in favor of emotional problems, whereas phrenologists, who were most familiar with the physical makeup of the body, developed explanations based on physical factors. Treatment theories and strategies have also evolved according to the interest and specializations of those using them. As Trojanowicz noted (1978, pp. 264–265), "Sociologists usually take a 'social engineering' approach to delinquency prevention and treatment, while psychologists treat the individual. In other words, sociologists attempt to determine the conditions of the social structure that breed delinquency, while psychologists emphasize the individual and his interpersonal dynamics… The social worker, then, translates the theories and assumptions of both psychological and sociological theory into action."

The concept of treatment of juvenile offenders, as opposed to "punishment," has passed through a number of developmental variations. As juvenile behavior was analyzed by psychologists and psychiatrists in the years after 1920, it came increasingly to be viewed as a manifestation of underlying emotional illness, to be diagnosed and "cured." This "medical model" of delinquency treatment reached the height of its popularity in the 1960s, when elaborate efforts were undertaken to analyze each child's "illness," and various treatments were undertaken to effect "cures." The ever-increasing tide of delinquent behavior and the high rates of recidivism among juvenile

© Springer Nature Switzerland AG 2020
P. C. Kratcoski et al., *Juvenile Delinquency*,
https://doi.org/10.1007/978-3-030-31452-1_16

offenders caused juvenile justice system treatment personnel to take a long second look at the medical model. In the 1970s, it began to be abandoned or downplayed in favor of treatment methods that hold that a youth is responsible for his or her own behavior and should be actively involved in attempts to change it, and they look to environmental factors as strong influences in the production of delinquency.

Since the first edition of this book appeared in 1979, opinions on the appropriate response to juvenile delinquency have changed considerably. Increases in serious violent offenses have motivated revisions in state juvenile codes that emphasize custody and control rather than treatment and, as evaluations of various types of treatment programs have revealed little or marginal improvement in the offenders' behavior, the focus of treatment has shifted. Although the concept of providing treatment has not been abandoned, it has been refocused. Currently, a majority of treatment programs combine the element of holding a youth responsible for his or her actions with discovering and dealing with factors that may have precipitated the deviant behavior. Treatment techniques such as positive peer culture, guided group interaction, reality therapy, and behavior modification continue to be used because they combine personal responsibility with treatment. There is also a growing emphasis on treatment that focuses on special problems such as substance abuse, sex offenses, or violent behavior.

Treatment programs may also involve some degree of punishment or sanctioning. Glaser (1994, pp. 712–723) maintained that treatment and punishment are compatible if their application is grounded in a sound theoretical base. He noted that in Massachusetts, where the institutional commitment rate for juvenile offenders is very low, with the majority of youths being placed in community supervision and treatment type programs, recidivism rates are much lower than in California, which institutionalizes a much higher percentage of its youth offenders. However, for youths who become chronic offenders, handling in community-based treatment programs is less successful, and both the community and these youths are best served by their placement in and institutional settings. He concluded that the development of appropriate combinations of punishment, community service, restitution, house arrest, and confinement with treatment will protect the community, satisfy the public's desire to have offenders punished, and lead to positive change.

In the 1990s, the National Center for Juvenile Justice and the National Council of Juvenile and Family Court Judges sought to identify effective programs. Juvenile court judges, probation administrators, and court workers nominated more than 1000 programs in 49 states and 425 of those were selected to be included in a directory titled, *What Works: Promising Interventions in Juvenile Justice* (Montgomery & Landon, 1994). The successful programs proved to have certain things in common. They combined offender accountability, graduated sanctions, and service provision. Various approaches and types of interventions were used, including skill development; inividual, group, and family counseling; and mentoring. Aftercare (parole) was also important. The majority of the programs served fewer than 50 clients and were community based. Staff training was also emphasized.

This chapter will focus on the treatment techniques and programs currently in use in juvenile justice that have been found effective in addressing the particular characteristics and special needs of today's juvenile offenders.

16.2   Treatment Personnel and Definition of Treatment

A large segment of juvenile justice system personnel is designated as "treatment staff." Whether these people work with children who have been referred to a diversion program as a result of a minor offense or with hardcore delinquents in a secure institution, they are expected to "treat" the young people under their supervision. Treatment personnel attached to a juvenile court might include probation officers, family counselors, social workers, and psychologists. Treatment staff members in a juvenile correctional institution might consist of social workers, group counselors, activity supervisors, and youth leaders. Those assigned to treatment positions typically hold degrees in fields related to the study or analysis of human behavior such as psychology, social work, sociology, criminal justice, or human services. Paraprofessionals are also frequently involved in treatment programs. Individualized treatment plans are designed to provide youths with the amount of support, direction, and supervision necessary to turn him or her away from socially unacceptable modes of behavior.

Treatment may involve intermediate sanctions, such as short term incarceration, electronic monitoring, or mandated substance abuse counseling and treatment. For juvenile offenders, the strategies chosen are designed to help the young person move toward acceptable behavior and cope with his or her problems. Gibbons (1977, p. 305) stated that treatment in a justice system setting involves the use of "explicit tactics or procedures deliberately undertaken to change those conditions thought to be responsible for the violator's misbehavior." Gibbons (1977, p. 306) also noted that since the treatment is undertaken because of unacceptable behavior that is believed to stem from certain factors or conditions in the offender's life, it should be designed to change some or all of these conditions.

After the treatment process begins, it proceeds through various stages, which have been characterized by Newman (1975) as an investigation, diagnosis, and treatment supervision. In the investigation phase, the causes of the manifested unacceptable behavior are sought. An important part of this phase is the use of the case study—a detailed report on a child's personality and physical characteristics, developmental history, home situation, family, school performance, recreational interests and activities, and current or past problems. This information, which is frequently made available to the judge at the time of the dispositional decision in the form of a social investigation report, is supplemented and correlated by treatment personnel in looking for reasons behind a youth's unacceptable behavior.

The diagnosis stage involved the organization and analysis of what has been learned in the investigation. A treatment plan, referred to as a case management plan, is developed that has practical, attainable goals. For example, treatment investigation revealing that a child has persistently run away from home because of intolerable domestic conditions that are not likely to change might lead to a diagnosis that the treatment goal for this child should be development of self-reliance to the point where an independent-living placement, away from his or her parents, could be worked out.

The third phase, treatment supervision, was described by Newman (1975, p. 63) as the "elaboration of knowledge about the individual through the process of communication, so that the individual through the process of communication, will gain a more realistic appraisal of his behavior, thereby enhancing his own ability to function more acceptably in the community." Ideally, the treatment plan finally recommended for each child is grounded in discovery of what appear to be the causes of current behavior.

Effective implementation of treatment may involve both direct interaction with the client and interaction on his or her behalf with community agencies that can offer assistance. A probation officer may be as successful in this "brokerage" role as in direct interaction with the young person. An effective treatment worker must also be aware of the social milieu within which the young person under his or her supervision operates, either in the community or within an institution, and adapt treatment strategies to the realities of the youth's situation. For example, a probationer who is sleeping on a bare mattress in a room with four siblings may not be an appropriate candidate for individual counseling and analysis of emotional needs until his or her basic physical needs are met. Although a treatment worker need not alter his or her own value system and ways of looking at things, the worker must recognize that other systems and outlooks exist and must develop an understanding of how adaptation to life in a social setting different from his or her own can be related to effective treatment. Finally, treatment personnel and policies must function within the bounds of a professional code of ethics and adhere to the regulations set by the department or agency by which he or she is employed.

16.2.1 The Application of Management Principles to the Implementation of Treatment Programs

The children who appear before the juvenile court represent the whole spectrum of the juvenile population with regard to age, gender, and racial and ethnic backgrounds. Some have committed extremely serious acts; others have been involved in minor offenses. Some are negative, antisocial, and bitter in their attitudes; others are scared, despondent, and remorseful. Some have strong family support to fall back on, but many do not.

On the assumption that most organizations can apply common management principles to improve their effectiveness, juvenile justice agency administrators usually have a coordinated plan under which the specific goals for each operation are established. It is not the unique character of the programs developed that accounts for the success any particular court experiences in its attempts at delinquency control and the rehabilitation of offenders, but rather the skillful utilization and integration of the many resources within the courts and the community.

Often, the number of programs developed by an agency has little relevance to solving problems confronting it, because the programs are implemented in a haphazard way as funds become available, without sufficient thought being given to the underlying purposes and goals the administrators hope to achieve through these programs. Some administrators in the juvenile justice field are ill prepared in management skills, and this condition is reflected in their failure to efficiently use the resources available to them. Successful administrators have systematically developed and coordinated each program in the light of the needs of the youths involved, the community's interest, and the resources available to them. Through a skillful use of community resources: juvenile justice agency administrators can provide the maximum service to these being treated while avoiding duplication of services.

16.2.2 Management of Treatment Programs

Before any treatment strategy can be developed and implemented, the underlying goals and philosophy of the treatment agency are established and communicated to all the various levels of personnel who will be involved in the program.

Too often, juvenile treatment personnel are required to participate in lengthy, seemingly endless series of "client-centered" sessions that have long ago lost their meaning. The sessions become reviews of probation requirements, rap sessions, forums where the clients can vent feelings (positive or negative) about the treatment personnel, or merely "booster shots" in the sense that at each meeting the worker gives the client some positive feedback and encouragement to make it through. Expected outcomes such as better ego strength, improved interpersonal relations, acceptance of self, or learning self-discipline are vague and different to measure.

In contrast, efficient justice agency management, like business management, insists on accountability. Filtering it through the system, administrators hold management accountable, management holds line staff workers accountable, and justice system members hold the youths accountable. Accountability is measured in terms of results rather than in time and effort. If after 6 months in a diversion program, probation, or institutionalization a youth is still burglarizing homes, the result is unacceptable and the victims of the child's delinquency should hold the juvenile justice system accountable.

Management by objectives is one approach to accountability in a result-oriented system. Objectives are identified as clear, concise tasks, with timelines where possible, and they emphasize working toward a goal. A goal is defined as an ideal behavior to be achieved. Goals are not readily attained or easily measured for success.

Sound management principles can be applied at the organizational level by the administrators and managers of an agency or by an individual practitioner in the case management of an offender.

Use of management by objectives in case management involves clear definitions of attainable goals and the objectives that can be used to achieve them. For example, the goal of a particular youth's treatment might be to be released from probation and the agreed upon objectives to reach the goals would be a series of tasks to be completed. For example, a young person who was adjudicated delinquent for stealing money from a neighborhood house might have the following behavioral objectives:

1. I will apologize to the victim by next week and offer to work out restitution.
2. I will attend at least 95% of my classes and keep a record for the probation officer.
3. I will not steal from anyone (objective: 100%).

The probation officer will measure the results of the objectives, perhaps monthly, and will delete and any as appropriate. The supervisory staff and administration should also set objectives for themselves, such as: conducting monthly evaluations of staff and treatment objectives, and the administration should establish a plan to measure the success of the supervisory staff's objectives for the entire justice agency.

In summary, management by objectives involves a high degree of accountability. The results are tangible measurements, not estimates. The rewards are built into the system. If an objective is met, a feeling of accomplishment results. Additional rewards may ensure for the juvenile that might include early release from probation. Especially the administration, benefits by being recognized in the community for having an efficient.

16.3 Interviewing: The Initial Contact

The purpose of the initial contact is to obtain information about a juvenile offender that will be used to determine the course of action to be taken by the agent of the juvenile justice system. For example, a police officer may have several options, depending on the nature of the offense and the circumstances pertaining to the offense. After obtaining enough information from the youth in an interview, the officer might decide to divert youth from the juvenile justice system by simply giving the young person a warning and releasing him or her to the custody of parents.

If the officer determines the seriousness of the offense, as well as other information obtained from the interview, requires official juvenile justice action, the officer might transport the youth to the juvenile court facility. If the youth is in need of emergency shelter care he or she is taken to a foster facility. The caretakers there will need any information about the youth's special needs.

If a youth is referred to the juvenile court, during the initial intake interview information will be obtained by the interviewer that will be used in making a decision on the appropriate course of action for the court to take (diversion, formal processing).

According to Mauer (2005, pp. 31–32) the objectives of the initial interview are as follows:

- To establish a good working relationship with the client;
- To obtain information about the client's background;
- To provide information about what to expect during the interview.
- To identify the general nature of the client's problems;
- To obtain a detailed history of the facts leading up to the present problem and any factors that may have contributed to the problem the client is facing; and

- To ask follow-up questions on areas in which the information provided is not complete or fully understood when necessary.

In order to achieve these objectives, the interviewer, to be effective, must develop several interviewing skills (Shearer, 1993, p. 15), including the following:

- The interviewer must have empathy, that is, be interested in the welfare of the person being counseled.
- The interviewer must focus on concrete experiences, needs, and changes that will lead to the adjustment of the person being counseled.
- The interviewer must know how to adjust the speed and pacing of the interview so that the counseling is given in a timely manner.
- The interviewer must know how to summarize the information provided by the person being interviewed, as well as the information provided by the counselor.
- The interviewer must know when an immediate response is needed, such as in a crisis situation, and have the skills to draw out the response.
- The interviewer must know when to confront the person being interviewed, particularly when it is apparent that the person is "playing a game" or not taking the counseling session seriously.
- The interviewer must be assertive when the situation demands assertiveness.

16.4 Types of Interviewing

In addition to the information gathering interview, other types of interviews are completed for a variety of reasons. These include the:

16.4.1 Cognitive Interview

The focus of cognitive interviewing is to have the respondent recall the incident or event and the thoughts and feelings about the event and perhaps to bring a different perspective on the matter, Kratcoski (2017, p. 198) noted, "In cognitive interviewing, the interviewee is often asked to provide information sought in a different time sequence. Instead of asking the person to start at the beginning and provide information on everything considered important until the time reached when the event occurred, the interviewer might start at the end point and ask the person to go back in memory to the starting point. The interviewer must keep the person on track, occasionally probe, or ask for clarification." The cognitive interview is often used in crisis intervention, or in situations in which the person being interviewed is in a state of panic or shock resulting from being physically harmed during an incident of violence in which the person was involved.

16.4.2 The Motivational Interview

The motivational interview is more focused on using methods and questions during the interview that will stimulate the person being interviewed to become motivated to change those behaviors that have created problems. The interviewer might use some of the same methods used in the cognitive interview to uncover the events or incidents that seem to be related to the source of the problem. During the interview, the person being interviewed is given support, particularly if there is some evidence that the person has been making an effort to make positive changes and is moving toward the desired goal. However, the interviewee is also confronted when it appears that the person has not been sincere in his or her desire for change. Motivational interviewing is used with youths in a wide range of setting, including alcohol and drug abuse treatment, in institutional facilities, and in private practices.

16.4.3 The Counseling Interview

The counseling interview is the most common type of interview used in the counseling and treatment of delinquent youths. It consists of an information gathering process and the application of treatment techniques. Kratcoski (2017, p. 199) states, "The counseling interview in corrections is used to obtain information that will be useful in developing a case management plan for the offender and for use in the actual counseling of the client. Depending on the personal characteristics of the client, the environmental setting, the type of information needed, and the changes in the client desired, the specific approach to the interview may differ."

16.5 The Decision to Use Individual or Group Treatment

The decision on the type of treatment to follow is based on many factors, including the type and seriousness of the youngster's most recent offense, the success of previous attempts at individual or group treatment, if the juvenile is a repeat offender, the range of group treatment programs available at this particular court, and the possibilities for placement in a specific program, and, most important, whether individual or group treatment seems to offer the best hope of securing help for the child.

A juvenile's initial entrance into the juvenile justice system takes place in a one-to-one situation, with an intake officer or judge talking with or questioning the child. Group treatment may enter the picture if it is decided that crisis intervention or counseling of the entire family over a period of weeks offers the best solution.

Another type of group treatment occurs when a probation officer meets with his or her probationers in small groups rather than individually. The group sessions are helpful to officers with large caseloads and are also beneficial to youngsters with problems related to subcultural (gang) delinquency. Those with problems related to the inability to relate well to peers, or to resist the influence of delinquent peers, may also be helped by group treatment. Some justice system personnel combine individual sessions (possibly weekly) for clients with a monthly group session that may involve recreation or cultural enrichment.

The obvious advantage of group treatment is that it is less expensive and allows an officer to increase the number of contacts with youths within the same time frame. It may prove impractical because of scheduling difficulties or because certain juveniles have problems that can best be handled in individual treatment sessions. Group discussions may allow youngsters to open up and make comments that they would not make without the group's presence and support. Peer pressure can be utilized to help a child conform to the group's expectations. Young people who have never had peer discussions or involvement may experience a sense of relief in a group situation and discover that their problems and fears are common to many other youths.

16.6   The Role of Treatment Personnel

Juvenile justice treatment personnel may assume a variety of roles in the course of their interaction with young people. They may serve as listeners, observers, information disseminators, service brokers, givers of emotional support, supervisors, behavior regulators, and imposers of sanctions. The roles they assume and the type of direction they give are dependent upon the needs of the juveniles, as ascertained by the treatment personnel. The counseling given may range on a continuum from nondirective to highly directive. Nondirective counseling is characterized by listening, giving information, and offering advice, without placing pressure on the person being counseled to choose a certain course of action. Vocational counseling is frequently of this type. Directive counseling, in contrast, involves activity ranging from strongly worded advice to commands and demands. In directive counseling, the counselor takes charge of the pace and the direction of the interview and even the content of the interaction. Highly directive counseling might occur when a youth who has violated rules or conditions of probation is told that unless he or she behaves in a certain way or conforms to certain ultimatums the probation will be revoked. Work with juveniles who have become involved in juvenile justice system will typically use a more directive type of counseling relationship, since the youth is placed under a supervisor and has been directed to follow a set of rules, or the family has not sought help voluntarily and the youth becomes involved in counseling because of court orders. Directive counseling involves an element of supervision or control. This supervision, which may be defined as a limited control through the exercise of the authority and sanctions of the court, involves assisting the child and perhaps the entire family to develop internal control of their behavior in order to conform to societal norms. Helping them to develop such inner controls may include the use by the counselor of external controls in the form of behavior contracts, conditions of probation, enforcement of strict adherence to a schedule of visits, or other requirements.

The counseling-supervision process may entail simple, short, infrequent meetings or more detailed and frequent sessions, depending upon the types and seriousness of the behavior that has brought the child under the supervision of the court. Ideally, even with juveniles who are not regarded as needing elaborate counseling supervision plans, the process, typically the counseling, involves developing empathy and trust between the juvenile and the counselor, formulating and implementing a behavior condition as the goal, and an assessment of the success or failure of the counseling. In the case of the details and extended counseling sessions, the counselor draws the youth to explore the causes of the problem, exploring possible solutions, definite goals, and develop specific behavioral activities that can be measured as working toward these goals. Once the counselor and the youth agree on and accept the goals set, they begin certain strategies to achieve them. The youth's progress is continually monitored and evaluated during this step until termination of the counselor–juvenile relationship. Even after the formal sessions are concluded, follow-up, in terms of recidivism checks or progress reports, is helpful to the counselor in gauging the effectiveness of the helping process.

16.7   Specific Treatment Techniques

16.7.1   Psychotherapy

The theories of crime and delinquency causation developed by Freud and his followers in the area of psychoanalysis placed the roots of deviant behavior within the personality. The general term "psychotherapy" is used to designate a variety of treatment techniques that are derived from the assumptions underlying psychoanalysis developed by Freud and his successors extends to reality therapy, which tends to be an eclectic, common-sense approach to therapy. As with other types, the goal of psychotherapy is the alleviation of the emotional or personal problems that are believed to be the cause of misbehavior.

Insight psychotherapy is a specialized area that requires training beyond the education of the typical juvenile justice system counselors. Psychologists or psychiatrists attached to juvenile institutions or to courts may attempt psychotherapy in certain cases or may refer children to specialists for such treatment. The effectiveness and applicability of psychotherapeutic techniques for most juveniles referred to the justice system have been questioned and most juveniles are not considered to have difficulties requiring such extensive treatment. A number of the therapies that are popular and widely used today do, however, attempt to incorporate some form of personality or behavior analysis.

16.7.2   *Reality Therapy*

Those who became somewhat disillusioned with psychotherapy as a general treatment approach for the majority of clients developed a new treatment alternative, *reality therapy*. Reality therapy (Rachin, 1974, pp. 52–53) states that a person's disruptive behavior stems from feelings of being unloved and of having no one to love, of not being worthwhile to oneself or others. Such a person is irresponsible. The goal of reality therapy is to make the person become responsible. Responsibility is defined as fulfilling one's own needs without depriving other people of their needs.

Many of the principles of reality therapy are applications of common sense; its value as a treatment technique lies in this fact. It is easy to learn, does not require preparatory training in sophisticated theories, and can be employed in only a fraction of the time needed with more conventional therapies. Workers in the juvenile justice field can apply and develop the reality therapy approach rather easily because it does not involve collecting a great deal of historical social data, but rather begins where the child is now and proceeds from there. Both professional and lay workers are able to utilize reality therapy because goals are clear. It requires the counselor to get involved, to care about the people being counseled, to let them know that he or she cares, and to help them fulfill their needs by helping them reject unacceptable behavior.

Making a person responsible is the aim of reality therapy and one becomes responsible by overcoming an identity with failure. A quick accomplishment is a good start towards a success identity. Developing a sense of worthiness increases a belief in self and helps the child see that her or she has a stake in the system. The goal of reality therapy is to act responsibly, not to be happy, although happiness and a feeling of well-being may be by-products of behaving responsibly.

Critics of reality therapy maintain that the assumptions underlying it are too simplistic to be applicable to all human behavior and that it does not take into account factors such as emotional disturbance, hyperactivity, or cultural influences that present a youth with a value system in conflict with that of the larger society. Also, the therapy is heavily dependent on the individual therapist's or counselor's interpretation of what constitutes "responsible" behavior. Certain children, particularly those who have turned to delinquent behavior because they could not meet the continually stated expectations of teachers or parents, are unlikely to respond favorable to a therapy that uses basically the same approach. Another danger is that "caring about the client" and therefore doing what is best for the client may be misinterpreted by some counselors. Rather harsh sanctions could be imposed under the principle of "doing it for the child's own good." With certain exceptions, however, reality therapy does offer an approach that can prove useful in working with many types of offenders.

16.7.3   Brief Therapy

According to the National Institutes of Health (Center for Substance Abuse Treatment, 1999, Chap. 3, p. 1) brief therapy is, "a systematic focused process that relies on assessment, client engagement, and rapid implementations of change strategies." Brief therapy techniques can be applied when the therapist is following one or a combination of several therapies, including cognitive-behavioral therapy, brief strategic interactional therapies, brief humanistic and existential therapies, brief psychodynamic therapy, short-term family therapy, and time-limited group therapy. When used in correctional counseling, it is appropriate for both juvenile and adult offenders. Kratcoski (2017, p. 239) noted that various other labels have been used to describe what is essentially brief therapy. They include reality therapy, crisis intervention, brief family therapy, and others. Also, the number of sessions required for the person being counseled may be just one or several, depending on the selection and type of problems the person being counseled has to be solved. There are many situations in which a person may have a crisis situation that needs immediate attention.

The main difference between brief therapy and therapy that comes about in a situation where the client needs immediate counseling as a result of some unexpected tragedy is that brief therapy is planned and time limited, ranging from 5 min to a more than six half-hour therapy session. The extensiveness of the assessment will depend on the nature of the intervention. Brief therapy may be administered by a wide range of professionals, while other types of therapy require specific training in that modality, and materials such as booklets or computer programs may be used.

16.7.4   Crisis Intervention

Roberts (1991, p. 3) defines a personal crisis as "An acute disruption of psychological homeostasis in which one's usual coping mechanisms fail and there exists evidence of distress and functional impairment." There may be a number of reasons why a "crisis" may occur in a person's life, but in general the cause of a crisis is related to a traumatic stressful situation, engagement in a hazardous event, or involvement in a situation for which the person cannot control the outcome or feels he/she does not have the skills to determine the outcome. Roberts (1991, p. 3) states, "A crisis often has five components: a hazardous or traumatic event, a vulnerable or unbalanced state, a precipitating factor, an active crisis state based on vulnerable or unbalanced state, a precipitating factor, an active crisis state based on the person's perception, and the resolution of the crisis." Crisis Intervention, as the name implies, involves immediate attention to the misbehavior of the child, within hours of its occurrence. It may involve the young person only or may include the entire family in efforts to determine immediately the cause of the youth's problems and activate efforts to alleviate them.

Crisis intervention therapy is based on the belief that at the time of a crisis, a child or the family may be more open to suggestions for assistance than they would be at a later time. Crisis intervention centers are operated by certain juvenile courts, which summon members of the family to a consultation session as soon as possible after a young person is apprehended and work with the family in setting up goals and methods of dealing with the problem. There are many situations, including loss of a parent, the loss of employment of a parent, illnesses in the family, involvement of the parent in crime, and others that may cause the youth's family to experience a crisis situation.

Child abuse has been associated with the cause of certain stresses or crises in the lives of the abusing parents. A portion of delinquency can no doubt be attributed to comparable family crises. It parents and youths may be more open to and willing to accept help at the time of a crisis, it must be is this segment of the cases that can best be served by crisis intervention techniques. Even though it must be remembered that crisis intervention must frequently be followed up with other types to prevent the recurrence of delinquent behavior after the crisis atmosphere is over.

Crisis intervention counseling can be applied in a variety of settings. The specific setting and nature of the crisis will determine the type of immediate response to the crisis that the counselor or caregiver will take. One of several model can be followed. For example, in the Training Guide for Crisis Intervention written by the Michigan Department of Community Health (1985, p. 2), it states that crisis intervention may be used "to provide for self-defense or the defense of others, to prevent an individual from causing self-harm, to stop a disturbance that threatens physical injury to any person, to obtain possession of a weapon or any dangerous object that is in possession of the individual causing the crisis, or to prevent 'serious' property destruction."

16.7.5 Assertiveness Training

Some young people become involved in delinquent activities because they are passive and easily led by peers. When they are placed in situations that involve pressures to engage in illegal acts, they "go along with the crowd," even though they know that what they are doing is wrong. They do this because they are afraid that they will lose the friendship of peers if they do not.

Children may become nonassertive and easily led as a result of conditioning at home or in school. When a child has been physically punished or verbally reprimanded by adults for expressing opinions or ever asking questions they judge to be inappropriate, he or she may fall into a pattern of refraining from contributing ideas and simply going along with what others suggest. Passivity may be reinforced when a child who is submissive and nonassertive is praised by parents or teachers for being "good." A child who develops a pattern of over conformity because he or she believes this is a way to please parents or teachers is also likely to overconform to gain the approval of peers. Another basis for lack of assertiveness on a child's part is inexperience with certain social situations and lack of opportunity to observe the proper ways to behave. In school situations, the leadership of peers who appear to "know the score" can be very strong. In addition, passivity, particularly for girls, is regarded as a virtue in some cultural or ethnic settings and a child may assume this posture as an ascribed status.

Assertive behavior involves informing others of one's needs, wants, and opinion without criticizing, threating or putting down the other person. It also takes the form of standing up for one's rights without violating the rights of others. According to Galassi and Galassi (1977, pp. 3–4), "Assertiveness involves three categories of behavior: (1) expressing positive feelings (giving and receiving compliments, carrying on conversations), (2) self-affirmation (standing up for one's rights, refusing to do certain things), and (3) expressing negative feelings (annoyance or anger that is justified by another's behavior)."

Assertiveness training for juveniles may involve an assessment of the types of situations in which they are most likely to go along with the suggestion of peers even though they may not really wish to, or situations in which they are unable to express their feelings or desires to parents or teachers. Assertiveness training sessions generally begin with a discussion of the rights and responsibilities of the juvenile in these types of situations. Youths are taught to analyze the short- and long-term consequences of various ways of acting and then decide how to behave.

16.7.6   Behavior Modification

Treatment programs grounded in behavior modification principles are often described as using "common sense" to bring about behavioral change. Most parents use a form of behavior modification in the rearing of their children. They assume that if a child is rewarded for "being good" and punished for "being bad," the child will be motivated toward "being good," that is, obeying the parents. Not being mean, nasty, and demanding, and not getting into trouble to receive the rewards given by the parents such as praise, special privileges, and affection are viewed as appropriate behaviors. However, Kratcoski (2017, p. 207) notes that parents as well as children do not always act rationally in their relationships with each other. At times, they tend to let their emotions control their responses, rather than basing their responses on a rational judgment determining the best course of action to follow. A parent who has become extremely irritated as a result of listening to a child complaining, refusing to cooperate, obey commands, and being extremely annoying, might "let off steam" by yelling at the child and by using derogatory labels to release the frustration. This this type of response may make the parent feel better, but eventually the parent may experience feelings of guilt. The emotional response by the parent might result in the child becoming uncertain as to how to interact with the parents and how the parent will respond in certain situations.

Brown, Wienckowski, and Stolz (1976, p. 3) explained the difference between behavior modification principles and the use of common sense by stating, "Behavior modification, (unlike common sense) like other scientific approaches, imposes an organization on its subject matter. While common sense often includes contradictory advice (both out of sight, out of mind, and absence makes the heart grow fonder), the principles of behavior modification codify and organize common sense, showing under what conditions and in what circumstances which aspects of 'common sense' should be applied." The authors go on and explain that mothers who use their common sense to reward and discipline their children for their behavior may not apply the positive rewards and negative sanctions consistently (punishing the child for an act on one occasion and ignoring the act on another occasion).

The basic concept underlying behavior modification theory is *operant conditioning*. Cherry (2016, p. 1) developed a definition of operant conditioning, stating, "Operant conditioning (sometimes referred to as instrumental conditioning) is a method of learning that occurs through rewards and punishment for behavior and a consequence for that behavior." Cherry (2016, p. 2) expanded the definition by noting that, "Operant conditioning relies on a fairly simple premise—actions that are followed by reinforcement will be strengthened and more likely to occur again in the future." If this is true, it follows that actions that have undesirable consequences would be less likely to be repeated.

The basic principles of behavior modification are derived from Pavlov's conditioned-reflex experiments in which he rang a bell and provided a dog with a treat repeatedly until the dog would salivate at the sound of the bell even when no treat was forthcoming. Extensive animal experiments along these lines have been performed since about 1920. Later the techniques were applied to modifying the behavior of emotionally disturbed or retarded children, and behavior modification as a technique for changing the behavior of delinquent, criminal, or mentally disturbed people has been widely used since the 1960s.

Behavior modification may involve the use of positive reinforcement or aversion stimuli. In positive reinforcement, a subject is given some type of reward each time a desired behavior takes place. In an institutional setting, this might involve a point system, with increased privileges given for a certain number of points for school truants, a certain amount of money may be given for each day of prompt attendance at school each week. The reward (reinforcement) given is selected to appeal to the age and needs of the person whose behavior is being modified. A negative reinforcement is the use of aversion stimuli, so that some unpleasant occurrence is associated with improper behavior. For delinquents, this might be a fine or loss of points for misbehavior. In an institutional setting, it could take the form of s short period of isolation or restriction of privileges such as television viewing or sports participation.

Behavior modification, in terms of the use of positive rewards or aversion stimuli, has always been used by parents as a way of controlling and directing the behavior of children. Outside institutional settings, it is most frequently utilized in juvenile justice work through the use of *behavior contracts*. Behavior contracts are written agreements between two parties that certain stated regulations will be followed and that, in return, various rewards will be given. They also provide that if the regulations are not followed, rewards will be withheld or sanctions imposed.

The success of behavior modification depends greatly upon the subject's receiving the positive reinforcements when the desired behavior occurs or the negative sanctions if undesirable behavior takes place. In the case of behavioral contracts, this may mean impressing on parents the importance of strictly enforcing the rules agreed upon in the contract and faithfully reporting even minor violations to the probation officer. For example, a juvenile who is adjudicated delinquent and placed on probation must agree to abide by the condition of probation (rules). A behavioral contract that might be set up between a probation officer and a youth, with the consent and cooperation of the child's parents, may specify special conditions of probation such as strict compliance with the curfew established by the parents, not missing school without a valid reason, and not frequenting "off limits" places or establishments.

Although the limited comparative research on the success of behavior modification indicated that it is useful as a delinquency treatment technique, a number of criticisms must be noted. Some have claimed that it has a dehumanizing quality and reduces regulation of human behavior to the same level as training an animal. Particularly in regard to aversive stimuli, questions have been raised about the morality of such devices as electric shock or drugs. These have not been widely used with juveniles, but are sometimes used in behavior modification programs for drug abusers, offenders who have mental health issues, or with or alcoholics. Civil libertarians have argued that some types of behavior modification border on "mind" or "thought control." Another expressed fear is that behavior modification can be used in institutions as a punitive rather than a therapeutic measure, either rewards withheld or aversive stimuli applied to strengthen control over the residents rather than to aid in the modification of their behavior in a therapeutic sense. Certainly, any use of behavior modification in a setting of total control and involuntary participation should be carefully monitored. Finally, longitudinal studies should be conducted to those who have completed behavior modification programs to determine whether the subjects returned to their former behavior patterns after the positive and negative reinforcements offered in the program were withdrawn for a period of time.

16.7.7   Milieu Therapy

Milieu therapy may be defined as the involvement of all aspects of a youth's environment in treatment and efforts to change his or her behavior. This group-oriented therapy can obviously be performed most easily in a controlled environment such as an institution, but it can also be utilized in community-based treatment centers such as group homes, even though outside influences in such settings may prevent the creation of a total-milieu treatment plan. In milieu therapy, everything in a young person's surroundings is manipulated or designed to assist in changing his or her behavior and leading the youth toward a more satisfactory way of behaving. Once this is accomplished, the changes in behavior, attitudes, or outlook must be internalized so that when the child leaves this closed setting, he or she will be able to function without reverting to old behavior patterns. Its obvious drawback is the difficulty inherent in transferring the youth's reactions to this artificial setting to the realities of life outside the institution or community treatment facility. Milieu therapy is frequently a prelude to other types of treatment that help a youth readjust to life in the community. It is often attempted with youths whose previous environments are considered to have contributed greatly to their delinquent behavior.

16.7.8   Group Work

We noted earlier that the decision whether to use individual or group treatment is an important one to be made by the counselor. In some cases, as in group work with gangs, the group already exists and the counselor must adapt his or her methods to its structure. This is also true of group work with family units. A counselor or probation officer who decides to use group formation can work out various combinations of youths that he or she believes will result in effective operation of the group process. Some background information or even diagnostic testing may be undertaken before the group is able to function in a way that is productive.

Vinter (1974) described group work as a form of therapy in which the desired ends are sought through interaction of the group members and the counselor, rather than through one-to-one counseling between a youth and a counselor. The group is both the context in which the group work takes place and the means by which treatment is given. Processes occur in a group setting that can be valuable in promoting identification of problems, goal setting, and movement toward solutions. The counselor uses the process of social interaction that occurs in the group setting as a means of bringing about the changes needed in the juvenile's life. In some groups, a counselor may play a very passive role, with the group members doing most of the problem identification and analysis; in others, the members may need to be prodded through the use of role playing to get the group process working effectively. The worker's skill in guiding the group toward the desired goals is all-important if the method is to succeed.

Kratcoski (2017, p. 229) identified some of the advantages the use of group treatment in counseling juveniles has over individual counseling. These include its cost effectiveness and the possibility that it can reduce the influence of the inmate subculture, since the group members can develop loyalty and pride in being involved in a group that is working to promote positive behavior. Group members will be encouraged to change by other group members, and the group discussions may result in possible solutions to problems of individual members, since other members may have dealt with similar problems in their lives. Many types of group work can be conducted by regular staff, without extensive training, and group members may even take the lead in self-help situations.

A problem that might interfere with the effectiveness of group work is the presence of an inexperienced group leader who does not have the skills needed to guide the group to its goals. Also, the group meetings can become "talkathons" or gripe session and not achieve anything positive, or one or more group members might dominate the discussions and ridicule or intimidate other members to the point that they feel uncomfortable or feel they have no opportunities to express their opinions.

16.7.9   Guided Group Interaction and Positive Peer Culture

The key element of guided group interaction is that the group members themselves are agents in changing behavior; they are agents of change for themselves and for each other. The members become a cohesive group, providing support for each other in working toward treatment goals—specifically, the goal of being able to live successfully in society—and they feel responsible as a group if an individual member fails. A therapy technique that has many similarities to guided group interaction is known as positive peer culture. It was developed by Vorrath and Brendtro (1974, pp. 17 and 18) and first applied at a Minnesota training school for delinquent boys. Small groups (9–10 members) were formed, with a staff group leader present to guide the members' interaction. Members of a group were committed to helping and being concerned about each other. They learned to accept responsibility for their own actions and those of other group members.

The designers of positive peer culture developed a "universal language of problems" for use in the group discussions. It allows those involved to label and define their difficulties in terms that are easy to understand. The language comprises three general problems—low self-image, lack of consideration of others, and lack of consideration of self—and nine specific problems and gives measurements for deciding when a problem is solved.

The group evaluates the behavior of each member and decides whether each has been successful in solving his or her defined problems. The group opinion is crucial at the time a youth appears to be ready to be terminated from a positive peer culture group. The group itself is responsible for recommending release from therapy. Its recommendation has great importance when this therapy process has taken place in an institution. When a member requests release, the group meets; evaluates his or her values, self-concept, and efforts and success in helping others; and votes on a decision. If the decision is in favor of release, it is referred to a staff team for final action.

16.7.10   Family Counseling

Realizing that a substantial portion of delinquent behavior is a result of malfunctioning of the family unit, family counseling agencies broke with the tradition of singling out the misbehaving child for treatment and instead began offering treatment for the family as a unit.

Family therapy is not merely one more method of treatment to be added to individual and group therapy. Its focus is not on changing a person's perceptions or behavior, but rather on changing the structure of a family and the sequences of malfunctioning behavior within it. The living situation of the troubled child is the target for positive change.

Since a large majority of youths who are under juvenile court supervision come from dysfunctional families, family counseling is often recommended or mandated as part of a youth's disposition. In many cases, the juvenile offender may have been victimized by a family member or close relative, through physical or sexual abuse or neglect, and in these instances one of more family members may be required to take part in counseling. If the juvenile was involved in substance abuse, runaway behavior, or sex offenses, the family is often involved in the treatment strategies, setting limits and applying needed sanctions.

Conjoint family therapy is an action-oriented form of treatment that emphasizes change in the dynamics of the family. Underlying this approach is the important concept that the family is a system, more dynamic and complex than the mere sum of its component parts, each of which is still an entity in itself. Satir (1972, pp. 569–579), identified five communication patterns in family interaction: the placater, the blamer, the computer, the distracter, and the leveling person. From these she developed the "family categories schema"—an attempt to categorize family systems, thereby allowing a consistent, systematic investigation of the family unit. Through the application of perceptual, conceptual, and executive skills, the therapist recognizes, describes, and helps the family evaluate the interaction patterns taken by the family members, and their effects on the family as a whole. The therapist assesses the strengths and weaknesses of the family unit in problem solving, affective expression and involvement, communication, role behavior, autonomy, modes of behavioral control, and problem areas. The interaction patterns developed by Satir are communicated to the family members and they are asked to try and identify these patterns in themselves and other family members and to use this knowledge to aid in positive, open communication.

16.7.11   Anger Management

Hollenhurst (2000, p. 350) states that anger management has "earned face validity as a reasonable treatment alternative for domestic abusers, child abusers, animal abusers, substance abuses, aggressive juveniles, scandals, perpetrators of hate crimes or road rage, and other violent offenders." Anger management programs for delinquent youths may vary in content and structure, but they all have the common goal of teaching those who are participating in the programs how to control their responses to anger provoking situations. Skills closely associated with the development of anger management are conflict resolution and violence prevention. The main focus of all these programs is to teach the participants to think of the consequences before they act.

Anger management treatment is grounded in cognitive behavior theories. It emphasizes that one's response to anger-provoking situations is shaped by socialization and a learned pattern of response. Anger management treatment usually takes place in a group setting and begins with a lecture on understanding the nature of the anger, that is, what types of stimuli cause a person to become angry, the biological and physiological changes anger produces, and how the anger is associated with aggression. Anger management training is a re-socialization process, geared toward changing inappropriate behavior response patterns to appropriate ones. During the sessions, participants are urges to "open up," to reduce their defensiveness, and come to understand how anger-induced responses intensify the possibility of aggression and violence.

16.8   Treatment Techniques for Specific Types of Offenders

While the techniques discussed up to this point could be used with a wide range of juvenile offenders, certain specialized treatment modalities are needed for offenders whose problems are focused in a specific behavior area. These include substance abusers; sex offenders; and serious, violent offenders. There may also be an inter-relationship of these behavior patterns. For example, a sex offender may also be violent and aggressive. In the treatment of the special offender types, some programs are grounded in a very specific treatment modality that focuses on what may be considered the root cause of the misbehavior, but the majority of them tend to be eclectic; that is, they use several approaches. These may include behavior modification, psychological counseling, employment skills development, self-esteem building, assertiveness training, art therapy, and therapy that focuses on cognitive distortions (errors in thinking). Group, individual and family counseling may be used (Kratcoski, 2000).

16.8.1   Art Therapy

A large proportion of the youths who are processed through the juvenile courts have experienced physical abuse, sexual abuse, and other forms of maltreatment from parents and other adult authority figures. Many of these youthful offenders are highly suspicious of all adults and unwilling to communicate with them in conventional types of therapy. Those involved in working with such youths have discovered that children who may be reluctant to express their feelings, emotions, wishes, or fears verbally will project them through their art work.

A student intern who was working with the director of a juvenile detention center (Brown, 2002, p. 8) described how a 13-year-old girl who had been involved in sexual activities with members of a gang revealed information about her relationships with members of her family through drawing.

> Rod [the director] wanted her to draw to see if she would express herself through drawing, particularly if she would draw about her relation to gang life or about her family. I told her that she could draw a picture about anything she wanted to draw about, not the typical five subjects that the juveniles are required to draw on. She chose to draw about her family, which was not a surprise to me. She drew her father, mother, brother, sister, and herself. Her

mother she drew with large hands and larger feet and her father with a large mouth. She drew her brother and sister very normal, with more emphasis on their features, for instance, moles and birthmarks. She drew herself very small, barely recognizing that it was her. Rod, the director, explained what those characteristics meant on each person she drew. I do not want to go into grave detail about each person that Sue drew about. However, I would like to talk about the characteristics of her mother. The large hands on her mother symbolized physical abuse and the large feet symbolized sexual abuse. The large mouth on her father symbolized that he was verbally abusive to her.

16.8.2   Treatment Programs for Sex Offenders

Some of the behavior of juvenile sex offenders may initially be regarded as normal or acceptable for a sexually developing adolescent. A large number of youths who are referred to juvenile courts as sex offenders have also been involved in other types of delinquency. Because the sexual deviance may be only one aspect of the youth's offense patterns, an eclectic approach to treatment is generally followed. Treatment modalities may include behavior modification, victim empathy, anger management, and confrontation. They often focus on breaking down denial and rationalization and concentrate on bringing the offender to accept responsibility for his or her actions (Knopp, 1982).

Denial is an important aspect of sex offending, with the perpetrator refusing to admit that the incident occurred or to accept blame for it. Consequently, confronting and breaking down the denial factor is a key part of the treatment process. To accomplish this, a group setting may be used to lead the offender to critically examine what has occurred. This may include probing, challenging, and role playing.

Because this involves thoughtfully examining what has taken place, it is unlikely to be successful with persons who are emotionally disturbed or who possess limited intelligence (Borzecki & Wormith, 1987, pp. 30–44).

16.8.3   Programs for Substance Abusers

Use of alcohol and drugs by adolescents is very prevalent in our society. Self-report studies (Johnston et al. (1999) revealed that 54% of all high school seniors had tried to illicit drugs. Marijuana was by far the most used drug, with 23% of the seniors reporting they had used it on 20 or more occasions in the previous 30 days. Thirty-one percent of the seniors had drunk alcohol in the last month, and even 25% of eighth graders had used alcohol in the last month prior to the survey. A study of youths in three cities (Denver, Pittsburgh, and Rochester, New York), conducted over a 5-year period Greenbaum, 1994, p. 3), found that half of the youths in the study were using alcohol regularly by age 16, but marijuana use began somewhat later, and only about 10% of the youths in the sample ever became involved in harder drugs.

Police officers and juvenile court personnel believe that, regardless of the specific charge, the majority of arrests of juvenile offenders are related to substance abuse in some way. Research has shown that involvement with drugs was associated with delinquent behavior. Among all the age, gender, and ethnic groups, the more seriously involved in drugs a youth was, the more seriously that a juvenile was involved in delinquency, and vice versa. It is fairly routine for those youths being held in detention or being formally processed through the juvenile court system to receive a substance abuse evaluation. Such assessments examine the following areas of a youth's background (Ellis & Sowers, 2001, p. 715): "history of alcohol or drug use, history of over-the-counter drug use, medical history, mental health history, school history, sexual history, peer relationships, gang involvement, inter-personal skills, leisure activities, neighborhood environment, and home environment."

Substance abuse is rarely the only problem in an adolescent's life. Instead, substance abusers are likely to be multi-problem youths who may require attention to their family situations, educational needs, and personal adjustment problems. Many juvenile courts have established a systematic approach to detecting substance abuse of those youths brought before the court. A summary of the program implemented by the Portage County Juvenile Court, Ohio (2019, p. 1) states "The Substance Abuse Awareness Program conducts substance abuse assessments on all substance related offenses forwarded to juvenile court and makes recommendations for treatment based on the results. Youth may be handled formally or informally within the department. The officer also coordinates placement for residential treatment opportunities and provides case management services for youth involved in treatment programs." The approach used by Portage County and those similar to it are preventive in that by using a screening for drug use of any youth coming before the court in which drug or alcohol use is suspected provides an opportunity for early involvement. It also provides various forms of differential treatment for those in which the tests confirm substance abuse, the treatment modality being determined by the needs of each youth who tested positive. The treatment for such abusers is designed to combine various approaches. It may be provided in secure or open settings, operated by private or public groups or agencies, and be residential or nonresidential. Depending on the severity of the youth's problem, it may involve detoxification or monitoring by urinalysis or be predominantly educational in nature.

16.8.4   Drug Courts

Creation of drug courts for juveniles and family drug courts has become more prevalent since juvenile justice and social services administrators and workers have realized that substance abuse and dependency are interrelated with deviant behavior of juveniles. Drug courts for juveniles were begun for the purpose of offering an alternative to formal juvenile court processing. Referral to drug court may be an option for youths who have some substance abuse problems but have not committed serious violent offenses that would make them a danger to the community. They must voluntarily agree to complete the treatment program. Although the drug treatment may be administered by professional therapists, the juvenile court judge still maintains control of the case. If a youth successfully completes the program, the initial charges are often dropped and the young person will not have an official delinquency record (National Association of Drug Court Professional, 1997, p. 7).

The family drug court is structured in a similar way. However, the major focus of this court is on parents who face criminal prosecution for substance-related abuse related offenses that have been shown to have detrimental effects on their children. After acceptance, those families that enter the family drug court program receive intensive interventions, with the goal of changing a dysfunctional family into a stable, productive family. A family drug court director gave this profile of the clients: "Participants in the Family Drug Court are of both genders, come from many different ethnic and socioeconomic backgrounds, use every kind of drug... and face other complicating factors... Often women in the program have personal histories of child and adult sexual or physical abuse. Their continued tendency to make poor choices in male companions has a direct impact on their sobriety and success in the programs... Many children suffer from birth defects associated with prenatal alcohol exposure. Often the mother also has defects associated with her mother's alcohol abuse" (McGree, 2000, p. 555).

The family drug court process frequently involves continued contact with and mentoring of the parents for long periods of time. As reported by McGree (2000, p. 555). "Substance abuse treatment programs identified as successful vary widely in their approaches. Such programs generally offer services for juveniles who have some involvement with drug court or alcohol-related charges and have a history of substance abuse. Nonresidential programs assess each youth and make referrals to community agencies, provide intensive casework testing, and use graduated sanctions for failure to meet required behavior. Some programs use group living in a non-secure residential setting. Treatment follows the 12 steps used by Alcoholics Anonymous, and living, communication, and social skills are emphasized. Following residential treatment, follow-up services may be provided."

Because substance abuse is involved in a great deal of delinquent behavior, the Office of Juvenile Justice and Delinquency Prevention (Sweet, 1990, pp. 16–18) sponsored the development of a training program for juvenile justice professionals that would assist them in identifying youths who have substance abuse problems. A 12-step program was suggested. The program is shown in Box 16.1:

Box 16.1 12 Steps for Identifying Youths with Substance Abuse Problems

- Take a drug history, using structured questions about prior drug involvement.
- Perform a preliminary prescreen, using questions, observation, and asking the juvenile to perform simple tests.
- Examine the eyes. Certain drugs will change the appearance or functioning ability of the eyes.

- Administer the divided-attention psychophysical tests. These involve activities that check balance and coordination.
- Perform the dark room examination. This checks the size of the eyes' pupils and their reaction to light.
- Examine vital signs. Certain drugs raise blood pressure and heart rate or cause rapid breathing.
- Examine for muscle rigidity, since some drugs cause muscles to become hypertense and rigid.
- Look for injection sites. Scars or tracks may be found on the arms, legs, or neck.
- Interview the juvenile and make observations.
- Form an opinion, based on the evidence and observations.
- Request a toxicological examination, since chemical tests can provide evidence to substantiate the conclusions reached. Once substance abuse is identified as a problem, court personnel must decide whether the youth needs to receive special intensive treatment for the abuse, of if a more general type of treatment and supervision is indicated.

16.9 Treatment Effectiveness

While most administrators of treatment programs for juvenile delinquents can describe success cases associated with their programs and provide statistics to back up their claims that their particular approach is effective, they must also concede that there are failures. Claims of great program success are met with skepticism in many instances and the flaws in the methods used to evaluate the treatment programs include concerns about the length of time used in the evaluation and the lack of a control group of youth with comparable characteristics. The influence of other factors that may have contributed to the positive results and the failure to provide measurements of success and failure are common criticism of program evaluations. In response to the criticisms given above, new instruments to measure the potential risks of juveniles recidivating and their needs during treatment have been developed. The large majority of juvenile justice agencies now use some form of a standardized assessment and classification instrument. For example, most juvenile courts will use risk and needs assessment tools to make decisions on the most appropriate dispositions for offenders, including probation, or community residential or institutional placement. These instruments are used to determine the level of supervision needed for those placed in probation or community supervision programs, and they are also used to help determine if the case management plan is successful. For example, if a youth is provided with drug treatment counseling and does not relapse, but continues to engage in delinquent behavior, an evaluation instrument can place this youth on a continuum ranging from complete success to complete failure.

Youths who are given a disposition of institutional placement are classified to determine the appropriate institution (maximum, medium, or low security), the appropriate living quarters within the facility (high, medium or low security), and the appropriate programming (substance abuse counseling, individual counseling, anger management). The effectiveness of these instruments can be empirically tested.

Often treatment programs are not effective because a youth is given a type of treatment to which he or she is not likely to respond. VanVoorhis (1995, p. 13) contended that the manipulative, exploitative, asocial type of offender, often labeled untreatable, can be reached effectively in a program that is designed to alter antisocial value systems and behavior, if the treatment is applied in a positive peer culture setting. She maintained that this type of offender will respond to confrontational therapy. In contrast, this type of approach is unlikely to be effective if it is used with juveniles who are neurotic or have personality disorders.

16.10 Summary

In this chapter, the characteristics of treatment and the process by which it is implemented were examined. The importance of effective planning and management in producing the best treatment possible and discovered that many types of individual and group treatment have been used by juvenile justice agencies was emphasized.

Because of the pressures of large caseloads and tight budgets, many agencies have been forced to search for new methods of handling juveniles referred to them for treatment. Group work has increased in popularity, as have the "action" therapies, which involve the use of volunteers and paraprofessionals. Interface (cooperation and communication) with other community agencies has enabled the juvenile courts to divert some youthful offenders to other sources of treatment rather than handling them within the justice system. The movements toward community-based treatment and deinstitutionalization have also highlighted the importance of cooperation with various local agencies for maximization of treatment potential. The key position of the counselor in the treatment process cannot be overemphasized. The helping person must be well versed in the particular techniques, able to relate to the juveniles (and parents) assigned to his or her care, and capable of measuring the effectiveness of various approaches and abandoning those that prove ineffective.

A wide variety of treatment techniques has been used with juvenile offenders. *Psychotherapy* may involve insight therapy to uncover the reasons for behavior or action therapies to improve psychological functioning. *Reality Therapy* involves analysis of behavior with the goal of becoming responsible. While such therapies may be applied over a period of weeks or months, *crisis intervention* is immediate attention to misbehavior, with both the offender and his or her family usually involved. The crisis event is seen as an occasion when parents and youths can come to acknowledge the need for help and agree to accept counseling. *Assertiveness training* is recommended for young people who may have been led into delinquency by peers because they lacked the courage to refuse to become involved. *Behavior modification* is a "cost and rewards" approach to behavior, with the person being treated receiving positive or negative reinforcement, according to the behavior that occurs. *Milieu therapy* attempts to involve all aspects of a youth's environment in efforts to change his or her behavior.

In addition to individual therapies, group work is also used in treating delinquents. In *guided group interaction*, the members of the group itself work to change each other's behavior. In a similar program, *positive peer culture,* members of the treatment group are committed to helping and being concerned about each other. They learn to accept responsibility for their own actions and those of other group members. *Family counseling* seeks to change family interaction patterns that have resulted in juvenile misbehavior. In *family therapy*, the family is examined and treated as a system and the positions of various members of the family are analyzed. *Anger management therapy* seeks to teach youths how control their responses to anger provoking situations and think of the consequences before they act.

An important trend in juvenile offender treatment is the development of techniques designed for offenders whose problems are focused in a specific behavior area. These include sex offenders, substance abusers, and serious violent offenders. The treatment may include group, individual, and family counseling, which may be applied in the institutional or community setting. The therapy combines elements of various treatment approaches to address the offenders' problems. Art therapy is useful when working with youths who are withdrawn, noncommunicative or depressed as well as those that are hostile and aggressive.

The best hope for treatment success appears to lie in a careful selection of treatment techniques, dedication and skill on the part of the treatment workers, and evaluation of methods to determine if they are achieving results or should be supplemented of replaced. Also, actively involving the juvenile in his or her own treatment must be stressed.

16.11   Discussion Questions

1. Discuss the underlying assumptions of the "medical model." Why has it been downplayed in favor of other treatment approached in recent years?
2. The management by objectives approach to juvenile treatment focuses on results. Do you feel that the results of treatment can be effectively measured? How do case management approaches that use management by objectives define or measure treatment effectiveness?
3. Discuss the factors that are considered in making decisions to use group or individual treatment for juveniles. Which types of offenders seem to respond most positively to group treatment?
4. Behavior modification is frequently used in delinquency treatment programs. Discuss the positive facets of behavior modification. What are some negative aspects?

5. What is the first step in treatment therapy for sec offenders? Why do you think a confrontational approach in a group setting is frequently used with sex offenders?

6. Describe the process followed when using brief therapy with delinquent youths. What types of situations are the most appropriate for use of brief therapy?

7. Why are art, drama, music, and dance programs so successful when dealing with juveniles housed in secure facilities, such as detention or correctional facilities?

8. Discuss the process followed in anger management counseling. Discuss whether it would be appropriate to combine anger management and family counseling.

9. Guided group interaction and positive peer culture are two forms of group therapy often used in secure facilities housing delinquent youths. Describe the key elements of these treatment approaches.

10. Discuss the process followed in identification of youths with drug abuse problems in a typical treatment process.

References

Borzecki, M., & Wormith, J. (1987). A survey of treatment programs for sex offenders in North America. *Canadian Psychology, 28*, 30–44.

Brown, B., Wienckowski, L., & Stolz, S. (1976). *Behavior modification: Perspectives on a current issue.* Washington, DC: National Institute of Mental Health, U.S. Department of Health, Education and Welfare, U.S. Government Printing Office (Reprinted in Kratcoski, P. *Correctional counseling and treatment* (5th ed.) pp. 367–404, 2004. Long Grove, IL: Waveland Press, Inc.

Brown, K. Y. (2002, October). *Internship paper* (pp. 1–18). Stark: Kent State University.

Center for Substance Abuse Treatment. (1999). *Brief therapy in substance abuse treatment* (pp. 1–11). Rockville, MD: National Institute of Health. Retrieved April 15, 2016, from http://www.ncbi/nim.nih.gov/books/NBK6-4943

Cherry, K. (2016). "What is operant conditioning and how does it work?" in Psychology, very well. Retrieved 7/18/2019 from https://www.verywell.com/operantconditioning-a2-2794863

Ellis, R., & Sowers, K. (2001). *Juvenile justice practice.* Belmont, CA: Brooks Cole.

Galassi, M. D., & Galassi, J. P. (1977). *Assert yourself.* New York: Human Sciences Press.

Gibbons, D. C. (1977). On the nature and forms of treatment. In R. G. Leger & J. R. Stratton (Eds.), *The sociology of corrections.* New York: Wiley.

Glaser, D. (1994). What works, and why it is important: A response to Logan and Gaes. *Justice Quarterly, 11*(4), 712–723.

Greenbaum, S. (1994). Drug, delinquency and other data. *Juvenile Justice, 2*(1), 3.

Hollenhorst, P., (2000). What do we know about anger management programs? Kratcoski, P. (2000) Correctional counseling and treatment, 4th Edition. Prospect Heights, Ill. Waveland Press: pp. 350–376.

Johnston L,, O'Malley, P. & Bach;man, J. (1999). *National survey results on drug use from the monitoring the future study: 1975–1998, Vol. 1: secondary school students.* Rockville, MD: National Institute on Drug Abuse.

Knopp, F. (1982). *Remedial intervention in adolescent sex offenses: Nine program descriptions.* Syracuse, NY: Safer Society Press.

Kratcoski, P., (2000). Special areas of correctional counseling, Correctional counseling and treatment, 4th edition. Prospect Height, Ill, Waveland Press: pp. 535–616.

Kratcoski, P. (2017). *Correctional counseling and treatment* (6th ed.). Cham: Springer.

Mauer, T. (2005). *Pre-trial* (6th ed.). New York: Aspen Publishers.

Mc Gree, C. (2000). Family drug courts: Another permanency perspective. In P. Kratcoski (Ed.), *Correctional counseling and treatment* (4th ed., pp. 553–557). Prospective Heights, IL: Waveland Press.

Michigan Department of Community Health. (1985). *Crisis intervention: Providing residential services in a community setting.* Retrieved April 25, 2016, from http://www.michigan.gov/mdch

Montogomery, I., & Landon, M. (1994). *What works: Promising interventions in juvenile justice.* Washington, DC: Department of Justice. Fact Sheet #20, p. 1.

National Association of Drug Court Professionals. (1997). *Defining drug courts: The key components.* Washington, DC: Office of Justice Programs.

Newman, C. (1975). Concepts of treatment in probation and parole supervision. In E. Peoples (Ed.), *Readings in correctional casework and counseling* (pp. 51–53). Pacific Palisades, CA: Goodyear.

Portage County Juvenile Court Department of Youth Rehabilitation. (2019). *DYR department overview: Substance abuse awareness.* Ravenna, OH: Portage County Juvenile Court.

Rachin, R. (1974). Reality therapy: Helping people help themselves. *Crime and Delinquency, 20*(1), 51–53.

Roberts, A. (1991). Conceptualizing crisis theory and the crisis intervention model. In A. Roberts (Ed.), *Contemporary perspectives on crisis intervention and prevention* (pp. 3–17). Englewood Cliffs, NJ: Prentice-Hall.

Satir, V. (1972). *People making.* Palo Alto, CA: Science and Behavior Books.

Shearer, R. (1993). *Interviewing in criminal justice* (2nd ed.). Action, CA: Copley Publishing Co..

Sweet Jr., R. W. (1990). Drug recognition techniques: A training program for juvenile justice professionals. *NIIJ Rep, 221*(Summer), 16–18.

Trojanowicz, R. (1978). Juvenile delinquency, 2nd ed. Englewood Cliffs, N.J.: Prentice Hall.

VanVoorhis, P. (1995). *Efficient applications of differential treatment to correctional treatment settings* (pp. 1–15). Paper presented at the Annual Meeting of the Academy of Criminal Justice Sciences, Boston, MA, March.

Vinter, R. (1974). The essential components of social group work practice. In P. Glasser, R. Sarri, & R. Vinter (Eds.), *Individual change through small groups* (pp. 10–11). New York: Free Press.

Vorrath, H., & Brendro, L. (1974). *Positive peer culture.* Chicago, IL: Aldine.

Index

© Springer Nature Switzerland AG 2020
P. C. Kratcoski et al., *Juvenile Delinquency*,
https://doi.org/10.1007/978-3-030-31452-1